Also by Richard J. Barnet

THE ALLIANCE:
America-Europe-Japan
Makers of the Postwar World

REAL SECURITY:
Restoring American Power in a Dangerous Decade

THE LEAN YEARS:
Politics in the Age of Scarcity

THE GIANTS:
Russia and America

GLOBAL REACH:
The Power of the Multinational Corporations
(with Ronald E. Müller)

ROOTS OF WAR:
The Men and Institutions Behind U.S. Foreign Policy

THE ECONOMY OF DEATH

INTERVENTION AND REVOLUTION

AFTER TWENTY YEARS
(with Marcus Raskin)

WHO WANTS DISARMAMENT?

THE ROCKETS' RED GLARE

WHEN AMERICA
GOES TO WAR

The Presidents and the People

RICHARD J. BARNET

SIMON AND SCHUSTER

New York London Toronto Sydney Tokyo

Simon and Schuster
Simon & Schuster Building
Rockefeller Center
1230 Avenue of the Americas
New York, New York 10020

Copyright © 1990 by Richard J. Barnet

Designed by Nina D'Amario/Levavi & Levavi
Manufactured in the United States of America

1   3   5   7   9   10   8   6   4   2

Library of Congress Cataloging in Publication Data
Barnet, Richard J.
The rockets' red glare: when America goes to war—the presidents and
the people/Richard J. Barnet.
p.   cm.
Includes bibliographical references.
1. United States—History, Military.   2. United States—Military policy
—Public opinion.   3. United States—Foreign relations—Public
opinion.   4. Public opinion—United States.   5. War—Public
opinion.   I. Title.
E181.B37   1990
327.73—dc20   89-22044
CIP
ISBN 0-671-63376-7

To the free citizens, past and present, who inspired this book
and
To my family and friends who made it possible to write it.

ACKNOWLEDGMENTS

I have learned so many things from so many people in writing this book that I am unable to list them. In the formative stages Shoon Murray was a brilliant research assistant, and in the final stages Leslie Rose and Peter Andreas provided invaluable help. Gar Alperovitz, Milton Cantor, James Chace, Joan Garces, Walter LaFeber, Saul Landau, Anna Nelson, Marc Raskin, and Michael Shuman were most generous in taking the time to give a close reading to the manuscript. Jill Guetling, Farhana Khera, Jane Godfrey, and Joan Drake helped at various points with the project. I am grateful to Patricia Miller, who was the copy editor on the manuscript. This is the sixth book on which I have benefited from Alice Mayhew's editorial judgment and encouragment.

CONTENTS

Introduction: The People's Will and the National Interest   11

Part One
A REPUBLIC IF YOU CAN KEEP IT   21

Chapter 1   Passionate Attachments   23

Chapter 2   Jefferson's Coup and Madison's War   52

Part Two
EMPIRE OF LIBERTY   71

Chapter 3   Popular Democracy and the Enemy Within   73

Chapter 4   The Politics of Expansion   92

Chapter 5   The Politics of Adventure   118

Part Three
THE BURDEN AND GLORY OF WORLD POWER   139

Chapter 6   The American People and the War to End War   141

Chapter 7   The Fight for the League of Nations   163

Chapter 8   "The Good War": Getting In   186

Chapter 9   "The Good War": Getting Out   216

Part Four
NATIONAL SECURITY IN THE AGE OF ANXIETY   247

Chapter 10   Clearer Than Truth   249

Chapter 11   The Cold War Consensus   285

Chapter 12   The Consensus Unravels:
From Korea to Vietnam   308

Chapter 13   The Politics of Feelings   352

Conclusion: Battleground of Democracy   399

NOTES   415

BIBLIOGRAPHY   429

INDEX   443

INTRODUCTION

The People's Will and the National Interest

American foreign policy is conducted in the name of the people, but what difference have the people made? The Republic was founded on the idea that the just powers of government are derived from the consent of the governed. Ever since, the United States has been engaged in a continuous struggle to reconcile the profound mistrust of central government on which the nation was founded with the making of foreign policy, which throughout history has been the sport of kings. The struggle to define the national interest of the United States through the disorderly process of electoral politics has set the limits of American democracy. The tension between the calculations and feelings of elected leaders and the interests and sentiments of ordinary citizens has put its special stamp on American diplomacy in many ways, but the tension is most palpable when the nation goes to war. This book is the story of the role the American people have played in the critical decisions of war and peace.

Since the founding of the Republic public opinion has been the mystery that has legitimated the authority of the state. Other nations operate on different myths. All sorts of leaders assert that they embody the will of the people by virtue of their warrior skills, their royal blood, their religious zeal. But in the United States the actions of government, especially on vital questions of national security, cannot for long violate the strong feelings and desires of citizens when large numbers are aroused and make their feelings known. Ordinary citizens usually have little to do with making foreign pol-

icy decisions, especially critical ones, but they can act as execution-
ers if the decisions go badly.

American presidents, seeking to wrap their foreign policy initiatives in the legitimating mantle of "public opinion," are engaged in
a continuous struggle to define public opinion. Most of them assume the existence of a "silent majority" of support. For the most
part they have believed it neither possible nor desirable to be guided
by what "We, the People" actually wanted. They have understood
that floating popular sentiment, even when it is widely shared, is
not a serious challenge to their policies. On the other hand, the
opinions of a very small number of people who care passionately
about a matter on which most people have no opinion at all can
have a decisive impact.

Since the "voice of the people" is the source of democratic legitimacy, there have always been oracles to tell us what it says. But
different oracles hear different voices. Over the years the voice of
the people has been sounded in many different ways. At times it is
the roar of throngs, even mobs in the street. Sometimes it is the
murmur of unhappy bankers or the siren songs of merchant dream-
ers. Sometimes it is little more than the squeals of excited newspaper columnists. People who read foreign news in the papers or
watch the network evening roundups are deemed to belong to what
social scientists call the "attentive public." Those who influence the
opinion of others beyond their immediate family qualify as "opinion
leaders," and they become the special targets of the spin doctors,
the choreographers of the telling photo opportunity, and the relentless marketers of official truth. Despite the passivity of most
citizens most of the time with respect to the great issues of war and
peace, George Washington and all his successors have exerted considerable effort to manage public opinion. In the Cold War years,
selling American foreign policy to Americans became one of the
principal tasks of the presidency.

The ballot is the only instrument specified by the Constitution by
which citizens participate in the making of foreign policy. Every
four years the candidates for commander in chief must present
themselves to the electorate. In the last fifty years, a time of continuous war, hot and cold, foreign policy issues have played a more
important role in domestic American politics than ever before. Unfortunately, preelection rhetoric about war and peace is notoriously
unreliable. Woodrow Wilson, Franklin Roosevelt, and Lyndon
Johnson all campaigned on the implied promise to stay out of war;
in each case, thousands of Americans were dying in battle within a

year of their inauguration. Richard Nixon pleaded for votes by hinting that he had a "secret plan" to end the Vietnam War with honor, a plan that did not exist. At the same time no one who voted for him could know that they were voting for normalization of relations with China.

By the same token the message that the voter communicates to the successful candidate by his vote does not provide a reliable guide to the sort of foreign policy he wants. There has never been a national election that was a clear plebiscite on an issue of foreign policy. Too many other issues are invariably involved, and even where there is an overriding public concern about a foreign policy issue, as on the eve of the two world wars, the candidates have not presented a clear choice on the issue of war and peace. The president and members of Congress take public positions on hundreds of issues between elections. All the voter is saying with his vote is "I trust you more than the other candidate." Or "I don't."

This journey into the American past is an inquiry into the mysterious role of public opinion in the choice of war and peace. In two hundred years the United States has evolved from a collection of quarrelsome colonies into a world empire. To what extent have the people been important actors in this extraordinary drama? Or merely bit players? When have the people refused to consent to their leaders' vision of the national interest? With what result?

Since 1945 American presidents have wielded power over national security and foreign policy beyond the dreams of tyrants. One American alone has had the authority to launch nuclear war and risk the death of the nation, even of civilization itself. For almost every one of the forty-five years since the end of World War II, presidents have ordered American soldiers into battle somewhere. The United States has fought two major Asian wars, but the last time Congress met to declare war was December 8, 1941. If the president need not consult either the people or their representatives on such life-and-death decisions for the nation, what role is left for the people in setting the nation's course?

Presidents have generally believed that they could protect the nation only if national security is exempt from the sort of political scrutiny to which domestic policy is often subject. International society is a jungle. In order for the nation to survive and maintain its power, the executive cannot escape doing things in the name of the people that square neither with the cherished myths of democracy nor with the self-image citizens have of themselves as moral beings. In pursuit of democracy, presidents support dictators. In the pursuit of peace, they plan wars of mass destruction. In the pursuit of justice, they supply arms for repression. In the pursuit of world order, they break international law. And so, a long succession of foreign policy experts has said, it must be. To serve the interests of domestic tranquillity it is better that citizens *not* know too much of what the president does to provide for the common defense.

The collective actions and feelings of the mass public influence the decisions of political leaders only when they are perceived by those in power to be an organized or potentially organizable force.[1] In the nuclear years the president's power over foreign policy has grown dramatically, but the impact of public opinion has also grown. Over the last two generations the organization of popular sentiment has forced even popular presidents to change direction. Millions of people demanded rapid demobilization in the fall of 1945, defying what America's leaders thought best for the nation. Popular disaffection forced the termination of American involvement in two Asian wars. To placate public anger over Indochina Richard Nixon ended the draft in the midst of a war. Even as constitutional limits on their power to make war have eroded, modern presidents have been destroyed by foreign policy disasters. Although he left office as personally popular as ever, Ronald Reagan's presidency was seriously damaged in its last two years because of a secret deal to trade arms for American hostages and to generate secret funds for a covert war that Congress had voted not to support. Jimmy Carter was severely hurt because he appeared impotent when Ayatollah Khomeini's zealots seized more than fifty American diplomats and military personnel and held them hostage for more than a year. A few years earlier Harry Truman and Lyndon Johnson abandoned the White House because of costly, unpopular wars in Asia they could neither win nor end.

During these fifty years the architects of America's global strategy have made extraordinary demands on the American people that would have been inconceivable in earlier times. Citizens have been asked to support permanent mobilization, relentless taxes, and a mountain of debt without any promise of defense in the literal sense. American leaders offer the people no serious prospect that the shadow of nuclear war will be lifted, whatever the sacrifice. Deterring wars has become almost as expensive as fighting them, and thus the acquiescence of the taxpayer has become ever more important. But consent has its price. In order to secure continued public support for a significant increase in military spending during the Reagan administration, the Pentagon's highest official issued the "Weinberger Doctrine," an official acknowledgment of the veto power of public opinion. The armed forces, the secretary of defense announced, will not fight wars that the American people will not support.

The official view of the American public that has normally prevailed in the White House and in the State Department is not a flattering one. Former secretary of state Dean Acheson once wrote that if you did what the people wanted in foreign policy, "You'd go wrong every time."[2] In the State Department Acheson and his associates "used to discuss how much time that mythical 'average American citizen' put in each day listening, reading, and arguing about the world outside his own country. Assuming a man or woman with a fair education, a family, and a job in or out of the house, it seemed to us that ten minutes a day would be a high average."[3] In periods of high international tension, issues of foreign relations arouse more powerful emotions than domestic issues. Alexis de Tocqueville's observation that democracy tends "to obey its feelings rather than its calculations" is taken so seriously in the White House that presidential advisers have elevated the monitoring and manipulation of public opinion into an art. The guardians of the nation's security have often looked upon a free press, the right of dissent, and the need to persuade the public as serious handicaps in the struggle with America's enemies.

In his *Democracy in America,* an admiring look at the United States in the year 1831, Tocqueville thought that the conduct of foreign relations could turn out to be the Achilles' heel of the American system, for "in the control of society's foreign affairs democratic governments do appear decidedly inferior to others."[4] More than a hundred years later, Dean Acheson, who more than anyone else was the architect of postwar United States foreign policy, came to a similar conclusion. "The limitation imposed by democratic political practices makes it difficult to conduct our foreign affairs in the national interest."[5] For two hundred years observers of American society have worried that democratic leaders who must sway the crowd to get into power often end up as prisoners of popular sentiment. Unable to do unpopular things in the pursuit of the national interest, or to resist doing foolish things that are popular, the democratic leader finds himself immobilized.

No thinker claiming to be a democrat has ever put the case against the people's role in foreign affairs more strongly than Walter Lippmann. "The unhappy truth is that the prevailing public opinion has been destructively wrong at the critical junctures." The public is a "willful despot," a "dangerous master of decisions when the stakes are life and death." The people "have imposed a massive veto upon the judgments of informed and responsible officials," compelling them "to make the big mistakes that public opinion has insisted upon."[6] More recently, neoconservative writers have attributed the decline of American power in the world to an "excess of democracy."[7]

Yet if democracy were really as antithetical to the pursuit of the national interest as so many writers assert, how did it happen that a handful of colonies on the Atlantic coast managed in two hundred years to become the mightiest nation of modern times? The obvious answer is that as far as foreign policy is concerned the United States has never been a democracy. There are plenty of people who believe this. For every elitist like Lippmann who sees the crowd as a terrible despot before whom presidents cower, there is a frustrated populist who sees America as a nation of sheep snookered by demagogic politicians and, depending upon one's political outlook, by the "liberal" media or the "military-industrial complex." But that is too simple. The need to persuade the public—if only after a decision has been taken—has profoundly influenced American foreign policy at every stage of our history. What Walter Lippmann called "the manufacture of consent" has left its mark on virtually every political and cultural institution. But, as we shall see, sometimes the consent is withheld.

The power of the people over foreign policy has grown over the years. Whether one considers this a positive or negative development depends upon the assumptions one makes about the educability and common sense of the people and the wisdom and rationality of leaders. Do leaders make better or worse decisions when they feel the need to seek the consent of the governed? Democratic ideology answers yes. Elite wisdom answers no. Diplomats, strategists, and politicians usually look upon democracy as something to promote in other countries but not in their own. By and large they believe with Edmund Burke that the task of a leader is to maintain the "interest" of the people against their "opinions," in short "to be a pillar of the state, and not a weathercock."[8]

Since the founding of the Republic public opinion has enjoyed a decidedly mixed reputation. The tradition of blaming the passengers rather than the captain when the ship of state runs aground goes back to some of the Founding Fathers. Alexander Hamilton, surely the most hostile to democratic tendencies of all the architects

of the Constitution, argued that governments in the thrall of popular feeling find themselves propelled into war. "There have been,
if I may so express it," he wrote in *The Federalist*, "almost as many
popular as royal wars. The cries of the nation and the importunities
of their representatives, have, upon various occasions dragged their
monarchs into war, or continued them in it, contrary to their incli-
nations, and sometime contrary to the real interests of the state."[9]
Far from being peculiarly peace-loving, Hamilton argued, democracies are especially prone to war because of popular passions and
the anxieties of the population about losing commercial advantage.

How responsible have the people been? How educable? Presidents invariably insist and usually believe that they are acting in
accordance with the people's will, but what they really are responding to is their own conception of the national interest. Elected
officials are the ultimate interpreters of their mandate—at least
until the next election. On foreign policy matters they enjoy considerable freedom of interpretation because public opinion is more
difficult to fathom than on issues closer to home.

Sometimes what "the people want" is quite unknowable because
most citizens are only dimly aware of the issues and many have
never even heard of them. Often opinion is sharply divided. Public
sentiment for or against a war, a treaty, or a foreign commitment
can appear strong, but it can evaporate with a shift in the headlines.
Moreover, Americans often seem to be asking our leaders to pursue
irreconcilable goals. We yearn for security, power, deference, the
world's highest standard of living, and the prestige of being "Number One," but we also want to do good, to be admired, and to be
noninvolved all at the same time. We react to events in far-off
places not on the basis of knowledge, which a barrage of polls keeps
showing is embarrassingly scanty and inaccurate, but on the basis
of pictures in our heads, usually pictures of pictures from the TV
screen. The less direct experience we have of another people or
culture, the less knowledge we have of their struggles, their hopes,
the weight of their histories, the real choices they face, the more
likely it is that our reaction will be guided by our outrage, disgust,
or fear. The less direct knowledge citizens have about what is happening in the outside world the more susceptible they become to
the comfortable simplifications of official truth.

A succession of critics has observed that the American people get
the foreign policy they deserve. Most citizens do not pay enough
attention to world affairs to understand the implications for their
own lives of the policies their government pursues abroad. On most

foreign policy issues only about 25 percent of the electorate is sufficiently knowledgeable to have an informed judgment; 30 percent are likely to have no opinion at all.[10] Intimidated by the complexity and scale of the problems, most citizens cannot even imagine how alternative policies might work. Struggles in remote places that most Americans cannot find on a map do not arouse much interest unless there is an American connection, and even then the national attention span is not long. Foreign policy can be safely left to the "experts" except when it ceases to be foreign, that is, when significant numbers of American troops are involved, American economic interests are clearly challenged, or when the national honor is thought to be at stake.

The history of the people's role in the choice of war and peace is inextricably intertwined with the successive revolutions in the technology of communications and in the arts of persuasion. As the composition of the electorate has changed, so have the techniques for influencing and tabulating public opinion. Today the measurement of public opinion is still largely impressionistic despite great advances in the technology of polling. In earlier periods there was no pretense that public opinion could be scientifically measured. The widespread use of public opinion sampling dates only from the administration of Franklin D. Roosevelt. Polling creates opinion in the process of monitoring it. Citizens with only the fuzziest notion of an issue will stand up and be counted when confronted by a pollster. In response to multiple-choice questions posed on Tuesday they will adopt an opinion they did not know they had on Monday, and it may well be forgotten by Friday. But a substantial proportion of citizens does eventually form firm judgments on highly publicized foreign policy issues, and these shifts can be detected by conducting repeated polls over several months or years.

Before the advent of modern polling, presidents and their advisers used to divine the public mood from letters people wrote, from audiences with petitioners, from the political slant of the popular newspapers, from the reports of trusted friends around the country, even from the sort of hats citizens wore. And, hats aside, they still sniff out the public mood in much the same ways. But there are times when people make their views on foreign policy known more dramatically by marching, rioting, and burning presidents in effigy. Just as there is a long tradition of foreign governments seeking to influence American opinion—the British Lobby in the early decades of this century and in recent years the Israeli Lobby—so, as we shall see, there is also a tradition of American citizens conducting their own foreign policy in private.

As the United States faces the new century and a new post–Cold War world, the nation is becoming integrated into a world economy over which it exercises less and less control. The fragile membrane that separates "foreign" and "domestic" affairs is fast disappearing. The role of warfare in international politics is changing. Yet the lack of serious public debate about these historic developments is striking. Politicians running for office are largely silent about the most crucial choices facing the nation, almost as if it were impossible to say something sensible about the fundamentally new challenges facing the country on the threshold of the new century and still get elected. Is the United States inhibited by our domestic political system from adapting to the demands of a radically new global environment? For two hundred years the managers of United States foreign policy have looked upon the American people much as a lawyer regards a difficult client who gets in the way of the case. This book is the story of how that critical relationship has evolved.

PART ONE

———

A REPUBLIC
IF YOU CAN KEEP IT

CHAPTER 1

Passionate Attachments

1.

In the earliest years of the Republic Americans cared passionately about foreign affairs. Four months after George Washington took the oath of office as president the electrifying news arrived that the Bastille had fallen. For the next four years citizens congregated on the streets of Philadelphia, Charleston, and New York, and in the coffeehouses, taverns, and courthouses, to argue about whether the bloody French Revolution was a glorious rage for liberty or "Cannibal's Progress," as one Federalist pamphlet termed it. Even in Puritan Boston where the clergy thundered from the pulpit against the antireligious ideas making their way from France, citizens put on a "civic feast" in the style of revolutionary France, an orgy of rum punch and roasted ox with fiery political speeches under flickering lanterns decorated with scenes of the Bastille in ruins. In this celebration of liberty and equality sixteen hundred loaves of bread were consumed.[1]

Far more than the modern-day television viewer, Americans felt themselves to be participants in the political drama beyond American shores, not just a passive audience. Citizens were excited about what was happening in Europe and active in pressing their views directly on government because the upheavals of the Continent were not seen as foreign affairs. European powers still controlled major North American outposts and rivers, and the vulnerability of the new nation to foreign attack was obvious. In the age of George Washington the Revolutionary spirit was still alive; men who had only recently disrupted their lives and risked them to fight the tyrant

George III were suspicious that the new American aristocracy now in power was trying to re-create Britain in America.

If the political debates of Washington's time sound petty, vicious, and even more personal than the negative campaigns of our own day, the difference reflects the wariness of post-Revolutionary Americans. Citizens, that is the roughly 5 percent of the total population who voted, did not assume that the men whom they elected to high office would discover the national interest disinterestedly, as if by revelation. It went without saying that personal loyalties, personal fortunes, political debts, and class interests would affect their decisions. It was a duty of citizens to honor their elected leaders, and to watch them.

Many Americans had been born in Europe and most still thought of themselves, as Thomas Jefferson did, as Virginians or as having primary allegiance to some other former colony rather than to the national government waiting to move to a Federal City not yet built; being American was a tentative identity based on powerful hopes and an ambiguous past. During the eight years of the Articles of Confederation, the United States was more a collectivity of duchies than a nation. The British foreign minister refused to send an envoy to the infant Republic with the cutting observation that he could not afford to send thirteen. With a barely functioning central government, the economy of the United States was threatened by the massive war debt, and its social fabric was still frayed by the lingering antagonisms between Revolutionary patriots and loyalists to the Crown.

In the infancy of the Republic there was nothing foreign about the wars of Europe. The continued independence of the territory wrested from the British Crown was by no means sure, for Britain, France, Russia, and Spain still held large chunks of North America. Nine years after the British had surrendered at Yorktown, the Republic still faced enemies on all sides. The British held seven military posts in the Northwest Territory, including Fort Niagara and Detroit. To the north the governor of Canada talked of turning the entire territory between the Great Lakes and the Ohio River into a satellite Indian state that would include a substantial bite out of Vermont and New York. To the south the Spanish had possession of Florida and Louisiana and controlled navigation at the mouth of the Mississippi. But their hold on the New World was weakening, and Secretary of State Thomas Jefferson worried, as he wrote Washington on July 12, 1790, that the British would take over Spanish possessions and upset the balance of power in the New World.[2]

The United States would then face a British squeeze from all directions, land and sea. If the British ever consolidated their hold over the territories bordering the thirteen states, the very survival of the new nation would be in jeopardy.

Foreign policy was a burning issue in the infant Republic because it was a metaphor for the political struggle to define what the United States was to be. It was not only that people who identified themselves as republicans felt a strong emotional attachment to France and its heroic efforts for liberty and those who called themselves Federalists still considered themselves in some sense English, but the two radically different European models of society forced choices in domestic American politics. England and France acted as polar pulls on America, each seized upon as a symbol of a whole worldview. The Jeffersonian vision of the United States was an agrarian society of small farmers. Not only did France symbolize democracy even as England was the embodiment of monarchist tyranny, but France was also the prime market for the agricultural goods of the South. For Hamilton, economics and blood dictated an everlasting tie with England. He passionately believed in a strategy of economic development based on manufacturing under the guiding hand of a strong, activist central government. England was the key to this strategy. He wished to see the gardens, the stately homes, and all the other aristocratic amenities of British civilization transplanted to the New World. After all, as he put it, "We think in English." Most important, he considered British capital and British technology indispensable to the growth of industrial capitalism in America. To the merchants and shippers on the eastern seaboard it made perfect sense to cultivate ties with Britain.

But George Washington wished to steer clear of entanglements with either France or Britain. The cornerstone of his foreign policy, as he put it years later in the Farewell Address, was the avoidance of "passionate attachments" to any other nation. This strategy of political detachment was much like the nonalignment policies articulated by the leaders of newly liberated nations emerging from colonization after World War II, and it was rooted firmly in the colonial past. In 1776 Thomas Paine in *Common Sense* had succeeded in arousing strong public sentiment for independence by arguing that dependence on Great Britain "tends directly to involve this Continent in European wars and quarrels. . . . As Europe is our market for trade, we ought to form no partial connection with any part of it."[3] The desire to be isolated from Europe, not only politically but spiritually—"to shake off the dust of Babylon," as

Increase Mather had put it—was a strong American sentiment from the first.[4] Washington understood that the security of the new nation required it to remain aloof from Europe's wars and to obtain assistance from several great European powers so as not to be beholden to any one of them. All this demanded a cool calculation of interests, agile diplomacy, and that show of strength on which the survival of the weak depends.

In no event would it have been easy to play the game of nations against the British and Spanish monarchs and the revolutionary regime in France, but the United States, having been invented as an expression of popular sovereignty, had a special problem. To establish stable relations with other nations it needed the consent of the governed. Washington and Jefferson could feel the hot breath of public passion as men brawled in the streets of America over what was happening in Europe, or better, what they thought was happening.

For the Jeffersonians—who to the confusion of future generations began to call themselves Republicans and then Democrats— the French Revolution revalidated the original democratic ideals of the American Revolution. "All the old spirit of 1776 is rekindling," Thomas Jefferson wrote in excitement to James Monroe.[5] America could not survive if France failed, Catherine Macauly Graham exclaimed in a letter to her friend Samuel Adams. Such extreme expressions of solidarity were uncommon, but no one doubted that the fate of the young Republic was intertwined with the social and political struggles of Europe. The contagion of liberty spreading across Europe would create a congenial climate for the fragile roots of republicanism to take hold in America. Unlike today, when "democracy" has been appropriated by all manner of authoritarian regimes, the word did not have motherhood status in the eighteenth century. Even so enthusiastic a supporter of popular sovereignty as Thomas Jefferson hesitated to use it as the name for the party he led because the word smacked of mob rule.

In the years just after the French Revolution it was not uncommon for a crowd to gather at the dock when a French vessel arrived and, depending on its political beliefs, harass or defend the visiting sailors. If you were pro-French, you wore a crimson silk "liberty cap" or a tricolored French cockade or you hoisted such headgear high onto a "liberty pole," daring the promonarchists to knock it off. (At the height of the Reign of Terror five hundred enthusiasts of the French Revolution gathered daily at the Tontine Coffee House in New York to keep a crowd of furiously anti-French Americans from capturing the liberty cap.) When the citizen army of France beat back the monarchs of Europe in 1792, Americans danced in the streets. Soon Philadelphians and Charlestonians began addressing one another as "Citizen" and "Citizeness" in the manner of revolutionary France, even using the titles in marriage announcements and death notices. In Boston Royal Exchange Alley became Equality Lane.

Washington, Hamilton, and the other Federalists who dominated the cabinet counted on the bloody reports from Paris to dampen some of the dangerous democratic impulses that the French Revolution had encouraged in the New World. When the news reached America that the king of France had been beheaded, some Americans began to have second thoughts about the revolution in France. But others openly rejoiced. In Philadelphia, one disgusted journalist reported, the king was guillotined in effigy twenty or thirty times a day. On the anniversary of the execution a dinner was held in that same city at which a pig was decapitated at the table, and the guests, decked out in liberty caps, attacked the severed head, shouting "Tyrant!" But all through the United States the killing of the king shocked even convinced republicans, for regicide was an assault on order itself. In Providence, as the strongly pro-French *National Gazette* reported, the people "fell into an immediate state of dejection."[6] The ladies of Philadelphia, Jefferson noted, were "openmouthed against the murder of a sovereign." It was not only the upper classes who recoiled in horror. In the "beer houses, taverns and places of public resort," one outraged Philadelphia citizen wrote, "our good allies, the French, are branded with every felonious epithet."[7]

Church bells tolled throughout the nation for the king who had made himself a friend of revolution in the New World without a thought that it could spread to the Old. Fearful that the Reign of Terror was making monarchists out of the shocked citizenry, Jeffersonians became apologists for all things French, including the bloodshed. "Everything was conducted with the greatest decency," the *Connecticut Gazette* assured its readers.[8] Jefferson wrote Madison that making "monarchs amenable to punishment like any other criminal" was progress.[9] But Tory papers like John Fenno's *Gazette of the United States* reprinted lurid accounts of the execution from the British press along with heartrending poems about the royal martyr.[10] On the other hand, in New York the theaters competed with one another to produce plays in celebration of the event— *Tyranny Supressed*, *The Demolition of the Bastille*, and *Louis XVI*

—and they all played to cheering audiences. "By a strange kind of reasoning," Oliver Wolcott, Hamilton's chief assistant at the Treasury, wrote, "some suppose that the liberties of America depend on the right of cutting throats in France."[11]

In 1793 the French proclaimed a "war of all people against all kings," and crowds in American cities broke into cheers at the news. Britain was soon drawn into the Coalition of the Kings to crush the French Revolution. Five years earlier under the Articles of Confederation the United States had signed a defensive alliance with France, and Britain began to treat its lost colonies as a hostile power. British ships searched American vessels on the high seas, seized American sailors, even chased American ships into U.S. harbors. At the news angry mobs poured into the streets of Boston, and the wardens of Christ's Church, hearing the outrage in their voices, quickly took down a bas-relief of George III from the front of the church. Men "staggered out of the beer-houses to shout imprecations on a government that would not war on England."[12]

Then the British stepped up the pressure on the United States. Orders in Council were passed in London directing His Majesty's navy to treat any neutral ship carrying goods to the French West Indies as a prize of war. A number of American merchantmen were quickly seized and their cargoes were confiscated. The purpose was to keep American food from France. In New York the popular actor John Hodgkinson appearing on the stage as a British officer had to interrupt the drama and explain that he was playing "a coward and a bully" before the angry crowd would let him go on. To the unabashed Anglophilia of Hamilton's supporters the Philadelphia *Daily Advertiser* responded with a bit of doggerel typical of the day:

From the speechification of Sedgewick and Ames
Some might think that they both had drank deep of the Thames

Despite the treaty of alliance with France, Washington issued a Proclamation of Neutrality, because he feared that the public pressure for war against England might become irresistible. This unleashed a storm. It "wounds the national honor," wrote James Madison, "by seeming to disregard the stipulated duties to France" and "wounds the popular feeling by a seeming indifference to the cause of liberty."[13] Alexander Hamilton wrote a series of newspaper articles defending neutrality, signing them "Pacificus," which fooled no one. James Madison, alias "Helvidius," wrote a series of stinging rebuttals. ("For God's sake, my dear Sir," Jefferson had written his friend, who was then the leading member of the House of Representatives, "take up your pen, select the most striking heresies and cut him to pieces."[14] To be pro-British, Madison argued, was to appeal to those "who hate our republican government." Washington's assertion that the executive alone could proclaim neutrality despite treaty obligations to France was to import the "royal prerogatives" of England. Hamilton thought Jefferson had a "womanish attachment to France"[15] and suspected that his antipathy to England was traceable to the fact that, like many southerners, he owed money to London banks. The Jeffersonians accused the secretary of the treasury of being a close friend of the British minister, George Hammond, which was true, and of having "a heavy investment in English funds," a charge that Commodore Nicholson, president of the New York Democratic Society, said he could prove and would publish the instant Hamilton announced for public office.[16]

Political parties in the United States were conceived in the growing discord over foreign policy. The Republican Party was organized first in Virginia and then in other states by using as a rallying point the popular opposition to Washington's Neutrality Proclamation. "In Connecticut, as elsewhere," the historian Alexander DeConde writes, "differing views on foreign policy provided the issue which split the people into two political groups or parties. . . . To Jefferson and other Republican leaders the unanimity of sentimental appeal offered by the French Revolution . . . presented political opportunities which they did not fail to utilize for party purposes. . . . In Pennsylvania, too, foreign policy split the people politically; year after year the governor referred to foreign policy in his message to the state legislature."[17]

George Washington believed, as the diplomat and writer of the day William Vans Murray put it, that "a wise govt. will never, in a free country go to War against the feelings of the People—but it will often refuse to go to war to indulge the heat of the public mind."[18] Willing to risk the public outcry that the Proclamation of Neutrality was virtually certain to arouse, the president issued it just two weeks after the arrival of Edmond Genet, the ambassador from revolutionary France. Citizen Genet, as he insisted upon being addressed, had come with the avowed object of stirring up popular support for France. A child prodigy who never grew up, impulsive, romantic, an eloquent speechmaker and good company, he managed to charm the crowds on his well-publicized journey north from Charleston. But his activities went considerably beyond campaigning. Having raised the money from sympathetic Americans, he bought two sailing ships and outfitted them with American crews to attack British shipping. His mission was to establish a base in the United States for privateers to fight the British on the high seas and to make raids on the Spanish possessions of Louisiana and Florida, in short to pull America into the war against England. In furtherance of this strategy he was offering commissions to Americans in the "French Army of the Mississippi."[19] The Revolutionary War hero George Rogers Clark, who had been grabbing land through corrupt dealings with the Georgia legislature, eagerly accepted one. When the Federalists complained of Genet's unconventional activities, he threatened to go over the head of the president and put his case directly to the people.

While Washington, Jefferson, and Hamilton debated whether to receive this "upstart," as Gouverneur Morris, Washington's envoy in Paris, called him, the French minister was met everywhere by enthusiastic throngs. Church bells sounded. French flags fluttered. Crimson liberty caps were thrown high in the air and "La Marseillaise" rang out all along his route as the elegant diplomat's carriage made its way to Philadelphia. Leading citizens of Philadelphia threw a fabulous dinner for him—at the enormous sum of four dollars a plate—and most of the crowd went wild. "What hugging and rugging! What mountebanking!" recalled one who didn't.[20] Washington decided to receive the envoy, but with calculated coldness in a room in which portraits of the recently executed Louis XVI and Marie Antoinette were prominently displayed. Genet, who had written his superiors in Paris of "the enthusiasm and entire devotion of our brothers in the United States," reported that "old Washington envies me my success."[21]

Years later John Adams wrote Jefferson how vividly he still remembered "the terrorism excited by Genet in 1793, when ten thousand people in the streets of Philadelphia, day after day, threatened to drag Washington out of his house, and effect a revolution in the government, or compel it to declare war in favor of the French revolution and against England."[22] Captivated by Genet, excited citizens seemed to pay scant attention to the stubborn facts of American weakness. Old grievances against England still rankled: discrimination against American shipping, encouragement of secessionist sentiment in Vermont, connivance with the Indians. Most important, the British were not carrying out the terms of the peace treaty concluded in Paris after the end of the Revolutionary War.

There were too many disturbing signs that Britain was not yet reconciled to the loss of the colonies.

Congress appropriated money for a six-ship navy, and for the
fortification of the port cities of the Atlantic coast. Grocers, bakers,
sailmakers, lawyers, and all sorts of others rushed to organize themselves into voluntary work brigades to help put up the battlements.
Congress voted a partial and temporary embargo, and individual
citizens took it upon themselves to enforce it. Resolutions for trade
retaliation against the British flooded Congress. The cry for war was
especially strong in the South, where plantation owners and dependent communities were heavily in debt to the British. "Compared
with New-England," the Federalist Fisher Ames exclaimed, "the
multitude in those towns [Norfolk and Baltimore] are but half civilized."[23] Governor Moultrie of South Carolina openly defied the
Neutrality Proclamation by allowing a privateer to be outfitted in
Charleston for service in the French cause. When federal authorities complained, he made an elaborate show of chasing it with two
impossibly slow sailing vessels.

"You cannot imagine," John Adams wrote his wife, Abigail,
"what horror some persons are in, lest peace should continue. The
prospect of peace throws them into distress."[24] Every day the war
spirit grew stronger. "Even the Monocrat [Jefferson's term for Fed-
eralist] papers are obliged to publish the most furious Philippics
against England."[25] The same issues that wrenched Washington's
cabinet were leading politicians to heap insults on one another in
legislative assemblies and crowds of ordinary citizens to curse pro-
English politicians at mass meetings and to burn them in effigy.
The House of Representatives, in control of Republicans after the
elections of 1792 (though party labels were not yet used), adjourned
in pandemonium when Abraham Clark of New Jersey, an aged
signer of the Declaration of Independence, shaking with rage, accused a Maryland congressman of being a British agent. The Boston
Centinel, a Federalist paper, promptly called Madison a French
agent.[26]

When Tocqueville almost two generations later wrote of the "tendency of a democracy to obey its feelings rather than its calculations," this was the time he had in mind. However, the enthusiasm
for fighting England, which was most pronounced in the South,
was rooted in more than a belief in the Rights of Man and a sense
of obligation for French help in the revolution. For the nation as a
whole, trade with Britain was far more lucrative than trade with

France—three-quarters of all foreign commerce was with Britain—
but France bought far more of the agricultural produce of the
South than England did. Some southerners, as Federalists charged,
wanted to fight England to get compensation for the slaves that the
British had captured during the war. Genet had been skillful in
playing to the economic interests of the South, proposing that the
American debt to France from the Revolutionary War now be used
to finance purchases of flour, rice, ships, and arms. This, as one
interested Virginian wrote the French envoy, would make it possible to combine "exertion in the Cause of Freedom" with "the
prospect of accumulating wealth."[27]

Then suddenly two things happened to turn public opinion
against Genet. The French had captured the British brig *Little
Sarah*, and the energetic ambassador had it outfitted as a privateer
and was arranging to send it out from Philadelphia harbor to attack
British shipping in open defiance of Washington's proclamation.
"Genet has totally overturned the republican interest in Philadelphia," a prominent anti-Federalist reported to Jefferson.[28] Madison
now declared that the Frenchman who so recently had been the
symbol of republican hopes was exhibiting the conduct "of a mad-
man." Washington demanded his recall, but Genet decided not to
risk his head by returning. Instead, he married the daughter of New
York's Governor Clinton, abandoned all revolutionary fervor, and
settled down to life as a country squire on the Hudson.

At this point the British took steps to cool the war hysteria by
allowing American trade in the Caribbean to resume and even paying compensation for confiscated cargoes. Although Washington
was pleased that these British moves had for the moment "allayed
the violence of the heat," the Federalists in power felt that they had
narrowly escaped being swept into a disastrous war by unbridled
popular passion. "*Le peuple souverain*," John Adams wrote in despair, "as proud and as inflammable as kings [are] continually committing some intemperance or indiscretion or other, tending to
defeat all our precautions."[29]

2.

The Federalists in office were terrified by angry crowds because they
had so recently felt their power. In the last years under the Articles
of Confederation it was not uncommon for citizens to take direct
action against government. In Rhode Island debtors took over the
legislature and started issuing paper money. The New Hampshire

legislature was surrounded by several hundred men demanding tax relief and easy money. In Northampton, Springfield, Worcester, and Athol farmers took up guns to prevent the collection of debts and land foreclosures. Daniel Shays marched on Boston with a thousand men. "I was once as strong a republican as any man in America," wrote Noah Webster after the outbreak of Shays's Rebellion. "Now, a republican is among the last kinds of government I should choose. . . . I would sooner be the subject of the caprice of one man, than to the ignorance and passions of the multitude."[30]

But republican sentiment was growing. Political clubs, anti-Federalist in their politics and known both as "democratic societies" and "republican societies," began to spring up in Philadelphia; Norfolk, Virginia; Lexington, Kentucky; and other major cities. By 1800 there were close to fifty of them. Tracing their lineage from the Sons of Liberty and the Patriotic Societies of pre-Revolutionary times, the political societies were discussion groups where philosophical works—of Paine, Rousseau, and Locke—were passionately debated. Leading citizens participated. In Philadelphia, for example, David Rittenhouse, a celebrated astronomer and scientific instrument maker, Benjamin Franklin Bache, Ben Franklin's grandson, and Charles Biddle, a prominent Quaker merchant, were members. Their purpose was to oppose what they saw as the aristocratic, centralist tendencies of George Washington's government, to fight changes in state constitutions that threatened to reduce popular representation, and to keep alive the issue of "taxation without representation" that had sparked the Revolution. "There is a disposition in the human mind to tyrannize when cloathed with power," declared the circular announcing the German Republican Society of Philadelphia, the first of the political societies. "Men therefore who are entrusted with it, should be watched with the eye of an eagle."[31]

Study groups on the Constitution were set up in Vermont and Pennsylvania. The United Freemen of Mingo Creek distributed laws passed by the Pennsylvania Assembly so that citizens could study them and recommend "capable persons" to serve in the legislature. The New York Democratic Society with the help of Albert Gallatin, later secretary of the Treasury, prepared an exposé of Federalist "intrigue and artifice" at the Constitutional Convention. "But let the people be led to the means of deliberate, unbiased investigation, and they will decide rightly," declared Elias Buell, president of the Democratic Society of Rutland, Vermont, in a Fourth of July oration in 1796.[32] Everywhere these clubs pressed for free education, protection of free speech and inquiry, and led the attack on the Alien and Sedition Acts of 1798—which were in no small measure directed at them.

The purpose of these societies, as one historian of the movement observes, was not so much to intervene directly in elections but to change the political culture, that is, "to alter the national political scene from one where popular involvement was low and factional politics still possible into one where public opinion rather than intrigue would be the vital factor in elections. The Federalists would then lose their advantage."[33] At times the societies resorted to direct action; at least three of them were involved in planning the Whiskey Rebellion of western Pennsylvania, a riot against Alexander Hamilton's excise tax on strong drink to support his economic program and to raise an army, neither of which the farmers wanted. But their principal purpose was to promote civic education, to agitate against the "obsolete phraseology" in which lawyers cast the laws to keep the people in the dark about what their representatives were deciding, and to propagandize and lobby on the great issues of the day.

Foreign policy was almost always a concern, because every local issue was mixed up in some way with foreign affairs: matters of trade; navigation on the Mississippi, the St. Lawrence, or rivers farther to the west held either by Britain, France, or Spain; dealings with Indian tribes; and frontier security. For the first generation of citizens of the United States of America, foreign policy was inseparable from domestic politics. Politics excited the interest of traders, bankers, shippers, and landowners because it was the arena for the calculation and pursuit of economic interest. But for a larger number of free men who had the rights of citizens, politics was sport, not spectator sport as it has become, but a form of self-expression that was as much a part of daily life as eating.[34]

The Federalists regularly attacked the societies, arguing that clubs made up of people who "set themselves up as umpires between the people and the government" had no legitimacy under the Constitution. "By clubbing together," the leading Federalist newspaper warned, a few citizens actually could usurp the powers of government, "set[ting] at nought the vote of a citizen who minds his own business and joins no dark meetings."[35] George Washington was opposed to the whole concept of political clubs. He dissuaded his nephew Bushrod from supporting Patrick Henry's plan to establish societies in Virginia to "instruct" the delegates to the legislature on how to vote. Such "self-created" citizens' clubs posed a threat to orderly government.

Unlike Hamilton, Madison, and Jefferson, Washington engaged in little abstract theorizing about public opinion. His views were tempered in the heat of battle. He accepted the fact that the country, though divided, was predominantly pro-French, but he thought that that was precisely the reason not to give in to public opinion, that it was better to bend over backward not to provoke Great Britain into war even if such a stance had its political risks. His standard reply to critics was to argue that the Constitution had given the treaty-making power to the president and the Senate, and they, "without passion [and with the best means of information]," would assemble "those facts and principles upon which the success of our foreign relations will always depend." As president his duty was "to overlook all personal, local and partial considerations . . . and to consult only the substantial and permanent interests of our country."[36]

The Federalists stressed the sinister connection between the unwelcome political activists in America and the bloody Jacobins of Paris, calling the democratic societies "nursuries of sedition." (A political club in Charleston did accept membership in the Jacobin Club of Paris.[37]) But having characterized the anti-Federalist activists as a "secret aristocracy" of nobodies, a few avowed aristocrats decided to form a club of their own. The arch-Federalist Fisher Ames credited the Federalist club in Suffolk County for his surprise electoral victory over Samuel Adams, who was much better known. But normally the Federalists, wishing to do nothing to legitimate the idea of popular participation, gathered in secret.

About 10 percent of the white population, Jackson Main has estimated in *The Social Structure of Revolutionary America*, were rich landowners and merchants, and about half the country's wealth, he calculates, was in their hands. But while the democratic clubs had merchants, doctors, lawyers, and public officials as members, the largest groups in the Charleston and Philadelphia societies were made up of tanners, blacksmiths, shotmakers, scriveners, coachmakers, bakers, and the like.[38] When the clubs came under attack, some of the more influential members dropped out, leaving only "the lowest order of mechanics, laborers, and draymen," as one prominent New York Federalist put it.[39] The Tammany societies in New York, begun as benevolent organizations for veterans of the Revolutionary War too humble in origins to get into the aristocratic

Society of the Cincinnati, turned to politics and attracted people near the bottom of American society. But blacks and women were out altogether, and because the clubs were in the cities for the most part, few farmers in outlying rural areas participated. Eighty percent of the population was still engaged in agriculture.[40]

One hundred and fifty years before the age of the Gallup Poll, when taking the country's temperature became a scientific and profitable undertaking, the visible activities of the political societies provided the Federalists in office with a window on public opinion. The press offered another. "The most important newspapers in the generation after the Revolution," writes the historian Allan Nevins, "were small dingy once-folded sheets which printed fragmentary commercial and political intelligence, some advertisements, and long editorials."[41] These newspapers were nothing other than political instruments, for there was little information in them, and they were entertaining only when some public figure was being skewered. (John Adams blamed his retirement on the "collection of libels" written about him by the prominent editors of the day.) Alexander Hamilton helped Noah Webster, later famous for his *Compendious Dictionary*, to set up *American Minerva*, a newspaper to promote the Federalist cause. John Fenno, another Hamilton protégé, published what he himself liked to think of as the "court journal," which shamelessly fawned on the rich and wellborn who were then running the government.

But Thomas Jefferson got his own paper first. He helped James Madison's penurious Princeton classmate Philip Freneau, the fiery "poet of the Revolution," who was even more passionate a republican than Jefferson himself, to start what became the leading newspaper of the Jeffersonian cause, the *National Gazette*. He appointed Freneau clerk for foreign languages in the State Department at two hundred fifty dollars a year and told Madison that he was willing to offer him "the perusal of all my letters of foreign intelligence and all foreign newspapers" and to subsidize the *Gazette* by letting it publish "all proclamations and other public notices within my department, and the printing of the laws."[42] The early American newspapers were filled with agitated letters from irate citizens, but for the most part these were carefully selected to serve as the chorus for the editor's song. Washington read the opposition papers regularly. Freneau made a point of making sure that two copies of the *Gazette* were put on the presidential desk. Each week there were virulent attacks on Hamilton, the president, even Martha Washington. But Washington did not take Freneau's editorials as evidence of public opinion, preferring to rely on friends around the country from whom he regularly solicited more congenial reports.[43]

The best way to tell what people were thinking and feeling in those days was to watch what they did on public occasions. Politics spilled into the churches. Broadsides were pasted up on the walls. Ushers would pass out political tracts. Few Sundays would pass without a hellfire sermon on the godless French. An alliance with France, ministers warned their parishioners, was a pact with the Devil.[44] The Federalists packed the theaters and whipped up the audience by getting it to sing "Hail, Columbia" and the "President's March," which were really Federalist hymns. When republicans in attendance objected and demanded pro-French tunes, even bribing the musicians to stop playing the Federalist songs, the rest of the audience rose from their seats and began pelting the musicians and breaking their instruments.[45]

3.

When Thomas Jefferson was ferried across the Hudson to take charge of the foreign policy establishment of the United States (five employees including a part-time translator in an office on Broadway with a budget of $8,000), he found himself clashing with Alexander Hamilton, the secretary of the treasury, over virtually every issue of domestic and foreign affairs. Of all the men around Washington, Alexander Hamilton was the clearest about what he thought of popular sovereignty. Government should be in the hands of "the rich and well-born"—to whose ranks he had arranged to be admitted despite his own humble beginnings—for "the people are turbulent and changing; they seldom judge or determine right."[46] He had argued before the Constitutional Convention that the president and the Senate should be chosen for life, and he was always frank to say that he had no use whatever for public opinion.

The secretary of state, a tall, sandy red-haired Virginian with a "loose shackling air" and a "rambling vacant look," as one senator described him, found almost every aspect of the Hamiltonian vision —big government, centralized authority, public debt, aristocratic style—offensive, wrong, or subversive. And he resented nothing more than that this man of lowly birth and studied elegance who abhorred the French Revolution but came to admire Napoleon should keep interfering in foreign affairs. (The British minister, who became Hamilton's personal friend, made a point of reporting to the secretary of the treasury instead of the secretary of state.) For Jefferson, France, despite the excesses of the Revolution, was to be honored for her enemies, "the confederacy of princes against human liberty."[47]

Despite his insouciant talk of watering the tree of liberty with blood every twenty years or so and his celebration of political passion—the American Revolution was the work of American "hearts," the "pulsations of our warmest blood"[48]—Thomas Jefferson, the most radical democrat among the Founding Fathers, shared his friend John Adams's fear of "mobs . . . debased by ignorance, and vice."[49] His argument for self-government rested on principles of human nature, but these he modified in the light of experience. As Garry Wills has shown, Jefferson believed that "common sense" and "moral sense" are widely distributed in the population. Just as some men may be born blind, he argued, "it would be wrong to say that man is born without . . . sight. The want or imperfection of the moral sense in some men . . . is no proof that it is a general characteristic of the species."[50] Negroes he considered inferior in intelligence but equal to whites in "benevolence, gratitude, and unshaken fidelity."[51] Theoretically, they possessed the moral sense justifying equal treatment as citizens, but he preferred the idea of freeing the slaves en masse and deporting them. Women he considered "too wise to wrinkle their forehead with politics."

What men did and where they lived were more important than their natural endowments. Though even in the lowest classes there were talented individuals to be "raked from the rubbish," he was contemptuous of artisans and mechanics as a class, considering them to be "the panders of vice and the instruments by which the liberties of a country are generally overturned."[52] He had a pronounced distaste for cities, which he talked of as if they were malodorous rabbit warrens. "The mobs of great cities," he once exclaimed, "add just so much to the support of pure government, as sores do to the strength of the human body."[53] The North, he thought, represented the nation's head; and the South, its heart; and since he preferred even the vices of the heart (being "fiery, voluptuary, indolent, and unsteady") to those of the head (coldness, calculation), even in the White House he could never bear being with icy New England bankers and preachers.[54]

Jefferson and Hamilton did agree on one thing: The new nation must not become involved in Europe's wars. The reasons were self-evident. The regular army consisted of 672 officers and men. In the fall of 1791 Washington had sent the whole army reinforced by about fifteen hundred volunteers into battle against the Indian village of Maumee, near what is now Fort Wayne, in order to put up an American fort there. (The Americans feared that the British were about to incite the Indians to attack.) But this first major battle had ended in disaster; after an ambush almost half the force was killed or wounded. The navy was in no better shape. After the Revolutionary War it had been completely disbanded. The Barbary pirates were preying on American merchantmen, seizing their crews and turning them into galley slaves or throwing them into deep dungeons. Secretary of State Jefferson told Congress that the choices were "war, tribute, and ransom." Congress voted for ransom, appropriating $2,000 a head, a considerable sum at a time when Jefferson's own annual salary was $3,500. Captain John Paul Jones was entrusted with delivering the cash to the pirates, but death spared the naval hero from carrying out so inglorious a mission.

As crowds in America shouted the famous cry "Millions for defense but not one cent for tribute," an American vessel docked at Algiers with twenty-six barrels of dollars of ransom money. After he became president in 1801 and the navy had been rebuilt, Jefferson sent warships to the Mediterranean and broke the pirates' hold on American commerce. But the humiliations of the 1790s caused many Americans to want to strike out at their array of tormentors in the Old World. The Federalists in office, well aware that public anger at England played into the hands of the Jeffersonians, decided to take a decisive step to defuse the popular rage and the rising pressure for war.

The Jay Mission to London was from the start a political move to shore up the sagging fortunes of the Federalists. John Jay, who had been secretary of foreign affairs under the Articles of Confederation, was now Chief Justice of the United States. He was a tall, courtly man with a view of democracy that accorded perfectly with Hamilton's. "That portion of the people who individually mean well," he once wrote, "never was, nor until the millennium will be, considerable."[55] Not only did his demeanor betray his contempt of the crowd but his pro-English sympathies were a matter of public record. He had written a secret report to Congress when he was running foreign affairs under the Articles of Confederation arguing that England was justified in holding on to the frontier forts in the Northwest, and over a glass of port he shared these views with the British consul in New York. The disclosure did not encourage the British to abandon the forts, and when Jay's opinions and indiscretions became public knowledge, they did nothing for his reputation. Madison wrote Jefferson that the Jay appointment was causing "the most powerful blow ever suffered by the popularity of the President."

Still, when Jay set sail for London on May 12, 1794, a thousand people assembled at Trinity Church to escort him to the ship, though the militia refused to parade in his honor. In his pocket he carried instructions prepared by Hamilton and endorsed at a secret conference of Federalist party leaders. Hamilton's economic policy depended upon peace with England, and the fate of the Federalist Party was riding on Jay's mission. In the House of Representatives James Madison rose to denounce the British for having seized 250 commercial vessels on their way to and from France. His anti-British rhetoric made good politics, for not only was it a way to attack the foundation of Hamilton's economic development strategy but it was also a way to attract the shipping interests into what would soon be known as the Republican Party. Playing to this constituency, Madison asked what sense did it make to be pro-British. The British, he reminded the House, sold the United States twice as much as they bought, while the French purchased seven times as much as they sold.[56]

Lord Grenville, the British negotiator, had, unbeknownst to Jay, a crucial piece of information as he sat down with the American minister. The Americans had little bargaining power other than the threat to join the Armed Neutrality Convention that Sweden and Denmark had organized to protect the rights of neutrals against British depredations on the high seas. But Hamilton had given secret assurances to the British minister in Washington that under no circumstances would the United States take such a step. Once again in possession of information about the private thoughts of leading American officials, the British gave barely an inch, and the result was what the diplomatic historian Samuel Flagg Bemis called the most humiliating treaty to which an American has ever put his signature. Jay had been instructed by the Federalist politicians to open up the West Indies trade, but the treaty permitted only the smallest American vessels to call at the island ports and prohibited all American vessels from carrying molasses, sugar, coffee, cocoa, and cotton to *any* port in the world outside the continental United States.

Yet the principal objective of the negotiations, getting the British to abandon their Northwest frontier posts, was achieved, and Great Britain and the British East Indies were opened to U.S. merchant vessels. By 1801, 70 percent of all trade with India was carried in American ships. Thus historians such as Samuel Eliot Morison have concluded that under the circumstances the Jay Treaty was not a bad deal. But that was by no means the contemporary view. Even Hamilton considered it an "execrable thing," though the anger of the crowd made him determined to see it ratified.

Washington considered not signing the humiliating treaty even if the Senate should consent to its ratification, particularly since the British began seizing American ships again even while Congress was deliberating on it. For the president to put his name on the document, one opponent argued, would bring down on his head "commotions, which would not only be extremely dangerous to the community, but would probably be attended with his own political destruction."[57] The president was hoping at least to threaten the British with repudiation of the treaty to get them to stop seizing American ships, but unbeknownst to the public, he was being blackmailed by His Majesty's government because of an indiscretion of a cabinet member. Letters implicating Jefferson's successor as secretary of state, Edmund Randolph, in an intrigue with the French had fallen into British hands, and they threatened to make them public if Washington did not go through with the treaty.

For eighteen days the Senate met in secret to debate ratification while public apprehension grew. A bare two-thirds voted to approve the Jay Treaty. Madison blamed what he took to be a serious defeat on the bribes and threats of "banks, the British merchants, the insurance companies," but the Jay Treaty won critical votes in the West because Washington eased its passage with a treaty with Spain to keep the Mississippi open. Others voted for the unpopular treaty because they feared dissolution of the Union. Several states, including New Jersey, announced their decision to secede if the treaty was not ratified.[58]

Fearing the public response, the Senate voted to keep the contents of the Jay Treaty secret. However, Senator Stevens Thomson Mason of Virginia struck a blow for the people's right to know and, incidentally, for Republican fortunes by giving the text to Benjamin Franklin's grandson, B. F. Bache, the editor of the *Aurora*, who immediately published it. The news rocked the country. A crowd snaked its way toward Washington's home in Philadelphia, but the cavalry was drawn up in front of the mansion, ready for the angry citizens as they surged into the street. Facsimiles of the treaty and effigies of Jay were burned in the major cities. A mob surrounded the British minister's house and broke a few windows. Speaking to what he thought was a friendly crowd by Trinity Church in New York, Alexander Hamilton was struck by a stone. In Boston the crowd was more decorous; fifteen hundred citizens poured into Faneuil Hall to consider the treaty, but not one was for it. Washington worried that public agitation against the treaty not only risked war with England but also threatened to make his government a permanent hostage to the French, who would benefit from "the spirit which is at work . . . to keep *us* and G. *Britain* at variance."[59]

By this time Hamilton had also left the cabinet, and Washington, under mounting personal attacks, could not wait to leave. His mail was tampered with. Forgeries of incriminating letters he had supposedly written were widely circulated. Anger at Washington's foreign policy was so strong that it even penetrated the armor of his heroic reputation. In the *Independent Gazetteer* "Atticus" noted that the "services of the president, during the revolution" could no longer "neutralize our indignation." Gratitude could not be expected to "put a seal upon our lips," particularly since the president had defied public opinion by signing the treaty "*after the general sentiments of his country had been made known to him, in opposition to it.*"[60] The evidence suggests that Washington would have refused a third term in any event, but the editor William Cobbett, an enthusiastic supporter, believed that "the true cause of the general's retiring was . . . the *loss of popularity* which he had experienced" principally over the Jay Treaty "and the further loss he apprehended from the rupture with France, which he looked upon as inevitable."[61]

In the election of 1796, as Samuel Eliot Morison has written, "the Jay Treaty was the central issue of the campaign." There were specific economic reasons to be for it or against it. For shippers dependent upon the West Indies trade it was a small but welcome window of opportunity. For those, in the South, especially, who depended more on France, the treaty was a disaster. The French had already made it clear what their reaction would be should the United States, after renouncing its alliance with the French Republic, move even in a modest way toward a rapprochement with the British Crown. Washington persuaded himself that it was unlikely that "the great body of Yeomanry has formed an opinion on the subject," but he knew that the treaty raised powerful emotional issues, for it reflected an American weakness in bargaining power that many Americans could not accept.[62]

The Federalists organized local birthday celebrations for George Washington wherever they could, knowing that even somewhat sullied, the reputation of the first hero of the Republic was their biggest political asset. The Republicans, on the other hand, campaigned on what they called Washington's betrayal. As one broadside in the *Jersey Chronicle* put it, "the nation has been secretly, I will not say treacherously, divorced from France, and most clandestinely married to Great Britain; we are taken from the embraces of a loving wife, and find ourselves in the arms of a detestable and abandoned whore, covered with crimes, rottenness, and corruption."[63]

Although the Federalists narrowly won, their base of support had been seriously eroded. The Jay Treaty was the first metaphorical use of a foreign policy issue in domestic politics. Many Americans took what they saw as a virtual capitulation to Britain as something more than just ill-considered foreign policy. For the Federalists to have pushed the treaty through in the face of popular opposition was a statement of Tory contempt, not just for republican values but for public opinion itself. A fight for the political control of the United States and the character of its institutions and civic culture had begun in the guise of a debate about foreign policy

4.

The public anger sparked by the Jay Treaty subsided, and Anglo-American relations improved. The episode had dramatized the problems of conducting foreign policy when the issues aroused popular emotions. John Adams, Washington's successor in the presidency, had complex, contradictory views of the role of the common man that he had inherited from European philosophers. He was caught in the contradictions between the promise on which he and the others had made a revolution and the confusing reality he saw about him. "In theory the only moral foundation of government is the consent of the people," John Adams wrote, but the "rude and insolent rabble" pursuing their private interests were often incapable of understanding, much less pursuing, the common good.[64]

Still, he never forgot the town meetings to which his father had taken him as a boy, where he had watched citizens make decisions. The "extraordinary engagement of the inhabitants of Braintree and her sister communities with the world that reached far beyond the boundaries of the town"[65] made him believe in popular government, and his own later experience in the Massachusetts legislature and in the Continental Congresses convinced him that "Government was a plain, simple, intelligible thing, founded in nature and reason, and quite comprehensible by common sense."[66] Public serice was a sacred duty, and participation in politics brought out "courage, fortitude, and enterprise, the manly, noble, and sublime qualities in human nature." But public opinion was something else, "a chaos, a Proteus—anything, everything, and nothing," he wrote his wife. The people were a force for "anarchy, licentiousness, and despotism." Adams felt the power of the Enlightenment; in theory human beings were no longer at the mercy of nature or the whims of tyrants. Yet as Voltaire himself had written in 1771, "More than half the habitable world is still populated by two-footed animals who live in horrible condition approximating the state of nature, with hardly enough to live on and clothe themselves, barely enjoying the gift of speech, barely aware that they are miserable, living and dying practically without knowing it."[67] How could such men act as citizens?

For Adams, like the other eighteenth-century rationalists who made the American Revolution, belief in the goodness, rationality, and teachability of the common man was an article of faith. Though he considered Rousseau and Helvétius confused by "naive optimism,"[68] Adams was strongly influenced by Locke, Montesquieu, Hutcheson, and Ferguson. Man is born free; he consents to the chains of despotism and he can break the chains. Kingly power corrupts; only the people know what is in their own interest. This radical myth of popular sovereignty, which was used so effectively to establish the rule of the few over the many, as Edmund Morgan has shown, was the main political weapon of the rising middle classes in the New World as well as the Old.[69] It was the foundation of Revolutionary War propaganda.[70]

But the people must be educated; otherwise self-government would be "as unnatural, irrational, and impracticable as it would be over the elephants, lions . . . and bears in the royal menagerie at Versailles."[71] But here too Adams was ambivalent. Universal education was no panacea. Greater knowledge, he argued with Benjamin Rush, would as easily make people skilled in defending their wrong opinions as in discovering the truth. Having property was surely an indispensable qualification for citizenship; "very few men who have no property, have any judgment of their own. They talk and vote as they are directed by some man of property, who has attached their minds to his interest."[72]

The Washington administration had done an ineffective job of managing public opinion because the Federalists could not disguise their contempt for both the "rabble" and the "mobocrats" who cur-ried favor with the crowd. But they taught future administrations with considerably more democratic flair an important lesson about running foreign policy. Public unhappiness about what some foreign power is doing can produce disorder, but it need not produce a change of policy. There is little the public can do if the government stands firm. In any event, memories are short. The passions of the moment are quickly forgotten. As well they should be.

Relations with England improved, but relations with France predictably worsened. The French Directory now in power in Paris considered the Jay Treaty a virtual Anglo-American alliance, and their navy stepped up its attacks on American shipping, capturing more than three hundred vessels. "Red-bonneted ruffians," Samuel Eliot Morison writes, "who represented France in the West Indies made an open traffic of blank letters of marque [authorization of the French government to seize American ships and cargoes]. Frenchmen at Charleston secretly armed American vessels to prey on American commerce." In 1796 a French general, Victor Collot, sailed down the Ohio and the Mississippi on a reconnaissance mission for a possible pincer attack on the United States to be carried out once the Directory had forced Spain to cede Florida and Louisiana to France. Meanwhile Quebec was being encouraged to declare itself a French republic, and the chief of the Creek Indians was commissioned a brigadier general in the French army. Though a French invasion was not entirely implausible, the Republicans did not swerve from their pro-French position. (When the U.S.S. *Constitution* got stuck on the ways in Boston as it was being launched, Philip Freneau wrote a poem celebrating the event. Better the ship should stay on shore than sail off to fight France.[73])

Now the Federalists became the war party. The Directory in Paris had refused to receive the new American minister, Charles Cotesworth Pinckney, a Federalist from Charleston. Oliver Wolcott, Fisher Ames, and other party leaders immediately called for a response to this insult, a rapid military buildup, and an end to all diplomatic contacts with France. For the Federalists France made the perfect enemy. (Ames later wrote—in this case he was thinking of Mexico—that the United States needed "as all nations do" some formidable foreign threat "whose presence shall at all times excite stronger fears than demagogues can inspire the people with towards their government."[74]) Hamilton, however, for the sake of uniting the country for the war he thought was coming but wished to avoid, thought one last effort should be made to reason with the French, and that a prominent Republican should be part of the mission. He proposed his two archenemies, Jefferson and Madison, certain that the mission would not enhance the reputation of either.

However, Adams chose the Massachusetts politician Elbridge Gerry to lead the mission, and as he arrived in Paris in October 1797, the Federalists, building on the growing anti-French sentiment in the country, launched a bitter campaign against the Republicans. The chief target was Thomas Jefferson, who was now vice president. William Cobbett's *Porcupine's Gazette* called him "mean and cowardly." Franklin was a "contaminated" plagiarist; Tom Paine, a debauched traitor. But as the months passed and no word from Paris arrived, the public began to turn against the war measures passed by Congress. Even in pro-British Cambridge the town meeting adopted a resolution condemning the arming of American merchant vessels to fight France.

On March 8, 1798, the explosive news arrived on President Adams's desk. Talleyrand, the French foreign minister, President Adams's envoys reported, had sent three agents to see them with a demand for a bribe: fifty thousand pounds sterling and a "loan" of $10 million as compensation for presidential "insults." Though hardly an unknown practice in those days—Britain was on the verge of paying the French 450,000 pounds a year earlier to grease the peace negotiation and Portugal was supposed to have paid a million pounds for peace with France—Adams had no intention of paying, for the country would be split open by another humiliation at the hands of a European power.[75] The president, fearing that public disclosure of what had happened to his peace mission would push him into a war he did not want, decided to withhold the incendiary information from Congress. He merely informed it that there was "no ground for expectation" that the mission would succeed.

There were cries of bad faith from the pro-French faction in Congress, and then the Republicans walked into a trap. Completely ignorant of their contents, the Jeffersonians demanded to see the dispatches from Paris. Hamilton, now a private citizen in New York, knew what they said; Thomas Jefferson, vice president of the United States, did not. Adams sent the dispatches to Congress with the letters X, Y, and Z substituted for the names of Talleyrand's blackmailers. The galleries were cleared and the doors were locked for three days while Congress debated in secret about whether and how widely to publish the inflammatory documents. Over the objections of the Republicans fifty thousand copies were printed and a wave of anti-French sentiment swept over the country, carrying

President Adams and the Federalists on its crest. John Adams basked in his new popularity, standing on the steps of his Philadelphia home in full military regalia, sword by his side, as he denounced France to the enthusiastic crowd. But later, having received a letter warning that the city would be burned, Adams had his servants bring arms and ammunition into the presidential mansion by the back door and waited for the attack of avenging Republicans that never came. Instead a prowar mob broke windows of the most prominent Republican editor and daubed Ben Franklin's statue with mud.

War hysteria grew. French invasion plots were discovered almost daily. Judges delivered perorations on the French threat in charges to juries, stern warnings that the Negroes would be armed, women ravished, and churches burned. From his Manhattan law office Hamilton drew up plans to conquer Florida, even Mexico. He and Adams, though of the same party, had become implacable political enemies. The Massachusetts aristocrat considered "the bastard brat of a Scots peddler" to be "stark mad."[76] The Republicans, tarred with the XYZ scandal, were now under full attack. At dinners in Boston, the Federalists entertained one another with anti-Jeffersonian toasts: "The Vice-President—May his heart be purged of Gallicism in the pure fire of Federalism or be lost in the furnace."[77]

In Congress the Alien Act of 1798 was pushed through by the Federalists, aimed primarily at the boatloads of Irish who were arriving in great numbers, most of them penniless, ready to serve as the "shock troops" for the Jeffersonian party. The law was a Federalist rejoinder to the attempted insurrection in Ireland that had produced what they considered to be a flood of "United Irishmen, Free Masons, and the most God-provoking Democrats this side of Hell." The Sedition Act made it a crime to write or speak against the president or Congress with intent to defame, and a congressman and several Republican editors were put in jail or given heavy fines. (For inciting the citizens of one Massachusetts town to put up a liberty pole, the "apostle of sedition" David Brown got a four-year sentence.)

In the angry mood of the moment Congress passed military appropriations far above what Adams had proposed. The legislation provided for a buildup of the navy and the strengthening of coastal defenses. That much the president wanted and the public seemed to want it too. Boston raised $125,000 in public subscriptions in a matter of weeks to build two frigates, and similar citizen initiatives in New York, Portland, Portsmouth, Charleston, Salem, Philadel-

phia, and Baltimore quickly followed. But Adams was against en-
larging the small army. (Under Major General "Mad Anthony"
Wayne the army had managed to redeem itself in 1794 by returning
to the village where it had been ambushed and this time defeating
the Indians so badly that they ceded a large chunk of the Northwest
Territory along with Vincennes, Detroit, and Chicago in return for
annuities worth about $10,000.)

Adams was worried about the expense of excessive war preparations, and he was fearful of being pushed by his supporters into a
fight he was convinced was against the national interest. Congress
had taken the initiative, against his judgment and sometimes without any consultation, to declare void all treaties with France, to
raise taxes and incur debt beyond what he considered wise, and had
come within a few votes of actually declaring war. For two years the
U.S. Navy with the help of private vessels carried on an undeclared
war against France, capturing more than eighty French privateers,
mostly in West Indian waters. The Federalists tried to squeeze the
full measure of popularity from the surge of patriotic feelings provoked by the French. A sailor's ditty of the day caught the new
mood:

> Now let each jolly tar, with one heart and one voice
> Drink a can of good grog to the man of our choice;
> Under John, the State pilot, and George's Command,
> There's a fig for the French and the sly Talleyrand.

With great fanfare Washington had been called from retirement
to command the American army to resist the French invader. But
John Adams saw no reason to increase the ground forces. "At present there is no more prospect of seeing a French army here, than
there is in Heaven,"[78] he wrote the secretary of war. He suspected
Hamilton of wanting a large army to put down domestic violence
but thought that high taxes for the unnecessary military forces
would actually provoke insurrections. The move was "altogether
desperate, altogether delirious." Like most of the American revolutionaries, he was against standing armies on principle and enough
of a politician to know that "the army is unpopular, even in the
Southern states."[79]

Events proved Adams right. High taxes and heavy-handed recruiting officers cooled public passion for war. The levying of taxes
to support the army sparked an insurrection of farmers in Pennsylvania. "Millions for defense" went the famous cry, but the bankers

were exacting their own tribute, patriotically financing the military buildup at interest rates three percentage points above the prevailing rate. Thousands of petitions poured into Congress calling for a disbanding of the army and repeal of the Alien and Sedition Acts. Thomas McKean won the governorship of Pennsylvania, Adams noted, by declaring himself "decidedly against a war with France."[80] Because the imposition of high taxes had stimulated antiwar sentiment, the Federalists did much less well than they had anticipated in Maryland and elsewhere in the elections of 1798. Foreign policy, not local issues, was decisive in several contests.

Pro-French feelings surfaced again when word leaked that the Directory was now ready to resume negotiations. Adams took note of the French cockades that "paraded before my eyes, in opposition to the black [read red, white, and blue] cockade" and ascribed the rebirth of enthusiasm for revolutionary France to the "popular eloquence of the editors of the opposition papers" with their "scoffing, scorning wit," and that "malignity of soul" exemplified in the writings of Tom Paine.[81] Several members of his cabinet took their orders from Hamilton, who was against resuming negotiations, but Adams himself wanted to explore the possibility, though not before making an impressive show of military might. "An efficient preparation for war"—the words of the presidential message to Congress sound familiar to twentieth-century ears—"can alone insure peace."[82]

In the fall of 1798 Adams felt himself being pushed by opposing waves of public opinion, both of which made him uncomfortable, one pushing him toward negotiations faster than he wanted to go, the other pushing toward war. A friend of Jefferson's, the Philadelphia Quaker George Logan, undertook a private mission to Paris at his own expense, an example of what today we would call citizen diplomacy. On his own he visited Talleyrand and convinced himself once more of what he already believed: A deal could be struck. Peace could be preserved with honor. Word of his trip leaked. The Federalists, furious that all pressure for war would be dissipated and that the army they had just begun to put together at great expense and difficulty would be disbanded, launched a campaign of vilification against Logan. The Quaker was falsely accused of giving Talleyrand a negotiating paper and passing it off as an official U.S. position. The Logan Act prohibiting private meddling in the foreign relations of the United States was passed. It is still on the books, and though its use has been threatened, particularly during the Vietnam War, no one has ever been convicted under it.

The Federalists wished to destroy Logan to get at Jefferson. They were enraged that Elbridge Gerry, the Republican member of the negotiating team, had remained in Paris when the mission had collapsed after the bribery incident. His wife, waiting for him at their home in Cambridge with the children, was terrorized by hideous catcalls in the night. Bonfires were set under her windows, and one morning as she looked out there was a miniature guillotine smeared with blood in front of the house.[83] The Federalists were even more angry when Gerry finally returned with the news that negotiations were still possible. Jefferson saw Gerry's report as a way to limit the political damage of the XYZ affair, and he urged that a précis be prepared, "stating everything . . . short, simple, and leveled to every capacity," which could be "printed in handbills, of which we could print and disperse ten or twelve thousand copies under cover letters, through all the United States by the members of Congress when they return home."[84]

Camping in the unfinished White House during his final months in office, John Adams was trying desperately to avoid war. His cabinet, made up largely of Hamiltonians, tried every maneuver to block negotiations, even sending a delegation of powerful Federalist senators to dissuade him. "I know more of diplomatic forms than all of you," Adams retorted. "It was in France that we received the insult, and in France I am determined that we shall receive the reparation." Once again the peace mission sailed off to Paris. "I have no doubt (uninformed as the public are)," Henry Knox, a former secretary of war, wrote the president, "that their entire reliance on your superior knowledge of the state of Europe and wisdom . . . will be perfectly satisfactory to ninety-nine persons out of a hundred."[85] Adams had a less sanguine view: "in general the people are ignorant, strongly prejudiced, vindictive in their resentments, incapable of being influenced except by their fears of punishment." He wrote his wife that he had sacrificed his chances for a second term. Perhaps his peace policy would appeal to moderates, but most of the voters, blinded by passion, could not discern the true interests of the country.

Federalist candidates did well in New York, Massachusetts, and throughout the South in 1800, but Adams, as he predicted, was voted out of office. The Federalist era was over. To his dying day Adams was convinced that his peace policy had been his undoing. Yet he considered his resistance to domestic political pressures the "most disinterested and meritorious action of my life." Like most successful revolutionaries, Adams was convinced that he knew what was best for the nation, and he took pride in his ability to manipulate the views of key members of Congress and other leading citizens all the while resisting the influence of "public opinion." Years later he wrote, "I desire no other inscription over my gravestone than: 'Here lies John Adams, who took upon himself the responsibility of the peace with France in the year 1800.' "[86]

CHAPTER 2

Jefferson's Coup and Madison's War

1.

For twelve years Washington and Adams had managed to keep the new nation from becoming embroiled in Continental wars. Public passions rose and fell as the European empires, now England, now France, challenged the sovereignty of the United States. Neutrality had proved to be a bumpy course, but when Thomas Jefferson became the third president, he was determined to keep to it. Despite the waves of public passion in favor of military action against England and France, both of which continued to harass American shipping on the seas, the logic of avoiding war was still irresistible. As he entered the White House, Jefferson knew that he could count on important constituencies to see that logic, particularly the traders and bankers of the East and the planters of the South.

The most insistent public pressure on American diplomacy, however, came from the West. All through the first decade of the Republic the Federalists had done little to deal with the security requirements of the frontier. Spain's possession of Florida and Louisiana gave that aging empire claim to all the land stretching from western Georgia to the Mississippi, and its control of New Orleans was a potential stranglehold on Mississippi River commerce and a brake on westward expansion.

Vocal frontier politicians like Tennessee's William Blount were heavy land speculators. The value of their millions of acres depended upon driving the Spanish out and pushing the Indians west. The Federalists in Washington, as Blount's protégé Andrew Jackson kept insisting, were paying little attention to their problems. The 1795 treaty with Spain had not secured navigation rights to the Mississippi and the Adams administration had not made the Indian threat a priority. Indeed, to the frontiersmen the administration seemed more sympathetic to Indian rights than to the needs of the West.

So important was the issue of navigation rights on the Mississippi that it threatened the survival of the United States even as it had hastened the breakup of the compact among the states under the Articles of Confederation. The Bill of Rights of the Tennessee constitution declared: "The free navigation of the Mississippi is one of the inherent rights of the citizens of this state." The God of Nature, the Democratic-Republican Society of Frankfort, Kentucky, insisted, had given the Mississippi to America. "Attachments to governments cease to be natural when they cease to be mutual. If the General Government will not procure it us, we shall hold ourselves not responsible for any consequences that may result from our own procurement of it."[1] A widely circulated letter read at town meetings and at court openings just before the Constitution was adopted called for the raising of twenty thousand troops "to drive the Spaniards from their settlements at the mouth of the river. If this is not countenanced in the East, we will throw off our allegiance and seek elsewhere for help."[2] In 1788, the year he arrived in Nashville, Andrew Jackson joined with some of the leading planters of the Cumberland settlement in a proposition to Spain. The failure of the central government under the Articles of Confederation to protect the settlement from Indian attack suggested the need to "seek a more attractive connection."[3] But the intrigues of frontier politicians did not stop once the Union was formed. James Wilkinson, for example, schemed with the Spanish for more than a decade to detach Kentucky from the United States, and remained in the pay of the Spanish long after he was appointed the ranking general of the United States Army. Jefferson felt the pressure of the frontiersmen more than Adams had for they were his natural constituency.

Not only was the president worried that Napoleon might get control of the Spanish territory and pose a mortal threat to the infant nation, but he also believed that the democratic society of yeoman farmers on which his hopes rested depended upon acquiring the territory. Small farmers in his view were the ideal citizens for a democracy, "the chosen people of God, if ever He had a chosen people, whose breasts He has made his peculiar deposit for substantial and genuine virtue."[4] Farmers could govern themselves because their affairs were simple, their communities self-contained, and their environment predictable. But a nation of spread-out communities of small farmers required an abundance of land. The people would remain virtuous, he wrote Madison right after the Constitutional Convention, "while there remains vacant lands in any part of America."[5] However, without the chance to spread out as the nation grew, Americans would find themselves "piled together upon one another in large cities, as in Europe," and then "we shall become corrupt as in Europe, and go to eating one another as they do there."[6] Jefferson was also struck by how the conflicting interests of the eastern and western states in the continuing confrontation with Britain and France had given "a new proof of the falsehood of Montesquieu's doctrine, that a republic can be preserved only in a small territory. The reverse is the truth. Had our territory been even a third only of what it is, we were gone."[7]

The new president felt popular pressure for expansion, but these sentiments were completely in accord with his own. He was greatly impressed with the idea that the population of America would explode. "However our present interests may restrain us within our limits," he wrote Monroe in 1801, "it is impossible not to look forward to distant times, when our rapid multiplication will expand it beyond those limits, & cover the whole northern if not the southern continent, with people speaking the same language, governed in similar forms, and by similar laws."[8] He was not alone among the Founding Fathers in worrying about elbowroom. As early as 1751 Benjamin Franklin raised the issue of inadequate living space in the colonies in a pamphlet anticipating Malthus entitled *Observations Concerning the Increase of Mankind*.[9] Jefferson strongly supported the attempt to take Canada in the Revolution, and the chance to try again was an important consideration when he urged war on Madison in 1812. "We must have the Floridas and Cuba," he was quoted by a visitor in his last days in the White House.[10] He once advised against establishing a penal colony for Negro criminals in some Caribbean island because, who knows, the United States might some day wish to annex it.

In 1800 Spain secretly agreed to cede Louisiana back to France in a trade for the Kingdom of Tuscany, but the deal was never completed. Napoleon saw no great reason why he should not take possession of Louisiana and keep Tuscany as well. But as he prepared to take the vast territory, the Spanish closed the port of New Orleans to American and all other neutral shipping and revoked the valuable privilege previously accorded American traders to deposit their goods at the port duty free. From the West came cries of war. "There is on the globe one single spot," Jefferson warned, "the possessor of which is our natural and habitual enemy. It is New Orleans, through which the produce of three-eighths of our territory must pass to market."[11] To deny American traders the use of the most important waterway in America was not just a commercial disaster but an affront to national dignity. Jefferson worried that the "fever" of the western mind and the "ferment" it was creating in the country would push him into taking the country to war. "The day that France takes New Orleans fixes the sentence," the president wrote Robert Livingston, the American minister in Paris. "It seals the union of two nations who in conjunction can maintain exclusive possession of the ocean. From that moment we must marry ourselves to the British fleet and nation."[12]

Though pessimistic himself about avoiding war, he wished to do nothing to inflame popular feelings. He set about making war preparations in secret. Neither Congress nor the public knew that despite his warning against "entangling alliances" in his inaugural address, he was considering one with Britain. Nor was it public knowledge that he had threatened Napoleon with war. He instructed the American minister in Paris to tell Talleyrand, the French foreign minister, that "a French take-over in Louisiana will cost France, and perhaps not very long hence, a war which will annihilate her on the ocean."[13] While he negotiated privately with both Spain and France, western legislatures were passing angry resolutions demanding the immediate dispatch of troops to New Orleans. "The measures we have been pursuing being invisible," Jefferson wrote to a friend, "do not satisfy their minds. Something sensible therefore has become necessary."[14]

By then the dispatch of a prominent individual on a highly publicized peace mission had become a tradition. To quiet talk of war and secession in the West, Jefferson announced that James Monroe, a Virginian who also was a large landowner in Kentucky and popular with westerners, would go to Paris to negotiate with Napoleon. He was authorized to pay $10 million for New Orleans and West Florida. At the same time, even though his party held both the Senate and House, Jefferson kept his diplomatic plans absolutely secret, making only a fleeting reference to Louisiana in what Alexander Hamilton called his annual "lullaby message" to Congress. But Jefferson's own party demanded the documents concerning the threat to Mississippi River commerce, and the House went into secret session to consider them. After two months the Senate passed a resolution approving the president's diplomatic efforts, but it also voted to activate eighty thousand militia for military action in Florida and New Orleans.

The Federalists kept agitating for war: "They insult our national flag . . . seize our merchantmen . . . abuse our seamen . . . yet honorable gentlemen cry out peace, peace, when there is no peace. If this be peace, God give us war!"[15] Jefferson was suspicious that the Federalists' strategy was "to force us into war if possible, in order to derange our finances, or if this cannot be done, to attach the western country to them, as their best friends, and thus get into power."[16] War talk had its effect. The Spanish minister, citing "the impulse of public opinion," urged his government to restore the right of duty-free deposit at New Orleans before the French took possession. Otherwise, "the clamor . . . will force the President and the Republicans to declare war against their wish."[17] The monarchist diplomats of Europe assumed that the republicans in office in America shared their own terror of the mob.

On June 28, 1803, a ship from Le Havre put in at Boston harbor with extraordinary news. Monroe and Livingston had signed a treaty in Paris acquiring the entire province of Louisiana. "From this day the United States take their place among the powers of the first rank," the American minister had declared as he signed. Earlier that morning Napoleon's two brothers had burst in on the emperor in his bath begging him not to give away Louisiana, but he had angrily splashed them in the face. He had lost fifty thousand troops in Haiti the year before and had yet to put down the slave revolt in that outpost of the French Empire in the Caribbean. Secretary of State James Madison had secretly aided the revolutionary leader, Toussaint L'Ouverture, believing that without the island and its sugar Napoleon would lose his taste for colonies in the New World, including Louisiana. As he signed away his huge wilderness in the middle of North America, Napoleon took satisfaction over the blow he was striking against his great enemy. "I have just given England a maritime rival that sooner or later will lay low her pride."[18]

The bewildering first report of the most momentous event of Jefferson's presidency was known on the wharves of Boston five days before official word arrived at the White House. When it did, the president was stunned. He had expected to buy the island of New Orleans and perhaps a slice of Florida, and he had been offered almost half a continent. Jefferson arranged to release the good news in time for the July 4 newspapers. But there were two problems. One was that the French did not have good title. Napoleon had not fulfilled his part of the bargain with Spain. Nor had he consulted his own legislature as the French constitution required. Moreover, under the French-Spanish agreement the king of Spain retained the right to approve the transfer of any territory to any third nation. The Spanish were now threatening war. Jefferson had no idea of exactly what had been purchased, so vague was the description of the territorial boundaries. "I asked the minister [Talleyrand] what were the bounds of the territory ceded to us," Livingston reported. "He said . . . I do not know."[19]

The second problem with annexing Louisiana was that Jefferson feared it exceeded his constitutional authority. He wrote a friend, Senator Wilson Cary Nicholas of Virginia, that the grant of power to Congress to admit new states into the Union applied only to what was considered American territory at the time the Constitution was adopted. The purchase raised a fundamental issue of what the American Union was to be. "I do not believe it was meant that they might receive England, Ireland, Holland, &c. into it."[20] Gouverneur Morris, who had participated in the drafting of the provision in the Constitution on the admission of new states, offered his view: "I always thought that when we should acquire Canada and Louisiana it would be proper to govern them as provinces and allow them no voice in our Councils."[21] Jefferson thought about asking for a constitutional amendment but was dissuaded; his closest advisers warned him that the treaty would be rejected by the Senate if he raised constitutional doubts. So, while acknowledging that meticulous observance of written laws was "a high duty," he argued— using words not unfamiliar to twentieth-century ears—that it was not the highest. Having made his political reputation by preaching strict construction, he now urged the Congress not to be distracted by the "metaphysical subtleties" of the Constitution. "The laws of necessity, of self-preservation, of saving our country when in danger, are of higher obligation. To lose our country by a scrupulous adherence to written law, would be to lose the law itself."[22]

The Federalists accused the president of "tearing the Constitution to tatters," and wasting money. (One editor of an opposition paper calculated that the $15 million Monroe and Livingston had agreed to pay Napoleon would fill 866 wagons with silver dollars or make a stack of coins three miles high.[23]) But since the Federalists had been courting the westerners by demanding a war for New Orleans, they were hardly in a good position to attack the bloodless acquisition of an empire. The members of the Senate immediately saw the political implications of what Jefferson had done; there would be new agricultural states carved from the vast new territory, and the manufacturing and commercial interests of the eastern seaboard could look forward to being outvoted. A Delaware senator pronounced the purchase to be "the greatest curse that could at present befall us."[24] Outside of New England, where Jefferson could do little right, Americans were excited about the vast opportunities that the new land acquisition seemed to offer. Most people, however, knew little of what was happening.

This suited Jefferson perfectly. In August he wrote his attorney general, Levi Lincoln, that Congress should "do what is necessary *in silence.* I find but one opinion as to the necessity of shutting up the country for some time."[25] Having doubled the size of the Republic almost overnight, beset by doubts that he had the legal power to do it, Jefferson dared Congress to undo his work. In a letter to Senator Breckinridge he compared himself to a guardian investing the money of his ward: "I did this for your good. I pretend no right to bind you: you may disavow me, and I must get out of the scrape as I can: I thought it my duty to risk myself for you."[26]

Members of Congress were stunned. "Darkness and mystery overshadow this House and this whole nation. We know nothing, we are permitted to know nothing. We sit here as mere automata," declaimed one New York representative.[27] Fearing that a public debate would upset his delicate negotiations with Napoleon, Jefferson arranged to call Congress back into special session just two weeks before Napoleon's offer was to expire. It was a tense time, for there were rumors that Napoleon was having second thoughts. The vote to ratify the most successful foreign policy accomplishment of the nineteenth century and to incorporate a people with a different religion, a different language, and a different legal system into the United States was taken after four days of debate in the Senate, less time, as one New Hampshire senator put it, than would have been allowed on "the most trivial Indian contract."[28] The treaty was approved 24–7.

In public Jefferson basked in triumph, but he was privately worried about the deal that had just been approved. Since he was not at all certain that the Spanish would transfer title to the French and get out, he did not know until Christmas whether he had purchased a great territory or a war. But the gamble paid off. Both Napoleon and the Spanish abandoned Louisiana with the result that the Jeffersonians, by now known as Democrats, did well at the next election. "Never have mankind contemplated so vast and important an accession of empire by means so pacific and just," proclaimed the

National Intelligencer, a leading Jeffersonian paper.[29] In a show of unity John Quincy Adams attended the dinner to honor Jefferson for his Louisiana coup, but always in character, he left early, claiming that the food was bad and the toasts boring.

The Louisiana Purchase changed the way Americans thought about Europe and the way they thought about themselves. At a stroke the greatest immediate threat to national security had been lifted. As American dominion spread west, the Atlantic Ocean seemed to widen. Jefferson had given the new nation an internal project to consume its energies. Being American now had more to do with mastering a continent and developing a frontier culture than with the stance toward Europe, as in the Federalist period. The passionate identification of Americans with distant kings or distant crowds was fading as a national consciousness began to grow. Even as early as 1797 Louis-Guillaume Otto, who had been French *chargé d'affaires* in the United States, had observed the phenomenon. There was now in addition to the "French party and the English party" a much larger "American party . . . which loves its country above all and for whom preferences for France and England are only accessory and often passing affections."[30]

2.

In 1803 war broke out between England and France, and Britain soon began seizing American sailors in international waters and impressing them into the British Navy. Faced with forty-two thousand British desertions during the first Napoleonic war, the British stepped up their recruiting efforts by boarding vessels on the high seas and impressing sailors deemed to be British subjects. If an American sailor was lucky enough to talk through his nose, he might be pronounced a Yankee and be left alone. But many, who were deemed to be subjects of the Crown, were dragged off to the floating hell of a British man-of-war. The commander of the boarding party was the court of last resort for determining the niceties of citizenship. About ten thousand indisputably American sailors were impressed into British service and many died—under the lash, poisoned by contaminated food, or killed in combat. The stories of the humiliation and suffering of American sailors made the British campaign against American shipping vivid and personal for citizens of the United States. Britain proclaimed a blockade of France. Napoleon also tried to starve his enemy, but he could not match British sea power. The United States was the largest supplier of imported food for both belligerents, and the British and the French now began seizing merchantmen flying the Stars and Stripes in large numbers and confiscating their cargoes. In 1806 the British fired a shot across the bow of a U.S. merchantman and managed to hit the boom which fell on the mate and killed him. The vessel limped into New York where the mangled body, raised on a platform, was paraded through the streets.[31] Public anger reached new levels the following summer when the British escalated their attack on American shipping by firing on the man-of-war *Chesapeake*. British sailors boarded the vessel, killed three Americans and wounded eighteen more, and then forcibly removed four individuals they claimed were deserters. When the wounded hulk arrived back in Norfolk, as the *Federalist* of Washington described it, "All parties, ranks, and professions . . . cried aloud for vengeance." British officers on shore leave rushed back to their ships to escape the mobs. The governor of Virginia called out the militia. Jefferson wrote his friend Du Pont de Nemours that he had not seen the country "in such a state of exasperation" since the Battle of Lexington.[32]

Jefferson was determined to maintain neutrality despite the rising public demands for vindication of national honor. He considered peace, as he wrote his friend Du Pont de Nemours some years later, "the *summum bonum* of our country." But only for the next twenty years. "At the end of that period we shall be twenty millions in number, and forty in energy, when encountering the starved and rickety paupers and dwarfs of English workshops."[33] But Jefferson knew that he had to do something. Since England and France both depended upon American food shipments, he thought that if the shipments stopped, the war would have to be settled. In December 1807, over Federalist opposition, he forced through Congress an Embargo Act more sweeping than any preceding effort to limit trade. In effect, the export of all goods from the United States by land or sea was prohibited. Eastern seaboard ports became ghost towns overnight. Ships rotted. Proud New Englanders committed suicide, went bankrupt, and even suffered the humiliation of soup kitchens.

Citizens along the Atlantic coast raged at Jefferson not only for bringing the nation to the brink of war but for his arbitrary exercise of presidential power. The president, so the saying went, had cut their throat to cure a nosebleed. Of course they had all screamed at the British outrages, but the canny shippers knew that if one out of three cargoes got through, they could still turn a respectable profit. The embargo put them out of business altogether, and therefore it was conspicuously violated. Several New England legislatures announced a right of "interposition," asserting their power to declare the federal law inapplicable to the citizens of their states. Jefferson "felt the foundation of the government shaken under my feet by the New England townships." Three days before he left office the embargo was repealed. But the cry for war grew stronger, particularly in the West and Southwest where frontiersmen saw a fight with England and her ally, Spain, as an occasion to expand west into land still controlled by the European powers and the chance to eliminate the last of their military posts on the frontier. The British, it was widely believed, were arming and inciting the Indians. Others saw war with Britain as a pretext for conquering Canada.

James Madison, who became president in 1809, had believed for almost twenty years that the British stranglehold on American trade had to be broken, but he wished to stop short of war. He was a soft-spoken little man with small features who usually dressed in black, thus prompting Washington Irving's contemptuous description of him as "a withered little apple-john."[34] More than most of his successors, he worried about how to pay for wars. In 1792 he had written an article on "Universal Peace" in which he argued that if every generation had to bear the expense of its own wars, fewer would be fought.[35] He also believed that "the management of foreign relations appears to be the most susceptible of abuse of all the trusts committed to a Government."[36]

By the time he moved into the White House, he feared that war with Britain could not be avoided. After two years in office, he was certain it could not be. His fate was to lead the nation into its most unpopular war until the twentieth-century debacle in Indochina. The War of 1812 was "Mr. Madison's war" just as the war one hundred fifty years later was Lyndon Johnson's war. He was the first of a series of presidents of pacific mien—McKinley and Wilson also come to mind—to sound the drumbeats of war.

Madison worried that the "common passion" of the people would result in the "tyranny of the majority" just as it had in earlier republics. The "virtue" of the people lay in their "intelligence to select men of virtue and wisdom." He wished to protect the body politic from the "distresses and vice of overgrown cities" by insulating legislatures insofar as possible from public opinion. "No member of this Convention could say what the opinions of his Constituents were," he argued at Philadelphia.[37] It was hard to ascertain what people thought and harder still to guess what they would think if they had the information available to their representatives. (Madison was much less sanguine than Jefferson about the merits of public education.) He was struck by how easily "public opinion may be influenced by government." The bigger the territory, however, the harder it was to counterfeit majority sentiment. His hopes for democracy in America rested on the vastness of the American expanse. In a big country with diverse interests there was less to fear from the tyranny of any single "faction." But at the same time he was concerned that in a spread-out society each individual becomes "the more insignificant . . . in his own eyes." Citizen apathy was also a path to tyranny.[38]

Madison, who had loved being in the House of Representatives, was expert in manipulating what he called the "leading opinions" in that body. But at the same time, ironically, he created unwelcome pressures for himself from the public at large. He was pushed toward war faster than he wanted to go because he was so maladroit in his maneuvers to protect American commerce. In these efforts Madison, the brilliant architect of the Constitution and an experienced diplomat—he had been secretary of state for eight years—was dogged by bad judgment and more than a dash of bad luck. His secretary of state, Robert Smith, was misled by David Erskine, the amiable British minister with an American wife, into believing that Britain was prepared to back down in the dispute over shipping rights and resume normal relations. Madison announced that agreement had been reached and that trade with Britain could be resumed. But after hundreds of ships bound for British ports put to sea, George Canning, the British foreign secretary, disavowed the agreement and a number of the ships were seized.

To add further insult, the British recalled their sympathetic minister and sent an overbearing servant of the Crown by the name of Francis James Jackson, who quickly became a hated figure in the United States, the regular target of newspaper articles demanding that he be tarred, feathered, and horsewhipped. He was an enthusiastic propagandist for the British cause but an inept one because he could not disguise his contempt for the American people, who were "more blackguard and ferocious than the mob in other countries." He had a budget of seven hundred pounds for his campaign "to correct the Public Mind." But it was clearly not enough, and as he became the focus of public anger, he received a letter of dismissal from London.[39]

Now it was Napoleon's turn to mislead Madison. On the very day the emperor ordered the American ships he had seized at Naples sold off to help pay for his war against England, his minister of foreign affairs was assuring the American envoy that "His Majesty loves the Americans." In slippery words that only wishful thinkers would take to be a promise, the French minister suggested that France might well stop harassing neutral shipping provided the British would do the same. Congress had passed a law providing that if either of the belligerents would agree to respect American rights on the seas, the United States would resume trade with it and stop all intercourse with the other. Napoleon's objective was to take enough pressure off the United States to lure it into his Continental system, in short to secure American help in his plan to starve England to its knees. ("A trap to catch us into a war with England," as John Quincy Adams had warned.) Now having gotten what he wanted, the emperor had no intention of letting American vessels freely sail the seas. He continued seizing ships flying the Stars and Stripes and selling them off in secret.

The presidents are thought to have been duped by foreign potentates, Americans are likely to turn first against the foreigners and then against their victimized leader. Madison had managed to earn both French contempt and British anger, and because he had allowed himself to be treated so shabbily, people felt humiliated. Feelings ran especially strong in the West. Ironically, the farther away from the sea a citizen lived, the greater the outrage at the English and French acts of piracy and the greater the contempt for President Madison. On the frontier the code of honor was clear and honor was prized above other virtues. Men were quick to take offense and quick to seek satisfaction. The cool calculation of interest of New Englanders, who saw no good reason to go to war with the British fleet when the country lacked an oceangoing navy, struck men in buckskin as stunted patriotism, the "low groveling parsimony of the counting room," as Henry Clay put it.[40]

Madison tried to use the rising public anger as a negotiating weapon against foreign powers. He instructed the American minister, William Pinkney, to tell the British that "public irritation . . . constant heart-burning . . . a deep and settled indignation" was leaving him no choice but to move toward war.[41] The British could read papers like the *Baltimore Federal Republican*, which referred to the president as a "political pimp," and get a sense of the rising pressure. The *Essex Register* declared that "the voice of every American is FOR WAR," but it had no way to measure public opinion. It was merely expressing the sentiments of the owner, no doubt concealing his regret that these were not more widely shared. In Boston the *Columbian Centinel* lashed out at the firebrands of the West whose "pretended skill in maritime jurisprudence" was pure hypocrisy since where they lived the "country furnishes no navigation beyond the size of a ferryboat or an Indian canoe."[42]

Madison's position within the Republican Party was not strong; by no means had he been the universal choice to succeed Jefferson, and his cabinet was an uneasy alliance of men who were loyal to others or had presidential ambitions of their own.[43] As 1812 approached, his election to a second term was not a foregone conclusion, so angry was the public becoming at British and French interference with American shipping. Westerners were also becoming alarmed at the efforts of two Indian leaders, the twin brothers Tecumseh and Tenskwatawa, the latter known as the Prophet, who were trying to create a separatist movement among the Indians. These two remarkable men had for several years been putting together a confederation to protect the remnant of the North American tribes from the incursions of the settlers. Their strategy was not to make war against the white man—they had fewer than four thousand warriors in the entire region bounded by the Great Lakes, the Mississippi, and the Ohio—but to withdraw from contact with him, rejecting his culture in general and alcoholic beverages in particular. Not only was there nothing on the frontier more un-American than prohibition, but it was widely assumed that so daring an idea could not have originated in the mind of a red man. The British must be behind Tecumseh's movement. On November 7, 1811, U.S. regulars under the command of William Henry Harrison, who years later parlayed that modest victory into the presidency, engaged Indian tribes near the Wabash River at a place called Tippecanoe, and when the Indians were dispersed, the battlefield was littered with new British weapons. The rumor quickly spread that the British were paying six dollars apiece for white American scalps. In their campaign to arouse more public anger the war faction now spliced the two slogans: "Look to the Wabash!" and "Look to the impressed seamen!"

The congressional elections of 1810 had helped to crystallize opinion on the issue of war. When the new Congress took its seat, almost one-half of the membership was new. A number of the new members were "war hawks," as John Randolph tagged them. These "pepperpot politicians" from the new frontier states were men in their thirties and forties who had campaigned on the code of the frontier, fervent nationalists all, too young to have had the cautionary experience of the Revolutionary War. Those historians who say that Madison was pushed into war by popular clamor rest their case on the election results of 1810, but recent historical research casts doubt on the thesis.[44] The war hawks in Congress were vocal, and applauded eagerly as their Speaker, Henry Clay, himself only thirty-four, denounced the "tranquil and putrescent pool of ignominious peace"[45] in which the nation was wallowing while Britain and France trampled American rights. But they did not have the votes to force a war. What they did have was a rousing issue with which to attack a vacillating president and to build a strong congressional party. "We are going to fight for the reestablishment of our national character," cried Andrew Jackson, "misunderstood and vilified at home and abroad."[46] But all during the 1811–12 session of Congress, which voted for war in June 1812, Madison, James Monroe, his secretary of state, and Henry Clay "gave direction to the war movement, and shaped its content and timing."[47]

Virtually all Federalists were still pro-British and they opposed another war against George III on principle. But some of their more Machiavellian politicians in New England were privately urging His Majesty's government to make no concessions to Madison in the hope that the crisis of impending war would get rid of the Republicans in 1812. They would be forced, as one historian has put it, into "disgraceful retreat or a demonstration of wartime incompetence."[48] Madison was under increasing pressure from his own advisers. The former minister to France, John Armstrong, who knew that Napoleon had been deliberately deceiving Madison, threatened to make public the diplomatic correspondence, then resigned. "We are a nation of quakers," he fumed, "without either their morals or their motives."[49] President Madison feared that Armstrong was conspiring with Robert Smith to take control of the Republican Party. The former secretary of state, the man whom the British had so successfully deceived, now circulated a pamphlet attacking the president for failing to maintain "the rights of our much-injured and insulted country."[50] Madison was sure Smith was planning to run against him. At July 4 celebrations the "malcontent" Republicans, as the anti-Madisonians were known, pointedly refused to drink to the president's health, and plotted to secure the nomination for DeWitt Clinton.

Once again "whiffling Jemmy," as his growing throng of enemies called him, lost his footing. In March 1812 he released some letters of a man by the name of John Henry, a British agent who had been hired by the British governor-general of Canada to explore and encourage rebellious sentiments among leading Federalists in New England. Madison had paid $50,000 for these letters, and he hoped that the expensively procured revelations, which turned out to be mostly Boston dinner-table gossip, would whip up popular feelings against the Federalists. But since no Federalist politicians were actually named and anyone who wasn't a Federalist assumed that Federalists were disloyal anyway, the public relations campaign backfired. The Federalists accused Madison of wasting money, and most of the public anger, to the consternation of Madison, who was not yet ready to ask for war, was directed at the British.

Finally, on June 1, 1812, Madison asked Congress to declare war on Britain. In his message the president intimated that he was being forced by public anger to put the "solemn question, which the Constitution wisely confides to the Legislative Department of the Government." But Madison knew how balanced the prowar and the antiwar interests in the country were. The president believed that the national interest demanded war, but he also knew that the future of the Republican Party depended upon its ability to make a strong national appeal. The vindication of national honor was a politically compelling argument for war. A second war with Britain could not only free American commerce but help keep the Union together.

Those who might have been expected to be most for war, the seafaring people of the East Coast, were for peace, and the westerners, whose hearts purportedly burned with indignation over the treatment of American sailors on the high seas, regularly voted down the appropriations to build a navy. It was Republican doctrine that navies were evil, "engines of power, employed in projects of ambition and war," as one congressman declaimed. Shippers were not eager to go to war, especially without a navy, for war would hardly be less injurious to commerce than either the embargo or the depredations of the British. Southerners were ready to go to war because they held Britain responsible, for no particularly good reason, for the precipitous decline in cotton and tobacco prices.

Far more decisive than the ebb and flow of popular feeling was the president's own judgment, backed by the unanimous opinion of his closest advisers. No one in his cabinet saw any alternative to war. Secretary of State James Monroe was particularly forceful in urging military action. Madison's mentor, Thomas Jefferson, had come to believe that "war or abject submission are the only alternatives left to us."[51] Both Jefferson and Monroe were politicians who were attuned to the public mood and took it no less seriously than geopolitics. They understood that the greatest enthusiasts for settling scores with Britain were those who saw it as an opportunity to digest a chunk, perhaps all, of Canada while the British were fighting for their lives against Napoleon. Jefferson himself held this view, and so did Andrew Jackson. Others cast covetous eyes on Florida. Public opinion on the frontier would support a war of conquest in any event, these politicans calculated, but city people would accept a second war with Britain only if there were no other way to vindicate national honor.

For three days after Madison's war message Congress deliberated behind closed doors. As Henry Adams explained the unusual secrecy, "Henry Clay and his friends were weary of debate and afraid of defeat."[52] The House voted for war by a margin of thirty votes, but in the Senate the war resolution passed by only six votes. Congress divided on party and sectional lines. Southerners and westerners, who saw the opportunity to annex territory, voted for war, but the Middle Atlantic shipping states, New York and New Jersey, did not, nor did any New England state join the war faction save landlocked Vermont. In the states voting for peace the Federalists were in control. In his *History of the United States* Henry Adams called the claim of the politicians who voted for war that they had no choice but to bow to the voice of the people hypocritical nonsense. The so-called war fever was "intermittent and imaginary." Ironically, just as the country was going to war the British were offering concessions. The French had seized more ships than had the English. But the pent-up feelings caused by two decades of British attacks on American commerce convinced enough of the doubters in Congress that they would be politically destroyed if they failed to stand up as defenders of the national honor.

Deep disagreements over the wisdom and justice of the war remained, however, and these severely hampered its conduct from the outset. At the news of war, flags were put at half-mast all through New England as funeral bells tolled. The governors of Massachusetts, Rhode Island, and Connecticut refused to call the state militia into national service. For all the belligerent talk that had preceded it, the war elicited surprisingly tepid support. Henry Clay had boasted that he could conquer Canada with the Kentucky militia alone, but in 1812 only four hundred Kentuckians showed up for service. The War Department was unable to build up the regular army to even one-half its authorized strength.[53] The best educated in the population, the ones with the most military experience, were Federalists, but since they were against the war and their loyalty suspect, Madison was slow to offer them commissions. Many prominent Americans, including Chief Justice John Marshall, opposed the war throughout. Congressmen who had voted for it were hooted at on the street.

While the war dragged on, John Lowell, a founder of the Massachusetts General Hospital, the Atheneum, and other venerable Boston institutions, seized the opportunity to propose a new constitution for the United States. His idea was that the original thirteen states should renew their compact free of the ignorant hordes who had illegally come into the Union as a result of the Louisiana Purchase. In short, it was a plan, in Samuel Eliot Morison's words, to "kick the West out of the Union!" At Harvard the antiwar sentiment that gave rise to Lowell's secessionist scheme was widely shared, and "Crazy Jack," as the local Jeffersonians called him, was awarded an honorary degree at the commencement exercises in 1814.

The War of 1812 ended, much as it began, in confusion. Caleb Strong, the Federalist governor of Massachusetts, author of *Piety and Patriotism*, was secretly negotiating with the British for a separate peace. By late 1813 the British were ready to negotiate to end the war. In April 1814, Napoleon was finally defeated, and eight months later the British signed the Treaty of Ghent, which ended the war. Two weeks after this ceremony Andrew Jackson won a brilliant victory at New Orleans. The news of the two events arrived together, creating the impression, which Jackson did nothing to dispel, that the one had to do with the other.

But the war ended in stalemate. The conquest of Canada, which Jefferson had said would be "a mere matter of marching," failed; indeed the British were occupying Maine. New England had come perilously close to seceding. Boston merchants and bankers loaned money to the British to finance the war.[54] The British burned the Capitol and the White House, and the First Family had to flee to the hills across the Potomac. Almost everyone agreed that the war had been miserably mismanaged. The peace treaty was silent on the one issue for which the young Republic had ostensibly gone to war; the British made no promise to abandon their practice of seizing American sailors on the high seas and impressing them into His Majesty's service. And even after peace returned to Europe, British ports in the Western Hemisphere remained off limits to American shipping.

Still, the United States had survived in a war against the winner of the European wars, now the greatest empire on earth, and in so doing had established itself at last as an independent and formidable actor in international politics. If the war had accomplished nothing

else, it convinced the British that the Revolution could not be un-
done. Despite the strains, the Union had managed to hold together.

Having threatened secession and treated with the enemy, the
Federalists were destroyed as a political party. Madison's experience
generated a new respect for the power of public opinion. Popular
passion had not forced the president to go to war, but the ambivalence about the second war with Britain hampered the war effort
and forced Madison to settle for a less advantageous peace than he
would have liked. Perhaps most important, his record of vacillation
and mismanagement shattered the aura of infallibility that had surrounded the Founding Fathers. They had never, of course, been
immune from attack, but the accumulation of executive blunders
during the War of 1812 emboldened Congress and fed a growing
populist feeling that republican aristocrats did not always know best.

PART TWO

EMPIRE OF LIBERTY

CHAPTER 3

Popular Democracy and the Enemy Within

1.

E very political theory needs what Walter Lippmann called an "inscrutable element" at its heart, a mystery that serves to legitimate the rule of one individual or a group over the rest. In the twilight of absolute monarchy the legitimating mystery was called "the divine right of kings," which, as Keith Thomas puts it, "was cunningly used by the Commons to weaken the monarch's power rather than to strengthen it." Since the king could do no wrong and his sacred authority could not be delegated, Parliament attacked the legitimacy of the king's ministers in the name of the king, thereby establishing its own.[1]

The doctrine of popular sovereignty, according to Edmund S. Morgan, was invented in the middle of the seventeenth century not as a response to the clamor of the masses but as a myth to support the claim of the gentry in Parliament against royal authority. In Thomas's words, "The few were attempting to enlist the many against the rest of the few."[2] Public opinion became the new legitimating mystery. The sovereignty of public opinion is still the commanding idea on which democracy rests. How the people actually make their will prevail, however, remains a mystery that, as Lippmann suggested, cannot withstand much empirical examination without destroying its power.

From Jefferson's time to the late nineteenth century, as the intellectual historian Stow Persons writes, American political theorists had "virtually nothing to say" on the theory of popular sovereignty.[3] American politicians and political philosophers stopped grappling with the theoretical questions that had fascinated Adams, Jefferson, and Madison, preferring to finesse the issues posed by public opinion—what is it? why should it guide policy?—in order to concentrate on improving the machinery of popular government and the techniques for tabulating opinion. The mystery lay undisturbed.

At the beginning of the nineteenth century the idea of popular sovereignty made it possible to create the new entities we call nation-states and to expand their power and domain by making war on a grand scale hitherto unknown. The historian Eric Hobsbawm points out that "the 'nation' is an historically novel construct, characteristic of the period since the late eighteenth century," in which the overlapping loyalties of feudal times—duchy, family, tribe, village, church—are replaced by a single overriding loyalty, that of "nationality."[4] The rationale of the modern nation-state was security, and its boundaries were established by war. The new industrializing nation-state could neither fight modern wars nor pay for them without greater mass participation. France, for example, though the richest and most populous of the European powers, had never fielded an army greater than 100,000 men before the Revolution. By 1813 the now prevailing myth that government was the expression of the general will helped make it possible to draft 2.3 million men for Napoleon's campaigns.[5]

The expansion of suffrage not only enabled rulers to exact more from their citizens, but it was also a way to shore up the authority of government as nation-states became increasingly centralized. With the dying of old myths like the divine right of kings and the obligations of hereditary fealty, people could no longer be fit neatly into their feudal niches. Breathing the free air of the city, as Max Weber called it, citizens were harder to control. They were also a much greater potential cause of trouble for government than when cities were small and most men were busy all day on the land. "The complex market economies that emerged from the industrial and commercial revolutions . . . ," as the political scientist Benjamin Ginsberg observes, "were far more sensitive to mass violence and disruption than their preindustrial predecessors."[6] In America direct citizen action against unpopular acts of government—the Boston Tea Party is one of the more nonviolent examples—was a venerable tradition, even an honored one. (It was a tradition L'Enfant was well aware of when he provided broad avenues for Washington, D.C., so that the artillery would have a good field of fire in case mobs should attack the White House or the Capitol.) As the caravans moved across the plains, the territory under the uncertain control of the federal government expanded, and so also did feelings of vulnerability to popular unrest. Channeling of popular feeling became increasingly important to the stability of government.

Andrew Jackson was the first popular figure to gain the presidency without the authority of having been one of the Founding Fathers. When Jackson died in 1845, President James Polk called him "the greatest man of the age in which he lived."[7] Years later when Nathaniel Hawthorne saw Raphael's painting of Julius II in Florence, his first reaction was a fervent wish that the master could have painted Old Hickory. Like Washington, Lincoln, the Roosevelts, and Reagan, Jackson was a focus of controversy while in the White House, but he towered over the politicians of his day by being able to touch the feelings of millions of citizens at a deeper level than any contemporary.

Jackson was an American man of action, the first war hero in the White House since Washington. His victory at New Orleans helped obliterate three years of defeats. His military exploits after the war continued to boost his political fortunes. Two years after the victory at New Orleans he was authorized by President Monroe to chase the Seminole Indians into Spanish territory. This he did with a vengeance, seizing every Spanish post in Florida except St. Augustine, deposing the Spanish governor after reluctantly deciding not to hang him, confiscating the Spanish royal archives, and declaring the revenue laws of the United States in force throughout all Florida. He summarily executed two British subjects whom he had charged with inciting the Indians, "unchristian wretches," he reported to the secretary of war, "who by false promises delude and excite an Indian tribe to all the horrid deeds of savage war."[8]

President Monroe and most of the cabinet were shocked. But Secretary of State John Quincy Adams, no admirer of Jackson, publicly supported his action in the strongest terms in the hopes of getting the Spanish out of Florida. Henry Clay, on the other hand, eager to destroy a future rival for the presidency, organized a Senate investigation of Jackson's conduct to determine whether he had exceeded his authority. The deliberations went on for twenty-seven days, the galleries so packed that men tripped over the cuspidors in the aisles and overturned them. The senators began carrying weapons after Jackson reportedly threatened to cut off their ears. (Known for a terrible temper, he went to the White House with two dueler's bullets in his body.) The four resolutions condemning him were soundly beaten. In effect, he was acquitted by the crowd. "Old and young speak of him with rapture," reported *Niles' Weekly Reg-*

ister.[9] Tammany Hall passed a resolution: "We highly approve of the manly spirit of the American general." It was a classic American drama of initiative, courage, and boldness in the face of a triple threat. With one decisive thrust Jackson had bested the Spanish, the British, and the Indians, and had become a popular hero for it. Adams told the Spanish minister that "Spain would not have the possession of Florida to give us" unless it moved fast. Thus did Adams skillfully use Jackson's great mass popularity as a warrior to induce the Spanish to sell all of Florida for "virtually no money and the surrender of no actual U.S. interest."[10]

By 1828, the year Andrew Jackson was elected president, property qualifications for voting had been removed in every state except Rhode Island, Mississippi, and Virginia (where a third of the white population still had no vote even after the reform of 1831).[11] The new political system of the Jacksonian age—Jackson himself was the beneficiary, not the instigator, of the democratization movement—changed the way parties functioned and the way elections were fought. The electorate was now almost double what it was in Washington's day. Though 800,000 more people voted in 1828 than four years earlier, the 1,155,340 white males who cast a ballot still represented less than 9 percent of the total population.[12] Printed ballots were replacing voice vote, but the balloting was not exactly secret; it was not uncommon to require the voter to pick up a party ballot, each with its own distinctive color. In all but six states presidential electors were now selected by the voters at large rather than by state legislatures, as had been the standard practice in the Federalist era.

The population seemed to explode. Americans would win their future wars "in the bedchamber," warned the British foreign minister, Lord Castlereagh, as the War of 1812 ended.[13] By 1820 there were as many people living in new states created after 1789 as in the original thirteen. As the population grew, so also did the proportion deemed to be citizens. But the meaning of citizenship changed. The expanding frontier was not like the New England townships where the few who acted as citizens held public affairs to be a public duty. Politics was becoming a profession, and the role of ordinary citizens was no longer to engage in the sort of deliberation celebrated by Jefferson so much as to participate in electoral rites. Just as the nation turned its attention inward, away from Europe, so individuals turned inward toward their own affairs. In a society that was at once increasingly urbanized but more and more spread out, there were fewer opportunities for citizens to govern themselves in the manner of the Braintree town meeting of John Adams's time. The political culture was entrepreneurial and libertarian; the dominant thrust, as Marvin Meyers puts it, was "an effort to pull down the menacing constructions of federal and corporate power, and restore the wholesome rule of 'public opinion and the interests of trade.' "[14]

The gap between the voter and his representative widened. As the young Republic grew, the distances between where citizens lived and the seat of the federal government expanded and so did the number of constituents each representative served. Though it became easier in Jackson's time for the common man to vote, it was no simpler for a poor man to win office. The campaign of 1824, which had ended in a dead heat between Andrew Jackson and John Quincy Adams, produced a minority president and a compelling political lesson: A winning majority could not be garnered by the sort of gentlemanly, low-key campaign that all the aspirants, including Andrew Jackson, ran that year. By 1828 the costs of campaigning had pushed the price of a congressional seat to $3,000, which only the well-to-do could afford.

Political parties in the United States now made less of a pretense of either ideological consistency or subtlety. As constituencies grew and the electoral process became more impersonal, the prime function of the party was to simplify issues rather than to debate them, and to market personalities for public office. As these new machines for seeking power were perfected, political rhetoric became more confrontational but the policy choices were deliberately blurred. Faced with the need to mobilize a larger electorate, candidates outdid one another in courting the broadest possible constituencies, flattering the masses and buying votes, whiskey being the common currency.

Character evisceration became the stock-in-trade of every successful politician. The campaign of 1828 is widely considered the dirtiest in American history. Typical of the era was Isaac Hill's list, which he published in the *New Hampshire Patriot* in 1832, of the twenty-one reasons why Henry Clay should not be president, the definitive one being that "he spends his days at the gaming table and his nights in a brothel."[15] Wealthy landowners like Jackson advertised their log-cabin origins, and the Jacksonian revolution ushered in a wholesale assault on aristocratic manners. The cult of equality made a deep impression on Tocqueville all during his visit.

Yet the result of the new politics was far from "mobocracy," the Hamiltonian nightmare. Wealth remained the key to political power, but it was now the wealth of the "self-made man."

The political energies of citizens, which in the Federalist time had gone into deliberation, organizing, and lobbying, making use of the political clubs and the coffeehouses, or into direct action in the streets, now increasingly went into the creation of voluntary associations, the number and diversity of which fascinated Tocqueville when he visited America in the year 1831. Far more people were eligible to participate in the democratic process, but now participation was set by the rhythm of election campaigns. Two famous foreign visitors to Jacksonian America came away with diametrically opposite impressions. Tocqueville was struck by the high level of citizen participation. "To take a hand in the regulation of society and to discuss it is his biggest concern and so to speak, the only pleasure an American knows."[16] On the other hand, Harriet Martineau, an acute British observer who spent two years in America—from 1834 to 1836—detected an alarming "apathy in citizenship." Having heard in England that Americans were "always talking politics, canvassing, bustling about to make proselytes abroad . . . buried in newspapers . . . hurrying to vote," her interviews with a congressman, a professor, a naval officer, a minister, and many others shocked her, for she found that Americans were reluctant, sometimes actually afraid, to get involved in politics, even to the extent of voting. A passionate enthusiast of democracy, Martineau lamented the "almost insane dread of responsibility" that had taken over the Republic.[17]

Citizens no longer confronted presidents directly as they had over the Jay Treaty, and especially not on matters of diplomacy as in the Napoleonic era, for the struggles of Europe became more and more remote as citizens focused on the enormous changes taking place on their own continent and in their own lives. With the end of the War of 1812 the nation was at last free of foreign threat. There would not be another European war to challenge American commerce for a hundred years.

Politics was becoming a public show. Ten thousand visitors poured into Washington to see Old Hickory take the oath of office, thereby doubling the population of the capital overnight. Carts, wagons, and carriages followed the sixty-two-year-old figure erect in the saddle as he made his way up Pennsylvania Avenue to the White House. The crowd kept following, surging into the East Room, spilling punch, breaking glasses, putting muddy boots on damask chairs. The president was forced to escape his admirers by a rear window and take refuge at Gadsby's tavern. The skeptics of democracy had predicted it all. The tradition of cultivated manners is lost, Charles Carroll of Carrolton, the last surviving signer of the Declaration of Independence, lamented in his interview with Tocqueville. "Society is less brilliant and more prosperous."[18]

The new president symbolized the end of old family rule. Though he always had powerful patrons, and some were relatives, he did not become rich or famous because of his family name. Andrew Jackson's career was a map of the new road to power. Acquire land. (Jackson took his lawyer's fees in land whenever possible.) Choose your friends wisely. Develop an imposing public presence. He epitomized the virtues and rewards of self-reliance, a free man, a father figure in whose hands the Republic could be safely left while the individual tried his hand at becoming rich. Old Hickory was the made-to-order politician for the American individualist. Tocqueville defined "individualism," a word he himself coined, as "a calm and considered feeling which disposes each citizen to isolate himself from the mass of his fellows and withdraw into the circle of family and friends; with this little society formed to his taste, he gladly leaves the greater society to look after itself."[19]

Andrew Jackson was the first American politician to build a political machine on a national network of friendly newspapers. There were now almost a thousand newspapers in the United States. "It is a testimony to the strength and purity of the democratic sentiment in the country," wrote Harriet Martineau, "that the republic has not been overthrown by its newspapers." The press was as good, she thought, at circulating falsehoods as at suppressing truth. In the 1830s every serious candidate had to have at least one newspaper editor in his pocket, for most of the country read nothing but newspapers, and a single newspaper at that. Buying editors, as John Quincy Adams discovered to his disgust, was expensive. Jackson had a coterie of sympathetic editors around the country, "a chain of newspaper posts, from the New England states to Louisiana, and branching off through Lexington to the Western States," as the National Republican organization charged.[20] His closest political advisers were newspapermen. His famous Kitchen Cabinet was comprised of Amos Kendall, former editor of the Frankfort, Kentucky, *Argus*; Kendall's associate, Francis P. Blair; and another newspaperman, John C. Rives. Jackson was the only president to start his own organ of news and opinion, mostly the latter, while in the White House. Edited by his crony, Francis Blair, financed by government printing contracts, and devoured by foreign governments for clues as to what was going on inside the presidential head, the *Globe* immediately flourished.[21]

The press did much to market Jackson's heroic reputation. James Gordon Bennett's description of Jackson's first inaugural was typical of the style of the day: "The Chief Justice of the United States then administered the oath of office; and thus, in the sight of Heaven and the surrounding multitude, was Andrew Jackson declared the chief of the only free and pure republic upon earth. . . . The very marble of the pediment seemed to glow with life—justice, with a firmer grasp, secured her scales. . . . What a lesson for the monarchies of Europe! The mummery of a coronation, with all its pomp and pageantry, sinks into merited insignificance, before the simple and sublime spectacle of twelve millions of freemen, imparting this Executive Trust to the man of their choice."[22] In the Jacksonian age the press became a critical instrument for manufacturing consent. "It is no secret," Martineau wrote, "that some able personage at Washington writes letters on the politics and politicians of the general government, and sends them to the remotest corners of the Union, to appear in their newspapers; after which they are collected in the administration newspaper at Washington, as testimonies of public opinion in the respective districts where they appear."[23]

The Jacksonian brand of nationalism suited the temper of the times. For a people constantly on the move the president provided a vision of national security that afforded limitless opportunity without the heavy hand of federal authority. Jacksonian democracy, in Samuel Eliot Morison's words, "was antinational in rejecting Henry Clay's 'American System.' That is, it wanted roads, canals, and (in a few years) railroads to be chartered and aided by the states, but no federal government messing into them or sharing the expected profits."[24] Every foreign visitor of the time was struck by the rootlessness of the Jacksonian American. "Speaking generally," one English traveler put it, "every farm from Eastport in Maine to Buffalo on Lake Erie, is for sale."[25] The pull of the West turned "Ohio fever," as one migrant put it, into "Missouri fever." Tocqueville was also impressed by the cyclical character of American lives—rags to riches and back to rags, fortunes made and lost and won again with dizzying rapidity. Between 1840 and 1860 more than 4.2 million immigrants poured into the cities of the East, and many of the earlier settlers pushed on relentlessly toward the Rockies and beyond.

The abundance of vacant land, which the historian George Bancroft in the tradition of Jefferson called the "safety valve of our system," did not entirely avoid controversy. Cheap land in the West was a magnet that created a labor shortage in the East and drove up wages. Westward migration, John Quincy Adams's secretary of the treasury had openly declared, was against the interests of manufacturing capital.[26] Jackson, however, believed that migration would serve the interests of the East as much as the West. Cheap land in the West would eventually absorb the thousands who abandoned their farms on the Atlantic seaboard. This would keep the multitudes from flocking to the mill towns of New England and turning them into the Dickensian horrors of Manchester or Birmingham.

Andrew Jackson saw a manifest destiny for America long before the phrase was coined. A continental republic with a great national market expanding from sea to sea could be built by the energies of a footloose people. The task of the federal government was to remove the impediments to expansion. For the first twenty years of the Republic the great issue had been national independence, fundamentally a matter of foreign policy. Now and for the next eighty years the overriding issue was continental expansion. In the American mind the conquest of the frontier was a matter of exploration and emigration, not foreign policy. Yet every thrust west toward Oregon and California or south toward Mexico involved confrontation and conflict with either a European power or an Indian nation.

2.

Andrew Jackson was widely admired in his time as a successful diplomat, and he skillfully used foreign policy issues to build his personal popularity. He came to the White House with a reputation as a man who could be counted on to "breed you a quarrel," as Jefferson once put it. But he surprised his critics. He successfully induced the British to open up trade in the West Indies by charming the Foreign Office with his unexpectedly moderate demeanor. With France, however, he reverted to type by threatening to seize French property if France did not pay a debt it had refused to honor. The French demanded a presidential apology and dispatched a squadron to the West Indies. "The honor of my country shall never be stained by an apology from me," Jackson declared in a message to Congress. His truculence produced cheers from enthusiastic supporters across the country, but the Whigs, the opposition party, played on the fear of war. Stocks fell. Insurance companies served notice that they would not insure cargoes if hostilities broke out. Finally, the British stepped in to arrange mediation, and both sides backed down. But Jackson had enhanced his reputation as a leader who could "demand the respect of all Europe."[27]

The most controversial national security issue of the Jacksonian era concerned Indian removal. It is the story of how a president was able to persuade the American people to acquiesce in a massive violation of human rights. Land distribution was at the very heart of economic planning and social theory in Jacksonian America, and the presence of the Indian on valuable acreage was seen as the principal constraint on economic development. In 1790 two-thirds of the American population lived within fifty miles of the Atlantic. Within the next fifty years 4.5 million Americans crossed the Appalachians, and by 1850 the western states were the most populous in the nation. In 1820, 125,000 Indians lived east of the Mississippi; by 1844 there were fewer than 30,000 left. Most had been forcibly relocated to the west. About a third had been wiped out.[28]

The very existence of the Indian challenged the American identity in two ways. America was the future, and the Indian stood for the primeval past. America was limitless possibility, and the very existence of the Indians posed limits. Since most of the tribes were hunters and wanderers, the borders of Indian land were uncertain. The primitive, collectivist ways of Native Americans were completely at odds with the new commonwealth that the European settlers were committed to building in America, a commercial society of individual opportunity based on science and industry. At the same time what to do about more than 100,000 people seen to be in the way challenged the American self-image at the deepest level. Hamilton had argued that the American state, in contrast to the shadowy beginnings of the European kingdoms, was built on "reflection and choice" rather than "accident and force."[29] But ever since 1622, the year of the first Indian massacre of the settlers at Jamestown, the white man and the Indian had been at war with one another in North America. In the Massachusetts Bay Colony Governor John Winthrop ordered punitive raids on Indian villages; he declared the land to be a "vacuum" as far as legal title was concerned, for the Indians, not having "subdued" the land, had only a "natural," not a "civil," right to it. Thus the virgin forests and plains were there for the taking by anyone prepared to put them to civilized use. As Roger Williams had put it, "All men of conscience or prudence ply to windward, to maintain their wars to be defensive," and so the deeply religious Puritans, who were determined to build their City on the Hill, successfully denied that two of the City's foundation stones were force and fraud.

In the French and Indian War and in the Revolution most Indian tribes had fought against the colonists, and this lent plausibility to the idea that Native Americans were ever willing instruments of foreign powers. American farmers and pioneers thought of Indian fights as a form of proxy war against England or Spain. "Confronting the Indian in America," Winthrop Jordan has written, "was a testing experience, common to all the colonies. Conquering the Indian symbolized and personified the conquest of the American difficulties, the surmounting of the wilderness. To push back the Indian was to prove the worth of one's own mission, to make straight in the desert a highway for civilization."[30] So intense were popular feelings about the Indians that, as Michael Rogin notes, five of the ten major candidates for president between 1824 and 1852 had won their reputations either as generals fighting the red man or as secretary of war, whose major task in those years was maintaining control over the Indians. None had made a fiercer reputation as an Indian fighter than Andrew Jackson, and his enthusiastic support for Indian removal helped him to sweep the southern states in the election of 1828.

In the Federalist era the federal government had taken a paternalistic approach to the Indians. Tribal lands were guaranteed by treaties with tribes beginning with the 1790 compact with the Creek nation. The United States agreed to furnish domestic animals and help regulate Indian trade in the hopes that they would become "herdmen and cultivators instead of remaining hunters." By law Indians were protected from attacks by whites. They were exempt from taxes, unless they chose to become citizens, which they were free to do if they left the tribal lands. The red men were the "children of the forest" and the Great White Father in Washington was their protector. Those who faced the Indians on the frontier, many of them immigrants, were impatient with the high-sounding sentiments embodied in the Indian policy. Not only did they flout the provisions of federal laws and treaties for the safeguarding of Indian rights, but their resentment steadily grew against what they considered the legalistic pieties of the Massachusetts and Virginia patricians whose ancestors had long since vanquished their own Indians.

For Thomas Jefferson the Indians raised profound moral and philosophical problems. In his *Notes on the State of Virginia* Jefferson confronted Buffon, the French *philosophe* who provided an elegant scientific patina for the prevailing prejudices in America:

The Indians were physically inferior—"feeble . . . small organs of generation . . . no ardor whatever for his female . . . no vivacity, no activity of mind . . . "—and morally inferior—" . . . they love their parents and children but little; the most intimate of all ties, the family connection, binds them therefore but loosely together; between family and family there is no tie at all . . . their heart is icy, their society cold, and their rule harsh. . . . Nature, by refusing him the power of love, has treated him worse and lowered him deeper than any animal."³¹ If the Indian lacked moral sense, then for Jefferson the whole theoretical underpinnings of democracy were shaky. He set out to refute Buffon's ideas with anthropological observations. Indian warriors, Jefferson argued, show their love for one another by the fierceness they show their enemies. The low birth rate is not to be explained by a subhuman lack of sexual ardor but by the hard life of Indian women, which takes its toll on childbearing. Jefferson's arguments seem almost frantic, as if the very existence of the Native American was challenging the philosophical premises of the new society.

Initially, Jefferson thought the answer to the Indian problem was their domestication as farmers. But when the Cherokees, possessors of fifteen million acres of Georgia land, successfully adapted to an agricultural life and took on the accoutrements of civilization, the white man's dress, an alphabet, a newspaper, the *Cherokee Phoenix*, a smattering of Christianity, some English, even slaves, all such efforts at assimilation did nothing to make the existence of the Cherokee nation within the state of Georgia any more acceptable to the Georgians.³²

Jefferson himself was the original architect of Indian removal. He gave the order for tribes to be moved across the Mississippi, believing that the presence of large numbers of red men in the Louisiana territory would encourage Napoleon to give it up.³³ In his 1803 draft of a constitutional amendment to legitimize the Louisiana Purchase he proposed making a land exchange with the Indians, giving them some of the new western land in return for "lands possessed by Indians within the U.S. on the east side of the Mississippi." After exploring the territory, Meriwether Lewis wrote the president that removal would be of "primary importance to the future prosperity of the Union."³⁴ But the Cherokees strongly resisted, and the matter was dropped. Monroe revived the idea, but said it would have to be done without the use of force, for such would be "revolting to humanity and entirely unjustifiable."³⁵ Since the Cherokees had made it a capital crime for any of their number to cede territory to the United States government, Monroe's call for peaceful removal was not only an oxymoron but an impossibility. This his successor John Quincy Adams understood, and though he had no feelings of guilt whatever that his Massachusetts ancestors had driven out the Indians—"What is the right of a huntsman to the forest of a thousand miles, over which he has accidentally ranged in quest of prey?"[36]—as president he believed that legal obligations to the Indians must be scrupulously observed. And so he too called for voluntary removal, which meant that the Cherokees would stay where they were.

The line between foreign and domestic policy is often murky; it was especially so, as we have seen, in the Federalist period when the new nation was still so politically and psychologically entwined with Europe. Then as now, there were powerful emotional reasons not to think of the Indian question as a foreign policy matter. If the Cherokee nation were a foreign nation like Britain or Holland, then certain standards of international law and custom would have to be observed. After all, the colonies had proclaimed their independence by appealing to the decent opinions of mankind. "The Indians being the prior occupants," Secretary of War Henry Knox had written George Washington, "possess the right of soil. It cannot be taken from them unless by their free consent, or by the right of conquest in a just war."[37] Explicit treaty promises made Indian land claims seemingly inviolate.

The confused legal status of the Indians reflected deep moral ambivalence. Americans were taught that Indians were beyond the reach of civilization and its law, "in a state of infancy, weakness, and the greatest imperfection," as an early school text described them. Their stubborn belief in the superiority of their primitive ways made Indians seem altogether unregenerate. But it was equally unthinkable that Indian tribes could establish permanent nations inside American territory subject to no law but their own. Yet it had been expedient to make treaties with Indian tribes as if they were foreign nations, and on several occasions Indian delegations invited to Washington for negotiations were treated with all the diplomatic pomp reserved for foreign ambassadors.[38]

Just as Jackson took office the states of Georgia, Alabama, and Mississippi theatened to enforce recently enacted laws asserting state sovereignty over the Indian lands. The Cherokees insisted upon their own sovereignty with a new assertiveness that enraged the whites. Jackson immediately began putting pressure on the Cherokees to move, warning them that if the states attacked them, they would get no help from the federal government. In his inaugural address Jackson promised "a just and liberal policy and to give that humane and considerate attention to their rights and their wants which is consistent with the habits of our Government and the feelings of our people."[39]

Public opinion in the North presented a problem for any plan to push Indians out of their lands in the South, for virtually all church groups had been strongly against removal of the Indians and church backing had been important to Jackson in the 1828 election. Jackson sent an old friend to the Cherokees to persuade them how much it was in their interest to move, but when gold was discovered on Cherokee land in the summer of 1829 it became harder to present the land grab as philanthropy. Whites rushed in with picks and pans and began putting up log cabins. The secretary of war instructed the southern governors to tell the squatters that they would be "forcibly removed and their Cabins destroyed." Relations with the Indians were to remain "quiet and peaceful." Even "the appearance of harshness toward the Indians" must be avoided.[40] The federal government would not forcibly remove the Indians from the South until there had been a shift in public opinion.

The strongest political opposition to Indian removal was from the American Board of Commissioners for Foreign Missions, a Boston missionary society that was the chief recipient of federal funds for civilizing the Indians. The Cherokees represented the great success of their efforts, for by settling down on their fifteen million acres they had proved that Indians could abandon the hunt and live like Christian farmers. Humanitarian organizations all over the North supported them. Jeremiah Evarts, a Congregationalist leader, wrote a series of articles under the pseudonym William Penn denouncing removal as an attempt "to *drive* the Indians by *force* from their country," a stain on the national honor. In the Senate, Theodore Frelinghuysen led the fight against removal and later became president of the American Board. In the House, Davy Crockett of Tennessee, famous for his own love-hate relationship with the Indian and for loathing Jackson, rose to denounce removal. The Indians were "a sovereign people." Forcible removal was "oppression with a vengeance."[41] The American Peace Society called the Cherokee nation "an American Poland." Jackson was behaving with all the perfidy of the czar, adding only "the hypocrisy of a claim to republicanism."[42]

Beyond those who felt that the moral issue of Indian rights was a battleground of the American soul were others like Henry Clay who saw it as a made-to-order political issue to break the Jackson coalition and win the presidency. The hard-drinking dueler, gambler, and womanizer from Kentucky considered the Indian to be "essentially inferior to the Anglo-Saxon." The red man was "destined to disappear" within fifty years. But once the Removal Act was passed in 1830, he called for public meetings across the nation to condemn "that abominable law" and to circulate petitions for its repeal.[43] The opposition to Indian removal was particularly strong in Ohio and Pennsylvania where Quaker influence was still considerable.

Jackson had adopted an Indian boy and brought him into his home, but this did nothing to alter his reputation in the North as a cruel Indian fighter and an enemy of the race. Thomas L. Mc-Kenney, on the other hand, the leading bureaucrat in charge of Indian affairs since 1816, was known as a humanitarian who understood the red man and his ways. He too had raised a Choctaw boy as his son while serving as Superintendent of Indian Trade. As head of the Indian Bureau he had improved living conditions and was considered the Indians' best friend in government. Better still for the task he was about to perform, he had opposed Jackson in the election. McKenney had long believed that the Indians could be "civilized" and become part of "our great American family of freemen." But while visiting the Cherokees and other tribes he had experienced a "sudden change" in his "opinions and hopes."[44] The Cherokees in fact were doing well. But McKenney, dependent as he was on his government salary and not in the best of health, made a public confession of his conversion just as the Jacksonians were about to take over and to institute the practice of using government jobs to reward friends and punish enemies. McKenney suddenly saw the handwriting on the wall. If the Indians did not emigrate, "they *must perish*."

He was put in charge of marshaling public support for removal. Having first tried to enlist the Episcopal bishop of New York, who turned him down, he managed to persuade Stephen Van Rensselaer, president of the Missionary Society of the Dutch Reformed Church, to form a new organization called the New York Board for the Emigration, Preservation, and Improvement of the Aborigines of America. It was to do battle with the American Board, the established missionary organization, which opposed removal. Funds originally appropriated for Indian education were diverted to pay for tracts arguing the case for removal. "This sort of machinery can move the world," McKenney exulted in his report to Secretary of

War Eaton. "I think the blow is struck that will silence all opposers."[45] The Baptists endorsed removal at their General Convention, and their magazine, *Columbian Star and Christian Index*, became part of the ground swell for saving the Indian by dispatching him to the wilderness beyond the Mississippi. Others with long experience in Indian affairs, who had been reluctant to press for forcible removal, climbed aboard. Lewis Cass, a former territorial governor of Michigan and a leading Indian fighter, wrote an influential article in *North American Review* supporting removal as "the only means of preserving the Indians from that utter extinction which threatens them."[46]

Three contradictory images of the Indian had entered the American popular culture and these helped seal his fate. First, most citizens saw the original Americans as foreigners in their midst. Though few would have followed Tocqueville's curious reasoning, the young French visitor's conclusion that the Indians were un-American because they represented the past was instinctively shared. Tocqueville compared the Indians to the Germanic ancestors of the Europeans. "He thinks hunting and war the only cares worthy of man. Therefore the Indian in the miserable depths of his forest cherishes the same ideas and opinions as the medieval noble in his castle, and he only needs to become a conqueror to complete the resemblance. How odd it is that the ancient prejudices of Europe should reappear not among the European population on the coast, but in the forests of the New World."[47]

The second image of the Indian has persisted down to our own day in Westerns, an image of savage, irrational violence. Long before he had become the chief propagandist for removal, Thomas McKenney was impressed by how deeply the image of the Indian as alien monster had penetrated the American consciousness: "Which of us has not listened with sensations of horror to nursury stories that we are told of the Indian and his cruelties? In our infant mind he stood for the Moloch of our country. We have been made to hear his yell; and to our eyes have been presented his tall, gaunt form with skins of beasts dangling around his limbs, and his eyes like fire, eager to find some new victim on which to fasten himself, and glut his appetite for blood."[48] For many who grew up on the frontier there were formative memories of hiding under the bed to escape an Indian raid. One Tennessee senator said that the first thing he remembered from his childhood was watching his brother being scalped. Indian violence licensed whites to shed the niceties of civilization. The frontiersmen became scalpers themselves.

Lewis Cass remembered as a child seeing his father returning home with a clump of Indian scalps. The doctor who had attended the dying Seminole warrior Osceola "hung the Indian's skull on the bedpost to frighten his misbehaving children."[49] Such stories revolted easterners, confirming their judgment that the frontier Americans were less than civilized, but the stereotype of the crazed, murderous Indian was widely accepted.

The third image was the very opposite of a national security threat, but it served equally well to justify removal. To save the Indian from inevitable extinction he must be banished from civilization and resettled in the forest. The red man was the Vanishing American. Unwilling to give up a life of "listless indolence" for "the stationary and laborious duties of civilized societies," as Lewis Cass put it, he would continue to die off.[50] While the picture of savage freedom and idyllic innocence might occasionally excite envy in the breast of hard-driving American frontiersmen, the stubborn defiance of American commercial values could not be permitted to block the march of civilization. As Francis Parkman put it, "The Indian is hewn out of rock. You can rarely change the form without destruction of the substance. . . . He will not learn the art of civilization, and he and his forest must perish together."

The ravages of nature and disease would continue to take their toll. But now the Indians faced a new threat. The tribes were on a collision course with the states. For thirty years Georgia had been chipping away at the Indian lands. Now state authorities asserted complete control, including the right to forbid whites from entering Indian land. Samuel Worcester, a missionary in the employ of the United States on Indian land, was arrested by the state of Georgia and put in prison for not having a Georgia license. John Marshall declared the Georgia law asserting jurisdiction over Indian territory unconstitutional because it violated Indian treaties, which, according to the Constitution, were the supreme law of the land. The Court had ruled that the issue of Indian rights was a matter of foreign affairs. But the federal government did not have legal authority to enforce the order until the Court issued a writ of habeas corpus or used its contempt power, and this it did not do. It is not certain whether Jackson ever actually said, "John Marshall has made his decision. Now let him enforce it." But he did say that the decision "has fell still born" and nothing was to be done about it.

As the election of 1832 approached, Worcester and other missionaries were still in prison, and the case made good propaganda for the anti-Jackson forces: "Will the Christian people of the United

States give their sanction . . . to the conduct of a President who treats the ministers of the Christian religion with open outrage?"[51] Though Van Buren, Jackson's running mate, estimated that they had lost perhaps ten thousand votes in New York because of sympathy with the Indians and the missionaries, the incumbents were reelected by a large margin. Once the Removal Act was passed and Jackson was safely assured of a second term, the Chickasaw, Creek, Choctaw, and Cherokee nations were doomed. During his second term the opposition of the missionary societies weakened as they competed with one another for government contracts to educate the tribes in their new homes on the far side of the Mississippi River.

In his Farewell Address in March 1837, Jackson dropped the humanitarian rhetoric with which he had originally cloaked his Indian policy. "The states which had so long been retarded in their improvement by the Indian tribes residing in the midst of them," he reported, "are at length relieved from the evil." He hoped that "the unhappy race" would prosper in its new faraway land. But in case it did not, the Removal Act provided for the reversion of the new Indian lands to the United States should the tribes become "extinct." After leaving office Andrew Jackson recollected that Indian removal had been "the most arduous part of my duty." The bill to bring it about was considered by supporters as "the leading measure" of the Jackson administration and by those who opposed it, such as the Massachusetts congressman Edward Everett, as "the greatest question that ever came before Congress, short of the question of peace and war."[52]

The actual task of removal Jackson left to his handpicked successor. In the first year of Van Buren's presidency the tribes were rounded up at gunpoint by five regiments of regulars and four thousand militia and volunteers under the command of Major General Winfield Scott and marched to the west. Seventeen thousand Cherokees crammed into 645 wagons, the rest marching alongside, arrived at the Mississippi by December. Van Buren reported to Congress that the Cherokees were now settled in their new homes with "the happiest effects," but almost a quarter of them had died on the way.[53] Ralph Waldo Emerson had tried to head off the forced removal with a stirring letter to the president: "The soul of man . . . from Maine to Georgia, does abhor this business." Henry Wadsworth Longfellow and James Fenimore Cooper also wrote sympathetically of the Indian but acknowledged, as one historian has put it, "that they had to make way for the American dream."

The removal of the Indians is one of the darkest chapters in

American history. During the Jackson–Van Buren years forty-six thousand Native Americans were forced to relocate and the United States acquired 100 million acres of land for approximately $68 million dollars.[54] During these same years the abolitionist movement against slavery was gathering strength. How did it happen that public indignation could be effectively mobilized against slavery but not against the barbarous treatment of Native Americans?

I would suggest three reasons. First, unlike the case of slavery, which abolitionists could argue was becoming obsolete, thanks to economic changes and advances in agricultural technology, the very existence of the Native American threatened the white man's vision of progress. Even in the abolitionist North the huge expanse of Indian land to the south was understood to be a precious national asset; slave labor was not. Second, Britain had outlawed the slave trade by 1807 and slavery itself throughout its empire by 1833. Elsewhere in Europe there was a gathering movement that demanded the elimination of bondage and serfdom. But with respect to the treatment of "savages" encountered in the quest for empire, there was no such progressive consensus. Wherever settlers confronted native tribes—Africa, Australia, Latin America, at the fringes of Europe itself—the same murderous costs of civilization were exacted. Third, for many Americans the humanitarian arguments that Andrew Jackson advanced in support of removal and that he himself believed were convincing. "I tell you that you cannot remain where you now are," Jackson had told the Cherokees. "Your peculiar customs . . . have been abrogated by the great political community among which you live. . . . Your condition must become worse and worse, and you will ultimately disappear, as so many tribes have done before you."[55] The false assurance advanced by Jackson, that the Indians were living beyond the Mississippi "in plenty,—and happy under their own laws and customs," encouraged Americans to forget what had been done in their name.[56]

───── CHAPTER 4 ─────

The Politics of Expansion

1.

The Monroe Doctrine, which was proclaimed in 1823, had helped to create a new national consciousness. By declaring that the New World was now closed to further colonization by the European powers, the feisty young Republic had drawn a line, and to a man, so the myth went, the wicked kings of Europe dared not cross it. From the first the Doctrine, though actually invoked rather erratically, served as a political icon, the very touchstone of Americanism. (Mary Baker Eddy, the founder of Christian Science, a peculiarly American religion, once explained that her creed was based on her strict belief in the Monroe Doctrine, in our Constitution, and in the laws of God—in that order.[1]) Exactly what America was, what its society would turn out to look like, how big it was to be, were still uncertain, but the one thing that held the United States together was pride in keeping Europeans from encroaching further on the New World.

There was now a certain bumptiousness to American nationalism. Travelers from Europe and observers of Americans abroad picked up on what Tocqueville called the "irritable patriotism" of early-nineteenth-century Americans. The poet Shelley, for example, was once invited aboard an American clipper schooner docked at Leghorn, and under the Star-Spangled Banner went out of his way to offer a gracious toast to Washington, who "was righteous in all he did, unlike all who lived before or since." According to Shelley's companion, the Yankee replied, "Stranger, truer words were never spoken; there is dry rot in all the main timbers of the Old

World, and none of you will do any good till you are docked, refitted, and annexed to the New."[2]

James K. Polk, a Tennessee politician whose gift for oratory won him the nickname "Napoleon of the stump," embodied the new spirit of nationalism. He was the original "dark horse" candidate for the presidency. Having just been defeated for reelection as governor of Tennessee, not an obvious qualification for higher office, he was pushed by the ultraexpansionists and received the Democratic nomination for president in 1844. Much like John F. Kennedy in 1960, he combined the image of youth with a promise to get the country moving again. According to his enthusiastic supporter, the *United States Journal*, the "triumphant election" of a forty-nine-year-old man—Polk was the youngest ever up to that time to ascend to the presidency—was inspired by "Young America, awakened to a sense of her own intellectual greatness by her soaring spirit. It stands in strength, the voice of the majority. . . . It demands the immediate annexation of Texas at any and every hazard. It will plant its right foot upon the northern verge of Oregon, and its left upon the Atlantic crag, and waving the stars and stripes in the face of the once proud Mistress of the Ocean, bid her, if she dare, 'Cry havoc, and let slip the dogs of war' "[3] Unlike the political favorites of the day, Van Buren and Clay, both of whom recoiled from taking Texas into the Union for fear of dividing the country further over slavery, Polk courted politicians of the West and the South who considered the Lone Star Republic already part of the Union.

The new president provoked a war with Mexico for the primary purpose of adding California to the Union. The great prizes were the thirteen hundred miles of Pacific coast and the magnificent harbor of San Francisco, which could then comfortably accommodate all the navies of the world.[4] But until the outbreak of war, as the historian Norman Graebner notes, "California's acquisition had never been a topic of public and congressional discussion at all."[5] Nonetheless, Polk had no trouble believing that he was responding to the will of the people, for he read his election as a mandate for conquest somewhere.[6] Americans seemed to be itching to go to war with Britain over Oregon. "Fifty-four forty or fight," the popular Democratic Party slogan calling for the annexation of a sizable chunk of British Vancouver, reinforced Polk's belief that war with Mexico to acquire Texas, and in the process California as well, carried no serious domestic political risks.

But Oregon itself was another matter, because a war for the northwest territory would require confronting the most powerful empire on earth. Southern cotton growers, exaggerating British dependence on their product, jeered at the thought that Britain would fight for Oregon. However, the stalwarts of the Whig Party, supported by merchants of the eastern seaboard, did not think Her Majesty's government was prepared to abandon its holdings on the Pacific coast. War would be a disaster; the U.S. Army was little more than eleven thousand strong. After the British rejected the American demands and began mobilizing thirty warships for a fight, Polk made a few rousing speeches about the Monroe Doctrine, quietly negotiated with the British, and then turned the matter over to the Whigs in Congress to ratify the compromise. With Calhoun's help, Daniel Webster shepherded the Oregon treaty through the Senate, exulting over this unusual delegation of presidential power. "Here is a treaty negotiated by the Senate, and only agreed to by the President."[7] But in fact Polk was happy to have the Senate take responsibility for the concessions to the British that were bound to disappoint the public.[8]

Polk believed that war with Mexico was a more promising route to expansion, but he was well aware that the country was divided about whether to annex Texas. For more than twenty-five years the United States had been trying to purchase the vast territory from Mexico. In 1819 Secretary of State John Quincy Adams had offered the Spanish one million dollars, and Andrew Jackson had raised the offer to $5 million. (Jackson did not care what Mexico did with the money, he had explained to his envoy. It could be used as a bribe "for the purchase of men" or it could go "to pay the public debt."[9]) But Mexico, having recently won its independence from Spain, was in no mood to sell.

Shortly before their ouster in the Mexican War of Independence in 1823 the Spanish had awarded a pioneer by the name of Moses Austin a large tract of land in Texas on the understanding that he would settle no more than three hundred families on it. By 1835, however, thirty thousand white settlers had made their home there. A new Mexican government under General Santa Anna took exception to the settlement and abolished the Texas legislature. When the Mexican general brought a large military force into Texas to restore control, the Americans—men like the rough-and-ready Sam Houston and James Bowie, inventor of the eighteen-inch knife known affectionately as the Arkansas toothpick—led a revolt. At the Alamo two hundred Texans held off five thousand Mexicans for twelve days, until on March 6, 1836, the last defender, Davy Crockett among them, was dead. Three weeks later a Texas force made

up of recent volunteers from the United States surrendered at Goliad, and three hundred of the prisoners were killed. Refugees from
Texas crowded their way north to the border. "Remember the
Alamo" became a rallying cry throughout the United States. A few
weeks later at San Jacinto the Texas army scored a victory as crushing as the defeats at the Alamo and Goliad. The Texans captured
Santa Anna and forced him to sign a treaty withdrawing all Mexican
forces and extending the Texas frontier one hundred fifty miles to
the south. Once back in Mexico City, however, Santa Anna repudiated the agreements he had signed to save his life and vowed to
recover the disputed territory.

Agents from Texas were untiring in their efforts to stir up public
opinion. As far away as Maine volunteers offered themselves to fight
for Texas's freedom. Mass meetings to raise money for the Texas
cause were held in every large city. Many volunteers were lured
south by the promise of land, and under the banner "Texas and
Liberty" they marched through Alabama to the border. The Texans
immediately offered their huge expanse to the United States, an
annexation that would be accomplished in two steps. First, the
United States would recognize the independence of the Lone Star
Republic, and then it would accept its petition to be gathered into
the Union.

An election was drawing near, and Jackson was determined to see
his protégé Martin Van Buren installed as his successor. A vocal
segment of the American public, mostly in the South, favored annexation. "The men under 35, *and all the women*," Chief Justice
Catron of the Tennessee Supreme Court wrote Jackson, "are for
having St. Anna shot, and the *Texas Eagle* planted on his capitol." [10]
But in New England particularly, the events in Texas were viewed
with the greatest suspicion. The sudden rush of American settlers
to Texas smelled of a conspiracy to create a huge new slave-owning
southern state to shift the electoral balance. Though most Americans felt that Texas was engaged in a noble struggle, Texans were
not universally admired. "Gone to Texas" was a euphemism for
hiding out from creditors, "the Botany Bay" of the New World, one
Savannah paper snorted. [11] In the North the Texas struggle brought
out not only abolitionist sentiments but snobbery. The call for volunteers for the Texas army elicited mock enthusiasm in Boston.
"What a capital chance for large cities to get rid of their loafers,"
observed the *Transcript*. "What man in his senses would volunteer
in a Texas Expedition who could earn an honest living at home?"

By 1844, the year Polk was elected, Texans and their partisans in the United States, to encourage the United States to annex the vast territory, were planting rumors that the British were about to take Texas. (The expansionists also spread stories that the British were about to take over California as well. The British minister to Mexico favored the idea, but the Foreign Office never considered it seriously.[12]) By conducting large-scale raids into Texas the Mexicans fed annexationist sentiment throughout the United States. Upon taking office, Polk sent John Slidell on a secret mission to Mexico City to purchase California and make one last effort to acquire Texas without war. Polk's passion for secrecy suggests that he may not have been quite so sure of his expansionist mandate as his diaries suggest. The Mexicans sent Polk's secret agent packing. "Be advised that nothing is to be done with these people," he informed the president, "until they shall have been chastised."[13]

Polk had urged the Texans themselves to occupy the disputed territory in the hopes that the move would provoke the Mexicans and justify a U.S. war of conquest under the pretext of protecting the new Americans. But some of the Texas leaders would not go along with the scheme. Now the president was determined to create his own pretext for an invasion. He secretly ordered a contingent of regulars under the command of General Zachary Taylor to cross into a strip of Texas territory that he knew Mexico considered its own. The general, charged with defending the Rio Grande as the Texas boundary and the new southern frontier of the United States, took up positions opposite the Mexican city of Matamoros and threatened to starve the city into submission if the Mexicans did not yield the disputed territory. "It looks as if the government sent a small force on purpose to bring on a war, so as to have a pretext for taking California and as much of this country as it chooses," Colonel Ethan Allen Hitchcock, a West Pointer who commanded one of General Taylor's regiments, wrote in his diary. "My heart is not in this business."[14] Newspapers like the Washington Union had no such scruples. "The road to California will be open to us. Who will stay the march of our western people? . . . A corps of properly organized volunteers . . . would invade, overrun, and occupy Mexico."[15]

At a Saturday-afternoon cabinet meeting on May 9, 1846, the day after his secret agent returned, the president informed his advisers that he intended to ask Congress for a declaration of war the following Tuesday. "The country," he said, "was excited and impatient on the subject, and if I failed to do so I would not be doing my duty." That same evening the not unexpected news arrived that two of Zachary Taylor's companies had been ambushed by a Mexican detachment that had crossed the Rio Grande into territory claimed by Texas. Three Americans had been killed. Polk immediately decided to speed up his timetable and ask for war on Monday. It went against his Scotch Presbyterian conscience to work on Sunday, he wrote in his diary, but he interrupted his work on the war message long enough to go to church.[16]

Mexico, the president charged, has "passed the boundary of the United States, has invaded our territory and shed American blood upon the American soil. . . . The cup of forbearance [is] exhausted." The immediate reaction of the Whigs, notably Henry Clay, and powerful members of the president's own party like John Calhoun and Thomas Hart Benton, was to oppose the war as unjust and dangerous. The Rio Grande was not the recognized border between Texas and Mexico. The territory on which blood had been shed was in dispute. Polk insisted, however, that Congress recognize the state of war and authorize him to prosecute it to a "speedy and successful termination."

No previous president had ever committed the country to a major war on his own responsibility as James Polk did in May 1846, and none would do so again until Harry Truman dispatched American forces to Korea in 1950 without even informal consultation with Congress. The Whigs charged that it was Polk himself "who began this war" by sending American forces into battle without the knowledge of Congress, but the president had the opposition in his power because Congress had no choice but to reinforce American soldiers who had been attacked by the Mexicans and were said to be in danger of being wiped out. Even those in Congress who hated the war, such as the freshman Illinois representative Abraham Lincoln, felt forced to give eloquent speeches against it, and then vote the appropriations.

The war bill was passed in two hours in the House and the next day by an even more lopsided majority in the Senate. Men like Stephen Douglas and Jefferson Davis welcomed the war as a vehicle for expanding American dominion to the Pacific Ocean. But Calhoun, who said he would rather plunge a dagger in his heart than vote for the lie that Mexico was the aggressor, did not vote. And neither did Daniel Webster. The antiwar faction opposed Polk's adventure for many different reasons besides moral revulsion at provoking a war of conquest against a weak neighbor. The antislavery Democrats feared that the extension of American dominion over the Southwest would add more slave territories to the United

States. Calhoun, though he favored annexation of Texas, thought the war with Mexico was unnecessary and dangerous because it might give the British a pretext to intervene on Mexico's side.

There was plenty of war fever in the newspapers well before the border skirmish. "LET US GO TO WAR," bellowed a New York *Journal of Commerce* editorial. "Nine-tenths of our people would rather have a little fighting than not," said the *Morning News* without the slightest substantiation for its claim. The Richmond *Enquirer* was also certain that Americans were all for "a full and thorough chastisement of Mexican arrogance and folly." Had some of the martial fantasies of the Mexicans been more widely known in the United States, the war fever might have been even greater than it was. How could the Yankees, having blundered in their efforts to take Canada, be a threat to Mexico? Degenerates, braggarts, and moneygrubbers, the Americans were no match for the Mexican Army—on paper five times bigger than the U.S. Army. Mexican officers boasted that they planned to drive into Louisiana, arm the slaves, and incite the Indians.

However, there is no evidence other than his own assertions at the cabinet table about public opinion that Polk was pushed into war. No organized political force was pressing for war. Ten years had elapsed since the Alamo. Unlike the agonizing years leading up to the War of 1812, or the protracted public debates as the United States groped its way to war in World War I or was led to the brink of war in 1941 even before the Japanese attack at Pearl Harbor, the United States was in the Mexican War before the public knew it. The public was being asked to support a *fait accompli*.

Nevertheless, many, probably most, Americans greeted the news of war with enthusiasm. Large rallies in support of the invasion of Mexico were held in New York, Baltimore, Indianapolis, and dozens of other cities. "A military ardor pervades all ranks," Herman Melville wrote to his brother. "Nothing is talked of but the 'Halls of Montezumas.'" Walt Whitman echoed the cry, "Mexico must be thoroughly chastised." "Our people are like a young man of 18," Calhoun wrote to his fellow South Carolinian Thomas G. Clemson, "full of health and vigor and disposed for adventure . . . but without wisdom or experience."[17] In New York City this first foreign war was celebrated in patriotic plays. *The March of Freedom*, in which General Zachary Taylor played opposite the Goddess of Liberty, was billed as a "grand national drama." In Philadelphia a play commemorating the destruction of Matamoros was put on within five hours of the receipt of the news—which turned out to be untrue.

Nathaniel Hawthorne compared the "chivalrous beauty" of the volunteers heading for Mexico to the "spirit of young knights." For thousands of volunteers the grueling months in Mexico forged a sense of national pride, for this was a war to "regenerate Mexico" and bring it into the modern world. Many others, however, were cured of their taste for glory by the tarantulas, scorpions, and dust. Contemporary chronicles of the war were immensely popular, and on the long march, soldiers eagerly read cheaply bound "novelettes" recounting the adventure, glory, and exotica of the war to the south.[18]

To many Americans the war against Mexico was Manifest Destiny. This quintessentially American ideology rested on three legs: the logic of geography (a vast expanse empty of all but savages), the blessings of technology (the steam engine and the telegraph, God-given sinews of a continental nation), and missionary spirit (The Temple of Freedom beckoning backward peoples to enlightenment and prosperity). The man who coined the term in 1845 was John O'Sullivan. A lawyer, a literary critic, the publisher of early works of Poe, Hawthorne, and Whittier, a regent of the University of New York, and later minister to Portugal, O'Sullivan was a romantic visionary who believed that the United States was destined to expand across the continent not by force of arms but because its freedoms would attract all the peoples of North America. The United States would "never be the forcible subjugator of other countries." But he soon came to believe that arms could be of considerable help. He became a soldier of fortune in Cuba, recruiting a private army to liberate the island when President Polk balked at sending in the marines.

The expansionist sentiments of the day were reflected in the "penny press." With the invention of the revolving-cylinder press, a machine that could throw off ten thousand papers an hour, metropolitan dailies began developing large circulations in Boston, Philadelphia, New York, and Baltimore. Thanks to the telegraph and faster transportation, smaller papers all around the country began reprinting articles from the big-city newspapers. Creating public opinion by planting articles in the press became more feasible. The penny press was the first commercially successful news medium. Of course every major political party still operated its own newspaper, but because of their mass circulation some of the large dailies could make themselves somewhat independent of party patronage. The dominant ideology of these papers was "manifest destiny." In their quest for circulation, editors shamelessly supplied their readers and

advertisers with what they took to be their own opinions and prejudices—American nationalism and the righteousness of conquest—
served up in overheated prose. "It would be as easy to stay the
swelling of the ocean with a grain of sand upon its shore," cried a
typical expansionist editorial in the *Boston Times* in 1844, "as to
stop the advancement of this truly democratic and omnipotent
spirit of the age."[19] If Harriet Martineau had been appalled by the
newspapers of the 1830s, she would have been rendered speechless
by the journalism of the 1840s. In the *New York Tribune* Horace
Greeley wrote eloquently of peace, social reform, and the evils of
slavery, but the market for social uplift was weaker than for jingoism, and he soon found that he had to raise his price to two cents a
copy.[20]

In 1846 virtually all Americans believed that the United States
should and would expand its territory, its influence, and its power.
It was a process as natural as the progression of the seasons. But as
to the extent and character of that expansion and the means by
which the nation would expand, there emerged deep differences.
Thus the Mexican War provoked bitter dissension within President
Polk's own party as well as in the principal opposition party, the
Whigs. One source of fury was the widespread belief, surely not
wrong, that Polk had staged the war, that he had "literally provoked" it, as Representative Stephens put it, and thus in the words
of one Whig congressman "usurped the power of Congress." To
which the president retorted, much as future presidents would answer their critics in the next century, that such a wrongheaded view
of the honorable struggle against the Mexicans lent "aid and comfort" to those who were shooting at American boys.

The concern that slavery would extend its domain over the
Southwest was not entirely allayed by Representative Wilmot's
amendment that declared slavery illegal in any of the territories
conquered in the war. Some opponents of the war used racist arguments to support their position. The warning of a Georgia newspaper was typical: The conquered Mexican territories—New
Mexico, California—would prove indigestible, and the nation
would choke on "a sickening mixture, consisting of such a conglom-
eration of Negroes and Rancheros, Mestizoes, and Indians, with
but a few Castilians."[21]

Perhaps more than any other save the Civil War, the Mexican
War raised fundamental questions of national identity. Could the
United States remain a republic if on his own the president could
commit the nation to a war of conquest? "Has the world ever known

a Republic," Horace Greeley wrote in the *New York Tribune*, "which extended its boundaries by the subjugation of diverse and hostile races without undermining thereby its own liberties?"[22] What about national honor? That was a question Americans on both sides of the war asked. For some, preying on a weak nation was the antithesis of morality; for others, bringing progress and enlightenment to backward peoples was a moral imperative. For patriotic Americans who considered the war of conquest abhorrent, the drive deep into Mexico "to extend freedom" was a hateful sham. "You [Mexicans] must have the same degree of freedom which we enjoy, whether you are fit for it or not," the *Richmond Whig* thundered. "If you refuse, we will ravage your fields, hang you up by the neck until you are dead . . . and leave your towns in smoking ruins."

Within weeks of the outbreak of war Polk's secret plans to annex large chunks of Mexico became clear. Colonel Stephen Kearny's Army of the West marched into Santa Fe and proclaimed that the Mexican province of New Mexico now belonged to the United States. The commander had secret orders to establish civil government in California, part of Mexico's richest lands. The American explorer John Charles Frémont along with Commodore Robert Stockton captured Santa Barbara and Los Angeles and the commodore proclaimed himself governor of California.

Expansionists had seen a happy connection between Texas and California ever since the days of Andrew Jackson; California was the sweetener to help abolitionist New England swallow Texas. Bankers and merchants on the eastern seaboard were as enthusiastic about extending federal authority over California as they were suspicious of taking in Texas. Boston traders had been engaged in the hunt for sea otters off the California coast ever since the 1790s, and by the 1820s their interest had turned to California hides. A Boston firm, Bryant & Sturgis, established an office in Santa Barbara in 1829 and later in Monterey, and several of its employees, most notably the travel writer Richard Henry Dana, played an important role in arousing public excitement about the Far West in the cities of the East.[23] Southerners, on the other hand, eyed California as part of a southern confederacy should secession prove unavoidable.

The war created a public opinion problem for all sides. Events had proved that Whig skepticism about Polk's real motives for starting the war was justified, but the opposition did not wish to denounce brilliant American victories that were undeniably popular.

So while the Whigs voted the military appropriations, they criticized Polk for lying about the war and for mismanaging it. Not unlike the Korean War, a little more than a hundred years later, the Democratic president was held responsible for the casualties and the cost, while the victories were laid at the feet of the two leading generals, both of whom were Whigs. By the end of 1847 Winfield Scott had landed at Vera Cruz and occupied Mexico City. (The fabled Duke of Wellington had said it could not be done.) Zachary Taylor, outnumbered four to one, won a smashing victory at Buena Vista.

As Winfield Scott sat in Mexico City, avoiding combat and casualties, waiting for the Mexicans to surrender, a strange thing happened. Despite the battlefield triumphs, more and more Americans were turning against the war. After a while the news of each victory below the Rio Grande evoked more anger than cheers. A brief war had been promised, and the conflict was now in its second year. A limited war had been proclaimed, and now the expansionists were calling for the annexation of all Mexico. The center of opposition to the war was in New England, particularly Boston, home of the American Peace Society and the Anti-Slavery Society. Ralph Waldo Emerson wrote in his journal, "The United States will conquer Mexico, but will be as the man swallows the arsenic, which brings him down in turn. Mexico will poison us."[24] But though the most popular lecturer of the day, he said nothing publicly about the war. "Better mind your lamp and pen," he advised himself, "interfering not with Politics." His friend Henry Thoreau, on the other hand, spent a night in jail for refusing to pay a tax that went to support the war, and, to his puzzlement, became famous for it. James Russell Lowell wrote satirical poems attacking the war, and Herman Melville, celebrating America's mission of freedom, reminded his readers, "It is not freedom to filch."

But the cities of the East and Middle West were also the centers of the "All Mexico" movement. Newspapers talked hungrily of the silver mines and the narrow Isthmus of Tehuantepec, so ideal for building an American canal to link the oceans. "The [Mexican] race is perfectly accustomed to being conquered," the New York Sun assured its readers, "and the only new lesson we shall teach is that our victories will give liberty, safety, and prosperity to the vanquished."[25] The New York Herald thought that all of Mexico would be "gorgeously" happy as a conquered province. "Like the Sabine virgins, she will soon learn to love her ravisher."[26]

How widely shared these views were among the general public is not so easy to determine. The historian Frederick Merk argues in his *Manifest Destiny and Mission* that while acquisition, by force if necessary, of particular pieces of real estate such as Texas and Oregon had wide public support, the doctrine of "continentalism"—incorporation of all North America into the Union—was never supported by more than a "small minority of a minority." The brewing storm over slavery had produced a strong movement for states' rights, which served as a check on rampant nationalism. Ironically, the same racist feelings that fueled the war, causing the *Illinois State Register* to disdain the Mexicans as "but little removed above the Negro" and the House Committee on Foreign Affairs to dismiss them as "a semi-barbarous people," also served to dampen enthusiasm for absorbing too many Mexicans. The *Democratic Review* thought that the "glories of enlarged dominion" could be purchased at "too great expense."[27] Yet at the same time a powerful theological argument in favor of annexation was gaining strength. "Divine Providence," so went a letter written in 1847 to the Washington *Daily Union* typical of such views, is calling the nation to a "glorious mission . . . to civilize and christianize, and raise up from anarchy and degradation a most ignorant, indolent, wicked and unhappy people."[28]

By 1847 the frustration of the American people with the Mexican War reached the boiling point. The great victories were over. Vast areas of Mexico were occupied, including the capital, but the Mexicans still refused to negotiate. Whig politicians and newspapers stepped up the moral arguments against land grabbing and the practical problems of trying to swallow all of Mexico with its "wretched population." As the war dragged on, the costs were of increasing concern. The president should be impeached "for the loss of the 15,000 lives, which have been sacrificed in Mexico," declared an Indiana paper that had earlier supported the war. Edward Everett, later famous for sharing the platform at Gettysburg Cemetery with Abraham Lincoln, complained to the British foreign secretary, "We are paying about 100,000,000 dollars for the luxury of conquest."[29] Even O'Sullivan, the prophet of Manifest Destiny, was having second thoughts about the war. "I am afraid it was not God that got us into the war, but that He may get us out of it is the constant prayer of yours very truly."[30]

In September 1847, Santa Anna fled after American reinforcements arrived, and a new Mexican president came into office determined to make peace. In the midst of the rising debate in Congress about whether the U.S. should press on and absorb "All Mexico" into the Union and the growing disillusionment with the war across the country came surprising news. Nicholas Trist, whom Polk had picked as his secret emissary in Mexico City, had negotiated a peace treaty. With the support of Generals Scott and Taylor but in defiance of the president's explicit instructions to return to Washington, he had signed it on behalf of the United States at the village of Guadalupe Hidalgo, just outside Mexico City. Mexico was relieved of Texas, California, and New Mexico, and was given a little more than $18 million, a punishing loss but considerably less than what U.S. military power could eventually have exacted had the war gone on. Although the peace terms were remarkably close to what he had originally instructed his agent Slidell to negotiate, Polk was outraged by Trist's insubordination and conspiracy with the Whig generals. The young diplomat was dismissed without pay. (Trist lived in poverty for more than twenty years until President Grant decided to make him postmaster in Alexandria, Virginia.) Having punished the peacemaker, Polk presented his peace to Congress as a *fait accompli*—just like the war.

Public opinion had operated as a modest brake on American conquest. Polk was not concerned about his own political future, because he had promised not to run again, but he worried that the gathering power of the All Mexico movement could split the country in two. This concern made him eager to grab the peace. "The popular passion for territorial aggrandizement is irresistible," reported William H. Seward, a brilliant New York politician with an insatiable appetite for distant tracts of land. "A more perfect Union, embracing the Whole of the North American continent," cried Senator Dickinson as he raised his glass at a Jackson Day dinner. Yet the anger of the Whigs was as great as the enthusiasm of the expansionists. The Boston *Atlas* went so far as to observe that it would be "a sad and woeful joy, but a joy nevertheless, to hear that the hordes under Scott and Taylor were, every man of them, swept into the next world."[31]

In the second major conflict fought by the United States under the Constitution the American people once again proved impatient with war, even a successful one. Polk believed that conquering California and Texas for future generations of Americans was an act of self-sacrifice, and indeed, within four months of leaving the presidency he was dead. But his triumphs brought tragedy. General Ulysses S. Grant wrote in his memoirs that the Civil War "was largely the outgrowth of the Mexican War," and it is a judgment to which many historians would subscribe.[32] The young Abraham Lincoln's concern in 1848 about what Polk's arrogation of war-making power would do to constitutional government itself was prescient:

> Allow the President to invade a neighboring country whenever *he* shall deem it necessary to repel an invasion, and you allow him to do so, *whenever he may choose to say* he deems it necessary for such purpose—and you allow him to make war at pleasure. Study to see if you can fix *any limit* to his power in this respect, after you have given him so much. . . .
>
> The provision of the Constitution giving the war-making power to Congress, was dictated, as I understand it, by the following reasons. Kings had always been involving and impoverishing their people in wars, pretending generally, if not always, that the good of the people was the object. This our Convention understood to be the most oppressive of all kingly oppressions.[33]

James Polk's war did not impoverish the American people. Quite the contrary. But the price of conquest was the usurpation of powers that under the Constitution rightfully belonged to the people and their representatives.

2.

In the decade before the Civil War, talk of Manifest Destiny was becoming extravagant. America, said the Philadelphia *Ledger* in 1853, was bounded on the East "by the sunrise, North by the Arctic Expedition, and South as far as we darn please." In New York the *Herald* struck the same note. "National glory—national greatness —the spread of political liberty on this continent, must be the thought and action by day, and the throbbing dream by night, of the whole American people, or they will sink into oblivion."[34]

American statesmen now consciously played to the new nationalist enthusiasms in the hopes of keeping together a Union that had begun to unravel over the slavery issue. When the Austrian government complained about the demonstration of American sympathy for the Hungarian Revolution of 1848, Secretary of State Daniel Webster made a point of responding with words "which should touch the national pride." The possessions of the House of Hapsburg, he pointed out in a feisty note addressed to the Austrians but meant for the American voter, "are but as a patch on the earth's surface" as compared with "the power of this republic . . . spread over a region one of the richest and most fertile on the globe." As Webster explained in a private letter, the justification for sending a communication so calculated to infuriate the Austrians was to make anyone in the United States "who should speak of disunion"—and there were many of course by the 1850s— "feel *sheepish* and look *silly*."[35] The next year the Hungarian revolutionary Louis Kossuth became a national craze as he toured the Midwest in triumph, making fiery speeches. Kossuth clubs, Kossuth hats, and Kossuth beards became briefly fashionable as ladies took off their diamonds and thrust them upon the handsome Magyar for his noble cause. "We shall rejoice to see our American model upon the Lower Danube," cried Daniel Webster at a banquet in Kossuth's honor. But when Kossuth began urging active U.S. intervention to bring down the Hapsburg empire, American enthusiasm for his project evaporated, and all traces of revolutionary ardor promptly disappeared save Kossuth County in Iowa. Stripped of his stardom, the bewildered Hungarian liberator sailed back to Europe.[36]

Though expansionist talk was common, the growing conflict over slavery served as a restraint on expansionist adventure. Every acquistion, whether inside the continental limits or beyond, raised the issue whether the new territory would be slave or free. Southerners, disappointed that their region had not gained territory in the Mexican War in which to grow more cotton, to spread what they euphemistically called the southern way of life, and to redress the deteriorating balance of power in the Union, were the most insistent expansionists. A secret society, the Knights of the Golden Circle, was formed with the purpose of spreading slavery throughout the Gulf of Mexico; by 1860 it boasted sixty-five thousand members, including three state governors and several members of President James Buchanan's cabinet.

In the pre–Civil War decade the southern expansionists focused their attention on Central America and the Caribbean. It was a time when private citizens without lawful authority could make foreign policy out of public view, the age of the filibusterer, "displaced men—adventurers, desperadoes, disappointed gold-seekers, ex-soldiers who could not settle down in civilian life . . . losers at home seeking wealth and glory in underdeveloped countries."[37] These soldiers of fortune hired private armies and intervened in foreign struggles for reasons of high principle and personal enrichment. A leading filibusterer of the day was William Walker, a wisp of a man weighing scarcely one hundred pounds, who carried out three expeditions in Central America and became the virtual owner and dictator of Nicaragua for two years. The gray-eyed man of destiny, as the newspapers called him, was an idealistic reformer who had tried to bring his notions of democracy to Mexico. He briefly became an enthusiasm of southern Democrats who pushed through a plank in the 1856 party platform celebrating his efforts to "regenerate" Nicaragua.

The principal focus of expansionist dreams in the pre–Civil War years was Cuba. American statesmen had had their eyes on the Pearl of the Antilles since Jefferson's day. (Jefferson told Calhoun in 1820 that the United States "ought, at the first possible opportunity, to take Cuba."[38]) Over the years there had been periodic fears that either England or France would try to take the island from Spain. Secretary of State John Quincy Adams believed that American annexation was "indispensable to the continuance and integrity of the Union itself" so great a risk would British or French occupation of the island pose. His successor, Henry Clay, warned away the French in 1825 when they sent a squadron into Cuban waters; the U.S. would not permit Havana harbor, the crossroads of the Caribbean and Gulf trade routes, to fall into the hands of a strong European power that could use that strategic position to bottle up American ports on the Gulf of Mexico or even to close the mouth of the Mississippi.

There had been American filibustering expeditions to Cuba since the first revolt against Spain in 1823 and the laws on the books against them were rarely enforced. Southerners were fascinated by Cuba because the colony had slaves and could comfortably fit as a new slave state in the Union. Conversely, if the U.S. did not act quickly to take the island, the Spanish might well be forced to free the slaves there, and that could spark slave revolts in the American South.[39] But northern Democrats too were interested in Cuba. The party was strongly under the influence of a populist, racist faction called Young America. Its leading figure was Stephen A. Douglas of Illinois, who believed that the United States was like a growing child; "mere 'red lines' on maps" could not restrain the inexorable push either to the north or to the south.[40] Franklin Pierce, who became president in 1853, was from New Hampshire, but he was beholden to Young America and he had many southerners in his cabinet. In his inaugural address he had made it clear that "my Administration will not be controlled by any timid forebodings of evil from expansion." A year later Pierce's secretary of state, after trying unsuccessfully to buy Cuba, gave an order to the U.S. minister in Madrid to work up a plan "to detach" Cuba from Spain.

While European diplomats watched in amazement, Pierce's ministers to London, Paris, and Madrid met in Belgium and wrote a confidential dispatch to the State Department, which was immediately leaked to the press; "by every law, human and divine, we shall be justified in wresting [Cuba] from Spain" to prevent the "Africanization" of the island. The public outcry in the North against what the *New York Tribune* called a "manifesto of brigands" was so great that Congress published the dispatches, but minus Pierce's own incriminating instructions. The publicity about the Ostend Manifesto, as it was called, derailed the efforts to take Cuba. The affair strengthened the antiexpansionists and loosened the grip of both southerners and Stephen Douglas Democrats over United States foreign policy.

The same year Franklin Pierce suffered another rebuff when he tried to annex the Hawaiian Islands. This man of such modest attainments that not even a full-length biography by Nathaniel Hawthorne could rescue him from obscurity found himself once more out of phase with public opinion. The British and the French had been making abortive efforts to seize Hawaii, and earlier administrations had warned the European powers away, in effect extending the Monroe Doctrine to the Pacific territories. Pierce, however, wanted to secure an American hold on the islands by granting them statehood, not realizing that for most Americans the idea of acquiring a multiracial state in the middle of the Pacific Ocean was bizarre.[41] Pierce was ahead of his time by about a hundred years.

For all the expansionist talk, no additional territory was conquered at all during the 1850s. The southern slice of Arizona and New Mexico was purchased from Mexico for $10 million, but even the Gadsden Purchase, as it was called, evoked howls in the Senate. Senator Thomas Hart Benton called it so desolate a piece of real estate that "a wolf could not making a living on it." The shadows of the coming struggle darkened the political landscape. Northerners could take little satisfaction in wresting some new territory from a European power, for victory would only mean another fight over slavery. As southerners saw their plans to preserve the Old South through expansion blocked, war became the only path. As the historian Walter LaFeber puts it, "Foreign policy issues were a central cause of the Civil War." Lincoln believed that the only way to avert the conflict "would be a prohibition against acquiring any more territory."[42] However, his secretary of state, William H. Seward, recommended precisely the opposite course. On April 1, 1861, less than a month after taking office, he presented the president with a plan to provoke a war with Spain and France, possibly with Great Britain and Russia as well, in order to divert attention from the domestic crisis and head off the Civil War.[43] Sadly, Lincoln shook his head. Eleven days later the forces of the Confederacy opened fire on Fort Sumter.

During the war, anti-British feeling ran high in the North. The British favored the Confederacy for many reasons. The British aristocrats who ran Queen Victoria's government felt closer to the landed gentry of the South than to the "gibbering mob" in the North, now more and more composed, as one of them put it, of the "scum of Europe."[44] Jefferson Davis, the London *Times* reported, does not chew tobacco and is "neat and clean looking, with hair trimmed, and boots brushed," a pleasant change from the man *Blackwood's* called the "imbecile executive" in the White House. British conservatives feared that a victory of the North was a victory for democracy, and they feared democracy because of the stirrings in their own country. After a series of Union reverses, the *Times* announced that the people of Britain could breathe more freely than at any time in the last thirty years. If the South won, England could extend its balance-of-power diplomacy to the New World, and, by playing the North against the South, restore some of its former influence in America. Much of this was well known in the United States, as was the fact that the British textile industry depended heavily on southern cotton. It was a time of turnabout, a United States blockade of Britain, and it nearly provoked active British intervention on the side of the Confederacy. All this was remembered when the war was over.

The four terrible years of the Civil War soured the public on martial glory. Binding up the wounds consumed American energies, and there was not much left over for imperial adventure even had there been more of a popular taste for it. The South, the section that had been the most interested in expansion into Latin America, lay wounded and mute. But William Seward stayed on as secretary of state after Lincoln's death, his zeal for foreign expansion undiminished by the recent ordeal. "Our population is destined to roll its resistless waves to the icy barriers of the north," he wrote, "and to encounter oriental civilization on the shores of the Pacific." Within a few months of the war's end, he tried to acquire the Dominican Republic, Cuba, Puerto Rico, and Hawaii. But politicians of both parties, attuned to the public mood, were not prepared to support conquests, nor were they enthusiastic about any more major purchases. Territorial acquisitions across the continental expanse were popular with Americans, but not overseas empire. The one was seen as a natural process of expansion. The other was acting like England.

Frederick Merk points out that Alaska was literally thrown at the United States by the czar in 1867. Many Americans were for throwing it back. (Nobody, on the other hand, objected to the acquisition the very same year of the Midway Islands, scene of the famous World War II battle, presumably because they were there for the taking.[45]) But the treaty of purchase solemnizing "Seward's Folly," the bargain of the age at $7.2 million, would probably not have been ratified had not Secretary of State William Seward launched a careful "campaign of education." He produced enthusiastic letters of endorsement for buying Alaska from prominent people all over the United States, which he then planted in leading newspapers along with extravagant hints of the riches to be found in that vast domain, about which almost nothing was known. Seward even had a clerk copy some of the foolish comments that the opponents of the Louisiana Purchase had made in 1803 and sent these to the newspapers. He was charged with trying to bribe the press into creating a ground swell for the treaty, but he swore that the budget for the whole campaign came to no more than $500.

Once approved by the Senate, however, the purchase ran into trouble in the House, which was in a position to block it by refusing to appropriate the purchase money. A number of congressmen resented the fact that they had not been consulted in advance by Seward. Many agreed with Representative Washburn of Wisconsin when he advised the president to buy his white elephant in Siam at a fraction of the cost. Others thought Alaska would eventually come free after Canada fell like a ripe apple into America's outstretched hand.

The Russian government was so eager to unload Alaska—mainly because the Russian American Company, which administered the region, was bankrupt and the czar's advisers worried that holding on to that indefensible territory would lead to war with either Britain or the United States—that the Russian minister, Édouard de Stoeckl, eventually resorted to bribery to grease the transaction. At first he retained ex-senator Robert J. Walker to lobby for the appropriation and paid him the enormous sum of $30,000, and when his efforts did not yield fruit, he proposed that the czar offer Alaska as a gift and shame the Americans into coming up with the money. Finally, after the czar turned down this novel approach, the Russian minister offered money directly to certain congressmen for their vote, and, according to Russian state documents, about $73,000 changed hands.[46]

For most of American history, presidents have been able to have their way on foreign policy matters far more easily than on domestic affairs. As Tocqueville noted, "It is chiefly in foreign relations that the executive power of a nation finds occasion to exert its skill and its strength. If the existence of the American Union were perpetually threatened, if its chief interests were in daily connection with those of other powerful nations, one would see the prestige of the executive growing, because of what was expected of it and what it did."[47] The president, he said, "possesses almost royal prerogatives," but because he presided over an agrarian republic separated from all powerful enemies by a great ocean, Andrew Jackson, the president of Tocqueville's day, "had no occasion to use them."[48]

More recent presidents have seen the office in a different light. They have been tempted by the powers of the presidency in foreign affairs but frustrated by the limitations imposed by public opinion. They will "cheerfully follow wherever you may . . . lead," an enthusiastic citizen assured President Ulysses Grant's secretary of state in 1873. It was self-evident that once the president decided what he thought, his ideas would automatically *become the views of our best men.*"[49] But Grant discovered a different reality. Impressed by the plans of some American speculators, promoters, and naval officers who were casting acquisitive eyes on the Dominican Republic, he became obsessed with the idea of annexing it. Yet there was so little public enthusiasm for the idea that Charles Sumner, chairman of the Senate Foreign Relations Committee, who considered Grant "a colossus of ignorance," successfully blocked the treaty of annexation. Grant shook his fist at Sumner's house when he drove by in his carriage. But for the majesty of his office, he exploded to a friend, he would challenge the arrogant senator to a duel. The Dominican Republic did not, however, become part of the Union.

By the last two decades of the nineteenth century new currents of public opinion had produced an extraordinary mood shift in the United States. When it was complete the United States had become a far-flung empire. Never again would a president be denied a territorial acquisition. The American people were now ready for the adventures of the twentieth century—at least enough of them to carry the day.

Nothing touches the American nerve quite like the accusation of imperialism. To accept the idea that the United States even resembles a colonial empire violates the American self-image in two ways. The American Republic was born an anticolonial nation. How could it have colonies? The United States was created as a reproach to the kings of Europe. How could it play their game? In the United States, as in every expanding nation based on popular consent since ancient Athens, the tension between democracy and empire has raised fundamental questions of priorities and purpose.

From a collection of settlements on the east coast of North America the United States has become a continental power with bases, protectorates, and clients around the world. For most Americans, ideology has served to explain territorial acquisitions and to justify them. Manifest Destiny can be either the hand of God or, in its secular version, the inevitability of history or the logic of geography —empty land and heathen people waiting for the developer's hand and the missionary's word. The individuals who decide to invade other people's territory or to dominate their societies are merely looking for security. Acting on the deeply ingrained impulse of self-defense, they are instruments of fate. Every modern empire explains its expansionist itch in similar ways. Britain assumed the White Man's Burden. France undertook the *mission civilizatrice*. The American empire has been gathered in the name of "extending the area of freedom" and "national security." Resting firmly on an idea as old as John Winthrop's celebration of the City on the Hill, America's democratic sensibilities and practice have made American expansionism legitimate to most (but by no means all) Americans. America's conquests are not like the conquests of other countries, because the conquered are in fact liberated. Given the views of progress that dominate modern society, few today would deny that the descendants of the Hawaiian natives who managed to survive the diseases of civilization are "better off"—richer, freer, and more secure from invasion—than they would be if they were still independent. Karl Marx made the point with respect to Mexico, wondering whether "it was such a misfortune that glorious California has been wrenched from the lazy Mexicans who did not know what to do with it."[50]

But what role did the people play in these conquests? Following in the footsteps of Alexander Hamilton, some contemporary historians ascribe the dramatic rise of imperial sentiment, confrontational policy, and overseas acquisition to the pressures of mass opinion. In his study *Imperial Democracy* Ernest May concludes that in the 1890s elite opinion was divided and uncertain, and that in taking the nation into the Spanish-American War President

McKinley was responding not to a well worked out strategy, because there was none, but to the public mood. The United States, he writes, "had greatness thrust upon it" largely because the people demanded an empire.[51] It was a plausible explanation in Europe for the sudden and threatening emergence of the United States as a world power. "Let us remember," the *Journal des Débats* stated in 1899, "how McKinley, who has no will of his own, came to annex the Philippines. Public opinion demanded it, and he was about as much master of the situation as a log drifting downstream."[52] The events leading up to the Spanish-American War have also persuaded historians of very different views that populist pressures provided the steam behind the drive for empire. In *The Roots of the Modern American Empire* William Appleman Williams puts much emphasis on the demands of farmers for foreign markets for agricultural surpluses. Thus "yeoman imperialism" was the force for expansion at a time when the bankers of Wall Street were dead set against it.

Without doubt, the potpourri of ideas percolating through the universities, the churches, and the popular press in the 1880s and 1890s helped to foster a new imperial mood. In *The Descent of Man* Charles Darwin had offered flattering scientific corroboration for American exceptionalism. The "wonderful progress of the United States, as well as the character of the people" were the results of natural selection.[53] In 1885 the American historian John Fiske carried the idea a bit further in *Harper's*; the Anglo-Saxons, being the survivors in the battles of evolution, were now "destined to go on until every land on the earth's surface that is not already the seat of an old civilization shall become English in its language, in its religion, in its political habits and traditions. . . . The race thus spread over both hemispheres, and from the rising to the setting sun, will not fail to keep . . . sovereignty of the sea and . . . commercial supremacy."[54] Clergymen, such as Josiah Strong, believed that the Anglo-Saxon race had been ordained by Providence to spread religion, enlightenment, and civilization to those lesser breeds fit enough to survive—and merciful death, by measles mostly, to those who were not. Captain Alfred Mahan of the Naval War College wrote eloquently of the need for big navies and far-flung bases. All these new ideas were widely circulated. Strong's book *Our Country* sold 170,000 copies. Mahan wrote regularly in *Atlantic Monthly* and *Harper's* and his books on sea power quickly became world famous. Economic imperialists like Albert Beveridge saw colonies as the answer to the terrible depression of 1893. ("The trade of the world must and shall be ours."[55]) Charles A. Conant argued in *North American Review* that developed countries needed "an outlet for their surplus savings, if the entire fabric of the present economic order is not to be shaken by a social revolution," thus setting out in defense of expansionism the very theory Lenin would use to attack capitalism as a reactionary and dying system.

"The active carriers [of American imperialism]," writes Arthur Schlesinger, Jr., "have been politicians, diplomats and military leaders."[56] Revelations of "vital American interests" in other people's countries flash before the eyes of a few strategically situated individuals who then act to change not only the behavior of the nation but to create the climate of opinion that will support its adventures. If the United States had greatness "thrust upon it" in the 1890s, the mass of ordinary citizens did very little of the thrusting. The expansionists of the late 1890s, men who did not distinguish the quest for security from the quest for power and glory, presented the American people with a new worldview and began to act on it before the people had a chance to assess what they were doing, much less to reject it.[57] As the new breed of expansionists saw it, it was impossible for the United States to remain untouched by the new encroachments of England, France, and Germany into what we now call the Third World, for they were closing doors of opportunity—not just foreign markets but sea-lanes, strategic minerals, and naval bases. To grab off the possessions of the weakest of the aging European empires was tempting, for it offered young men adventure and the chance of riches. Why should the United States hold itself aloof from the responsibilities and pleasures of empire?

Seeing themselves as trustees for the nation, the enthusiasts of empire skillfully avoided serious popular scrutiny or orderly political debate for their radical notions, even though the implementation of their theories required a fundamental departure in national policy with far-reaching consequences for the Constitution itself. Surely it was not self-evident that "national security" required taking Hawaii and the Philippines, for the argument depended upon the logic of preemption. "If we shrink," as Theodore Roosevelt put it, " . . . then the bolder and stronger peoples will pass us by, and will win for themselves the domination of the world."[58] But though the pace was now quickening, the European powers had been grabbing colonies ever since the United States was founded. The nation had survived for more than one hundred years without joining the race, and in those years it was far more threatened and more vulnerable than in the 1890s, when it had become the most powerful industrial economy on earth. There is little doubt that "national security" buttressed by the creed of Manifest Destiny was the dominant argument advanced in favor of empire. The question is why the concept of national security was so broadened and the cry for security so shrill at a moment when the United States had never been less vulnerable.

The story of the sea change in the American mood begins with the last act of renunciation of imperial acquisition. In 1893 the Americans on Hawaii—missionaries, whalers, planters, and businessmen, whose families had been on the islands since the early decades of the century—threw the islands at the United States with no less force than that used by the czar to propel Alaska in the American direction. But this time there was a president in office who refused to catch it.

For years the American families in control of the Hawaiian sugar industry were happy with the state of affairs on the islands. They had managed to lobby through Congress some of the privileges of statehood; sugar from the islands came to the mainland duty free. But by 1890 the Louisiana sugar interests finally succeeded in removing these concessions, and the Hawaiian planters now saw no way to get equal access to the American market other than annexation. Moreover, growing opposition to their dominant position by smaller growers and a resurgent nationalist movement under Queen Liliuokalani, who came to the throne in 1891, prompted the American business elite on the island to reach out for American protection.

The planters formed a secret organization called the Annexation Club and hatched their plans in close collaboration with American naval officers and the American minister, John L. Stevens. The leader of the Annexation Club, Lorrin Thurston, came to Washington, informed the secretary of the navy and the secretary of state that the club was about to create a pretext for annexation, and arranged for pro-annexation articles to appear in journals pushing the expansionist line, such as the *New York Tribune* and the *Review of Reviews*.[59] "The Hawaiian pear is now fully ripe," the American minister informed the secretary of state. In January 1893, the Hawaiian queen attemped to put through a new constitution by edict under the slogan "Hawaii for the Hawaiians." This was quite enough for Stevens, who ordered an American force of a hundred and fifty men onto the island to "protect American life and property," a task that turned out to require imprisoning the queen.

A treaty of annexation was prepared with dizzying haste but not fast enough; the Republican administration of Benjamin Harrison had only two weeks left. The next president was Grover Cleveland, the ponderous former sheriff of Buffalo who had already served one term in the White House. Enthusiastic about acquiring foreign markets but not faraway uncivilized islands, the new president withdrew the treaty of annexation from the Senate after five days in office. While the San Francisco dailies, the *Chronicle* and the *Examiner*, were strongly for annexation, as were virtually all California businessmen, some of Cleveland's strongest supporters, such as the New York *Evening Post*, the Boston *Herald*, and the Chicago *Herald*, and influential businessmen of the East and Midwest were opposed.[60] Cleveland concluded that although public opinion would probably support annexation, he was free to make his own judgment. It was evident that the circumstances under which Hawaii was being served up to the United States were, to say the least, irregular. The president sent James H. Blount, a former Georgia congressman, to Hawaii to investigate. When he reported the sordid story of the "revolution" and his estimate that the Hawaiians were overwhelmingly against annexation, Cleveland refused to resubmit the treaty. Down came the American flag in Honolulu as Blount stood at attention while the Royal Hawaiian Band, intending only to honor him, played "Marching Through Georgia."

In his decision Cleveland was supported by leading Democratic newspapers; whether or not they were troubled by the moral issues, most Democrats were against taking responsibility for that "dusky country." The United States had been in a twenty-year depression as a consequence of the huge postwar production boom, and the big banks were nervous that the country could get into a war with Britain or Japan over Hawaii with devastating effects on the economy. Other powerful economic interests, especially the beet sugar lobby, which feared that duty-free Hawaiian sugar would flood the country, also vigorously opposed annexation.

Americans, as the political scientist Walter Dean Burnham points out, split over their religious worldview as much as, probably more than, over class interests.[61] These differences in religious outlook affected attitudes on foreign policy. The mainline Protestant churches were strongly for annexation. Hawaii was, according to John Mott, a prominent missionary leader, "a great lighthouse and a base of operations for the enterprise of universal evangelization."[62] But some Christian leaders expressed strong moral objections. "Stealing an island from a poor old colored woman is not a great national achievement," declared the editor of the *Christian*

Enquirer; "it belongs to the cheat-your-washer-woman style of diplomacy."[63]

The overwhelmingly Protestant Midwest divided between what the historian Richard Jensen calls the "pietist" branch and the "liturgical." The former, more numerous in the center of the country, were more likely to support the Republican Party, but not its military adventures. Some strains of pietism, like the Mennonites, the Brethren, and the Quakers, had a clear pacifist tradition, but even those that did not object to organized violence tended to reject earthly crusades of all sorts. As Burnham points out, the church helped to politicize the electorate in the second half of the nineteenth century and was responsible in large measure for the high levels of mass participation in elections. But with regard to imperialism and expansionism, American Protestantism was split down the middle, and this in part explains the coolness toward the Hawaiian pear in the panic year of 1893. But Henry Cabot Lodge, Theodore Roosevelt, and the other imperialists regrouped for another day.

CHAPTER 5

The Politics of Adventure

1.

I t is not possible to understand the shift in the public mood that took place in the second half of the last decade of the nineteenth century without seeing its relationship to two closely related developments in domestic American politics. One was a shift in the nature of political parties and the other the transformation of the economy. To Americans in the post–Civil War decades, being a Republican or a Democrat was like being a member of a church. "To its massed and devoted partisans," as Walter Karp puts it, the party offered not only "creeds and slogans . . . and holiday outings," but it was also "a standing army perpetually arrayed for battle, an army whose orders men gladly obeyed, whose rudest tricks its partisans cheered . . . a kind of end in itself."[1] The Republicans, the party of Lincoln, spoke for the winners in the late war. Outside the South, being a Democrat and being a traitor were considered sufficiently akin by enough voters to keep Republicans in the White House. In this system, as Walter Burnham has pointed out, class antagonisms played a relatively unimportant role.[2]

By the 1890s the era of issueless politics began to change in response to the rise of Big Business and the devastating consequences of industrialization on farmers, small-business men, and factory workers, a process of economic restructuring that the economist Joseph Schumpeter once called "creative destruction." In the years between the panics of 1873 and 1893 the United States became the most formidable economy on earth. In the second half of the century the population doubled, reaching 71 million by 1900. Wheat production almost tripled. Coal production was up 800 percent, steel 500 percent, and oil 2000 percent. As the new industrial giant challenged the European powers in world markets, other countries like Russia, Argentina, and British India were outcompeting U.S. farmers in cotton and grain. American agriculture was becoming more dependent on exports, but the prices on the world market were falling. (Wheat was $1.90 a bushel in 1860; 57 cents in 1895.) The roaring factories produced more than could be sold, and there were riots in Brooklyn, San Francisco, and other large cities. In addition to the bloody Haymarket Riot of 1886 and the Pullman strike of 1894 there were almost twenty-four thousand other strikes in the United States between 1881 and 1900. Hobo armies were taking to the streets.[3] In 1892, the year five hundred banks closed and sixteen thousand companies went bankrupt, a populist movement of debt-ridden farmers determined to fight Wall Street, the big banks, and the trusts organized itself into the People's Party. The two major parties were now forced to deal with massive popular discontent or find themselves dislodged from power by a radical third party.

Faced with the panic of 1893, the Democrats in office for the first time since the Civil War sought to defuse the populist movement by co-opting it. This they did by ignoring the hard-money views of their leader in the White House and embracing the inflationary remedy demanded by the debt-ridden farmers and small-business men—the free coinage of silver to increase the money supply. With the lure of reform symbolized by the rising star of William Jennings Bryan, the Democrats successfully brought the populists back into the fold and the People's Party soon disappeared. The Republicans, however, were in no position to follow suit, for the Grand Old Party was beholden to large banks and trusts. Republicans considered inflation a form of leprosy. Buying off the masses by mortgaging the nation's future was the height of irresponsibility. There had to be another way.

The politics of foreign adventure served the interests of the Republicans because it seemed to be a way to shift the political agenda. Theodore Roosevelt's own story of how he turned himself from an asthmatic youth into cowboy, crime fighter, warrior, and big-game hunter thrilled the country, and his enthusiasm for "the strenuous life" was infectious. Roosevelt believed that "oversentimentality, oversoftness . . . and mushiness are the great dangers of this age and this people."[4] Americans could not afford to "be content to rot by inches in ignoble ease within our borders, taking no interest in what goes on beyond them . . . the nation that has trained itself to a career of unwarlike and isolated ease is bound, in the end, to go down before other nations which have not lost the manly and adventurous qualities."[5]

As Roosevelt and others celebrated the "life of strife" and "the barbarian virtues" without which "the civilized ones will be of little avail," Americans were looking for adventure in all sorts of new ways. Sports suddenly became the rage—basketball, football, and baseball. In 1901 Bernarr MacFadden's book *The Power and Beauty of Superb Womanhood* appeared. Instantly popular, its message was that women needed well-developed muscles. Men began riding bicycles on the highways and women showed up on the tennis courts, the golf courses, and the racetracks.

On June 1, 1895, the chairman of the Republican National Committee was quoted in the *New York Tribune* as saying that the chief issue in state and local elections should be Cleveland's "weak foreign policy."[6] Cleveland was vulnerable because the panic of 1893 had occurred in his administration. But the Republicans doubted that their hard-money policy would go down well with the voters. E. L. Godkin, the editor of the New York *Evening Post*, was convinced that the Republicans wanted "to get up a foreign war if possible" because "they have tremendous and urgent domestic questions to confront and settle, but find the work dangerous politically."[7] The new breed of Republicans such as Roosevelt and Lodge consciously set out to commit the Republican Party to what Lodge called a "large policy," making the pursuit of American power and prestige the supreme national purpose around which to unite the country. In the process of nation building via foreign policy the Republican Party could wrap itself in the flag and recover the presidency.

There was an irresistible logic to the attempt to shift the voters' gaze from increasingly divisive domestic economic questions. The Republican expansionists and some of the Democrats saw the political dividends of foreign triumphs that could diffuse the dangerous ideological polarization around domestic economic questions. The 1892 Republican platform called for "the achievement of the manifest destiny of the Republic in its broadest sense."[8] The process of educating the public to its larger destiny began. In 1891 the secretary of the navy declared that "colonies are the greatest help" in gaining "a preeminent rank among nations."[9] Theodore Roosevelt favored a war with Spain, but he was aware that the public was not for it. "Our people are not yet up to this line of policy in its entirety and the thing to be done is to get whatever portion of it is possible at the moment."[10] A small, successful war would serve to inoculate the public. The leading Republican newspaper, the *New York Tribune*, had made a similar sort of argument for the annexation of Hawaii. It would help overcome "the traditional hostility of the United States toward an extention of authority, if not of territory, among the islands near our coasts." It would, as a Philadelphia paper put it, "familiarize the public mind with the acquisition of other territory."[11] Some Democrats were thinking along the same lines. A war with England, as one Texas politician put it, could lance the "pus [from the] anarchistic, socialistic, and populistic boil."[12]

The "system of 1896," as the historians of electoral politics in America call the realignment of the political parties of that year, created a new political arena. What had been the "most thoroughly democratized" of any political system in the world in the mid-nineteenth century was converted into what Burnham calls "a rather broadly based oligarchy."[13] Before the shift, voter participation was high. Party loyalty was intense, and therefore landslides were rare. The realignment of 1896 brought with it two crucial changes. First, sectional politics became more important, not just the traditional North-South conflict but a sharpening split between the agrarian West and the rapidly industrializing North and Midwest. Second, party loyalty declined precipitously and the hold of the parties on their potential supporters loosened dramatically. The consequence, Burnham argues, was an extraordinary drop in voter turnout that, despite a few surges, has continued to the present day.

The radical shift in the American political system and the radical reorientation of American foreign policy occurred in the same years. How much did the one have to do with the other? International conflict, as more than one writer has noted, is a continuation of domestic politics by other means. (The political scientist Bruce Russett in a study of twenty-three industrialized countries going back into the nineteenth century found that democratic countries are more likely to threaten or to actually engage in foreign military action in hard times than in periods of prosperity.[14]) The real fight between the Democrats and the Republicans was over industrialization, not foreign policy. The Democratic Party in the age of William Jennings Bryan spoke for an agrarian past, an America of family farms and small business. The Republicans spoke for the massive accumulation of capital and thoroughgoing industrialization, a process of development that has had cruel and disruptive consequences in every country, irrespective of political system. Before the Civil War the infant Republican Party had been outspokenly anti-imperialist; Republicans were no more ready to rule over dark-skinned people than to make slaves of them. After the war the attitude of party stalwarts toward foreign adventure remained skeptical. The complaint of a Boston stockbroker to Henry Cabot Lodge was typical: "If we attempt to regulate the affairs of the whole world we will be in hot water from now until the end of time."[15] But in defusing the crisis of the 1890s, imperialism served the interests of both parties in the difficult task of managing the fear and outrage of millions of potential voters.

Grover Cleveland, the first Democrat to reach the White House since the Civil War, was strongly in favor of expanding American commerce, but he considered the annexation of distant islands to be "a perversion of our national mission."[16] Making war for colonies was even worse. Yet two years into his second term he took the nation to the brink of war with Britain over a piece of distant real estate no one thought of annexing. The pressing issue was the Venezuela–British Guiana border, a foreign quarrel if ever there was one, but a test, so Secretary of State Richard Olney argued, of the Monroe Doctrine. "Today the United States is practically sovereign on this continent," Olney wrote in what the president called a "twenty-inch gun" note, "and its fiat is law . . . not . . . because wisdom and justice and equity are the invariable characteristics . . . of the United States . . . [but] because . . . its infinite resources combined with its isolated position render it master of the situation and practically invulnerable."[17] ("Only words the equivalent of blows would be really effective," said Olney, in defending his lawyerly rendering of might makes right.)

In the decades following the Civil War, twisting the lion's tail, even tweaking its nose, became an almost irresistible rite of the political culture. To sell their candidate in the election of 1896 the Republicans distributed vast quantities of a pamphlet entitled "How McKinley is hated in England." The British cabinet had favored the South in the Civil War, and this was not forgotten in the North. Moreover, Britain was the world's leading advocate of the gold standard, while American populists saw "free silver" as the answer to the financial distress of the debt-ridden classes. (One free-silver pamphlet declared that a war against England would be the most "popular [and] just war ever waged by man."[18]) The cities on the eastern seaboard were teeming with recent Irish immigrants who regarded the British with the same degree of detachment present-day Cubans of Miami display toward Castro. Until the very end of the nineteenth century, elections were close, and Republicans and Democrats outdid one another in playing to Irish Anglophobia, courting the swing votes that might tip the balance. Disputes over fishing rights with Canada added fuel to the fires of anti-British feeling. "Whenever the American flag on an American fishing smack is touched by a foreigner," cried Congressman Henry Cabot Lodge in 1887 as the Canadians began arresting American schooners, "the great American heart is touched." While the Detroit *News* thought that "the Canadian provinces will make elegant States in the Union," the South was not ready to support what one of its sons called "another war all for the sake of a few hundred Yankee fishermen and a few stinking codfish."[19]

In 1895 Grover Cleveland was losing the fight within his own party for a sound money policy. William Jennings Bryan was becoming the most popular Democrat by marching under the banner of free silver. Being anti-British was one way for Cleveland to appeal to the populists in order to maintain his ebbing power. Besides, he had a personal score to settle. During his campaign for re-election in 1888, when he attacked the Republicans for their high protective tariff, he had been accused of having been "bribed" by British gold. (How else to explain why he was not attackable for his "free silver" views like other Democrats?) Republican campaign literature regularly pictured him under a fluttering Union Jack. So concerned with their pro-British image were the Democrats in 1888 that the administration took pains to keep news of the engagement of the daughter of Cleveland's secretary of war to the famous British politician Joseph Chamberlain a state secret until after the election.

Despite all such efforts, however, Cleveland became the victim of a political dirty trick that damaged him in the eyes of millions of voters and may well have cost him that election. A Californian by the name of Osgoodby, representing himself as a naturalized citizen of British birth, wrote the British minister in Washington of his concern about where the president stood with respect to the mother country. Sir Lionel Sackville-West wrote back, assuring him that Cleveland was at heart splendidly pro-British. The letter was turned over to the Republicans and the big cities were blanketed with copies a few days before the election. "THE BRITISH LION'S PAW THRUST INTO AMERICAN POLITICS TO HELP CLEVELAND," screamed the headline in the New York *World*. The minister, who became an overnight celebrity (receiving an offer of $2,000 a week to appear at the Hippodrome), was ordered out of the country, but it was too late for Grover Cleveland.

Now seven years later, having staged a comeback and recovered the presidency, Cleveland felt himself under special pressure to stand up to the British. The Venezuelans were laying claim to about half of British Guiana, strategic territory with gold on it, and about forty thousand British subjects. Venezuela was demanding that the dispute be put to arbitration in the expectation that it might get half of its extravagant claim. The Venezuelan minister kept reminding Americans of "the immortal Monroe." Americans had no choice, he argued, but to intervene against British imperialism. But of course they did have a choice. The United States had declined to invoke the Monroe Doctrine on five occasions between 1850 and 1865 when Venezuela clashed with one or another European power. Nonetheless, Cleveland formally suggested arbitration and the good offices of the United States and was not pleased when the British turned down his offer cold.

The Venezuelans hired a former American minister to their country, William L. Scruggs, as their propagandist. (Scruggs had made profitable use of his time in Venezuela and had been fired by President Harrison for improper financial dealings.) His pamphlet "British Aggressions in Venezuela, or the Monroe Doctrine on Trial" went through four editions. Republicans like Lodge were calling for war if the British refused to arbitrate. Finally, after both houses of Congress passed a resolution demanding arbitration—"Heavenly Father, let peace reign. . . . Yet may we be quick to resent anything like an insult to this our nation," the chaplain of the House prayed as the vote was taken—President Cleveland delivered an ultimatum to Engand. The United States would now itself decide what rightfully belonged to Venezuela and would "resist by every means in its power" if Great Britain did not accede to those rights.

The eminent Harvard psychologist William James deplored the "fighting mob-hysteria" that had brought a leader of moderate and independent views to such a point.[20] James marveled that with a single threat of war the president could undo the "peace habits of a hundred years." The psychologist was awed by "the power of the war-demon when once let loose," but though he himself opposed war on that occasion and later the Spanish-American War as well, he considered the "obedience to the executive," which the public had demonstrated to be the foundation "of all national safety and greatness."[21] Despite the fact that Britain had thirty-two battleships to five for the United States, twenty-eight governors supported the idea of going to war. Senators from silver states thought this was the moment to rid the country of "English bank rule."[22] But the New York Chamber of Commerce passed a resolution attacking the "war craze," and the stock market greeted the presidential war threat by declining a half billion dollars. Upon hearing the news, Theodore Roosevelt condemned the "patriots of the ticker" and urged the country to support Cleveland's ultimatum. He derided Harvard professors and students, most of whom opposed going to war, as believers in "the cult of nonvirility" who would "put monetary gain before national honor"[23] He wrote Henry Cabot Lodge that the "clamor of the peace faction has convinced me that this country needs a war."[24]

War was averted because the German kaiser suddenly decided to oppose the British in South Africa after they had suffered a setback in the Transvaal. The fear of war with Germany prompted the British to back off their collision course with the United States. In early 1897 the British signed an arbitration treaty with Venezuela, but even though the British went to considerable lengths to smooth ruffled feelings in the United States, the treaty fed the muscle-flexing mood because it was widely hailed as an American victory.

2.

The "splendid little war," as Secretary of State John Hay called the Spanish-American War, started off in a ground swell of public enthusiasm and, like all of America's wars with the exception of World War II, ended with the country divided. The domestic political reasons that had prompted one of the nation's more pacific presidents to risk a confrontation with the British Empire remained. What the New York *Journal of Commerce* had called the "artificial patriotism being carefully worked up at the present time . . . hanging the flag over every schoolhouse and . . . giving the boys military drill" was now part of the cultural landscape. The diplomatic historian Thomas Bailey argues that the United States needed a war somewhere. Certainly that was Theodore Roosevelt's view. The Democratic oligarchy in the South, concerned that the grass-roots "free silver clubs" would shake the foundation of their power, became increasingly exercised about the revolution in Cuba, which had achieved such success by 1895 that the *insurrectos* had established a Provisional Government. As the Richmond *Dispatch* put it, there were advantages to "swapping off the free coinage of silver for the Cuba question." [25]

William McKinley scarcely looked like the public relations pioneer he actually was. No one would have accused this Republican politician who had risen to prominence by dutifully serving the ironmongers and sheep raisers of Ohio of having an ounce of charisma. Yet from the neck up he looked every inch a president. His dark eyes were famous for their kindly twinkle. He wore a carnation in his lapel, and on at least one occasion presented it to a petitioner as he turned down his request, thus earning his eternal gratitude. He would countenance no unseemly language in his presence, would jump up from the cabinet table to perform little errands of mercy for his invalid wife, and in general behaved, as the historian Ernest May puts it, like a character out of Louisa May Alcott. He invariably insisted upon being photographed in what he considered his presidential pose, always affecting the same austere look. An enigmatic figure who left little trace in a hundred volumes of personal papers of his real feelings or the evolution of his thought, McKinley remains a puzzle to historians. Was he the passive instrument of the imperialists? Was he, as others argue, an exceedingly cunning politician with an imperial vision no less grand than Theodore Roosevelt's who preferred to dissemble rather than to exhort? [26] Or was he a weak man who was pushed into a war he did not want by the hysteria of the people?

McKinley was the first president to understand the power of the mass media. His was the first inauguration to be preserved on film. When he moved into the White House the entire presidential staff consisted of six typists and clerks, one of whom was assigned to the First Lady. McKinley tripled the staff and created the post of secretary to the president, which was largely a public relations job. Unlike his predecessors, McKinley cultivated the press. He attended the press corps' annual Gridiron Dinner, invited editors and reporters to receptions, and encouraged them, particularly the Washington representatives of the newly expanded national wire services, to call on him and his cabinet for information. The White House began to put out regular press releases. McKinley kept track of public opinion with a scrapbook of clippings from newspapers around the country that his secretaries prepared for him each day. [27]

When he came into office in March 1897, Cuba was not yet a burning issue. The latest insurrection against Spanish rule had been going on for two years. Filibustering activities were flourishing despite their being officially discouraged as violations of the U.S. Neutrality Act. The Coast Guard succeeded in stopping most of the expeditions, but there were more than thirty vessels that were regularly supplying the insurgents from Florida. When the Spanish fired on what they believed to be one of these ships, the newspapers began their cry for war. The American flag had been insulted, said the New York *Sun,* and the Spanish government "requires a sharp and stinging lesson at the hands of the United States."[28]

For most Americans the insurrection in Cuba became a compelling emotional issue because of Spanish violations of human rights on the island. A Spanish force of 150,000 troops rounded up Cuban civilians by the thousands and put them behind barbed wire in concentration camps. Because of this brutal policy perhaps as many as a quarter million Cubans died. For two hundred years foreign oppression has aroused American sympathies and anger. Appeals to American public opinion because of human rights violations in foreign countries began, as we saw, with the French Revolution. In the Greek War of Independence in the 1820s Harvard and Yale students collected money for the rebels. American citizens protested the pogroms of czarist Russia. Just as the crisis over Cuba was about to heat up, American outrage reached new heights because of the massacre of some ten thousand Armenians by the Ottoman Empire. William Lloyd Garrison, Julia Ward Howe, and the Congregational Church launched a successful campaign to arouse public opinion in behalf of the Armenians. At public meetings jingoist speakers cried out that the United States had a Christian obligation to use its power to promote justice—by the sword if necessary. As Ernest May argues, Armenia was a dress rehearsal for Cuba. The popular outcry demonstrated "that public opinion could be mobilized . . . for a moral crusade."[29]

A crusade for human rights in Cuba involved no great risks, for Spain was a tottering empire, even weaker than when it was stripped of its continental possessions in North America almost one hundred years earlier. Americans treated the Spanish with undisguised contempt. They were, as the early American historian Jedidiah Morse had put it, "naturally weak and effeminate."[30] Encouraged by the jingoist press and by the adroit propaganda efforts of the junta, or central committee, of the Cuban rebels, demonstrations and rallies denouncing the Spanish and raising money for the insurrection were held in Chicago, Kansas City, Cleveland, Providence, and many other cities and towns. William James, trying to understand the surge of interest in Cuba, doubted whether the average person was all that excited by the fiery preachers. Nor was all the pious talk about "raising and educating inferior races" anything more than "mere hollow pretext." Imperialism, he finally decided, was catching on because it had become a "peculiarly exciting kind of *sport*."[31]

The philosopher's intuition was shared by the great press lords of New York. William Randolph Hearst's legendary promise to his illustrator, Frederic Remington—immortalized in *Citizen Kane*—that if he would produce the pictures, the publisher would produce the war, was more self-promotion than history. Neither Hearst nor his archrival, Joseph Pulitzer, publisher of the New York *World*, produced the war, but they tried. No question, they used the war to build empires of their own. (Ironically, Pulitzer had played a key role in damping down public hysteria in the Venezuela affair.) Hearst's New York *Journal* had a circulation of 150,000 in 1896. Over the next two years, during which the paper played up the insurrectionary war in Cuba and agitated for the United States to intervene, the circulation climbed to more than 800,000, and this phenomenal growth was almost entirely attributable to the sensational coverage of events in Cuba. In the race for readers the *World* kept pace. Pulitzer, according to his biographer, "rather liked the idea of war, not a big one, but one that would arouse interest and give him a chance to gauge the reflex in his circulation figures."[32]

The other New York dailies and major papers across the country like the Chicago *Tribune* and Hearst's San Francisco *Examiner* joined in the drumbeat for war. They carried huge banner headlines denouncing the Spanish and ran human-interest stories of Americans—often their own correspondents—caught in the war. (The Spanish executed one reporter and threatened to try another.) Spanish attacks on American ships suspected of supplying the guerrillas were featured. While editorials sounded the war cry, the front page featured atrocity stories. "The skulls of all were split down to the eyes. Some of these were gouged out. . . . The bodies had almost lost semblance of human form." For more than three years "eyewitness accounts" like these by James Creelman of the *World* or those by the *Journal*'s Richard Harding Davis describing the cruelties visited on the island by the Spanish were spread across the front pages, accompanied by Remington's lurid sketches, and denounced in shrieking headlines. The Spanish were indeed carrying out a cruel pacification campaign, pioneering counterinsurgency techniques that the U.S. Army itself would use in the Philippines a few years later. But liberties were taken with the facts in virtually every news story out of Cuba and some of the accounts were outright fakes. Terrorist acts of the *insurrectos*, who were extorting protection money from American plantation owners in Cuba, were glossed over or not reported.[33]

Not content with reporting the news, the *Journal* made news. A young woman by the name of Evangelina Cisneros, whose father had been sent to the Spanish prison colony on the Isle of Pines for some modest complicity with the insurgents, was also arrested, allegedly because she defended her virtue against a lecherous Spanish officer. "Enlist the women of America," William Randolph Hearst is reported to have cried as he launched a public relations crusade to free Señorita Cisneros. The publisher induced Mrs. Jefferson Davis to sign an appeal to the queen regent of Spain and persuaded Julia Ward Howe, famous for writing the words to "The Battle Hymn of the Republic," to send off a letter to the pope. The *Journal* was able to persuade twenty thousand women to join its crusade, including President McKinley's mother. Hearst then dispatched one of his correspondents to rescue the señorita, which he did by climbing the roof of the house next to the ancient jail, taking a crowbar to the rotting window bars, and lifting the young woman out. "The Rescued Martyr in her Prison Garb" was spread across the front pages, and *Journal* headlines took credit for what months of diplomacy had "FAILED UTTERLY TO BRING ABOUT."[34] Send five hundred reporters and free the whole island, the governor of Missouri suggested.

The nature of the press had changed once more. With the arrival of the penny press in the 1840s, newspapers had become a profitable business, but in the period 1850–90 journalism was still primarily a vehicle for serving up selected facts with a heavy dose of ideology in behalf of political candidates and political parties. Horace Greeley's *New York Tribune*, for example, was, as Walter Dean Burnham notes, "indispensable to the Republican mobilization in the 1850s."[35] Politicians used newspapers to get their ideas across. The level of political debate and discussion in their pages was high, and the reportage and analysis were sophisticated. (Greeley's European correspondent was Karl Marx, whose style would never make it in *USA TODAY*.) In the 1890s the possibilities of mass circulation now prompted another shift in the news industry. Papers loosened their ties with political parties. The boredom of industrial work and the new leisure of city life were creating a market for entertainment. The technology of journalism, mass circulation presses, wire services, and photography, offered new opportunities to reach that market. Thus, despite the fact that educational levels in the country were rising, the emphasis of the press shifted perceptibly in the

1890s from information and political persuasion to the marketing of adventure and fantasy. This change would have a lasting effect on both electoral politics and foreign policy.

William McKinley did not want war with Spain. He feared that the cost of war would undermine the dollar and stall the economy just as the twenty-year depression appeared to be ending. He did not want to annex Cuba; the country needed no more blacks. He was enough of a traditionalist to believe that the Constitution followed the flag. The United States should annex no territory which it was unwilling to grant statehood. His interest was to protect American property on the island and exert American influence without taking responsibility for a miserably poor country. His strategy was to use the threat of war to persuade the Spanish to put down the rebellion and to grant reforms. In his secret negotiations with the Spanish the president emphasized the pressure of Congress and public opinion, which were forcing him to take stern measures. But actually when his ultimatum was delivered to the Spanish on September 18, 1897—the Spanish had until November 1 to give the American minister in Madrid "such assurance as would satisfy the United States that early and certain peace can be promptly secured" —neither his scrapbooks of newspaper articles nor his personal mail revealed that he was under any such pressure.[36] He was in fact deliberately protected from the "yellow press" by his press secretary, who considered these "products of degenerate minds" unworthy of presidential attention. In the last six months of 1897, according to one scholar who went through the presidential files, McKinley received exactly three letters from the public on Cuba.[37] "The impression I got on crossing the continent," the publisher Whitelaw Reid wrote McKinley a little more than a month before war was declared, "was that the more intelligent classes are not greatly affected by the sensational press; . . . I have never seen a more profound or touching readiness to trust the President, and await his word."[38]

McKinley knew that powerful interests in the country divided on the issue. When he took office, magnates such as John D. Rockefeller, J. P. Morgan, and George Pullman were against risking war.[39] So were most business organizations, from the Boston Merchants Association to the Baltimore Board of Trade. But the people seemed more jingoist than the bankers and the railroad barons who bankrolled the Republican Party. In 1896 there had been rallies in small towns from New Jersey to Iowa where the Spanish general in command in Cuba, "Butcher" Weyler, was burned in effigy. Civil War veterans in GAR posts throughout the North were aching to send the next generation to war. The Cigarmakers' Union, to which many Cubans belonged and from whose ranks had come Samuel Gompers, head of the American Federation of Labor, was equally ready to take on Spain. Blacks were sympathetic to their brothers fighting in Cuba, and the organization of white upper-middle-class Americans that had been formed to carry forward the spirit of Lincoln, the Union League Club, considered it a duty to fight for the Negroes in Cuba. The Cubans themselves energetically marketed atrocity stories, collected millions of dollars, and lobbied for votes.

With the country divided, the president decided to say almost nothing about Cuba and let public opinion develop on its own. The cry in Congress to recognize the belligerent status of the rebels and even to intervene militarily was increasing. The atrocity reports were beginning to be read on the Senate floor. In just three weeks "American Friends of Cuba" gathered 300,000 signatures for recognizing Cuba. More mass meetings were held around the country, and by the end of 1897 young men were enlisting to fight in Cuba. Of course, only a small part of the population took part in these activities, and their importance was exaggerated by the newspapers pressing for war.

McKinley delivered an "appeal to the people" for patience while he waited for the concession he still hoped to extract from Spain, the granting of "autonomy" for the island. The president was neither concerned that the public would push him into war—he believed that the expansionists in Congress did not have broad public backing—nor worried that the public would shrink from war if he sounded the call. But he wanted such overwhelming public support that if war broke out he would be free to conduct it without criticism or controversy.

By January 1898, it was evident that the Spanish would not, probably could not, meet the American terms, for when they offered to give the Cubans autonomy, there were riots in Havana, instigated by Spanish army officers. On January 20 the Senate passed a resolution recognizing the Cuban rebels as having the status of a belligerent under international law, a declaration without legal effect but clearly a hostile message. About forty or fifty Republican members of the House threatened to turn on the president if he did not move to war. Republican politicians worried that William Jennings Bryan would campaign against him two years later for not rallying to the banner of human rights in Cuba. The president in fact was deeply moved by the plight of the Cubans and sent an anonymous gift of $5,000 to a humanitarian organization working for the victims in

Cuba, but it still appeared that he wished to avoid war. Assistant Secretary of the Navy Theodore Roosevelt let his friends know that he considered the president to be a "white-livered cur" with "no more backbone than a chocolate eclair."[40]

On February 9, 1898, the *Journal* succeeded in raising the temperature further. The paper procured a confidential letter from the Spanish minister to Washington recounting his hostility to the negotiations and published it. The minister called McKinley a "low politician catering to the rabble,"[41] an indiscretion that may have had as much to do with making war inevitable as the blowing up of the battleship *Maine* in Havana harbor six days later.

The explosion and the loss of 253 Americans was the biggest single news event since President Garfield's assassination eighteen years before. McKinley had the secretary of the navy announce that there was no "cause for alarm" and "no indication of anything but an accident."[42] A Court of Inquiry was appointed, which deliberated in secret, while the *Journal* and the *World* conducted their own investigations, which resulted, not unexpectedly, in "proof" of Spain's responsibility. (TR was of course totally convinced. "I would give anything," he wrote in a private letter, "if President McKinley would order the fleet to Havana tomorrow. . . . The *Maine* was sunk by an act of dirty treachery on the part of the Spaniards."[43]) But the Court of Inquiry was unable to fix blame and most historians doubt that the Spanish, who had every interest in not provoking the United States, were behind the explosion.[44] The captain of the *Maine* himself considered it an accident. Many contemporary newspapers came to the same conclusion but said the Spanish were "responsible" anyway since the ship was in their harbor.

McKinley used the Court of Inquiry to focus public attention and to deflect some of the pressure from the newspapers and from Congress to go to war. He kept hinting about the imminent release of the court's finding and teased the press into reporting it as less than the anticlimax it actually was. He made a point of giving small scoops to the wire services, and was rewarded by their almost consistent support. His scrapbook began to fill with laudatory editorials approving his prudence and diplomatic skill, and 90 percent of his correspondence, according to his press secretary, was "an endorsement of the President's course." The public favored war, his press secretary reported, only "as a necessity and for the upholding of the national honor."[45]

On March 17, 1898, McKinley's close friend Senator Redfield Proctor of Vermont, who had opposed going to war, made a speech shortly after returning from a visit to Cuba in which he announced that he had changed his mind. War was now the only way to protect American property and to keep leftist revolutionaries from taking over. A week later the president received a telegram from W. C. Reick, a political confidant in New York: "Big corporations here now believe we will have war. Believe all would welcome it as a relief to suspense."[46] McKinley now knew that the "business pacifism," which so infuriated Roosevelt, had weakened, and that indeed no substantial segment of public opinion would oppose him, whatever he did. He set April 6 as the date for sending his war message to Congress, then waited five more days to permit Americans to evacuate Cuba. Meanwhile, the Spanish offered concessions, and the president in a more or less parenthetical sentence said he hoped Congress would give them "just and careful attention." But the mood in Congress was now more in keeping with the advice of the New York *World*, which suggested, "Negotiate afterward if negotiation is necessary."

In the cloakroom and lobby, Congressmen were singing "Dixie" and "The Battle Hymn of the Republic" as the heated debate on the war resolution proceeded on the floor. Books were thrown, reported the London *Times*. "Members rushed up and down the aisles like madmen, exchanging hot words, with clenched fists and set teeth."[47] Eight days later Congress passed a joint resolution directing the president to use armed force to free Cuba. Any intention to annex the island was specifically disclaimed. The Senate had wanted the president to recognize the revolutionaries, but McKinley did not want to commit himself to support of the *insurrectos*, whom he distrusted. He insisted on maintaining presidential control of foreign policy and faced the Senate down. Because McKinley, in William Allen White's words, combined "the virtues of the serpent, the shark, and the cooing dove," he was able to carve out for himself more freedom to set his own foreign policy than his immediate predecessors had enjoyed.[48] He was strengthened greatly by the fact that the generation-long economic crisis was coming to an end.

The war was short, spectacular, and victorious. "Divine favor seemed manifest everywhere," McKinley declared when it was over. Five days after the declaration of war Commodore George Dewey sailed into Manila Bay and destroyed the Spanish fleet. On February 25, almost two months before the president's war message, Acting Secretary of the Navy Theodore Roosevelt had cabled secret orders to Dewey to begin "offensive operations in Philippine Islands" in the event of war with Spain. (The secretary of the navy was away for the afternoon. "Do not take any such step . . . without consulting the President or me," he admonished his subordinate upon his return. "I am anxious to have no occasion for a sensation in the papers."[49] The president later claimed that when he received word that Dewey had taken the Philippines, he could not have located "those darned islands" on a map. But the secretary of the navy had on two occasions discussed with the president the orders that his brash assistant had sent to Dewey in February.[50]

Roosevelt's ideological friends knew exactly where the islands were and how important they could be. On the day war was declared Albert Beveridge of Indiana, a leading expansionist, cried, "The Philippines are logically our first target." Roosevelt had written his friend Senator Lodge the previous September, "Our Asiatic squadron should blockade, and if possible, take Manila." Cuba, not the Philippines, was in the headlines. Most Americans had never heard of Manila, although the New York *Sun*, a strongly expansionist paper, kept mysteriously predicting that an American attack would soon take place there.[51]

It is now clear that the imperial strategists like Roosevelt and his friend Captain Mahan saw the Philippines as crucial to the expansion of American power in the Far East. The American minister to China, a railroad lawyer by the name of Charles Denby, saw the Philippines as a stepping-stone to the markets of China. These men had a clear-eyed view of the war against Spain, and they saw themselves as guardians of the American national interest. But the war they sought and the war they succeeded in winning had almost nothing to do with the cause in the Caribbean that had aroused popular feelings. It was once said that France had its conquests and Napoleon his. The United States had also had the experience of the people's representatives declaring one war and the nation fighting another as well.

The surprising, painless victory was of course immensely popular. "HOW DO YOU LIKE THE JOURNAL'S WAR?" Hearst's headline crowed. McKinley publicly ordered the capture of Havana, but it was not until June that an American force was able to land near the port of Santiago. On the first of July Theodore Roosevelt, wearing a blue Cavalry uniform ordered from Brooks Brothers, led his Rough Riders up San Juan Hill. The rest of the Spanish fleet was driven out to sea where an American flotilla was waiting to destroy it.

The war had the three indispensable ingredients to insure public support. It was a moral crusade. It was blessed by victory. It was short. But even as the victory was celebrated, the public reaction was mixed, for the news was not all good. The same yellow press that had lambasted the government for not getting into the war now reported how badly it was taking care of the recruits. They were not getting enough to eat, and they were coming down with yellow fever, malaria, and typhoid. (There were fewer than four hundred battlefield casualties, but four times that number died from disease.) Local papers demanded that the "army of convalescents" be brought home immediately.

William McKinley professed to having given not a thought to the Philippines before the war, but within hours of Dewey's victory he ordered ten thousand American troops sent eleven thousand miles into the far Pacific to occupy the islands. As soon as he heard the news of Dewey's victory, he made up his mind to keep Manila Bay as a naval base. But in the flush of victory there were all sorts of good reasons to hold on to the entire archipelago. An indemnity for the war, said Secretary of State Hay. If not taken under an American wing, the islands would fall prey to the British, French, German, or Japanese empires. McKinley is perhaps best remembered for a piece of presidential cant, his heartfelt confession to visiting Methodist clergymen that he "walked the floor of the White House night after night" and on his knees heard Almighty God tell him to take the Philippines "to uplift and Christianize them." And besides, he added, "we could not turn them over to France or Germany" and it went without saying that they were "unfit for self-rule."[52] Although he was worried about the insurrection on the islands that had flared up against the Spanish, he concluded that Manila could not be secure unless the United States had control of all the islands.

But public opinion was split. The religious press strongly supported annexation "in the interest of human freedom and Christian progress," as the *Presbyterian Banner* argued. However, the old arguments against straining the Constitution still had a powerful hold on the Democrats. In the fall of 1898, just before the congressional elections, McKinley took a swing around the Midwest to test the waters. "His entourage took notes on the relative levels of applause," Ernest May writes, "indicating that annexation drew louder handclaps."[53] But McKinley, according to another historian, "seemed more concerned about the public's apprehension about accepting new responsibilities."[54] The United States had come to a watershed. Here for the first time the United States was acquiring territory that by virtue of climate, customs, and race was widely assumed to be unsuitable for admission into the Union as a state.

The treaty signed with Spain on December 10, 1898, ended Spanish sovereignty over Cuba and ceded the Philippines, Puerto Rico, and Guam to the United States for which the Americans agreed to pay $20 million, just a little more than what Mexico had been paid for California and New Mexico fifty years before.

The peace treaty with Spain was almost defeated. William Jennings Bryan, who two years later would run for president on a platform condemning imperialism, played a critical role in persuading seventeen senators to vote for it. Any two of them could have blocked it. Had the issue of holding on to the Philippines come up by itself, the Senate would have voted against taking the islands as a colony.[55] The anti-imperialists still were a formidable force in the Senate. Imperialism would mean the end of American democracy, some said. It would compromise the moral superiority the United States enjoyed over the land grabbers of Europe, said others. It would, as Andrew Carnegie tirelessly preached, sacrifice the great advantage the United States had as a peaceful commercial nation. The anti-imperialists did not shrink from using racist arguments: The mission of the United States is democracy, and democracy cannot flourish among dark-skinned peoples in hot climates. There were powerful figures in American life against imperialism, including two ex-presidents, Harrison and Cleveland. But their arguments and those of fellow members of the Anti-Imperialist League, Harvard professors such as Charles Eliot Norton, publicists like E. L. Godkin, and maverick businessmen like Carnegie began to sound old-fashioned in the face of the new reality created by the war. As the vote in the Senate was about to be taken, word reached Washington that Filipino insurgents had fired on American troops.

William McKinley had no ambivalence about annexing Hawaii. By the time he took office a quarter of the population on the islands was Japanese. The white planters were resisting further Japanese immigration and the Tokyo government had sent two warships to Hawaiian waters. But the Senate would not vote annexation. As soon as news of the battle at Manila Bay was received in May 1898, however, McKinley pushed through annexation by a joint resolution of House and Senate. The anti-imperialists were literally outflanked by Dewey's victory in Manila. Hawaii now became a "bridge" to the Pacific, a necessary base to support the military operations in the Philippines. "Manifest Destiny says, 'Take them in,'" so went a typical congressional speech of the day. "The American people say, 'Take them.' Obedient to the voice of the people, I shall cast my vote to take them in."[56] Large majorities in Congress heard the same voice, and the "consummation," as McKinley called it, of the Americanization of Hawaii quickly followed. American dominion was soon thereafter extended over Puerto Rico, Guam, and the eastern half of the Samoan Islands. The effort to buy the Virgin Islands was launched.

Commodore Dewey had transported Emilio Aguinaldo and some of his exiled insurgents back to the Philippines in U.S. Navy vessels, and was rebuked for it by McKinley three weeks after his famous victory. What Dewey thought was a good deed was in fact aiding the enemy. Aguinaldo, who did not agree that his people needed civilizing, announced the creation of a Philippine republic in January 1899. The United States fought for four years, using 120,000 troops to put down the insurgency, suffering more than 4,000 battle deaths, and inflicting perhaps as many as 200,000. General Arthur MacArthur, the father of the great World War II general Douglas MacArthur, commanded the American force, and George C. Marshall, the top U.S. military officer in World War II, was a young staff aide. "Of course we can thrash the Filipinos," Henry Adams wrote, "but it will cost in one season at least fifty thousand men, fifty millions of money, and indefinite loss of reputation." It was an underestimate of the financial and human cost—but also of the shortness of collective memory.

America's first offshore guerrilla war dragged on until 1902. McKinley imposed censorship, but stories of torture by American troops filtered through and were widely broadcast by the Anti-Imperialist League. The nation was being asked "to puke up its ancient soul, and the only things that gave it eminence among the nations," lamented William James. He pronounced the pacification war "one protracted infamy towards the islanders, and one protracted lie towards ourselves." Aguinaldo lived long enough to collaborate with the Japanese in driving Arthur MacArthur's son from Corregidor in the early days of World War II.[57]

In the election of 1900 William Jennings Bryan tried to turn the contest into a referendum on imperialism. While McKinley sat home on his front porch in Canton, Ohio, his running mate, Theodore Roosevelt, went around the country defending annexation. As the anti-imperialists warned against "the incorporation of a mongrel and semibarbarous population into our body politic," TR said that if morals required the nation to "surrender American territory" in Asia, the United States might as well give Arizona back to the Apaches. Bryan abandoned his foreign policy arguments midway into the campaign. Because the country was emerging from a twenty-five-year depression McKinley's slogan "Let Well Enough Alone" carried the day. The election of 1900 was not a referendum on imperialism but a vote of confidence in the McKinley prosperity and a rejection of Bryan's nostalgic vision of an agrarian America. Yet foreign policy had played a crucial role in transforming domestic politics.

PART THREE

THE BURDEN
AND GLORY
OF WORLD POWER

CHAPTER 6

The American People and the War to End War

1.

When war broke out in Europe in August 1914, Woodrow Wilson called in the White House reporters and lectured them. "Of course, the European world is in a highly excited state of mind, but the excitement ought not to spread to the United States." Reporters should not print rumors or do anything else to inflame public opinion. In a speech to the nation the president declared: "The United States must be neutral in fact as well as in name. We must be impartial in thought as well as in action."[1] He immediately ordered his remarks translated into four languages and displayed in post offices across the country.

For more than a year there had been war scares out of Europe, but the reaction in the United States when the first shots were fired on August 2 was shock and foreboding. It would be "the bloodiest war ever fought on earth," a *New York Times* editorial declared, "and the least justified of all wars since man emerged from barbarism."[2] It is hard now even to imagine the innocence of that time. In the days just before World War I, military conflict was thought to be so destructive, so irrational—for the victors no less than the vanquished—that it simply would not happen. Norman Angell's best-selling book *The Great Illusion* made that point for a wide audience on both sides of the Atlantic. In 1910, four years before the outbreak of the Great War, Andrew Carnegie had established a $10 million endowment for the abolition of war. That same year Woodrow Wilson joined the American Peace Society. Two years earlier William Bayard Hale, a *New York Times* reporter, had had

an extraordinary two-hour interview with Wilhelm II that was littered with the kaiser's bellicose observations about the other nations
of Europe and bloodcurdling celebrations of war. ("Jolly good fighting" was healthy for the state and good for Christian souls.) So
alarmed was the owner of the *Times*, Adolph Ochs, that he sent
Hale to Washington to show the incendiary interview to President
Theodore Roosevelt. "I don't believe the Emperor wanted this stuff
published," said Roosevelt, shaking his head in disbelief, and he
strongly advised the *Times* not to run it. Ochs agreed, and it was
only six years later that the American public began to be aware of
the man who would soon be known in the press as the Beast of
Berlin.[3]

Nor had it sunk into the public consciousness how involved in
global affairs the United States already was as a result of the Spanish-American War and the diplomatic intrigues over the building of
the Panama Canal. Most citizens were not aware of how seriously
Wilson had involved the United States in the effort to avert the war.
Only a few had paid much attention as the president's closest confidant, Colonel Edward House, shuttled back and forth among the
statesmen of Europe in the spring of 1914, and no one knew that
what he had in mind was an alliance of sorts that would bind Germany, Britain, and the United States.

So the shock in America was enormous. The nations of Europe
had "reverted to the condition of savage tribes roaming the forests
and falling upon each other in a fury of blood and carnage to
achieve the ambitious designs of chieftains clad in skins and drunk
with mead," came the cry of the *New York Times*. The lamps were
going out all over Europe, the British Foreign Secretary Edward
Grey mourned, and all civilization was being plunged into darkness.
The coming of war dealt a terrible blow to the myth of progress, to
the rationality of man, in short to the instinctive beliefs and intellectual underpinnings of most secular Americans. The psychoanalyst Franz Alexander reported the profound impact that the
memory of the outbreak of war still had on his patients in the early
1920s. "It was an immediate vivid and prophetic realization that
something irreversible of immense importance had happened in
history."[4]

Everyone expected a short war; the destructiveness of modern
warfare precluded a long one. Neutrality was the obvious American
response. A month after the outbreak of war the country's most
famous hawk, Theodore Roosevelt, who believed that "no triumph
of peace is quite so great as the supreme triumphs of war," wrote in

praise of neutrality.[5] The former president congratulated the country for having kept itself free from the "bitter and vindictive hatred among the great military powers of the Old World." Even the British ambassador, Sir Cecil Spring-Rice, wrote Colonel House of his hope and belief that "at any rate one part of the world will keep out of it."[6] The only serious suggestion of intervention came from Charles W. Eliot, the former president of Harvard, who proposed an immediate alliance with Japan and the European powers fighting Germany "to rebuke and punish" Germany. Wilson took Eliot's letter seriously enough to read it to the cabinet, but he refused, as he told Congress, to be "thrown off balance by a war with which we have nothing to do, whose causes cannot touch us, whose very existence affords us opportunities of friendship and disinterested service."[7]

Woodrow Wilson, so austere a figure that he would not dance at his inaugural ball, loved baseball and vaudeville, told dialect jokes, and wrote limericks. An eloquent, devout, and distant man, he had been a popular professor, a brilliant orator, a leading scholar of government, president of Princeton, and governor of New Jersey. As a scholar, he understood that the closing of the American frontier had catapulted the United States into world power. The closing of the American frontier and the transformation of America's world role as a result of the Spanish-American War meant that "foreign questions became leading questions again," and "in them the President was of necessity leader."[8] Wilson believed in a strong presidency. Early in his career he understood that international crisis strengthened the president's hand; yet he had forebodings about what another war would do to constitutional government.

Wilson was one of the least sensitive to public opinion of American presidents. He was often impatient with Congress, although in his early years he was quite skilled in getting the legislative branch to fall into line. By nature, according to Robert Lansing, his wartime secretary of state, he "resisted outbursts of popular passion. . . . He had the faculty of remaining impervious to such influences, which so often affect the minds of lesser men."[9] He paid little attention to White House mail or to the newspapers. He came to the White House with a strong sense of mission and a deep conviction that America's role was to inspire and the president's task to teach.

Wilson was certain that other nations would turn more and more to America "for those moral inspirations which lie at the basis of all freedom."[10] But despite House's efforts at secret diplomacy, Wilson remained convinced that the United States should stand aside from all foreign conflicts so as to end up as the "moral arbiter" of the competing empires. If the United States stayed above the fray, at the right moment its power could be used to usher in a new world order, "a universal association of the nations to maintain the inviolate security of the highway of the seas . . . and to prevent any war."[11] His first secretary of state, William Jennings Bryan, was by now a pacifist, and Woodrow Wilson himself, though willing to use the United States Army to intervene in the Mexican Revolution and teach the Mexicans "to elect good men," was close to that position himself. He feared particularly the terrible consequences of war to American society. "Every reform we have won will be lost if we go into this war."[12]

In 1914 American public opinion was also overwhelmingly for keeping out of the war. To be sure, many of the eastern bankers and lawyers who were most active in diplomacy and commerce, many of British descent themselves, were close to London banks and tended to be sympathetic to British legal institutions. Woodrow Wilson, a southerner of Scotch-English ancestry, had written admiringly of the parliamentary system and, like most educated Americans, felt drawn to British culture. "You and Grey [the British foreign minister] are fed on the same food," the British ambassador told Wilson shortly after the outbreak of war as they discussed Wordsworth sonnets together. The ambassador reported to London that there were tears in the president's eyes.

British writers, such as Lord Bryce, whose celebratory book *The American Commonwealth* had gone through many editions since its publication in 1888, Rudyard Kipling, John Galsworthy, J. M. Barrie, and H. G. Wells, were popular in America; contemporary German writers, for reasons of language alone, much less so. American newspapers covered the events of Europe mostly from London, employing a largely British staff, and were heavily influenced by British viewpoints all through the war since their cables were censored.[13] The exaggerated reports of German atrocities in Belgium, including wholly fabricated stories of crucifixions, "corpse factories," and Belgian babies with their hands cut off, were widely believed despite the fact that American correspondents traveling with the German Army sent a joint cable to the Associated Press declaring the reports "groundless."[14] Americans were ready to believe that the kaiser was the Beast of Berlin, but few wanted to fight him. Theodore Roosevelt, who was soon to lead the drumbeat for war on Germany, was one of the few to sound a note of caution.

Anger at the Germans, that "stern, virile, and masterful people," would not help the Belgians.

At the same time there was considerable pro-German sentiment among Americans of German descent, most of whom were in the Middle West. When war was declared, German-language papers such as the *New-Yorker Staats-Zeitung*, the *Cincinnatier Freie Presse*, and the *Westliche Post* (St. Louis) cheered the kaiser, predicted a glorious victory for his cause, and reminded all German reservists to report to the nearest consulate. On the day war broke out, German-Americans marched at a Bavarian *Volksfest* in Harlem River Park and sent off a congratulatory telegram to King Ludwig of Bavaria. That same Sunday in Chicago there was a war in miniature as marching Slavs and marching Germans clashed in the streets. In Cincinnati Russian Jews began forming a regiment of volunteers to join with German reservists in fighting the czar.[15] "America is no nation," the British ambassador reported, "just a collection of people who neutralize one another." More than a quarter of the population, according to the 1910 census, was either born abroad or had two foreign-born parents. Wilson believed that public opinion precluded any course other than neutrality, "since otherwise our mixed populations would wage war against each other."[16] There were more than one million unnaturalized German and Austrian males of military age in the United States in 1914.

Pro-German sympathies were more strongly represented in Congress than in the country as a whole. The head of the Foreign Relations Committee, Senator William J. Stone, came from St. Louis, which had a large population of German descent, a center of what increasingly were derided as "hyphenated Americans." There were many German clubs in the United States, the largest and most powerful of which was the National German-American Alliance. Theodore Roosevelt was popular with German-Americans and was an honorary member of several of the German societies. As the war spread, these groups agitated against every measure to aid the Allies, including loans. The *New York Times* and other newspapers played up the danger of the German-Americans. The *Times* publisher, Adolph Ochs, was himself a target of a hate campaign on account of his German-Jewish origin and always felt the need to prove his Americanism. (Late in the war, after the *Times* had printed an editorial suggesting that Austrian peace feelers be seriously pursued, an unpopular idea when total victory seemed near, he sent his top editors to Colonel House to assure the administration of his patriotism.[17])

The great waves of immigration at the turn of the century had stoked the fires of xenophobia. Wilson himself was concerned about what the German-Americans would do in the event of war. House advised him that there would be no "organized rebellion or outbreak, but merely some degree of frightfulness in order to intimidate the country."[18] The president was quite prepared to play on popular feelings to score political points against the Republicans. He pandered to prowar sentiment, just enough, he hoped, to avoid war. Though few German-Americans proposed that America fight on the German side and a very small number engaged in actual subversion, Wilson warned Congress in his 1915 State of the Union message that foreign-born Americans were pouring "the poison of disloyalty into the very arteries of our national life," and to great applause promised that his hand would "close over them at once."[19]

Unlike Franklin D. Roosevelt, a generation later, Woodrow Wilson saw public opinion not as a restraint on military action but as an angry beast that would drag prudent leaders into war. The problem for Wilson was not, as for Roosevelt, how to arouse public opinion, but how to tame popular passions. "Once lead this people into war," the president told Frank Cobb of the *World* shortly before he delivered his war message to Congress, in April 1917, "and they'll forget there ever was such a thing as tolerance. To fight you must be brutal and ruthless, and the spirit of ruthless brutality will enter into the very fibre of our national life, infecting Congress, the courts, the policeman on the beat, the man in the street."[20]

Isolationism was not an issue in America when war broke out in Europe. It was simply in the air Americans breathed. True, American troops had landed on foreign shores more than one hundred times since the founding of the Republic. American power had spread across the continent, far into the Pacific, and into the Caribbean. But the consequences had yet to sink in. Woodrow Wilson had two goals with respect to public opinion. He wished to prepare public opinion for participation in an "association of nations" in the postwar world, and he ran for reelection in 1916 on this theme. "A disentangling alliance," he quipped. "We are participants whether we like it or not in the life of the world . . . the day of isolation is gone." At the same time he wished to reassure Americans of his intention to stay out of the war in Europe. And he ran on the slogan "He kept us out of war!"[21]

For Wilson as late as the autumn of 1915 war was literally unthinkable, and he gave the order to fire any officer who dared to think about it. The *Baltimore Sun* had reported that the General

Staff was putting together contingency plans for a war with Germany.[22] If true, demanded Wilson, "trembling and white with rage," as Henry Breckinridge, the acting secretary of war, remembered it, every officer on the General Staff was to be relieved on the spot and ordered out of Washington! This remarkable scene took place eighteen months before the United States went to war against Germany.

When war broke out in 1914, the United States had been in a depression for more than a year. That year there occurred the largest number of business failures in the nation's history. Factories were operating at 60 percent capacity in many places, and there were nearly a million unemployed.[23] As eager as it was to preserve strict neutrality and to avoid war, the Wilson administration was strongly for taking advantage of the war to expand exports. Domestic economic considerations encouraged the president to take risks. In six months exports of explosives jumped 1500 percent; iron and steel manufactures expanded ten times in the same period. When the Austrians protested the arms shipments to England and France, the administration took advantage of the occasion to make a vigorous defense of the arms traffic to the American public. "You will observe in reading it," Secretary of State Lansing reminded the president, "that [the U.S. diplomatic response] is presented in a popular rather than a technical manner because I think it will be more valuable for the public here in the United States than for its effect upon Austria-Hungary. . . . It is our first opportunity to present in a popular way the reasons why we should not restrict the exportation of munitions of war."[24]

Though German complaints grew increasingly bitter as U.S. arms shipments to the Allies mounted, for the first six months of the war the United States actually had more serious conflict with Britain than with Germany, for it was the British who were taking action that threatened American trade. Protests poured into the State Department from all over the nation when the Royal Navy began searching U.S. merchantmen on the high seas and in some cases seizing members of the crew who were German reservists. The governor of Texas, evoking memories of the War of 1812, demanded that "American ironclads" be sent to "England's door" to enforce the rights of American shipping.[25] The British "blockade" stopped American vessels on the high seas even when their destination was a neutral port deemed near enough to Germany to be a "conduit pipe." (Technically, it fell short of a true blockade, but the British naval net designed to strangle the German economy was popularly known as such in the United States.) The British were

extravagantly stretching international law, and in the process out-
raging Wilson's cabinet despite the fact that every member but
Bryan was staunchly pro-British. The United States sent stiff notes
of protest. But Walter Hines Page, the U.S. ambassador in London,
was so charmed by the British and so eager to have the United
States enter the war on their side that after reading the official
protest, he offered to help the British foreign secretary answer it.
On another occasion when the British decided to intercept a vessel
that was carrying cotton for Germany and was displaying the American flag, the ambassador advised the British to arrange for the
French to seize it since it would go down better with American
public opinion.

Former secretary of state Elihu Root, a prominent Wall Street
lawyer who still had great influence over his protégés in the State
Department, was unreservedly pro-British. In a letter to Lord Bryce
he described his worries that "the men who were deprived of profits
[from shipping contraband to Germany] would stir up the Press,"
and he recounted how he had "asked the State Department to send
for the newspaper correspondents . . . and impress upon them the
public duty of discouraging all sensational publications."[26] The British carefully monitored public opinion in the United States, for the
object of British diplomacy, as Sir Edward Grey wrote, "was to
secure the maximum of blockade that could be enforced without a
rupture with the United States."[27] The British ambassador reported
to London in late 1914 that "the American conscience is on our
side, but the American pocket is being touched. Copper and oil are
dear to the American heart and the export is a matter of great
importance . . . the howl may become very furious soon."[28]

On May 7, 1915, the Germans rescued Anglo-American relations.
One of their submarines sank the luxury liner *Lusitania*. Swept into
the sea forever were 1,198 persons, among them 128 Americans.
Crowds formed in front of newspaper bulletin boards crying for
war. Among the sudden converts to a prowar stance was John Wanamaker, the Philadelphia merchant who had lost one of his shoe
salesmen on the ill-fated voyage. In a thousand newspapers across
the country editors fulminated. The sinking was "deliberate murder," "a massacre," "an outrage," an act of piracy." Yet less than six
out of one thousand, as one hasty count showed, were actually
calling for war.[29] Wilson, "aware that the feeling of the country is
now at fever-heat," was, nevertheless, convinced that at the moment the crowd would "move with me in any direction I shall sug-

gest." But he doubted, as he told his press secretary, Joseph Tumulty, that the mood of the fickle crowd "would last long enough to sustain any action I would suggest to Congress."[30] Therefore, he would take no "radical action now based on the present emotionalism of the people." When Ambassador Page wrote him that the United States "must declare war or forfeit European respect," Wilson burned the dispatch.[31]

The president elected to calm the nation with the rhetoric of redblooded pacifism. America was "too proud to fight." Upon hearing that famous phrase, Major General Leonard Wood, the former chief of staff, exploded, spluttering in his diary: "Rotten spirit in the *Lusitania* matter. Yellow spirit everywhere." Theodore Roosevelt wrote Senator Henry Cabot Lodge that "the iniquitous peace propaganda . . . has finally had its effect." It would take years to offset it.[32]

William Jennings Bryan, on the other hand, thought that the American note to Germany regarding the sinking was unduly provocative, and resigned as secretary of state. Two weeks later, as an estimated seventy thousand people were turned away, he spoke at a huge rally at Madison Square Garden under the auspices of the United German Societies of New York. Even as the German-Americans courted the former secretary, who was also the leading advocate of Prohibition, by sacrificially forgoing wine at the dinner in his honor, they were mightily offended at Bryan's suggestion that they could or would influence the German government. "*Überflüssig*," scolded the *Germania-Herold*.[33]

For the next two years while the kaiser's ministers built submarines, their most cost-effective weapon, and the diplomats and admirals in Berlin argued about how much provocation the United States would take, the Germans became alternatively belligerent and conciliatory as they gauged American opinion. Anti-German sentiment was running high, but "it now may be regarded as certain that neither the President nor the American people want a war with Germany," Count Bernstorff, the German ambassador, reported to Berlin after the furor over the *Lusitania* had subsided.[34] Now the British unwittingly helped the Germans in the fight over American opinion. More than a year after the *Lusitania* incident, the British blacklisted eighty-five U.S. firms and individuals suspected of giving aid to Germany, and Woodrow Wilson exploded. "I am, I must admit," he wrote to House, "about at the end of my patience with Great Britain and the Allies."[35]

2.

The war for American public opinion intensified on all sides. Jane Addams had helped launch the Women's Peace Party in January 1915 and later that year held an international conference in The Hague calling for mediation of the conflict. Rosika Schwimmer, a well-known Hungarian feminist and pacifist, convinced Henry Ford that he should do something dramatic to strengthen the peace movement. In early December of 1915, to almost universal derision, Henry Ford's Peace Ship, the *Oscar II*, sailed for Europe "to get the boys out of the trenches by Christmas." The newspapers played up the buffoonery. One peace delegate, the governor of North Dakota, explained that actually he was for more military spending, "preparedness," as it was called, but he was taking the Peace Ship to visit some relatives in Sweden, while a distinguished judge, who was also along, was heard to cry, "Oh God, why am I here!" as the Ark of Peace pulled away from the dock.

The peace movement was split because people opposed the war for so many different reasons: Christian pacifism, revulsion at the slaughter, and fear of what war would do to the United States. Many people of wealth and their representatives in Congress opposed the war because they knew it would mean a stiff graduated income tax, though J. P. Morgan insisted that it wouldn't be necessary because the patriotic rich would lend the necessary money. Congressmen from the South worried that drafting blacks into the army would disrupt the southern way of life. As the German submarine warfare campaign intensified, prominent people defected from the peace movement. The established peace organizations, such as the Carnegie Endowment, were openly pro-Ally and discouraged antiwar activities, and the American Peace Society, which received its money from the Endowment, abandoned its militancy and earned congratulations from prowar newspapers for being a "good loser."[36]

A number of peace organizations such as the American Truth Society and the American Humanity League were working for the Germans, surreptitiously financed by the German military attaché, Captain Franz von Papen, who as chancellor seventeen years later was instrumental in bringing Hitler to power. The official German propagandist, Dr. Bernhard Dernburg, had been sent home after the sinking of the *Lusitania*, and the German government quietly hired the former *Times* reporter William Bayard Hale to counter the stream of pro-Ally propaganda. Books and articles by British and French correspondents on life in the Allied trenches were finding an eager audience, and the Germans wanted their side presented. But Hale's propaganda efforts were not inspired. His wife launched a humanitarian drive against the export of American horses for use in the battle zone and prepared a film script about a retired fire-engine mare "who, after her years of noble service to humanity, was dispatched to a miserable end upon the fields of Flanders."[37]

Another German propagandist, Dr. Heinrich Albert, left his briefcase on the Sixth Avenue "L" and two Secret Service agents who had been trailing him picked it up and turned it over to Wilson's son-in-law, Secretary of the Treasury William G. McAdoo. The stolen papers revealed German plans to subsidize writers and speakers in the United States, an attempt to buy up munitions factories secretly, a letter from someone offering to foment strikes in behalf of Germany, and a proposal to buy up one of the smaller U.S. wire services for the *Vaterland*. McAdoo, who strongly favored the Allied cause, gave the stolen documents to the editor of the *World*, swearing him to secrecy as to the source, and the whole story of the mysterious briefcase did not come out until fifteen years later.[38] The documents created a sensation.

The Germans did engage in actual acts of sabotage on American soil, most notably smuggling firebombs into the holds of vessels carrying munitions to the Allies.[39] But their hostile activities were greatly exaggerated in the American press, and their propaganda efforts were bumbling. Even so they were enough to convince Wilson, as he wrote House, "that the country is honeycombed with German intrigue and infested with German spies."[40] The German spy scare, which Dr. Albert's carelessness did much to feed, was deliberately fanned by the editor of the *Providence Journal*, who kept revealing incriminating coded messages from Berlin. These were not received on his wireless, as he claimed, but sprang directly from his head. Anti-German sentiment rose further when a man named Erich Münter managed to get into J. P. Morgan's home brandishing a revolver in each hand. Morgan, who in the 1930s would be questioned by the Nye Committee as a leading "merchant of death" for his zealous promotion of munitions financing and war loans, needed to get the feel, his visitor explained, of what it was like to face the murderous machines he was doing so much to promote. Then he would repent and work for peace. Unfortunately, the guns went off accidentally, and the banker was slightly wounded. The umlaut in the dangerous visitor's name was quite enough to set off headlines about a vast German conspiracy.

The political forces in the country favoring American intervention in the war against Germany were gathering strength as the 1916 election approached. Shortly after the outbreak of the war Theodore Roosevelt abandoned his support of neutrality. He told British Foreign Secretary Sir Edward Grey that "the bulk of our people do not understand foreign policy" and promised to devote his energies to arousing the people "to an active sense of their duty in Europe." (Public opinion, he once said, is "the voice of the devil, or what is still worse, the voice of a fool."[41]) The former president went about the country preaching the "virile strength of manliness." He had personally seen the war plans of two of the belligerents, he told Princeton students, and they called for seizing the coastal cities of the United States and holding them for ransom.[42]

Roosevelt and other associates in the Progressive Movement had been calling for a preparedness campaign for years. The United States Army in 1914 had fewer than 100,000 men, smaller than some Balkan powers. The navy, with thirty-one obsolete battleships, was perhaps the third- or fourth-strongest in the world.[43] Modernizing, rationalizing, and augmenting the meager military forces of the United States was as necessary, the Progressives believed, as domestic reform. TR's old comrade in arms from Rough Riders days Major General Leonard Wood took the lead in the campaign for preparedness. In the summer before the war broke out Wood organized what became known as the Plattsburgh Movement. At a camp in Plattsburgh, New York, young men, mostly businessmen, lawyers, even an Episcopal bishop, were assembled to take military training together and pay $100 for the privilege. For many the experience was formative and socially helpful. "It seemed to me that all the right people went," John J. McCloy recalled seventy years later.[44] Not much could be done with these ardent green recruits "in the way of detailed military instruction," General Wood admitted, "but . . . a great deal can be done in the implanting of a sound military policy."[45]

By election year 1916 the preparedness movement was in full swing. A book, *Defenseless America*, by Hudson Maxim, the brother of the inventor of the famous Maxim machine gun then efficiently mowing down young men in the trenches on both sides of the line—the body count was about five thousand a day—warned that America could be taken over by 100,000 raping and pillaging troops from Europe. The humor magazine *Life* printed on its cover a map of the United States now renamed New Prussia.[46] *Electra: The National Preparedness Magazine* devoted itself to the contribution that the electrical industry was prepared to make to the national defense, and the editors promised to enlist their readers in the "National Spiritual Reserve of the United States." It was the first of its genre, journals to celebrate the accomplishments of defense contractors and the ever-greater need for ever more of their wares. The author of the book on which the famous film "The Birth of a Nation" was based produced a cautionary tale entitled "Fall of a Nation" and Victor Herbert supplied the music.

Established organizations lobbying in behalf of the armed forces, such as the Navy League, now gathered in reinforcements. The National Security League, founded in the fall of 1914, had prominent men like the mayor of New York, the international lawyer Frederic R. Coudert, and Cornelius Vanderbilt on its letterhead and had more than seventy branches across the country. The pro-preparedness organizations multiplied—the American Defense Society, Council of National Defense, the National Protective Society —but most were small and not well funded. Indeed, in 1916 the League to Enforce Peace, which stressed international organization, not armaments, had a budget more than twice as big as that of the National Security League.

Wilson derided the scary fantasies of the propagandists for preparedness; imagining the horrors of war befalling the United States was "good mental exercise" perhaps, but the U.S., he argued a year and a half before delivering his war message in April 1917, should wait until the end of the war to build up the navy; it was simply good sense to get the benefit of other people's wartime experience. Even if Germany won the war, it would be exhausted; it would take years before the German Empire could pose a challenge to America. He would not be thrown off balance "by a war with which we have nothing to do," Wilson told Congress "because some among us are nervous and excited."[47] Colonel House, who privately favored rearmament, thought it prudent to tell the president what he wanted most to hear. When the war is over, "public opinion in this country will applaud you for not being carried away by the excitement of the moment."[48]

However, as the election of 1916 approached, Wilson was under increasing pressure within his own government to build up the military establishment. The assistant secretary of the navy, Franklin D. Roosevelt, shared the views of his cousin Theodore. So did the secretary of war, who warned that any first-class military power "could pulverize our small regular army and punish us to a humiliating degree."[49] The American ambassador in Berlin told Wilson that because of our military weakness the Germans "call us cowardly bluffers." In August 1915 Joseph Tumulty, Wilson's private secretary, had argued that the Republicans would make an issue of defense in the upcoming presidential election unless the president took the issue away from them by devising a "sane, reasonable, and workable" preparedness program of his own. Just as the presidential campaign got under way Wilson signed the National Defense Act of 1916, "a fake preparedness bill," the leading advocate for rearmament in the Congress called it, but it was the most ambitious armaments bill since the Civil War, and it passed by overwhelming majorities. However, Wilson refused to accept compulsory military service, and the secretary of war resigned over the issue.

Preparedness, as Wilson had come to believe, was the popular alternative to war. In the Preparedness Parade held on May 13, 1916, crowds kept marching down Fifth Avenue until late into the night, fourteen thousand from Wall Street firms alone, battalions of clergymen ready for battle, Thomas A. Edison, Elihu Root, William K. Vanderbilt, and other distinguished members of that citadel of wealth and Republicanism, the Union League Club, which put up a large electric sign: ABSOLUTE AND UNQUALIFIED LOYALTY TO OUR COUNTRY. The marchers may well have thought preparedness and getting into the war were the same thing, and so did the pacifists like Henry Ford, but for the electorate at large, Wilson was sure, the best policy was peace through the appearance of strength.

In the 1916 election, the Republican candidate, former Supreme Court justice Charles Evans Hughes, though he tried to court the "hyphenated Americans" and at the same time attack Wilson for not being more forceful in dealing with the kaiser, took a position that was virtually indistinguishable from the president's. Though Wilson kept warning that a Republican victory would mean war, both candidates were already committed to the same policy: If the Germans were to resume unrestricted submarine warfare against American vessels, war would be unavoidable. Wilson's famous election slogan, "He kept us out of war," was actually neither a promise nor a prediction but a message designed to reassure the still overwhelming antiwar sentiment in the country without provoking the defeat that a pacifist position would surely have produced. Yet as the campaign began, Wilson hedged on the promise implied in his

instantly popular slogan. There could come a time "at any moment
. . . when I cannot preserve both the honor and the peace of the
United States. Do not exact of me an impossible and contradictory
thing."[50]

Less than a month before the election Wilson received Count
Bernstorff, the German ambassador, at his home in New Jersey, an
"unusually pleasant" visit, Wilson thought, one that reinforced his
ambivalence: "I wish someone would tell me what the Allies are
fighting for."[51] But German U-boat warfare was steadily arousing
growing anti-German feeling in the country. Not long after his
pleasant visit with Count Bernstorff a German U-boat sank six merchantmen off Nantucket Island. Still, there was considerable anti-
British sentiment to offset the cry for revenge against the Germans,
particularly among the Irish and in the cotton states where the
people felt the effects of the British blockade. (Cotton was then
important in the manufacture of munitions.)

As the campaign approached its climax, Jeremiah O'Leary, who
a year or so earlier had lent his own services to German propagandists, attacked the president for "truckling to the British Empire."
Wilson rose to the bait. Some of his advisers had been telling him
to portray his opponent as "the German candidate." So the president shot off an angry public telegram: "I would feel deeply morti-
fied to have you or anybody like you vote for me. Since you have
access to many disloyal Americans and I have not, I will ask you to
convey this message to them."[52] House was delighted by Wilson's
move. "The best thing so far in the campaign," he cheered, not
realizing that the telegram would lose New York for the president.
O'Leary did as he was told and spread the word among the Irish
who controlled Tammany Hall and the New York Democratic
Party. The president's suggestion that being anti-British was the
same as being un-American elicited the predictable reaction. As it
turned out, however, all the mistake cost was a night's sleep. With
New York lost to the president, Hughes went to bed thinking he
had been elected, and TR went to bed proud that his country had
repudiated the "sissy" schoolmaster. But in the morning when the
returns from the West rolled in, Wilson had won by a margin of
twenty-three electoral votes.

Wilson took the election results as a vindication of his policy of
avoiding war. He now stepped up his efforts to bring about a negotiated peace, conducting secret talks with the British and German
governments and calling publicly for a "peace without victory." The
German government, reflecting its own internal split, encouraged

the peace effort but also announced on January 31 that beginning the following day German submarines would sink without warning all ships venturing into European waters. Three days later Wilson broke diplomatic relations. Yet he still hoped to avoid war. He asked Congress for authority to arm merchantmen, and when a group of antiwar senators blocked the measure as Congress was adjourning, Wilson discovered the authority elsewhere and went ahead.

Armed neutrality was of course difficult to maintain. Though the Allies had been violating American rights "more consistently and persistently than Germany" ever since the war began, as Thomas Bailey concludes, British military operations took American property while German attacks took lives.[53] Germany was not only an ideological enemy symbolized by the spiked helmet and the kaiser's imperial strut, but that militaristic autocracy was throwing down a challenge to American export industry and to individual Americans who wished to travel. Finally, at the end of February the British scored an intelligence and propaganda triumph. They produced a decoded telegram sent by the German foreign minister, Arthur Zimmermann, to the German minister in Mexico proposing an alliance against the United States in which Mexico with German support would "reconquer the lost territory in Texas, New Mexico and Arizona."[54] The American connection to the European war was now there for all to see.

When the Germans on March 18, 1917, sank three American merchantmen without warning, Wilson decided within twenty-four hours that war was unavoidable. A substantial minority of newspapers was now demanding it. Yet as Wilson's biographer Arthur S. Link puts it, the decision was in his hands, "so divided and distraught were the American people."[55] The advice from the military was that armed neutrality made war inevitable anyway. "In Wilson's agonized mind," writes Link, ". . . the war could not last beyond the summer of 1917. And belligerency would give Wilson what he wanted most passionately—a seat at the peace table."[56]

So less than a month after his second inauguration on March 4, 1917, Wilson, still uncertain, decided to lead a divided nation into the greatest war of history. The president called Congress into extraordinary session. As a thousand militant pacifists bearing white tulips boarded trains to Washington determined to keep the nation at peace, Wilson was preparing to go to Capitol Hill to ask for a declaration of war against Germany. Just before noon Senator Henry Cabot Lodge agreed to listen to an angry young man who had come with a delegation of constituents to protest the war. The sixty-seven-year-old senator, incensed by the "degeneracy and cowardice" of the pacifists, floored the young man, who was not altogether nonviolent, with a single punch to the nose and briefly became a national hero. At the Metropolitan Opera in New York that evening the crowd broke into cheers at the news that war had come, and the orchestra, disregarding the management's insistence that opera must be "neutral," spontaneously struck up the national anthem. A visiting German soprano fainted onstage, and the opera went on without her. That evening in the White House Tumulty remembers the president saying, "My message today was a message of death for our young men. How strange it seems to applaud that." Woodrow Wilson put his head down on the cabinet table and wept.[57]

3.

The Great War, as it was known before it became necessary to number the global explosions of the twentieth century, was the occasion for America's first effort to create an official culture. Less than two weeks after his war message Wilson established the Committee on Public Information, a vast bureaucracy for managing public opinion on a massive scale, and put the journalist George Creel in charge. Creel had organized some of the most famous writers in the country, such as Frank Cobb, Kathleen Norris, Lincoln Steffens, and Ida Tarbell, to write pamphlets for Wilson's re-election campaign. He had been editor of the *Rocky Mountain News* and a bit of a muckraker himself. As the nation went to war the Wilson administration faced a formidable morale problem. The nation had entered what Raymond Aron was to call the Century of Total War. For the first time the industrial economy, the educational system, the entertainment and information industries, indeed the whole country, had to be mobilized for war. Four million men were drafted and uprooted. Women went to work in war industries. Hundreds of thousands of blacks migrated north looking for war work. Within a few months family relations, race relations, and relations between the sexes had all been shaken by the great mobilization. The increasing intrusion of government into almost every phase of American life was transforming the very meaning of being American.

Though Creel clamped tight controls on the export of news by cable and wireless, newspapers themselves were not censored. They were asked to censor themselves. To be accredited as war correspondents individuals had to swear that they would behave "like a gentleman of the press," divulge their travel plans, promise not to disclose information that could aid the enemy, and post a $10,000 performance bond.[58] While the war was on, the only real controversy it sparked in the press was how to pay for it. Papers in the Middle West put forth the populist argument that if "the masses fight the battles, wealth should pay the bills." The *Wall Street Journal* was not impressed. Punitive burdens on corporations, the *Journal* retorted, would penalize "small estates held in trust for widows and children." Taxation of everyone with a thousand dollars of income or more would "bring home the war to all the people."[59]

The challenge, as Creel saw it, was how to manage opinion without destroying the democracy for which the nation was fighting. The committee, he insisted, was an advertising agency—his book describing his wartime activities was called *How We Advertised America*—not "an agency of censorship" or "machinery of control or repression." Nonetheless, as Americans grew impatient with the war, Creel experimented with some of the repressive techniques of totalitarian regimes. He placed advertisements in *The Saturday Evening Post* and other mass magazines calling on readers to report to the Justice Department "the man who spreads pessimistic stories . . . , cries for peace or belittles our effort to win the war."[60] The task of mobilizing consent to the changes of wartime life was particularly difficult because this was a distant war for which many Americans had no enthusiasm. No dramatic event like Fort Sumter or the *Maine* or Pearl Harbor had galvanized the population; the United States had inched its way into the war. American citizens were going to be asked to make sacrifices in behalf of the nation beyond anything government had demanded since the Civil War. The war effort would require high taxes—by the spring of 1918 the top tax bracket was up to 77 percent—food shortages, dislocations of private lives, and the loss of loved ones. Many citizens—socialists, some "hyphenated Americans," and pacifists, especially—remained unconvinced about the righteousness of the cause or the necessity to get involved.

While the Creel Committee organized "positive" propaganda, opinions that challenged official truth were dealt with harshly by other agencies. The Espionage Act, passed two and a half months after the declaration of war, permitted the postmaster general to exclude magazines from the mail for expressing views deemed embarrassing or offensive. *Masses, International Socialist Review,* and other journals that opposed the war were barred from the mail, but so also was the *Freeman's Journal and Catholic Register* for quoting Thomas Jefferson's opinion that Ireland should be an independent republic. The postmaster general, a former Texas congressman by the name of Burleson, invited local postmasters to send him all unsealed mail that might "embarrass" the government. In May 1918 a Sedition Act was passed making it a crime to say anything "scornful or disrespectful" of the government, the Constitution, the flag, or the uniform. There were two thousand prosecutions and eight hundred convictions under the two acts. The most prominent defendant was Eugene V. Debs, Socialist candidate for president, who was sentenced to ten years for opposing the war. A movie producer, Robert Goldstein, was also sentenced to ten years (later reduced to three) and fined $5000 for including a scene in his Revolutionary War epic that showed British soldiers bayoneting women and children. Facts are facts, Judge Bledsoe admitted as he pronounced sentence, but the film could cause people "to question the good faith of our ally, Great Britain."[61] Prosecutions, as they always tend to be, were arbitrary. Theodore Roosevelt, who regularly took potshots at the president all through the war, could accuse Wilson of betraying the nation without running afoul of the Espionage Act.

The Committee on Public Information developed a large and effective propaganda machine. Its Civic and Educational Corporation Division produced propaganda pamphlets for schools and universities written by historians such as Charles Beard and Sidney B. Fay. The Bureau of State Fair Exhibits targeted the farmers. The Labor Publication Division made sure that workers received patriotic literature. The Pictorial Publicity Division under Charles Dana Gibson, famous for the Gibson girl, prepared posters, including the classic recruiting poster UNCLE SAM WANTS YOU. The Bureau of Cartoons bombarded the cartoonists with patriotic suggestions and the Division for Work with the Foreign Born made special efforts to inculcate enthusiasm for the war effort in the hearts of what was widely assumed to be a suspect group.

The war required conscription, but the American tradition was against it. The Allies were crying for more men; they had suffered a million casualties in the offensive that began in the spring of 1917. But the United States could put no more than 500,000 men under arms during the first year of war, and only 200,000, a large number of them still trainees, could be sent to Europe. To sell conscription, the opinion specialists advised Secretary of War Newton Baker, you must make going into the army an exciting, festive occasion. On July 20, 1917, the secretary, appropriately blindfolded, reached into a fishbowl, and as the flashbulbs popped, he selected the "winning" number of America's first twentieth-century conscript, who turned out, happily for the feature writers, to be a peanut vendor at a New York baseball stadium. Even the name "Selective Service" was carefully chosen to suggest, as Wilson put it, that the process was "in no sense a conscription of the unwilling" but indeed "selection from a nation which has volunteered en masse."[62] The actual induction of recruits was preceded by parties, rallies with balloons and streamers, and pretty girls in generous numbers. The stirring send-off given the contingent from Hollidaysburg, Pennsylvania, was typical. As the recruits prepared to board the train, a bonfire of German books crackled and the band played "Keep the Home-Fires Burning." Red Cross ladies were at the station to hand the boys apples and cigarettes as the train pulled away.

Three-quarters of a million copies of the pamphlet "Why America Fights Germany" were distributed around the country. It was a call to enlistment backed by a graphic picture of what Germany would do if its troops ever landed on American shores: "They pass through Lakewood. . . . They first demand wine for the officers and beer for the men. Angered to find that an American town does not contain large quantities of either, they pillage and burn the Post Office. . . . Then they demand $1,000,000 from the residents. One feeble old woman tries to conceal $20 . . . she is taken out and hanged (to save a cartridge.)" The writer was a Stanford English professor. Booth Tarkington, Mary Roberts Rinehart, and John Erskine were enlisted for more subtle efforts.

The most ingenious suggestion came from a Chicago businessman, Donald M. Ryerson. His idea was to use the network of movie theaters that had recently sprung up across the country to reach captive audiences for short patriotic speeches. By Armistice Day he had enrolled seventy-five thousand "Four Minute Men" in an army of orators. (The name was picked to evoke patriotic memories of the battles of Concord and Lexington in the Revolutionary War but also to assure the moviegoers that the speakers were limited to four minutes.) Well-known authors like Samuel Hopkins Adams and the actor Otis Skinner became Four Minute Men, but the "General Instructions" from Washington advised local organizers to avoid famous people, who usually talked too long, in favor of young lawyers and businessmen, who will "abide by the standard instructions of the department . . . [and] present *messages* [as opposed to rambling speeches] within the four-minute limit."[63]

The messages emphasized the patriotic duty to register for the draft: "The man who stands back now is lost; lost to the ranks of citizenship; lost to the mother who bore him; lost to the father who gave him a name; lost to the flag that protects him."[64] The case for buying Liberty Bonds was starkly put: The alternative was to watch the kaiser's soldiers "goose-step along Pennsylvania Avenue." Americans could lend their savings to the government at 3.5 percent interest or wait for the kaiser to take them. Other messages emphasized the importance of conserving food so that it could be shared with hungry allies. "They are not whimpering, the Frenchmen, they are not that kind, but . . . if we fail them with our 'grubstake' they will S-T-A-R-V-E."[65]

Much of the work of the Creel Committee was aimed at changing the popular sentiments that had made the American people so reluctant to get into the war. These attitudes, as we shall see, did not become casualties of the war but reappeared in the 1920s and 1930s as cynical reflections on the war to end war. One widely held view that was regularly combated by the Four Minute Men was the conviction that Germany and Britain were equally at fault. Traditional Anglophobia was attacked in places where England could not be openly defended by making anti-British Americans feel that they were being victimized by German propaganda. Similarly, the rather widely held idea that it was "a rich man's war" started by the financiers and arms profiteers was also ascribed to German propaganda.

The Germans were active in planting rumors of all kinds, but their efforts were clumsy and easily countered. To deal with a German campaign to convince churchgoing blacks that they should rise up and support the kaiser because he invoked the Deity in his speeches and Wilson did not, prominent Negro speakers were enlisted to specify the variety of ways the kaiser had broken every one of the Ten Commandments. German propaganda, as Bernstorff wrote after the war, "showed a complete lack of understanding of American national psychology. . . . The outstanding characteristic of the average American is a great, even though superficial, sentimentality. There is no news for which a way cannot be guaranteed through the whole country, if clothed in a sentimental form. Our enemies have exploited this circumstance with the greatest refinement in the case of the German invasion of 'poor little Belgium,' the shooting of the 'heroic nurse,' Edith Cavell, and other incidents."[66]

Germany was regularly attacked in official American propaganda as being "feudal," "dictatorial," and exhibiting "an ancient, outworn spirit." On the evil of the German people official propaganda had to steer a difficult course. The traditional distinction of war propagandists between the wicked enemy government and the innocent people victimized by their leaders was usually maintained, but although the president privately deplored the excesses of anti-German fanaticism, the committee encouraged it. Some of its propaganda was calculated to fan the hatred of all things German that was sweeping large areas of the country. German *Kultur* itself was a target since that was the banner under which the Germans were fighting. Patriots soon learned to call hamburgers "liberty steaks." German was dropped in the public schools in many places, and opera companies canceled performances of Wagner for fear of riots. The speaking of German, TR proclaimed, has no place in America.

─── CHAPTER 7 ───

The Fight for the League of Nations

1.

The fight for the League of Nations is perhaps the most dramatic example in American history of a presidential failure to persuade the American people to support a radical change in foreign policy to which the leader himself was passionately, even obsessively, committed. Not only did Woodrow Wilson fail, but the fight destroyed him at the height of his popularity. The story has often been told as a morality play: A leader with a noble vision is betrayed by his people because they cannot scale the heights from which he glimpses the future. Alternatively, it is recounted as a duel of personalities, a contest between a principled but flawed leader and a few "willful men" bent upon humbling a popular political figure.[1] Why did the American people not follow Woodrow Wilson in the hour of victory?

No president had ever heard such cheers echo in his ears. Against the judgment of his close advisers, Woodrow Wilson had gone to Paris to negotiate the peace without victory that would end war. As he rode down the streets of the port city of Brest on the first leg of the journey to the French capital, enormous crowds waved flags under huge banners: "HAIL THE CHAMPION OF THE RIGHTS OF MAN." "HONOR TO THE APOSTLE OF INTERNATIONAL JUSTICE." "HONOR AND WELCOME TO THE FOUNDER OF THE SOCIETY OF NATIONS." Paris was the triumphant climax to the democratic pageant. The presidential carriage proceeded slowly down the Champs-Elysées under a shower of flowers, and the crowds screamed Wilson's name as women wept.

"I saw Foch pass, Clemenceau pass, Lloyd George, generals, returning troops, banners," the journalist William Bolitho wrote of
that moment, "but Wilson heard from his carriage something different, inhuman—or superhuman. Oh, the immovably shining,
smiling man!" The carriage passed under the Arc de Triomphe and
the premier of France exclaimed, "I do not think there has been
anything like it in the history of the world."[2]

For six months the president fought with America's three European allies, Clemenceau of France, Lloyd George of Britain, and
Orlando of Italy, for the idealistic peace he had promised the American people. "Of course I'm an idealist," he once retorted. "That's
how I know I'm an American." His wife saw him grow thin, gray,
and irritable as he came up against politicians of Europe with neither the inclination nor the political space to experiment with Wilsonian idealism; the voters in England, France, and Italy wanted to
see Germany punished. As months of negotiations passed, disappointment turned to frustration and anger. He became suspicious
of his old friend House, obsessed with the French servants whom
he thought were thieves and spies, and so overcome by violent
coughing that he had to sleep for three days. When he awoke, he
insisted on resuming the talks immediately, summoning the British,
French, and Italian prime ministers to his bedside.

In the end he failed to get the peace he wanted. The Versailles
Treaty was harsh, shortsighted, and full of inexplicable compro-
mises. Wilson's dream of a League of Free Peoples to keep the peace
was now embodied in a Convenant of the League of Nations, but it
had been purchased by honoring the commitments in secret treaties
to preserve the British and French empires and to divide the spoils
of war. "I never knew anyone to talk more like Jesus Christ and act
more like Lloyd George," Clemenceau sniffed."[3]

Wilson returned to the United States to enthusiastic crowds, a
New York parade, a standing ovation at Carnegie Hall, and ten
thousand cheering people to welcome him back to Washington as
the late-evening train pulled into Union Station. But he was no
longer the immovably shining, smiling man. Nor was everyone
cheering. Wilson's old nemesis Theodore Roosevelt had died while
the president was in Europe, but a few months before, he had
helped start a new publication, *Harvey's Weekly*, the main purpose
of which was to attack Woodrow Wilson. (George Harvey, the editor, an owlish newspaperman who had helped gain Wilson national
prominence, now believed that patriotism dictated his destruction.)
Roosevelt, furious at the president's refusal to let him lead a division

to France, had attacked Wilson mercilessly all during the war, even accusing him of coming "dangerously near to treacherous diplomacy" in his efforts to arrange an armistice with Germany.[4] A few weeks before Wilson sailed for Europe Roosevelt's ally Senator Henry Cabot Lodge had secretly sent a memo to Henry White, the one Republican on the Peace Commission, asking him to show it to European politicians. The argument was simple: The American people would never support Wilson's League. Even on his deathbed Roosevelt was still plotting against the man who represented everything he hated. When the weary president returned from Paris, among the crowd at the White House was TR's daughter, Alice Roosevelt Longworth, making the sign of the evil eye and muttering hexes.[5]

Though he could be an electric speaker, Wilson's speech to Congress presenting the treaty was uncharacteristically flat. Senator William Borah had obtained a bootleg copy of the Treaty and read it into the *Congressional Record* before the president's appearance, so angry was he at the tight presidential control over information flowing from Paris. (Eight months after the armistice the government still controlled the transatlantic cable.) The Republicans did not applaud, one of their number pronouncing the speech merely "soap bubbles of oratory and soufflé of phrases," and another, Senator Warren G. Harding, dismissing it as "utterly lacking in ringing Americanism."[6] The president had spoken as if the ratification of the Treaty were a *fait accompli*. To many senators he sounded as if he were informing them, almost as if their advice and consent were a foregone conclusion. Still, Wilson had every reason to feel confident that he would prevail. Though the treaty ending the Spanish-American War was ratified by only two votes, no peace treaty had ever been rejected by the Senate. Moreover thirty-two state legislatures had passed resolutions endorsing the League and thirty-three governors were on record as favoring it.[7]

Wilson's archantagonist was Senator Henry Cabot Lodge. Scarcely a "pygmy mind" (Wilson's favorite characterization of troublemakers in the Senate), Lodge was brilliant, powerful, and experienced. As editor of the *International Review* he had accepted the first scholarly article Wilson ever published while the younger man was still a Princeton senior. No less adept than Wilson himself in patronizing his enemies—Wilson was "not a scholar in the true sense of the word"[8]—Lodge once told a friend he did not believe that he could hate a man so much. The president was a "shifty" fellow, always ready under high-sounding rhetoric, as Lodge's friend TR had said, "to sacrifice all patriotic considerations to whatever he thinks will be of benefit to himself politically."[9] Wilson once refused to sit on the same platform with Lodge. By the end of the war the two men were barely speaking.

In the congressional elections of 1918, held a few days before the armistice, Wilson had appealed for a Democratic victory in the name of patriotism. To vote any other way was to undermine the war effort: "The return of a Republican majority to either house of the Congress would . . . be interpreted on the other side of the water as a repudiation of my leadership. . . . I am asking your support . . . for the sake of the nation itself in order that its inward duty of purpose may be evident to all the world."[10] But the voters rejected his appeal, and Lodge became majority leader of a Republican Senate and chairman of the Foreign Relations Committee.

All through the summer of 1919 Wilson tried to enlist support by talking with—lecturing, some said—individual senators as they pressed him to answer the objections they were now making publicly with calculated passion. Article X of the Covenant of the League of Nations committed each signatory to go to the aid of every other in the event it was attacked, a permanent alliance for peace. Did that not mean, asked Senator Lodge, that American youth could be ordered to war by other nations? Did that not mean, asked the Missouri Democrat James A. Reed, that "Asiatic or European despotisms or monarchies" would now exercise control over the great controversies involving "the national honor and the national life?" Would we not have to apply to the League if we wanted to increase the armed forces, "asking the gracious permission of eight gentlemen, six of whom probably cannot speak our language and who have likely never set foot on our shores?" The United States would no longer be able to deal unilaterally with Mexico, surely "an astounding sweep of power" from American hands![11] There would be a "sort of international smelling committee" to inspect American industry to see whether the nation was manufacturing illicit arms. Moreover, the League would be dominated by the British Empire, which, Senator Hiram Johnson charged, would "demand American blood to subdue Ireland."[12] The League also attracted the hostility of other anti-British groups for whom the idea of a permanent alliance with the king of England was a supreme outrage. As the attacks on Britain mounted in the play for the Anglophobic vote, two prominent Republicans visited the British ambassador to assure him that nothing was meant by it all except domestic politics.[13]

Senator Frank B. Brandegee of Connecticut put some of the toughest arguments against the League to the president in a private meeting and told a newspaper the next day that he felt as if he had had "tea with the Mad Hatter." Lodge also pronounced the president "befuddled about many most important points."[14] Meanwhile the senator was showing exquisite contempt for the president by reading aloud the entire text of the treaty to an empty committee room, then inviting a parade of hostile witnesses to condemn it. With money from Henry Clay Frick and Andrew Mellon, Lodge began organizing a public education campaign to kill Wilson's treaty. It would be "Americanized" through amendments and reservations designed to assure that the United States would always remain the master of its fate.

Wilson was convinced that public opinion was with him. During the war the idea that there should be some sort of league to keep the peace in the postwar world was so widely endorsed that it was hard to find anyone against it. Even Lodge had been for it. In 1916 the senator had spoken before the League to Enforce Peace, a lobby organized by William Howard Taft, A. Lawrence Lowell, the president of Harvard, the Boston merchant Edward A. Filene, and other conservatives to get the United States to join a league of nations. "I do not believe that when Washington warned us against entangling alliances," said Lodge to the delighted audience, "he meant for one moment that we should not join with the other civilized nations of the world if a method could be found to diminish war and encourage peace."[15]

The notion of an association of nations to keep the peace was at least as old as Immanuel Kant. Disorder had produced the Great War, and especially for the lawyerly minds of the foreign policy Establishment of the day it made perfect sense to *organize* the peace once it was over. Prominent Republicans were on record as favoring an association of nations. Taft had endorsed the idea of a collective security organization as early as 1914, and even Theodore Roosevelt said he was for a "great world league for the peace of righteousness." Though Wilson himself had been toying with the idea of a league almost from the day the war broke out, these Republicans had spoken out before he did. (Two weeks after war broke out the president told his brother-in-law that he favored "some sort of an association of nations wherein all shall guarantee the territorial integrity of each."[16] When he did call for a "concert of free peoples" in his war message to Congress in April 1917, he evoked no controversy and little more comment when he spelled out the idea further in his enunciation of war aims, the Fourteen Points, which became the basis for the armistice.

In the winter of 1919 even the opponents of the League believed that they faced a losing battle. The *Literary Digest* reported that "the majority of our papers regard the experiment as tremendously worth trying." Not a single religious publication surveyed "opposes the League *in toto*."[17] After Borah made his first speech in February 1919 attacking the League as an affront to Americanism, Lodge congratulated him but pronounced it a "hopeless" task to defeat Wilson on the issue. "All the newspapers in my state are for it." Senator Warren G. Harding of Ohio was equally pessimistic. "Bill, I'd like to get in the fight against this League of Nations, but the people of my state are all for it I'm afraid."[18]

How did it happen that such a popular idea was so decisively rejected? Was it not precisely the popularity of the League idea as an abstract proposition that was the problem? "Everyone"—meaning everyone who commented publicly on public affairs—was for it while the war was on, for it seemed an obvious answer to the international anarchy that had produced the war. But everyone had a different view of what the League should be. In 1916 Randolph Bourne counted thirty-eight different plans for organizing the peace and assured his readers that it was not an exhaustive list. "Everyone has some scheme or plan or League, and all seem to differ profoundly," wrote Leonard Woolf in London, "so that the plain man is inclined either to lose himself in bewildering details, or to turn away in despair."[19]

Like most successful political leaders, Woodrow Wilson read the auguries with invincible optimism. The League issue raised fundamental questions of American identity as nothing had done since the Civil War, for unlike the Great War itself this was to be no mere expedition into the jungle of Europe but a permanent, transforming involvement. Wilson did not see or rather he refused to see the powerful political crosscurrents in which his treaty was caught.

2.

The years 1919–20, during which the debate on the League took place, witnessed a stunning outbreak of American nativism. There had been organized nativist groups in the United States ever since the 1840s when the Native American Party had been formed to block the takeover of the country by Catholic immigrants from

Europe. The party was dedicated to the election of native Americans, by which they did not mean Indians. No one born abroad should be eligible for elective office, the party declared, and no one should become a citizen until he had been a resident for at least twenty-five years. The Know-Nothing Party, as it was popularly known, did well at the polls in New York, Massachusetts, and Delaware in 1854. (The "Know-Nothings" were tagged with that name because their movement was made up of secret societies whose members would answer all questions with "I don't know.") Split by the slavery issue, the Know-Nothing Party disappeared, but a superpatriotism based on fear and loathing of the foreigner within and without has erupted periodically ever since.

The Great War was the first event since the earliest days of the Republic to dramatize how close the United States still was to Europe despite the watery expanse between them. Many Americans recoiled at the thought. Besides, the country was beginning to look too different too fast and in ways that were hardly reassuring. Many Americans felt either assaulted or mesmerized by the beginnings of a continentalwide national culture. In either case people whose prism for viewing the outside world had been limited to the local newspaper or what they might happen upon at the public library watched the silent movies from Hollywood, listened to the strange voices from Pittsburgh on the crystal set, or devoured the romance magazines from New York almost as if they were receiving messages from outer space. These were not the only intrusions. Strange people had moved to town, 600,000 of them of a different color. Loved ones returning from France had been touched by the experience of life beyond the United States and traces of war could be glimpsed in their eyes. The war boom had transformed factory life and brought the terrors of runaway inflation. Retail prices had more than doubled in a five-year period—even milk had gone from nine to fifteen cents a quart—and by the spring of 1919 the loss of purchasing power, as the Democratic national chairman told Wilson, was the number-one worry in the country. That same year the stock market briefly collapsed. By the fall of 1919, four million workers were on strike. More walkouts in the coal, steel, and rail industries threatened. Soldiers returned to find that black men had taken their jobs, and there were ugly race riots in Washington, D.C., and elsewhere. As if the war had not already shattered so many of the illusions on which American identity was based—isolation from a contaminating world, the prospect of living out their lives in familiar small-town surroundings, the right to be left alone—millions of new immigrants, refugees from the ravages of war, were arriving on American shores.

The upheavals of war continued into the bitter peace. The Russian Revolution of November 1917, proclaiming a world Bolshevik revolution, threatened to spread to defeated Germany, and revolutionary revolts broke out in Eastern and Central Europe. These events produced panic in America even as the homegrown radical movements were reeling from government repression. Eugene Debs, the Socialist candidate for president, was in jail along with leaders of the IWW for opposing the war. The fledgling Communist Party USA had neither a base in the American labor movement nor at the time any guidance or subsidy from the embattled revolutionaries in the Kremlin. (Ironically, that happened after the Red Scare of 1919–20 had passed.) But many Americans were afraid of a takeover by radicals. The secretary of labor declared that Bolsheviks and the IWW were behind the outbreak of strikes in the rail, steel, and coal industries. Senator Charles Thomas of Colorado warned that the country was "on the verge of a volcanic upheaval." Senator Poindexter of Washington thought that there was "real danger that the government will fall."[20]

The fears centered on tiny anarchist groups that began publishing scores of new journals, many in strange Eastern European languages, printed on cheap paper, sometimes barely legible, each with a minuscule circulation. They offered their immigrant readers radical fantasies and revolutionary prophecies. The United States was "on the verge of a revolutionary crisis."[21] Leading newspapers reprinted the scariest fragments from radical pamphlets and periodicals. Secretary of State Lansing was given a private memorandum, "The Spread of Bolshevism in the United States," which convinced him, as he wrote in his diary, that the country was in peril of revolution. The only evidence cited was a collection of inflammatory anarchist speeches.

By the summer of 1919, however, a series of mysterious highly publicized bombings had occurred to lend some credibility to the hysteria. In April the former mayor of Seattle, who had been stumping the country to warn of the Red Menace, received a bomb in the mail, which suspicious aides managed to defuse. A former Georgia senator who had led the fight to close off immigration received a similar brown package supposedly from Gimbels and his maid had her hands blown off. Discovered at the New York Post Office were sixteen more bombs intended for members of the cabinet and the two most famous symbols of American capitalism, J. P. Morgan and John D. Rockefeller. Barely a month later there were more bomb explosions, including one at the home of Attorney General A. Mitchell Palmer, which demolished the facade of Palmer's house and blew to pieces the man who set off the bomb. Nearby the dismembered body was a copy of a radical publication called *Plain Words*. On September 16, 1919, a bomb blast on Wall Street claimed thirty-four lives and injured more than two hundred passersby.

The perpetrators were never found. Nor were there any solid clues. But paranoia could serve as a substitute for evidence. "Alien radicals aided and abetted by naturalized radical agitators," declared a spokesman of the Bureau of Investigation, were behind this "revolutionary organization."[22] Palmer himself went further. "On a certain day of which we have been advised," he informed the House Appropriation Committee, the radicals, the Communists, and the anarchists were planning to "rise up and destroy the Government at one fell swoop."[23] (The total membership of the Socialist Party, the Communist Labor Party, and the Communist Party USA was at the most a little more than 100,000 members, one-tenth of 1 percent of the adult population.[24]) The attorney general, who thought that by playing on popular fears and getting rid of the foreign threat that inflamed them he might catapult himself into the presidency, decided to round up for deportation all alien Communists and anarchists. Under the wartime Sedition Act any foreigner could be expelled merely for having dangerous thoughts. On the night of January 2, 1920, his agents swept into meeting halls, offices, and homes around the country and arrested about four thousand individuals, many without warrants, who by virtue of looks or accident of place were assumed to be Communists. For good measure, authorities in Hartford arrested anyone who came to the jailhouse to visit a "Communist." The raids netted three pistols, but no explosives.

Though within five months the Palmer Raids were condemned in a devastating congressional report entitled "The Illegal Practices of the United States Department of Justice," and a resolution was introduced in the House calling for Palmer's impeachment, the attorney general kept on with his anti-Red crusade. The public mood that had made such police-state tactics seem politically plausible did not change. In March the *Literary Digest* polled 526 labor leaders and found that 293 of them "fully approved" of what Palmer had done to protect the Republic and 132 disapproved. Now as the attorney general distributed tens of thousands of propaganda leaflets about the country with pictures of scruffy-looking Bolsheviks, he reminded the twenty million holders of Liberty Bonds and the eleven million depositors in savings banks that a Communist takeover would mean the confiscation of all they owned.

This mood of hysteria and confusion was the ground on which the struggle over the League took place. Americans were feeling insecure about their savings in the face of inflation and about their jobs in the face of incomprehensible changes in the national labor market. In assessing the receptivity of the American people to his high-minded notions of international responsibility Wilson underestimated the trauma of war. "This country is still suffering from shell shock," said Senator Reed in August 1919. "Hardly anyone is in a normal state of mind."[25] The personal dislocations and intellectual confusions of war produced a spasm of superpatriotism.

Gordon W. Allport, one of the influential pioneers in the study of prejudice, argues that extreme nationalism is a device to which individuals often resort when they see the underpinnings of their personal world threatened by rapid, inexplicable change. In the Weimar Republic a few years later the psychological difficulty of accepting defeat and the terrors of finding their money worthless also stimulated ultranationalism. Something of the same sort happened again in the United States in the early post–World War II period when the dislocations of another war and the unprecedented fears of the nuclear age made it easy to create the culture of anti-Communism in which McCarthyism took root. The resurgence of American nationalism in the 1980s came in the wake of a frightening double-digit inflation. Allport notes that people who are susceptible to nationalist appeals are prone to see their nation as "an island of institutional safety and security" and the chief protection of the individual. "It is a conservative agent; within it are all the devices for safe living that he approves."[26]

The psychoanalyst Erich Fromm explained superpatriotism in terms of what he called "group narcissism," the myth of collective superiority of a nation or a race. Ultranationalism, the celebration of the triumphs and virtues of one's own group and the cultivation of hatred, fear, and contempt for outsiders, can help individuals overcome feelings of personal inferiority or worthlessness. Those who fail by the standards of their own society are peculiarly susceptible to jingoist appeals, as Hitler demonstrated when he courted the unemployed of Germany with messages of ultranationalism and hate. Nonetheless, group narcissism, as Fromm points out, continues to be more socially acceptable than individual narcissism. An individual who declares that he and his family are the only clean, honest, and intelligent people in town while all the rest are lazy, dirty, incompetent, or vicious makes no friends thereby, but the same sentiments can be expressed with respect to one's own nation and evoke tumultuous applause.[27]

This was especially true in the 1920s when group narcissism took bizarre and violent forms. At a victory loan gathering in Washington, D.C., in early 1919 a man refuses to stand for the playing of the "The Star-Spangled Banner." A sailor sitting behind him shoots him in the back, and, as the *Post* reported the next day, "the crowd burst into cheering and handclapping." An alien who made the mistake of yelling, "To hell with the United States," is assassinated, and a jury in Hammond, Indiana, takes two minutes to acquit the killer. A clothing store salesman in Waterbury, Connecticut, gets six months in jail for telling a customer that he considered Lenin "one of the brainiest of the world's political leaders."[28]

So just as Woodrow Wilson was preparing to take his case for the League to the country, his own secretary of the interior, Franklin K. Lane, was sponsoring a conference to promote the Americanization movement. One patriotic organization, the National Security League, claimed that it had a thousand study groups for teachers on how to inculcate "Americanism" in their foreign-born students—that "new and holy religion," as one enthusiastic Harvard official called it. The way to fight Bolshevism and all other foreign ideologies, he said, was to "instill the idealism of America's wars and that American spirit of service which believes in giving as well as getting." A senator from Iowa declared that "the time has come to make this a one-language nation," and the American Legion took up the cause. The language was American, not English.

It was a time to celebrate the heroes of the American past and to revere holy American texts. In January 1920 the originals of the Constitution and the Declaration of Independence went on display for the first time, and the Division of Foreign Intelligence of the State Department distributed movies of the ceremony to almost every town and city in the United States. Churches, the bar associations, and the Daughters of the American Revolution threw themselves into the Americanization campaign. The flag became a talisman. Aliens suspected of radical leanings were forced to kiss the Stars and Stripes in public.

The mobilization of public anger against the wartime enemy had helped to create a climate of fear. During the war, according to the attorney general, Thomas Watt Gregory, the Justice Department was receiving "as many as fifteen hundred letters in a single day suggesting disloyalty and the making of investigations."[29] For agitated Americans it was a small step to shift the focus of their fears from the Germans and German sympathizers within their midst to foreigners and un-American ideas. S. Stanwood Menken of the National Security League thought that there were at least 600,000 Communists in Connecticut alone. The American Defense Society, which during the war had run the American Vigilante Patrol to stop "seditious street oratory," now took the position that readers of "revolutionary" publications like the *New Republic* and members of the League of Women Voters and of the Federal Council of Churches obviously belonged on the list of subversives.

The experience of the World War changed the way Americans thought about their country. In the early years of the country, as Merle Curti has shown in his *Roots of American Loyalty*, the loyalties of Americans were evoked by the uniqueness of the American land, its climate, its physical beauty, its abundant harvests, and the blessings of liberty. Despite the myth of being a nation without an activist national government, the services that the federal government provided citizens across the continental expanse beginning in Hamilton's time—roads, canals, postal service, land-grant colleges—served as the mortar of patriotism. Feelings of national pride and loyalty were rooted in the positive virtues of the land and the society.

After World War I, however, the passion that a citizen could muster against enemies became the touchstone of one's love of country. Patriotism became powerfully identified with military virtues, suspicion of foreigners, and "my country right or wrong." To be sure, feelings of loyalty had from the beginning been strengthened by appeals to xenophobia and celebration of American exceptionalism but rarely had it been defined by them. As he prepared to inspire the country to a very different conception of patriotism, Woodrow Wilson, forgetting his own predictions, underestimated the impact of wartime fear and suspicion on the American psyche.

3.

On March 4, 1919, Henry Cabot Lodge announced that he had lined up thirty-seven senators to go on record against the League "as now proposed," more than enough to defeat the Covenant. The president saw no particular reason why cooler heads could not be enlisted to persuade the senators to see the light. That influential conservative, former secretary of state Elihu Root, "reactionary" though Wilson considered him, would be expected to help. For almost two decades Root had been pressing for the buildup of international legal institutions—arbitration, conciliation, and judicial settlement of disputes. He shared the optimism of the times, and had been rewarded for it by receiving the Nobel Peace Prize on the eve of the war. Democracy was on the march. Public opinion was gaining control over governments everywhere. In 1907 he had written that America was on the threshold of the "pathway that leads from the rule of force as the ultimate sanction of argument to the rule of public opinion." But Root always had reservations about how much American sovereignty to give up and when to give it up. The world was not ready for the Covenant of the League of Nations.[30]

Wilson was sure that the liberals would support him; after all, they claimed to be idealists too. In 1918 a liberal lobbying organization to influence public opinion had been formed. Originally called the Committee on Nothing at All, it was known during the years of the fight over Wilson's Covenant as the League of Free Nations Association. In 1921 it became the Foreign Policy Association. The league was the pantheon of American liberalism. All the famous names were inscribed on its rolls: Charles and Mary Beard, Felix Frankfurter, Walter Damrosch, Will Durant, John R. Commons, Ida Tarbell, Learned Hand, and Herbert Croly. The group's manifesto appeared to embrace Wilson's "new diplomacy" with its emphasis on removing the drives to aggression and war through "cooperative nationalism" and a "peace without victory," which would stop the cycle of revanchist wars. Though the word was not used, the group considered imperialism to be a root cause of the war, prompting the New York Times to label it Marxist and pro-German. "League for the Resuscitation of German Commerce at the Expense of the Allies" would be a better name for the organization, the Times editorial writer suggested.[31]

The New Republic, which had moved reluctantly from an antiinterventionist to a prowar position in the years before the American entry into the war, now reversed course. It had supported the idea of a League during the war, and when the Covenant was published, the liberal magazine hailed it as "The Constitution of 1919." Within a few weeks, however, it launched an attack on the Covenant for excluding defeated Germany and Bolshevik Russia. How could you have a world organization and leave out the two greatest potential disturbers of the peace? The editors rejected Article X out of hand, for it would "guarantee the mistakes made at Paris." As the gap between Wilsonian promises and the realities of the Versailles Treaty became apparent, the *New Republic* stepped up its criticism. The weekly published John Maynard Keynes's devastating critique of the Versailles Treaty, which he later brought out as *The Economic Consequences of the Peace.* Yet it always equivocated and never advocated total rejection.

The *Nation,* on the other hand, which took a pacifist position and never supported Wilson's decision to go to war, had nothing good to say for the Versailles Treaty. It was nothing more than a "Covenant with Death" that would consign the German people to "chattel slavery." There were at least a hundred injustices imbedded in the treaty to cause idealistic liberals to recoil, injustices of result —Why was China being stripped of Shantung?—and injustices of principle—Why should the United States promise to go to war to guarantee the rotten status quo of Europe? So liberals split over the issue, and the group of American citizens who were expected to be the most ardent supporters felt betrayed and confused. As the director of the leading liberal lobby wrote President Wilson after the League was defeated, "The concessions made to European National Interests cooled the ardor of American liberals toward the Treaty."[32]

The Protestant Church was also split, though the mainline denominations were with few exceptions League supporters. The Federal Council of Churches proclaimed the League "the political expression of the Kingdom of God on Earth."[33] Was not Woodrow Wilson "an Ambassador of God?" the *Christian Register* (Unitarian) exclaimed. Quakers took out ads in the Philadelphia subway in behalf of the League, and the Church Peace Union spent more than $100,000 in the fight for ratification, most of it from Andrew Carnegie. Churchmen who were unsympathetic to liberal theology and the social gospel opposed the League as the false path to peace, which was to be found only in the converted hearts of individuals. Extreme fundamentalists condemned it as secular millennialism; men in striped pants in Geneva could not be expected to do Christ's work on earth. The revivalist Isaac M. Haldeman, pastor of the First Baptist Church in New York, warned that the League was "getting the world ready for the coming of the Anti-Christ." By which he meant the pope.

Irish-Americans could not forgive Wilson for not having secured Ireland's freedom. Many were ready to believe the charge of the die-hard opponents that the League could order American boys of Irish descent into battle against Irishmen fighting for freedom. The president of the Irish "revolutionary assembly," Eamon de Valera, escaped from a British jail and toured the United States in the spring and summer of 1919 to stir up enthusiastic crowds of Irish-Americans against the Treaty. Fiorello H. La Guardia, then president of the New York City Board of Aldermen, tirelessly organized Italian-Americans against the Treaty because Wilson had not supported Italian claims to the port of Fiume. There were Poles, Czechs, Jews, Chinese, and Japanese who were disaffected because of one or another of the Paris decisions to remake the world.[34] German-Americans, for the most part patriotically silent during the war, now held mass meetings to condemn the humiliations of Versailles.

The most vocal antagonists of the League worried about the loss of sovereignty. It was the best issue for working a crowd, for it played on popular feelings going back to the Jay Treaty; American negotiators always get tricked by European sophisticates and end up selling their birthright. "If I were an Englishman, a Frenchman, or an Italian, I should want this League," George Harvey thundered in his *Weekly*. "But I am an American." A Kentucky editor and a New York inventor teamed up to organize the League for the Preservation of American Independence. Keep the armed forces strong, and America has no need to "place herself under an international protectorate." The American Club of Minneapolis was typical of many organizations springing up across the country. Some were for a strong military. Others were for disarmament. But they were united by the conviction that nothing must ever be allowed to dilute American sovereignty over decisions of war and peace.

4.

"Where am I on this fight?" Woodrow Wilson asked a group of senators he had invited to the White House in the summer of 1919. "Mr. President, you are licked," Senator James E. Watson replied. The only way to get the Treaty was to "accept it with the Lodge reservations." "Never!" Wilson exploded. He never would agree to anything so prominently identified with "that impossible name." It was morally wrong to compromise further. He would take his case to the people, an appeal to Caesar, as he called it.[35]

He had been stirring audiences ever since his Princeton days when his lectures were always jammed. If he lacked the histrionic art of repackaging popular feelings as political wisdom, like Lincoln or Franklin D. Roosevelt, he knew how to present himself as the embodiment of principle and reason. He said once "that it was the men talking in the grocery stores of a thousand towns who formed American public opinion."[36] These good people believed that they had already made the world safe for democracy by winning the war. He had to wake them up. He was sure that the people would rise to their responsibilities once he explained what was at stake.

His physician begged him not to go. It was obvious that he was ill. He knew it, but he believed that the fate of the world was resting on his shoulders. If America did not join the League, there would be another war to "sear" the planet. Setting off with his wife, aides, and secret service agents in a seven-car train, the president traveled nearly ten thousand miles, from the Canadian border almost to the Mexican frontier, twenty-six major stops, ten speeches a day. Even as his voice gave out he would keep making the same points over and over. "And when this treaty is accepted, as it will be accepted, men in khaki will not have to cross the seas again. . . . Shall we or shall we not sustain the first great act of international justice? . . . What difference does party make when mankind is involved?"

The crowds were always curious, usually respectful, but enthusiasm was sporadic. How Wilson was received depended almost entirely on local conditions, usually what local politicians and newspaper editors had said about the League. In heavily Republican Iowa the president received a tumultuous welcome; the *Des Moines Register* was strongly for the League. At his appearance at the Indiana State Fair thousands came to gawk, but no one could hear what he was saying and the crowd kept moving on to other exhibits. In Nebraska the largely German population was unmoved. Upon finally reaching the Pacific coast, the president found himself on friendly soil. Thirty thousand people gave him an "uproarious welcome" in Tacoma. Although California Senator Hiram Johnson was one of the leaders in the fight against the League, Wilson had a good reception in the state. In San Diego, where both Republican papers strongly backed the League, the audience was estimated at fifty-thousand. "I am the attorney for these children," he would say as fathers held up their young children along the route of his motorcade. The splitting headaches were getting worse. After ten speeches a day the exhausted president tossed and turned all night.

The crowds buoyed his spirits, but the news from Washington was not encouraging. William Bullitt, a twenty-eight-year-old member of the American delegation at Paris, subpoenaed before Lodge's committee, read the senators his notes about what Secretary of State Robert Lansing had said when the treaty was being negotiated. The League was "useless." The American people would "unquestionably" defeat the pact if they "ever understood what it lets them in for."[37] Wilson was furious at this act of betrayal. But the more vigorously he carried his fight to the country, the more it seemed to galvanize the opposition. Democratic politicians were coming to believe that public opinion was turning against Wilson. The crowds were not big enough and the president's performance was clearly faltering. There were only twenty-seven Democrats in the Senate who were prepared to support the president's position on the League, which was all or nothing; no reservations, no amendments accepted.

By summer the euphoria of victory had subsided. Wilson was no longer the war leader or the symbol of democratic hopes as he was in that golden moment when his carriage passed under the Arc de Triomphe, but a contentious, arrogant lame duck. A Democratic senator observed, "We may be winning elections about 1940 on the strength of Woodrow Wilson's memory, but not in the near future."[38] Senators from Wilson's own party began breaking ranks, announcing that they would support reservations to the treaty. Senator Hiram Johnson, pursuing his presidential ambitions, was stirring up crowds in Lincoln, Nebraska. "Shall American boys police the world?" In Chicago William Borah denounced the president as a "quitter" who had gone to Paris preaching "open convenants" openly arrived at and had stayed to make secret agreements to remake the map of the world. "Impeach him! Impeach him!" the crowd roared.[39]

The presidential caravan headed back east. In Cheyenne the president stumbled on the way to the podium and looked as if he were about to collapse. In Pueblo he pleaded for the League with tears in his eyes and received a ten-minute standing ovation, but in the night he became so ill that the tour was abruptly canceled and the train sped back to Washington. A few days after returning to the White House, Woodrow Wilson collapsed in the bathroom. A cerebral thrombosis left him paralyzed.

For two weeks the president hovered between life and death. Even as he slowly grew stronger, his wife and doctors kept him incommunicado in the White House; the demands for his resignation would be irresistible if his enemies could see him. As upbeat bulletins on the president's recovery issued from the White House, the president lay in a darkened room while clerks and assistants a

few feet away literally fought over possession of urgent letters requiring presidential attention. Mrs. Wilson's scribbles on scraps of
paper provided the only clues to the rest of the government of what
was going on in the president's head. Colonel House wrote urging
the president to compromise with Lodge to head off a total defeat.
There was no reply.

On September 10 the Foreign Relations Committee reported. It
proposed forty-nine amendments to transform "the entangling alliance" into a geniune "League of Peace." The United States Congress would continue to decide when to make or to honor
commitments to other nations. On November 19, 1919, the amendments were defeated and so was the Versailles treaty. "The greatest
victory since Appomattox," Borah exulted. Wilson's dream was
dead. But the proponents of the League refused to give up. Representatives of twenty-six national organizations all favoring the treaty
in some form, boasting a membership of more than 20 million descended upon Lodge. They pointed out that polls taken in colleges
and universities showed that there was still overwhelming support
for the League. They appealed to the senator, who considered himself the preeminent scholar in politics, to listen to the intellectual
leadership of the country, which was solidly pro-League. Lodge,
who had a much more interventionist vision of national security
than the Midwestern isolationists, began working on a compromise
amendment with the leader of the moderate Democrats, modifying
somewhat his all-out opposition to Article X. Pro-League opinion
was still so strong in the country that the Senate, it was now clear,
would be forced to take another vote. However, Senator Borah
threatened to organize a campaign to depose Lodge as majority
leader if he went against the dominant sentiment of the party, and
the Massachusetts senator abandoned his compromise efforts.

The president was determined to rid himself of the doubters and
the compromisers and to put the great moral decision cleanly before
the Senate. He had recovered sufficiently to fire Secretary of State
Lansing. "Nothing . . . justifies your assumption of Presidential authority . . . I must say that it would relieve me of embarrassment,
Mr. Secretary, if you would give your present office up."[40] "WIL-
SON'S LAST MAD ACT" ran the Los Angeles Times headline. The
president made it clear that no loyal Democrat could vote for com-
promises. "Either we should enter the league fearlessly . . . or we
should retire as gracefully as possible from the great concert of
powers by which the world was saved." All or nothing.

On March 19, 1920, the Senate voted for the second time. The verdict was again negative. Ironically, 80 percent of the senators were for the League in some form, but twenty-three Wilson loyalists refused to compromise and the compromisers on both sides were divided. Had seven of the loyalists switched their vote and joined the other Democrats willing to compromise, they could have saved Wilson's tattered dream. "Governor, only the Senate has defeated you," said Joseph Tumulty, his old political retainer, as he brought him the bad news. "The People will vindicate your course." Then he read out loud from Wilson's own *History of the American People* about how George Washington had been vilified until the very end of his term when the country realized it was about to lose him. The president wept.

Still he would not give up. He convinced himself that despite his illness and the gossip swirling about the White House—the president had gone mad and the First Lady was running the country— he could be nominated for a third term. When his illusions were punctured and the Ohio newspaper publisher James Cox received the nomination along with Franklin D. Roosevelt as vice-presidential nominee, the new leaders of the party paid a courtesy call at the White House. Wilson asked that the campaign be made "a great and solemn referendum" on the League. "We're going to be a million per cent with you and your Administration, and that means the League of Nations," said Cox, gazing down at the vacant-looking face peering up from the wheelchair and the thin, white neck with the shawl draped about it, and there were tears in both their eyes.

In fact the 1920 election campaign, though it was solemn enough, was neither great nor much of a referendum on any specific issue, certainly not on the League of Nations. Cox, fired up from his encounter with Wilson, started off a crusader for Wilson's League, then waffled and said he would favor a reservation to Article X, much like Lodge's. The Republican candidate, Warren G. Harding, said he was not for "Wilson's League" but rather for "an association of nations," which he had yet to conceive, but once elected he would get "the best minds" working on it. On October 7 he came out unequivocally for "rejection" of the Versailles Treaty, whereupon Elihu Root, Herbert Hoover, Charles Evans Hughes, and other Republican leaders, ignoring their maladroit candidate, issued a statement a week later promising that a Republican administration would take the United States into the League.[41]

To predict what either candidate would actually do on the basis of the contradictory things they said a voter would have had to be clairvoyant. But the Harding subtext was very clear. The country wanted no more war, no more parades, no heroics, no dreamy internationalism, just a "return to normalcy." Two days after his landslide victory Warren Harding declared that the League of Nations was "now deceased" as far as the United States was concerned.[42]

5.

Psychohistorians have been fascinated by the story of how the fight Woodrow Wilson believed he could not lose and his fiercest opponents believed they could not win went the way it did. Sigmund Freud himself teamed up with William Bullitt to probe the psychopathology of Woodrow Wilson, a man who at every turn seemed to do the wrong thing to accomplish what he most wanted in his life. A willingness to compromise at almost any point would have resulted in American membership in the League. Clearly, Wilson's illness aggravated the very character traits that isolated him and crippled his political judgment. Much has been made of the personal animosity between Wilson and Lodge, but jealousy and bad feelings are commonplace in politics; they do not usually determine great national debates. Nor did they in this case.

Historians have drawn all sorts of contradictory lessons from the story of the rejection of the League. In the 1930s and 1940s the episode was widely taken as proof of the inability of the United States to conduct its foreign policy in the national interest. Looking back on 1920 from the vantage point of World War II, anyone could see that a historic mistake had been made. Had the United States risen to the obligations imposed upon it by its great power, there would have been no Hitler, no war, perhaps no nuclear weapons. Much of this argumentation was advanced to promote the idea of the United Nations, a warning that isolationism leads to catastrophe. Yet it is of course not at all clear that American membership in the League would have made any difference. Woodrow Wilson admitted that the obligations of the Covenant were primarily "moral." In the climate of the thirties, as we will explore in the next chapter, the will to oppose Hitler was lacking in Europe, and Roosevelt lacked clear objectives and a practical strategy for inserting American power into the European struggle. Though history does sometimes appear to turn on the want of a nail, it is fanciful to think that an American ambassador sitting in Geneva would have made the crucial difference.

Nor can it be said that the judgment of the American people was firmly set against participation. Indeed, to the very end, a majority of the people who thought about foreign affairs at all, and more than three-quarters of their representatives in the Senate, were for membership in a League of Nations, at least in principle. Americans were perplexed by the notion of the League, not adamantly against it. No wonder the voters were confused when none of the so-called experts seemed to agree. Unlike the end of World War II, no clear consensus on defining and protecting national security in the postwar world ever emerged—except by default. The Covenant had been put together in ten days by an American president who had given it little thought. ("You helped write these points," Colonel House sounded almost desperate when he finally located young Walter Lippmann in Paris on the eve of Big Four talks on Wilson's famous Fourteen Points. "Now you must give me a precise definition of each one. I shall need it by tomorrow morning at ten o'clock."[43]) The League had been agreed to by European statesmen with little heart for it in order to get Wilson's support for their territorial and economic objectives. Wilson never faced the implications of what he was asking, and the advantages to the United States were not obvious.

Wilson's dream was caught in three quite different political struggles that engaged American passions far more than the League itself. One had to do with separation of powers. When the passions of the people's representatives appeared to be aroused over the intricacies of Article X, they were actually more concerned about their own prerogatives. War, as indeed Wilson had predicted, shifts and transforms the power of government, concentrating more of it in the hands of the executive. After every war the people's representatives fight back to regain lost prerogatives. It happened again in 1946 after World War II though, largely because of the Cold War, with different results. In 1917 the Republicans had demanded— without success—that Wilson share power by appointing a bipartisan war cabinet or at least a joint committee of Congress, a demand that Lincoln had also resisted in the Civil War. The politicians in the Senate regarded Wilson's treaty not merely as the embodiment of a softheaded internationalism for which they had no sympathy but a political device to circumvent Congress's role in foreign affairs. Their concerns were justified. As the post–World War II experience made clear, when the executive commits the nation to international obligations, Congress loses some of its prerogatives in foreign affairs.

Second, the attacks on the League were part of a conscious strategy to break up a winning political coalition. When Woodrow Wilson was elected in 1912, he was only the second Democrat to reach the White House since the Civil War. He owed his election in 1912 to his bitterest enemy, Theodore Roosevelt, who split the Republicans by running as a third-party candidate. Twice Wilson had managed to keep intact the traditional Democratic base, the solid South and the expanding immigrant population in the cities, and to cobble a winning majority by adding Midwestern Progressives and the Far West. But the war split the "hyphenate" vote. Wilson had declared the mother country of millions of Americans to be their enemy, and as architect of the peace he had failed the nationalist aspirations of Irish, Italians, Slavs, and many more. Large numbers of immigrant Americans still identified with the struggles of Europe, but many more turned away from the chaos of the Old World as wartime prosperity opened up new economic opportunities for them and they became super-Americans. In either case they shrank from the Wilsonian vision. Being American did not require saving the world. There had been enough talk of America's great mission to humanity. Humanity was not grateful. The neighbors were not lovable. "We were a nice prosperous nation when we were just for ourselves," said the letter from a constituent to a Missouri senator, not untypical of much public sentiment in the summer of 1919. "Now, if some blatherskite is not working up some sort of 'drive' for money, old clothes, or nighties for the 'down-trodden' . . . some other thimble-head is kicking and screaming for internationalism."

Finally, the debate over the League raised fundamental questions about American identity at the very moment when nationalist symbols were being skillfully manipulated by powerful political interests for domestic purposes. The League symbolized a tolerance for foreigners, a willingness to work with them, and to share their problems. But this set of attitudes clashed head-on with the antilabor campaign of American business. The climate of reform engendered by the Progressive Movement had emboldened radicals like the International Workers of the World to challenge the economic status quo. The Wobblies also used the symbols of Americanism—the Constitution, Jefferson, Lincoln—to argue for workers' rights, greater equality, and an assault on privilege. The radicals in the labor movement wanted not merely better wages and hours. They had vague ideas about workers participating in the design of the economic system itself. That was not "playing the game respectably," as the editor of The Survey had put it in 1912.

The outbreak of war had made it possible to mobilize patriotism against social change, radical or otherwise. After 1917 many in the labor movement were excited about what was happening in Russia, and a few radicals openly proclaimed their allegiance to Russian Bolshevism. This was quite enough to inspire propaganda campaigns financed by wealthy men to tar the entire labor movement as subversive, disloyal, and foreign dominated. The flag was deployed as a weapon in the defense of capitalist values. The Sedition Act, which was modeled on the Montana IWW statute, was used to prosecute 184 leaders of the IWW. By 1920 thirty-five states had enacted legislation similar to Montana's, which allowed for the crackdown on "disloyal, scurrilous, or abusive language about the form of government of the United States," or to the Colorado statute, which severely limited organized activities designed to affect "governmental, industrial, social, or economic conditions."[44] Corporations invested heavily in patriotic organizations like the National Security League and the American Defense Society, which flourished as long as the corporations kept backing them. The National Clay Products Industries Association, by no means the biggest of the industry lobbies, sought new subscribers with the claim that "we co-operate with over 30 distinctly civic and patriotic organizations . . . 'trailing the reds' . . . has been a paying proposition for our organization."[45] The temptation to stigmatize the call for unions, labor organizing, and strikes as a foreign ideology promoted by the "foreign born" was irresistible. It was too tempting not to lump moderate labor leaders like Samuel Gompers with the radicals. So the fight against things foreign—which put the League into a long list that included Catholics, Jews, immigrants, pacifists—was used as a powerful metaphor in the fight against social reform and labor rights. In the battle against social change the great weapon was nationalism. The prime target was labor, but in the attack idealistic internationalism suffered collateral damage.

———— CHAPTER 8 ————

"The Good War": Getting In

1.

World War II was "the Good War," to use the ironic title of Studs Terkel's oral history. It was morally unambiguous. The Nazis and the Japanese militarists had struck first. Total war ended in total victory. The "arsenal of democracy" crushed the aggressors and emerged from the carnage as the number-one nation, its economic prosperity restored by the very struggle that had crippled enemies and allies alike. The war showered the American people with all sorts of benefits, a scientific and industrial explosion, a sense of national purpose, even, despite rationing, fourteen pounds more meat on the table for the average citizen than in the Depression years. Years later, as Terkel's collective memoir shows, World War II was still remembered as the Good War. Two hundred ninety-six thousand Americans died in battle; 680,000 suffered wounds from enemy fire. But for millions of other Americans it was the high point of their lives, a time of excitement, commitment, and camaraderie, a moment of testing never again to be equaled, or perhaps just a God-given opportunity to escape the life of a sharecropper or being bored in a small town. Almost fifty years after the attack on Pearl Harbor Americans still remember World War II, despite all its horrors, as the just war, the inevitable war, the war that worked.

In the 1930s the memories of World War I could not have been more different. When Walter Millis's book *Road to War: America 1914–1917* appeared in 1935, Americans made it an instant best-seller, so ready were they for the story, as the book jacket put it, of how "a peace-loving democracy, muddled but excited, misinformed and whipped to frenzy, embarked upon its greatest foreign war." The lessons of the Wilson era were clear. "Read it and Blush!" invited the publisher. "Read it and Beware!"

In hindsight World War I had come to be seen as a failure, just as a century before, the War of 1812 had come to be seen as a victory. An entire school of revisionist historians had succeeded in raising doubts in retrospect about the moral superiority of the Allies and the war guilt of the kaiser. Stories of British propaganda campaigns in the United States—even the great Lord Bryce had been a British agent in the secret campaign to push the United States into the war—were calculated to make Americans believe that once again they had been outwitted by wily Europeans. A parade of witnesses before the Nye Committee recounted how the House of Morgan and the "merchants of death" had done their best to get the United States into the war, making huge profits by sucking American boys onto the battlefields of France. The months of tendentious hearings trivialized the history of America's road to war in 1917, but much of what was said there was not actually false. It was hard for Americans not to be cynical about international affairs. Wilson's dream of the United States becoming the moral arbiter of the nations had long since come crashing down. Despite being the preeminent economic power on earth, America exerted little influence over the democracies of Europe shaken by Depression and beset by doubt, and none at all on the fascist regimes of Italy and Germany, which had risen up to challenge them. To top it all, the ungrateful Allies did not pay their war debts. In 1935, a year before he went to Spain to cover the civil war, Ernest Hemingway, in an article called "Notes on the Next War," wrote that "never again should this country be put into a European war through mistaken idealism." That was the interventionist position. Ninety-five percent of the American people, according to a poll of the American Institute of Public Opinion taken a year later, thought the United States should not get into a future European war for any reason.[1]

The most damaging case against democracies for their conduct of foreign affairs has been made by the historians of the era of appeasement in the 1930s. The failure of public opinion in the European democracies and in the United States to see Hitler for what he was and to support leaders like Churchill who wished to stand up to the German dictator when he made his first aggressive moves and before he had built himself an awesome military machine was a piece of monumental folly. This public misperception of the national interest, so it is widely asserted, not only made World War II inevitable, but made it far more terrible than it needed to be, thereby creating the colossal ruin that gave rise to the Cold War. The pacifism and defeatism of Europe in the 1930s are still cited as an object lesson to show how fragile morale in democracies can be when they are faced by ruthless dictators, and therefore how insulated from the public mood sensible national security strategies need to be.

The indictment rests on two rather different counts. One is as old as the Spartans, who believed that the life of Athenian democracy was so comfortable that citizens would not fight for their empire or even their own freedom. The contemporary version of the argument, made by writers like Jean-François Revel in his *How Democracies Perish*, is that the people in democracies are so self-indulgent and obsessed with their individual affairs that they will not sacrifice for the nation.[2] Hitler taunted the democracies for being "soft," a challenge that was adroitly used in domestic propaganda in America to step up war production, enlistments, and war bond sales. Nikita Khrushchev made a similar jab when shortly before the Cuban missile crisis of October 1962 he told the poet Robert Frost that he considered the United States "too liberal to fight."

Walter Lippmann emphasizes a somewhat different point. Democracies are not naturally pacific, much less cowardly. Indeed they can be ferocious. But they cannot be "aroused to the exertions and sacrifices of struggle" unless they are "incited to passionate hatred" or "intoxicated with unlimited hope."[3] A democratic society, as Lippmann saw it, operates on inertia. If it is at peace, it will say no to war. If it is at war, it will say no to anything short of the enemy's surrender.

The experience of World War II—the process of getting into it and the extraordinary circumstances of its ending—transformed American society from top to bottom, and in the process it altered the role of public opinion in the making of foreign policy. In the two-hundred-year story of the people's part in American foreign policy, World War II is the great watershed. Four place-names associated with that war have become etched in our national consciousness. These national security metaphors have set the parameters of political debate for fifty years: Munich. Pearl Harbor. Yalta. Hiroshima.

In the story of how World War II changed forever the relationship between the people and the president and the role of government in society there is one towering figure: Franklin D. Roosevelt.

His leadership of the American people into World War II still stirs enormous controversy, not just because powerful contending forces in the United States have a great deal riding on the historic reputation of this now mythic personality, but primarily because the view one takes of the crisis period 1933–42 buttresses a host of diverse views about the postwar world. How much secrecy, how much candor, how much deliberate manipulation of public opinion, or how much bypassing of public participation on issues of national security one favors depends a good deal upon one's reading of the Roosevelt period.

"He lied us into war because he did not have the political courage to lead us into it." Clare Boothe Luce's assessment of FDR has been shared by those who wanted to get into the war earlier and by those who wanted to stay out. James MacGregor Burns, a Roosevelt admirer, is harsh in judging Roosevelt's inadequate efforts to mobilize public opinion in support of the anti-Hitler coalition. His "policy of pinpricks and righteous protest,"[4] from Hitler's invasion of the Rhineland in 1936 to the attack on Pearl Harbor in December 1941, showed hesitancy in the face of strong isolationist sentiment and failure of leadership. Other admiring biographers reflect the same impatience felt by members of his own cabinet, Henry Stimson, Frank Knox, and Harold Ickes, at the spectacle of a leader bobbing, weaving, and sugarcoating unpleasant truths because he dared not share his real concerns with the electorate. Roosevelt apologists make the same assumption that public opinion constituted a powerful veto on presidential action. Robert E. Sherwood, the playwright who became Roosevelt's speech writer, admits flatly that on occasion Roosevelt misled the electorate about his feelings and his plans with respect to the European war, but he defends Roosevelt's "cautious policy of one step at a time" and his avoidance of a head-on fight with the isolationists on the grounds that he might well have lost, thus signaling to the British "that their cause was hopeless and that they had no choice but surrender."[5] In 1943 the State Department published a review of the previous decade of diplomacy, concluding that misguided popular sentiment had acted as a brake on the development of national policy.[6]

The pro-isolationist historians turned the argument inside out. Agreeing with the interventionist critics that Roosevelt failed to educate public opinion, they attack him for "professing a policy of isolation and neutrality while actually conspiring with Churchill to lead the nation into war."[7] The extreme Roosevelt haters, some of whom were liberals and pacifists who felt betrayed by FDR, such as

Charles A. Beard, the most famous historian of his day, charged the president with the greatest possible deception of the American people, a deliberate provocation of the Japanese attack on Pearl Harbor in order to take the choice of war or peace out of their hands.[8]

World War II has inspired an abundance of conventional wisdom for our own time. If what actually happened in those years is anything like what is commonly asserted to have happened—that is, that popular ignorance and cowardice imposed an almost suicidal veto on the leader's efforts to protect the nation—the story of America's road to war in 1941 is indeed a devastating indictment of democracy. In a time of national peril it appears that a leader has only three stark choices: to deceive public opinion, to fight the uphill battle to change it and risk losing everything, or to be bold enough to act in defiance of the popular will. The question is whether the brutal lessons so many have learned from that time are the right ones.

2.

For Franklin D. Roosevelt, like most of our presidents before and since, foreign affairs were not a primary interest. His experience was limited, his firsthand knowledge shallow. It is hardly surprising that he spent much of his presidency groping his way as he tried to reconcile the shattering events of the 1930s with what he had learned in a lifetime of New York politics. True, he had been assistant secretary of the navy during World War I and had played a minor role in the Paris Peace Conference. When Wilson invited him to lunch aboard the *George Washington* and told him that the United States had to join the League "or it will break the heart of the world," the young Roosevelt became a convert. In his race for vice president in 1920 he subscribed to all the principles of Wilsonian idealism, but characteristically he defended them before the voters as good politics. Wilson had "slipped one over" on Lloyd George, he said in a campaign speech. The United States would end up with more votes than the British Empire for surely the Latin-American republics "will stick with us through thick and thin."[9] (He then boasted that he had personally written the constitution of Haiti in the Navy Department.)

By the time he was elected president, Roosevelt had reverted to his original feelings about collective security. (His first reaction to the League before talking to Wilson was that it was just "a beautiful

dream.") To get the support of the archisolationist William Randolph Hearst in his race for the Democratic nomination in 1932 he
issued a statement opposing American "participation in political
controversies in Europe or elsewhere," denounced the League, and
later, under Hearst's further pressure, the World Court as well.[10]

Roosevelt's isolationist stance was not merely a piece of political
opportunism. Roosevelt was a leader who aroused worshipful feelings among ordinary people because he could identify with the
popular yearnings of his time. In 1933 Americans wanted peace
every bit as much as they wanted economic security. In the spring
of that year twenty thousand students from sixty-five colleges and
universities participated in a poll organized by the Brown University
campus newspaper in which 72 percent voted against serving in the
armed forces even in wartime, almost half of the respondents refusing to bear arms even if the United States were invaded! The following April twenty-five thousand students walked out of their classes
to participate in antiwar demonstrations, and in 1935 sixty thousand
students carried out an antiwar strike across the country. "Life is
Short Enough," "Build Schools—Not Battleships," the placards
read. Religious and pacifist groups campaigned to eliminate ROTC
units.[11] The Kellogg-Briand Pact of 1928 to "outlaw" war had been
supported by 90 percent of the press. "It is a thing to rejoice over, it
is superb, it is magnificent," said the Boston *Herald.* Senator Borah
had persuaded the National Grange to push the idea of making war
illegal, and though one senator dismissed the treaty as an "international kiss," the State Department reported that it was receiving
almost five hundred enthusiastic letters a day.[12] The popular literature of the day reflected the depth of antiwar feelings. John Dos
Passos's *1919* with its bitter description of the burial of John Doe—
"Where his chest ought to have been they pinned the Congressional
Medal"—Hemingway's *A Farewell to Arms,* Irwin Shaw's *Bury the
Dead,* and Remarque's *All Quiet on the Western Front* held up a
mirror to war that disillusioned Americans found credible and moving.

How does one account for this burst of pacifism so soon after the
spasm of superpatriotism at the end of World War I? In part it
reflected disillusionment with that war, disillusionment with Europe. But it was also the product of a growing disillusionment with
war propaganda, a growing realization that public officials, often
allied with private interests, had deliberately manipulated the fears
of the American people. If there has always been a nativist virus
lurking in the American consciousness, it has been kept from rav-

ishing democratic institutions by the antibodies that, fortunately, it seems to activate. Suspicion of things foreign coexists with suspicion of government, especially the federal government. When it began to dawn on Americans that neither the federal government nor any more of Europe had fallen to the Reds, that the unions were not in the hands of the Wobblies after all, and that indeed President Coolidge was reportedly napping away his afternoons, the atmosphere of crisis subsided. Americans reflected on the excesses of the Justice Department, and public pressure forced William J. Burns, whom Palmer had made head of the Justice Department's Bureau of Investigation, into lucrative retirement. (The fear he did so much to arouse in office helped create a market for the William J. Burns International Detective Agency.)

The credibility of peace groups was boosted by revelations of the lengths to which the government had gone to discredit them. The efforts of private organizations like the American Legion and the DAR to paint Midwestern church ladies pink if not scarlet began to look silly, but the involvement of the War Department in the campaign seemed clearly un-American. In 1923 General Amos Fries, head of the Chemical Warfare Service, had commissioned the librarian of the unit to circulate the Spider Web Chart, which purported to show that all women's peace organizations in the United States had secret ties to the Bolsheviks.[13] Four years later the American Civil Liberties Union pronounced the War Department and the "Professional Patriots," as such organizations as the American Legion and the American Defense Society were increasingly derided, to be the "principal purveyors of intolerance in the country."[14] On reflection, as in the McCarthy era, many Americans began to feel a bit ashamed for being so ready to accept the abandonment of constitutional principles so easily, and they were angry at the government's efforts to mislead them. Though such things as "confidence in government" were not measured in the late 1920s, the awareness that they had been propagandized by the government undermined the credibility of official "patriotic" messages.

The Depression of course completely changed the ways ordinary people thought about security. How to feed the family without having either a job or a bank account, how to save the farm or the house, were the questions on people's minds, not dangerous ladies preaching peace. Money from the corporations to fund super-Americanism was drying up, and most of the professional patriotic organizations went out of business. In the 1930s Americans had little interest in supporting what the playwright Sidney Howard called "patriotic clashes" with liberalism, unionism, or child labor reformers. On the contrary, people wanted government to promote economic reform. Conservatism had failed, and it could no longer wrap itself in the flag.

In his first years in office Roosevelt fanned the isolationist sentiment not just because he was telling the public what it wanted to hear, but, as the historian Robert Divine convincingly argues, because he believed it himself. At least on some days. On Armistice Day, 1935, he declared that "the primary purpose of the United States of America is to avoid being drawn into war." The next year, after he had been renominated, he gave a passionate antiwar speech at Chautauqua in which he sounded virtually every theme in the isolationist litany, the "fool's gold" of the arms trade, the need to make a choice between "profit or peace." ("The Nation will answer —must answer—'we choose peace.' ")

> I have seen war. . . . I have seen blood running from the wounded.
> I have seen men coughing out their gassed lungs. I have seen the
> dead in the mud. I have seen cities destroyed. I have seen two
> hundred limping, exhausted men come out of line—the survivors of
> a regiment of one thousand that went forward forty-eight hours be-
> fore. I have seen children starving. I have seen the agony of mothers
> and wives. I hate war.

This emotional speech was drafted by William Bullitt, who remembered first hearing the phrase "I hate war!" shortly after the declaration of war in 1917 when a tearful Woodrow Wilson had theatrically seized both Bullitt's hands and cried out the words as they met alone together in the president's office. Roosevelt no doubt saw the speech as a bid for isolationist support, but it must have had special meaning for him because he gave away inscribed copies to his friends the following Christmas.[15]

In those years FDR was a "big navy" isolationist. With its economic power protected by the fleet, the United States could and should stay aloof from the political struggles of Europe and Asia. He loved ships, had pictures of them on his walls, models on his desk, and even in the prewar years of low military budgets he tried to take special care of the navy. He had never shared Wilson's pacifist leanings. As assistant secretary of the navy he had been almost as eager to get into World War I as his cousin Theodore. He thought "dear, good people" like his boss Secretary of the Navy Josephus Daniels were hopelessly unrealistic in thinking that the

U.S. could keep out of the European war. "I just *know* I shall do some awful unneutral thing before I get through," he had written his wife in April 1915. A year earlier he had asked to be part of an invasion fleet he hoped would be dispatched to punish Mexico for Pancho Villa's "banditry."[16]

Like many Americans, he had come out of World War I with considerably less enthusiasm for war than when the United States went in, flags flying. In the 1920s, recovering from polio, he rethought many things. His religious feelings deepened, and he became more conflicted about when and where the United States should use military force. Still, when he turned his attention to Hitler's challenge in the early years of his presidency, his first impulse was to call on the navy. On April 10, 1935, eleven months before Germany occupied the Rhineland, he wrote a letter to Colonel House telling him that he was considering American participation in a joint military and naval blockade to seal off Germany's borders. "A boycott or sanction would not be recognized by us without Congressional action but a blockade would fall under the Executive's power after establishment of the fact."[17] These private musings went nowhere; no statesman of Europe was prepared for such an initiative.

But two years later Roosevelt again brought up the idea of a blockade—he preferred the word "quarantine"—this time aimed at Japan, which had just attacked and sunk British and American gunboats on the Yangtze River. In a conversation with the British ambassador on December 16, 1937, Roosevelt suggested drawing a line somewhere in the Pacific and instituting a blockade as a response to Japan's next act of aggression. "It would not mean war," he insisted, "and it was within his presidential rights."[18] The British, who wanted an immediate show of Anglo-American naval power in the Pacific, a proposal that FDR turned aside, were shocked at the president's insouciance about using the navy in this way. Blockades are indeed acts of war. Prime Minister Chamberlain concluded that the president was mostly talk, a conviction that was borne out when Roosevelt's emissary to the Royal Navy confirmed that American public opinion in 1937 was hardly prepared for the risks of a blockade.

Roosevelt was not an appeaser. There is nothing to suggest that he ever thought Hitler's appetite could be satisfied by feeding it. He was not "taken in" by the German dictator, as historians like A. L. Rowse charge. Indeed, his private letters show that he saw the danger of Hitler early. But in the years 1935–39 he was perplexed and often naive as he tried to figure out the meaning of Germany's challenge and what to do about it. Principally preoccupied with domestic affairs, Roosevelt was guided by the prevailing views of his time, most notably the conviction that the roots of wars are economic. But unlike most of the business community of the day, he did not believe that rearmament would imperil economic recovery. (He considered the 1934 naval appropriation to be a splendid public works bill.) His most influential adviser and friend, Harry Hopkins, was by instinct pacifist and isolationist, and Eleanor Roosevelt was close to the peace movement. The idea that a single evil individual would gamble with the future of civilization itself, the thought that has been at the center of the postwar nuclear nightmare, or that Hitler could be stopped only by challenging him in a test of will was much too brutal, too pessimistic for the times. Roosevelt confronted the world of the late thirties with the confusing lessons of World War I. Not one of his advisers in his inner circle was telling him in the early years of Hitler's rise to play a more confrontational role in European diplomacy, or to begin serious rearmament. His secretary of state, Cordell Hull, in whom he reposed almost no confidence, was an internationalist in the sense that he wanted the United States to play a more active moral and political role in world politics, but at every turn he counseled caution in the threat of force.

Meanwhile Hitler was growing stronger and more belligerent. In 1935 Congress passed the Neutrality Act, imposing an embargo on exporting munitions to warring nations. Roosevelt signed it reluctantly and called for a largely ineffective "moral embargo" when Italy invaded Ethiopia. The purpose of American policy, he said, was to make sure that the United States did not "become involved in the controversy."[19] After the Japanese attack on the American gunboat *Panay*, cruising down a river in China, and the outbreak of war between Japan and China, Roosevelt and Hull began talking with the British about an international peace conference, which, Foreign Secretary Anthony Eden reported to the cabinet, the Americans wanted "for educating their public. They did not know what step they might be able to take next, but they hoped the Conference would gain more energetic public support for them." However, despite the urgings of Admiral Francis Leahy, the president's senior naval adviser, and Secretary of the Treasury Henry Morgenthau, Jr., Roosevelt refused to order the Pacific fleet to put to sea.[20]

It is a tradition of American diplomacy ever since Washington's time for presidents to use the constraints of public opinion to justify policies they themselves wish to pursue. In Roosevelt's case he used public opinion to certify his own reluctance to act. In October 1937 he gave a speech in Chicago that appeared to call for a "quarantine" of aggressors, as if they were the carriers of a contagious disease, warning that if the forces of "international lawlessness" should win in Europe "let no one imagine that America will escape, that America may expect mercy." There was no security to be found in "mere isolation or neutrality."[21] The speech provoked a howl of protest from the isolationist press, but a less negative reaction, as Roosevelt wrote House at the time, than he had expected. What disappointed him were not the attacks, which he had anticipated, but, as Under Secretary of State Sumner Welles put it, "the failure of certain members of his Administration and of certain Democratic leaders in the Congress to come out with courageous and vigorous statements supporting his speech and clarifying the purposes he had in mind." In the light of the heated reaction to his speech the president decided at a press conference the next day to minimize its significance. "It's a terrible thing," he told Samuel Rosenman, "to look over your shoulder when you're trying to lead—and to find no one there."[22] He told the reporters that he was just expressing "an attitude." He didn't have a program to go with it, but he was looking for one.

Public opinion polls revealed that many people in the country were considerably more positive than the Chicago *Tribune* or isolationist politicians like Senator William Borah about what they heard as the anti-Hitler and anti-Japanese tone in the president's speech.[23] (The German, Japanese, Italian, and Soviet governments, however, all responded in identical fashion: the president must have had some other country in mind.) Roosevelt's words had not been calculated as a trial balloon; they were merely an expression of his own ambivalence. He wanted to strike a moral posture, but he intended to do nothing that would increase the risks of America's involvement in war. In this regard he was being swept along by the strongest undercurrents of popular feeling. The Philadelphia *Inquirer* reflected them perfectly with an editorial professing equal enthusiasm for the president's denunciation of "international gangsterism" and his determination "to keep this country out of war."[24]

Politicians are of course not constrained by public opinion itself but by their perceptions of public opinion. In 1937 the polling industry was just getting under way. A year earlier the *Literary Digest*, which had been featuring opinion polls on important questions, had predicted a Republican landslide in the 1936 election and had become such a laughingstock that it promptly went out of business. George Gallup, whose predictions had been more or less right, found himself famous; a new era of scientific polling had arrived. Roosevelt was an avid reader of polls. Soon the White House began receiving in advance of publication confidential analyses of Gallup polling data from Dr. Hadley Cantril, who ran the Office of Public Opinion Research at Princeton.[25] Later, the president was even invited to submit his own quesions in secret, and through an intermediary, his friend Anna Rosenberg, he did. But Roosevelt did not look to polls for guidance as to what to do so much as for what to say. They could be used to probe attitudes and test rhetoric without requiring one to take it all as seriously as did Dr. Gallup himself. "Since the views of the majority in a democratic society must be regarded as the ultimate tribunal," the founder of the polling industry once wrote, public opinion sampling could function as the "pulse of democracy." Here was a channel of continuous communication between the government and the governed that made it possible for any day to be Election Day. Although the British government at the time was horrified at the thought of soliciting "uninformed opinion," as if peppering a few hundred people with questions could ever elicit suitable guidance for Oxford and Cambridge men in positions of responsibility, Roosevelt saw the possibilities at once. Polling could take some of the risks out of politics.

In the years 1937–39 most polls showed that a majority of Americans had isolationist impulses, but there were unmistakable signs that many Americans had warring feelings within them about how to protect America. In this they were no different from Roosevelt himself. Much less fixed in their views and more educable than the strident editorial writers, Dr. Gallup's respondents kept shifting their opinions in clear response to the headlines. Again, much like the president, indeed like people anywhere who digest experience and learn from it. In September 1938, at the time of Munich, only 34 percent were willing to sell military equipment to England and France; by March 1939, after Hitler had torn up the Munich Pact and occupied Czechoslovakia, 66 percent were ready to take this step.[26] By September 1939, 76 percent believed that the United States "will be drawn" into the European war. There was no "illusion of neutrality" held by the men and women picked for Dr. Gallup's scientific sample.

But to the question asked a week after Hitler invaded Poland— "Should we declare war and send our army and navy abroad to fight

Germany"—94 percent answered with a resounding NO! The answer was neither surprising nor significant, for the president himself neither wanted nor expected at that moment to do either. And the last thing the military services wanted to do was to go to war. (Even on the eve of Pearl Harbor, after two years of rapid military buildup, the U.S. Navy was still telling the president that it needed six months more before it would be ready.) Even someone as strongly committed to stepping up defense efforts and increasing aid to Britain as Henry L. Stimson, the Republican lawyer whom Roosevelt appointed secretary of war in 1940, after the fall of France, did not believe that American participation in the war was inevitable when he joined the cabinet in April, and he only came to that conclusion at the very end of that year. Not until the spring of 1941 did he think the United States should take active steps to enter the war. There were angry differences in Roosevelt's cabinet about what to do at each step of the way, but no one favored getting into the war until quite late in the day. Indeed, those who were charged with running American foreign policy were somewhat more optimistic about avoiding war than the general public, at least more so than Dr. Gallup's respondents. The record of the prewar years strongly suggests that the American people were ready to be educated by events and to follow the president whenever he chose to lead.

Yet is is clear that despite what the polls said, Roosevelt, and Hull particularly, felt "the isolationists" to be a formidable political force with which they were locked in combat every step of the way on the road to war. It was not the public's reaction to his educational effort that worried Roosevelt so much as the counterattack it provoked from those who were determined to educate the people in exactly the opposite direction. Public opinion was not an organized political force to constrain a president but a battleground over which the president and his divided opposition struggled.

The "quarantine" speech and the scare over the *Panay* actually had the effect of loosening the Ludlow Amendment from the grip of the House Judiciary Committee where it had been bottled up for three years. This amendment to the Constitution, the brainchild of a Democratic congressman from Indiana, now received new support from those in both parties who wanted to punish Roosevelt for even the slightest shift away from his isolationist stance. The amendment would have established a popular veto; Congress could not declare a state of war until the people had approved it in a national referendum. Roosevelt pleaded that it would "cripple any President in his conduct of our foreign relations," and it was barely defeated by a complicated parliamentary maneuver.[27] But the point had been made. In the battle for public opinion the president faced formidable forces.

Who were the isolationists? The German ambassador, Hans Heinrich Dieckhoff, had it more or less right in the analysis of American opinion he prepared for Weizacher, head of the Political Section of the German Foreign Office, on December 7, 1937. Americans were against foreign entanglements, he wrote. These "pacifists" were not pro-German—there was much less of that than in World War I—but "large elements of the population, especially in the Midwest, who are indifferent to foreign policy . . . whose only wish is to be left in peace." These people along with peace organizations, "particularly those drawing support from labor and liberal circles," now held the interventionists in check. However, he warned, "If they should ever be roused out of their lethargy or arrive at the realization that their doctrinaire concept is either un-workable or will help the opponents of liberalism and democracy, the jump from a policy of isolation to one of intervention will not be very great. . . . In a conflict in which the existence of Great Britain is at stake, they will throw their weight on the English side of the scale."[28] In assessing the strength of "internationalist senti-ment" in the United States the ambassador was aware that large American corporations, including Du Pont, Standard Oil, and Union Carbide, were secretly collaborating with firms in Nazi Ger-many. In the mid-1930s Ford and General Motors subsidiaries were producing half the tanks for Hitler's *Wehrmacht*.[29]

When Franklin Roosevelt and his advisers plotted their strategy of response to Hitler's aggression, it was neither the faceless crowd nor the magic of polling data that impressed them. It was particular faces of particular men, each of whom was touching a different current of opinion. Charles A. Lindbergh was the spokesman for the defeatists. The great aviator, who had seen Hitler's mighty air force, could throw a pall of gloom over any dinner party in Wash-ington, New York, or Chicago by offering his expert opinion: The next war was as good as won by the efficient, goose-stepping tech-nocrats who represented the "wave of the future." Lindbergh tapped into the fashionable antidemocratic intellectual currents of Europe. The argument had been succinctly stated by the influential French writer Anatole France: "Those people who are governed by their men of action and their military leaders defeat those peoples who are governed by their lawyers and professors."[30] Lindbergh received a medal from Goering for his political acumen, and he managed to send it back by registered mail only a few days before Pearl Harbor.

General Robert E. Wood, the chairman of Sears Roebuck who became the head of the America First Committee, which was the leading keep-out-of-war lobby, represented conservative isolationism. When war broke out in Europe he wrote the president that the "only possible way of preserving our own institutions is to stay out of the conflict at any cost."[31] Wood had gone to West Point, served in the Philippines, been in charge of supplies for the building of the Panama Canal, and he was no pacifist. But he believed that war could ruin the American economy and turn the New Deal into a permanent socialist dictatorship. Other conservatives, including the Democratic leader of Queens, William J. Goodwin, considered Roosevelt's cautious anti-Hitler rhetoric to be an attempt "to line up on the side of Stalin in the European war which now seems to be threatening." It throws a "startling light upon some of the past actions of the present administration," he hinted darkly. What better way to launch a Communist dictatorship in America than to concentrate power in the WPA?[32] The president, "having shot his bolt and missed the bull's eye" with his New Deal nonsense, warned Amos Pinchot, was out "to gain support by the tom-tom and war dance method."

Isolationism flowered on the Left in many varieties. Communists and those who took their signals from them were interventionists as long as Stalin was trying to put together an anti-Hitler coalition, and when those efforts failed and he made his near-fatal deal with Hitler, the Communists became just as passionately antiwar. Twenty months later they were interventionists once more when Hitler attacked Russia. Some of the most powerful antiwar novels of the period, such as Dalton Trumbo's *Johnny Got His Gun*, were written by leftists. Norman Thomas spoke for much of the non-Communist Left when he pleaded that "if we show it is possible to improve and keep democracy and settle better than the dictatorships have ever settled the problem of jobs and the cries of poverty, no dictator could keep Europe under his thumb." Going to war would bring fascist dictatorship to America. In this fear he was joined by the conservative Senator Robert A. Taft, who was equally convinced that "a war to preserve democracy . . . would almost certainly destroy democracy in the United States."

The New Deal isolationists differed in only one respect. The Securities and Exchange Commissioner, Jerome Frank, who coined the battle cry of the isolationists in his 1938 book *Save America First,* was not as worried as the conservatives about entrusting war powers in the hands of Franklin D. Roosevelt, but he believed, along with Robert Hutchins and other pro-Roosevelt intellectuals, that America's salvation lay in continuing the New Deal and that meant keeping out of war. Of some influence in these circles was Charles A. Beard. The famous historian, who counseled that America's destiny was confined to the American continent, had been an interventionist in World War I, because he had been appalled by German militarism when he had been a student there in prewar days, but he had become even more disturbed by the hysteria and reactionary politics that the war had brought to America. He understood history to be primarily a matter of economics; presidents, in his view, when faced "by the difficulties of a deepening domestic crisis and by the comparative ease of a foreign war" had invariably chosen the latter. There was no reason to believe that FDR would prove to be an exception.[33] The garden needed tilling at home. "Let Dorothy Thompson settle the problems of Europe," he growled to an interviewer. (The foreign correspondent was a well-known Cassandra who kept warning that Europe was going to explode.) "I can't."

The Axis powers employed their own propagandists to persuade Americans not to get into the fight against them. The Japanese hired Ralph Townsend, a former U.S. consul in China, to make the case that in Asia the Japanese were "fighting the white man's battle" against China.[34] William Dudley Pelley organized a small band of native Nazis into the Silver Shirts, but the American storm troopers aroused the interest of few Americans other than the FBI and the columnist Walter Winchell. George Sylvester Viereck, who had been a propagandist for the kaiser, wrote enthusiastically once again about Germany being the peacekeeper of Europe, but unlike World War I, German-Americans, far from being a sympathetic constituency, were outraged and ashamed at what Hitler was doing to the Catholic Church and to the Jews. Though serving Hitler's cause, Viereck made much of his independence. In his New York apartment he hung photos of Freud and Einstein next to Hitler's.

Father Charles E. Coughlin had, like Roosevelt, a voice made for radio, "a voice of such mellow richness," said the writer Wallace Stegner, "such manly, heart-warming, confidential intimacy . . . that anyone tuning past it on the radio dial almost automatically returned to hear it again." He began broadcasting sermons from a Detroit radio station in 1926, and by 1934 his idiosyncratic blend of populism, anti-Communism, promotion of family values, and denunciation of the Versailles Treaty was bringing in ten thousand letters a day and a flood of cash contributions.[35] He had been an enthusiast of the New Deal—he called it "Christ's deal"—and had helped Roosevelt to fight off Al Smith for the Catholic vote in the 1932 Democratic Convention. In celebrating the New Deal in his weekly radio sermon Roosevelt's popularity had rubbed off on him and he was now the biggest thing on the air, as *Fortune* put it, invited to address the Massachusetts legislature, a guest at the White House. In late 1934 he suddenly turned on Roosevelt for being a capitalist after all and took up Hitler's cause. Though he criticized Germany occasionally, he embraced the major tenets of fascism, the corporate state, anti-Semitism, and the old populist standby, Anglophobia. In 1935 he played a key role in getting the United States to reject membership in the World Court, which Roosevelt had proposed, because it meant an alliance with "internationalism," by which he meant the world Jewish conspiracy. He overreached himself in 1936 by running his own pathetic candidate against Roosevelt and thereafter declined precipitously in influence, but he remained a nuisance and a symbol in the White House of the power of those volatile, irrational forces still lurking in the country, waiting for another demagogue.

As far as the Roosevelt White House was concerned, the publicists, the professors, and the businessmen who were fanning public passions on war and peace were the supporting cast. The major players in the battle for public opinion were in the Senate, which would have to approve any major shift away from isolationism. Roosevelt saw William E. Borah of Idaho, who had been a leader of the "battalion of death" in the Senate that had defeated Wilson's League, as his great antagonist in the gathering battle over foreign policy. Borah, a central casting senator with a shaggy silver mane, leonine face, and a declamatory style he had been developing ever since he ran away from an Illinois farm to join a traveling Shakespeare company, represented in his own serenely confident person several different strains of isolationism. Originally a free silver populist, he supported much of the New Deal and was no friend of Big Business. Borah insisted that he was an internationalist in matters of commerce and humanitarian aid. But, as he had put it in 1934, "in all matters political, in all commitments of any kind or nature, which encroach in the slightest upon the free and unembarrassed action of our people, or which circumscribe their discretion and judgment," the United States was isolationist and should forever remain so.

3.

It was the evening of July 18, 1939. As he looked up from the couch by the fireplace, flashing the famous smile, holding out his hand to Senator Borah, President Roosevelt was trying his hardest to be charming. He had invited a half-dozen Senate leaders from both parties along with Vice President Garner and Secretary of State Hull—neither a Roosevelt favorite—to his study on the second floor of the White House. The president's political stock was at an all-time low. He had failed in his scheme to "pack" the Supreme Court. The country was still in the recession that had brought the New Deal recovery to a halt in 1937. He had staked the prestige of his office on the 1938 election primaries by personally intervening to purge conservative Democrats, and he had lost. Now it seemed he was about to lose again.

Roosevelt had taken no public action in response to the dismembering of Czechoslovakia at the Munich Conference in September 1938. Sitting by the radio with Harry Hopkins in his railroad car on a siding near the Mayo Clinic, waiting to hear the results of his son Jimmy's operation, he listened as Hitler ranted and the crowds roared. Shortly afterwards he decided to send Hopkins to the West Coast to make a secret survey of the capacity of the aircraft industry to make warplanes. But almost four months went by before he said anything much publicly about the gathering storm in Europe, and then only to hint that there were "methods short of war" that could be used to bring home "to aggressor governments the aggregate sentiments of our own people." What they were he didn't say.

Then two months later a friendly senator put forward a bill prepared by the State Department to revise the Neutrality Act to permit belligerents to buy arms from the U.S. if they would pay cash and carry them in their own ships. "Cash and carry" arms trade, an idea Bernard Baruch had been pushing on Roosevelt, was designed to favor Britain and France, both of which were naval powers with a large merchant marine, and was crafted with public opinion in mind. The measure carefully took account of what everyone believed were the forces that had propelled the United States into World War I. This time American munitions makers would not be allowed to send American ships to the war zone to be sunk and force a choice between dishonor or war. This time there would be no loans, no debts. This time no House of Morgan would have a financial incentive to involve the nation in other people's quarrels.

Roosevelt carefully avoided a personal endorsement of the bill. Secretary Hull would act as the lightning rod. A majority of congressmen and senators, including many Democrats, refused to budge. Some attacked the "vast discretionary powers" that the bill would give the president. Others denounced it as an "un-American, 10 Downing Street bill" to "defend stolen colonies with the blood of our youth."

The president had agreed to meet Borah in a last-ditch effort to get the Neutrality Act repealed, and only after reluctantly being talked out of denouncing him to the nation. The isolationists, he had intended to say in the undelivered speech, deserved "only the utmost contempt and pity of the American people." But all such feelings were pleasantly masked as the president set about to soften up the senator. Borah, however, proved as impervious to Rooseveltian banter about how to make old-fashioneds as he was to Hull's alarmist arguments. Finally, the president tried the persuasive technique perfected by his successors in the postwar era. There was secret information he had to share. "I must tell you," he warned, "that according to intelligence in the hands of the State Department, war in Europe is imminent." Hull predicted war by the end of the summer and stated flatly that if the embargo in the Neutrality Act were removed, the chances of war would be cut by at least half. A change in U.S. law on arms shipments might just give Hitler pause. "It is our last chance to avoid war."

"Mr. President, my feeling and belief is that we are not going to have a war. Germany isn't ready for it," Borah interrupted. "So far as the reports in your Department are concerned," he said turning to Hull, "I wouldn't be bound by them. I have my own sources of information which I have provided for myself, and on several occasions I've found them more reliable than the State Department." Hull was close to tears. "Captain, you haven't got the votes, and that's all there is to it," said the vice president. Roosevelt made sure that the meeting ended with a joke, but he was furious. At a press conference three days later he accused the Republicans of destroying his last chance to avert war.[36]

Just before dawn on September 1, 1939, German troops in Polish uniform "invaded" Germany, triggering Hitler's long-planned response. Waves of German tanks began rolling across the Polish countryside. The greatest war of all time had begun. Roosevelt went on the radio two days later to promise that "as long as it remains within my power to prevent, there will be no blackout of peace in the United States." Unlike Wilson, he did not expect Americans to be neutral in thought, but he would "seek to keep war from our firesides by keeping war from coming to the Americas." The speech articulated perfectly the feelings of the American people as his adviser, A. A. Berle, Jr., had summed them up a few months before: "Americans want two inconsistent things at once: to stay out of war, and to damn the side they disagree with."[37]

The blitzkrieg against Poland in September 1939 now made it possible to do what Roosevelt had failed to achieve three months earlier. The Non-Partisan Committee for Peace through Revision of the Neutrality Act was hastily organized by members of the old League of Nations Association under the leadership of William Allen White, the Republican editor who had been a national institution for almost fifty years. "The sage of Emporia," a red-faced pudgy man, so exquisite a literary craftsman that he could write a riveting biography of Calvin Coolidge, knew all the presidents of his time. Made famous by Mark Hanna, who reprinted millions of copies of his editorial attacking William Jennings Bryan, captivated by Theodore Roosevelt, who tried to make an expansionist of him back in 1896, White had made a career of celebrating the gold standard and the Republican Party. Nonetheless, he was fascinated by Franklin D. Roosevelt, and they became good friends. "What worries me, especially," Roosevelt wrote White in December 1939, after Poland had fallen, "is that public opinion over here is patting itself on the back every morning and thanking God for the Atlantic Ocean (and the Pacific Ocean)." Of course the president fully expected "to keep us out of war," but "my sage old friend, my problem is to get the American people to think of conceivable consequences without scaring the American people into thinking that they are going to be dragged into this war."[38]

Roosevelt won an overwhelming victory. By more than two to one the Senate voted for the "cash and carry" amendment. Its job done, the Non-Partisan Committee for Peace went out of business. In making his case to the people the president had been deliberately misleading. The measure to permit England and France to buy American weapons, he assured the country, "offers far greater safeguards than we now possess or have ever possessed to protect Amerian lives and property." A step toward belligerency was thus presented as a measure to avoid war.[39]

In May 1940, Hitler invaded the Low Countries and France. With the encouragement of the administration White revived his committee, changing its name to the Committee to Defend America by Aiding the Allies. "No munition-makers' money, no international bankers' money, and no money from the steel interests," White insisted. The Committee to Defend America soon had chapters in almost nine hundred cities and towns across the country. (Adlai E. Stevenson was chairman of the Chicago branch.) The committee regularly put on coast-to-coast broadcasts featuring, in addition to White himself, Henry Luce, James B. Conant, the president of Harvard, and to Roosevelt's great delight, even Colonel Lindbergh's mother-in-law. White was no great Anglophile. Great Britian was a "mangy, sore-eyed" lion that had let loose on the world "an avalanche of blunders," but, make no mistake, the war was not "a contest of imperialist nations struggling for power. It is a clash of ideologies." The committee battered away at the idea that the situation in Europe bore any resemblance to that of World War I. This time the moral differences between the belligerents were so clear that no believer in democracy could afford to say, "A plague on both your houses."

CBS foreign correspondents like William L. Shirer and Edward R. Murrow, who brought the horrors of Hitlerism and war into American living rooms every day, were powerful allies in Roosevelt's campaign to alert the American people. Listening to Murrow describing the Battle of Britain with the sound of bombs bursting in the background, or noting Shirer's professionally controlled outrage as he reported on the latest Hitler speech, Americans, whether they were sitting in their kitchens or driving in their cars, wondered whether there was any place to hide. The inevitable Movietone newsreel at the local movie house reinforced the ostrich instinct, but as the weeks went by and more countries were engulfed by war, escape seemed increasingly improbable. If thirty years later the news industry dramatized Vietnam as the unnecessary and unwinnable war, in World War II it provided the most potent antidote to isolationist illusions.

The White Committee's message was welcomed by such leading Republican newspapers as the *New York Herald Tribune* and the *Des Moines Register*, which had attacked most of Roosevelt's domestic policy, but which now supported his efforts to aid the Allies. Most columnists were with him, and Robert E. Sherwood, who had written popular plays attacking totalitarian dictatorship, wrote a full-page ad for the committee, which appeared on June 10, 1940, the day Italian forces swept into France for the kill. Under the banner "STOP HITLER NOW" the advertisement pulled no punches: "Anyone who argues that the Nazis will considerately wait until we are ready is either an imbecile or a traitor."[40]

White and his friends inaugurated a new art form in American politics, the "independent" committee to say things in behalf of the White House that the president did not yet dare to say himself. "I never did anything the President didn't ask for, and I always conferred with him on our program," White later explained. "Why didn't you call me pusillanimous?" the president grinned when a committee member brought him a mock-up of a full-page newspaper ad attacking the administration for its excessive caution. But White was impatient with Roosevelt. As France was about to fall, he shot off a telegram to the White House: "You will not be able to lead the American people unless you catch up with them."[41]

The leading isolationist lobby was the America First Committee. It was started by two Yale students, R. Douglas Stuart, Jr., the son of a high Quaker Oats executive, and Kingman Brewster, Jr., who many years later became president of Yale. The two young men went to both political conventions in 1940 and drummed up interest in the idea of a national organization to combat interventionist propaganda and to resist Roosevelt's moves toward war. Senator Robert Taft and his colleague from Montana, Burton K. Wheeler, were enthusiastic. Most of the leadership of the America First Committee, such as William Regnery, the publisher of conservative books, were Roosevelt-hating right-wingers, but liberal isolationists such as Chester Bowles, William Benton, and Robert Hutchins were also attracted to the committee. Douglas Stuart's father persuaded General Robert Wood to become chairman. The leadership discouraged pacifists and called for a strong defense. It was against "foreign" wars, by which it meant wars in Europe fought alongside cynical, ungrateful allies. Despite the distances involved, some isolationists took the position that the war in Asia was less "foreign," and they were all for giving Chiang Kai-shek American aid. The key difference was that China was a ward, not an ally. Once Japan was stopped, they assumed that the United States would have a free hand in the Pacific.

At its height the committee had about 850,000 members, and considerable funds.[42] It was dogged by the charge that it was anti-Semitic, since some of the most vocal isolationists took the line that Roosevelt was being pushed into war to save European Jewry. Sensitivity to the power of anti-Semitism in America had been a major factor in the Roosevelt administration's disgraceful hesitation to welcome refugees from Hitler when there was a chance to save them. Breckinridge Long, an assistant secretary of state, waged a successful fight to keep out the refugees, whom he considered, as he wrote in his diary, "just the same as the criminal Jews who crowded our police court dockets in New York and who could never become moderately decent American citizens."[43] The national leadership of the America First Committee tried to distance the organization from anti-Semitic groups, and for a time managed to get Wood's business associate at Sears, Lessing Rosenwald, on the board. But the group's most prominent spokesman, Charles A. Lindbergh, not only accused American Jews of "agitating for war" but, echoing *Mein Kampf,* threatened that "they will be the first to feel its consequences."[44] Sensing that the hero had now gone too far, the administration moved to cut him down. Roosevelt compared Lindbergh to Clement Vallandigham, a traitor to the Union cause in the Civil War, and Stephen Early, Roosevelt's press secretary, observed that there was a "striking similarity" between what the aviator was saying and "the outpourings of Berlin in the last few days."

4.

In the struggle to bring the power of America to bear against Hitler Roosevelt fought four major battles. In each he confronted the problem of public opinion in a different way. The first battle was the hardest. Five days after Winston Churchill became prime minister on May 10, 1940, the Former Naval Person, as he would call himself in cables to Roosevelt all during the war, pleaded for a "loan" of the World War I destroyers that the U.S. Navy had just reconditioned. The fall of France was imminent. The evacuation of British forces from Dunkirk was about to go into final planning stages. The next six months would be critical. The American ships could make the difference in stopping Hitler's invasion of the British Isles. Roosevelt replied with sympathy but said that he could do nothing about the destroyers because it would take "a specific act of Congress." Churchill, who knew how to use weakness as a weapon, cabled back a veiled threat. His public position was supreme confidence: "We will never surrender." But he would not let Roosevelt forget that defeatism had paved the way for the Nazis in France and Norway.

> If members of the present Administration were finished and others came in to parley amid the ruins, you must not be blind to the fact that the sole remaining bargaining counter with Germany would be the Fleet, and if this country was left by the United States to its fate

no one would have the right to blame those then responsible if they made the best terms they could for the surviving inhabitants. Excuse me, Mr. President, putting this nightmare bluntly. Evidently I could not answer for my successors, who in utter despair and helplessness might well have to accommodate themselves to the German will."

Three weeks later Churchill applied more pressure. "I understand all your difficulties with American public opinion and Congress," he began his argument, but "a pro-German government" willing to make the British islands "a vassal state of the Hitler empire" might well hand over the British fleet to Hitler. "If we go you may have a United States of Europe under the Nazi command far more numerous, far stronger, far better armed than the New. . . . The sending of . . . 35 destroyers . . . will bridge the gap."[45] On July 31, the cabinet having agreed to offer British bases in return for the destroyers, Churchill's tone grew desperate. "Mr. President, with great respect I must tell you that in the long history of the world this is a thing to do NOW."[46]

An interventionist group daring enough to make White's Committee look moderate now appeared. A Virginia gentleman by the name of Francis Miller—so ardent an Anglophile that he and the American woman he had met in England had recrossed the Atlantic to get married in an Oxford chapel—prepared a Manifesto calling for American ships and planes to "join in the protection of the British Isles and the British Fleet." At a dinner at the Century Club he persuaded Henry Luce, Walter Millis—a plum for the committee, given his views on World War I—Dean Acheson, Elmer Davis, James Conant, and Allen Dulles to sign on. But William Allen White would not go that far. He was busy trying to get the Republicans not to pass an isolationist plank at their 1940 convention and to push the candidacy of Wendell Willkie.

Roosevelt sensed that he was at a great turning point. The destroyers, he was persuaded, might make the crucial difference between saving Western civilization and ushering in a thousand years of a dark new order as Hitler promised. A fight in Congress would involve hopeless delay. Senator David I. Walsh, chairman of the Senate Naval Committee, was a fervent isolationist who considered the transfer an act of war, an opinion that a weekend on the presidential yacht did nothing to alter. The president decided to go ahead and trade fifty destroyers for bases in Newfoundland, Bermuda, Bahamas, and other places in the Western Hemisphere, and on the strength of a highly elastic opinion of the attorney general, to do it by Executive Order, without consulting Congress. He told Colonel "Wild Bill" Donovan, a Republican but an interventionist, that he expected to lose the election because of what he was about to do. "Congress is going to raise hell," his secretary Grace Tully remembers him saying, "but even another day's delay may mean the end of civilization."[47] So after repeatedly pooh-poohing the thought of such a thing when asked about it at press conferences, Roosevelt had the White House announce the deal on September 3, 1940. The day before, "fortuitously," said the president, the British government had made a public pledge never to sink or surrender the British fleet.

The presidential campaign was in full swing. Willkie, the Republican candidate, attacked Roosevelt "for the most dictatorial action ever taken by any President." But though he attacked the dictator, he did not attack what the dictator had done. At White's urging Willkie had privately agreed that if he got the nomination, he would not make an issue of the destroyer deal. Roosevelt was also encouraged by a Gallup poll taken two weeks before. Sixty-two percent of those who claimed to know what the pollsters were talking about favored selling the destroyers to Britain. Getting the bases, Roosevelt realized, made the deal that much better.[48]

At a press conference he defended the destroyer swap as an act of "continental defense" in the tradition of the Louisiana Purchase. He gave the reporters a long off-the-record lecture on what Jefferson had done. "There was never any treaty, there was never any two-thirds vote in the Senate, and today Louisiana is about one-third of the whole of the United States." The letters and telegrams pouring into the White House were overwhelmingly favorable. Constitutional lawyers were more impressed with the attorney general's ingenuity than with his regard for the Constitution. Edward S. Corwin, the most eminent constitutional scholar of the time, concluded that the transaction violated two statutes and "represented an exercise by the President of a power that by the Constitution is specifically assigned to Congress."[49] Some international lawyers complained, but their quibbles were generally considered academic. Under the pressure of events the fateful assertion of presidential prerogative in foreign affairs was widely accepted.

Until the last two weeks of the campaign Wendell Willkie avoided sharp attacks on Roosevelt's foreign policy. He appeared to be riding high. The tradition against a third term for presidents was working for him. The press was overwhelmingly for the Republican candidate, who was being statesmanlike and even above party on foreign policy. He promised to keep Cordell Hull as secretary of state. Then as the election approached and Roosevelt—"the Champ," as Willkie called him—took to the campaign trail, the Republicans grew desperate. Willkie was persuaded to play to the American fear of war. The nation would be at war within five months if Roosevelt won, he cried in his hoarse voice. The boys were already on the transports. Echoing one senator who charged that Roosevelt was about to plow under every fourth American boy, Willkie kept painting Roosevelt as a warmonger who in his drive to build "socialism" in America had neglected the national defense. From Democratic National Headquarters came the message relaying the thousands of letters and telegrams pouring in from citizens and party professionals around the country: "Please, for God's sake, Mr. President, give solemn promise to the mothers of America that you will not send their sons into any foreign wars. If you fail to do this, we lose the election!"[50]

The master rhetorician in the White House was put on the defensive. The crowds liked it when he lashed out at the isolationists, naming them in a euphonious chant, "Martin, Barton, and Fish," but they liked it better when he echoed their antiwar sentiments. In the midst of the election campaign, faced with the presidential duty of launching Selective Service by drawing the number of the first registrant out of a fishbowl, Roosevelt scrupulously avoided the words "conscription" or "draft." This was a "muster," a word to evoke memories, as the speech writer Robert Sherwood put it, "of the rugged farmers of Lexington and Concord taking their flintlock muskets down from above the fireplace." Using a letter from Cardinal Spellman to keep the interventionists happy—the prelate warned against "a peace whose definition is slavery or death"— Roosevelt walked the tightrope. By Election Day he had succumbed completely to his nervous political advisers. He had said "again and again and again" that American boys would not be going into any "foreign wars." On November 2 in Buffalo, a few days before the election, he stated flatly, "Your President says this country is not going to war."[51] The campaign was, in Sherwood's words, "a dreadful masquerade, in which the principal contestants felt compelled to wear false faces, and thereby disguised the fact that, in their hearts, they agreed with one another on all the basic issues." The 1940 campaign ushered in the era of the "bipartisan foreign policy," the first of many campaigns featuring fraudulent rhetoric and blurred issues.

Once reelected, Roosevelt moved more aggressively but still cautiously against Hitler. In his efforts to assist the British war effort Roosevelt risked three more confrontations with the isolationists in Congress. By the time of the vote, public opinion, as reflected in the polls, supported all of them. The first was "Lend-Lease," which was a euphemism for a massive military aid program for Britain designed to avoid a "war debt" that would have made the unpaid bills of World War I allies look trivial. It was like lending a neighbor a garden hose to put out a fire next door before the flames spread to your own front porch, the president explained in a fireside chat. After the fire is out, you get the hose back. No, said Senator Taft, what was being proposed was more like lending someone a piece of chewing gum. It was not something you wanted back. Democratic managers in the House worked it so that the Lend-Lease Bill bore the patriotic number HR 1776. The administration won easily, and would have won by an even larger margin had Lend-Lease not evoked a second fear almost as powerful as the fear of war. The act gave the president enormous discretion to aid any country whose defense he happened to think was vital to American security. Congress was being asked to dispense with its advice and to consent in advance.

On August 12, 1941, the House passed by one vote an extension of Selective Service which provided for the first time that peacetime draftees could be sent outside the Western Hemisphere. The isolationist cause had been helped by Hitler's attack on Russia in June. The war was no longer ideologically neat; there were now dictators on both sides. In Buffalo the America First Committee proposed a national referendum to find out whether Americans wanted to fight alongside the Communists. Many of those who voted against the draft four months before Pearl Harbor did so because of their not inaccurate belief that Hitler's attack on the Soviet Union had saved Britain and made an eventual attack on the United States much less likely. Senator Harry S. Truman expressed a common feeling when he remarked: "If we see that Germany is winning, we ought to help Russia, and if Russia is winning we ought to help Germany and that way let them kill as many as possible. . . . Neither of them think anything of their pledged word." [52]

The last battle Roosevelt fought with the isolationists before the Japanese preempted the decision to go to war by bombing Pearl Harbor was over acts of war in the North Atlantic. Once again Churchill pressed Roosevelt to take another step. Lend-Lease supplies were flowing to Britain, but German U-boats were destroying 500,000 tons of shipping a month. The British lacked the escort vessels to protect the cargoes. Frank Knox, the Republican publisher of the *Chicago Daily News*, whose blistering editorials attacking Roosevelt's spineless response to Hitler had won him an appointment as secretary of the navy, urged Roosevelt to put the newly created Atlantic squadron to work convoying vessels to Britain. Roosevelt refused, saying that "public opinion was not yet ready."[53] Instead he gave the order to extend American naval patrols halfway across the Atlantic and secretly arranged to report to the British fleet the presence of German ships. When the president announced the "patrol"—it was not a "convoy," as there was a resolution pending in the Senate forbidding the president to authorize convoys—he said nothing about the most significant aspect of the new policy. Providing target information for British warships was, as Secretary of War Stimson told Roosevelt, "a clearly hostile act to the Germans." The American people were being deliberately misled. Ickes was convinced that Roosevelt's purpose was to provoke Germany into a hostile act that would justify openly using the U.S. Navy to convoy ships to Britain. In August 1941, after Roosevelt and Churchill met on an American warship in the North Atlantic, the prime minister reported to the cabinet: "The President . . . said that he would wage war, but not declare it, and that he would become more provocative. If the Germans did not like it, they could attack American forces. Everything was to be done to force an 'incident' that could lead to war."[54]

By this time Morgenthau, Stimson, and Ickes thought it was imperative for the United States to get into the war and for the president to be forthright in making the case to the American people. But that was not Roosevelt's way. On May 27 he made his toughest speech to date, promising "all additional measures necessary" to get the critical war supplies to Britain. "They're ninety-five percent favorable," he exulted as he showed Sherwood baskets of a thousand telegrams or more that had come to the White House after the speech. "And I figured I'd be lucky to get an even break on this speech." Yet the next day at his press conference he appeared to take back most of what he had said. He wasn't planning to use the navy for convoy duty. The Neutrality Act was just fine the way it was. Sherwood concluded that while the isolationists' campaign "had failed to blind American public opinion to the huge accumulation of events, . . . it certainly had exerted an important effect on Roosevelt himself: whatever the peril, he was not going to lead the country into war—he was going to wait to be pushed in."[55]

The push came in the North Atlantic. A German submarine fired

a torpedo at the American destroyer *Greer*, which had been following the U-boat for three hours and broadcasting its location to British ships in the area. Though the German torpedoes missed,
Roosevelt tried his best to make an atrocity of the incident. Hence-
forth, the U.S. Navy would escort "all merchant ships . . . of any
flag" to protect them against "the rattlesnakes of the Atlantic." In
mid-October a German torpedo hit the destroyer *Kearny* near Ice-
land. "America has been attacked," declared the president. "Very
simply and very bluntly—we are pledged to pull our own oar in the
destruction of Hitlerism." Americans waited breathlessly by their
radios for the president's call to war, but all he asked for was the
revision of the Neutrality Act to remove all restrictions on American
commerce in the war zone. That was more than enough for Senator
Taft. Revising the Neutrality Act, he said, would remove the last
impediment to war.

In his speech Roosevelt made much of a secret map "made in
Germany by Hitler's Government—by planners of the new 'world
order,' a map that "makes clear the Nazi designs, not only against
South America but against the United States itself." The map was
in fact a brilliant forgery concocted by Section M of the British
Security Coordination in Ottawa, which passed it to the FBI. Sir
William Stephenson, the British intelligence agent known as "In-
trepid," had been "discovering" a number of mysterious documents
designed to get the United States excited about Nazi plans for the
Western Hemisphere. He remembered well that the "Zimmermann
telegram" had been helpful in getting America into World War I
and so a handwritten note appeared on the margin of Hitler's secret
map discussing possible Mexican participation in Nazi plans for
Latin America. When one of the American operatives used by the
British in the operation learned of the forgeries in 1984, he said that
he felt "as if a member of my club had been passing bad checks." [56]
Isolationist senators at the time said the map was a fake. But it
accomplished its purpose. The amendments to the Neutrality Act
passed by slim majorities.

A month before Japanese planes took off for their bombing run
over Pearl Harbor Roosevelt was telling his cabinet that he wished
he could poll the people on whether to go to war. The cabinet was
unanimous in telling him that the people would support him. It
would be popular to go to war with the Japanese, Attorney General
Biddle said, because Americans don't like Japanese, and it would be
a naval war, which the country prefers to slogging in the mud. Army
cryptographers had broken the Japanese Purple code, and the inter-

cepts, known as Magic, allowed the White House to follow Japan's inexorable moves toward war. Ickes urged Roosevelt to use Japan as the way to get into the war against Hitler, but as late as November 23, Ickes concluded, the president "had not yet reached the state of mind where he is willing to be aggressive as to Japan."[57] On December 5 Roosevelt and the cabinet knew that the Japanese fleet had put to sea. In the evening of December 6 Roosevelt received a thirteen-part intercept from Tokyo, and after he and Hopkins read it, Roosevelt said, "This means war." But the crucial paragraph referring to a surprise attack on Pearl Harbor had been dispatched in a low-priority code, and American cryptographers did not get around to translating it until after the bombs had fallen on Hawaii. Thus on December 7, 1941, the White House expected an attack, but it did not know where. No one in Washington credited the Japanese with either the daring or the skill to pull off a knockout attack on Pearl Harbor. When Hopkins suggested a preemptive attack on the Japanese fleet, Roosevelt shook his head. "No, we can't do that. We are a democracy and a peaceful people."[58]

As the bombs fell on Pearl Harbor it was still unclear whether public opinion would ever permit Roosevelt to declare war against Hitler. The Nazi dictator resolved the problem by declaring war on the United States four days later. Roosevelt subsequently expressed the view that the United States would not have joined the war in Europe had not Hitler taken this step. But FDR's success in taking the nation to the brink of war even before Pearl Harbor suggests otherwise.

CHAPTER 9

"The Good War": Getting Out

1.

American participation in World War II produced a bureaucratic revolution that has been transforming the nation ever since. The experience of war changed the shape, character, and style of government and led to a radical shift in the balance within the executive branch between those bureaucracies promoting "domestic tranquility" and those providing "for the common defense." In 1939 the federal government had about 800,000 civilian employees of whom 10 percent worked on national security. At the end of the war the figure approached four million, of which more than 75 percent were engaged in war-related activities. The last premobilization defense budget for fiscal year 1938 was about 1.4 percent of the gross national product. Defense spending never dipped below 6 percent in the postwar period even when the GNP reached $4 trillion.[1]

Not only did the balance of power shift from domestic agencies to national security bureaucracies but within the foreign policy establishment the military became the dominant force. The State Department had already lost its traditional near-monopoly on foreign affairs in the New Deal years when Roosevelt ran his own foreign policy. It never regained its former power, and in wartime it was effectively sidetracked as the military establishment under the political direction of the president was given the task of defining the substance and scope of national security.

The United States came out of the war with a global network of bases, a formidable intelligence capability (the OSS, which became the core of the CIA), a large military assistance program, a permanent agency to conduct overseas propaganda, and what President Eisenhower called a "military-industrial complex." This new set of relations between industry, "a scientific-technical elite," and the military enabled the country to maintain its forces in a permanent state of readiness. The changes in the priorities of the federal government wrought by war became permanent conditions of American life in the postwar world.

The lessons of the thirties became the wisdom of the forties. The United States would never go back to having a small army or a low profile. In 1943 when Stalingrad was under siege and only the liveliest imagination could have conjured up a future Soviet military threat to the United States, Pentagon planners were drawing up blueprints for a large permanent military force—based on the assumption that the Soviet Union would be an ally, not an enemy. Practices once considered un-American by the high-minded lawyers and career officers who looked after the nation's defense in the interwar years were now the foundations of national security planning. When he was secretary of state in the Hoover administration, Henry L. Stimson is reputed to have observed, "Gentlemen do not read each other's mail" as he dismissed a proposal for a national intelligence agency. (This was the same prehistoric era when a top general could veto plans for a new bomber on grounds that it was "immoral" to design a plane to bomb civilians.)

Nothing had been considered more un-American than for the federal government to get into the business of propagandizing the American people. Though presidents had been "educating" the public to their point of view since the beginning of the Republic, to set up bureaucracies to merchandize policy and manipulate the feelings and opinions of citizens, using their own tax money to do it, was to imitate Hitler and Goebbels. The last wartime propaganda effort of George Creel and his committee had left a bitter taste. A generation later he was remembered for having whipped up blind hatreds and empty enthusiasms for an unnecessary, even fraudulent, war. Yet by the end of World War II, the federal government had developed elaborate machinery for manufacturing consent, and some of it in altered form remained in the postwar years.

World War II was the most powerful educational experience since the Civil War. For Americans it was a collective as well as an isolating experience. At the end, the people of the United States had a more coherent self-image and worldview than when the war began. The average citizen's angle of vision shifted perceptibly under a bombardment of battlefront reports, pictures, and sounds of war interpreted by the rapidly expanding news industry, the entertainment industry, and, most notably, by the president himself. As sophisticated techniques of opinion management and new theories about the role of public opinion were developed under the pressure of war, the relationships between the individual and government in the United States underwent subtle but lasting changes.

The shock of Pearl Harbor brought the appearance of instant unity. "My first feeling was of relief," Stimson recalled, "that the indecision was over and that a crisis had come in a way which would unite all our people." Unlike World War I, the overwhelming majority of Americans accepted the necessity of the war and the righteousness of the cause. Even Charles A. Lindbergh said he would have voted for war had he been in Congress on December 8, 1941.[2] There were exceptions, to be sure. The pacifist Jeannette Rankin cast the sole vote against war in the House of Representatives. Fifty-two thousand Americans were conscientious objectors. Six thousand more refused to cooperate with the military as a matter of principle.

Yet the war disrupted and divided the nation even as it presented Americans with a common purpose and homogenizing experience. There was no moratorium on partisan politics. "The New Dealers are determined to make the country over under the cover of war if they can," Senator Robert Taft wrote a friend seven weeks after Pearl Harbor. Another conservative, Daniel Reed, who had just won the nomination for a House seat, explained his victory, "I went after the Roosevelt foreign policy with just as much vigor and venom as though there were no war."[3] The only beneficiaries of such attacks, Ed Flynn, the Democratic national chairman declared, were in Tokyo and Berlin.

Even in peacetime the president of the United States is a king without a crown. He is Head of State. He is the only individual in the nation who in his person represents the flag. In crises he becomes a father figure. Franklin Roosevelt played the role to the hilt, for he knew how to use the miracle of radio to project his reassuring voice into the American home. When Orson Welles once visited him, the president told him that there were two great actors in America, and it was a fine thing that they had now met. Roosevelt had grasped the power of radio ever since his days as governor of New York, and he understood that in wartime the power was greater than ever. Because the president was the most credible source of information about the extraordinary sweep of world events in which all Americans were now caught, he was the Interpreter of Last Resort. Roosevelt's personal authority grew in the war years. Republicans worried that the permanent world crisis would mean a permanent Roosevelt presidency, and though there were certain political risks in striking at the father figure in the White House in wartime, they saw no alternative but to keep reminding the country from time to time that Franklin Roosevelt was just a clever politician with dictatorial leanings.

While the president was protected by the special aura that attaches to the commander in chief in wartime, the benefits did not extend to his party. The issues that had brought the Democrats to power in 1933—unemployment and poverty—were dissolving in the new prosperity brought by military spending, and the political cast of the Democratic Party was changing. In the 1942 election the Democrats lost nine Senate seats and forty-six seats in the House. This stunning defeat of liberals, which was taken in the White House as a sign of public frustration over the way the war was going, left the Democratic caucus in the House and Senate in the control of conservatives from the southern and border states.

The coalition between Republicans and southern conservative Democrats, which has been the rudder guiding the postwar bipartisan foreign policy consensus for more than two generations, was forged in wartime. Democrats from the southern and border states with safe seats, a region that has usually been readier than the rest of the country to support an interventionist foreign policy and the use of military power, became the chairmen of the major committees in charge of mobilization, military affairs, and oversight of the war effort. Conservatives who had been at odds with much of the New Deal now became the powers in the president's party. When the president declared that Dr. New Deal had been replaced by Dr. Win the War, he was not merely reassuring conservatives in an appeal for unity. He was stating a political fact.

Selling the war to the American people was a different problem in World War II from what it had been in the fight against the kaiser. After Pearl Harbor no one could make the case that war could have been avoided. (The issue did not arise with respect to Germany either, since Hitler had declared war on the United States.) But the American people did have to be convinced that the enemy was formidable enough to require an enormous sustained effort and yet not so formidable as to be unbeatable. The administration had two great public relations problems. One was to establish that the burdens of war were being shared equitably at home, that slackers, war profiteers, and labor leaders were not taking advantage of the national emergency to feather their own nests. But inevitably, all of that was happening, and it did nothing for patriotic fervor. The other, which is the concern of this chapter, was to convince the public in the face of a substantial body of contrary opinion that the administration's strategy for winning the war and organizing the peace was the right one.

2.

The twentieth century is the Age of Propaganda. To be sure, since the beginning of history, kings, chieftains, and priests have been simplifying reality for their followers, supplying them with soothing cover stories, and turning the enemies they mark for destruction into subhuman hate figures. Psychological warfare is at least as old as Genghis Khan, who had a large contingent of secret agents to spread defeatism among the peoples whom the Mongol armies were about to attack. But in this century, propaganda has gained unprecedented importance because of two developments, one political and the other scientific.

In the twentieth century the foundations of political legitimacy were shaken as kings lost their thrones and the authority of churches was displaced by the new authority of science. The myths of democracy successfully competed with myths of the past—the divine right of kings, the infallibility of the church—though the older myths persisted in new dress. Twentieth-century constitutions, such as the one Stalin drew up in 1936, provided for more political participation and the enumeration of more citizen rights, mostly economic rights, than were prescribed in the American Constitution of 1787, but the political rights were sham. The legitimacy of government now rested solidly on universal suffrage. But in such one-party countries voting became a coerced ritual. The 99 percent yes vote in plebiscites and elections was the new symbol of the "divinity that doth hedge a king," replacing the symbol of hereditary rule, the Crown. With the expansion of literacy and popular education there was now a mass culture in every advanced industrial country. The control of that culture, as the Nazi experience showed so clearly, was a key to effective rule. The propaganda ministry became an indispensable instrument of orderly government, though some governments used a more cunning name. But once public sentiment was stated to be an important legitimating principle of government, whether demonstrated by rigged elections or crowds roaring themselves hoarse in the Nuremberg stadium, the government had to keep selling itself to the people. As the United States went to war in 1941, the greater ability of totalitarian societies to use propaganda to mobilize their own people was regarded in Washington as a major advantage of the Axis powers.

By that time, psychological theory had further undermined traditional views about public opinion in democracies. Eighteenth-century theories of democracy rested on optimistic assumptions of human rationality and educability. Though the private opinions of the Founding Fathers were, as we saw, more realistic than some of their more extravagant public pronouncements, the model citizen on which Jefferson and Madison's theories were based was rational and educable. Human beings were not altruistic, but they could be counted on to perceive and pursue their best interests. Therefore political institutions could be devised to contain the clash of contending interests so that parochial concerns could be transcended for the benefit of the whole community. Perhaps the most influential intellectual advance of the first half of the twentieth century was Freud's exploration of the human subconscious and his attempt to map the vast reaches of the irrational behind the everyday masks of rationality. As early as 1908 Graham Wallis was challenging the rationalist model in his *Human Nature and Politics*. Freud's theories provided scientific authority for the pessimism about human beings on which Walter Lippmann built his elitist view of public opinion.

> The mass of absolutely illiterate, of feeble-minded, grossly neurotic, undernourished and frustrated individuals, is very considerable, much more considerable there is reason to think than we generally suppose. Thus a wide popular appeal is circulated among persons who are mentally children or barbarians, people whose lives are a morass of entanglements, people whose vitality is exhausted, shut-in people, and people whose experience has comprehended no factor in the problem under discussion. The stream of public opinion is stopped by them in little eddies of misunderstanding, where it is discolored with prejudice and farfetched analogy.[4]

In the interwar years the study of public opinion and its management became a social science discipline. The unflattering model of the public offered by the new psychology—a mass of emotionally labile individuals, easily confused, dangerously susceptible to propaganda—led academic analysts such as Harold Lasswell to a logical conclusion: "Government management of opinion is an unescapable corollary of large scale modern war."[5] At the same time the techniques for managing opinion were becoming more sophisticated. Edward L. Bernays, Sigmund Freud's nephew, developed public relations into an applied science that he defined as "the engineering of consent." For private clients he put psychological insights to profitable use. He helped turn pork scraps into a staple of the American breakfast table by arranging to have the Prince of Wales photographed at the Waldorf-Astoria eating bacon. For the Rockefeller family he set about systematically raising the value of their Renaissance art collection by placing critical articles on selected painters in the right journals.[6] Thanks to the genius of Ivy Lee, John D. Rockefeller shed his robber-baron image and became known as a kindly old man who gave away dimes. The same techniques, Bernays argued, could be used by government. Democracy would be strengthened thereby, for the more effective the arts of persuasion, the less government needed to resort to coercion.

Congress, however, remained skeptical about letting the president hire press agents. As early as 1912 the Senate had refused to appropriate money to hire an "advertising agent" for the Marine Corps.[7] After World War I more and more former newspapermen landed jobs as public affairs, public information, and press liaison officers in the growing federal bureaucracy, but the legislative branch always insisted—wartime aside—that the distinction between "public education" and "propaganda" be scrupulously observed. In practice, however, the line between information and advocacy became harder and harder to maintain.

At the outset of the war, the Republicans worried that Roosevelt would exploit the crisis to make the Democratic Party permanently unbeatable. Not only was the president the greatest radio personality of his time and his wife a syndicated columnist with her own radio show, but in the New Deal years the administration had used tax dollars to create a national culture. In the 1930s the WPA had sponsored theater, artists, music, and film. The war gave Washington bureaucrats seemingly unlimited power to influence what Americans thought and felt. (So allergic were members of Congress in those years to the PR efforts of the administration that some Republicans even accused Surgeon General Thomas Parran of trying to manipulate public opinion when he wrote an article in the *Reader's Digest* on stamping out syphilis.[8]

Roosevelt understood how sensitive the issue of opinion management was. In 1940 and 1941 he resisted strong pressure to create a superagency to "educate" the people about the war and the growing American responsibilities and involvements that it was causing. The power of Hitler's propaganda had made a deep impression in the United States. The precipitous fall of France, the nation with the largest army in Europe, was attributed to defeatism and the failure of national will. The vulnerabilities of that society had been skillfully manipulated by an insidious Nazi propaganda campaign, and it was foolish complacency to think that something of the sort could not happen in the United States. As the European war got under way, the United States was the only major power without a propaganda agency. Members of Roosevelt's cabinet, such as Ickes, Stimson, and Knox, pressed for a major official effort to shape public opinion. "I do not believe armaments will be much use to us," Ickes wrote Roosevelt on April 28, 1941, "if we do not have the will to use them and an understanding of why we are expected to use them."[9]

Roosevelt, however, turned aside the proposal for a Public Relations Administration, which the Joint Army-Navy Board had approved. Instead, in the years before Pearl Harbor, he experimented with various efforts to "stimulate patriotism."[10] He began with the Office of Government Reports, a small, deliberately low-key operation designed to spread good news only about the defense effort and to inform the executive branch about public opinion on defense-related issues. He put Henry Wallace in charge of another abortive propaganda effort, and New York mayor Fiorello La Guardia was enlisted for still another. The mandates of these overlapping agencies were unclear and the extent of their bureaucratic turf was deliberately left in doubt. The president was afraid that a single strong information agency would bring charges from Congress that he was propagandizing the American people into war. Some prominent intellectuals like Archibald MacLeish argued that the ideological issues underlying the global conflict be put before the American people in a clear, forceful way. Morale depended upon a free people seeing clearly that the entire system of values undergirding the nation was at risk. But Roosevelt was not prepared to take on an ideological campaign of that sort while the nation was still at peace. He worried about arousing chauvinism, hysteria, and intolerance as Creel's efforts in World War I were widely thought to have done.

Instead the emphasis would be on building morale by creating opportunities for citizens to get involved themselves in supporting the military buildup. Thus morale building was the principal reason for the "defense bond" program in which even first graders brought pennies to school to buy "defense stamps" (soon to be "war stamps"). The academic advisers called such government programs to encourage voluntary participation "propaganda of the act." Get the people to take a step, and the hearts and minds will follow. Six weeks before Pearl Harbor, Roosevelt put MacLeish in charge of another propaganda agency with an Orwellian name the president himself conceived, the Office of Facts and Figures. The office would put out "actual and accurate information," but, as La Guardia wrote approvingly to Roosevelt, the information would be spiced with "sugar coated, colored, ornamental matter, otherwise known as 'bunk,' but very useful."[11]

When war came, the greatest challenge was to conceal the actual sights, smells, and sounds of war from the American people, especially from the families of the men who were fighting it. The immediate problem was how much to tell the public about the Pearl Harbor disaster itself. The opinion analyst Hadley Cantril urged Roosevelt to tell the public the truth, a position repeatedly taken by journalists like James Reston, who wrote in the New York Times that the people had to know that the military situation was desperate before they would make the necessary sacrifices. But the military services were adamantly against revealing the extent of the damage, for it would expose the Pacific forces to great risks if the Japanese knew how badly they had hurt the fleet. Navy officials, acutely embarrassed at having had so many ships and planes destroyed in their home base, also argued that civilian morale would plummet if the American people knew the truth. Indeed psychological warfare had been one of the prime purposes of the attack. Admiral Yamamoto Isoroku, the principal planner of the Pearl Harbor bombing, who had been naval attaché in Washington, believed that the blow would leave both the U.S. Navy and the American people "so dispirited they will not be able to recover."[12] The true dimensions of the disaster did not come out until after the war.

In June 1942 Roosevelt created the Office of War Information and persuaded Elmer Davis, the famous radio commentator, to head it. "You know who I mean," the president struggled for the name, "the one with the funny voice. Elmer—Elmer something."[13] Davis's commentaries on CBS, delivered in Hoosier twang, were popular because they sounded calm and sensible. There were a half-dozen or so network commentators on whom Americans became dependent in the war years for interpreting the whirlwind of events. Each became enormously influential. There was authority in the clipped, pompous, somewhat Germanic cadence of H. V. Kaltenborn and the spooky-voiced analyses of Raymond Gram

Swing. There was relentless cheer even on the darkest days in Gabriel Heatter's inevitable report, "There's good news tonight." All of them had helped shift the public mood by bringing home the horror of a war from which no escape was physically or morally possible. But Elmer Davis seemed the most reassuring because he was not professorial, nor was he a Cassandra, a propagandist, or a blowhard. In short, he was the least threatening individual the president could find to run the wartime propaganda effort. But he was far from an American Goebbels, as his critics charged, for he was a man of strong democratic principles without either political power or developed bureaucratic skills.

The war clearly needed selling. In the summer of 1942 at least a third of the people interviewed by OWI pollsters indicated their willingness "to negotiate a separate peace with the Germans."[14] A year later about a third of the respondents still said that they had no "clear idea of what this war is all about."[15] But this was true all through the war for the fighting men themselves. "The Marines didn't know what to believe in," *Life* correspondent Robert Sherrod reported from Tarawa, "except the Marine Corps." As one American private at the Anzio beachhead put it, "if we killed, we could go on living. Whatever we were fighting for seemed irrelevant." In the final week of the war in Europe an infantryman wrote his mother, "If you could only see us kids killed at eighteen, nineteen and twenty fighting in a country that means nothing to us, fighting because it means either kill or be killed not because you're making the world safe for democracy or destroying Nazism."[16] All through 1942 and for much of 1943 the news from both Europe and the Pacific was almost unremittingly bad. While the level of participation of ordinary citizens was high—18 million served in the armed forces and 25 million workers bought war bonds—despite the carefully cultivated appearance of unity, the mobilization produced some deep internal strains. As blacks migrated north to take the jobs vacated by white workers going off to war, the resulting racial tensions sparked serious race riots in Detroit. Workers wanted their fair share in the new prosperity, and full employment gave unions the bargaining power to push much more ambitious wage demands than in the thirties. There were more strikes in the war years than at any comparable time span in American history, about fourteen thousand of them involving almost seven million workers.[17]

In theory, OWI was to be an agency to get out the sort of information to the public that would focus their energies on the war effort instead of their personal struggles. There would be no high-powered, inflammatory propaganda such as George Creel's committee had put out. And unlike World War I, the agency, hoping to deflect the hostility from the press that had descended on Creel, would not be in the censorship business. There was another agency for that. OWI continued and expanded the work of the Bureau of Intelligence that had been set up in the Office of Facts and Figures. As one government study described it, "The Bureau of Intelligence, mainly following the technique of market research and the Gallup poll technique . . . developed a system to pre-test government campaigns and program material in order to determine whether the public reached reacted to this material in the manner the government desired."[18]

Hadley Cantril, who ran a private opinion analysis project at Princeton, had direct access to the White House through presidential assistant David Niles. He invited Roosevelt himself to suggest questions for Gallup and *Fortune* polls. "We can get confidential information on questions you suggest . . . and provide you with the answers to any questions ever asked," he had volunteered in the months leading up to the war. His polling data was then being used by the interventionists to prod the president, because it showed the public readier for war than was generally believed. After the United States got into the war, Cantril kept pushing data on the White House about Roosevelt's political strength, resorting, as he wrote the president's assistant Anna Rosenberg, to "a nefarious stunt." He persuaded Gallup to run a poll that he correctly predicted would show an eight-point drop in presidential popularity and then tried (unsuccessfully) to use it to get Roosevelt's attention and an audience to push his theories. On a later occasion he told Niles that he had "tried to influence poll results by suggesting [to Gallup] issues and questions the vote on which I was fairly sure would be on the right side."[19]

Like most of the politically connected social scientists of the time, Cantril was frustrated that there was so "little connection between the information all of us gather and policy formation."[20] The wartime government was an irresistible laboratory for testing the theories of the new social science. While anthropologists like Margaret Mead, psychologists, psychiatrists, and all sorts of experts on human behavior were welcomed to official Washington for the first time, bureaucrats and politicians often treated the eager academics with less awe than the professors considered their due. Harold Lasswell, for example, had made perhaps the most ambitious claims for what he called "the policy sciences" and suggested that experts in propaganda should actually sit in the highest councils of government to help make policy. "Policies are not safely formulated," he had written in his book on propaganda, "without expert information on the state of that opinion upon which they rely for success."[21] It did not happen that way. Yet politicians and national security bureaucrats proved to be quick learners in applying the insights of public opinion research.

The wartime effort to shape public opinion suffered from problems very different from those of the Creel Committee in World War I. Indeed they were a legacy of that experience. The overselling of idealism in 1917–18 had had a boomerang effect a few years later. This time war aims would be set more modestly. Most official propaganda about what America was fighting for was high-minded but vague. The president was reluctant to say much himself about the postwar world until victory seemed assured, for he did not want to give his enemies something to shoot at.

Meanwhile, other prominent Americans were offering competing visions of the postwar world. In early 1941 Henry Luce had written an editorial in *Life* celebrating the dawn of "The American Century." It would be a Pax Americana, a humanitarian order built on the rock of capitalism, not utopian dreams of social reform. He expanded these ideas in pamphlets and newspaper advertisements during the war—and for the rest of his life. Vice President Henry Wallace answered him with "The Century of the Common Man," a celebration of democracy, a world begun anew in the spirit of freedom and cooperation, a New Deal for all humanity. In 1943 Wendell Willkie wrote *One World*, a report of his world tour with a meditation on postwar international cooperation, and it became the best-selling book in history up to that time. The philosopher John Dewey argued more modestly that it was enough to sell the war as a fight to erase fascism. But Roosevelt was reluctant to give leadership on the issue. Feeling vulnerable to the charge that he was trying to extend the New Deal across the seas, Roosevelt took pains not to appear "ideological." Though he articulated the Four Freedoms—freedom of religion and speech, freedom from fear and want—so eager was he to avoid the appearance of another Wilsonian tilt at the windmills of Europe that government propaganda, whenever it was identifiable as such, tried to present the war as an exercise in self-defense. But behind the scenes, the OWI, as we will see, was pushing a more ideological line.

By 1943, conservatives in Congress were accusing the OWI of using its propaganda capability to support Roosevelt's political fortunes. The target was the Domestic Branch, which was headed by a Republican, Gardner Cowles. "The type and character of the domestic propaganda foisted on the American people through publications printed and distributed at government expense by the Office of War Information is a stench to the nostrils of a democratic people," cried Congressman Joe Starnes of Alabama as he demanded that all domestic activities be cut. America "needs no Goebbels sitting in Washington" to guide opinion on domestic affairs. The Republicans attacked Davis's loyalty, pointing out that he had been a member of the left-wing American Labor Party, and accused the agency of imparting "a distinct State socialist tinge" to its propaganda for the purpose, as another congressman put it, of promoting "the fourth term of the President and a continuance of the bureaucratic control in Washington and the unwise policies of the New Deal."

The Republicans saw the OWI as the soft underbelly of the Roosevelt administration. The ideology of the OWI was left-wing New Deal, a view of the world in which democracy was the highest value and free trade the world over was no less sacred a principle, a blend of Wendell Willkie's "one world" and Henry Wallace's "century of the common man." (The maverick Republican, who was planning to run again in 1944, was more progressive on race relations than most of the New Dealers.) According to one OWI manual supplied to filmmakers, the war was not only a crusade against fascism— "there can be no compromise with Satan"—but a battle for democracy all over the world. Freedom would "always be in jeopardy in America" unless democracy triumphed everywhere.[22] Any nation fighting by America's side was by definition democratic, including imperial Britain and Stalin's Russia, for how could the war be a crusade for democracy if they were not democratic?

Almost everything about this view of the world invited Republican attacks. Besides, there was something un-American about propaganda anyway, and the confusion about the agency's legitimate functions made it even more vulnerable. Pamphlets for domestic consumption designed to unify the nation and build morale actually exposed the cleavages in American society. A pamphlet entitled "Negroes and the War" drew particular fire. Designed to counteract Japanese propaganda that blacks had no stake in American society, the effort was attacked by southerners as glorifying Negroes and by Republican northerners and some black leaders for patronizing them. The writers of primers on inflation and taxation were attacked as New Deal apologists. The agency decided to stop its domestic pamphlet program, and a group of writers denounced the harried agency and resigned.

Creel had called his propaganda mill an advertising agency, but the domestic operations of OWI twenty-five years later were much more directly influenced by Madison Avenue. Executives from CBS, Coca-Cola, and Hollywood studios, most of them marketing and advertising experts, were brought in to create punchy slogans for public service announcements on radio about war bonds, collecting waste paper, and the like. Inside OWI, to the anger of the disgruntled writers and professors who thought the public deserved better, the operative slogan was "a truth a day keeps Hitler away." The grim posters of Ben Shahn were banished, replaced with the surefire nostalgia of Norman Rockwell. But the propaganda of the hucksters was syrupy, not stirring, and probably reinforced the complacent attitudes they had been hired to shake up.

The serious progaganda was done by private industry. Newspapers. Magazines. Radio. Film. Every two weeks the Domestic Branch met with the program directors of the networks and provided them with priority themes for the coming fortnight, which were to be incorporated into public service announcements or woven less obstrusively into dramatic sketches.[23] OWI also distributed a manual to every film company laying down the official line. Control of Hollywood's output was easy; during the war years the film industry was still under virtual monopolistic control of a handful of major Hollywood film studios. OWI had ideas on how to portray the enemy, what to show about allies, and what dreams about the postwar world to sell.

3.

No task of persuasion was more important than to arouse feelings against the enemy strong enough to sustain years of struggle, and no target audience was more critical than the GIs on whose morale the whole war effort ultimately depended. Unlike World War I, American propaganda did not declare a cultural war on all things German but concentrated on the Nazis. Hollywood film director Frank Capra prepared a series of orientation films entitled *Why We Fight*, which millions of soldiers were required to see. Roosevelt liked one of the films so much that he urged it be shown in movie theaters for the general public. "Let our boys hear the Nazis and the Japs shout their own claims of master-race crud," Capra declared, "and our fighting men will *know* why they are in uniform."[24]

In his book *War Without Mercy* John Dower shows how differently American progaganda treated the Germans and the Japanese. Germany was an enemy because it had fallen into the grip of Nazi fanatics. Japan was an enemy because the people, as *Time* magazine put it in its first issue after Pearl Harbor, were "yellow bastards." The Japanese, according to the treatment for another Capra propaganda film, were to be presented as "an obedient mass with but a single mind." Japanese soldiers were "as much alike as photographic prints off the same negative."[25]

The American hatred of the Japanese was rooted in primitive racist feelings and ran very deep, so deep that there was little stir when 110,000 American residents of Japanese ancestry, two-thirds of them citizens, were rounded up and sent to relocation centers in desolate places surrounded by barbed wire.[26] By the end of the war at least one leading American official was publicly calling for genocide. Paul V. McNutt, chairman of the War Manpower Commission, said in April 1945 that he favored "the extermination of the Japanese in toto," and he made it clear that he meant the people, not just the militarists, because "I know [them]." Admiral Leahy considered Japan "our Carthage," and Elliott Roosevelt told Henry Wallace that he thought victory would require more and more bombing "until we have destroyed about half the Japanese civilian population."[27]

When the war was over, the historian Allan Nevins wrote, "Probably in all our history no foe has been so detested as were the Japanese." It was easy to whip up feelings against the Japanese with stories of their atrocities, the Bataan Death March, *kamikaze* raids, disembowelings and torture, and fanatical racist pronouncements found in captured letters of Japanese soldiers. Nevins compared the feelings Americans had toward the Japanese during the war with the "emotions forgotten since our most savage Indian wars."

The very language of America's military leaders encouraged a special hatred of the Japanese. "Kill Japs, kill Japs, kill more Japs" was Admiral William Halsey's famous cry. When three of the fliers shot down after a daring raid over Tokyo were executed, there was a roar of rage across the United States at the "uncivilized," "inhuman," and "barbarous" behavior. The British Embassy reported to London that the "stimulus of national anger and humiliation . . . makes of the Pacific front permanently a more burning issue than [the] European front is ever likely to be."[28]

The intensity of feeling against the Japanese was understandable. As Dower's study of both Japanese and American wartime propaganda makes clear, the Pacific war was sold to the public on both sides in explicitly racist terms. Moreover, in the first year of the war, until the landings in North Africa in late 1942, virtually all the American combat was in the Pacific and by far the greater number of casualties was at the hands of the Japanese. It was the Japanese, not the Germans, who had dealt the United States its most humiliating defeat and done it by an act of treachery.

Yet the intensity of feeling about the Japanese presented a political problem for the administration. The strategic priority had been made at the outset of the war to defeat Germany first before concentrating on Japan. The decision was politically controversial. General Douglas MacArthur, commander of the Pacific forces, was not reconciled to having his theater declared a secondary priority. He was close to powerful members of the Republican Party, some of whom wanted him to run against Roosevelt in 1944. The isolationist wing of that party had always differentiated between Europe and the Pacific, and its creed was simple. Europe had its own politics, its own wars, and no American interests could be served by getting involved with either. But Asia, apart from the militarists in Japan, had no important political actors of its own. If the European powers could be forced to give up their colonies in the East, the United States, the great anticolonial naval power, would control the fabled markets and resources of the region. Some of the "Asia first" faction, which became the core of the China Lobby after the war, were sons of China missionaries and had a strong sentimental attachment to that exotic land teeming with potential converts and customers.

Since the war plans called for postponing the major land war against Japan for years, it would have been logical in the early years of the war for American propaganda to whip up popular feelings against Germany rather than Japan. But, on the contrary, the administration, mindful of the excesses that had occurred in World War I, took care not to do that. It did not assume the disloyalty of German aliens—there were 264,000 of them—but encouraged them to participate in patriotic demonstrations. Twenty-six "native fascists" were indicted under the Espionage Act of 1917, but after the trial dragged on for seven months the government moved for dismissal. Even during the war the Supreme Court overturned the conviction of George Sylvester Viereck, the veteran German propagandist, and reprimanded the prosecutor for his inflammatory charge to the jury.

German crimes committed in Eastern Europe, such as the eradication of the Czech town of Lidice, were public knowledge, but except for some Czech-Americans the hundred killed there and the millions butchered by the Germans in less publicized places did not carry the emotional impact of the execution of three American airmen in Tokyo. By the beginning of 1943 the contours of the "final solution" to Hitler's "Jewish problem" were becoming clear. Yet except for a few veiled references the existence of the extermination camps was kept secret from the American people.

Hollywood had been a favorite target of the isolationists. On September 9, 1941, almost exactly two months before Pearl Harbor, a subcommittee of the Committee on Interstate Commerce had convened in the Caucus Room of the Senate to investigate the motion picture industry's "propaganda for war." Burton K. Wheeler, a leading opponent of Roosevelt's foreign policy, was chairman. Senator Gerald Nye, the arch-isolationist architect of the "merchant of death" hearings of the thirties, was the chief prosecutor of the movie industry, and Wendell Willkie was the industry counsel. Nye openly charged the movie studios, which were largely controlled by Jews, with churning out propaganda to get America to step in and save the Jews of Europe. It was "quite natural," he said, disavowing any thought of anti-Semitism, "that our Jewish citizenry would willingly have our country and its sons taken into this foreign war." But the wiles of the Hollywood moguls had to be exposed. "When you go to the movies, you go there to be entertained. . . . And then the picture starts—goes to work on you, all done by trained actors, full of drama, cunningly devised. . . . Before you know where you are you have actually listened to a speech designed to make you believe that Hitler is going to get you."[29]

Actually, as Clayton Koppes and Gregory Black have shown in their history of the film industry in World War II, Hollywood was slow to attack Hitler and Mussolini. As late as 1940, according to the industry censorship czar Will Hays, only 27 of the 530 feature films related "in any way" to political happenings. In those years, when Hollywood had a near monopoly of the global market, studio executives wished to avoid offending Hitler and Mussolini for fear of losing access to the theaters of the expanding Nazi and fascist empires. Once Hitler moved to outlaw American films as "Jewish" and "decadent," some of the studios grew notably bolder in attacking him. Nevertheless, films like *Confessions of a Nazi Spy* and *The Great Dictator*, and indeed all U.S. films on Nazi Germany made through 1941, carefully distinguished between bad Nazis and good Germans. It was part of the Production Code of the Hays Office, the industry self-censorship board, that "hate films" be avoided. *Beast of Berlin* had caused riots in some American cities when it was shown during World War I.[30]

Hollywood moved toward intervention in 1941 for two reasons. The major reason was that the market now supported it. Public opinion polls and best-seller lists clearly showed that a mood shift was occurring. A larger proportion of the country was expecting war and was becoming psychologically ready for it. It was devouring books by such openly interventionist war correspondents as Quentin Reynolds, Vincent Sheean, and William Shirer. With the 1930s the age of mass culture had arrived: Coast-to-coast radio. Movie-house chains. Mass opinion shapers like *Time, Life,* and *Reader's Digest.* The successful market strategies of the major media offer important clues to popular sentiment on foreign policy issues. Unlike polls, for which pollsters are paid irrespective of the results, a film that touches a political subject represents a major investment in a particular assessment of public opinion. The gambles that pay off at the box office tell us more perhaps about the popular sentiment of that time than any other measure. A movie, unlike an encounter with a pollster, is an intense experience, and in the 1930s and 1940s going to the movies was as much an American habit as church attendance had been for earlier generations. In the Darwinian world of mass entertainment, timing is all-important. The survivors in the box-office wars need to be as attuned to shifts in public opinion as politicians, and, if anything, even more conservative in not getting ahead of the prevailing mood. This was especially true when a few competing studios supplied all the movie houses. By the 1940s great sums were being risked on hunches that the public was finally ready to buy something other than the standard isolationist view of reality. Glimpses of other nations and foreign struggles about which most Americans had given little thought of their own were produced in the expectation that hundreds of thousands of moviegoers would accept them as their own dreams for eighty-four minutes.

Explicit government pressure was also a factor in Hollywood's shift toward interventionism. In 1940 a film on the life of Pastor Niemöller, the courageous former U-boat captain who became an outspoken foe of Hitler, which the Hays Office considered "avowedly British propaganda," finally got its seal of approval because the distributor was James Roosevelt, the president's son. The First Lady appeared in the prologue. (France was collapsing and London was under the blitz, but no major studio had wanted to battle the Hays Office for permission to distribute the film.) A year later Franklin Roosevelt personally helped to promote *Sergeant York* by inviting the World War I hero to the White House just as the film about him opened at the Astor Theater. The story of the pacifist hillbilly turned warrior, played by Gary Cooper, was a metaphor for a peaceful America now aroused to heroism by the menace of Nazism. General Lewis B. Hershey, the director of Selective Service, attended the premiere so that everyone would get the point, and the army prepared an eight-page recruitment pamphlet based on the resurrected World War I hero.

While some studios went out of their way to support the Roosevelt foreign policy—Warner Brothers offered to make shorts on preparedness free of charge, and Darryl Zanuck, a reserve colonel, once rounded up studio employees for an interventionist rally at the Hollywood Bowl—the administration was not above encouraging more patriotism in the film colony by using favors and threats. In August 1940 Roosevelt personally asked Nicholas Schenck, the head of Loew's, to make a film on defense. Schenck's brother Joseph, head of Twentieth-Century Fox, was then awaiting sentence for income-tax evasion, and Roosevelt asked the attorney general to let the filmmaker off with a fine. Nicholas produced *Eyes of the Navy* in time for a mid-October release in the midst of the presidential election campaign, but the attorney general, Robert Jackson, insisted on a jail sentence, and Joseph Schenck served four months in jail before the Parole Board ordered him back to the studio.

In 1938 the administration had filed an antitrust suit against the five major production and distribution companies, and the threat—which was actually carried out after the war—gave the administration more than a little leverage. As Lowell Mellett, then the presidential assistant in charge of media relations and later the principal bureaucrat in charge of film propaganda, wrote the president in March 1941, the industry "is conscious of the Justice Department."[31]

The right answers to "why we fight" were elicited by showing the enemy as hate figures. After the United States entered the war the "good German" began disappearing from the screen. The OWI was concerned that even after the Casablanca Conference in late 1943, when the goal of "unconditional surrender" was proclaimed, almost a third of the respondents to the agency's poll thought a separate peace with the German Army was possible because the *Wehrmacht* "was pretty much like the German people and not at all like Hitler."[32]

The war effort also required the generation of warm feelings for America's allies. Delayed fury against the British and French had been at the heart of the revisionist view of World War I. Countering traditional Anglophobia was relatively easy. The British, pounded nightly under the German blitz, were now the underdog. At their head was a larger-than-life figure, Winston Churchill, whose inspired rhetoric and bulldog looks made him an instant hero in the United States. For good measure he was half-American, a point he unfailingly reiterated on his many wartime visits to the United States.

During the thirties, Americans, disapproving and enthralled, devoured books and flocked to films about the British upper classes. The snobbery and rigid class divisions that they portrayed reinforced American feelings of moral superiority. All during the war Roosevelt and Hull kept putting pressure on Churchill to loosen the bonds of the British Empire, especially to end the system of imperial preferences, which discriminated against American goods. The economic issues raised by the imperial system were not part of the public debate, but the symbolism of the British Empire in a war for Roosevelt's Four Freedoms posed a problem for American opinion managers. Lowell Mellett, chief of the OWI Bureau of Motion Pictures, prevailed upon RKO not to rerelease *Gunga Din* with its classic British imperial stereotypes. The agency was much more enthusiastic about *Mrs. Miniver*, a Greer Garson film about the struggle of an upper-middle-class British family during Britain's darkest hours, because it showed democratic tendencies breaking through the stuffiness of the British upper crust. (Mrs. Miniver, a successful architect's wife, actually has conversations with the stationmaster who names a rose after her.) Give us a Mrs. Miniver of China, an OWI official implored. (Selling Chiang Kai-shek's China with its legendary corruption was not all that easy.) OWI bureaucrats exerted considerable pressure on MGM to make script changes in *The White Cliffs of Dover*, a syrupy rendering of a best-selling poem, but eighty pages of changes were not enough to make the film acceptable to OWI. (The critic James Agee likened *White Cliffs* to "cup after cup of tepid orange peko at a rained out garden party.") The agency had no power to keep it off the screen in the United States, but it did control the export market. The film was declared unfit for overseas distribution, except to Britain where it was a huge success.

Soviet Russia presented a far greater problem for the administration. By the middle of 1941 the hopes of the democracies centered on Soviet resistance to Hitler's invasion. Yet the American people were strongly anti-Communist. For the first sixteen years after the Bolshevik Revolution the United States and the Soviet Union had maintained no diplomatic relations whatever. With support primarily of American business leaders who saw the possibility of vast markets in Russia, Roosevelt had agreed to establish relations in 1933 on the basis of certain Soviet promises, most importantly a pledge to refrain from engaging in Communist propaganda in the United States. Though American firms did undertake projects in Russia, economic benefits from the new relationship in the Depression years were disappointing. The Moscow purge trials and the takeover of the Baltic states in 1940 aroused anger among Americans of East European origin, most of them Catholics, and among a few disillusioned intellectuals. Most Americans, however, gave little thought to Russia. In 1937 Eugene Lyons, a writer for the *Reader's Digest* and a former enthusiast of the Soviet regime, wrote *Assignment in Utopia*, the first of the "god that failed" genre that became so popular in the early Cold War years. This devastating attack on Stalin's Russia by a former left-winger became a bestseller. That same year 59 percent of the respondents in a Gallup poll said that they would prefer to live under Hitler than Stalin.[33] Yet the next year 82 percent said that in a war between the two they would rather see Russia win. Stalin was no less evil than Hitler, but he was less of a menace to the United States.

Westbrook Pegler, the columnist who was the leading antagonist of Roosevelt, organized labor, and anything even suspected of veering in a leftward direction, regularly branded the New Deal a pale-pink version of Stalin's Russia. As war clouds gathered, he also made a point of lumping Stalin and Hitler. Writing in *American Legion* magazine four months before the Hitler-Stalin Pact of August 23, 1939, he compared the enmity between the dictator of the Right and the dictator of the Left to the "mock feuds between radio comics. It's just an act." The Hitler-Stalin Pact, which took not only the American Communist Party but most liberals by surprise, appeared to validate the idea that there was a single opponent of democracy loose in the world—"Hitler bolshevism." The term "totalitarian" had not yet become current. The pact produced two views in the press. Republican newspapers openly exulted that the Popular Front was over and that the Roosevelt administration had been tarred in the process. "Mr. Roosevelt's great Russian liberal democratic friend," said the Chicago *Tribune*, its glee undisguised, had "turned despot." Isolationists echoed the view of the New York

Daily News about the sudden turnaround. "The whole thing should teach us once more that we have no business in Europe."[34]

When Soviet tanks crossed the frontier into Finland in November 1939 and the Finns mounted an unexpectedly brave and fierce resistance in snowy passes and on frozen lakes, feeling against Russia in the United States reached new heights. Finland was the one nation of Europe to pay its World War I war debts. Stalin edged out Hitler as *Time's* Man of the Year for 1940—"The World's Most Hated Man." A year later Stalin was back on the cover. Roosevelt was Man of the Year, but the Soviet leader hovered above him at one side, Churchill at the other, to symbolize the new alliance in the making. Two years later Stalin was back again, this time by himself, looking saintly.

The rehabilitation of Stalin's Russia began on the day the Germans invaded. In a masterly speech delivered a few hours after the German attack, Winston Churchill welcomed the Soviets to the democratic alliance. The man who had sought, as he said, to strangle Bolshevism in its cradle now declared that "the Russian danger is . . . our danger and the danger of the United States." After finishing off Stalin, Hitler would turn on Britain and then America. "No one has been a more insistent opponent of Communism than I have. . . . I will unsay no words that I have spoken about it. But all this fades away before the spectacle that is now unfolding. The past with its crimes, its follies, its tragedies flashes away." Carefully distinguishing "the dulled, drilled, docile, brutish masses of the Hun" from Russian soldiers "guarding their homes, where mothers and wives pray . . . where maidens laugh and children play," Churchill's blessing helped to transform the Soviets from robbers into cops virtually overnight. Because he was a hero in the United States, burdened by none of the political baggage he carried in Britain, Churchill was a supreme authority figure.

Most of the American press echoed the dominant sentiment reflected in the public opinion polls. George Gallup summed it up this way: "Russia, even if she won, would not invade the United States, whereas Germany probably would." There were dissenters, of course, who were reluctant to embrace the Soviet dictator. "The American people know," said the *Wall Street Journal* three days after Hitler's attack, "that the principal difference between Mr. Hitler and Mr. Stalin is the size of their respective mustaches. An alliance with either would be at the price of national self-respect." Yet most conservative publications, including *Reader's Digest* and *American Mercury*, took the position that Soviet resistance was crucial. However the war turns out, some of the anti-Communists argued, it would spell the end of Communism. Either it would be crushed by Hitler or abandoned by Stalin in order to save Russia. Revisionists rushed into print with new understanding of Stalin's purges and the twists and turns of Soviet foreign policy. Russia's system, Walter Duranty, the Soviet expert of the *New York Times* explained, could not be bad because it was not really socialism but state capitalism. Stalin, the photographer Margaret Bourke-White reported in *Life*, was fond of American cigarettes. [35]

The leading revisionist work was Joseph E. Davies's *Mission to Moscow*. A well-connected figure in the Democratic Party who had married the heiress to the Post Toasties fortune, he had been made ambassador to the Soviet Union in 1936. George Kennan, counselor of the U.S. Embassy in Moscow under Davies, writes with the contempt of the unheeded expert of the ambassador's efforts to give Soviet-American relations "the outward appearance of being cordial, no matter what gnashing of teeth might go on under the surface." The ambassador attended one of the infamous purge trials in 1937, the counselor acting as his interpreter and fetch. (Kennan would be sent out for sandwiches during the recesses.) Davies, Kennan later wrote, "placed considerable credence in the fantastic charges leveled at these unfortunate men." [36]

The book *Mission to Moscow*, which reflected a rosy view of Stalin's Russia throughout, sold 700,000 copies in hardcover and was translated into thirteen languages. It was serialized in *Life*, and when a twenty-five-cent paperback was issued, news of the publication was a page-one story in the *New York Times*. At a White House dinner Franklin Roosevelt appealed to Harry and Jack Warner to make a film of the book. Michael Curtiz, of *Casablanca* fame, was hired as director, and the writer was Howard Koch, who was experienced in fantasy, having written the script of Orson Welles's famous 1938 broadcast of the Martian invasion of New Jersey. Davies, who was granted script control, met with the president twice in the fall of 1942 to keep him informed of the film's progress.

The film, one of at least twenty-five features that were intended as pro-Soviet propaganda in the service of the war effort, had everything in it to guarantee its becoming a prime target once the political climate changed. (It is now almost impossible to find a print.) Stalin appeared avuncular and mellow, and Roosevelt and Davies, clairvoyant. The archvillains were the Republican isolationists. "If I had to choose between Hitler and Stalin," one of them says to Davies, "I'd choose Hitler. Germany and Japan are good customers."[37] In the film the improbable and the outrageous were neatly spliced. Churchill applauds the Hitler-Stalin Pact. Davies toasts Stalin as a "great builder for the benefit of the common man," and when Vyshinsky exacts confessions from Bucharin and the other old Bolsheviks, Davies pronounces it a triumph of justice. "Based on twenty years' trial practice, I'd be inclined to believe these confessions." The original print included a scene showing Trotsky actually conspiring with Ribbentrop to sell out the Soviet Union, but OWI, which called the film "a magnificent contribution to the Government's War Information Program," drew the line at that point and the scene was cut when the film was released.

The overselling of Russia was a peculiarly American campaign. The sort of *Realpolitik* exhibited by Churchill, who said that he would have a good word for the devil should he ever join the anti-Hitler coalition, was not in the American grain. Across the planet, war had been making strange bedfellows for centuries. But the United States, so Americans were encouraged to believe, took up arms only in a moral crusade—to extend the area of freedom, to reclaim the land from savages and to save the red man from himself, to make war to end war. The war for democracy would be exposed as a sham unless the Soviet Union, the member of the coalition bearing the brunt of the fighting, could be accorded honorary status as a member in good standing of the community of democratic nations. Almost everyone, including Roosevelt, looked for signs that the Russians were really "like us." The president wrote Thomas Lamont in late 1942 of his hopes for good relations based on the growing convergence of the two systems. He quoted Soviet Foreign Minister Litvinov as saying in 1933 that at the time of the Bolshevik Revolution "you were one hundred percent capitalist and we were at the other extreme—zero. In those thirteen years we have risen on the scale to, let us say, a position of twenty. You Americans [thanks to the New Deal] have gone to a position of eighty. It is my real belief that in the next twenty years we will go to forty and you will come down to sixty."[38] Roosevelt seemed to approve Litvinov's argument that as ideological differences narrowed, possibilities of genuine cooperation would grow.

In the Cold War the thrust of American propaganda from both official and commercial sources would be to dehumanize the Soviets; in wartime, Americans felt it almost a patriotic duty to paint the Soviet Union with a human face, even sometimes a false one. In *American Hebrew*, William Zuckerman declared that anti-Semitism had been "literally wiped out." Stalin's Russia did not "know the meaning of anti-Semitism." Ignatius Kelly, writing in *Ecclesiastical Review*, detected in the Soviet resistance "buried and perhaps long forgotten Christian holiness." In the *Ladies' Home Journal* Ella Winter wrote rapturously of Soviet life. "For those who don't like commercials in radio, Russia would be a paradise." CBS commentators re-created a reassuring picture of an active Soviet public opinion—the very antithesis of Hitler's "dulled, drilled, . . . brutish masses." "Well, Larry," said Walter Kerr in an interview the day after Stalin dissolved the Comintern, the official international apparatus for spreading Communism, "I'm sure that right now men and women are talking about this near Pushkin Square, in Gorki Street, in Moscow's famed subway, out in the Park of Culture and Rest, and probably at the ballet between the acts. I think you will agree with me that they are glad to hear about the dissolution of the Communist International. The people in Moscow are tired of that sort of thing."[39]

On September 24, 1942, two hundred of the top businessmen in the country met at the Banker's Club in New York to hear Robert A. Lovett, formerly of Brown Brothers Harriman and now assistant secretary of war, praise the Soviet Union. In Washington another gathering of notables was held at Tregaron, the Davies estate, where Vice President Henry Wallace declared that "Stalingrad is Chicago's line of defense." In New York a mass meeting for Soviet-American Friendship was held in Madison Square Garden on November 8, 1942, and Mayor Fiorello La Guardia proclaimed it "Stalingrad Day."

The new relationship with the Soviet Union presented the propagandists in Washington with two major problems. Stalin's Russia was welcomed as an "ally," but in fact it was a cobelligerent operating independently rather than as part of a coordinated alliance of the sort the United States had forged with Britain. The difficulties involved in securing even minimal cooperation in military matters were concealed from the public as indeed was the perennial suspicion in both Washington and Moscow that the comrade in arms across the water was about to make a separate peace with Hitler.

The biggest problem concerned the issue of a second front. Almost immediately upon arriving at the White House in late May 1942—to be put up in the Roosevelt family quarters, an honor rarely accorded to any foreign dignitary and never before to one who carried a pistol and a roll of sausage in his briefcase—Foreign Minister Molotov began pressing Roosevelt to mount a second front across the English Channel to take pressure off the Russian front.

A few days later Roosevelt and Molotov issued a communiqué stating that "full understanding was reached with regard to the urgent tasks of creating a Second Front in Europe in 1942." Churchill flew to Washington as soon as Molotov had departed and argued strongly that an attack on Fortress Europe was premature. On July 30 the decision was made to invade North Africa instead. The following August, after the Soviets had recovered two-thirds of the territory lost to the Germans, American and British military chiefs approved a contingency plan for a cross-Channel invasion in 1943, but only if the Germans appeared to be winning or about to collapse. The proposed operation had the code name Rankin and it was designed, as a Joint Chiefs of Staff Memorandum put it, to achieve two basic aims: "(1) to destroy the German domination of Europe, and (2) to prevent the domination of Europe in the future by any single power (such as the Soviet Union), or by any group of powers in which we do not have a strong influence. If we do not achieve *both* these aims, we may consider that we have lost the war."[40] Thus, as the historian Mark Stoler notes, a second front "could be used to aid the Russians militarily and block their expansion at the same time."[41] Both Generals George Marshall and Dwight Eisenhower favored a cross-Channel invasion in 1943. As early as January 22, 1942, Dwight Eisenhower, then the chief of the army's War Plans Division, had written in his diary, "We've got to go to Europe and fight—and we've got to quit wasting resources all over the world—and still worse—wasting time." Marshall planned an emergency invasion for 1942 with the code name Sledgehammer while he developed plans for the major American effort to take place in the spring of 1943, an operation designated Roundup.[42]

Despite all this planning, the invasion was postponed until June 6, 1944, two years after Roosevelt had publicly pledged to assault Western Europe. Stalin, whose paranoid suspicion was often triggered by much less, assumed that the delay was a deliberate attempt to bleed the Soviet Union. The friction over the timing of the attack on the western front had more to do with the subsequent souring of relations than anything else that was decided during the war, except possibly the dropping of the atomic bomb. Even today few Americans are aware that more than 90 percent of the casualties suffered in the European theater during World War II were borne by the Soviet Union.

In early 1942 the question of a second front became a public issue in the United States. Wendell Willkie called for a cross-Channel invasion, and within months *Time, Life,* and the *New York Times* added their voices to the demand that the Allies invade Western Europe before the end of the year. The argument that delaying the invasion of Europe would work to Hitler's advantage was taken up at mass meetings by the CIO, but George Meany, secretary-treasurer of the AFL, fearing that the Communists were trying to use the issue of a second front to gain power in the labor movement, insisted that "the question of when, where, and how a second front will be established" was for "our commander in chief and our military experts."[43] Some conservative Republicans argued against any second front to help Russia until the Soviets started a second front against Japan.

But public agitation was embarrassing because it focused attention on the deep divisions and ambivalence within the alliance. OWI went to work to quiet the public clamor. "Popular pressure for action on this front or that," the release to the media issued on August 7, 1942, stated, "can serve no useful purpose." Within a week, as one scholar has been able to document, editorial demands for a second front declined "precipitously."[44] As in the decision to drop the atomic bomb in 1945, concern with saving lives was a crucial argument in the deliberations with respect to a second front and was taken as a critical constraint on strategic planning. Civilian morale in the United States was shaky in 1942 and for much of 1943. There was too much bad news. An American president in 1942 did not have the political option, as the leaders of Britain and France had in 1914, to throw wave upon wave of cannon fodder into the front. The lessons of that war sobered democratic politicians who had lived through it, and Roosevelt and Churchill knew the importance of minimizing casualties. It was an American tradition that even in war the state treated soldiers as citizens, not cannon fodder, although there were Civil War battles in which the distinction was scarcely maintained. Had the cross-Channel invasion been successfully carried out in 1943, the westward advance of the Soviets might have been stopped and U.S.–Soviet relations might have been better. Had he been in Roosevelt's shoes, Stalin could have taken the gamble. Roosevelt could not.

4.

The decision of the Roosevelt administration not to attempt to save millions of Jewish victims by bombing the gas chambers, crematoria, and railheads of Auschwitz was subtly influenced by concern about anti-Semitism in the United States. By June 1944 a thirty-page eyewitness report describing "the camp's geographical layout, internal conditions, and gassing and cremation techniques" was available to the United States and British governments.[45] Nahum Goldmann of the World Jewish Congress and other Jewish leaders appealed to President Roosevelt on several occasions to bomb the camps and the railways leading to them. Assistant Secretary of War John J. McCloy, the highest civilian official involved in the decision, believing that the military should not be involved in "refugee matters," accepted the military view that planes could not be spared. However, no study was ever done to determine whether this was true, and indeed on August 20, 1944, as the historian David Wyman writes, "127 Flying Fortresses, escorted by 100 Mustang fighters, dropped 1,336 500-pound high-explosive bombs . . . *less than five miles* to the east of the gas chambers."[46] There is no evidence that Roosevelt, unlike Churchill, was personally exercised about the mass deportations and gassings. (Churchill told Foreign Secretary Anthony Eden in July 1944 that the death camps were "the greatest and most horrible crime ever committed in the whole history of the world," and he gave the order, "Get anything out of the Air Force you can, and invoke me if necessary."[47] But no bombings of the camps ever took place.)

Jewish officials working for the Roosevelt administration, with the exception of Secretary of the Treasury Henry Morgenthau, Jr., avoided the issue. Judge Samuel Rosenman argued that Roosevelt should not involve himself in the plight of the European Jews because it would increase anti-Semitism in the United States. Elmer Davis killed two plans for a campaign to circulate news of the extermination because it was too "controversial"—meaning that it might provoke public demand for action. The mass media treated the extermination as minor news. Thus, on July 2, 1944, the *New York Times*, "Jewish-owned but anxious not to be seen as Jewish-oriented," as Wyman puts it, printed on page 12 the story that 400,000 Hungarian Jews had already been sent to their deaths and 350,000 more would be killed in the next three weeks. The enormity of the Holocaust made it hard to believe, and the memories of exaggerated atrocity stories from World War I still lingered.[48]

During the war the Roosevelt administration periodically sampled public opinion to test the reaction of citizens to military initiatives. For example, on March 1, 1944, David Niles, the White House assistant in charge of minority groups, asked Hadley Cantril to predict what the reaction of American Catholics would be to the bombing of Rome, which was scheduled to take place two days later.

(Sixty-six percent of Catholics approved provided "our military leaders believe it will be necessary."[49] From time to time pollsters also tested public attitudes about the postwar world. In 1942 and 1943 when the fate of the struggle hung on the Russian resistance, a majority of respondents, but never as much as two-thirds, were hopeful that good relations with the Soviet Union could be maintained in the postwar world. Expectations fluctuated with official pronouncements, principally the invariably upbeat but Delphic communiqués from major conferences with Soviet leaders. Soviet gestures, such as the dissolution of the Comintern, helped Soviet ratings.

By 1944, however, pro-Soviet sentiment in America had peaked, and the strains in the alliance were showing. Upper-class, better-educated respondents were likely to be much more favorable to the Soviet Union than those at the bottom of the economic scale, roughly a quarter of whom disclaimed any opinion whatever. (However, class consciousness being un-American, 98 percent of the respondents described themselves as belonging to "the middle class.") Catholics at all income levels were significantly more skeptical than Protestants or Jews. Republicans were more wary of Russia than Democrats, but in September 1943, 36 percent of the respondents to a Gallup poll who said they voted Republican favored a military alliance with the Soviet Union after the war (as opposed to 45 percent of the Democrats). Of all the regions of the country the South, traditionally the most interventionist, was strongest in its support for a permanent military alliance with the Communist colossus (40 percent).[50]

American sympathy for the bravery and sacrifice of the Russians was deep and genuine. The National Committee of Soviet-American Friendship, which had chapters in twenty-eight cities across the country, could arouse strong feelings by showing the awesome spectacle of Soviet resistance, Russian bodies frozen in the snow, German tanks stalled forever. In 1942 women who had been knitting sweaters for the plucky Finns now knit for their invaders. The mass media, notably *Life*, made it easy for millions of Americans with little interest or knowledge in foreign affairs to repress information about the Soviets that was inconsistent with the artfully packaged image. The image polishers could count on two psychological devices to assist them in their task. One was "cognitive dissonance." According to this well-known psychological theory, human beings, at least Westerners uncomfortable with Zen or Marxist contradictions, faced with two seemingly incompatible ideas will reject one or the other. Russia was heroic and was saving American lives. Communism was an evil system. Ergo, the Russians were not Communists. (After the war the same device worked equally well in the opposite direction: Communists have no interest in peace or normal relations. The Russians are Communists. Ergo, war of one sort or another is inevitable.) The other device might be called the patriotic suspension of disbelief. Goebbels wants you to think ill of the Soviets. Ergo, it is playing into the hands of the enemy to do so.

By 1944 the alliance was already splitting. The common danger had passed. Victory was inevitable. The dominant question was the shape of the postwar world. The issues that have continued to dominate the remainder of the century were being discussed within the administration and in a few publications intended for elite "opinion makers"—how much power should the United States share with the Soviet Union and how should power be exercised—but most Americans knew nothing of the fateful choices then being made to reorganize the postwar world. Until late in the war Roosevelt had encouraged the idea that it was somehow illegitimate to talk about the postwar world except in heartwarming generalities. The very meaning of being American had been changed by the war, but Americans were unaware of what had happened. Even the partial vision of America's leaders of the new world in the making was not shared with the people. The tough issues concerning conflicting interests were avoided until it was too late for moderation or compromise. The unpreparedness of the American people for peace was a major contributing factor in the coming of the Cold War.

PART FOUR

NATIONAL SECURITY IN
THE AGE OF ANXIETY

CHAPTER 10

Clearer Than Truth

1.

The war had been over for almost five months, and American soldiers stationed in the Philippines, twenty-thousand strong, advanced on command headquarters at Manila City Hall demanding immediate release and return to civilian life. In Frankfurt four thousand GI demonstrators were stopped at bayonet point as they descended on the Supreme Commander, General Joseph T. McNarney, screaming, "We want to go home!" In Yokohama a mob in khakis greeted Secretary of War Patterson with the same cry. Had the Articles of War been enforced, there would have been no room in the stockades.

Impatient servicemen in Guam suddenly began to act like citizens again; hundreds took up a collection to place full-page ads in fifteen leading newspapers in the United States. Across the nation more than two hundred "Bring the Daddies Home" clubs were organized by the wives of servicemen, and to make their point they distributed pairs of booties to members of Congress. "Be a good Santa Claus and release the fathers," Senator Edwin C. Johnson implored the secretary of war as he sent along his booties to the Pentagon. More than half of all congressional mail in the early postwar months contained complaints about the pace of demobilization; hundreds of thousands of telegrams demanding a speedup were unloaded on the desks of congressmen and senators.[1] In Tokyo General Douglas MacArthur, to the delight of GIs and the irritation of the Pentagon, volunteered that he could get along with fewer occupation troops.

The Truman administration reacted with alarm to the mounting public pressure. Pentagon planners had anticipated that the traditional American view of war—an interruption of life to be ended as soon as possible—would cause problems once the danger had passed. There were signs everywhere. As the war was coming to an end John Wayne strutted out onto a stage in Iwo Jima, pistol in belt, struck a macho pose, and was booed by the troops. There had been enough gung ho in their lives. With the Nazi and Japanese danger gone, citizens in uniform had little patience with the strange, sometimes Kafkaesque efforts of the military to fill their time. Stories of military make-work—a platoon of GIs is ordered to cut grass with bayonets—were now splashed across the pages of American newspapers. In the fall of 1945, after three years and nine months of total war, temporary corporals, sergeants, and captains saw no reason why they should not get on with their lives. The job had been done.

In May 1945 there were 12.3 million men and women in the military services, more than 7.6 million stationed overseas, most of them in the army; ten months later the army was down below 1.5 million. This was a million men below what the Pentagon considered the bare minimum for occupation duty and for the unspecified world responsibilities to which the new Chief of Staff, General of the Army Dwight Eisenhower, alluded in a speech to Congress on January 15, 1946. You don't fire the firemen just because they are waiting around playing checkers, he said. "They may be vitally needed a few minutes later."[2] The melting away of the military forces dismayed the professional military and frightened senior officials of the Truman administration, for they all believed that the peace of the postwar world would rest on American military might.

The military "wish list" was formidable. The army wanted a capability to mobilize ground forces of 4.5 million within twelve months. The navy wanted to keep 600,000 men, 371 major combat vessels, and its own "little air force" of eight thousand planes. The Air Corps was demanding that it be made a separate service with a seventy-group force and 400,000 airmen.[3] For the first time in the history of the Republic, American strategy envisaged a large permanent standing army. It was not aimed at the Soviet Union; the most plausible enemies were a resurgent Germany or Japan. Indeed, postwar plans assumed that the Soviet Union would be an ally, not an adversary. But the United States was now the keeper of the peace. Appeasement and weakness had brought on the war, and only military strength could prevent another.

Franklin Roosevelt, the memories of his battles with the isolationists in the prewar years still fresh, had worried whether the voters were ready to pay the price. He was skeptical that public opinion would support the maintenance of the military power necessary for the United States to carry out its responsibilities as the first among what he called the "Four Policemen." In 1943 at Teheran he had proposed to Stalin a continuing alliance of the United States, Soviet Union, Britain, and China operating through an international organization to enforce the peace. For Roosevelt it was unthinkable that public opinion would permit the permanent stationing of American forces abroad in the postwar world.[4] "I do not want the United States to have the postwar burden of reconstituting France, Italy, and the Balkans," he wrote the acting secretary of state on February 21, 1944. "This is not our natural task at a distance of 3,500 miles or more. . . . I can only add that political considerations in the United States makes my decision conclusive."[5] Usually a better poker player, at Teheran he volunteered to Stalin that United States forces would be out of Europe within a year or two of victory. He said that "if the Japanese had not attacked the United States he doubted very much if it would have been possible to send any American forces to Europe."[6]

The same pessimism about the political obstacles to the maintenance of a large American military establishment in the postwar world was behind his schemes for enforcing the postwar peace with air power. The United Nations, as Roosevelt once explained it to a journalist, would maintain bomber bases around the world to deter the rise of another Hitler; "outlaw" nations would be bombed. It would be a relatively cheap security arrangement that would risk few American lives. At the same time, like Woodrow Wilson at the end of World War I, he wished to break down the venerable tradition that conscription in peacetime was un-American. Four months before his death, in April 1945, he had proposed a permanent program of universal military training just as Wilson had done in 1920. It was an idea as old as the early-twentieth-century Progressive Movement. An obligation for every citizen to spend time preparing to defend the nation would be a way to educate the voters to the realities of maintaining power in a dangerous world. As a side benefit Americans would learn discipline, acquire marketable skills, and feel part of a great national effort.

No idea could have been less popular in the weeks following the Japanese surrender. By January 1946 men and women were being discharged from the armed services at the rate of twenty-five thousand a day. The country is "going back to bed at a frightening rate," Secretary of the Navy James Forrestal wrote his friend Ralph Bard in October 1945, "which is the best way I know to be sure of the coming of World War III." In 1945 almost everyone in the national security establishment shared Forrestal's concerns. At a cabinet meeting held on January 11, 1946, Forrestal proposed a public relations campaign to relieve the pressure behind the "frenzied demobilization," as Truman called it, which was leading to the "disintegration" of the armed forces.[7] "I said that I thought the President should get the heads of the important news services and the leading newspapers—particularly Mr. Sulzberger of the *New York Times*, Roy Roberts, Palmer Hoyt, the Cowles brothers, John Knight, plus Roy Howard and Bob McLean of the AP—and state to them the seriousness of the situation and the need for making the country aware of its implications abroad," Forrestal reported in his diary. "I said these were all reasonable and patriotic men and that I was confident that if the facts were presented we would have their support in the presentation of the case." He also suggested making a presentation at the "weekly luncheon" of the Association of Radio News Analysts.[8] Truman had nodded assent. But candor had its problems. When Forrestal suggested that "the President ought to acquaint the people with the details of our dealings with the Russians," Secretary of State James Byrnes firmly opposed the idea of telling the American people how badly relations with the Soviets had deteriorated. Stalin would consider the campaign provocative, and it might end any chance whatever of making satisfactory peace treaties on Germany and Eastern Europe. (A few months later Byrnes changed his mind, and after Truman fired him, he sounded the tocsin about the Soviet threat in his memoirs, *Speaking Frankly*, even suggesting that the United States might have to drop the atomic bomb on the Russians.)

Truman's own political instincts also made him hesitate. The resurgence of prewar isolationism seemed inevitable. In October 1945 not more than 7 percent of Americans, according to a Gallup poll, considered foreign problems to be the "most vital" facing the country.[9] The new president had been an artillery captain in World War I, and like most Democrats of his generation the "lessons" of World War I were almost as important as the "lessons" of the war that had just ended. "This is my second round trip into war, peace, and the aftermath," the financier Bernard Baruch wrote Secretary of the Navy Forrestal, "and already I can see nothing but a repetition of what took place after the last war."[10] Truman, seeing exactly the same thing, was reluctant to confront headlong the complacency and confusion of the American people about the extraordinary events that were transforming the world about them. In 1919 an American president had gone to Paris to rewrite the map of the world and had come back full of certitudes only to face rejection and defeat. In 1945 and all through the next year another president, inexperienced in governing and largely uninformed on foreign policy, was undergoing a dizzying education himself. There were good political reasons not to share what he was learning with the public.

Ironically, Truman felt trapped by the success of the wartime public relations effort. Thanks to the prodigious campaign of the war years, the hopes of the American people in the possibilities of continued cooperation with the Soviet Union remained high. The fears and difficulties that had plagued the ambiguous alliance from the very beginning had not been shared. As a result, though residual suspicion of collectivist, atheistic Russia remained all through the war, by the time of the Yalta Conference in February 1945, 55 percent of those polled by Gallup's American Institute of Public Opinion were optimistic about U.S.–Soviet relations, and the optimism continued into the next year even as the pessimism within the foreign policy Establishment deepened.

"The tide of public opinion was impossible to stem," Truman once told an interviewer. "Every momma and poppa in the country had to have her boy home right immediately, and every Congressman, of course, wanted to be re-elected."[11] The pressure for demobilization confirmed what Truman suspected. The American people were not ready for the American Century. "The country was being flooded with isolationist propaganda . . . ," he recalled in his memoirs, "and many of us were apprehensive lest the isolationist spirit again become an important political factor."[12] In the fall of 1945 a close reading of public opinion polls suggested that the American people attached even less importance to international problems than they had during the late 1930s.[13] Speaking to the Maryland Historical Society in November 1945, Assistant Secretary of State Dean Acheson reflected the elite pessimism of the day. "I can state in three sentences what the 'popular' attitude is toward foreign policy today. 1. Bring the boys home; 2. Don't be a Santa Claus; 3. Don't be pushed around."[14] Despite his carefully cultivated populist image, Truman himself was no less an elitist when it came to foreign policy. "Our Government is not a democracy, thank God," he told the Association of Radio News Analysts in May 1947. "It's a republic. We elect men to use their best judgment for the public interest." [15]

2.

The two years between the death of Franklin Roosevelt in April 1945 and the announcement of the Truman Doctrine in March 1947 was one of the fateful turning points of the twentieth century. Never before had an American president had to make so many decisions so quickly. The decisions taken over those two years still shape our lives. Amidst tumultuous change an inexperienced president was evolving a worldview, guided by a foreign policy elite that had been disillusioned by Woodrow Wilson's shattered peace, hardened by the war against the Nazis and the Japanese, frustrated by the ambivalent alliance with Russia, and fearful that the American people themselves would keep the nation from seizing its historic moment.

Harry S. Truman was a hardworking senator from Missouri, moderately liberal on domestic issues, who had had almost nothing to do with foreign policy before he became president. He had never been to the White House map room, Roosevelt's nerve center for keeping up with the war. He was unaware of the atomic bomb project. His gut reactions reflected Midwestern skepticism about foreign dictators; he strongly supported cooperation with the Soviet Union during the war, but, as he wrote in his diary shortly after becoming president, "I've no faith in any totalitarian state, be it Russian, German, Spanish, Argentinian, Dago or Japanese. They all start with a wrong premise—that lies are justified." [16]

Whereas Roosevelt appeared supremely, maddeningly confident and seemed to delight in keeping his advisers guessing, Truman was dependent on them. A man who felt that "the moon, the stars and all the planets" had just fallen in on him, as Truman put it upon hearing the news of Roosevelt's death, was open to the advice of more experienced men. The investment bankers and corporate lawyers Roosevelt had brought in to manage the war effort now became the core of a new and enduring national security Establishment and the architects of a new American foreign policy. [17]

The men around Truman—Dean Acheson, Robert Lovett, Averell Harriman, James Forrestal, John McCloy, and the two leading Soviet specialists in the State Department, George Kennan and Charles Bohlen—shared a basic assumption about America's new world role. Although they differed among themselves about the nature of the Soviet threat and how to deal with it, they all assumed that the United States would be the guiding power of the postwar order. Its economy restored by the same war that ravaged ally and enemy alike, producer of half the world's goods, holder of the world's gold reserves, and sole possessor of the atomic bomb, the United States was not only first among the world powers but first in a way that had never been equaled. But how to exercise that power was not clear. Roosevelt's model, the Four Policemen, an idealistic facade behind which the world balance of power would be maintained by the wartime allies, was altogether too cunning. Moreover, it had been overtaken by events. By 1946 Stalin did not look like a policeman. Roosevelt had at times during the war seemed to be moving toward a U.S.–Soviet condominium, ganging up with Stalin against Churchill. (Churchill, wounded by Roosevelt's cavalier attitude toward British power, had roared at him at one of their meetings, "Do I have to beg, like your dog Fala?"[18]) Now as Truman took over, the prime minister was pressing for a postwar Anglo-Saxon alliance as a counterweight to Russia.

The remarkable men who designed the postwar strategy became the leaders and progenitors of an enduring American foreign policy Establishment. A qualification for membership was to wrinkle one's nose at the term. (Nonetheless, in 1968 when McGeorge Bundy arranged for the aging stalwarts of the Truman administration to advise President Lyndon Johnson on how to get the country behind the Vietnam War, he entitled his memorandum "Backing from the Establishment."[19]) The bankers and lawyers came to their duties in Washington with large personal fortunes or from hugely successful professional careers. They were early achievers. Dean Acheson had already resigned as undersecretary of the Treasury by age forty. They lived their lives in a rarefied world—Groton, Skull and Bones, Porcellian, the Metropolitan Club, Council on Foreign Relations— that bore only somewhat more resemblance to the America in which most citizens were struggling to make a living and raise a family than the court of Louis XVI bore to prerevolutionary France. For this the Wise Men, as they have been called, were at times targets of populist envy and rage. "I watch his smart-aleck manner and his British clothes and that New Dealism," Nebraska senator Hugh Butler fumed after one of Dean Acheson's virtuoso performances in the Senate, ". . . and I want to shout, Get out, Get out. You stand for everything that has been wrong with the United States for years."[20] ("Shave it off," Harriman once demanded of Acheson, referring to his famous reddish-gray bushy mustache, which gave off an aura of British colonels and London clubs. "You owe it to Truman."[21] Men like Acheson were resented because they were perceived, wrongly, to be Anglophiles, when actually they were creating a role for the United States modeled on British diplomacy that was designed to replace Britain as the orchestrator of world politics.[22]

The United States would devote its resources to the maintenance of a balance of power in Europe. That required a permanent alliance with the nations of Western Europe and a commitment to halt the spread of Soviet power outside Europe. In the climate of 1946, balance-of-power diplomacy seemed impossible to sell to the American people. Popular opinion would support either isolationism— the United States would look after itself—or possibly a Wilsonian mission of reform if it didn't cost much. Both isolationism and missionary zeal were in the American grain, but "power politics" so far as the public understood it was a wicked European practice.

The architects were ever mindful of Roosevelt's struggles to mobilize the country for war. As they looked about them, they saw a hostile, expansionist Soviet Union, the possibility—for some the inevitability—of another war, and a complacent American electorate. The gulf between the emerging consensus within the Truman administration about how to exercise American power and the hopes and feelings of the American people in 1946 was immense. As Acheson himself later put it, the postwar consensus that evolved over twenty months beginning in early 1947 constituted nothing less than a "complete revolution" in American foreign policy.[23] NATO, the Truman Doctrine, and the war prevention strategy called deterrence were revolutionary because they committed the United States to permanent mobilization, entangling alliances, twilight war, foreign aid, and the renunciation of a protectionist American economy. The new national strategy, a multiple affront to cherished American traditions and what had so recently been strong majority opinion, was designed to minimize congressional interference and to short-circuit domestic debate.

During the war the chief planner in the Treasury had warned that "it would be ill-advised, if not dangerous, to leave ourselves at the end of the war unprepared for the stupendous task of worldwide economic reconstruction."[24] Stimson was worried that the reluctance of the American people to support a huge program of postwar aid represented the "chief danger" to the country, and he wrote Roosevelt recommending "a great effort of education" to convince the American people where their real interests lay.[25] The United States would have to provide the capital to finance the expansion of trade. War-ruined economies would not have the dollars to buy American goods. The success of the postwar vision depended on the skillful deployment of American largess—the use of loans as political leverage and the liberal circulation of dollars to finance expanded trade. The ideas had the support of some of America's most successful bankers and traders, but such ideas fell on conventionally conservative ears not as sophisticated *Realpolitik*, which is what they were, but as a highly suspect mélange of Keynesian pump priming and New Deal do-goodism.

The war was barely over when Herbert Hoover, who had become famous for running relief efforts after World War I, declared that domestic American needs should take precedence over aid to Europe. Bernard Baruch, who thanks to the prodigious efforts of the publicist Herbert Bayard Swope had the reputation of being the elder statesman of the Republic, agreed with the former president. Congress tacked an amendment to the Lend-Lease program prohibiting the use of any such funds for postwar reconstruction. Faithful to the will of Congress, Harry Truman abruptly terminated Lend-Lease one week after the surrender of Japan. At the dawn of the postwar world it seemed all but impossible to elicit public support for the "giveaway programs" that the postwar planners believed were now the principal instruments of American power.

Although Pentagon planners assumed that the postwar peace would rest, as Forrestal put it in 1943, on the military might of the United States, the idea that postwar American policy should be grounded in the "containment" of the Soviet Union took shape slowly. No question, the Soviet Union was not playing the role assigned to it in American postwar planning. Not only was it resistant to opening up the Soviet Union to the world market and participating in a world economic order dominated by the United States, the outline of which had been drafted at Bretton Woods in 1944, but it was using its military power to close out Western influence in Eastern Europe. Most significantly, it appeared to be challenging the very idea of an American Century. Within days of taking office Truman received universally pessimistic reports about Roosevelt's dealings with Stalin. At Yalta the deal on Poland had been struck. The Poles would have "free and unfettered elections," but the Soviets could count on having a "friendly" nation on its border. The vivid memories of centuries of Russian-Polish warfare in both nations meant that the Yalta formula was an exercise in squaring the circle. In 1945 no freely elected Polish government would have been "friendly" to the Russians by anyone's definition and certainly not Stalin's.

In the early months of the Truman administration the national security elite, outwardly cool, cautious, and sober men, seemed to be in the grip of near panic. Ambassador Averell Harriman, returning from the U.S. Embassy in Moscow six days after Roosevelt's death, sounded the alarm. Europe faced a "barbarian invasion from the East." The "outward thrust" of Communism was not dead, and the United States "might well have to face an ideological warfare just as vigorous and dangerous as Fascism or Nazism."[26] These attitudes were quite at variance with Roosevelt's optimism about working things out with Stalin and his more limited view of America's role in postwar Europe. But Harriman's warnings resonated with and served to reinforce the growing concerns in the Pentagon and in the Office of Strategic Services about a civil war and possible Communist victory in France. As early as February 1944 Pentagon planners were revising their postwar planning documents. The postwar enemy would not be a revanchist Germany but Soviet Russia. The State Department had a number of professionals who considered that war with the Soviet Union was inevitable. In May 1945, the month the war in Europe ended, Under Secretary of State Joseph Grew wrote in his journal that totalitarian Russia would constitute "as grave a danger to us as did the Axis."[27]

As a group, men like Acheson and James Forrestal talked a great deal about "educating" the public, but in these months they were educating themselves even as they educated the new president. They had a clear view of what the world should be, but not about how to bring it into being. In September 1945 Dean Acheson recommended at a cabinet meeting that the atomic secrets be shared with Stalin, saying that he could not "conceive of a world in which we were hoarders of military secrets from our Allies, particularly this great ally."[28] Yet only a few months later he was the moving force behind a hard-line policy toward the Soviet Union. Soon he would be calling the United Nations "messianic globaloney." But his initial reaction on hearing of the dropping of the first atomic bomb was different. He wrote one of his daughters on the evening of August 6, 1945: "The news of the atomic bomb is the most frightening yet. If we can't work out some organization of great powers, we shall be gone geese for fair."[29] Truman himself was uncertain how to deal with the Soviets. After he had been in the White House two months, he wrote in his diary, "I'm not afraid of

Russia. They've always been our friends and I can't see any reason why they shouldn't always be."[30] A few months later he was talking about testing Stalin to see whether he was really bent on starting World War III.

As they groped for a grand strategy, the men around Truman were reluctant to dash the people's hopes for peace. In the first two weeks of the new administration when Foreign Minister Molotov visited the White House, Truman's manner was so belligerent that more than one historian has described the meeting as the opening battle of the Cold War. "I have never been talked to like that," Molotov protested. Truman shot back, "Carry out your agreements and you won't get talked to like that."[31] Later he boasted to a friend about how he had given Molotov "the straight one-two to the jaw," then asked plaintively, "Did I do right?"[32] The contrast between this private meeting and the pageant that took place two days later on the River Elbe could not have been greater. As the advance patrols of the two great Allied armies caught sight of one another on the opposite banks, Russian and American soldiers clambered into the water, splashing, guzzling wine, and hugging one another. An opinion poll taken two months earlier showed that more Americans expected trouble with imperial Britain in the postwar world than with the gallant Soviet ally.

As world statesmen gathered in San Francisco to plan the new organization to secure the peace amid growing U.S.–Soviet tensions, some of the hard-line views floating about inside the administration found their way into the press. When Walter Lippmann heard Harriman tell journalists covering the San Francisco Conference on the United Nations that American-Soviet differences were "irreconcilable," he walked out of the room furious. The United States was trying to organize the United Nations to "police" the Russians. It would never work. The influential radio commentator Raymond Gram Swing went on the air to call for the resignation of officials who no longer believed in diplomacy. Senator Arthur Vandenberg, the leading Republican spokesman on foreign policy, a repentant isolationist now zealously courted by the administration, warned Harriman that his pessimistic analysis of Stalin's objectives would produce panic. "I would like nothing better than to have the people rise up in protest," Harriman retorted.[33]

"Last week the possibility of World War III was more and more in the horrified world's public eye," reported *Time* magazine on U.S.–Soviet wrangling at the San Francisco conference just two months before the end of World War II.[34] Truman worried about the public reaction to any policy that appeared to raise the risk of war. The American people had been fed a diet of idealism all during the crusade against Hitler and Japan, and there appeared to be a hunger for it. When the Dumbarton Oaks Conference to plan the United Nations opened in 1944 heralding a new era in diplomacy, Americans were quite unaware that even at that moment Churchill and Stalin were making a late-night secret deal over their respective spheres of influence in the Balkans. The successor to the League of Nations had not even been an issue in the election of 1944. A world organization to keep the peace had overwhelming bipartisan support. A study prepared by the Operations Division for the Joint Chiefs of Staff on March 14, 1946, noted that "we are at the present time embarking on a series of major unilateral acts . . . when it is certain we lack the military power (other than the bluff of the atomic bomb) and have only questionable public support to back up our stiff notes insofar as Russia is concerned." It recommended greater use of the United Nations "to take the onus . . . off the United States. . . . UNO in its present concept is impotent anyway."[35]

In February 1946 Stalin gave a speech laying out his analysis of world affairs and a ringing ideological challenge. "The Soviet social system has proved to be more capable . . . more stable, and a better form of organization of society than any non-Soviet social system."[36] The globe was now divided into "two camps" and conflict seemed inevitable. The liberal Justice William O. Douglas called the speech "the declaration of World War III." Secretary of State Byrnes immediately began to take a much tougher public position against the Soviets. When in March 1946 Stalin delayed the promised withdrawal of Soviet troops from Iran, the State Department's "Fortnightly Survey of American Opinion" noted that 71 percent of the respondents to a Gallup poll "disapproved" of Russia's foreign policy. The same poll showed that 60 percent thought the United States was "too soft" toward Russia.[37] Though influential commentators like Lippmann were still apportioning the responsibility for the breakdown of United States–Soviet relations on both countries, a large majority of ordinary citizens was now ready to lay the blame on Stalin. Byrnes, therefore, decided to make a public issue of the Soviet troop withdrawal even after the Soviets had privately indicated their willingness to withdraw in order, as the historian John Lewis Gaddis concludes, "to make clear to his critics at home that the United States had abandoned the politics of appeasement once and for all."[38] He told the French foreign minister that he was "very much impressed with the way opinion had rallied behind the American position."[39]

All through 1946 the administration continued to send mixed messages to the nation. Even as the Truman government began developing its grand strategy for what it saw as an inevitably divided and hostile world, the president and other senior members of the administration were still making optimistic speeches. Acheson, who believed that there were "real problems" in diplomacy and then there were "moral problems," and that law was irrelevant when the "survival" of the nation was at stake, had little use for the United Nations. But the administration continued to celebrate the United Nations in its public rhetoric.

To persuade an uninformed, complacent, and distracted people to support the national interest as leaders see it, Acheson believed, was a herculean task. Reality must be made "clearer than truth."[40] Kennan, Harriman, and particularly Forrestal, for whom the Soviets became central actors in a paranoid fantasy that eventually drove him to suicide, spent considerable time worrying about the mood swings of the public. As the navy secretary put it in a letter to Harriman in September 1946, he was "a little fearful that [public opinion] may swing too strongly the other way now" because of the American temptation to "see things precisely in black and white terms."[41] But the Truman advisers encouraged this human tendency because they felt unable to persuade any other way.

In the early Cold War years advisers with strong views inserted alarmist prose into top-secret state papers in order, as Acheson also noted, to "bludgeon the mass mind of 'top government.' "[42] Men like Dean Acheson and George Kennan knew how hard it is to change the direction of great bureaucracies. They understood the dangers of exaggeration even as they resorted to it. George Kennan's influential "long telegram," which he sent off to the State Department from the Moscow embassy on Washington's Birthday, 1946, brought him instant fame within the higher reaches of government. Drawing on his years of study and experience inside the Soviet Union, he stressed the ominous point that "Soviet power is impervious to the logic of reason, and it is highly sensitive to the logic of force." The Kremlin leaders had a "neurotic view of world affairs," one that assumed inevitable conflict with the West, and this view was reinforced by the "instinctive Russian sense of insecurity." Communist ideology was a "fig leaf" for Russian expansionism, but the Soviets would back down when faced with an adversary who "makes clear his readiness to use [force]."

Kennan's views were more nuanced than his portentous prose suggested, but the latter was critical in changing the public mood. His secret cable was leaked to *Time* and later a version was published in *Foreign Affairs*. The diplomat spent the rest of his life disowning the literal meaning of his message, which others, notably Secretary of the Navy Forrestal, amplified and distorted as a brief for a big military buildup and an across-the-board "get-tough" policy with Russia.[43] (Actually, Kennan favored abandoning Eastern Europe on the grounds that the split of Europe was inevitable. The United States, for all its justifiable moral outrage about what was happening in Poland, had no power to prevent it. He later opposed the rearmament of Germany and the "militarization" of U.S. foreign policy.)

By the time of the congressional elections of 1946, public opinion had shifted sharply against the Soviet Union. But even as wartime hopes were dashed, an anxious, conservative, and isolationist mood emerged. This new wave of public opinion was opposed to every major element of the national security strategy then taking shape within the government. The armed forces were shrinking by popular demand. In 1946 one-third of American exports were being financed through various programs of economic assistance and the Council of Economic Advisers worried that "a drastic reduction in public outlays plus the rapid demobilization of our armed forces, would lead to heavy unemployment and business dislocation for a substantial period of time."[44] But conservatives, divining the public mood, were gearing up to block the "giveaway programs" on which the administration's economic and political strategies depended. Impassioned oratory about unpaid World War I war debts echoed through the chamber of the House of Representatives. According to a Gallup poll, a majority of Americans favored high tariffs.

Conservatives like Senator Robert Taft and former president Herbert Hoover, though strongly anti-Soviet, called for retreat into what would later be called "Fortress America." Europe should look after itself. To complicate Truman's problems, the conservative isolationists advocated exactly the reverse in the Pacific, a war, if necessary, to save China from Communism. At the other end of the spectrum, the opponents of the anti-Soviet policy, though no longer supported by a majority of Americans, were becoming more vocal. Secretary of Commerce Henry Wallace gave a foreign policy speech in Madison Square Garden denouncing "the get tough with Russia policy." Truman at first said that he had approved the speech, which was an attack on his foreign policy, then at the insistence of the secretary of state he fired Wallace. Around this mercurial and misunderstood personality now coalesced a movement of frustrated New Dealers, liberals, internationalists, Communists, and fellow travelers, all concerned by the anti-Soviet thrust of American foreign policy and determined to challenge Truman in 1948. During the 1946 campaign, Truman, whose approval rating had fallen to the historic low of 32 percent, did not make one appearance in behalf of Democratic candidates, for the mere mention of his name elicited boos.

In 1946 the United States seemed unable to marshal the extraordinary power that had fallen to the world's mightiest nation. It was self-evident that public opinion now had to be taken much more seriously in the conduct of American foreign policy than ever before. Permanent preparation for war in time of peace required a permanent campaign to mobilize consent. The confrontation with the Soviet Union, neither war nor peace, was completely different from anything in the national experience. Most Americans thought of their history as long periods of peace interrupted by war. Now the lines were blurred, perhaps forever. While foreign policy issues remained peripheral to most citizens, wars, revolutions, and political struggles in distant places were like the rumble of approaching thunder. Via radio, and, for a growing minority, television, sounds and images of the outside world crashed relentlessly into American living rooms day after day. The Cold War was a call to arms, and every citizen was now a combatant. There was no place to hide, least of all in the inner space of private fantasy. The dominant public response was still apathy, but the foreign policy managers worried that the fears and passions of the crowd could one day erupt in such a way as to tie their hands.

During the war, the State Department had set up a Public Studies Division that published a fortnightly survey of opinion data for top officials in the department. Acheson was impatient with the new fascination with opinion polling inside the government. He dismissed this "mass temperature taking" as a form of "hypochondria."[45] Nevertheless, by 1947 he was spending most of his time worrying about public opinion, testifying before Congress, and defending the administration's new course. The principal task of the State Department was no longer conceiving foreign policy but selling it. As one of Dean Acheson's associates once explained it, "almost 80 percent of your time, if you are on a policy job, is management of your domestic ability to have policy, and only 20 percent, maybe, dealing with the foreign."[46]

The fortnightly survey prepared by the Public Studies Division for internal use only was based on published polls, confidential surveys initiated by the department, selected comment of editorial writers, radio pundits, and other "opinion leaders," as well as excerpts from letters from concerned citizens. It provides the best clue we have as to how the professional opinion watchers in the foreign policy Establishment perceived the state of public opinion in the early postwar years. In October 1945, 71 percent of college-educated respondents, the segment of the population that elicited the most attention and concern inside the State Department, were still optimistic about U.S.–Soviet relations and opposed to a tougher policy toward Stalin.[47]

The atomic bomb presented another public relations challenge. Despite the fact that America alone possessed the weapon that was credited with bringing the victory over Japan, the early apocalyptical pronouncements of leading opinion makers were not inspired to make people feel more secure. Within eight hours of the White House announcement on August 6, 1945, that an atomic bomb had been dropped on Hiroshima, the dean of radio commentators, H. V. Kaltenborn, warned, "For all we know, we have created a Frankenstein! We must assume that with the passage of only a little time, an improved form of the new weapon we use today can be turned against us."[48] The victory weapon had produced only the "most grimly Pyrrhic of victories," declared *Time*'s issue marking the end of the war in August 1945. One could be grateful that World War II was over, but the conflict had shrunk to "minor significance" in comparison to the awesome new threat facing all nations.[49] The initial public reaction to the atomic bomb was in the same vein, more perceptive than Secretary of State Byrnes's assumption that it was a "winning weapon" to bring the Soviet Union to heel. Ordinary people seemed to understand intuitively that the flash over two Japanese cities spelled the end of American invulnerability. The military analyst for the *New York Times*, Hanson Baldwin, offered cold comfort. Civilization could go underground. "Consider the ant, whose social problems much resemble man's. . . . Constructing beautiful urban palaces and galleries, many ants have long lived underground in entire satisfaction."[50]

The atomic bomb preceded the theories of deterrence in the name of which large nuclear stockpiles were later assembled. Truman insisted on several occasions that Big Boy and Fat Man, the two bombs dropped on Japan, were just improved artillery weapons. Nothing had really changed in warfare. In August 1945 that was also the working assumption of the Air Force, which prepared a study within days of the attacks on Hiroshima and Nagasaki calling for the dropping of every available bomb on the first day of the next war to achieve "immediate destruction of the enemy centers of industry, transportation, and population." But the first official word of "The Bomb," as it was immediately dubbed in the press, sent the public a very different message. The atomic bomb "is a harnessing of the basic power of the universe," Truman announced after the Hiroshima bombing. "The force from which the sun draws its power has been loosed against those who brought war to the Far East." Newspapers described the explosion as "cosmic power," "hell-fire," and "Doomsday itself."[51]

In September 1948, the National Security Council approved NSC 30, which concluded that "in the event of hostilities, the National Military Establishment must be ready to utilize promptly and effectively all appropriate means available, including atomic weapons, in the interest of national security." This first top-secret planning document on the use of nuclear weapons stressed the fact that public opinion was "a factor of considerable importance." Great care must be exercised to avoid "placing before the American people a moral question of vital security significance at a time when the full security impact of the question had not become apparent." NSC30 concluded that if "this decision is to be made by the American people, it should be made in the circumstances of an actual emergency."[52] This was a piece of bureaucratic obfuscation, since a national referendum or even congressional debate in the midst of a crisis about whether to drop the atomic bomb was implausible, to say the least. In the midst of the 1948 Berlin crisis the United States communicated a nuclear threat by leaking the news that sixty B-29 "atomic bombers" were being dispatched to bases in England from which they could strike the Soviet Union. In fact, the planes were not configured to carry atomic bombs. (The United States had fifty bombs in the stockpile.[53]) It was an effort to bluff the Soviets, but it was also a public announcement to the American people. The decision to base the defense of the United States on the *first* use of nuclear weapons—that is, against a nonnuclear provocation—had been made, without congressional debate or public discussion of any kind.

The ideas of Bernard Brodie, William T. R. Fox, Albert Wohlstetter, and others articulated the radical new strategy of nuclear deterrence: This weapon, unlike all others in history, was not designed to win wars but to prevent them. Peace could be kept by the threat of nuclear retaliation. Security demanded that the United States stay ahead in an unending arms race. American survival depended on the sureness and swiftness of the retaliatory strike. In the arcane language of the deterrence theorists, nuclear punishment must be "credible." Credibility depended not only on having enough bombs to strike back no matter what the enemy did but also on "national will." The president's determination to risk nuclear war in the defense of "vital interests" had to be beyond doubt. If the Soviets should ever believe that shrieking mobs in the streets might stay the president's hand in a crisis, the nuclear deterrent would be undermined. The nerves of the American people were now to be permanently deployed as weapons.

3.

On February 21, 1947, the British first secretary called on the director of the U.S. State Department's Office of Near Eastern and African Affairs and the deputy director of European Affairs and handed these two senior Foreign Service officers a note. What the note said was that Britain could no longer maintain its forces in Greece or continue its economic support to that nation. What the note meant, as the director of Public Affairs comprehended it, was that "Great Britain had within the hour handed the job of world leadership, with all its burdens and all its glory, to the United States." The State Department now had a theme to take to the country.

Greece was the one country in Europe facing a Communist insurgency, and Turkey had just been a target of Soviet political pressure. Stalin had consigned the Hellenic peninsula to Britain in his negotiation with Churchill in 1944, and he actually tried to discourage Tito's support for the Greek resistance. Milovan Djilas, then a top aide to Marshal Tito, the Communist leader of Yugoslavia, remembers Stalin telling the Yugoslav leader, "The uprising in Greece must be stopped, and as quickly as possible."[54] But this was not known in Washington in 1947, and the working assumptions were that Stalin was behind all Communists everywhere. Acheson quickly elaborated the policy that came to be known as the Truman Doctrine. But he understood that a policy of unilateral intervention in the Greek civil war on behalf of a right-wing government that the British had put in place would be hard to sell. In late February 1947, Joseph Jones, the head of the State Department Public Affairs Office, in a memo for Acheson compared the problem facing the country's leaders to the "situation . . . prevailing prior to Pearl Harbor: a powerlessness on the part of the government to act because of Congressional or public unawareness of the danger or cost of inaction."[55] The State Department's fortnightly survey had reported a few weeks before that 67 percent of Americans still considered the U.N. "the best chance for peace" and only 28 percent favored "trying to stay ahead of the Russians by building atomic bombs."[56] Thus as the Cold War was about to be declared, two of the pillars of the new foreign policy consensus—unilateral military action to keep the peace and nuclear deterrence—were in conflict with strong majority sentiment.

Truman's speech to Congress on March 12, 1947, in which he announced the Truman Doctrine, was developed with domestic politics uppermost in mind. Acheson saw the Greek civil war as a window of opportunity for mobilizing support for a broader program of foreign assistance. "If FDR were alive . . . ," Acheson observed, "he would make a statement of global policy but confine his request for money right now to Greece and Turkey."[57] These were the countries to start with in developing the European and eventually worldwide aid packages that came to be known as the Marshall Plan and Point Four Program. In Greece and Turkey the case could be made on the basis of anti-Communism rather than on the need to lubricate free trade with tax dollars. Anti-Communism was sure to strike a responsive chord; Congress had just gutted a relief appropriation for Europe on the grounds that some of the money was going to Hungary and Poland. The enunciation of the Truman Doctrine—"I believe that it must be the policy of the United States to support free peoples who are resisting attempted subjugation by armed minorities or by outside pressures"—set a direction for the United States that eventually led to the jungles of Vietnam in the 1960s and 1970s and to American participation in the "low-intensity wars" of El Salvador and Nicaragua in the 1980s.

Acheson and the team of speech writers and public relations specialists who worked on it had been severely shaken by the initial reaction of congressional leaders. General of the Army George Marshall, the new secretary of state, was perhaps the most respected figure in the country. He had run America's global war effort and was an incisive man who radiated authority. Thus it was all the more alarming that when he, Acheson, and Truman met a bipartisan group of House and Senate leaders in the White House to present the new strategy, it fell flat. Marshall made the mistake of talking about the security problem in the Balkans and Mediterranean the way people talked about it in the State Department. Britain was withdrawing. There would be a "power vacuum." There was a humanitarian obligation to provide aid. Frowns and puzzled looks greeted Marshall's low-key presentation. "Wasn't this pulling Britain's chestnuts out of the fire?" Acheson grew desperate. Convinced that his chief had "flubbed" his opening statement, he whispered for a chance to step in. "This was my crisis," he wrote in his memoirs. "For a week I had nurtured it. These congressmen had no conception of what challenged them; it was my task to bring it home." And this he did with lawyerly passion. Not since Rome and Carthage had there been such a polarization in the world. Only the power of the United States stood in the way of Communism. Eschewing the dry language of statecraft, Acheson likened the new menace to a disease. "Like apples in a barrel infected by one rotten one, the corruption of Greece would infect Iran and all to the east. It would also carry infection to Africa through Asia Minor and Egypt, and to Europe through Italy and France, already threatened by the strongest domestic Communist parties in Western Europe. The Soviet Union was playing one of the greatest gambles in history at minimal cost. . . . We and we alone were in a position to break up the play."[58]

Vandenberg bluntly told the president that to get the money he would have "to scare the hell out of the country" by dramatizing the menace of Communism.[59] The orchestration of the foreign aid program set a pattern for the future. First, an atmosphere of crisis was carefully engendered. For months the leaders of the administration had been aware that the British would have to pull out of the eastern Mediterranean, but the impression was created that the news had arrived as a bolt from the blue. It was a tactic to avoid the delay that had almost killed a loan to Britain a few months before. Second, the drafters made a point of not sharing the real thinking inside the State Department. The emphasis inside the department was on reconstruction and political consolidation of Western Europe, but the speech tried to create an atmosphere of imminent military crisis. Clark Clifford had written months before that aid could be an effective instrument for welding Western Europe into an anti-Soviet bloc, but it was premature to say this publicly. Clifford proposed educating the people to the strategic importance of the Middle East. If Communism spread to the eastern Mediterranean, Europe's access to oil might be cut off. The thrust of the Truman Doctrine was preemptive. Stalin was intimidating but not attacking Turkey, or Greece either. The real fear in Washington was that political and economic weakness would invite some future Soviet expansion into the region.

But Acheson vetoed the idea of talking about oil. "The American people were not accustomed to thinking . . . in strategic-military terms in time of peace." Too much emphasis on military aid to Turkey "might have been alarming to the point of defeating the [proposal]."[60] The underlying purpose of the Truman Doctrine, as Clark Clifford put it, was to serve as "the opening gun in a campaign to bring people up to [the] realization that the war isn't over by any means."[61] Truman's assistant George Elsey put the point no less starkly: "The only way we can sell the public on our new policy is by emphasizing the necessity of holding the line: communism vs. democracy should be the major theme."[62]

Walter Lippmann publicly attacked the Truman Doctrine for its strident tone and global pretension. Acheson and the columnist had an angry exchange about it at a dinner party and each jumped up from the table and "stalked off in opposite directions."[63] Kennan was also upset, not about giving military aid to Greece and Turkey but about the exaggerated expectations that would flow from the declaration of a worldwide war against Communism. When Acheson went to Congress to testify, he encountered sullen resistance from members who knew how much they were being manipulated to pass an aid bill for which they had little enthusiasm. He was forced to blur the anti-Communist thrust of the policy in his testimony in order to escape having to explain why the Truman Doctrine did not apply to China. After the overwhelming vote of approval for the administration's bill was taken, Congressman Francis Case wrote the president to complain, "The situation was regarded as an accomplished fact. You had spoken to the world. At least 75 members, I judge, would have voted against final passage, myself included, had it not been that we thought it would be like pulling the rug out from under you and Secretary of State Marshall.[64]

The Greek-Turkish aid bill was designed as the opening wedge of a much larger program of reconstruction for Europe. Will Clayton, assistant secretary of commerce, proposed asking for $5 billion, but said that "the United States will not take world leadership effectively unless the people . . . are shocked into doing so."[65] Members of the administration had been sending up trial balloons making use of influential columnists with whom they had close personal relations. Lippmann used to pass policy suggestions to high officials at lunch and then would write glowingly about them after they were adopted by the administration. It was he who hit upon the idea of having the Europeans draw up their own plan for reconstruction so that the United States could "respond" to Europe's carefully thought through need, a defense of the Marshall Plan against the Republican charge that the nation was meddling in a foreign morass. (The crossover of the line between critic and policy maker happened more than once. In January 1945, the columnist had collaborated with James Reston of the *New York Times* to produce the speech of Senator Arthur Vandenberg in which he renounced isolationism and presented himself as candidate for senior Republican partner in a bipartisan foreign policy. Reston hailed the speech as "wise" and "statesmanlike," and Lippmann too discovered good things to say about it in his column.[66]) The top officials had favorites to whom they would leak secret cables and memoranda. Acheson courted Reston. Forrestal supplied alarmist cables to Arthur Krock, a Princeton clubmate. Bohlen used Joseph Alsop of the *Herald Tribune*, a widely read columnist and a fellow member of Harvard's Porcellian Club.[67]

Having gotten the world's attention, Acheson and his colleagues were eager to mollify the opposition they had aroused. After a burst of support for the president and laudatory editorials supporting the new readiness of the United States to assume "world responsibilities," the critics spoke out. On the Left Wallace denounced the Truman Doctrine as "a curious mixture of power politics and international carpetbagging." America, he predicted, "will become the most hated nation in the world."[68] Wallace noted that what Truman had called "imperfect democracy" in Greece was really fascism. By supporting Greece's right-wing government just two years after Hitler's end the United States had switched sides. Conservatives, while welcoming the anti-Communism, worried that the Democratic administration was plunging unilaterally into expensive commitments. Among the old-fashioned Right in Congress, "Operation Rathole" was the preferred designation for foreign aid. Much of the editorial comment attacked the anti-Soviet and militaristic tone of the Truman Doctrine.[69]

For the men of the Truman administration the Cold War was above all else an ideological struggle that might or might not turn into a hot war. James Forrestal saw the daunting economic crisis in Europe in 1947 as the moment to strike a blow in the ideological war. The "central problem," he told Clifford, is "which of the systems currently offered in the world is to survive." Despite the overwhelming economic superiority of the United States and its nuclear monopoly, he and others within the national security elite had doubts on this score. Not only did they fear that capitalism was headed for another depression, but America's "open society" was a distinct disadvantage in fighting any war, especially a protracted one with uncertain goals. Added to the original economic reason for providing economic aid to Europe was an urgent political reason. Although Communists had already been expelled from the cabinets in France and Italy, Acheson and his associates in the State Department were worried about the strength of the Left in Europe. The specter of political stalemate and neutralism now haunted Europe, and the crisis called for emergency treatment. On top of all its other problems war-ravaged Europe was having the worst winter in more than a hundred years.

Acheson worried that Stalin could derail the emerging national strategy by playing on the people's hopes for peace. He told the Senate Foreign Relations Committee, "I think it is a mistake to believe that you can, at anytime, sit down with the Russians and solve questions."[70] To sell European aid the only way it could be sold, as an instrument of containment, it was important to close off avenues of hope that the problems of Europe could be settled through negotiation with Stalin. Once again, Stalin, belying his reputation as the master propagandist, cooperated. A little more than a month after the Truman Doctrine message, Secretary of State Marshall met with the generalissimo. Doodling wolves' heads in red ink as he listened to the secretary of state, Stalin seemed in no hurry to arrive at an agreement. Perhaps they would agree next time they met, he murmured, or maybe the time after that.

Dean Acheson, back at his law firm for a few months, organized the Citizens' Committee for the Marshall Plan, and he went about the country making speeches on its behalf to such groups as the National-American Wholesale Grocers' Association at their annual get-together at Atlantic City. When the representative of the National Farmers Union testified on behalf of what many Republicans were calling the "International WPA," he spoke the clipped phrases Acheson had ghosted for him.

George Kennan had been put in charge of drafting the Marshall Plan. He deplored "the hysterical sort of anti-Communism which, it seems to me, is gaining currency in this country," he said in a lecture at the Army War College.[71] The aim of the European Recovery Program, as he and Bohlen emphasized in the speech prepared for Marshall to give at Harvard announcing the initiative, was "not against country, ideology, or political party" but instead

"against hunger, poverty, . . . and chaos." But so "Platonic" a purpose, as far as Acheson was concerned, might move a few commentators and columnists, "but the bulk of their fellow citizens were
unimpressed."[72] The campaign to sell the unprecedented commitment to Europe could not elicit the support of the American people
unless it was aimed at a flesh-and-blood enemy.

4.

Even in the midst of total war there had been only a fitful semblance
of bipartisanship in foreign policy. Nor despite the ritualistic use of
the term by politicians of both parties in the early postwar years did
politics ever stop at the water's edge. In 1944 Franklin Roosevelt
had summoned home his key ambassadors, including Averell Harriman, to give campaign speeches for his fourth term. Harold Ickes
had made it clear that a vote for Dewey "would revive the fading
hopes" of Hitler and Hirohito. Truman declared that "the reason
our boys are now dying again on the battlefields of the world" was
Warren Harding's "failure."[73] The myth of the postwar bipartisan
consensus is that the same lightning struck Democratic and Republican statesmen at the same time, causing them to put aside partisan
quarrels in the face of an overwhelming external threat. What actually happened is less miraculous but more interesting. In return
for a share of the credit key Republican leaders offered qualified
support for the critical provisions of the foreign policy consensus
taking shape within the Truman administration. In turn, the rhetoric of the new foreign policy was carefully crafted not only to
please Republican politicians whose votes were needed on foreign
aid, loans, and military appropriations but also to win over their
constituents to the Democratic Party in the 1948 election.

In February 1947, the Truman administration's strategy for the
creation of a liberal international economic order was cast as a
strategy to win the Cold War in order to secure Republican support
and to sell the policy to the country. The Republicans had won a
smashing victory in the 1946 elections. The dominant figure in the
Senate was the isolationist Robert Taft, and in the House the key
personality was Joseph Martin; the object of Rooseveltian scorn in
the 1940 election was now sitting in the Speaker's chair. There were
two things the Republicans, hungry for power after fourteen years
in the wilderness, intended to stop. One was the Reciprocal Trade
Agreements Program, which offended them not only because it was
a program to reduce tariffs but also because it transferred important

powers from Congress to the executive. The second was foreign aid, which Speaker Martin said would be bad for the "war-stricken nations" themselves. Not unlike domestic welfare recipients, these foreign supplicants "may be led to rely too much on the United States and try too little to help themselves." The United States should be careful not "to be dragged down with them."[74]

Nor could the money be appropriated without overwhelming bipartisan support. In pursuit of Republican votes the Truman administration had a powerful ally, the vanity of Arthur Vandenberg, which Dean Acheson grew expert at massaging. "I marvel how you maintain your good humor, your strength, and your zest for the fray" went a typically buttery note. The most effective way to flatter Vandenberg was to stamp an administration proposal with "the Vandenberg brand," as Acheson called it, by accepting a meaningless change and calling it "the Vandenberg amendment." Thus in 1947, when Acheson was utterly skeptical of any positive contribution the United Nations could make to American foreign policy, he was happy to agree, on Vandenberg's insistence, that the world organization would take over the Greek-Turkish aid program whenever circumstances should permit. With the Soviet veto in the Security Council, circumstances would never permit, but the born-again internationalist could take credit for a good try. Acheson made sure that similar Vandenberg "brands" were applied to the European Recovery Program legislation in order to split the Republican opposition to the new worldview taking shape in the State Department.[75]

All through the New Deal and wartime years J. Edgar Hoover, the director of the Federal Bureau of Investigation, had been careful about jeopardizing his excellent relations with Roosevelt in pursuit of his favorite quarry, the Communist Party USA and its sympathizers. Although the Roosevelt haters such as Elizabeth Dilling published broad-brush attacks on the New Deal—in her 1934 publication *Red Network*, she charged that Interior Secretary Harold Ickes (along with Republican Senator William Borah and Mrs. Justice Brandeis) was an undercover Communist—Hoover did not attack the loyalty of highly placed officials even when he privately considered them dangerous leftists. But with the war over, Roosevelt gone, and clouds for another war gathering, he shifted tactics.

A few months after Roosevelt's death Hoover sent Truman a report on Harry Dexter White, based on revelations of a former Communist Party official, Elizabeth Bentley, stating that the high Treasury official, the principal author of the monetary arrangements put forward by the United States at the Bretton Woods Conference, was a member of a Communist espionage ring. Truman ignored the report and appointed White to be a governor of the newly created International Monetary Fund, thus infuriating Hoover. Truman, according to White House aide George Elsey, was "very strongly anti-FBI" and worried that Hoover might be trying to create a "Gestapo." On May 29, 1946, the FBI director sent the White House a list of names from a "source believed to be reliable" that included Alger Hiss, a former official of the State Department who had been with Roosevelt at Yalta, along with Henry Wallace, Dean Acheson, John J. McCloy, and others, all described as having "pro-Soviet leanings."[76] Once again Hoover's warning met with silence.

Although the reports that the director regularly forwarded to the White House were often wildly inaccurate—one of his "generally reliable" sources reported in November 1945 that Stalin had been deposed and Molotov was in charge—he was incensed when they produced no action.[77] By 1946 Hoover believed that war with the Soviet Union was imminent. When Truman refused to implement a tough program for screening the loyalty of government employees, Hoover decided to launch his own public campaign to force a change of policy.

In 1946 the Republicans had made the choice between "Communism and Republicanism" a major theme of the election, and the Democrats were dismayed at how effective the Red-baiting tactic had been. Now as 1948 approached, the Republicans had a powerful ally, the highest police official in the United States. Breaking tradition, Hoover agreed to testify before the House Un-American Activities Committee on March 26, 1947, just two weeks after the Truman Doctrine message. (In the past, out of loyalty to Roosevelt and a desire not to share the headlines with the committee, Hoover had always declined to appear.) But this time he struck every note in the right-wing litany and skillfully linked the issues of foreign policy and internal security. Hoover declared that there were seventy-four thousand members of the Communist Party in the United States and for each member another ten sympathizers. Playing on still fresh memories of Hitler's success in the use of propaganda and fifth columnists, secret Nazi sympathizers, and defeatists, Hoover denounced Communism as a crime. Communists were "masters of deceit" whether in the Kremlin, in schoolhouses in New Jersey, or in the State Department. He lashed out at the administration for not firing individuals whom the Bureau had identified as Communists. The problem was not only the machinations of the Kremlin but "the liberal and progressive who has been hoodwinked and duped into joining hands with the Communists. . . . Under the guise of academic freedom [Communists] can teach our youth a way of life that eventually will destroy the sanctity of the home, that undermines faith in God, that causes them to scorn respect for constituted authority and sabotage our revered Constitution."[78] Every Communist and Communist sympathizer was part of the Kremlin's fifth column. "Their allegiance is to Russia, not the United States."

Hoover encouraged the committee to launch a crusade against Communism. Attorney General Tom Clark warned in a Washington *Post* article about "the rising tide of totalitarianism that [is] coming to our shores." The connections were now clearly drawn and the implications clear. The United States could not do business with Stalin for he was just another Hitler—but armed with a more insidious and more salable ideology. Hoover wanted to enlist the public in exposing Communists so as to facilitate his plans for the Custodial Detention Program. This was a plan under which suspected Soviet sympathizers would be rounded up on the outbreak of the war with Russia that he considered certain. Pentagon planners recommended to the Joint Chiefs of Staff on April 12, 1946, that war plans operate on the assumption that in any war with Russia "the United States will be faced with serious internal unrest, particularly in the form of work stoppages and sabotage in key industries and facilities."[79] Hoover insisted that victory would be assured "once Communists are identified and exposed, because the public will take the first step of quarantining them so they can do no harm."[80] He also understood how swiftly the political culture could be altered by the skillful equation of dissent with disloyalty.

The headlines of the early postwar years lent credibility to Hoover's warnings. The issues of Soviet espionage in America and Stalinist foreign policy merged in the public mind. In June 1945 the FBI had raided the offices of *Amerasia*, a small magazine devoted to American policy toward Asia run by a left-wing editor, and discovered classified documents. In February 1946 the Canadian government announced that all during the war a Soviet spy ring had been stealing secrets relating to the atomic bomb. In early 1947 the House Un-American Activities Committee began calling former Communists, beginning with Louis Budenz, the former editor of the *Daily Worker*, to testify about Communist subversion in America. Many Americans were now ready to agree with Hoover that every Communist was a "corruptionist" skilled at talking peace "until his forces are sufficiently strong to rise with arms in revolt."[81] Every American who still hoped for good relations with the Soviet Union was a dupe or worse.

The Communist coup in Czechoslovakia in February 1948 raised the specter of war. A Gallup poll in April showed that 65 percent of the respondents now considered that preventing war was the most important issue facing the country. The domestic issues that had sustained the New Deal in its triumphant years had become, according to Gallup's reading, a priority for only 9 percent of the electorate. As the 1948 presidential election campaign loomed, Harry Truman appeared to be in deep trouble in large part because of public concern about how the administration was handling Russia and Communists in America. Forty percent of the public, according to private polls of the Democratic National Committee, was critical of the Truman foreign policy. A slightly smaller percentage approved, and most alarming for the Democrats, a slight majority thought the Republicans could do better. Truman was widely perceived as being "too soft" on the Russians, but at the same time 63 percent of the respondents favored a meeting with Stalin or some other bold stroke to reduce the danger of war.[82] Since the Republicans were likely to advocate a hard line and Wallace, who was about to announce his candidacy on a third-party ticket, was sure to promise more active diplomatic initiatives for peace, as 1948 began, foreign policy looked like a political trap for Truman.

Moreover, the Republican Congress threatened to paralyze the Truman policy. The Republicans remained skeptical of foreign aid and seemed to be moved only by anti-Communist appeals. But for Truman there were political costs in moving too far in that direction for Henry Wallace was gaining strength. In June 1947 Gael Sullivan of the Democratic National Committee warned Clark Clifford that Wallace was "hotter than a busted blowtorch," and would be a "major consideration" in 1948. In 1946 Truman had written in his diary shortly after firing Wallace from the cabinet, "the Reds, phonies and 'parlor pinks' seem to be banded together and are becoming a national danger. I am afraid they are a sabotage front for Uncle Joe Stalin."[83] Less than a year later, however, at least one prominent Democrat was speculating, as David Lilienthal noted in his diary, that they "may have to run [Wallace] for Vice-president yet."

In February 1948 a candidate pledged to Wallace ran in a special congressional election in the Bronx on the left-wing American

Labor Party ticket and soundly defeated the Democrat. Gallup reported that Wallace would carry anywhere from 13 percent to 18 percent of New York, enough to cost Truman the state and the election. As Gael Sullivan put it, there were only two choices: Since Wallace had "captured the imagination of a strong segment of the American public . . . action should be taken either to (1) appease Wallace or (2) pull the rug on him."[84]

In the first two postwar years Americans were, as public opinion specialists predicted during the war, caught up again in their own lives, worried about the uncertainty of career, education, and housing. The shock of peace was producing turbulence, not tranquillity. Millions of servicemen returned to find a housing crisis and their old jobs gone. These dislocations were compounded by severe strikes in the coal, steel, railroad, automobile, and meat-packing industries. The wave of unprecedented labor militance seemed to be part of a worldwide phenomenon that included Communist-led strikes against the Marshall Plan in Italy and France and even prolonged battles for workers' rights in French West Africa. Against the backdrop of insurrectionary movements in the Philippines, Indochina, and elsewhere in the collapsing British, French, and Dutch empires the labor unrest in the United States revived vivid memories of the class conflict of the thirties; the truce imposed by a global war appeared to be over. Leading American economists expected a depression. Unions had gained six million new members during the six years of World War II. Communists exercised an influence in the labor movement that far exceeded their numbers.

Now into this explosive brew, Forrestal and Hoover worried, the Soviet Union was about to throw a lighted match. In his Farewell Address the first president had warned that foreign powers would take advantage of the unique republican institutions of the United States in order to confuse American opinion. Now the twentieth-century totalitarians had perfected the means for doing it. Joseph Goebbels, Hitler's propagandist, and the Japanese "thought control" police had turned Germany and Japan into formidable military machines, not only by making automatons of their own people but by spreading the virus of defeatism to the nations they targeted for conquest. The Soviet Union had an even more formidable propaganda and subversion capability, and a significant cadre of loyalists burrowed within American society—an American fifth column far beyond anything Hitler ever controlled.

Domestic Communism was the crucial catalyst for transforming a Soviet Union that had no military means for attacking the United

States into a national security threat that could be understood by ordinary citizens. Franklin Roosevelt knew that the only way to mobilize the American people for war was to persuade them that "self-evident home defense" demanded it.[85] In a fireside chat a few months before Pearl Harbor he warned that "Hitler's advance guards—not only his avowed agents but also his dupes among us— have sought to make ready for him footholds and bridgeheads in the New World."[86] The exaggeration of Hitler's fifth column in the Americas a few years before made it easier for millions of Americans to believe that a few thousand of their card-carrying neighbors trudging off to Marxist study groups constituted a paramilitary threat. (By the time historians had burrowed into Nazi archives and ascertained that Hitler had few assets in the Americas and no discernible plans for a military attack on the United States only historians were interested.)

Forrestal was the high official most concerned about Communist efforts to mold American opinion, a subject he brought up periodically at cabinet meetings. He sought out editors and publishers to enlist their help in exposing and countering Soviet propaganda, a label he applied to any opinion that converged at any point with the Stalinist line. He wrote to Secretary of State Marshall, "The American press should be an instrument of our foreign policy, just as is the British press."[87] Forrestal was particularly concerned with Soviet success in generating popular pressure in the United States for disarmament, and he and Harriman called for a "centralized program of counterpropaganda."[88] Secretary of War Robert Patterson wrote Roy Howard, publisher of the Scripps-Howard newspapers, in August 1947 to complain of a series that eviscerated a bungling U.S. Army general. "We stand in need of a strong army and constant criticism of the demoralizing variety may cost the country dear."[89] In 1947 the army revoked the credentials of eleven correspondents and denied credentials to fifty more on the grounds that they had "Communist connections." Forrestal drew up plans for peacetime censorship, but the outcry from the news industry forced a hasty retreat. At the first meeting of the National Security Council, in December 1947, the newly constituted body approved NSC 4, which called for "covert psychological warfare" to counter the "vicious psychological operations of the USSR, its Satellite countries, and Communist groups to discredit and defeat the activities of the U.S. and other Western powers."[90]

By the end of 1947 the Truman administration had put in place the largest and best organized propaganda effort ever undertaken in peacetime. The problem, as Attorney General Clark saw it, was "to reawaken in the American people the loyalty we know them to have to the American way of life. . . . Our best defense against subversive elements is to make the ideal of democracy a living fact."[91] In his annual report for 1947 the Commissioner of Education, John Studebaker, said that "the single most important educational frontier of all" was the need "to strengthen national security through education." It was now the task of schools to cultivate patriotism. The commission announced the Zeal for American Democracy program and promoted it in several national conferences for educators. Study guides were prepared for schools at all levels to show how "the principles of democracy may be inculcated in children through percept and experience." Another explicit purpose of the program was to "reveal the character and tactics of totalitarianism."[92] Initially, the message of the Zeal for American Democracy program was somewhat mixed, for in addition to its anti-Communism it included a good deal of idealistic internationalism—what the Office of Education called "world-mindedness." This not only raised eyebrows in the Republican Congress but was out of step with the *Realpolitik* of Acheson, Lovett, Harriman, and Kennan. But by the end of 1947 anti-Communism became the focus, and the commissioner, as a *New York Times* headline reported, was calling for a "war on Communism" in the nation's schools.[93]

The Justice Department simultaneously launched its own program to redefine the limits of acceptable opinion. In late 1947 Attorney General Clark published a list of organizations considered to be "communist," "fascist," "totalitarian," or "subversive" under the authority of an executive order of the president that established a loyalty program for screening government employees. Congressional committees had published lists of suspect organizations in the past but never the Justice Department. The official purpose of the list was to assist the highly publicized effort Truman was now making in response to Republican attacks to weed out subversives from the government. We have "stolen their thunder," Clifford assured the president. "Our strategic objective," declared Tom Clark before the House Un-American Activities Committee in February 1948, "must be to isolate subversive movements in this country from effective interference with the body politic."[94] The Communists were mounting a strong campaign against the Marshall Plan and the other components of the new Cold War strategy, using front organizations that the administration sought to label as "subversive." Government employees who publicly opposed the

Marshall Plan were questioned by security officials.[95] As the Supreme Court later found, the listing of organizations "significantly impaired the effectiveness of the organizations . . . named."[96] Because the evidence for including an organization was secret, the existence of the list had a chilling effect on dissent that went far beyond the members of the organizations actually labeled. Citizens were reluctant to join organizations that *might* be listed, because membership risked loss of job, passport, or federally financed housing. In 1947 rumors were spread that Henry Wallace's Progressive Citizens' Association, which became the nucleus of the Progressive Party the following year, was about to be added to the list.

In May 1947 Clark sponsored a White House Conference on the Freedom Train that drew up plans for a tour of two hundred American cities. At each stop the Freedom Train, outfitted as a museum for displaying the Declaration of Independence, the Constitution, the Emancipation Proclamation, and the Truman Doctrine message, invited local citizens on board to instill what Clark called "an upsurge of patriotism." It was designed in part to build a constituency for the controversial and expensive Marshall Plan aid package then being debated in Congress. As the Freedom Train wound up its tour Thanksgiving week of 1947, government employees were given time off to participate in mass demonstrations where the crowd took the "freedom pledge" and sang "God Bless America." The celebration culminated in a patriotic speech by President Truman and a mock bombing run on the nation's capital.[97]

That same month Clark Clifford wrote Truman a forty-three-page memorandum on how to snatch victory from what appeared to be certain defeat in the coming presidential election. The handsome young lawyer with courtly manners and a political sixth sense advised Truman to move to the Left on domestic policy in the hope of keeping the old New Deal coalition—farmers, blacks, Jews, the urban ethnic vote, and organized labor—and to make the Cold War a major issue. The "battle with the Kremlin" was sure to work to the president's advantage in two ways. First, Truman could run as commander in chief and shed the image of former haberdasher and political hack. "The nation is already united behind the President" on getting tough with Russia. "The worse matters get, up to a fairly certain point—real danger of imminent war—the more is there a sense of crisis. In times of crisis the American citizen tends to back up his President." Second, focusing on foreign policy was necessary to defeat the Wallace movement. The way to do that was "to identify him and isolate him in the public mind with the Communists."[98]

The election of 1948 was a milestone of American politics for it solidified the bipartisan consensus and discredited the liberal critique of the Cold War. When it was over, the meaning of the words "liberal" and "internationalist" in American politics had shifted. Harry Truman proceeded to follow Clark Clifford's advice to the letter and to run as commander in chief. Stalin cooperated to the fullest. In February 1948 there was a Communist coup in Czechoslovakia that produced shock, black headlines, and considerable propaganda. "The atmosphere of Washington today," wrote the Alsop brothers in their syndicated column, "is no longer postwar. It is a prewar atmosphere."[99] There were some high officials who were themselves overcome with war fever. The Chief of Naval Operations proposed a campaign to "prepare the American people for war," and the secretary of the air force privately recommended dropping several "atomic bombs" on the Soviet Union if Stalin did not get out of Central Europe. Kennan was becoming horrified at the talk of the inevitability of war, and Marshall scribbled a note to Truman not to make an emotional speech, for it might "pull the trigger—start the war."

A week after Jan Masaryk, Czechoslovakia's pro-Western foreign minister jumped, or was pushed, out of a window in Prague, Truman appeared before Congress to deliver an appeal for the immediate passage of the European Recovery Program, the reinstatement of Selective Service, and universal military training. The crisis atmosphere in Washington had been stirred up by leaks of an alarmist cable from General Lucius Clay, the military governor of Germany. War, he wrote, could come "with dramatic suddenness." Actually, Clay did not believe that there had been any change in Soviet strategy to warrant the fear of imminent war. He was responding to a request from Army Intelligence for something that might get attention on the Hill.[100] Truman, however, used the crisis to push the Marshall Plan legislation, which had been stalled in Congress by Republicans who feared inflation more than they feared the Russians. The president of the United States warned that the Soviets had a "clear design" on the "remaining free nations of Europe." Within days the European Recovery Program legislation was on the president's desk awaiting his signature. On March 25 Clay held a press conference to assure the world that he was "not the least bit apprehensive about war" and that much too much was being made of the Czech crisis. The administration was following Clifford's script exactly. The people will rally behind the president —up to the point of "real danger of imminent war." The crisis of March quickly evaporated. The president of the United States had intentionally given the impression, contrary to the opinion of Secretary of State Marshall and the top military advisers, that Europe faced an imminent military threat and by so doing had produced a politically helpful public mood.

Clifford's second recommendation—to identify Wallace with the Communists "in the public mind"—originally struck Truman as distasteful, for he had once considered the former vice-president "an honest man and a faithful public servant."[101] However, when Wallace announced his candidacy, Truman authorized the publicity director of the Democratic Party to issue a statement declaring that "a vote for Wallace . . . is a vote for things for which Stalin, Molotov and Vyshinsky stand." But Wallace was gaining strength with important constituents of the Democratic Party, particularly because, unlike Truman, he had taken an unequivocal stand in favor of the establishment of a Jewish state in Palestine. The State Department was against antagonizing the oil-producing Arab world. "This is a serious matter of foreign policy determination," George Marshall lectured Truman's political advisers in what Clifford called a "righteous God-damned Baptist tone." Eventually, however, Truman's own sympathies, the appeals of Eddie Jacobson, his old haberdashery partner, and the warnings of the political strategists of the Democratic Party won out. After months of politically damaging equivocation the Truman administration became the first government to recognize the new state. "In all my political experience," Truman observed to a friend during the campaign, "I don't ever recall the Arab vote swinging a close election."[102]

Immediately after giving his crisis message to Congress on March 17, 1948, Truman flew to New York, and at a Saint Patrick's Day dinner that evening declared, "I do not want and I will not accept the political support of Henry Wallace and his Communists." Communists did indeed play a key role in the Progressive Party, but Wallace himself was a strong believer in free enterprise, free trade, and was squarely in the business pacifist tradition of Andrew Carnegie and Henry Ford. The comparative advantage of America, he was convinced, was the power of commerce, not war. But Truman put the prestige of the presidency behind a thinly veiled charge of disloyalty. By "reading Henry Wallace out of the Democratic Party," as Truman put it in his diary, he made Wallace a lightning rod to deflect Republican charges of softness toward Communism.[103] At the same time Truman's highly publicized Employee Loyalty Program blunted the impact of Republican Red-baiting.

The Democrats hoped to keep controversy over foreign policy out of the election and counted on the Republicans to join Vandenberg in "stopping politics at the water's edge." Other Republicans were eager to launch a full-scale attack on the Democrats' "failures" at Yalta and their softness on Communism. Thomas E. Dewey, the party's candidate, however, sided with Vandenberg. Believing the polls that showed him winning by a landslide, he was sure that he could afford to be statesmanlike. Once again Stalin helped Truman. On June 23, 1948, the day Dewey was nominated, the Soviets cut all rail, truck, auto, and barge traffic to Berlin. After rejecting the advice to send an armored column to relieve Berlin, the administration began an airlift. This daily pageant of American innovation, daring, and resolve worked greatly to Truman's advantage. The "little man" from Missouri was standing up to the Russians without plunging the nation into war. The crisis persuaded Dewey not to challenge Truman's Cold War strategy. The near unanimity on foreign policy left Truman free to mount slashing attacks on the Republicans as "mossbacks" on economic issues. As the historian Robert Divine has concluded, "The greatest asset that the Democrats possessed was their control of foreign policy during a time when the American people were obsessed with a sense of grave national peril."[104]

Bipartisanship was an enormous gift to the Democrats, because Truman actually remained quite vulnerable on foreign policy all during the campaign. The ambivalence that has characterized the public mood for the last forty years was evident in the first postwar presidential election. The polls kept showing that Americans wanted a tough posture toward Stalin, but they also yearned for peace initiatives. Two of Truman's speech writers, David Noyes and A. Z. Carr, noting that lines like "I wish for peace, I work for peace, and I pray for peace continually" brought crowds to their feet, suggested that the president announce that he was sending General Eisenhower on a goodwill mission to Moscow. Truman jumped at the idea but decided to send his old friend Fred Vinson, whom he had appointed Chief Justice instead of the war hero whose popularity he envied. After ordering the reluctant jurist to make the trip, the president booked airtime for a speech to announce the initiative. But when Secretary Marshall was informed, he insisted that Truman abandon the idea. The speech was canceled, but the story of the abortive initiative got into the press and was denounced by everyone but Henry Wallace. "In plain words," wrote Walter Lippmann, echoing an old theme of his, "Mr. Truman does not know how to be President."[105]

But in the end the initiative probably won Truman votes, for he could appear to be a peacemaker without abandoning a single element of his "get tough" policy. In the closing days of the campaign Dewey stepped up his charges that Truman's "vacillation" on foreign policy had allowed the Soviet Union to extend "its sway nearly halfway around the world." But what Dewey called a policy of "appeasement and bluster" worked for Truman. In Boston he declared that "the Communists will never forgive me" for stopping Soviet aggression, and in Brooklyn two days later, echoing Wallace, he proclaimed "a people's foreign policy . . . to win a people's peace." The following Tuesday he was reelected by a comfortable margin.

CHAPTER 11

The Cold War Consensus

1.

In carrying on the struggle with the Soviet Union the men of the Truman administration believed that one of the principal handicaps under which the United States labored was the very democracy it was defending. As late as 1950 they were doubtful of their ability to persuade the American people to support permanent mobilization for a strange, unending war for peace. In NSC 68, a top-secret strategy paper prepared under the auspices of the secretaries of state and defense in February and March of that year, one can detect more than a trace of envy for Communist regimes that do not have to put up with public opinion.

This comprehensive policy review was prompted by a series of alarming events. In the fall of 1949 the Soviet Union had exploded an atomic device and set up the German Democratic Republic, signaling its intention to hold on to a half of Hitler's Reich. The division of Europe had already happened. On February 14, 1950, Stalin signed a treaty of friendship with Mao Tse-tung, who had recently proclaimed the world's most populous nation a Communist "People's Republic." To Dean Acheson and Paul Nitze, the principal author of NSC 68, these were acts of confrontation verging on recklessness. Nitze, a protégé of Forrestal's at Dillon, Read, pushed by Kennan in the State Department, was a convert from prewar isolationism. Convinced that American power was all that stood between the dark forces of totalitarianism and the abyss, he spent his life planning Cold War strategy—from Truman's time to Reagan's.[1]

NSC 68 presented a stark Manichean picture of the world. The Soviet Union, "animated by a new fanatic faith, antithetical to our own . . . seeks to impose its absolute authority over the rest of the world."[2] Nitze was convinced that the Soviet Union was committed to the "defeat" of the United States. But he was personally convinced that Stalin was not "preparing to launch in the near future an all-out military attack on the West." (Pentagon planners did not think the Soviet Union would be ready for war for ten, possibly twenty years.) The immediate danger was political, not military. NSC 68 warned that the Allies in Western Europe might "as a result of a sense of frustration or of Soviet intimidation drift into a course of neutrality eventually leading to Soviet domination."[3] When the Soviets had the capability of delivering atomic bombs on the United States, they would step up their political and military pressure on Europe. The year of "maximum danger" would be 1954. Since the Soviet system was inherently evil, conflict with the United States was "endemic." The United States should, therefore, not merely contain the outward thrust of Soviet power but "foster the seeds of destruction within the Soviet system."

Faced with this challenge, the authors worried little about the implications for either the American economy or for democratic institutions. "The integrity of our system will not be jeopardized by any measures, covert or overt, violent or non-violent, which serve the purposes of frustrating the Kremlin design." Instead the concern was public opinion. Permanent mobilization would require a fourfold increase in military spending, from $13 billion to almost $50 billion. This would mean permanent high taxes. If the president needed tens of billions a year every year to defend the nation, he would have to make his case year after year. The new importance of money in the conduct of foreign policy meant a more important role in foreign affairs for the House of Representatives, where appropriations bills originate. Since House members must defend themselves to the electorate every two years, the making of foreign policy was now more vulnerable to the vagaries of public opinion than ever before.

In March 1950, while NSC 68 was in preparation, the assistant secretary of state for public affairs, Edward W. Barrett, reported on the department's weekly study of the media and public opinion polls. The surveys showed that while most Americans were "prepared for a period of protracted tension in East-West relations" and strongly supported a more vigorous anti-Soviet policy, nothing suggested that they were willing to pay for it. There was always a danger that a taxpayer revolt could frustrate the evolving national strategy. Harry Truman had gone on record in the 1948 campaign in favor of a $15 billion ceiling on military spending. In 1949 the United States was recovering from its first postwar recession, and most businessmen and legislators agreed with the conservative Democrat George Mahon, chairman of the Defense Appropriations Subcommittee, who told the House that "nothing would please a potential enemy better than to have us bankrupt our country and destroy our economy by maintaining over a period of years complete readiness for armed conflict."[4] Truman had selected as secretary of defense Louis Johnson, who espoused exactly the same philosophy. Nitze and the other drafters of NSC 68 believed the opposite. The economy was slowing, and a massive increase in military spending would be a shot in the arm. Leon Keyserling, chairman of the Council of Economic Advisers, thought that the United States could spend as much as 20 percent of its gross national product on arms, and the result would be prosperity, not bankruptcy. But military Keynesianism, soon to become the economic assumption on which the bipartisan national security consensus rested, was a radical notion in 1950, especially among conservatives. Receiving the paper a few weeks before the outbreak of the Korean War, Truman was convinced that public opinion would never support "doubling or tripling the budget, increasing taxes heavily, and imposing various kinds of economic controls."[5]

A second concern was that the American people might not have the staying power for protracted conflict. The great advantage that the Soviet Union enjoyed in the struggle was that the Kremlin leadership "does not have to be responsive in any important sense to public opinion." The problems of the Soviet Union were material; the Soviet economy might in the end prove incapable of supporting permanent war with the world's mightiest power. But the vulnerability of the United States had to do with the spirit of the nation. "Our fundamental purpose is more likely to be defeated from lack of the will to maintain it, than from any mistakes we may make or assault we may undergo because of asserting that will." The great question posed by NSC 68 was whether "our free society" would be able to resist "a foreign power so implacable in its purpose to destroy ours, so capable of turning to its own uses the most dangerous and divisive trends in our society." A democracy "can compensate for its natural vulnerability only if it maintains clearly superior overall power."[6]

Even as technology was turning the American people into essential combatants in the war to prevent war, skepticism about the public was growing. The Jeffersonian conception of a citizen— someone who is knowledgeable, educable, and rational—now seemed quaint. Civics-book optimism about American democracy —the idea that expanded suffrage, electoral reforms, and the spread of public education would make popular sovereignty work—no longer fit modern mass society. "If the voter cannot grasp the details of the problems . . . because he has not the time, the interest or the knowledge," Walter Lippmann had written in *The Phantom Public* a generation before, "he will not have a better public opinion because he is asked to express his opinion more often."[7] It was a "false ideal" to imagine that voters were "inherently competent" to give direction to public affairs. The book had provoked considerable outrage in 1925, but though long forgotten, its pessimistic message now seemed vindicated by the worldwide crisis of democracy of the 1930s and 1940s.

The memory of crowds screaming "Heil Hitler!," the Stalin worship in the Soviet Union, and George Orwell's 1949 fable of the postdemocratic age, *Nineteen Eighty-Four*, were the images that formed the political consciousness of the postwar generation. The Cold War began in the shadows of a post-Auschwitz world far removed from the pastoral innocence of Jefferson's republic. To encourage hope based on the capacity of the average citizen to govern was to promote dangerous illusions, for Hitler and Stalin demonstrated how easily populist yearnings turn into nightmares. José Ortega y Gasset's *The Revolt of the Masses* (1930) was the most influential of a whole genre lamenting the death of democracy at the hands of what he called "hyperdemocracy." Because of the rootlessness of modern life, the mob was now in control, crushing beneath it "everything that is excellent, individual, qualified, and select." In the 1930s, as Peter Drucker had put it, the masses had turned to the magician "who promises to make the impossible possible." Works such as these frightened influential Americans, among them Henry Luce, who vowed that his magazines would enlighten and instruct American opinion in the excellence of moderation.[8]

The unflattering view of public opinion in the highest reaches of government was reinforced by the new social science. Harold Lasswell, drawing on Freud's probings of the subconscious, had explored the psychopathology of politics: Both leaders and the followers who assent to their rule act out of personal psychological needs and anxieties, not rational deliberation and judgment. The consent of the governed is won in large measure by using political symbols to manipulate mass feelings, never more so than when the fate of the nation is at stake. The more apathetic the citizen, the more vulnerable he or she is to demagogic appeals and the more resistant to reason. Apathy increases with distance. (A shooting of one individual on the block arouses more interest than the deaths of hundreds of thousands in Africa.) Citizens are more easily subject to manipulation on issues of foreign policy than on local affairs for they are less able to test reality against personal experience. Because of the complexity and remoteness of world affairs, citizens feel a special need for official truth whenever, as at the dawn of the atomic age, foreign affairs become too threatening to be ignored. When citizens are confused and frightened, "insiders" with the mantle of authority and the claim of special information enjoy considerable latitude to engineer consent to whatever policies they wish to pursue, provided only that they can create a compelling simplification of a confusing world. In his influential wartime book *Escape from Freedom*, Erich Fromm offered a chilling psychological explanation for why people so fear freedom that they barter it for social order.

Theorists of public opinion contributed to the pessimism about the vulnerability of the public to mass manipulation. While George Gallup continued to argue that polling could make democracy function better, other analysts of polling data were coming to very different conclusions. Polling revealed how naive it was to assume that citizens could be informed enough to participate intelligently on complex issues of foreign affairs. In 1949 Martin Kriesberg, reviewing a variety of early postwar polls, sketched what he called the "dark areas of ignorance" of the American people; 30 percent of Americans were "unaware of almost any given event in American foreign policy." Forty-five percent of the population were "aware but uninformed," and less than 25 percent showed "knowledge of foreign problems."[9] (A conspicuous exception was the dropping of the atomic bomb. An astounding 98 percent, according to one poll taken after Hiroshima, claimed to have heard of the event.[10] Despite the preoccupation with Communism, few Americans could identify which countries were Communist and which were not. The polls also detected a high level of resignation about nuclear war. In the summer of 1946 Leonard Cottrell and Sylvia Eberhart found that more than half the respondents in their survey expected a nuclear war within ten years. When asked whether they were worried about the prospect, typical answers were: "What's the use?" "I'm not worried. It wouldn't do me any good," or, "No, I don't care. I got everything I need." Other academic analysts concluded that opinion on foreign issues was highly volatile. The answers varied dramatically depending upon how and when the questions were asked. Polling could provide guidance for the management of public opinion, but the voice of the people was too unsteady and too uninformed to provide guidance for policy. In his influential 1950 study, *The American People and Foreign Policy*, the Princeton social scientist Gabriel Almond summed up the prevailing view: "The American foreign policy mood is permissive; it will follow the lead of the policy elites if they demonstrate unity and resolution."[11]

Students of American character reinforced these views. While Americans celebrated individualism in their economic life, in cultural and political matters the habit of conformity was deeply ingrained. As early as 1835 Harriet Martineau had noted that the "worship of Opinion"—by which she meant the dominant opinion —"is, at this day, the established religion of the United States."[12] Even that celebrator of American democracy Lord Bryce noted that Americans demonstrate "a disposition to fall into line, to acquiesce in the dominant opinion."[13] In 1950, in *The Lonely Crowd*, David Riesman built a whole social theory on the idea that the post-World War II generation of Americans was "other-directed" and looked to the mass culture to define their values for them. The book, which became a best-seller, appeared just as Senator Joseph R. McCarthy was gathering enthusiastic popular support for an anti-Communist crusade.

Tocqueville had raised the question whether the citizens in a democracy had the "perseverance" needed for the conduct of foreign policy. Acheson was convinced that the chief character flaw of Americans was impatience. They call problems "headaches," he would say, as if you could dispatch them by taking an aspirin. Now for the first time, the United States had a chronic national security crisis, for the struggle with the Soviet Union and world Communism would last a generation or more. The great danger was that the American people would grow tired of the struggle and allow themselves to be seduced into defeat by threats and blandishments. Equally dangerous, the American people might be aroused by talk of "preventive war" into demanding a reckless policy. Several congressmen reported to the State Department that their mail reflected "increasing public pressure, which could become dangerous, for some sort of bold action." In the early postwar years there were voices in the land—among them the secretary of the navy—arguing that it was time to "get it over with" in the fight with Russia before Stalin got the means to deliver the bomb. The alternative to a real war was to be "nibbled to death" while pursuing expensive, inconclusive strategies for countering Soviet expansionism.

But preventive war, NSC 68 concluded, was no solution. Stating that there is a "powerful argument" that only "under the crisis of war" would the people support mobilization, the secret study concluded, nevertheless, that a strike at the Soviet Union would be "generally unacceptable" to Americans. The document noted, moreover, that an attack "with atomic weapons" on the Soviet Union "would not force or induce the Kremlin to capitulate and the Kremlin will still be able to use the forces under its control to dominate most or all of Eurasia." Because many Americans would doubt that this was a "just war" and many more in other countries would consider the American surprise attack repugnant, victory in battle, even if it could be achieved, would not bring "victory in the fundamental ideological conflict."[14] Thus the only alternative was to mobilize the country for what Robert Lovett, the deputy secretary of defense, called a protracted "mortal conflict" in which "death comes more slowly and in a different fashion."

2.

The concerns that kept State Department officials up late at night writing secret papers—power vacuums, nuclear deterrence, the fight against European "neutralism," and ideological jousting with the Soviets—meant very little to what Acheson called the mythical average citizen. The new consensus was buttressed by strong popular fear and the almost complete absence of credible alternative policies. By 1950 the only two plausible alternative directions to surface in American political debate had been discredited by a concerted national history lesson from pulpits, radio, television, editorial pages, and, most importantly, from the White House. The Fortress America policy favored by Senator Taft, Joseph Kennedy, and Herbert Hoover was tagged as the new "isolationism"; it had failed in the fight against Hitler and it would fail against Stalin. Henry Wallace's plea for greater emphasis on diplomacy and for more reliance on America's overwhelming economic power instead of the military was discredited as appeasement. Wallace himself, thanks to the key participation of old left-wingers in the Progressive Party and Truman's political strategy, had been tarred as a Communist dupe.

The glue of the new consensus was anti-Communism, for here was the issue that brought foreign policy home. As a result of massive education campaigns by government, business, churches, and the media, the issues of Soviet foreign policy and the influence of domestic Communism in American life were neatly merged in the public consciousness. It was entirely predictable that Russia and America, two great continental powers each imbued with missionary spirit, should have emerged from the war as rivals. (Tocqueville had predicted the competition of the two great land masses more than a hundred years before.) But it is not obvious why anti-Communist hysteria swept America in the late 1940s. Nothing of the sort occurred in France or Italy, two societies in the path of Soviet tanks, each with a large Communist Party. There were never more than 100,000 Communists in the United States, even in the Depression, and though conspiratorial in demeanor and beguiled by the totalitarian myths of Stalinism, few American Communists did anything illegal or disloyal. In its heyday the party put its stamp on American politics principally by union organizing, exerting a certain influence in Hollywood films, and providing energy to the civil rights movement, activities that were controversial but hardly treasonous. But the announcement by the FBI in early 1946 of the Communist spy ring in Canada and the allegations of spying in high places under the New Deal, culminating in the perjury conviction of Alger Hiss in January 1950, provided the crucial ingredient for branding left-wing activists traitors. Any American who for whatever reason favored policies supported by the Communist apparatus was also suspect. If Stalin was against the Truman Doctrine, the rearmament of Germany, and the atomic bomb, surely it was unpatriotic for loyal Americans not to be for them.

Every major institution in American life was now engaged in the effort to influence popular opinion in the direction of the new orthodoxy. The rapidity with which Americans changed their minds about fundamental national security concerns—the Russians, the United Nations, maintaining a large military, massive foreign aid, foreign military involvement—was attributable in large part to the extraordinary coincidence of imagery, rhetoric, and prescription employed by a wide variety of American opinion leaders. McCarthyism was the product of this remarkable elite consensus on the nature of the national security threat, not its source, but the extremism of the Wisconsin senator helped to solidify the consensus by making it appear moderate in comparison with his own recklessness. Before McCarthy gained national attention, opinion leaders in churches, unions, business organizations, and in the media had already delivered the essence of his message.

Although government agencies such as the FBI actively sought to shape public opinion, the new conformity was not orchestrated by the Truman administration and did not always serve its interests. How then can it be explained? The conventional assumption is that Stalin's behavior was so obviously threatening and his rule so immoral that the concerted response in America was inevitable. There are difficulties with such explanations. True, Russia under Stalin would, at the very least, have taken the place Britain held for most of our history. But it was not obvious that Stalin's Russia should have been so quickly and so universally feared as an evil empire bent on world conquest. To be sure, "Communism" was a dirty word in the United States even before the Russian Revolution; American officials applied the word to the Mexican Revolution of 1910. After the Bolsheviks came to power even the names of Communists assumed magical properties. An ordinance adopted in Cambridge, Massachusetts, in the 1920s made it a crime to shelve any book containing the words "Lenin" or "Leningrad." Communism challenged American ideas of private property, individual freedom, and religion. But it was not ordained that anti-Communism should become the organizing principle of American political life for two generations.

There were, of course, alternative ways to analyze the phenomenon of Communism. George Kennan's, for example. By 1950 the man who had coined the word "containment" had left government service, disillusioned by what he considered the hyperbolic response to Stalin and by the Cold War hysteria it was engendering. The other top Soviet expert in the State Department, Charles Bohlen, also believed that Stalin had neither the intention nor the capability to embark upon the Hitler-like plan for world conquest now automatically ascribed to him in secret planning documents and comic strips alike. It was not inevitable that either competition with Russia or antipathy to Communism should have produced the Truman foreign policy. (Kennan favored a "military facade to quiet the anxieties of the jittery Western Europeans" and negotiations for the "retirement of Soviet forces" from Central Europe, which could have been purchased at the price of the neutralization of Germany.[15] But no serious public debate on alternative strategy ever took place in 1949 either within the government or outside it.) The Cold War analysis, like any set of ideas about national security, was a simplification of reality. Official truth necessarily rested on selective attention to the extraordinary turmoil of the immediate postwar era and summary judgment about the significance of complex events. Crucial components of the official worldview were exaggerated. For example, the most alarming evidence that Stalin had plans for military aggression was the "fact" that he kept his vast armies more or less intact while the United States disarmed. But the Soviet leader actually demobilized his forces far more than American officials indicated at the time. The disparity between American forces and the Soviet Army was nowhere near so large as represented, and American Intelligence knew that Stalin was not ready for war.[16]

Conversely, some of the most disturbing facts about the Soviet Union were not widely known at the time. Stalin's greatest crimes, the liquidation of the kulaks in the 1930s and the massive scale of the purges, were unknown even to moderately well-informed newspaper readers in the United States until Khrushchev's revelations in 1956. (The exceptions were a few Soviet specialists, liberals concerned with human rights like John Dewey, and disillusioned former Communists who were caught up in the backwash of the Stalin purges.)

Moreover, the fateful implications of the new Cold War policy received little attention in public discussion. Thus the heart of the new policy was an alliance with West Germany and the rearmament of a society that had closed its eyes to the slaughter of more than six million men, women, and children in its midst. Why was American public opinion so ready to embrace a chunk of the former evil empire barely three years after the exposé of the Holocaust and the end of Hitler's war? Why did voices counseling caution and moderation in embracing the Cold War worldview fall silent so quickly? How was the new public mood in support of Cold War orthodoxy created?

The best answer to the last question is that the Cold War message was everywhere. A small child could begin the day with the comics and find Little Orphan Annie in the clutches of atomic spies working for Moscow and after school could watch the television show "The Atom Squad," which also fused the two political terrors of the day, The Bomb and The Reds.[17] At school these fears were driven home. As they hid under their desks after receiving the order to "Duck and Cover," the children were instructed in the importance of keeping calm during the blast. In 1951 the Federal Civil Defense Administration distributed twenty million copies of *Survival under*

Atomic Attack, and a film of the same name sold more prints than any film in history, up to that time.[18]

Fear of The Bomb preceded panic about Communism and the Soviet Union. Ironically, the nuclear panic that contributed to the Cold War hysteria was initially spread by groups seeking to shock the public into supporting the control of atomic energy. On the first anniversary of Hiroshima, the World Federalists sponsored a show on ABC radio that began with the wail of a small boy: "What's happening to my arm?" His mother shrieks, "Look! . . . his left arm is gone! And his right arm is slowly—Eeeee!" The agonized cry introduced a call to world federalism. The columnists Joseph and Stewart Alsop, along with other prominent publicists, tried to stir up public support for the Baruch Plan, the official disarmament proposals, with a scare article in *The Saturday Evening Post*, "Your Flesh *Should* Creep." Jane Fonda recalls a radio special, "The Fifth Horseman," which she heard as a child, because "it frightened me more than anything I can remember. . . . Because of that radio show I've always thought . . . we were playing God by creating such weapons."[19] Soon Conelrad, the emergency warning network, was periodically interrupting scheduled broadcasts. The scary fantasies merged into daily life.

Nuclear fear, to use the title of Spencer Weart's book on how images of The Bomb have shaped American consciousness, prepared the psychological ground for the anti-Communist panic. In the immediate aftermath of Hiroshima and Nagasaki, as Weart summarizes the polling data, "a majority of Americans foresaw a real danger of their families dying in atomic attacks, along with most of the people in the world's cities." By the end of 1946, however, the immediacy of the threat seems to have dissolved; the apocalypse became more hypothetical and distant. People responded with professions of confidence that the government, the scientists, or God would come up with some protection. But even a superficial probing revealed how hollow was the cheer and how deep the resignation and despair just below the surface.

As the realization grew after the failure of early disarmament efforts that The Bomb was here to stay, anxiety about it was displaced onto the Russians. The Bomb was something beyond human control. The Soviet Union was a flesh-and-blood enemy like Nazi Germany. The power of America and the justice of its cause had vanquished two totalitarian empires. With The Bomb at its command, it could handle a third. The most famous popular fantasy depicting nuclear triumph over Russia was the October 27, 1951, issue of *Collier's* devoted to "The War We Do Not Want," which showed in graphic detail a future American nuclear attack, invasion, occupation, and massive reeducation campaign to cleanse Russia of Communism.

The Bomb also became the most dramatic and concrete symbol of Soviet hostility. In the early postwar years Americans were preoccupied with the "secret" of the atom. Americans need not be concerned, insisted General Leslie Groves, the head of the Manhattan Project under which The Bomb had been built, because the Soviet Union would not be able to produce the atom bomb for years. But the mythic secret—some talked about the scientific knowledge behind The Bomb as if it were the forbidden fruit ripped from the Tree of Knowledge—was itself a myth. There were enormous obstacles to building nuclear weapons, but there was no secret once it had been demonstrated to the world that they could be made. Nonetheless, the espionage of Klaus Fuchs and others shortened the time it took the Soviets to explode their first nuclear device. In stealing "the secret," Stalin had seized the Promethean fire that the United States in its generosity had offered to give up to international control. In sentencing the convicted atomic spies Ethel and Julius Rosenberg in 1951, Judge Irving Kaufman, who had decided upon the death sentence even before their conviction, pronounced their crime worse than murder. They had given the weapon of annihilation to the enemy. Thus, he said, they bore responsibility for the Korean War.[20]

Each major institution of American life produced its own Cold War educators, for each had its own compelling reasons either to invest in anti-Communism or not to resist the wave of anti-Communist feeling. As the war ended, the business community was divided. Business leaders who had gone to work for the war effort, such as Donald Nelson, formerly of Sears Roebuck, and Eric Johnston of the Chamber of Commerce, were optimistic about trade with the Soviet Union. *Fortune*, also upbeat about the Soviet market, suggested that "Russia is in many ways not so very different from the U.S. under the New Deal." Coming from Roosevelt-hating Henry Luce, this peculiar assessment fell short of an enthusiastic endorsement. But sympathetic articles on the Soviet Union were to be found even in the Chamber of Commerce publication, *Nation's Business*, where one writer concluded that Stalin was up to nothing more sinister in Eastern Europe than the establishment of "security zones against political aggression."

The conservative wing of the business community, however, soon reverted to its traditional anti-Communist stance. Shocked by the wave of strikes sweeping through major American industries in the first two years after the war, the Chamber of Commerce organized a nationwide education campaign to alert the country to the menace of Communism. Francis P. Matthews, an insurance executive who had been head of the Knights of Columbus, became the chairman, and he recruited educators who could match his zeal. (Appointed secretary of the navy a few years later, he spoke out in favor of "preventive war." The United States, being the "repository" of the Ark of the Covenant and "custodians" of the Holy Grail, should initiate "a war of aggression" and "become the first aggressors for peace.") On October 7, 1946, he released a document originally written as a secret report to the U.S. Catholic bishops by Father John F. Cronin entitled "Communist Infiltration in the United States" and followed it up with charges that "about 400" Communists held "positions of importance in Washington." The campaign used the Communist issue effectively to discredit the New Deal, add weight to the rightward push in the political climate, and, most importantly, to launch a campaign against the militant unions. Communists had gained control of twenty major unions, the Chamber charged, and they operated as a "transmission belt" from Moscow. Whoever stirs up "needless strife" in American labor relations "advances the cause of Communism." One enthusiastic organizer for the Chamber wrote Matthews in January 1946, at the crest of the strike wave, "We will have to set up some firing squads in every good sized city and town in the country and . . . liquidate the Reds and Pink Benedict Arnolds." The Chamber pushed Truman to adopt a loyalty program, and while it supported the Truman Doctrine and the Marshall Plan, it used the Communist issue to agitate for an even tougher policy toward the Soviet Union and a crackdown on dissent from the new Cold War orthodoxy. In a five-month period the Chamber issued three reports with a combined circulation of almost one million copies.

The National Association of Manufacturers used the Communist issue to attack organized labor and the New Deal. "The trend toward Socialism in America has been the theme of more than sixty of my speeches during the last year," D. A. Hulcy, an NAM executive, reported proudly in 1952. "Socialism is junior-grade Communism looking for promotion." The NAM and the Chamber aimed their campaigns at small-business men and veterans hoping to become entrepreneurs. Associating the Wagner Act and other

prolabor legislation with Moscow's grand design helped build the
political climate for the Taft-Hartley law, which greatly cut back
labor's power and reversed the thrust of the New Deal in labor
relations.[21]

The business organizations worked closely with veterans' groups
in educating the American people to what they called the "realities"
of the Cold War. The American Legion, an organization with seventeen thousand posts and more than three million members, most
of whom were farmers, small-business men, and skilled workers,
had an Americanism Commission which campaigned throughout
the American heartland against unions, giveaways, and the U.N.
The Legion was an effective lobby for bigger military budgets and
for anti-Communist legislation. J. Edgar Hoover was a frequent
guest at Legion conventions. In 1950 to great applause he proposed
that all members of the Communist Party be interned and tried for
treason.[22]

Each private association was reinforcing Cold War orthodoxy because the Communist issue served its own institutional purposes.
The labor unions were no exception. Here was the one place in
American life where Communist influence at the end of the war
was considerable. Even before the Congress of Industrial Organizations (CIO) was formed in 1938, John L. Lewis had eagerly accepted the energy, drive, and skills of Communist organizers. It was
the time of the Popular Front, and Communist Party members and
loyalists were in a position to exercise control or major influence in
at least 40 percent of the CIO unions. Communist union officials
followed each twist of Soviet policy and attacked those who didn't
as tools of Wall Street. So when the war ended there was already a
history of conflict between the Communists and the non-Commu-
nists in the CIO. In 1946 the Communists controlled unions with
about 15 percent of the membership of the organized labor movement. But in that year union officials who depended upon Communist support were challenged by candidates running on an anti-
Communist platform, most notably Walter Reuther, who was
elected president of the United Automobile Workers. The next year
the United Electrical Workers and ten other Communist-domi-
nated unions were thrown out of the CIO for "disloyalty to the
CIO" and "dedication to the purposes and program of the Communist Party."[23] Under President Philip Murray, the CIO adopted
resolutions in support of the Truman-Acheson foreign policy. The
campaign against Communists within the unions was strengthened
by Cold War patriotism as the left-wing staffs in the education de-

partments of the unions were replaced by anti-Communists. Thus millions of American workers now heard much the same message that was being promoted by business groups. American workers should be against Communism not only to protect God, country, family, and the American way of life but also to express solidarity for repressed workers, for nowhere in Stalin's domain did a free labor movement exist. In 1948 American workers contributed thousands of dollars at the urging of their churches and the unions to defeat the Communist unions from taking political power in Italy.

For many Americans the Communist issue was brought home by the churches. The postwar era coincided with a boom in organized religion. By 1950, 57 percent of American families were church members; ten years later more than 63 percent of Americans so identified themselves. (At the time of the Civil War, church membership had been about 20 percent.) Between 1949 and 1953 Bible sales rose dramatically. Congress established a prayer room in the Capitol, and legislated the inclusion of "Under God" in the Pledge of Allegiance and the engraving of "In God We Trust" on every coin.[24]

The official promotion of what the theologian Will Herberg called "civic religion" was much more than a response to atheistic Communism. The war, the Holocaust, the postwar strains of family life, and the assault on small-town values as the country became a national market wired coast to coast by radio and television inspired a longing for the two great gifts of religion—solace and meaning. The upbeat nondenominational Protestantism of Norman Vincent Peale and the therapeutic message of Rabbi Joshua Loth Liebman offered the former. These popular clergymen emphasized positive American values and personal fulfillment and gave little attention to the Red scare. Peale's A Guide to Confident Living (1948) and his The Power of Positive Thinking (1952) were huge best-sellers as was Liebman's Peace of Mind (1946). The God of Norman Vincent Peale was a celestial uncle, kindly, brimming with optimism, and eager to reward hardworking and right-thinking Americans. Peale's uplifting message "How to Think Your Way to Success" was fortuitously timed to coincide with the mass marketing of paperback books.

Monsignor Fulton J. Sheen and the Reverend Billy Graham stressed meaning over solace. With his burning eyes and an orotund style leavened with flashes of wit, Sheen became one of the first television stars. His weekly program, "Life Is Worth Living," often drew a larger audience than did Milton Berle, the most popular comedian of the day. The program was a vehicle for attacking America's "spiritual vacuum" and for explaining how patriotism rooted in anti-Communism could give new purpose to life. Off camera, Sheen was also an influential participant in the anti-Communist crusade. He had converted Clare Boothe Luce and the two most famous reformed Communists, Louis Budenz and Elizabeth Bentley, who launched new careers as witnesses before congressional committees. In his book *Communism and the Conscience of the West* he exhorted Americans to take on the passion and commitment of the enemy.

Billy Graham was even better known. By the mid-1950s his radio show had twenty million regular listeners. "Either Communism must die, or Christianity must die," he preached.[25] He focused on the blasphemous appeal of Communism, not only its defiance of God but its heretical celebration of government. With great passion he called for a profound moral awakening. In late 1949 William Randolph Hearst, a collector of religious art but not a notably religious man, sent a telegram to all his editors, "Puff Graham."[26] Hearst had shed his isolationist leanings of the 1930s and was now a crusader against Stalin. The Los Angeles *Examiner* carried banner headlines and the Hearst empire—movies, newsreels, magazines as well as newspapers—fell into line, helping to make the evangelist a world figure. In February 1950 Graham met Henry Luce at the governor's mansion in South Carolina and they sat up half the night together. Luce, who had appointed the former Communist Whittaker Chambers as Foreign News editor, shared his view that the Soviet Union's primary purpose was the "conquest of the world." He saw his task as educating the American people for the American Century, alerting them to the inevitability of conflict and the perils of Communism. "*Time* and *Life* began carrying everything I did, it seemed like," Graham later recalled. "They gave me a tremendous push." In 1954 he appeared on the cover of *Time*.[27]

The most politically powerful Catholic voice in the fight against Communism was Francis Cardinal Spellman. In early 1946, according to an FBI memorandum of the conversation, he promised to help the Bureau "ferret out and eliminate the Communists and fellow travelers who are in positions of control in labor unions." His articles on Communism began appearing in *Cosmopolitan*, *Good Housekeeping*, and *Reader's Digest*.[28] It was he who arranged the Saint Patrick's Day dinner in 1948 at which Harry Truman denounced "Henry Wallace and his Communists."

The Catholic Church was more than a tireless educator in the fight against Stalin; unlike the mainline Protestant churches it was a combatant. Spellman was determined to enlist American opinion and American money in behalf of the beleaguered Church in Eastern Europe. In Yugoslavia, Tito had imprisoned Archbishop Stepinac of Zagreb for collaborating with the Germans during the war, and in Hungary, Cardinal Mindszenty had been condemned to death as part of Stalin's campaign to break the power of the Church. From the pulpit in St. Patrick's Spellman inveighed, "Help save civilization from the world's most fiendish, ghoulish men of slaughter."[29] In July 1949, Pope Pius XII issued a decree warning that Catholics who "defend and spread the materialistic and anti-Christian doctrine of Communism" would be excommunicated.[30]

The Federal Council of Churches in America, later renamed National Council of Churches, was much less hawkish than the Catholic hierarchy. "Our people should not rely on military strategy to meet Communist aggression," the Council declared in 1948. "Such reliance is more apt to bring war than prevent it." Two years later, just as the Chinese entered the Korean War, Henry Knox Sherrill, the president of the National Council, wrote Truman that a "preponderant majority" in the church leadership "reluctantly accept the necessity of military strength to serve as a deterrent to aggression," but "it is the prevailing opinion . . . that the government must resist the hysteria which would call for the use of the atomic bomb without regard for larger moral and political considerations."[31] Except for a small pacifist wing in both the Catholic and Protestant churches the increasingly authoritative voice of organized religion lent strong support to the emerging consensus. No church figure commanding a wide audience challenged the morality of basing the nation's security on the threat to use weapons of mass destruction.

In the climate of the late 1940s the universities were incapacitated from challenging the conventional wisdom and offering alternative views of world developments and how to deal with them. Thus American society was deprived of ballast at exactly the moment it was most needed. Government contracts and grants in the social sciences, the increasing role of classified research on the campus, and the need for government clearances to work on such projects meant that at the leading universities scholars became part of the government team; academic prestige in the social sciences was now measured by "relevance" to the gathering national security crisis and by "access" to power. Criticism of government in academia by no means disappeared, but the limits of acceptable criticism were narrow. Government money was flowing into area studies—for example, a large, classified Air Force project involving interviews of Russian defectors provided the major funding for Harvard's Russian Research Center—and promising careers as policy researchers and analysts depended upon having acceptable politics.

McCarthy and his admirers in state legislatures and in the U.S. Congress saw the universities as hotbeds of Communist subversion. Professors were hounded out of their jobs for their views, for past membership in the Communist Party, for being unwilling to "name names" of other radicals they had encountered in their brush with Stalinism. Communists, James Bryant Conant of Harvard declared in 1949, "are out of bounds as members of the teaching profession" because "conspiracy and calculated deceit have been and are the characteristic pattern . . . of regular Communists all over the world." The National Education Association declared that Communists, having surrendered their intellectual integrity, were unfit to serve as teachers on any level. Charles Seymour, president of Yale, bristled at the suggestion that academic freedom was being endangered by witch-hunts. "There will be no witch-hunts at Yale," he declared, "because there will be no witches."[32]

The Communist issue poisoned the atmosphere in universities. Even if one accepted the orthodoxy, that being a "card-carrying Communist" was conclusive evidence of unfitness to teach, the problem was not resolved. Obviously, the more conspiratorial the professor, the less likely he was to admit it. In the spring of 1949 the regents of the University of California voted to make all university employees swear that they were not members of the Communist Party. In Oklahoma, professors had to swear that they were not members of any organization deemed to be "subversive" by the attorney general or any "other . . . public agency of the United States."[33] By the late 1950s two-thirds of the states required similar oaths. In the universities, professors talked and wrote about "defending freedom" but few there were who felt free to challenge Cold War orthodoxy.

The national "media"—the word was not then current—magnified the fears that were gripping American society by simply mirroring them. This happened in several ways. Performers, writers, and musicians were blacklisted; two former FBI employees launched a newsletter to expose "Communists" in broadcasting. Its report, *Red Channels*, "cited" 151 individuals, including Leonard Bernstein and Orson Welles, for such traitorous activities as supporting Russian War Relief and voting for Henry Wallace. Radio personalities with "controversial" views lost their audience. William L. Shirer, the famous CBS war correspondent, was dropped as a prime-time radio commentator in 1947 because his sponsor, the J. B. Williams Company, and the advertising firm handling the account did not like his politics. Shirer had criticized the loyalty program and the Truman Doctrine and did not share the sponsor's enthusiasm for Chiang Kai-shek.[34]

It was in Hollywood, however, that the cultural sea change became most visible. In 1944 the actors Adolphe Menjou, John Wayne, and others had formed the Motion Picture Alliance for the Preservation of American Ideals, an organization to oppose Communism in general and the Hollywood unions in particular. As president, John Wayne worked for a law requiring all Communists in Los Angeles to be registered. These early efforts were not popular in the film community, for many saw them simply as antiunion, but by 1948 the actor Ronald Reagan and an A.F. of L. union organizer by the name of Roy Brewer formed two new anti-Communist organizations in Hollywood, the Labor League of Hollywood Voters and the Motion Picture Industrial Council, to certify the anti-Communist credentials of candidates for office and to mount a public relations campaign to convince the moviegoing public that Hollywood had rid itself of Communist influence. Reagan told the FBI, according to a November 14, 1947, Bureau memorandum, that the Council, which was headed by the industry's most powerful producer, Louis B. Mayer, was designed to "purge" the industry. This was a job the government should be doing by simply outlawing the Communist Party, he said, but in the meantime the industry would do its own policing.[35]

In November 1947 several producers suspended a group of writers who refused to cooperate with a House Un-American Activities investigation of Hollywood, the Hollywood Ten, as they came to be known, using the standard contract clause permitting dismissal on grounds of "morals." Reagan, now president of the Screen Actors Guild, declared that actors who had "so offended public opinion" as to make themselves "unsaleable at the box office" would not be supported by the Guild. Years later Reagan and the actor George Murphy, briefly a senator from California, denied that there ever was a Hollywood blacklist. "That was a lot of horseshit," said John Wayne. "The only thing our side did that was anywhere near black listing was just running a lot of people out of the business."[36]

Communists were now substituted for the Nazis and "Japs" of the wartime years. The industry also adapted the formula gangster films of the 1930s to the headlines and cast American Communists as mobsters, complete with molls, machine guns, and deluxe hideouts. In *Walk East on Beacon* (1952) the Al Capone figure is Gerhard Eisler, a Communist whose escape to East Germany had recently made headlines. He is shown eating caviar and sipping champagne as he explains to the FBI informant how "it's the way we're all going to live after the revolution," except of course that "the workers will ALWAYS be workers!" In such films as *I Was a Communist for the FBI* (1951) and *The Woman on Pier 13* (1950), moviegoers were shown the brutality, cynicism, and the five-o'clock shadows of the "slimy red," to use the epithet employed by the FBI hero in one film. In *Crime of the Century* (1952) the point was driven home that the freedoms guaranteed in the Bill of Rights were available only to "loyal Americans."[37]

While some Hollywood producers saw themselves as having a duty to propagandize in behalf of the American way of life—Jack Warner personally supervised a film designed for recruits in the armed forces called *Red Nightmare* showing what would happen to an average American family under Communism—most filmmakers saw anti-Communism as just another fashionable fear on which some money might be made. These films were generally panned for their art, though little was said about their politics, and they were not box-office hits. But they helped to complete the educational circuit by repackaging as entertainment the political message of the day.

Why were there so few prophetic voices to challenge the hysteria? Or were they there but simply drowned out in the institutional clamor? The most powerful intellectual voices in the land not only spoke out in support of the Cold War consensus but they shaped it. The dominant ideology of American writers, critics, and philosophers was either liberal or radical or, to use the peculiarly American term, progressive. The disillusionment of writers and artists with World War I, their sense of alienation from the banality and materialism of the roaring twenties, and, especially, the shock at the social failure of capitalism in the Great Depression had driven a number of America's most brilliant and eloquent writers to the Left. In 1931 the critic Edmund Wilson wrote an "appeal to Progressives" in the *New Republic* to vote Communist in the next election, and many rallied to the call. Liberalism, he argued, had failed. It was no longer possible to "bet" on reformed capitalism.[38] But unlike every other advanced industrial country there was no legitimate socialist party in the United States that was a serious contender even for a share in political power. Not since the People's Party had there been a mass movement in America dedicated to the radical transformation of capitalism. There was not even a labor party. Thus politically committed, radical intellectuals had the choice of joining a fringe party or remaining aloof from electoral politics and writing polemics.

By the end of the thirties the battle of the intellectuals was being carried on in "little magazines" like *Partisan Review*. Founded in 1934 by the Communist John Reed Society and reborn three years later as an anti-Stalinist publication, its circulation at the end of World War II was seven thousand. The *New Republic* (twenty eight thousand in 1939) was another important battleground for left-wing intellectuals trying to define a direction for American society and a role for themselves. The old categories seemed to make less and less sense; Stalin's "socialism" and Hitler's "national socialism" might hold out different utopias but the organization of the state and society were dishearteningly alike. By 1940 committed leftist radicals such as Max Eastman, James Burnham, and Sidney Hook had become equally committed anti-Communists. But on the role of intellectuals in the society they remained exactly where they had been. To those social critics who argued that intellectuals should stick to their last—criticize culture, not politics, and certainly not act like politicians—the former Stalinists and Trotskyites responded, though usually more elegantly, with the Stalinist slogan, "Ideas are weapons."

During the war, artists, writers, and academics had flocked to Washington to unravel enemy codes, write propaganda, control prices, and feel the exhilaration of being participants in great events. Because the Cold War was pronounced to be a clash of two secular faiths, there was suddenly a market for political ideologues to define and to defend the American faith. The old battles of the little magazines now found themselves on the editorial pages of the great newspapers. Those who had once espoused Communism could write most persuasively of its failures and its menace to American values and American hopes. Magazines like *Harper's* and *Atlantic* by the end of the war had circulations of about 150,000 and *The New Yorker* was up to 230,000 subscribers. The "serious" and "middlebrow" magazines went overwhelmingly to "opinion leaders" —the *New Republic*'s subscribers, according to its own market survey, were "upwardly mobile subscribers in their twenties and thirties" living in Washington, D.C., or in one of the "most politically significant industrial states."[39] If an article on the Cold War or the

Red menace in one of the smaller magazines was written with the right tone, it stood a good chance of being excerpted in the *Reader's Digest*, which had the largest circulation of all.

Since the Cold War started as primarily an ideological contest, many intellectuals saw themselves in the late 1940s as shock troops in the front lines. Reinhold Niebuhr, Arthur Schlesinger, Jr., and Kenneth Galbraith joined Hubert Humphrey and Eleanor Roosevelt in organizing Americans for Democratic Action, a response to the Wallace movement. Its purpose, as the historian Richard Pells puts it, was "to cleanse liberalism of any totalitarian taint." The hope for America was Keynesian economics and the reform of capitalism through the welfare state. The threat was the Soviet Union, and any American who did not see Stalin as the principal threat to peace was an enemy of liberalism.

The guiding intellectual spirit was the theologian Reinhold Niebuhr, whose powerful pen graced the pages of *Life* and whose austere face was the subject of a cover of *Time*. Once a Marxist, Niebuhr had a sense of irony that fit the times. "Man's capacity for democracy," he wrote, "makes democracy possible, but man's inclination to injustice makes democracy necessary." Jefferson could not have said it better. But democracy was under attack by the forces of totalitarianism precisely because the "children of light" had foolishly overestimated the capacity of human beings to surmount self-interest. Because they so feared power themselves, liberals had badly underestimated its lure. The "children of light" had denied the centrality of evil in human affairs, but the "children of darkness," the fascists and the Stalinists, understood the brutal realities. The survival of societies based on "openness," which became a Cold War watchword, depended upon appropriating "the wisdom of the shrewd without succumbing to their 'malice.' "[40] More than many whom he influenced, Niebuhr struggled with the contradictions in his analysis. He watched painfully as the Open Society he celebrated closed down on dissent in the name of battling the Closed Society. By the end of his life he was calling Lyndon Johnson "the Machiavelli in the White House" for the war in Vietnam. ("I am scared by my own lack of patriotism," he confessed in a letter to a fellow churchman in 1966. "For I take satisfaction in the embarrassment [of the United States] in a fantastic war."[41]

Niebuhr was not present in Berlin in June 1950, with Arthur Koestler, Arthur Schlesinger, Jr., Sidney Hook, Carson McCullers, Tennessee Williams, and James Burnham, at the founding of the Congress for Cultural Freedom, which got under way just as the news arrived that war had broken out in Korea. But he sent a telegram of endorsement. Organized by Michel Josselson and Melvin Lasky, one an alumnus of OSS and the other the editor of an American Information Service magazine in occupied Germany, the Congress in the 1950s and early 1960s was financed by the CIA. There may have been CIA money even at the outset, but the intellectuals were not pawns of government; they were enthusiastic volunteers in the ideological war, ready to replay on a world stage the old battles of the little magazines.

In Berlin, Sidney Hook sounded the theme of the Congress: ". . . instead of saying 'Neither-Nor' and looking for other viable alternatives, we must recognize an 'Either-Or' and take one stand or another."[42] To Europeans he was saying: Choose America or Russia. To Americans he was saying: Celebrate America, criticize at the margins, perhaps, but what you see is the best there is. Ironically, the very intellectuals who would in a few years proclaim the "end of ideology," advanced for themselves and for the society an ideological straightjacket. As Christopher Lasch has written, the intellectuals became anti-intellectuals, not daring to challenge their compatriots even to conceive of alternatives to a nuclear suicide pact and permanent mobilization for war.

CHAPTER 12

The Consensus Unravels:
From Korea to Vietnam

1.

The outbreak of war in Korea in June 1950 appeared to be a political opportunity for the Truman administration. Joseph Harsch of the *Christian Science Monitor* wrote that never had he "felt such a sense of relief and unity pass through" Washington.[1] Here was open military aggression, a clear and simple event that authenticated for anyone with a radio or a television set the apocalyptical worldview of NSC 68. Hitler had been dead only five years, and the familiar pictures were back: columns of advancing tanks, refugees with pushcarts, villages on fire. "By God," Harry Truman exploded to Dean Acheson as they rode together from Andrews Air Force Base to an emergency meeting at Blair House, "I'm going to let them have it."[2] Advised by Acheson not to seek prior congressional approval, Truman ordered General Douglas MacArthur to take on the North Korean invaders with the occupation troops on hand. Soon more U.S. troops were on the way. The United States Seventh Fleet took up positions near Formosa with the announced purpose of preventing a Communist invasion of that island or an attack on the mainland by the forces of Chiang Kai-shek. Secretary of State Dean Acheson, *U.S. News & World Report* noted somewhat prematurely, was now "off the hook on the Communist issue."

The support for the American military response was almost universal—the *New York Times*, the Joint Chiefs of Staff, Senator Joseph R. McCarthy, ADA, Walter Lippmann, Robert Taft, even Henry Wallace. George Kennan, now so dovish on most issues that he was about to leave the Acheson State Department, met Joseph

Alsop on a Georgetown sidewalk and did a little jig, so delighted was he that the United States, despite being a democracy, could "stand up in time of crisis."[3] Early public opinion polls revealed that 77 percent of Americans approved the prompt dispatch of American troops into the combat. Not a single major American daily expressed a word of disapproval.

Yet within weeks the consensus had melted away. The "police action," as a right-wing Republican senator enthusiastically dubbed it at the outset, had become, in Harriman's words, a "sour little war." How did this happen? By mid-July North Korean forces had pushed MacArthur's army back into a small perimeter around the post of Pusan. Columnists warned of an "American Dunkirk." The Republicans now sensed that they had a near-perfect issue on which to return to power. Suddenly the battle for democracy—legitimated by an overwhelming United Nations endorsement of the American response—became "Truman's war." The Korean War provided the perfect backdrop for Senator Joseph R. McCarthy. Serving notice that "Communists, fellow travelers and dupes . . . are not going to be able to hide and protect themselves behind a war which would not have been necessary except for their acts," McCarthy attributed the war and the failure to win it to the "Commiecrats," "homos," and "the pretty boys" in the State Department "with silver spoons in their mouths."[4]

Beginning in 1946 Acheson had toyed for more than two years with a policy designed to split Mao and Stalin; NSC 34, adopted on October 13, 1948, had taken the view that Mao was another Tito, the Yugoslav Communist leader who had just broken with Stalin, a tough nationalist even harder for the Kremlin to control because he had been "entrenched in power" ten times longer. Five months before the Korean invasion a State Department working group thought that "an effective split" might be no more than three years away.[5] In March 1950 Secretary Acheson told the Senate Foreign Relations Committee in executive session that the "very basic objectives of Moscow are hostile to the very basic objectives of China."[6] For Republicans who believed that Communists anywhere were part of the same world conspiracy this was heresy.

The idea that China and the Soviet Union might have conflicting national interests fit Acheson's predilections, for in the interests of limiting American commitments in Asia he wished to downplay the strategic importance of a Communist victory in China. The world balance of power would be decided in Europe, not Asia. For Acheson, Korea was a godforsaken, strategically inconsequential appendage to an Asian morass. In a speech delivered six months before the war, which every Republican politician would soon learn by heart, he had excluded it from the American defense perimeter. But now Korea had been transformed into a symbol. The Europeans would be watching to see whether the United States would stand up to Communist aggression. The American taxpayer could now be jolted by a real war in Asia into preparing for the hypothetical but far more important war in Europe.

Acheson badly underestimated the domestic political impact of all this, and in so doing unwittingly taught his successors the danger of having any China policy at all. The American people, or more accurately the small but influential segment responsive to the appeals of the China Lobby, were so caught up in their own fantasies for remaking China that they reacted to the communization of the mainland with all the fury of a spurned lover. (As Senator Kenneth Wherry had put it, American free enterprise could "lift Shanghai up and up until it is just like Kansas City.") It was not just that some of the most vocal opinion leaders like Henry Luce felt responsible for the soul of China because they had been born there of missionary families; the sense of responsibility was more widely shared. Otherwise, how could the absurd premise behind the Republican campaign charge that "Acheson lost China" have ever been accepted into American political discourse?

At one press conference after another McCarthy turned the State Department's confused response to the rush of events in Asia into a dramatic tale of conspiracy. When it looked as though MacArthur's forces might be pushed into the sea, McCarthy charged that American boys were dying because Acheson had given the Soviets "a green light to grab whatever it could in China, Korea, and Formosa."[7] Acheson's failure to apply the Truman Doctrine to China and to defend Chiang's hopeless cause in the late 1940s lent a certain plausibility to the conspiracy charges. If the administration was really dedicated to the containment of Communism, why did it sit back and let the world's most populous nation fall into Communist hands?

In the summer of 1950, political figures of all sorts sought to present the Korean War as a cautionary tale to illustrate a number of quite different points. "Korea brought Europe to its feet," John J. McCloy wrote, for it symbolized the possibility of an attack in another divided land. As High Commissioner for Germany he used the crisis to push German rearmament and the political and economic integration of Western Europe.[8] As badly trained American troops kept retreating down the Korean peninsula, the "primitives" in the Republican Party, as Acheson called them, stepped up their charges. Vandenberg was dying and no longer available to run interference for Truman. His colleagues had taken the lesson of 1948 to heart: Bipartisanship was a trap, for it would always favor the commander in chief. The GOP should never again let the "me-too" internationalists of the Willkie-Dewey stripe set its course. For the Republican Right, Korea represented the bankruptcy of the Establishment's obsession with Europe. The place to fight world Communism was Asia. To tie American interests to bankrupt, ungrateful European politicians was just what elitists like Acheson would do, but it was a terrible blunder, or worse. As the congressional elections of 1950 got under way, politics in the United States degenerated into volleys of Red-baiting. The Democratic Senator Millard Tydings, noting that William Jenner, an isolationist Republican senator from Indiana, had voted against the Marshall Plan, pointed out that "Joe Stalin and the *Daily Worker* and the Senator all vote the same way." Not to be outdone, Jenner thundered back: Tydings, who had just been boasting about his World War I medals, soon would be getting another from Stalin with a grateful message, "Thanks, from good old Joe, for a job well done."[9]

On September 15 Douglas MacArthur dramatically reversed the fortunes of war by staging a daring and risky amphibious attack at Inchon. MacArthur himself had called it a "5,000 to one shot" and the Joint Chiefs of Staff and the secretary of defense had opposed it. As the November elections approached, MacArthur's forces were heading toward the 38th parallel. It seemed as though the goal of freeing South Korea was about to be achieved. The battlefield triumph added new luster to Douglas MacArthur's reputation as the nation's number-one hero. The general, still nursing his wartime resentment that the war against Japan had been neglected by the Eurocentered New Dealers, believed even more strongly than most of his fellow Republicans that American destiny lay in Asia. Having already leaked a secret State Department memorandum instructing Foreign Service officers on how to put the best face on a Communist takeover of Taiwan (then called Formosa),[10] he now released a speech to the Veterans of Foreign Wars in which he attacked Truman's Asia policy. Taiwan was an "unsinkable aircraft carrier," a base from which Chiang—with American assistance—could retake China.

Political pressure was building to escalate the original war aim and to order MacArthur to cross the 38th parallel so that all Korea might be liberated from Communism. MacArthur himself took the lead in pushing for total victory in Korea. The Joint Chiefs of Staff had taken the position all along that the 38th parallel was not something to be taken seriously by an advancing army, which should be permitted to pursue the enemy and destroy him. This reasoning now commended itself to influential columnists, including Walter Lippmann and Joseph Alsop, who along with many others argued that the parallel was a "purely fictitious line" that should be ignored. A few weeks before the election, Republican Congressman Hugh D. Scott's campaign cry against the "Hiss Survivors Association down at the State Department who wear upon their breasts the cross of Yalta" sent shivers through the White House. Other Republicans charged that the administration was planning "to subvert our military victory by calling a halt at the 38th parallel."[11] John Foster Dulles, the principal foreign policy adviser of the Republican Party, suggested to Paul Nitze that the United States "obliterate" the 38th parallel. Acheson, though originally skeptical of courting a wider war, changed his mind a week before the Inchon landing. Stung by the charge that he planned to "cringe" behind the 38th parallel, he was desperate to find some way to win over public support. "This was worry number one with him," C. B. Marshall, a member of the Policy Planning Staff at the time, remembers.[12]

The success of Inchon made the lure of victory in Korea irresistible, for battlefield success could be used to neutralize the savage Republican attacks. A few weeks before the election, at a cabinet meeting to discuss the election, Acheson, painfully aware of how much of a political liability to the administration he himself had become, announced that the 38th parallel would soon be crossed and that Korea would be added to the list of countries—Greece, Turkey, Iran, and those of Western Europe—that the Democratic Party had saved from Communism. Korea, he said, would be "used as a stage to prove what Western Democracy can do to help the underprivileged countries of the world."[13] George Marshall, now secretary of defense, sent MacArthur an EYES ONLY cable approved by the president, "We want you to feel unhampered tactically and strategically to proceed north of the 38th parallel."

Two days before the election, Harold Stassen sounded the Republican campaign theme, denouncing the Democrats for "five years of coddling Chinese Communists, five years of undermining General MacArthur."[14] The charges of appeasement, even treason, hit their mark. Despite the upturn in the fortunes of war, on November 7 the Democrats lost six Senate seats and about two-thirds of their majority in the House. On election night Truman was deeply depressed. George Elsey, a White House aide, recalls that it was the only time he ever saw the president drunk.[15]

The decision to invade North Korea led to a military disaster for MacArthur and a political disaster for Truman from which neither recovered. As MacArthur pushed close to the Yalu River, which was the border with China, and he began to talk of bombing China itself, the Indian ambassador transmitted warnings to Acheson that the Chinese would intervene. These the secretary dismissed as "panicky vaporings." As he himself later admitted, Acheson had "the clearest idea . . . of the utter madness and folly of what MacArthur was doing up north," but he and his colleagues "sat around like paralyzed rabbits while MacArthur carried out this nightmare."[16] It was not only MacArthur's reputation as a military miracle worker that induced the stunned silence in the White House and the Pentagon, but, more importantly, their own sense of political vulnerability.

Here is one of the clearest cases where fear of a domestic political backlash drove a critical strategic decision. Despite the risks of Chinese intervention—on which the experts predictably disagreed —the explicit warnings from the acting head of the Chinese military forces, and the realization that the nation was unready for a major land war with China, Acheson did not dare call a halt to Mac-Arthur's plunge to the north. Polls taken in September had shown that more than 60 percent of Americans favored chasing the "Communist invading army" into North Korea even though 64 percent of the respondents believed that Russia and China would enter the war if the line were crossed.[17] Acheson of all people was not to be moved by so bizarre a mandate, but he knew that the anxious public mood was fertile ground for the "primitives" to plow. The confused state of public opinion was the source of their power. To halt a victorious MacArthur in mid-battle would bring the well-organized wrath of the people down on Acheson's head.

On October 8, 1950, Mao had ordered contingents of "volunteers" into Korea, and U.S. Intelligence began picking up indications that some sort of Chinese intervention was under way. MacArthur minimized it and announced an offensive on November 24 that would "have the boys home by Christmas." The next day the Chinese sprang their trap. Three hundred thousand Chinese Communist troops suddenly appeared, surrounding MacArthur's forces, shrieking, banging cymbals, and screaming, "Son of a bitch marine, you die!" In the first forty-eight hours the Americans suffered more than one thousand casualties and the Eighth Army was in headlong retreat. Official Washington was thrown into panic. The Joint Chiefs asked Acheson to negotiate a cease-fire, but the secretary turned aside the suggestion. "There is a danger of our becoming the greatest appeasers of all time if we abandon the Koreans and they are slaughtered." The World War II hero General Omar Bradley, now chairman of the Joint Chiefs, suggested that perhaps "we could come home and just forget the matter."[18] A few days after the disaster at the Yalu Truman wrote in his diary, "It looks like World War III is here." The Republicans in the House passed a unanimous resolution to which twenty Republican senators subscribed calling for the immediate resignation of Dean Acheson. By early January, 66 percent of the respondents to a Gallup poll favored pulling out of Korea; 49 percent thought it had been a mistake to intervene in the first place. Thirty-six percent thought Harry Truman was doing a good job as president.[19]

A far more dramatic and revealing test of public opinion now followed. As his troops were reeling back in late December, MacArthur made a secret request for authorization to drop atomic bombs on twenty-six targets.[20] The request was denied, but Bernard Baruch, Senator Owen Brewster, and Congressman Mendel Rivers publicly called for using the bomb. Senator Henry Cabot Lodge was all for using the weapon if it could be used "efficiently and profitably"; colleagues noted that Hiroshima had proved its effectiveness. The commanders of the four largest veterans' organizations demanded that MacArthur be given "such means as may be necessary" to bring about a victorious end of the war. At a press conference Truman said use of atomic weapons could not be ruled out; panic spread in Europe, and the British prime minister flew to Washington to plead for restraint.

Meanwhile MacArthur, having recaptured the capital city of Seoul and stabilized the battle line, wrote the House Republican leader Joseph Martin a stinging critique of the Truman policy of limited war in which he included the ringing phrase that would become the slogan of the Republican Right: "There is no substitute for victory." Six days after the letter was made public Truman decided to recall "our Big General in the Far East." MacArthur's titanic fury was all the greater for the humiliation of having to hear the news first on a public broadcast.[21]

Within forty-eight hours of the firing on April 11, 1951, the White House had received 125,000 telegrams, overwhelmingly negative: "Impeach the bastard who calls himself President"; "Impeach the little ward politician"; "Impeach the Judas." After being relieved of his command MacArthur returned to the United States for the first time since 1936 to the acclaim of millions who lined the streets as his motorcade passed. The MacArthur firing triggered a prolonged congressional investigation of the Truman foreign policy. A variety of polls showed that American opinion was more supportive of MacArthur than Truman.

Eventually MacArthur faded away, as he had promised in a histrionic televised speech to Congress, but the duel of the president and the general served to dramatize the depth of the public opinion problem that the managers of American foreign policy now faced. The pursuit of national security had become counterintuitive. The very idea of war without victory defined twentieth-century history, American tradition (unconditional surrender), and all conventional logic. The slogan of the Right—"Why not victory?"—was far more plausible than the prescription of "the Eastern Establishment" with its apparent willingness to endure indefinite war without resort to America's winning weapon. The Chinese had killed tens of thousands of American boys. Why should their homeland be exempt from retribution?

2.

Even as the consensus was unraveling in Asia the administration was seeking to solidify bipartisan support for its policy in Europe. The president was now committed to the permanent stationing of a large American army on the Continent, but his advisers thought that this would require considerable selling. Even before the Korean War Robert Lovett had urged the creation of "a much vaster propaganda machine to tell our story at home and abroad."[22] In the fall of 1950, after the Chinese had entered the Korean War, the need for an "education campaign" was greater than ever. The war made bigger military budgets politically possible, but it was not obvious that troops should be sent to Europe when American boys were retreating in Korea.

For John J. McCloy and the administration's Eurocentered strategists "an immediate increasing of American forces in Europe" was needed "to show that we intend to fight there."[23] But the administration itself was divided on what to do. At this point the president of Harvard, James Bryant Conant, the top wartime government scientist Vannevar Bush, and several others launched a campaign in behalf of sending a permanent American army to Europe. Conant, as he wrote a fellow university president, Henry Wriston, wanted a "million combat troops in Europe" and to that end wanted to "raise the armed forces to 3-5 million men." In December 1950, in the midst of the debacle in Korea, the Committee on the Present Danger announced its formation. At a private "Citizens' Conference" a few weeks earlier attended by "fifty industrialists, heads of many communication services—press, radio, newspapers, . . . — financiers, educators, heads of farm organizations, life insurance and railroad presidents," General Dwight D. Eisenhower laid out the reasons why the Committee on the Present Danger was needed. "The Soviet objective," he said, is "world domination" and the Russians "are willing to use armed force to win." A critical element in the present danger was American public opinion. "The American people are responsible for this country's present position. The moment the fighting ceased in World War II the cry was to bring Willie home. Now we are reaping the results." [24]

Modeled on the William Allen White committee to arouse public opinion in World War II, the committee prepared to do battle against the Asia-only isolationists and once again wake up the country. Billing itself as "nonpartisan" and "private," the committee took out newspaper ads, had a weekly radio program, and distributed a film, *Modern Arms and Free Men*, which showed Soviet tramp steamers mining American harbors with atomic bombs. [25] The committee lobbied strongly for universal military service, more foreign aid for Europe, and played a key role in assuring the success of the administration's request that 100,000 American troops be dispatched for permanent duty in Europe. On the day the Senate voted for troops to Europe, concluding the so-called Great Debate, Joseph Martin, the Republican minority leader in the House, read the letter from MacArthur that led to the general's dismissal. The fight between the Republican Asia-firsters and the bipartisan Eastern Establishment had only begun.

The Korean War dragged on for two more years as armistice talks began and then immediately bogged down. Public support for the war continued to decline until the truce was signed in July 1953. The polls showed a precipitous drop in public support when the entry of the Chinese made it apparent that the war would last a long time—down to 39 percent in the Gallup poll—but despite mounting casualties there was little further decline over the next two and a half years. A public judgment had been reached. In every Gallup poll but one over the next three years a majority of those polled said it had been a mistake to fight in Korea.

Opposition to the Korean War was much less vocal than the anti–Vietnam War movement fifteen years later, but the Korean War was almost as unpopular. In the climate of the 1950s, people were far more reluctant to take to the streets in the midst of a war than they were ten years later. Other than a Madison Square Garden protest rally organized by Stalinists four days after the invasion, which drew a crowd of ten thousand,[26] the largest antiwar demonstration, according to one study of opposition to the Korean War, was held on August 20, 1952, at Randall's Island. During three years of the Korean War, there were only two ads in the *New York Times* relating to the war. (In the first year after the escalation of the Vietnam War by the Johnson administration there were twenty-seven ads that listed a total of 9,476 names.[27])

While virtually every prominent intellectual rallied to the Korean War and avoided public criticism—in contrast to Vietnam—the public was unenthusiastic after the first few weeks. The majorities who continued to support the war when forced to choose by a pollster had no clear sense of what the conflict was about. Defending South Korea was not a compelling war aim. Polls suggested that supporters were more influenced by party loyalty and by a sense of patriotic duty than by a belief that American security was at stake. Even anti-Communism did not translate into support for the war. (One poll showed that a large majority of those who favored outlawing the U.S. Communist Party—by then composed heavily of FBI informants—were also for the immediate pullout from Korea.) Most Americans continued to believe that since the commander in chief had made the decision, he should be supported. But the public mood steadily soured as Korea looked more and more like a trap. Troop morale in Korea was low; for the men of the Eighth Army, made up of recalled World War II veterans and draftees, fighting a war, *any* war, so soon after the last one was a bad break, but especially this dirty little war for which the United States seemed to have no will to win.

The 1952 election was as clear a referendum on a war as any in American history.[28] The Republicans approached the election determined to make the Truman foreign policy the central issue of the campaign. The fear of immediate war that had worked to Truman's advantage in 1948 was gone, replaced by chronic frustration and anger at the stalemate in Korea. Senator Robert Taft advanced an "isolationist" foreign policy that was strongly rooted in Cold War ideology. The United States should not waste its resources in a vain attempt to impose a Pax Americana on the world but should build up its naval and air power; the atomic bomb represented "the best deterrent to war." On no account should the United States get involved in a ground war anywhere but should withdraw its troops from Europe as soon as the Europeans were in a position to defend themselves. At the same time Taft sought to defend himself against the charge of isolationism by calling for an ideological offensive against Communism, "an affirmative policy which will constantly extend the doctrine and the power of liberty."[29] He recommended that the United States launch a worldwide campaign of propaganda and subversion of Stalin's empire, "an underground war of infiltration in Iron Curtain countries."[30] These ideas he launched in the form of a fierce partisan attack on the Democratic Party, blaming its "sympathy toward communism" for the loss of Eastern Europe and China, and its appeasement policies for the tragedy of the Korean War.

The "internationalist" wing of the Republican Party pinned its hopes on General Dwight D. Eisenhower, the war hero with a reputation as a peerless military politician. The essential difference between Eisenhower and Taft was NATO. Ike had had a secret meeting with Taft in the spring of 1951 in which he offered to stay out of the campaign if Taft would support the principle of collective security in Europe. This Taft refused to do. Eisenhower entered the race and won the nomination by using his credentials as Cold War strategist to go after Taft as an isolationist who when it came to military matters didn't know what he was talking about. But the Republican Party and its candidate embraced the Taft policy and much of his rhetoric with the important exception of his position on withdrawing American troops in Europe.

Most of Taft's other ideas were taken over by John Foster Dulles, who was determined to serve as secretary of state whichever wing of the party emerged victorious. In an article in *Life* he attempted to reconcile old-fashioned conservatism and Cold War activism. To avoid "the twin evils of militarism and bankruptcy" the United States should rely on the threat of massive retaliation—presumably with nuclear weapons, though the point was not made explicit—rather than continue the expensive and futile policy of containment. At the same time the United States should promote the "liberation" of the nations that the Democrats had allowed to fall under the yoke of Communism. Like Taft he also proposed a massive radio propaganda campaign and the promotion "of a great new Declaration of Independence" for the satellites of Eastern Europe. Liberation could be achieved peacefully, Dulles insisted. There would be no need for "bloody uprisings." Emmet John Hughes, the *Life* editor assigned to the piece who later became an Eisenhower speech writer, described how we "would chase this proposition around and around and around but it never acquired substance beyond his affirming the desirability of it."[31]

At the Republican Convention in Chicago the Taft and Eisenhower forces agreed on a platform that accused the Democrats of "tragic blunders" in the past and "no hope of victory" for the future. Eisenhower thought the document "a bit savage,"[32] but Robert Humphreys, the Republican public relations director, developed a plan to sell Eisenhower as a man of "real leadership" who could get out the vote by playing on the international situation. The Democrats were now saddled with a war that was causing Americans "to fear for their national security and lives."[33] In February 1952 Harry Truman's approval rating had fallen to 25 percent, an all-time low. "Communism, Korea, and Corruption," so went the Republican campaign slogan, had produced the "mess in Washington." Mink coats and deep freezers had found their way into the homes of administration officials under suspicious circumstances, and these scandals—peccadilloes in comparison with what was to follow in future administrations—reinforced the notion that Truman was a small man surrounded not only by Communists and appeasers but crooks too. After losing the New Hampshire primary to a maverick senator, Estes Kefauver, the president announced that he would not run again.

Adlai Stevenson, the governor of Illinois, who won the nomination, tried to distance himself from Truman personally, but he eagerly embraced the administration's Cold War strategy. His Cold War rhetoric, though elegant at times, was thoroughly conventional: "the Soviet objective is one world—one Communist world." Indeed, to defend against the Republican charges, the Democrats pressed the Domino Theory, as it came to be known years later in the Vietnam War. Stevenson said that by fighting in Korea the United States had prevented World War III. From the back of his campaign train on the whistle-stop tour Stevenson had hoped he would not make, Truman heightened the rhetoric: The choice, he said, was to fight the Communists in Korea or in Wichita or in whatever little town the train happened to stop. Averell Harriman told a crowd in Boston that American withdrawal would "open the floodgates of Communist aggression to sweep down and across all of Southeast Asia and Formosa . . . and undermine the Middle East." At the Alamo Stevenson said the United States was in Korea because "God has set for us an awesome mission: nothing less than the leadership of the free world."[34]

It was not easy to sell the heartbreaking war in Korea with the arguments that persuaded Acheson—a show of determination to impress the Europeans and push them toward rearmament. In 1939 Franklin D. Roosevelt had told the American Society of Newspaper Editors—without any evidence for his assertion—that the Nazis would soon be able to put planes in Mexico and bomb Kansas. Now in 1952 the Democrats once again understood that support for what Americans in the heartland call "foreign wars" could only be mustered by dramatizing a direct threat to people's homes.[35]

The Republicans tried to make the rollback of Communism in Eastern Europe an issue. At Dulles's urging Eisenhower told the American Legion, "We must tell the Kremlin that never shall we desist in our aid to every man and woman of those shackled lands." But when Dulles became more specific, calling for the U.S. to encourage passive resistance and slowdowns in Eastern Europe to bring about "disintegration from within" of Stalin's empire, professors, syndicated armchair strategists, and European politicians grew nervous. Truman accused the Republicans of playing "cruel, gutter politics with the lives of countless good men and women behind the Iron Curtain."[36] Although local Republicans made much of the "Yalta sellout" before local Polish audiences, Eisenhower himself, except for one Pulaski Day speech, backed off the issue. (His adviser C. D. Jackson pointed out that voters of Hungarian descent liked Yalta—"what is Yalta poison for the Poles is Yalta meat for the Hungarians.")

The Eisenhower strategy was to hold the Republican base with a clear conservative message on domestic issues and to marshal a winning majority not by appealing to Democrats as Willkie and Dewey had tried to do, but by bringing in millions of new independent voters. For this purpose national security was the all-important issue to transcend traditional party politics. The general was a made-to-order candidate for the new age of television. He knew how to simplify complex issues; at each stop he would hold up an egg and begin to recite the sixty-eight taxes that had descended on the poor thing. Stevenson was a master of Wilsonian oratory, admired for his patrician wit by reporters and pundits who were appalled by Eisenhower's apparent inability to speak in complete sentences. They did not understand what the general knew intuitively, that instant communication by image was now a political requirement. Winning personalities moved crowds, not beautiful sentences.

It was only late in the campaign that Eisenhower's advisers began to see Korea as the key to the election. On September 16, Gerard Lambert, a Princeton public opinion specialist hired by Sherman Adams, Eisenhower's campaign manager, discovered that Americans ranked the Korea issue second only to government waste and inefficiency. After a special survey in twenty-seven major states Lambert found that Korea was the number-one issue with the independent voters, which the Eisenhower strategists most wanted to woo. The Roper survey indicated that 53 percent of the public wanted a new military offensive to win the war and 12 percent wanted to withdraw. No one was happy with the stalemated war and the endless truce talks. Sixty-seven percent of Gallup poll respondents thought that the general was the best man to handle Korea; only 9 percent thought Stevenson could do a better job. Eisenhower began to advance the policy that in a later war would be known as Vietnamization. The war was "a job for the Koreans," not "young farm boys" and "students" from America. "If there must be a war there, let it be Asians against Asians." On October 24 in Detroit Eisenhower delivered the speech that guaranteed his overwhelming victory. "The old Administration cannot be expected to repair what it failed to prevent." Only a personal trip to Korea could equip the next president to bring peace. "I shall go to Korea." Eisenhower offered no ideas for ending the conflict. He offered his persona, and that was enough. After his landslide victory a number of surveys corroborated what James MacGregor Burns and Philip Hastings found after interviewing Massachusetts voters: In voting for Ike, Americans were voting against the tensions of the Cold War and for the general's experience in foreign affairs. "He served as a symbol of national security," they concluded, "much as Roosevelt served as a symbol of economic security in the 1930's."[37]

3.

The Eisenhower administration spent eight years conducting an activist foreign policy all over the world, but the global fight against Communism resulted in no major war. For this reason during the fifties foreign affairs intruded into the consciousness of ordinary citizens much less than in the preceding decade. With respect to foreign policy, public opinion was permissive. By 1954 both the

Korean War and the rampage of Joseph McCarthy were ended. Eisenhower was slow to act against the demagogic senator not only because he wished to avoid "a pissing contest with that skunk," as he put it, but because he shared McCarthy's concerns about Communism in government—though he was made uncomfortable and occasionally angry by McCarthy's methods. Driven by success, the fascinated, favorable attention of a sizable chunk of the press, and alcohol, McCarthy began taking on the CIA, the Protestant churches, and the United States Army, all of which he accused of harboring Communists. McCarthy's recklessness now verged on sacrilege, and his attack on the military and mainstream religion inspired a burst of civil courage that resulted in a Senate vote to censure him—but only after he had managed to destroy himself on television by revealing who he was.

The tense atmosphere that had hung over the country since the Czech crisis and the Berlin blockade of 1948 now began to dissolve. Most citizens, happy to leave the task of defending American prosperity and power in General Eisenhower's experienced hands, rallied around a popular leader's vision of national security. The new president was convinced that he could not govern effectively until the unpopular war in Korea was ended. Although his military advisers were against agreeing to an armistice in place—they argued that the terrain a few miles to the north would be a better line to defend if war should break out again—Eisenhower insisted that domestic political considerations outweighed these military concerns. The war had to be ended without more heavy fighting and expense. When Secretary of State Dulles suggested that if the Communists in Korea did not agree to reunification the U.S. should resume the war, he responded, "The American people will never stand for such a move."[38] Within six months and six days of Inauguration Day an armistice was signed at Panmunjom ending the Korean War.

Eisenhower came into office with two deeply held, irreconcilable convictions. One was that the nuclear arms race was a dead end. Again and again in his personal correspondence and in impromptu remarks Ike revealed how deep was his revulsion at the use of weapons of such destructiveness. The United States had about sixteen hundred atomic bombs on the day he moved into the White House. He recoiled from the apocalyptical vision of NSC 68. It was "pure rot" to talk about a "year of maximum danger." The military always posed worst cases, always asked for too much. When Vannevar Bush argued the case at one of the presidential stag dinners "for scaring the people into a big tax program to build bomb defenses,"

Eisenhower, as his close friend Bill Robinson, who was present, noted in his diary, "became greatly spirited and said that our great advantage was spiritual strength—this was our greatest offensive and defensive weapon." In 1953 Eisenhower saw that the nuclear arms race was robbing a generation of hope. "Is this all we can do for our children?" he asked.[39] The new president worried that an unending arms race "would either drive us to war—or into some form of dictatorial government." Ever since the 1930s, according to his biographer Stephen Ambrose, he had worried about "how long a democracy would be willing to pay the cost of maintaining its defensive strength before it lashed out at the source of the threat and removed it."[40] Over the next two years Eisenhower on several occasions turned down requests by the Joint Chiefs of Staff to authorize the use of nuclear weapons against China and to save the French garrison at Dien Bien Phu in Indochina. Although he approved a public statement by Dulles threatening the use of tactical nuclear weapons in the event the Chinese attacked Formosa, he worried, as he wrote in a memo to the secretary of state, that the use of the atomic bomb would divide American public opinion and that the country would find itself "isolated in world opinion."[41]

To build domestic support for his national security policy in which arms control would play a major role President Eisenhower proposed an education campaign that came to be known as Operation Candor. Americans needed to be told the truth about nuclear weapons. "We've just got to let the American people know how terrible this thing is," he said to his aide Bernard Shanley after a few months in office. National strategy had to be based on something better than aimless drift toward nuclear war. "The individual feels helpless to do anything about the foreign threat that hangs over his head and so he turns his attention to matters of immediate interest." Eisenhower worried about creating stable, long-term support for a strong defense. Why should the citizen pay taxes for a "defense" that could not protect his home and family from nuclear destruction? He was eventually talked out of Operation Candor by the military and the Atomic Energy Commission, which saw no reason to hand the Soviets information about American weapons. But the most compelling argument was that "educating" the public would scare it even more. Indeed, the Atomic Energy Commission was so concerned in the 1950s that public anxiety would threaten the weapons testing program that some officials failed to warn citizens near the testing ground in Nevada to take elementary precautions against fallout. In 1953 an explosion at a test site in Nevada was televised nationally. Pointing to the radioactive cloud drifting off camera, Walter Cronkite remarked reassuringly, "It's not dangerous."[42] Not everyone believed him. Tom Lehrer's song "The Wild West" with its suggestion that visitors to Nevada take along lead underwear drew nervous laughter in college towns.

Eisenhower's dilemma was that he believed strongly in the need for deterrence by means of superior military power, feared nuclear weapons, but he feared the consequences of a "garrison state" economy even more. Profoundly distrustful of the Soviets, he once told a royal visitor that but for NATO and nuclear weapons we would have "no recourse except to try to accept the Communist doctrine and live with it." And he would not want to live or see his grandchildren living in such a world, because "you would pay too big a price to be alive."[43] He told the men selected for the cabinet right before the inauguration that "my whole picture of China is claws reaching at you because you looked like you had five cents."[44] Yet he was determined to cut military expenditures to balance the budget. "The defense of this country is *not* a military matter," he insisted. "The military has a very limited sector."[45] His solution was the New Look, a cutback on expensive manpower and conventional armaments and a greater reliance on cheaper nuclear weapons. The Eisenhower-Dulles era, which coincided with the rise of Nikita Khrushchev in the Soviet Union, was the age of nuclear bluff. It was also a time of massive nuclear buildup.

In eight years of coexistence with Stalin's successors the battle lines of the Cold War hardened, and, despite the urging of Winston Churchill for a grand settlement, no major political agreements other than the treaty neutralizing Austria were achieved. To humanize nuclear energy Eisenhower launched an Atoms for Peace campaign. What began as a propaganda exercise in positive thinking about nuclear fission and a challenge to the Russians to turn fissionable material over to the United Nations quickly led to the establishment of the nuclear power industry. By 1957 General Electric had distributed millions of copies of its comic book "Inside the Atom" and Walt Disney's *Our Friend the Atom* was shown on television and in schools. The animated cartoon showed how The Bomb could be turned into a friendly, obedient servant.[46]

Instead of Operation Candor the Strategic Air Command launched a public relations campaign to make Americans comfortable with The Bomb. Curtis LeMay, the SAC commander, cultivated Arthur Godfrey, the most popular radio personality of the day and already a TV star, who praised SAC on his show and asked his listeners to write their congressmen to demand higher military pay. Print journalists were welcomed to SAC bases, provided food, drink, and a kit with a feature article already written. Mock bomber raids were staged for radio and television. In 1955 the film *Strategic Air Command* showed a pilot patriotically choosing his B-47 bomber, the delivery vehicle for atomic bombs, over his wife. (The wife eventually threw in the towel and came to love The Bomb too.) According to the press release, the film would "build up our confidence in our protective devices and allay some of our uneasy feelings." Two years later the same basic plot was adapted to the next generation bomber in *Bombers B-52.*[47]

The Republicans came into office publicly committed to a more activist foreign policy than containment, which had been branded in the campaign as a suspect invention of Democratic Party appeasers. Ike had promised to restore the "initiative" in the fight with Communism, but the subliminal message that got him elected was a promise of peace. In the early months in office the Eisenhower administration undertook a supersecret review of national security strategy known as Solarium, because the review panels met in the White House indoor garden. Its purpose was to draft the Republican answer to containment. Reluctantly, however, Eisenhower concluded that there was none. They would have to keep doing what Truman and Acheson had begun but do it better. As Eisenhower's biographer puts it, "nuclear war was unimaginable, limited conventional war unwinnable, and stalemate unacceptable."[48]

The answer to the dilemma was covert action. The Central Intelligence Agency could fight and win the only battles that could be won, small operations of political significance in strategic places of American choosing. And it could be done without the extent and character of American involvement getting into the newspapers. Forgoing the pleasure of announcing victories was a small price to pay for hiding the inevitable defeats in the "back alley war" that Eisenhower thought would last at least a generation.[49] The capability for covert action was already in place under Truman. Now it would become the principal weapon for carrying on the Cold War.

4.

The national project of the thirties had been the New Deal; in the forties it had been war and Cold War. In the fifties the energies of the people, Eisenhower hoped, would be focused on building a prosperous America. The government would fight the Cold War.

That was its main job other than to facilitate a boom in production and consumption. A man of considerable political intuition, Eisenhower did not need polls to convince him that Americans had had enough social experiments and that their enthusiasm for international crusades was limited. They wanted a job or, better, a career, families, and a home. In short, after twelve years of World War II and threats of World War III, they wanted the fruits of a hard-won peace.

In the first postwar decade, government subsidized the pursuit of happiness on a scale unprecedented in American history. The GI Bill of Rights sent more than two million returning veterans to college. Thanks to VA mortgages, highway subsidies, and government-aided mass-produced housing, the returning veterans could afford to be homeowners in developments at the edge of town. By 1960 more than half of American families owned their own homes. The suburbs had been democratized. The prosperity sparked by the Korean rearmament launched the generation-long rise of the new middle class. (By 1970 the real wages of factory workers had risen 50 percent.)

In the Eisenhower years there was a production boom of all sorts —most impressively, of babies. Soon a dazzling array of new products was on the market—cars with automatic shifts, dryers, electric garbage-disposal units, freezers, air conditioners, TVs, hi-fis, long-playing records, gadgets and furnishings of vinyl and Styrofoam— to absorb the money, time, and energy of the progenitors of the Baby Boom generation. Some of the outward symbols of class disappeared as Americans left the family farm in droves and put on suits and ties to take office jobs. Citizens with modest incomes could not only buy a house in the suburbs but, thanks to the boom in consumer credit, an array of mechanical servants to keep it clean and neat, and the grass clipped. Despite an early attempt to cut the government payroll, the federal bureaucracy grew in the Eisenhower years and state and local government doubled.

Eisenhower once observed that Americans are " 'a happy people' doing exactly what they choose." Happiness was now defined more and more as the freedom to consume. To no small extent the ideological struggle with Communism was about consumption. Not only was Russia a slave society but it was a prison with only one brand of toothpaste. And no choice of household conveniences. Indeed, no house. The new American prosperity was built on large enterprises devoted to producing goods for consumption and a high-technology armaments industry. The Cold War was presented to the public as an inevitable and unendable struggle with international Communism, but one which, happily, required little sacrifice in either blood or taxes. Most of the actual battles were fought out of the public view.

Momentous national security commitments and decisions were made during the Eisenhower years without most Americans even being aware of what was happening. The destructive power of the hydrogen bomb stockpiles grew to staggering proportions and the military forces became dependent on nuclear weapons. There was no public debate in advance of these decisions and no public review. Only a few members of Congress were even familiar with the issues. By a vote of 410–3 in the House and 83–3 in the Senate the president in the so-called Formosa Resolution was given the unprecedented authority to initiate war against China wherever, whenever, and under whatever circumstances he deemed appropriate. In his fight to protect members of his administration against Senator McCarthy, Eisenhower proclaimed, in Arthur Schlesinger, Jr.'s words, "the most absolute assertion of presidential right to withhold information from Congress ever uttered to that day in American history."[50] Commitments to go to war in behalf of any one of a group of nations ringing the Soviet Union and China joined by the SEATO, CENTO, and other treaty arrangements and executive agreements designed to bypass Congress were made with no discussion of the implications for either American security or American democracy. In May of 1955 the Soviet delegation to the disarmament talks in London suddenly offered substantial acceptance of the American position, including on-site inspection. The administration, which had never considered the possibility that the Soviets would accept its proposals, withdrew them. But no serious political costs resulted. Too little attention was being paid; suspicion of the Soviets was too high. Except for the rising concern about nuclear tests in the atmosphere, there was no debate on the arms issue, not even in the election campaign the following year.

How did it happen that public opinion was so permissive? The popularity of the president and the unique credibility he enjoyed in national security matters were important of course. But even more important was the fact that the most controversial foreign policy initiatives were secret. Under the Truman administration the CIA had begun to carry on secret military operations inside the Soviet bloc, even inside the Soviet Union itself. No American citizens other than a handful of government officials were aware that U.S. and British intelligence agencies were parachuting guerrillas into

Communist Albania in the spring of 1950 or that from 1949 to 1953 American agents were being periodically dropped into the Ukraine to support the Ukrainian guerrilla movement fighting Soviet rule. In the political climate of the day a majority of Americans might well have supported these secret military involvements, but there would have been political costs to pay had the public known that both operations were doomed from the start because one of the top-secret planners, Kim Philby, was a spy for the KGB.

There were many other things the public did not know that were being carried on in the name of the national security that it would have liked less. People were not aware that their tax dollars were going to overthrow the government of Indonesia, to arm Tibetans, or to subsidize raids on China. They did not know that the CIA was opening mail of American citizens (Project HTLingual), using citizens as guinea pigs for experiments on mind-control drugs (Project MKUltra), or that money a conservative Congress would never have appropriated was being secretly funneled to the non-Communist Left in Europe, even to some who called themselves "socialists."[51] Eisenhower used secrecy not only to avoid controversy with isolationists, liberals, and others who recoiled from the idea of secret wars but also to sell his foreign policy to the hard-liners when he was unwilling to go along with their demands. In the privacy of the Oval Office Eisenhower, turning aside Senator William Knowland's call for a blockade of China, confided, "There is a very great aggressiveness on our side that you have not known about . . . on the theory of why put burdens on people that they don't need to know about."[52]

In 1953 American newspaper readers and TV viewers began reading about and watching a wild Iranian leader who had nationalized the holdings of the foreign oil companies, a gaunt man with wild eyes given to fainting fits who was usually photographed in his pajamas. Mohammed Mossadegh, a nationalist with a large popular following, a modernizer, was not a Communist, indeed was opposed to the Iranian Communist Party. The real issues had to do with nationalization, modernization, democracy, and control of national resources, but in American newspapers, and on television and radio, the official characterization of the issue prevailed: Mossadegh was a Communist or would soon be one. The country bordered the Soviet Union. It had a large Communist Party. Mossadegh had confiscated American property and was conducting trade talks with the Soviet Union. Nothing more was needed to turn the political struggle within Iran into a battle of the Cold War.

When the Shah of Iran fired Mossadegh and jubilant mobs marched in the streets of Teheran, Americans who cared at all about what was happening in Iran took it as a piece of fortuitous good news. Old "Mossy" was gone. They knew nothing about Operation Ajax, in which a senior CIA official engineered the coup by encouraging the Iranian Army to strike at Mossadegh, even hiring the mob that went into the streets to cheer the Shah. U.S. correspondents in Iran mirrored official truth in their dispatches. The *New York Times* correspondent Kennett Love went further and acted as a scout for the pro-Shah tank units, advising them of the weakness of the security arrangements at Mossadegh's house.[53] The seeds of the future tragic course of U.S.–Iranian relations are to be found in these events, unreported at the time in the United States and largely vanished into the American memory hole—but well remembered in Iran.

The next year a larger operation, called Operation Success, promoted a coup against the elected leader of Guatemala, who was also a populist, a nationalist, and a non-Communist, though he had two in his cabinet. The CIA trained a tiny, ragtag army of invaders and authorized the Nicaraguan dictator, Anastasio Somoza, to use two U.S.–supplied planes to bomb Guatemala City. All this convinced the Guatemalan Army that it had better support the American candidate, Castillo Armas, as president and persuaded Arbenz, the elected president, that it was time to leave the country. Thirty-five years later the army is still the dominant political force in the country, responsible for the longest and bloodiest record of human rights violations in the hemisphere. The Guatemalan episode became a model for later covert operations. So proud of it was the CIA that within months of the coup the Agency began leaking sanitized and exaggerated accounts of its triumph.

With the Iran and Guatemala operations a watershed was crossed. Here were major covert military campaigns that required for their success not just secrecy but the elaborate misleading of U.S. public opinion. "Ridiculous," snapped the State Department spokesman when Arbenz accused the CIA of conspiring to overthrow him. At the very moment, a secret CIA transmitter in Honduras beamed at Guatemala was broadcasting the inflammatory propaganda of the "Voice of Liberation." Edward L. Bernays, the public relations pioneer, had been working since 1949 on behalf of his client, the United Fruit Company, to discredit the Arbenz government and the reformist government that preceded it. Bernays convinced the American ambassador in Guatemala that the reason

Arbenz's government was putting United Fruit's Guatemalan operations to great expense by passing labor and social legislation was Communism. Bernays made the same point more strongly to Arthur Hays Sulzberger, the publisher of the New York Times, who recalled the Times reporter there and sent another who wrote so favorably about United Fruit and so unfavorably about the Guatemalan government that Bernays arranged to have these "masterpieces of objective reporting" quoted in Time, Newsweek, U.S. News & World Report, and Atlantic Monthly.[54]

Between 1952 and the spring of 1954, during which time Arbenz was nationalizing lands belonging to United Fruit, Bernays arranged a series of junkets for correspondents of Time, Newsweek, the Christian Science Monitor, and others who took the United Fruit Company guided tour of Guatemala and wrote sympathetic articles about the beleaguered company fending off the Communists of Guatemala. Thomas McCann, the company official in charge of the tours, wrote a repentant account of the campaign, which he called "a serious attempt to compromise objectivity" of the reporters.[55] Sydney Gruson, a New York Times reporter, was so unsympathetic to Arbenz that he had been expelled from the country and only readmitted at the insistence of the American ambassador. But when he later wrote that Guatemalans were resisting American pressure and were rallying around their leader, the head of CIA, Allen Dulles, phoned General Julius Adler, the Times business manager, to tell him that he had confidential information casting doubt on Gruson's "political reliability," whereupon the reporter was ordered to stay out of Guatemala.[56]

The nostalgia for the quiet fifties is mostly rooted in recollections of a scant three and a half years between the summer of 1954 and the fall of 1957. Korea and Senator McCarthy had disappeared from the headlines by Thanksgiving Day in 1954. Ike had decided against a major war in Indochina. The economy began to boom. While Cold War battles were being fought off camera, Eisenhower's efforts at achieving arms control were highly publicized and popular. Secretary of State Dulles viewed arms negotiations and improvement of the "atmospherics" in U.S.–Soviet relations with considerable suspicion. Relaxation of tensions, he said, was not necessarily a good thing for democracies because the people let down their guard. But for the first time since the onset of the Cold War a president was holding out hope of avoiding nuclear disaster. In 1955 the Democrats, seeking to use the national security issue against the Republicans in the way it had been used against them, charged

Ike with allowing a "bomber gap" to develop. The following year Adlai Stevenson, again running for president, accused Ike of being "dangerously dilatory" in building missiles. But none of this worked for the Democrats. Eisenhower was reelected by an even bigger landslide.

By 1957, however, the era of good feeling had come to an end. The Soviet space shot that launched Sputnik and a barrage of Khrushchevian boasts about Soviet technological and military superiority created an atmosphere of panic. Lyndon Johnson, the Democratic majority leader, called on the administration to admit "frankly and without evasion that the Russians have beaten us at our own game—daring scientific advances in the nuclear age." Edward Teller called Sputnik a greater defeat for the United States than Pearl Harbor.[57] Eisenhower tried vainly to calm the nation, saying that the tiny satellite flying over the United States several times each day didn't raise his apprehension "one iota." But Democrats and Republicans like Nelson Rockefeller rushed to denounce Eisenhower's parsimony in military spending.

Each leg of the Eisenhower strategy, except for covert action, now came under attack. General Maxwell Taylor wrote a book attacking the neglect of conventional forces, saying that the New Look left America no options but nuclear holocaust or surrender. A Council on Foreign Relations study written by Henry Kissinger said much the same thing. Both books became best-sellers. H. Rowan Gaither of the Ford Foundation headed a committee to look into national security and leaked its alarmist conclusions. The country needed a major military buildup, an acceleration of the missile development program, about which Eisenhower was not an enthusiast, and a $30 billion investment in fallout shelters. (Three members of the committee thought that the Soviet menace was so serious that the only answer was preventive war.[58]) The rhetoric of Khrushchev and Mao escalated as a result of their increasingly deep and public dispute over ideology and power. Khrushchev's boast, "We will bury you," provided ammunition for the proponents of big military budgets. The press played up Mao's declaration that China would defeat the American "paper tiger" even after sustaining 300 million casualties in a nuclear war.

All this created not only a loss of public confidence in American military strength but encouraged the gathering moral critique of the Eisenhower presidency. In the mid-1950s liberal and conservative social critics began to decry the emphasis on consumption, individualism, and private pursuits. The country was showing a

dangerous loss of spirit and in the face of a mounting Soviet challenge was going soft. Where was the sense of national purpose? The
Eisenhower response was to organize a Commission on National
Goals, but the belated convening of a committee of inspiration
could not deflect the mounting attacks. A new generation of politicians—Nelson Rockefeller in the Republican Party and John F.
Kennedy in the Democratic Party—was summoning the nation to
the New Frontier, a slogan coined by Rockefeller for a policy of
bigger military budgets and a more overtly activist foreign policy,
which John F. Kennedy adopted as his own.

The 1960 election campaign was dominated by the atmospherics
of foreign policy. The great issue, Kennedy declared, was America's
falling prestige. The Eisenhower administration, made up of mi-
serly old men, had stinted on the nation's defense and allowed a
dangerous "missile gap" to develop. The torch must now be passed
to the young and vigorous, who would fight the Communists with
the courage and subtlety so lacking in the quiet clubhouse atmosphere of the Eisenhower White House. Pressed by Rockefeller,
Nixon called for a military buildup almost identical to the one Kennedy asked for and largely obtained once in the White House. The
campaign featured the first televised debates. For Nixon, according
to his own account, the darkest hour of the campaign came when
he was trapped by circumstances into appearing "softer" on Fidel
Castro than Kennedy. The Democratic candidate, who had been
secretly briefed that plans for a covert operation against Castro were
under way, argued forcefully that the United States should take
strong measures to rid the hemisphere of the Communist "only
ninety miles away." Nixon, who was privy to the plans, was forced
in order to protect them to adopt a cover story and argue that
invading Cuba would be illegal and would offend world opinion.
Having to appear "statesmanlike" instead of "dramatic" and "forceful" did not go over with the voter, he later wrote.[59] This charade
set the tone for future television debates by making it clear to politicians that the medium rewarded posturing. (However, most commentators decided at the time that Nixon lost not because he was
soft on Castro but because bad makeup left him with a sinister-
looking five-o'clock shadow.) In his Inaugural Address Kennedy
sounded the theme of sacrifice—for the first time in years. He called
on the people to "pay any price, bear any burden, meet any hard-
ship," and shortly thereafter persuaded Congress to raise the defense budget and cut taxes. The sacrifice would be deferred.

In connection with the covert operation to topple Castro the CIA had set up its own public relations firm, Lem Jones Associates, run by the veteran intelligence agent David Atlee Phillips, in the hopes of choreographing U.S. press treatment of a risky and possibly controversial operation.[60] His purpose was not merely to disseminate cover stories to keep the extent of U.S. involvement out of the press but to encourage inflammatory articles about Cuba's repressive government and Soviet connections that would serve as a justification for the invasion. The *New York Times* and UPI had the story that a large, heavily guarded tract of land in Guatemala was being used to train an anti-Castro invasion force but, being unable to confirm it, published instead the denial by the president of Guatemala, which had been prepared and distributed by Lem Jones Associates. Richard Dudman of the St. Louis *Post-Dispatch* went to Guatemala, established that the airstrip and training facility did exist, and that there were Cubans there. Another reporter, writing for the Los Angeles *Mirror*, concluded that the operation was being funded by the United States. All this appeared in the press in December 1959 in scattered places and provoked one or two editorial raised eyebrows. In its issue of January 20, 1961, *Time*, having dismissed Castro's protests a week earlier as the "continued tawdry little melodrama of invasion," reported with approval that the anti-Castro Cubans were getting $500,000 from the United States. Twenty-four hours before the invasion the *Times* censored an exclusive account obtained by its veteran correspondent Tad Szulc indicating that an invasion was "imminent." The publisher, Orvil Dryfoos, decided to downplay the scoop because the story would either doom the invasion or cause its cancellation.

The passive role of reporters and editors in the 1950s and the ease with which they could be misled, manipulated by appeals to patriotism or flattered into cooperating with the men in power, had much to do with the permissive public mood of the Eisenhower and Kennedy years. An administration whose greatest asset was the credibility of the president but whose national security strategy depended heavily on secret wars, propaganda, and what the press called "dirty tricks" worried that public opinion might interfere with the strategy. In his September 1954 report on covert operations Lieutenant General James Doolittle had noted that in fighting the Cold War "hitherto acceptable norms of human conduct do not apply. If the United States is to survive, long-standing American concepts of fair play must be reconsidered. We must . . . learn to subvert, sabotage, and destroy our enemies by more clever, more sophisticated, and more effective methods than those used against

334] NATIONAL SECURITY IN THE AGE OF ANXIETY

us. It may become necessary that the American people be made acquainted with, understand and support this fundamentally repugnant philosophy."[61]

But by 1961 the philosophy did not seem especially repugnant to most Americans because neither the advantages nor the risks of covert operations were publicly discussed. For most Americans spying was patriotic adventure, an image that the Agency secretly cultivated while publicly claiming to be a rather dull organization of bureaucrats who clip newspapers and compile statistics. The Bay of Pigs invasion was widely lamented because it had failed, not because it was morally wrong, contrary to international law and treaty obligations, questionable on constitutional grounds, or even unwise policy. Kennedy took responsibility for the military failure on himself, reasserted the right to rid the hemisphere of Castro, and went to Miami to present a banner to the exile army, promising that one day it would wave over Havana. His standing in the public opinion polls shot up. On April 21, four days after the fiasco and Kennedy's graceful damage limitation speech before the American Society of Newspaper Editors, the editors took a straw vote and concluded 120–10 that "President Kennedy is doing a good job."[62]

Ironically, the credibility of the American presidency is enhanced exactly because the United States has no ministry of propaganda, owns no newspapers or television stations for domestic broadcast, and the commander in chief must do daily battle with a free press. Its official publications, except for tax forms, are not generally distributed. There are many explicit legislative prohibitions on propagandizing the American people. Unlike citizens in repressive and closed societies, who learn to discount what their leaders say, it has been a tradition that most Americans believe their president. In the age of TV the president, especially in foreign policy, has enormous resources for persuading the public. He can command prime time for a speech or a press conference. He can create news merely by saying something. On a foreign crisis he can usually have the first word. As the twentieth-century master of propaganda Joseph Goebbels wrote, creating the first impression of an event in the public mind is critical. No matter how many subsequent corrections may ensue, what people remember is the dramatic first announcement. The alchemy of presidential attention turns previously unnoticed countries into vital interests, foreign leaders with unpronounceable names into friends or enemies, and foreign struggles into American crises.

Although he neither pays the press for what it writes nor can he throw reporters and editors into jail, the president has other levers of power over the fourth estate. The gift of access—the hint of exclusive interviews, invitations to White House dinners, and leaks —encourages respectful treatment. And reporters know that only when presidential credibility is already shaky will TV viewers support tough questioning of the chief executive. Nor should the role of indolence be underestimated. Bill Moyers, a former presidential press secretary, once told the White House press corps that they were "the highest paid stenographers in Washington."[63] Reporting official truth or reinterpreting it in a column after a pleasant lunch at the Metropolitan Club or a dinner party with old friends is easier and for most of the press more congenial than probing mendacity or nonsense in high places. The relationship between the press and the national security Establishment became more adversarial in the 1960s. Nevertheless, the media's continuing dependence on officials for information, for instant newsmaking—the Sunday TV talk shows produce stories for Monday newspapers, which are notoriously hard to fill—and the human pressures not to make a scene or lose a friend, all conspire to limit reportorial curiosity and indignation.

Eisenhower was the first president of the television age. In the 1952 campaign Citizens for Eisenhower-Nixon aired the first TV political commercials. Ike was the first to hire a White House TV consultant, the actor Robert Montgomery. He was the first to hold televised press conferences. His impromptu answers were often so opaque that he delighted in the thought of how much he must be confusing intelligence agencies around the world. Columnists laughed at the wandering presidential tongue, but to the public it made the famous general seem human. Eisenhower was also the first president to exploit the pageantry of the medium. Near the end of his second term he traveled to India, Greece, Afghanistan, Iran, Pakistan, Turkey, and Italy, and pictures of enthusiastic crowds allowed Americans sitting in their living rooms to bask in their president's triumph. Here, the networks reported, was a vote of confidence in America from the people of the world.

But John F. Kennedy was a master of the new medium. His speech was cool, pithy, and rapid-fire, his face telegenic. His televised press conferences in the auditorium of the State Department gave him the chance to articulate familiar Cold War themes with style, humor, and grace. Having been elected by only 112,000 votes, Kennedy missed no opportunity to persuade through television. In November 1961, only 44 percent of the public, according to Gallup, favored resumption of nuclear testing in the atmosphere. After a televised explanation by President Kennedy for his decision to resume testing, support for the decision—despite wide publicity about the health hazards involved—rose to 66 percent.[64] Since foreign policy was his greatest interest, Kennedy's thousand-day presidency was an education campaign on national security.

After he had been in office two years, the Roper organization, which for twenty-two years had been surveying where Americans get their news, reported that for the first time more Americans relied on television than on newspapers.[65] (By the 1980s some surveys claimed that for 65 percent of Americans television is the sole source of news.) Despite their initial fears that American viewers would not sit still that long for talking heads spliced with shots of wars, hurricanes, and important people arriving at airports, CBS and then NBC expanded their fifteen-minute nightly news show to thirty minutes. By the end of the Kennedy era a window was opening on the world in millions of American households for twenty-two minutes interspersed with eight minutes of commercials.

5.

Lyndon Johnson once said that his grandchildren would be proud of two things: "What I did for the Negro and seeing it through in Vietnam for all of Asia. The Negro cost me 15 points in the polls and Vietnam cost me 20."[66] The Vietnam War ended the Johnson presidency and accelerated the collapse of the Cold War consensus. No foreign policy issue ever divided the country more deeply or over so long a period. There has never been a clearer case of a shift in public opinion producing a change in national strategy. Or more controversy about how it happened.

If there was one issue that still elicited strong bipartisan support at the beginning of the 1960s it was Indochina. Scarred by the savage Republican reaction to his attempts at subtlety in developing a China policy, Dean Acheson had taken a different tack in Indochina. His jottings in 1950 became a guiding principle for five presidents. "Question whether Ho [leader of the guerrilla movement fighting the French for an independent Vietnam] is as much nationalist as Commie is irrelevant." Since he was an "outright Commie," the United States had no choice but to protect IC [Indochina] from further COMMIE encroachments."[67] Eisenhower and Kennedy had both agonized over the strategy of keeping Vietnam out of Communist hands. Eisenhower had rejected both the use of nuclear weapons and the sending of American troops. But by 1961 Kennedy had decided to send armed Americans as "advisers" to organize the South Vietnamese pacification effort. More visible than Eisenhower's secret wars, the U.S. pacification campaign in Vietnam was still a remote, low-key affair. No attempt was made to mobilize wide support for the increasingly expensive effort. Indeed Secretary of Defense Robert S. McNamara thought that "the greatest contribution Vietnam is making—right or wrong is beside the point—is that it is developing an ability in the United States to fight a limited war, to go to war without the necessity of arousing the public ire."[68]

McNamara did not notice the gathering public concern about Vietnam because his eyes were fixed on the statistics of battle that guaranteed the United States would prevail. (In 1975, as the U.S. military effort was collapsing, a sardonic story was still making the rounds of Georgetown dinner parties. The war planners, having fed masses of data into the Pentagon computer—GNP, population, troop levels, tanks, planes, and the like—asked the electronic oracle, "When will we win?" and the computer replied, "You won in 1964.") The story of how "the best and the brightest" failed to persuade its Vietnamese allies or to break the will of its Vietnamese enemies has been told in many places.[69] Here we will concentrate on their efforts to shape American opinion.

In the 1964 election the Republicans picked as their candidate Barry Goldwater, an honest, blunt-speaking senator from Arizona, who was also an Air Force reserve general and the inspirational figure of the conservative movement in the United States. In his speeches and in his popular book *The Conscience of a Conservative* he posed what he considered the fundamental issue: Were enough Americans willing to die to keep Communism from taking over the world? Only by convincing the Communists that they were ready to die could Americans live in freedom. In the midst of the campaign he suggested using nuclear weapons to clear the jungles of Vietnam, and despite the generally horrified public reaction he stuck to his guns. The Johnson campaign responded with the prototype "negative" TV ad. Shown only once, the picture of a little girl picking petals off a daisy with a countdown in the background followed by a nuclear blast set the tone for a campaign to persuade the voters that Goldwater was a nuclear nut. But Goldwater's charges that the administration was making war in Vietnam and that it was doing so with neither a clear goal nor a willingness to tell the truth were on the mark.

Lyndon Johnson promised that he would seek "no wider war," but he stopped short of saying that he would never fight one. During the campaign, he made vague threats against North Vietnam; it was playing a "dangerous game." He understood that the American people would not vote for someone who was "ready for American boys to do the fighting for Asian boys." But Johnson did not want to give a green light to Hanoi with a flat rejection of further military options. His disavowals of wider war were always hedged with "for now" or "at this stage of the game." As much as he needed to appear as the peace candidate, he needed to protect himself from the charge that he was ignoring a Communist military threat to the American protectorate in Indochina. When Goldwater called for victory, Johnson knew that millions of American hearts stirred.

The announcement of attacks on two American destroyers in the Gulf of Tonkin and the retaliatory air strike on North Vietnam during the first week of August 1964 elicited nearly universal support. Opinion polls showed that 85 percent of Americans approved of the American response. But the attack on the first destroyer, the *Maddox*, was hardly "unprovoked," as charged; the *Maddox* was mapping North Vietnamese coastal and air defenses. The second attack never took place.[70] A number of senators were privately suspicious of the president's call for a resolution "to take all necessary measures . . . to prevent futher aggression." Had they known that draft resolutions granting presidential authority to make war in Southeast Asia already existed in a State Department safe, they would have been more suspicious. Only Senators Wayne Morse and Ernest Gruening voted against the Gulf of Tonkin Resolution. The rest, including senators like Richard Russell of Georgia who worried about another land war in Asia, responded as Johnson had hoped, "Our national honor is at stake. We cannot and we will not shrink from defending it." Armed with this bipartisan blank check, Johnson disposed of any vulnerability from the Right and played the role of "responsible" peacemaker right up to Election Day.[71]

Lyndon Johnson was doubly torn by the war in Vietnam. Unlike his two predecessors, his passion was domestic policy, not foreign affairs. The Great Society—an array of health, welfare, education, and urban renewal programs—was, as he put it, "the woman I loved," and it pained him to sacrifice her "to get involved with that bitch of war on the other side of the world." But he believed that if Communists came to power in South Vietnam "I would be seen as a coward and my nation would be seen as an appeaser." He was not "going to be the President who saw Vietnam go the way China did."[72]

Lyndon Johnson knew that the management of public opinion was a formidable problem. If Americans were going to be sent to die in Vietnam, then the case for the war had to be persuasively made. But at the same time he feared that if he aroused too much popular passion he would find himself pushed into a war with China, even a nuclear war. The "why not victory" school had not disappeared with MacArthur's retirement or Goldwater's defeat. When the course of steady escalation of the war began in February 1965 with the bombing of North Vietnam in retaliation for an attack on American bases in South Vietnam, Johnson's worries were focused on the Right. He was afraid that "all those conservatives in Congress" would use the war to kill the Great Society. American withdrawal, he believed, would lead to "Communist carnage" throughout Indochina and a right-wing backlash in the United States. In 1965 a third of Americans, according to the polls he carried around in his pocket, wanted to use nuclear weapons to end the war.

The military strategy adopted was a step-by-step escalation of the war, which Pentagon planners called the "slow squeeze." The "carefully calibrated" military operation to "punish" Vietnam, which ended up tearing American society apart and severely damaging the economy, was dictated by Johnson's assessment of the state of public opinion. The electorate would punish a president who walked away from Vietnam, but the people were not willing to pay enough taxes to support his ambitious plans for domestic reconstruction and a war for all-out victory at the same time. Johnson, despite warnings from economists, was reluctant to ask for the tax increases needed to avert inflation, because a draconian tax bill would have constituted a referendum on the war. Remembering Korea, Johnson knew that the polls he liked to show reporters were good for advertising support but not for assessing its stability. The enthusiasm of citizens demanding victory in Vietnam could either create a ground swell for risking global war or as easily evaporate as soon as the consequences became clear to them.

All the visible signs in 1965 indicated strong public support for making the maintenance of a non-Communist South Vietnam an American project. But of course the pollsters' questions never raised the matter of price. All through 1965 and into the middle of the next year, support for the war was stable as more troops were sent to Vietnam. Even as the casualties rose, public opinion rallied around the flag. By the end of 1965 there were 275,000 American fighting men in Vietnam. By the end of the following year, 385,000. By October 1967, when there were about 450,000 American troops, a majority of respondents for the first time answered Yes to the question: "In view of the developments since we entered the fighting in Vietnam, do you think the U.S. made a mistake sending troops to fight in Vietnam?"[73] By 1971 only 28 percent still thought that it had not been a mistake.

It is evident that public opposition to the Johnson war strategy played a key role in forcing the president out of office in 1968 and in forcing Richard Nixon, his successor, to try another, equally unsuccessful strategy to avoid defeat—American troop withdrawal and "Vietnamization" of the war. Less clear are the dynamics of the shift in public opinion. Why did the public come to reject both the Johnson strategy of controlled escalation and the Nixon strategy of controlled de-escalation? How did a large majority of the public come to decide that withdrawal in defeat was preferable to the risks of continuing the war? What had been an unthinkable, even traitorous proposal when put forward by a few who were considered pariahs even within the antiwar movement in 1965—Just Get Out! —became national policy ten years later. By then the overwhelming reaction was relief.

The role of the antiwar movement and television in altering the public mood still stirs embers of anger. Both Lyndon Johnson and Richard Nixon blamed television for sapping the people's will to win in Vietnam. In 1987 a U.S. Army officer still smarting from the defeat wrote in *Military Review*, "In our next war, the television cameras must stay home!"[74] In 1988 the actress Jane Fonda, a highly visible activist during the war, apologized to Vietnam veterans for posing behind a North Vietnamese antiaircraft gun on her trip to Hanoi twenty years before.

The antiwar movement began in the universities. The first "teach-in" was held on March 24, 1965, at the University of Michigan, six weeks after Johnson began the daily bombing of North Vietnam. In this first burst of antiwar activity professors and writers sailed forth onto campuses to do battle with the administration, challenging the president on facts and debating representatives of the State Department's Inter-Departmental Speaking Team on Vietnam Policy. Drawing inspiration from the success of the antinuclear testing movement a few years earlier, in which distinguished scientists like Linus Pauling had challenged official figures on the fallout from bomb tests and built public pressure for an atmospheric test ban, the teach-in movement disputed not only the content of official truth but the very idea of official truth. For the first time the premises of the national security state were being challenged. The presidential claim of secret information no longer deflected criticism, and the well-worn argument that complex matters affecting national security had best be left to the experts failed to intimidate the growing number of antiwar activists.

Although most of the teach-ins were conducted in a spirit of civility, Lyndon Johnson's unctuous manner generated public rage. Behind the pieties that earned him the sobriquet "Ole Cornpone" in Washington drawing rooms was an impulsively generous, infuriatingly contradictory personality who found it astonishingly easy to lie. Television magnified Johnson's hokeyness and revealed more about him than he wished, creating what came to be known as the "credibility gap." The relentless contrast between this large, rather old-fashioned figure as revealed by the implacable electronic eye and that of his cool predecessor fed the myth of Camelot. As the level of anger in the country rose, memories of his martyred predecessor grew fonder. Although Kennedy had made some of the critical decisions to escalate the war, forcing upon his successor the choice whether to try to redeem the sacrifice or write it off, to the growing antiwar movement it was "Johnson's war." The depth of the anger and sense of betrayal among many New York intellectuals was expressed in the poet Robert Lowell's public rejection of a White House invitation and reached the boiling point in the off-Broadway production of *MacBird*, a modern-day *Macbeth* in which Johnson orders the assassination of John F. Kennedy.

The president's men, unaccustomed to challenge, responded with an arrogance calculated to infuriate. McGeorge Bundy, Johnson's assistant for national security, answered letters challenging the assumptions of the Vietnam policy with unfailing condescension, ". . . if your letter came to me for grading as a professor of government, I would not be able to give it high marks."[75] In July 1965 Johnson's old friend and adviser Horace Busby passed along his worries about Secretary of Defense McNamara's image. "Frankly, I believe strongly the Secretary needs to make a speech revealing himself—what he believes, not what he computes." He recommended that the chairman of the Joint Chiefs, General Wheeler, make a speech with "a lot of 'peace' in it." Each cabinet member should take his appropriate slice of the electorate to educate: "Udall, before a liberal group; Connor, before a New York business group;

Wirtz, before a Midwestern audience. . . . Dr. Robert Weaver for a speech to a Negro audience. . . . John Gronouski, for a speech to an ethnic audience; maybe even ask [Chief Justice] Earl Warren to make a California speech denouncing the lawlessness evidenced in Vietnam."[76]

As the teach-ins gave way to demonstrations and then to acts of civil disobedience and finally bombings, the mood of the confrontation grew uglier. Robert McNamara shouted back at shouting Harvard students who were crowding around his car, "I'm . . . tougher [than you are]."[77] The antiwar movement, drawing into its orbit activists who had been politicized in the civil rights struggles in the south in 1963 and 1964, energized by the Students for a Democratic Society and other campus-based groups, which came to be known as the New Left, sought to frame the issues of the war in moral rather than conventional geopolitical terms. The war was wrong. The United States had no business in Vietnam, no right to destroy it. In 1966 a number of peace candidates ran for the House and Senate. Robert Scheer, who had more than one thousand students working for him, received 45 percent of the vote in a California House race on a "Get out of Vietnam" platform. The passion level rose. A Quaker from Baltimore, Norman Morrison, doused himself with gasoline on the steps of the Pentagon and lit a match; a few days later another pacifist burned himself up at the United Nations. Students around the country began burning their draft cards, and the famous baby doctor Benjamin Spock and four other antiwar activists were charged with a conspiracy to destroy the Selective Service system.

The turning point of the war was the Tet offensive. On January 31, 1968, seventy thousand Vietnamese Communist troops launched an attack in the course of which the basement of the U.S. Embassy in Saigon was occupied for six hours. Described by an American officer as a "piddling platoon action," this daring feat was not a victory for the North Vietnamese in strictly military terms, but after three years of escalating commitment, mounting casualties, and official predictions of "light at the end of the tunnel," the Tet offensive shocked the country. On TV screens Americans could see the dead bodies, the dazed GIs, and the unforgettable footage of General Nguyen Ngoc Loan, the South Vietnamese chief of police, putting a gun to the temple of a small man in black shorts with his hands tied behind his back and pulling the trigger. Johnson ordered General Westmoreland, the U.S. commander in Vietnam, to "reassure the public here that you have the situation under control." But the general's starched fatigues and official complacency seemed so out of sync with what was happening all around them that the press corps in Vietnam grew increasingly skeptical. Three and a half weeks after the Tet offensive, returning from a visit to Saigon, Walter Cronkite, a man whom the polls pronounced to be "the most trusted man in America," declared that despite official predictions of victory, it was "more certain than ever that the bloody experience of Vietnam is to end in a stalemate."[78] It was time to negotiate to get out, he said. Lyndon Johnson snapped off the TV in his office and is said to have told his aides, "It's all over."[79]

But Cronkite was resonating with public opinion, reinforcing it, perhaps, not leading it. The country had already turned against the way Johnson was conducting the war. In November 1967, 44 percent of Americans had favored gradual or complete withdrawal while 55 percent wanted to escalate the war. A poll taken in the midst of the Tet offensive showed that 53 percent of the respondents wanted a more vigorous prosecution of the war even at the risk of fighting Russia or China. Lyndon Johnson was reluctant to take actions such as bombing Hanoi and Haiphong or threatening the use of nuclear weapons because he feared it could spark World War III. At almost every turn the predictions of his senior military officers had been wrong. Why should he believe them now when the stakes were higher and the consequences of failure catastrophic? So Johnson felt caught between a war no one could tell him how to win and the mounting impatience of an increasingly divided people.

Both Lyndon Johnson and Richard Nixon blamed TV for the demoralization of the home front. Television journalism, Samuel Huntington charged in the Trilateral Commission report *The Crisis of Democracy*, published a year after the final American defeat in Vietnam, posed a serious problem for democratic rule because it undermined "governmental authority." Much of the attack on the press was pure scapegoating. Nixon's vice president, Spiro Agnew, went around the country attacking the "eastern Establishment media" as a sinister cabal of liberals out to destroy the administration, and when the investigative journalists of the *Washington Post* began unraveling the Watergate scandals, this only confirmed the suspicions of ardent Nixon supporters that the *Post* was trying to undo the 1972 election. To be sure, the *Post* had begun as a party newspaper; its pledge in 1877, when it began, was to "do what it can to uphold the Democratic majority in the House and the majestic Democratic minority in the Senate."[80] But a hundred years later its dominant concern, along with the rest of the major media, was not electing Democrats (or Republicans) but being a professional supplier of a commodity called "news" and the most popular entertainer at the breakfast table.

From time to time publishers continued to put their own spin on the news, as Luce did when he decided to turn against the Vietnam War, but in the late twentieth century, reporters respond primarily to the professional code of "responsible" journalism, which encourages skepticism about the ethics, words, and foibles of powerful political personalities but discourages the probing of their policies. Publishers respond to the market. Papers print what they think their readers want to read; TV airs what network executives think the viewers are ready to see (and the sponsors will not find objectionable). Television especially is organized to entertain, not to propagandize for or against government policies, but prudence dictates not striking at the king. There is entertainment value when White House correspondents appear somewhat confrontational in the presidential presence, dramatizing their role as watchdogs. How far they go in asking tough questions and pressing for answers, however, depends upon the president's popularity. (In the pre-Watergate days neither sponsors nor viewers would have tolerated Dan Rather's treatment of Richard Nixon. After the Iran-Contra scandal broke, the reverential aura that had hung over Ronald Reagan's East Room press conferences for almost eight years dissolved.)

The very structure of television news, as Neil Postman has argued, discourages not only real debate but thought itself. The grammar of the medium discourages reflection and the insight to be derived from making intelligent connections between seemingly unrelated events. Because they reinforce the atomistic picture of the world, the television networks, without meaning to, lend added credibility to the president of the United States as the Interpreter of Last Resort. The unfathomable snippets from around the world cascading onto the screen build support for official truth. Criticism is not reported until it is borne by a powerful political constituency. As Max Frankel, executive editor of the New York Times, described the coverage of the Vietnam War protest, "As protest moved from left groups, anti-war groups, into the pulpits, into the Senate . . . as it became a majority opinion, it naturally picked up coverage. And then naturally the tone of the coverage changed. Because we're an Establishment institution, and whenever your natural community changes . . . , then naturally you will too."[81]

In his study The Uncensored War Daniel Hallin concludes that the TV networks and the *New York Times*, whose Vietnam War coverage he monitored during the Kennedy-Johnson escalation, were "overwhelmingly favorable" to American policy in Vietnam in the years 1964 to 1968. None of the papers and television news operations most fiercely accused of undermining the government ever challenged the fundamentals of official truth even when it was so fatally flawed as to guarantee the failure of U.S. strategy. No one watching the networks and listening to their commentary had any reason to doubt that the mastermind behind the Vietnam War was China or that the consequences of "losing" Vietnam would be the communization of Asia. Until public opinion began to shift, the media presented escalation as the only responsible, indeed inevitable option. Headlines communicated the White House spin on the news. Thus the *New York Times* headline for April 25, 1965:

PRESIDENT PLANS NO MAJOR CHANGE IN
VIETNAM POLICY
He is Adhering to Firm but Cautious Course
With Talks with Reds a Main Goal

(Three weeks earlier, NSAM 328, approving "a change of mission [a larger combat role] for all marine battalions deployed to Vietnam," said that the policy should be implemented "in ways that should minimize any appearance of sudden changes of policy."[82] The second attack on the destroyer *Maddox*, the one that never happened, was billed by the Washington *Post* as "the gravest military confrontation since the Cuban missile crisis." North Vietnamese charges and denials were regularly dismissed as propaganda or simply ignored. This is hardly surprising. Despite the ethos of professionalism, reporters are naturally reluctant to credit their nation's designated enemies over the commander in chief.

In the days following Tet, lights burned late in the White House and State Department as Johnson's advisers wrote memos to one another on opinion management. John Roche, an academic whom the president had brought to the White House, wrote him a professorial one-page EYES ONLY suggestion that he avoid using the Tonkin Gulf Resolution to justify the war, keeping in mind "the historical fact that Americans really don't give a damn about treaties, congressional resolutions and other legalisms. . . . By and large, the American tradition assumes that when one is weak on facts, he talks about law." The president's task was to convince the people "1. That we are *right* in being there. 2. That we are going to *win.*"[83] It was a succinct and accurate statement of an insoluble problem. "Public affairs" specialists in the White House prepared a "plan to rally the homefront." Recounting past efforts to "sell the war," including "work with veterans organizations" and "formation of a committee of intellectuals-for-the-war," a March 3, 1968, top-secret draft plan for "people rallying" once again correctly assessed the challenge. "1. Prove that it is in our national interest. 2. Prove that we have a plan to win it." The problem was especially difficult because Americans "do not hate the enemy and emotions have not been aroused as they were in earlier wars. Consider that: We cannot talk about bombing Laos; We scrupulously avoid killing the enemy at home, and brag about it; We do not mine his harbor or blockade his coast. . . . We go to great extremes to avoid a confrontation of any nature with his . . . major supply allies."[84] When Johnson was forced by the signs of galloping inflation to call for a 10 percent tax surcharge, support for the war took a precipitous drop. The first big casualty lists had the same effect. "The weakest chink in our armor," Johnson told his staff when the polls dipped, "is American public opinion. Our people won't stand firm in the face of heavy losses, and they can bring down the government."[85]

The Vietnam protest movement spilled out of university auditoriums and into the streets. From the first it was a divided movement. The initial energy for the first big Washington demonstration came from the Students for a Democratic Society, and it was preceded by months of rancorous argument between radicals and moderates. But the young activists challenged the established peace movement on many fronts. Initially, they clashed on the issue of whether to welcome Communists into the leadership of the antiwar effort. Veterans of old battles of the 1930s in the labor movement, such as Bayard Rustin, who had organized Martin Luther King's March on Washington in 1963, were reluctant to risk tarring the new movement or let Communists stage a comeback by riding the war. But to the new activists it was a matter of principle not to succumb to Red-baiting and McCarthyism. Soon, however, SDS was becoming more radical in its critique and much more confrontational in its tactics. To radical critics, including a rising number of professors and prominent intellectuals, the war was not a mistake but a crime. For the few student activists who had grown up as "red-diaper babies" the war confirmed the violence and injustice of America that had hounded their parents and defined their world. But most thought of themselves as liberals who believed in an America that had now, as one SDS leader put it, broken their American heart.

As the nation's leaders seemed immovable in their passion for the war, the radical activists came to believe that the orgy of violence in Southeast Asia was neither an unfortunate accident nor an aberration of American life. The carnage in Vietnam was the inevitable consequence of capitalism and the profound corruption of American society.[86]

In the end the antiwar movement became a broad-based coalition of doves and hawks determined to end American involvement in a dirty, unwinnable war. But the early leaders of the movement, the ones who wrote the manifestos, organized the marches, gave the interviews, were young people, idealistic, passionate, manipulative, alternately elated and depressed by sudden fame, and confused. Far more than the civil rights movement and the peace movement of the 1960s, the campaign to end the Vietnam War was a student movement whose leaders rejected conventional American politics. Believing the promise of America, they came to see the seemingly confident, passionless generation in power as betrayers of the dream. Some of the denunciation of American life grew out of hastily learned (and quickly unlearned) Marxism. But Phil Ochs, Lenny Bruce, Dick Gregory, Mort Sahl, Allen Ginsberg, and the Beatles exerted a far deeper and wider influence than Lenin, Castro, or Herbert Marcuse. The comfort and anxiety of the Eisenhower era had stimulated the social critique of David Riesman, John Kenneth Galbraith, Daniel Boorstin, William Whyte, and Vance Packard, and the existential cry of the "beat generation" poets and novelists, notably Jack Kerouac. These critical themes were transformed into the black humor and songs of protest of the 1960s. American society was dehumanized, image-ridden, commodity-worshiping. Corporate-controlled America offered life without meaning, without community, without love. LBJ's motives and Hitler's were the same, said Norman Mailer. "No, no, of course one cannot compare Hitler with Johnson," said one prominent antiwar activist, "Hitler moved more slowly toward murder." The drug culture, the explosion of four-letter words, audacious sex, and loud music were the revenge of the Vietnam generation on the parents whom they blamed for the war and the sick society that could not stop killing poor Asian peasants.[87]

Some of the antiwar leaders had a theory: It would take draft-card burnings, desecration of the flag, and street theater to draw the TV cameras, shock the country, and build the movement; polite debate was useless. But most of the theater that Americans saw on their TV screens, however, was neither contrived nor theoretical. The spirit behind some of the rage is perhaps best captured in the remark of an SDS leader after students had just seized a dean at Columbia University and occupied a building in April 1968: "We've got something going here and now we've just to got to find out what it is."[88] The energy to build the protest movement was generated by the pain of destroyed illusions and a sense of moral urgency, a need to sacrifice one's self to stop "the machine." For the radicals anything less was to be complicit with the evil. The movement was a "liberated zone" where anguished, young middle-class Americans could break free of the homogenized society of Wonder Bread and foolish consumption to confront, as Norman Mailer told an antiwar rally, "that particular corrosive sensation so many of us feel in the chest and the guts so much of the time."[89] The war became the vehicle for mobilizing all manner of discontents and the movement itself a theater for acting out a variety of feelings about parents, plastics, gender, grades, sex, bureaucracy, hidden persuaders, and invisible government.

Most of the millions of Americans who opposed the war by expressing their feelings to pollsters, taking to the streets, supporting Eugene McCarthy, George McGovern, and other antiwar candidates were simply voting No to a war that had not been demonstrated to be vital to national security, an ugly conflict for which the administration had no plan to win. They were certainly not voting for the Vietcong or for socialism in the United States. Most but not all of those who "put their body on the line" were making a moral statement about what they saw on television—the naked Vietnamese girl running down the street in flames, trying to run away from the napalm burning her flesh, a GI setting fire to a thatched hut with a Zippo lighter, babies shot in a ditch at My Lai, South Vietnamese soldiers looting enemy corpses. Some were outraged, some merely uneasy about what was being done with their tax dollars in the name of America. The ranks of the antiwar movement were overwhelmingly nonviolent; most of the marchers, the letter writers, the anguished parents, were committed to the reclaiming of America, not its humiliation; to a cultural loosening and an overdue recognition of constitutional rights, not to a radical transformation of American society.

The largest group within the movement opposed the war on the ground that it was a failure. Many of the New Hampshire voters who surprised the world in March 1968 by voting in a primary for a quirky, relatively unknown senator in preference to a sitting president favored the war and were registering disapproval of Johnson's handling of it. When McCarthy dropped out, they transferred their support to the hawkish George Wallace, who promised a bigger, shorter war. The antiwar movement became a vehicle for the emerging women's movements, black movements, movements for new consciousness, new life-styles, and a counterculture; riding the same wave of protests, these activists sang songs together and headed off in different directions. While many who marched refused to see the Vietnamese as enemies, only a tiny faction within the antiwar movement with names like Committee to Aid the NLF identified itself as a solidarity movement with America's officially designated enemies. Unlike earlier anti-imperialist movements in the United States, this highly publicized fringe of the movement seemed more interested in celebrating the virtues of North Vietnam and in seeing their own country humbled than in ending the war. To television viewers, anguished over the mounting casualties, the screaming demonstrators waving Vietcong flags were more than just willing to see their country "cut and run." They seemed to relish defeat. As the country turned against the war, bumper stickers appeared everywhere: AMERICA: LOVE IT OR LEAVE IT!

The meaning of patriotism was now at issue. J. William Fulbright, who had guided the Tonkin Gulf Resolution through the Senate for his friend Lyndon Johnson, turned against the war a few months later. As chairman of the Foreign Relations Committee he held televised "educational" hearings in February 1966 at which prestigious critics of the war policy, George Kennan and Generals James Gavin and Matthew Ridgway, explained why the war could not be won and why it could escalate into a conflict with China. Johnson's supporters, responded with Fourth of July rhetoric. "I swell with pride," said Senator Russell Long, "as I see Old Glory flying from the Capitol. . . . My prayer is there may never be a white flag of surrender up there."[90] Fulbright, a soft-spoken intellectual who had been an important shaper of the foreign policy consensus since World War II, now denounced America's "arrogance of power" and endorsed the citizen's right to criticize dangerous foreign policies as a "higher patriotism." Blaming himself for his silence during the escalation of the war, he charged that it was "only when politicians join in a spurious consensus behind controversial policies, that the campuses and streets and public squares of America . . . become the forums of a direct and disorderly democracy."[91] Indeed, it was fear of public opinion that made it so urgent to speak. The patience of the American people, he said, "will give way to mounting demands for an expanded war, . . . a strike against China; and then we will have global war."[92]

The deepening division within the American elite legitimized the antiwar movement and gave it new strength. One by one, some of the nation's most prominent and prestigious figures came out against the war. General David Shoup, the former commandant of the Marine Corps, called for an end to the American involvement, and Martin Luther King announced that if he were of draft age, he would be a conscientious objector. "I could never again raise my voice against the violence of the oppressed in the ghettos without having first spoken clearly to the greatest purveyor of violence in the world today—my own government."[93]

In the 1980s it has been fashionable to assert that the antiwar movement may have even prolonged the war. George Weigel argues that the movement "played into the hands of the men it most despised"—George Wallace, who drew 13 percent of the vote in 1968, and Richard Nixon, who used the Vietcong banners on the Mall to enlist a Silent Majority behind his candidacy.[94] The disorder and calculated assault on American values, including patriotism itself, may have helped to elect Nixon in 1968 and to create a backlash on "social issues"—drugs, abortion, family values, pornography, "permissiveness" in criminal justice—that drove American politics to the right in the 1980s. But as we shall see, the antiwar movement had a lasting effect on the conduct of foreign policy.

By 1972 the Democratic Party was carrying the antiwar banner; it was now "Nixon's war." In 1976 the voters punished the disgraced Nixon by voting against his hand-picked successor who pardoned his crimes, but for more than a decade thereafter they punished the antiwar party even as they had patriotically punished the Federalists and the Whigs for having opposed the wars against England and Mexico in 1812 and 1846. But the disorder, the tearing apart of families, what John McNaughton, one of the Pentagon war planners, called "the worst split in our people in more than a century,"[95] made even those who hated the demonstrators want the war over. It was the split in the country, the damage to the economy, and the opposition of their own children that shook the confidence of "opinion leaders." It was the domestic impact of the war that convinced former hawks like Dean Acheson and Clark Clifford to advise Lyndon Johnson in March 1968 that he had no choice but to "deescalate" the operation in Vietnam. As Cyrus Vance, Johnson's deputy secretary of defense, had put it, "The divisiveness in the country was growing with such acuteness that it was threatening to tear the United States apart."[96] If such sober men had come to this conclusion, Johnson worried, "what must the average citizen in the country be thinking?" Later that month he announced that he would not run again.

Richard Nixon ran against the demonstrators but adopted their goal and promised the country peace at home as well as abroad. In the campaign he adverted to a "secret plan" to end the war. In his Inaugural Address he promised to "bring us together." By the end of his first term Nixon had pulled most of the American troops out of Indochina even as he widened the war by invading Cambodia, an event that precipitated a wave of campus protests, the shooting of students at Kent State, and a howl of anguish throughout America. The most visible antiwar activity declined as the war dragged on and the New Left radicals fractionated into warring sects and proceeded to self-destruct. The movement became more mainstream. A clear majority of Americans wanted the war over, and while many still wanted victory, fewer and fewer believed that victory was possible. It was no longer clear what victory would be.

Nixon searched vainly for a strategy to restore the broken consensus. "Vietnamization" was a strategy to keep the South Vietnamese Army fighting without suffering further American casualties. South Vietnam could not win, but with American aid it might postpone the humiliation of defeat. In the end the increasingly broad-based antiwar movement achieved its goal, because Nixon was too weak to stop it. Wounded by the Watergate scandals, the president could not prevent Congress in 1973 from cutting off military aid to the South Vietnamese government. The United States was now out of Vietnam. Only his forced resignation in August 1974 saved him from presiding over the frenzied evacuation of Saigon eight months later as the victorious North Vietnamese Army took over the city. The failure in Vietnam was not the sole cause, perhaps not even the primary cause, of the breakdown of the foreign policy consensus. The new vulnerability to Soviet missiles, the unacceptable costs of policing the world, and the growing economic competition with major allies in Europe and Japan dictated a rethinking of U.S. national security strategy. But the outcome of the Vietnam War was the most dramatic symbol of the growing gulf between ambitious but unexamined ends and limited means, between a dimming vision of a tired foreign policy elite and the rush of feelings of an anxious public.

CHAPTER 13

The Politics of Feelings

1.

By the mid-1970s the American political system was reeling from the pressures of the civil rights, antiwar, ecology, and consumer movements, the Watergate scandals, the disgrace of Richard Nixon, and the agonizing end game of the Indochina war. In 1976, the year of the bicentennial, Americans were caught up in what the social critic Walter Karp calls "a vast, chaotic upheaval that was mainly democratic in spirit, purely democratic in its outcome, and deeply threatening to the nation's political establishment, which watched with increasing anxiety as its power and authority eroded."[1] A populist counterattack against the imperial presidency, self-serving secrecy in government, harassment of citizens by the FBI and the CIA, and concentrated power in the backrooms of party politics and the boardrooms of the large corporations brought a season of reform: sunshine laws, a strengthened Freedom of Information Act, reform of the Democratic Party nominating machinery, investigations of the FBI and the CIA for spying on citizens, and an unprecedented vote in Congress against a CIA operation in Angola. These signs of democratic vitality were interpreted by prominent fashioners of opinion as symptoms of social disorder; there were few voices raised to defend the upsurge of populist spirit. In its front-page bicentennial essay the *New York Times* warned of "a wild disorientation about the state of American life, as though the national compass had been lost."[2] In the midst of the national celebration of American independence, pollsters reported a vote of no confidence in basic American institutions. In

1958, when the Institute for Social Research at the University of Michigan first began asking citizens whether they trusted the government, 73 percent said they always did or at least most of the time. By 1974, the year Nixon resigned, only 37 percent would admit to trusting the government more than occasionally. By 1980, the year Ronald Reagan was elected, only one in four Americans said they trusted the government to any substantial extent.[3]

More telling than the polls were the election returns. In 1976 the process of presidential nomination had become more democratic, but barely 54 percent of the electorate bothered to vote in the general election. The two national political parties had become phantoms, rising every four years to lick envelopes and collect money. The cohorts of old-time American politics—ward heelers, city bosses, precinct organizers, and reform clubs—were hardly to be seen. The biennial rituals for the transfer of power were changing, and the media consultants, impresarios of direct-mail campaigns, pollsters, and political action committees were taking control of the action. (By 1986 PACs raised more than $132 million for House and Senate races. The average cost of a campaign for Congress was $261,000, and a Senate race was ten times higher.)

At the same time there was a burst of new energy for greater participation in decision making throughout the whole society. The decline in the percentage of citizens who took their civic obligations seriously continued, but those who did participate were likely to be more active than in the 1950s and early 1960s. Hundreds of thousands took part in demonstrations of one sort or another during the 1970s and the numbers were higher in the 1980s. Thousands of Americans engaged in acts of civil disobedience and tax resistance in the 1970s and 1980s, and much larger numbers joined new organizations to educate, agitate, and lobby for electoral reform, consumer safety, environmental protection, and justice for women, blacks, Hispanics, Native Americans, the handicapped, and senior citizens. The bumper sticker "QUESTION AUTHORITY" caught the spirit of the times. The United States was in the throes of a cultural transformation. There was a new informality in manners, dress, and speech, a relaxation of discipline in the armed forces, government bureaucracies, and corporations, and a noticeable weakening of deference to age, rank, male gender, old money, small-town values, advanced degrees, and professional accomplishments.

All this inspired the same sort of fears for the Republic as in Andrew Jackson's day. The polls showed a loss of confidence in every institution, including the military, corporations, churches, universities, media, the medical establishment, even the Supreme Court. As a consequence there occurred, in Samuel Huntington's words, "a weakening of the coherence, purpose, and self-confidence of political leadership."[4] In post-Vietnam, post-Watergate America there was much apocalyptical talk about the "crisis of democracy." While it was fashionable to note that the collapse of "the imperial presidency" after Nixon's failure to subject the federal government to his personal control or to frustrate congressional investigation meant that "the system worked," it was equally fashionable to note that the crisis had occurred because the United States was now "ungovernable."[5] The presidency of Richard Nixon marked the high-water mark of the welfare state, "the revolution of rising entitlements," as Daniel Bell called it, but also the end of the extraordinary twenty-year growth spurt in the world economy that had made the welfare state possible.

In fiscal year 1960, foreign affairs, mostly the cost of supplying and maintaining the Department of Defense and the armed forces under its command, had accounted for 53.7 percent of the federal budget. That year the government spent on defense ten times what it spent on welfare. But in 1965, after successive cycles of boom and relentless growth and no major war since Korea, these budgetary priorities were no longer politically acceptable. Before he made Vietnam a major war, Lyndon Johnson made the War on Poverty a national project. By the early 1970s the Cold War, having served as the ideological glue for a generation, was suddenly out of fashion; indeed, in the early 1970s it was commonplace to pronounce it a thing of the past. Richard Nixon had responded to the rising demands in the country for education, medical care, environmental protection, increased social security benefits, and transfer payments to the poor all the while he was withdrawing American forces from Vietnam. By FY 1974 bureaucrats in Washington working for a Republican administration were spending more of the national wealth than ever before, but foreign affairs was taking only a little more of the federal budget than transfer payments, social security, and other social spending.

Nixon had run for reelection in 1972 by marketing his missions of peace to Moscow and Peking. On the foundations of "détente" with the Soviet Union and a trip to the Great Wall of China he promised a "generation of peace" to war-weary, middle-class American voters who wished to sacrifice no more of their sons in Vietnam or see them flee to Canada. Nixon ended Selective Service. In the midst of a war he knew he could not win but promised not to lose—the slogan was "peace with honor"—Nixon discovered that the talisman of "national security" had lost its magic. The mere invocation of the intimidating phrase had usually served to protect presidents in the Cold War years, but this time it failed to stop Nixon's pursuers, and his attempt to defend himself against impeachment by invoking the national interest merely increased public cynicism about government.

In April 1975, when the last United States Army helicopter lifted off the roof of the American Embassy in Saigon, Gerald Ford was in the White House. The first appointed president in history, he immediately undermined what little support he had—based mostly on being a genial American who in no way resembled Richard Nixon—by pardoning his disgraced predecessor. Not just the presidency but all the principal Cold War institutions were now under sharp attack. The Central Intelligence Agency was being investigated in both houses of Congress for its role in the overthrow of the elected left-wing government in Chile, for the planning of assassinations of Fidel Castro and other foreign leaders, and for its harassment of American citizens who opposed the Vietnam War. The armed forces of the United States, no longer able to conscript, faced not only the increased costs of a volunteer army but the prospects of lower budgets. Leading colleges and universities, reflecting the feelings of the Vietnam War generation, barred recruiters for the military and the CIA from their campuses.

The old foreign policy Establishment, derided as "the best and the brightest" in David Halberstam's popular book on America's tragic blunder in Southeast Asia, was on the defensive. The fundamental assumption on which Walter Lippmann had based his fierce indictment of public opinion no longer rang true. "The people," he had written in *The Public Philosophy*, "have imposed a veto upon the judgments of informed and responsible officials. They have compelled the governments, which usually knew what would have been wiser, or was necessary, or was more expedient, to be too late with too little, or too long with too much."[6] Now book publishers, television commentators, and investigative journalists, alive to the new market potential for stories of error, greed, and confusion in high places, offered a mirror of reality that turned Lippmann upside down. The leaders had been neither wise, moderate, informed, nor responsible. Mass opinion had imposed no veto on sending a half million troops to Vietnam. But the public had rejected the claim of five presidents that keeping Vietnam non-Communist was vital to

U.S. national security. And events had proved them more right than their leaders. No dominoes fell in Asia outside of Indochina itself. China, supposedly the real enemy in Vietnam, became a recipient of U.S. aid and invaded Communist Vietnam.

Secretary of State Henry Kissinger understood that the American Century as articulated in the Truman Doctrine was over. For him national power consisted of a web of appearances. The perception of power was what mattered, and in the wake of Vietnam, perceptions about American will and purpose seemed to be changing dramatically. The military balance had shifted. The Soviet Union could now destroy the United States and was ahead in numbers of missiles. The sharp rise in oil prices in 1973 produced panic. The revolution in Portugal the following year, which raised the specter of a left-wing government in a NATO ally, the electoral advances of "Eurocommunism" in Italy, and the rise of domestic violence in Western Europe brought forth a wail of Spenglerian pessimism from the secretary of state.

Kissinger, a media star as no previous foreign policy adviser had ever been, suddenly discovered that he lacked the personal credibility to persuade the country to support his new global strategy for the post–Cold War world. It was a subtle strategy combining limited cooperation with both China and the Soviet Union and continuing efforts to contain both by playing one against the other. Kissinger's approach depended upon increased reliance on surrogates, notably Iran, to play the role of "peacekeeper" in threatened regions and on the CIA to keep Communists from coming to power in places such as Portugal and Chile. Congress, however, reacting to the public disclosures of CIA operations and methods and to war weariness, voted in 1975 to cut off further support for a guerrilla force fighting to prevent the Soviet-supported MPLA movement from taking over Angola. In his writings Kissinger had often identified popular intolerance for the moral ambiguities of statecraft and the public's failure of nerve in moments of crisis as the great handicaps of democratic nations. The resistance of U.S. public opinion to the use of force in pursuit of the national interest, he warned, now threatened to hobble American leaders in the exercise of power and to serve notice on the rest of the world that it was safe to defy the United States.

In 1975 Kissinger's pessimism resonated with the mood swing of post-Watergate, post-Vietnam America. For many reasons, including the suddenly higher cost of energy, economic growth in the industrial nations ground almost to a halt in the 1970s even as inflation rose throughout the capitalist world. National magazines and TV commentators discovered the profoundly subversive idea that there were "limits to growth." The environment was not infinitely forgiving. The extraordinary prosperity of the first postwar generation had been purchased at the price of befouled air, poisoned water, depleted soil, and squandered minerals.

The global struggle with Communism had made the idea of a centralized, managerial state in America legitimate and built consent for policies quite at variance with the American past—permanent emergency, large standing armies, continuous military preparation, large-scale undeclared wars, covert operations, and high taxes to pay for it all. Every successful presidential candidate, irrespective of party, adopted Truman's 1948 election strategy and promised that even as the United States fought the Cold War the nation would become richer and afford its citizens greater equality, justice, and opportunity. In asserting its role as the people's protector every administration devoted its major efforts to building a world system for promoting American wealth and influence, in short an empire, though it had been years since the word had been admissible in American political debate to describe anything but the Soviet Union or what was left of British glory.

By the mid-1970s federal, state, and local governments were spending almost a third of the gross national product. Presidential promises to the electorate were being redeemed by an ever growing and more activist federal bureaucracy. But the swelling of the welfare state was producing big budgetary deficits, fears of inflation, and rising concern on the Right about the penetration of government into the social and cultural life of the nation. All this posed a mortal threat to Cold War liberalism, the bipartisan ideology. In theory, the welfare state was the stabilizer of the American system, the human face of democracy under arms. Public happiness now depended upon dreams of ever greater prosperity and growth, but by the mid-1970s the myth of never-ending economic progress no longer compelled belief. Polls detected that millions of Americans feared for their future. The harvest of the boom years was an accumulation of expectations. Each of the mushrooming entitlements—Medicare, food stamps, housing subsidies, job creation programs, pollution control, occupational safety, access for handicapped, and consumer protection—created its own constituency, each of which was prepared to fight the others for a share of the pie. And the pie was barely growing. Something would have to give. Inflation was the signal to the middle class that real growth had stopped.

The strategic premises of Cold War liberalism were also under challenge. World Communism was the wrong target because there was no such thing. Communists in Russia and China were seeking détente with America and fighting one another. The most pressing threats to U.S. security—dependence on foreign oil, declining hegemony in the world economy, environmental crisis—had little to do with either of the old adversaries. Moreover, Kissingerian *Realpolitik* had disturbed the ideological neatness of traditional Cold War rhetoric. It had been asserted since 1946 that the depravity of the Communist system made it impossible to have normal relations with the dictatorships of the Soviet Union and China. Yet Nixon and Kissinger had reached out to China when that whole society was being consumed by the cruel madness of the Cultural Revolution, and the administration was encouraging trade with Moscow even as it turned a deaf ear to the dissidents, refuseniks, and other victims of Brezhnev's repressive policies.

Before Vietnam, containment had been an easy policy to defend, because its success could be stipulated. Nuclear war had not happened. Russian tanks had not rolled over the German plain. No one could prove what, if anything, the level of U.S. defense expenditures had to do with either. But in Vietnam five presidents had asserted a "vital interest" and failed to achieve it. The failure elicited two fundamental critiques of the Kissinger foreign policy, one practical, the other moral. Realists pointed out that controlling the political and economic development of the Third World, whether by direct military intervention or by the use of surrogates, was no longer possible. The United States, as American leaders now made a habit of saying in foreign policy speeches, could not be the policeman of the world. Commitments and resources had to be brought into balance. The moralists argued that the means employed to fight the Cold War were corrupting the ends. If the American president was toasting Russian leaders in the Kremlin, all the while blinking at human rights violations and supporting murderous generals in Chile, Argentina, Korea, the Philippines, and Brazil, the very legitimacy of American power was thereby challenged.

Jimmy Carter tried to craft a new ideology to restore coherence to American foreign policy and attract a divided and confused electorate into a new consensus. In the 1976 election Jimmy Carter attempted to gather in the two groups that had broken with Kissinger, liberals who were repelled by his cynicism and amoral approach to foreign policy, and hard-liners who thought he had conceded too much to the Soviet Union. Attacking Kissinger for having "given up too much to the Russians and gotten too little in return," Carter promised a return to morality, a concern with human rights, and a determination to scold Free World dictators who ruled by torture.[7] The new president set as his goal "the elimination of all nuclear weapons from this earth," decried the "inordinate fear of communism" that had led the nation "to embrace any dictator who joined us in our fear," and set about to introduce the electorate to a new foreign policy agenda. Inexperienced in foreign affairs himself, his new approach reflected the shift in elite opinion. In 1972 the Council on Foreign Relations had put forward a new agenda, which it called the "management of interdependence." It was typical of many new ideas advanced by a variety of writers on foreign policy as the Vietnam policy collapsed. The defeat in Southeast Asia and the new world of the 1970s left in its wake demanded that the United States use its power more wisely and modestly, "leadership without hegemony," as one prominent Nixon adviser had called it.

That same year David Rockefeller, chairman of the Chase Manhattan Bank, organized the Trilateral Commission, a collection of bankers, corporate executives, former high government officials, and well-connected academics from the United States, Western Europe, and Japan. The commission had as its purpose the creation of a congenial transnational elite to counter the rising tide of nationalism that had overtaken the industrial world in the wake of the energy crisis and the world economic slowdown. These "leading citizens," as they called themselves, held well-publicized meetings to design coordinated policies for the increasingly interdependent market economies of the industrial world. But the timing was wrong. The Trilateral Commission soon became a lightning rod to attract precisely those nationalistic impulses it was designed to overcome. In the 1980 election amid cries of conspiracy the commission became a campaign issue. In its attempt to deal with the limitations on national sovereignty stemming from the late-twentieth-century reality that neither bombs, dollars, corporations, refugees, information, nor foul air are respecters of borders, Rockefeller's initiative ran up against what Walter Dean Burnham has called the "diffuse, spontaneous, and pervasive revolt among non-elites against the integrated, bureaucratized, 'cool,' and instrumentally rational world which is emerging in our time." If to the ordinary citizen the federal government in Washington now seemed unresponsive and uncaring, then a nonelected, unaccountable group of leading citizens making private deals with foreigners to manage "world order" was positively sinister.

Here was Jimmy Carter's dilemma. Seeing himself as a moral educator, he set about to explain why old Cold War simplicities would no longer do. But the new strategies called for real sacrifice instead of grandiloquence—lower expectations, changes in lifestyles, even the rethinking of the American credo of growth, bigness, and quick return on investment. Talk of sacrifice was inevitably explosive because it would open the question of how the sacrifice was to be shared.

Early in his administration Carter had expended considerable political capital to orchestrate a careful public campaign to secure the ratification of a treaty to turn the Panama Canal over to Panama in 1999. Negotiated under Johnson, Nixon, and Ford, the treaty enjoyed bipartisan support and enthusiastic endorsement of the Catholic Church, the National Council of Churches, the AFL–CIO, most of the media, even John Wayne, who had struck up a friendship with the Panamanian dictator Omar Torrijos. But Richard Viguerie, who was developing a direct-mail campaign to mobilize the conservative vote, saw the treaty as an opportunity to "raise America's consciousness about national security . . . win or lose." He later estimated that the Panama Canal debate yielded 250,000 to 400,000 new names for his computerized list of conservative activists that helped put the reigning spokesman of conservatism in the White House.[8] Running against Ford for the nomination in 1976, Ronald Reagan said of the Canal, "We bought it, we paid for it, it's ours, and we're going to keep it," and brought crowds to their feet.[9] Despite the broad organized support for the treaty, nine out of ten citizens told pollsters that they viewed the "Canal giveaway" as another retreat. Senator Orrin Hatch called it "the culmination of a pattern of appeasement and surrender."[10] Carter formed yet another committee of notables to educate the country on why turning over the Canal was good for the United States, and became the first president to appear on a special radio call-in show to answer questions of concerned citizens. The campaign succeeded, but the victory had its costs.

Nevertheless, Carter pressed on relentlessly in his educational efforts. Wearing a sweater on television to make the point that he had turned down the thermostat in the White House, the president called on Americans to conserve fuel, adopt less wasteful habits, stop speeding on the highways, and recognize that the real world imposed limits on the American appetite that could no longer be ignored. By the end of the 1970s the United States was dependent not only on foreign oil but foreign capital to finance the nation's deficit. To attract the capital, interest rates were raised, and as bank charges skyrocketed so did the cost of buying homes, cars, and vacuum cleaners. Jimmy Carter was caught up in the fashions of the 1970s, and his impulse was to pin the responsibility for the "governability crisis" on the people. He did not go quite so far as the British writer Barbara Ward, who reproached American babies for gobbling up five hundred times as much food, water, and minerals in a lifetime as Mongolian babies, but the president, despite his smile and twinkling blue eyes, came across to his countrymen as a scold.

To Americans watching the nightly news, not much seemed left of the American Century. As 1979 began, Iran, a centerpiece in Kissinger's post-Vietnam strategy, had an Islamic fundamentalist revolution fueled by anti-Americanism. The immediate consequence was higher gas prices and longer lines at the filling station. A leftist revolution occurred in Nicaragua. Inflation soared and Jimmy Carter's pollster, Patrick Caddell, and his media adviser, Gerald Rafshoon, brought word that the country blamed him for the gas lines and "stagflation." (The newly coined word made the point that the economic distress was without precedent in the postwar era, not only in its gravity but in its unknown causes.) Carter agonized for ten days and then made a speech blaming the people for their "spiritual malaise" and fired a quarter of his cabinet. This public relations fiasco produced waves of ridicule. Not long afterward, the president's fortunes sank further as the Iranians took fifty-three hostages at the American Embassy in Teheran and held them captive for more than a year. As the final year of his term was about to begin, the Soviet Union invaded Afghanistan.

2.

By the mid-1970s taking the American temperature had become a national pastime. Lyndon Johnson was the first president to carry poll results in his pocket and flash them in the face of skeptics, but Carter was the first president to have a pollster on the White House staff. Not only had politicians become utterly dependent upon oracles to monitor the mood swings of the American voter, but the voters themselves devoured stories about what they were supposed to be thinking. Pollsters happily reported poll results showing that

Americans liked polling. (Seventy-three percent of respondents told Gallup that they thought polls were good for the country and 68 percent thought that their results were "mostly right."[11]) At least someone was paying attention. Reading polls was like running your eye over the fashion pages, a chance to mentally try on opinions.

The networks, the major newspapers, and national magazines all began running regular polls and many had their own opinion experts. The increased interest in polls was a reaction to the demonstrated power of public opinion in the Vietnam–Watergate years. The feverish interest in public opinion by elected officials that began in the 1960s was triggered by their concern about having misread the national mood. It reflected not a celebration of public opinion but apprehension about mood shifts. Politicians were advised to consult these modern auguries not because they would find popular wisdom for guiding their policies but because marketing surveys were needed to craft a winning strategy. To govern a volatile, capricious, and largely uninformed public it was essential to keep closer watch on what was going on in their heads at any given moment. Public opinion polls had become indispensable devices for detecting political booby traps.

Between 1964 and 1980, according to a mass of polling data, there were two perceptible shifts in the public mood with respect to national security. In the first twenty years after World War II large majorities year after year had assented to the proposition that the United States should defend with military force almost any country identified by a pollster as an ally; usually no more than 10 percent of respondents thought the nation was spending too much on the military. Between a quarter and a third of respondents to a variety of polls favored using nuclear weapons to deal with the Communist threat.

But beginning in the late 1960s, at the height of the Vietnam War, there was a significant increase in the numbers who would answer Yes to such questions as "Should the United States mind its own business internationally and let other countries get along as best they can?" (Eighteen percent in 1964; 41 percent in 1974.) In the latter year 77 percent of the respondents answered affirmatively to the suggestion that the United States "shouldn't think so much in international terms but concentrate more on our national problems and building up our strength and prosperity here at home." (But this so-called "isolationist" response was always popular; in 1964 it was selected by 53 percent of respondents.[12]) Opinion experts, reading the mood of the country as it tried to absorb the "lessons of Vietnam," concluded that a "dovish consensus" had taken hold, particularly in the younger generation and within that generation most markedly among "citizens of upper socioeconomic status," who would be the "opinion leaders of tomorrow." In 1974, the last year of the Nixon administration, only 37 percent, according to a Potomac Associates poll, said that they would be willing to use military force to defend Japan; and according to a Louis Harris opinion survey, only 38 percent would support U.S. military involvement in the event of an invasion of Western Europe.[13]

Beginning in that same year, however, a growing countertrend was also observable. It was dubbed "the new nationalism" by some analysts of public opinion. Between 1974 and 1978 there was a 22 percent increase—from 33 percent to 55 percent—in support of the proposition that the United States "ought to play a more important role as world leader in the future." As the expectations of Nixon and Kissinger's détente—"a generation of peace" based on a managed arms race and a more passive Soviet foreign policy—failed to materialize, and the Soviets supported a series of revolutions and coups in the Third World—Ethiopia, Angola, Yemen—53 percent of those questioned in a CBS–*New York Times* poll said that the United States "should get tougher in its dealings with the Russians."[14] By the end of the decade, Iran, once the recipient of billions of dollars' worth of U.S. high-technology weapons, was threatening to try American diplomats taken hostage in the embassy, and the Soviet Union had finally done what the entire military effort of the United States was supposedly designed to prevent. By invading Afghanistan Soviet troops were rolling over an international frontier, defying the unstated rules that had kept the Cold War limited.

The succession of fifty-second glimpses of the outside world flickering across America's television sets, most of them menacing, reinforced the frustration citizens were already feeling about what was happening in their own country. Fueled by high interest rates, the overheated economy had produced "double-digit inflation." The "energy crisis" had dramatized the regional divisions in the country, between the prosperous energy producers of Texas and the shivering consumers of the Northeast. Millions of factory jobs were being lost to foreign competition and the major U.S. corporations joined in, moving more and more of their production out of the country. Every economic problem had a foreign dimension. The need to attract foreign capital to finance U.S. government deficits and domestic investment meant high interest rates. The unwillingness of

America's allies to inflate their own economies meant that American goods would continue to be uncompetitive and that more manufacturing jobs would be lost. A report to the New York Stock Exchange in the spring of 1980 warned that 68 percent of the American people thought the economy was in "a real crisis," not just a cyclical downturn.

No political leader, including the increasingly beleaguered President Carter, dared to explain that the increasing dependence of the U.S. economy on a world economy less and less subject to U.S. control was an inevitable consequence of long-term world economic trends assisted by America's own economic and political strategies.[15] Instead, politicians, sensing the mounting public anger, directed their fire to an assortment of foreign targets—Arab oil sheiks, Japanese traders, German banks, Middle East terrorists. But the president was blamed for being unable to stop them all from "pushing us around." Numerous polls showed the depth of feeling about the "loss of American prestige." The Soviets, one out of two Americans believed, invaded Afghanistan because "they now have military superiority over the United States and can get away with it." In emptying his prisons and putting his "undesirables" on little boats bound for Florida, Fidel Castro had used America's concerns with human rights to make us "look foolish," 62 percent of ABC/Harris poll respondents concluded.[16] Increasingly, Americans linked their own growing sense that they were losing control over their future to the machinations of foreigners.

Though anxious national security experts were quick to label cautious attitudes about allies or skepticism about the use of force abroad as resurgent isolationism, the public did not appear to believe that American withdrawal from the world was possible or desirable. But it was evident that more and more Americans were questioning whether military intervention to defend foreign governments or even in behalf of the NATO alliance still made sense. The nation should be readier to act on its own. Some of the earlier idealistic beliefs about the United Nations, international cooperation, and the American mission to bring development to the Third World had been battered in the 1970s thanks to the oil producers' cartel, Third World demands for a "new international economic order," highly publicized attacks on the U.N.—most notably by the United States ambassador to the United Nations Patrick Moynihan—wars, revolutions, anarchy, and terrorism in the nonwhite world. The press began giving more attention to the plight of underdeveloped countries, but the treatment of Third World politics, though somewhat more probing, was substantially more unsympathetic than in the 1960s.

The trend in public opinion was now unmistakable. In poll after poll, taken in 1980, majorities favored increased military spending, return of the peacetime draft, and renewed support for the CIA in its clandestine efforts "to weaken those forces that work against us" in other countries.[17] According to a *Newsweek* poll taken that year, 69 percent of Americans believed that the United States was falling behind the Soviet Union. In 1979, when the SALT II Treaty was being considered in the Senate, a "substantial majority" believed that the Soviet Union could not be trusted to live up to it. (Only five years before, positive feelings about the Soviets had been higher than at any time since World War II.) As the 1970s came to an end, large percentages of the much-polled American public thought that the Soviet Union was ahead in nuclear weapons, that it was growing more powerful than the United States. In the year Ronald Reagan was elected president 73 percent told their telephone interrogators that the Soviets were seeking "global domination" and more than a third thought the Kremlin "will risk major war" to achieve its aims. No more than 3 percent of Americans believed that détente had been a net gain for the United States.

What prompted these major shifts in public attitudes? The obvious answer is Soviet behavior. There is no doubt that Soviet intervention in the Third World became more active in the 1970s and that Soviet assistance in deploying Cuban troops to Africa and the invasion of Afghanistan had a cumulative effect on public attitudes toward the Soviet Union. Moreover, the public perception about who stood to gain more from détente was correct. The Nixon-Brezhnev agreements gave the Soviets what they most wanted, recognition of the division of Germany and the permanence of Soviet dominion over Eastern Europe. The Soviets offered nothing of equivalent importance. But American opinion, as usual, was influenced more by the official filters of events than by the events themselves. The clearest case of noncorrelation between Soviet behavior and public attitudes about the Soviet Union had occurred a few years before during the Vietnam War. By supplying the armaments that enabled the Vietnamese Communists to kill and maim large numbers of Americans and thereby frustrate the strategy of the United States, the Soviets inflicted more damage on American society than by anything else they had ever done. Yet official U.S. policy was to draw attention away from this fact. Johnson feared a public clamor to widen the war and court a nuclear catastrophe if he aroused popular feelings about the Soviet contribution to the American travail in Vietnam. Nixon believed that by adopting a posture of accommodation he could secure Soviet assistance in ending the war.

Trust of the Soviets took a sharp dip after the Carter administration announced in 1979 that it had discovered a Soviet brigade in Cuba and charged that its presence violated the understandings reached after the Cuban missile crisis of 1962. But the White House had made a mistake. The brigade had been there for twenty years, its presence acquiesced in by four administrations. There was no violation, but public opinion polls reacted as if there had been. Actually, this small but important incident, which helped destroy the prospects for the SALT II Treaty, was a product of domestic American politics. Frank Church, a liberal senator running for re-election in a conservative state, started the flurry. Having been confronted by his opponent with TV footage that showed Castro embracing him at the Havana airport, Church seized on the unverified rumor to prove to the people of Idaho that he was not soft on Castro.

Détente was vulnerable from the first, because it was given a false face. Nixon tried to create the impression that he had scored a diplomatic triumph. There would be a generation of peace because the Soviets had given up their most objectionable policies, encouraging revolutions in strategic places and aiming more nuclear missiles at the United States and its protectorates. But the Soviets never agreed to any such thing. Indeed, in making the case for détente before Soviet audiences Brezhnev argued that détente would give a boost to the "ideological struggle." Not surprisingly, the Soviets had no intention, nor did they signal any, of abandoning any weapons programs other than those they specifically agreed to limit. Since the SALT agreements set no disarmament obligations, merely ceilings on future weapons buildup, no immediate visible change in Soviet behavior was required.

The official mythology surrounding détente created unreal expectations and drew such powerful cries of denunciation on the Right that President Ford banned the tepid little French word from his campaign vocabulary. Three years later Carter's expression of shock and betrayal after the Afghanistan invasion completed the circuit. Most Americans now believed that the Soviets had taken advantage of American goodwill and offers of peace to spurt ahead in the arms race and use its military power to challenge the United States at a time of its greatest vulnerability. More accurately, the

Soviet Union, as at Yalta thirty years before, had taken advantage of ambiguous agreements that had been oversold to the American people. Ironically, détente had served to dramatize negative features of Soviet society that previously had been ignored by the American news industry. The partial opening of Soviet society made human rights an issue, and the publicity surrounding individual cases caught the imagination of American viewers and readers. The uncertain mood now made the management of American public opinion a much more difficult task.

Tocqueville predicted that presidential prestige and power would grow the more the executive directed his energies to foreign relations.[18] Not only has the prediction been borne out, but it has become part of the folk wisdom presidents themselves bring to the office. "It really is true that foreign affairs is the only important issue for a president to handle, isn't it," John Kennedy is supposed to have said. "I mean, who gives a shit if the minimum wage is $1.15 or $1.25?" Richard Nixon, who was not only fascinated by the game of international politics but understood the political advantages of playing the role of Leader of the Free World, especially when he was under attack, once dismissed domestic policy as "building outhouses in Peoria."[19] It is easier for presidents to cut heroic figures at the Berlin Wall than in Des Moines, and it is more tempting to gamble their historic reputation on a self-proclaimed military triumph, a diplomatic coup, or a bit of oratory to vindicate American honor than to wrestle with mundane matters like affordable housing and industrial decay. On the bridge of an aircraft carrier or at dinner at Buckingham Palace the president looks presidential. When he appears with teachers, farmers, local officials or tries to persuade various interest groups to support his conception of the common good, he is not the commander in chief. At best he comes across as an earnest manager.

But foreign policy is also a trap. American failure in war and diplomacy has ended two recent presidencies and severely damaged two others. The Vietnam debacle destroyed the presidency of Lyndon Johnson. The Watergate scandal destroyed the Nixon presidency. Watergate was a criminal effort to subvert the political process; in large part it aimed at limiting public dissent and congressional interference with the only part of his job Nixon really cared about: the conduct of war and diplomacy. The outhouses of Peoria would not have inspired Richard Nixon to compile an "Enemies List," order break-ins, or other impeachable offenses. Jimmy Carter was also the victim of foreign policy disasters. No leader could have been reelected in 1980 in the face of double-digit inflation, it is usually asserted, but the Iranian hostage crisis, the failed rescue mission, and the public perception of an "irresolute and wavering" president guaranteed his doom.[20] Exit polls taken in the 1980 election indicate that the loss of national "strength" in the Carter presidency was a reason a majority of voters gave for pushing the lever for Ronald Reagan.[21] Had the hostages been returned before the election, the results could well have been different.

By the end of his term, Jimmy Carter had lost the greatest source of presidential power. His role as Interpreter of Last Resort on world affairs was directly challenged, even within his own party. His competence was attacked by Senator Edward Kennedy, who ran against him in the primaries in 1980. Old-line Democrats who favored a tough Cold War posture, such as Eugene Rostow, former under secretary of state in the Johnson administration, and Henry Fowler, former secretary of the Treasury, joined with retired generals and hard-line Republicans in a new Committee on the Present Danger. Named for the elite bipartisan group that had promoted rearmament at the beginning of the Korean War, its driving figure was Paul Nitze, the author of NSC 68.[22] The committee was initially organized to alert the country to the dangers of the Kissinger détente and to create public pressure on the Democratic Party to erase all trace of the "McGovern foreign policy," which had called for modest cuts in the defense budget and a buildup of the domestic economy.

The Committee on the Present Danger became highly visible in the late Carter years when it spearheaded the attack on the SALT II arms limitation treaty.[23] Nitze had been one of the negotiators and resigned because he believed that the treaty would favor the Soviets and open up a "window of vulnerability" inviting Soviet "blackmail." The argument was complex, technical, and fanciful. But scary. It could be presented with graphs, and with photos of big Soviet missiles side by side much smaller U.S. missiles. It could use as authority the alarmed report of Team B, a group of hard-line Soviet watchers assembled by CIA Director George Bush to review and revise the CIA estimates on the missile balance. This "kangaroo court of outside critics all picked from one point of view," as former CIA Deputy Director Ray Cline called it, had credentials to match those of the administration for all the public knew.[24] Hardly anyone followed the intricacies of the argument. What came through to the public was the fact that the experts were split. This was a made-to-order moment for Ronald Reagan. In running for the presidency in

1980, as Garry Wills has noted, the former California governor was making as radical a hard-line critique of the administration's foreign and military policy as Goldwater made in 1964. But this time the challenger "had important parts of the 'permanent government' ready to support him."

3.

Ronald Reagan understood more clearly than any other politician of his time the symbolic importance of foreign policy in winning elections and in building presidential power. Reagan was unique among postwar presidents in not embracing foreign policy as the primary challenge of the office. He was neither a student of foreign policy like Nixon nor, like Kennedy, was he energized by matching wits with foreign leaders. The ineffective foreign policy record of Reagan's years in office, particularly the first term, when the "Reagan Revolution" was transforming the management of domestic affairs, was the product of presidential neglect and internecine combat within the national security bureaucracy. In the early years Secretary of State Alexander Haig proclaimed himself "Vicar" of foreign policy, but in fact no one was in charge; neither clear goals nor a clear strategy were agreed upon. Ronald Reagan's attention and interest were elsewhere.[25] He was passionately interested in reducing taxes, getting government "off the back" of business, and in cutting back on entitlements. Foreign policy made a good political backdrop. The new president knew how to use hard-line rhetoric to craft an image as a tough leader who could stand up to the Russians, but the accomplishments he had in mind had to do with the American economy and the American mood, not with the outside world.

Anti-Communism had been Reagan's launching pad throughout his political career, from his battles with the Hollywood Communists in the 1940s to his appearance before the Christian Anti-Communism Crusade in 1961, but his feelings about the Russians, the Cubans, or the "Marxist-Leninists" of Nicaragua were religious, not strategic. The very crudity of his anti-Communist analysis—there wouldn't be any "hot spots" anywhere in the world, he told the *Wall Street Journal*, if it were not for the Soviet Union—or the extreme character of his proposals—in the 1980 campaign he suggested a blockade of Cuba—meant that they could not serve as the basis of a coherent policy. But Ronald Reagan's celebration of America and denunciation of its enemies served brilliantly to mold the evolving nationalist mood to his own purposes. He was hardly the first president to use foreign policy as mood music. But he was the most adept of all recent presidents in employing the symbols of national security to restore the powers of his office and to establish his personal reputation as leader. In the first four years of the Reagan presidency enormous efforts were made to use the symbols of nationhood to unite a divided country behind its leader.

In the 1980 election Reagan's advisers had understood that their candidate could ride the wave of rising nationalism but that too hawkish a message would alarm the voters. "The rhetoric must *not* be strident or threatening," Reagan's pollster Richard Wirthlin warned him in a memo of August 9, 1980. "Rather than a 'defense posture' we should use the term 'peace posture.' " In his opening statement in the debate with President Carter held one week before Election Day, Ronald Reagan stated with great passion, "I believe with all my heart that our first priority must be world peace and that use of force is always and only a last resort, when everything else has failed. . . . I don't want to see another generation of young Americans bleed their lives into sandy beaches . . . or the muddy battlefields of Europe." The way to peace "requires strength." He ended the debate by asking, "Are you better off than you were four years ago? . . . Is America as respected throughout the world as it was?"[26] Taken together, the two statements accurately telegraphed what Reagan had in mind.

The United States would regain the respect of friend and foe by committing hundreds of billions of dollars to the military Establishment but would be exceedingly cautious in committing that force to any battle that could become another Vietnam. The polls suggested that the American people wanted to take some decisive, unilateral action to regain the control over world affairs that had been lost in the 1970s. The far Right and the neoconservatives, mostly former Democrats like Norman Podhoretz who believed that American self-criticism and self-doubt had produced a "culture of appeasement," favored a strong anti-Soviet and anti-Communist focus to foreign policy, but only a tiny fringe was actually willing to risk a nuclear showdown. Increased military spending and a more belligerent posture could do no harm, the Reagan team unanimously agreed, for the buildup would give a lift to the economy and produce jobs in a time of serious unemployment. Throwing money at national security seemed to be good politics, for it promised peace without appeasement and communicated a sense of hope to the voters. At last something was being done to reverse the negative trends in the world. The American arms buildup would induce Soviet caution and put them to such expense that they might agree to modify or slow down the arms race. However, throwing American troops into battle was quite another matter. The Reagan administration spent eight years trying to cure the American people of the "Vietnam syndrome," but the Pentagon never got over its own aggravated case.

Reagan's interest, as he said in his acceptance speech, was to unite the country around a vision of a new America in which government neither scolded the people, made them feel guilty, nor permitted the erosion of traditional "family values." The business of government was to encourage private enrichment to fuel economic growth, and the new administration had a clear strategy for achieving this goal. Reagan used the world beyond American shores as a set on which to stage his crusade to transform the federal government and its relationship to business. The drama of national security could be used to inspire hope and confidence, to build support for his leadership, and to reassert the president's role as the Interpreter of Last Resort.

Ronald Reagan rode into office on a genuine nationalist tide, which he saw as a source of presidential power. He understood, as Carter did not, that the hunger for a moral vision of America had to rest on national pride. Evoking the Mayflower Compact, John Winthrop's City on the Hill, and Tom Paine's radical secular faith —"we have it in our power to begin the world over again"—Reagan tried to revive the confidence of Americans in themselves and in the unique virtues of their society. He preached the old-time religion of American exceptionalism, an unfashionable faith at a time when intellectual analysis in the universities and in the press was focusing on the failure in Vietnam and America's new economic problems. The professors and columnists may have discovered that there were real limits to American power and growth, but the president denounced such "gloom and doom" talk. The only limit on American power was the failure of American will. He pronounced "malaise" to be a thing of the past. To criticize the nation's foreign policy was to join the "blame America crowd," and no real patriot could bring himself to do that.

Ronald Reagan played many parts in the White House, but above all he was a salesman, in Garry Wills's words "selling substance not appearance," always using his gift for self-projection to advance a cause or an ideology. He intuitively understood what a succession of Democratic Party challengers failed to grasp, that a political salesman aspiring to the presidency must be a therapist as well. Reagan was vague about what he might accomplish in foreign policy, but he understood that the symbols of foreign policy were crucial to creating an upbeat, permissive mood. Foreign policy failures and the endless talk of professors, columnists, and politicians about those failures—Vietnam, Iran, the energy crisis, the collapse of détente—had made Americans feel bad. Ronald Reagan, the moral educator, set about to bring back the certitudes of the Cold War years.

He was an accomplished storyteller who knew how to reinterpret the myths of nationhood to inspire—and indoctrinate—the people. "We are a nation that has a government—not the other way around. And that makes us special." (Inaugural Address.) The founders "gave us more than a nation. They brought to all mankind for the first time the concept that man was born free." The president painted a nostalgic picture of an America of small-town heroes, white picket fences, volunteer fire departments, and friendly neighbors. Once again, as in other times of great change, Americans were especially open to hearing stories of their roots that offered meaning, a sense of purpose, and hope for the future.

At his first White House press conference Ronald Reagan denounced the Soviets for their ideology, which he said gave them the "right to commit any crime, to lie, to cheat." Rhetorical fierceness reached its zenith when the president pronounced the Soviet Union to be an Evil Empire and the source of the world's woes, oddly at the very moment a reformer, Yuri Andropov, had come to power in the Kremlin and the most radical reformer the Soviet system has ever produced was waiting to take over. Nervous Europeans worried that the president was whipping up the country for war. But he was only trying to make the country feel better. Americans should stop blaming themselves and focus on the real source of evil. An end to the heresy of "moral equivalence!" (This was the slogan neoconservatives attached to any critical analysis of United States foreign policy.) At West Point Reagan declared that "the era of self-doubt is over. We've stopped looking at our warts and rediscovered how much there is to love in this blessed land."[27]

The celebration of the New Patriotism, as the press called it, gathered force all through the first term. Enlistments, flag-waving, parades, were up; self-criticism was down. The brand of patriotism based on righteous wrath against America's enemies was not only fashionable again but marketable. In the late 1970s, sales of war toys had plummeted, but between 1982 and 1984 they jumped 35 percent. Five of the six best-selling toys in 1984 were mechanical power fantasies for kids—one of them was called Masters of the Universe —and each was promoted by daily TV cartoons that showed the good guys evaporating, slugging, burning, or grinding to dust designated black hats. (There were eighty-three violent acts per hour in the cartoon to sell the best-selling toy Transformers, according to the National Coalition on Television Violence.)

Another indicator of the new public mood was the mounting attack on textbooks used in the public school system. In her analysis of history texts Frances FitzGerald traces the difficulties the writers faced in the 1970s. By the mid-1960s the classic nationalist message was obsolete. It was no longer possible to maintain the "tone of innocent wonder" that permeated the high-school history books of the 1950s. In those years the United States was almost invariably portrayed as the Mother Teresa of the nations, always educating, wiping out disease, saving humanity from fascism, Communism, and war itself. In no country are textbooks on its own national history notably self-critical, but FitzGerald, after reviewing nineteenth- and early-twentieth-century American history texts, concludes that the fifties represented a high point in chauvinism. In the late 1960s and 1970s, consonant with the mood shift of the times, history textbooks became somewhat more analytical. In some of them the existence of Native Americans and a hint of their fate was actually mentioned. Not all American wars were portrayed as crusades for freedom. What is radical about the 1970s texts, Frances FitzGerald observes, "is that they question the judgments of past Presidents and Administrations, and, in the process . . . foreign policy appears in textbook history as something less than a sacred revelation."[28]

But this modest reform of history textbooks became a target of a gathering right-wing backlash against the cultural currents of the 1960s. Indeed, an important source of the antigovernment feeling that helped elect Reagan was the growing anger of parents who were scandalized by what schools were teaching. Government was subverting traditional values in the classroom. Jerry Falwell, head of the Moral Majority, launched a campaign attacking textbooks for not "showing respect for our nation's heritage." In 1982 more than one-third of school librarians in the United States reported that individuals and, increasingly, organized groups were demanding the removal of books from school libraries. The biology texts were the principal targets, because they favored the theory of evolution over a Bible-based "creation science." But the new history texts did not escape attention. In 1982, under pressure from Norma and Mel Gabler, veteran activists against "moral lapses and erosion of traditional values" in textbooks, the Texas state board of education issued a proclamation, "Textbook content shall . . . emphasize patriotism and respect for recognized authority." The New Right, the ultraconservative groups, mostly religious, which took credit for electing Ronald Reagan, campaigned against the infiltration of "secular-humanist" ideas into the schools by "elitist" liberals, and education officials of the Reagan administration lent their support. American children must be told, Secretary of Education William J. Bennett declared, that their country is morally superior to the Soviet Union.[29]

The Summer Olympics of 1984 was an occasion for Reagan to celebrate and to identify himself with the "new patriotism spreading across our country." The Soviet bloc, with the exception of Romania, boycotted the games. The United States was the clear winner, and the television networks played the event as a great national victory and an occasion to celebrate patriotism. McDonald's built its advertising spots around the slogan "When the U.S. wins, you win." Evoking his role in the film *Knute Rockne*, the president called on the American "heroes" to win for family, country, and "for the Gipper." The Olympics ended in a burst of patriotic fervor in the midst of an election campaign. The presidential appearances fitted the reelection campaign strategy proposed by Reagan's adviser Richard Darman: "Paint RR as the personification of all that is right with, or heroized by, America," he wrote in a campaign strategy memorandum. "Leave Mondale in a position where an attack on Reagan is tantamount to an attack on America's idealized image of itself—where a vote against Reagan is, in some subliminal sense, a vote against a mythic AMERICA."[30]

The high-water mark of the New Patriotism was 1985, the year of Sylvester Stallone's movie *Rambo*. It was the story of how a muscular American loner, defying the culture of appeasement in the State Department and the CIA, had gone back to Vietnam and single-handedly refought the war, rescued American prisoners, and killed a lot of Communists thanks to American courage and high technology. The film was a huge box-office hit and for a season it spawned an entire industry. Rambo dolls, Rambo guns, Rambo vitamins, and Rambo high-tech crossbows. A nightclub called Rambose opened in Houston featuring waitresses in fatigues, a buffet laid out on a military stretcher, and a .50-caliber machine gun to make everyone feel safe. About twelve hundred people jammed into the club every night. "We ask everyone to raise their hand and give the one-finger salute to Russia," said the club manager. "Everybody's proud. That's part of the gimmick."[31] The U.S. Army pasted up Rambo posters outside recruiting centers to spur enlistments. Ronald Reagan invited Sylvester Stallone to the White House and announced that after seeing *Rambo* he would "know what to do next time" terrorists took American citizens hostage.[32] United States foreign policy was stalled on virtually every front in the real world, but under the leadership of a genial president Americans reveled in fantasies of power and revenge.

The patriotic mood inspired other Hollywood efforts—*Red Dawn,* a Soviet invasion of Colorado foiled by heroic high-school students; *Invasion; Missing in Action*—and TV shows such as "The A-Team," "Magnum, P.I.," and "Call to Glory." All of them depicted triumphant conclusions to fantastic wars or to real world struggles that had not gone quite so well on the nightly news— struggles against the Vietnamese, the Soviets, terrorists.

Rambo itself was more antigovernment than anti-Soviet. It was the story of America triumphing *despite* government, a favorite Ronald Reagan theme. It was a plea for respect for Vietnam veterans and a vague attack on self-criticism and diplomatic caution. National magazines ran cover stories trying to explain what the New Patriotism meant. Was it anything more than a marketable hunger for good news and for a revival of national pride and self-respect? Americans filed into movie theaters to watch Chuck Norris and Sylvester Stallone refight the Vietnam War, but large majorities kept telling pollsters that they wanted no such adventures in real life. The most popular song, Bruce Springsteen's "Born in the U.S.A.," celebrated a different sort of patriotism, an empathy with Vietnam veterans but without a trace of triumphal fantasy:

> Got in a little hometown jam
> So they put a rifle in my hand.
> To go and kill the yellow man . . .
> Come back home to the refinery.
> Hiring man says, "Son, if it was up to me . . ."

It was fashionable in the Reagan years to say that patriotism was "back." But for most Americans love of country had always been part of their life. What was new was the content of the New Patriotism. George Orwell once wrote that patriotism, which he defined as "a devotion to a particular place and a particular way of life, which one believes to be the best in the world but has no wish to force upon other people," could be an inoculation against "nationalism," which he defined as "the habit of assuming that human beings can be classified like insects . . . and can confidently be labeled 'good' or 'bad.' " Nationalism parading as patriotism always needs to be nourished by fantasies of power and glory and celebrations of moral superiority. The most striking feature of the New Patriotism was the defensiveness and self-doubt it betrayed. Plainly, there was a market for anything that made Americans feel good about their country; but the appeal was focused not so much on the democratic values that still inspired people around the world or on economic opportunity or on the physical beauty of the land, but on the nation's killing power. In the brief era of Rambo, American virtue was certified by the existence of the Evil Empire, and love of country was evoked by reminding Americans of how lucky they were not to live in the Soviet Union. In 1986 Royal Crown Cola produced a series of humorous TV spots featuring ranks of gray faceless Russians being admonished to drink the competitor's cola or being arrested for sneaking a nip of Royal Crown. A fast-food chain showed a comical Soviet fashion show in which there is only one dress that is recycled for every occasion; the viewer is promised a "choice" at Wendy's.

4.

From the first the Reagan presidency was even more internally divided on foreign policy goals and strategy than its unsteady predecessor as "ideologues" and "pragmatists" struggled to set policy. It was an article of faith of Ronald Reagan and his close advisers when they came into office in 1981 that the Vietnam War had been lost in the United States. Presidents would continue to have their hands tied by the bewildered crowd until they paid proper attention to the management of public opinion. Within days of taking office Reagan's secretary of state, Alexander Haig, began leaking highly alarmed (and inaccurate) stories in the press about how the Soviets and Cuba were engaged in a massive campaign to take over Central America. This was the war, he argued in the White House, to cure the country of the Vietnam syndrome. It was a war that could be won and won quickly. El Salvador, unlike Vietnam, was not ten thousand miles away but a two-day car ride from Texas and it had been claimed as America's "backyard" ever since the promulgation of the Monroe Doctrine. If ever there was a war that the American people would support, this was it. Jeane Kirkpatrick, the new U.S. ambassador to the United Nations, declared Central America to be "the most important place in the world for us," and Secretary of State Haig threatened to make war on Cuba, which he declared to be the "source" of the insurgencies in Central America. Under Secretary of Defense Fred Iklé relished the thought of a confrontation with the liberals in Congress, who, as one State Department planner put it, would be "reviled for losing Central America to the Communists" if the administration did not get its way.[33] But despite the enthusiasm of a small coterie of middle-level national security officials for a fight with Communism in the hemisphere, there never was a plan to win the war in either El Salvador or Nicaragua. Repeating the experience of the Johnson administration in Vietnam, the Reagan national security officials minimized their military and political problems in Central America and underestimated the opposition of the American people to military intervention.

Reagan's pollster, Richard Wirthlin, warned that talk of war with Cuba—in Haig's phrase "going to the source"—was frightening the public. In March 1982, according to a Harris poll, disapproval of Reagan's policy on El Salvador stood at 64 percent.[34] The president's political advisers, afraid that a war scare would drive away the political support they needed to carry through the far-reaching domestic program, counseled caution. In Michael Deaver's words, "A. you cannot win. B. the American people will not stand for a war in Central America."[35]

Suddenly El Salvador all but disappeared from the front pages as Chief of Staff James Baker's "low profile" strategy was put into effect. By 1984 pollsters had with rare exceptions stopped asking about El Salvador. The focus had shifted to Nicaragua or to Central America in general. While the public relations impresarios in the White House were exercising great care that the administration speak "with one voice," the State Department, the Department of Defense, the CIA, and the National Security Council often leaked their own stories, each pushing its own policy line. The internal disharmony and the gulf between what the administration was saying and what its warring bureaucratic baronies were actually doing was much greater than in previous administrations because the president exerted so little personal control. Emboldened by presidential rhetoric, these bureaucrats worked tirelessly to make Ronald Reagan's dreams of triumph real.

The administration, though it secured hundreds of millions of dollars all through its years in office to support the Salvadoran government's counterinsurgency campaign, never succeeded in convincing the American people that the tiny, war-ravaged land of few resources and an overabundance of desperately poor peasants posed a national security threat to the world's most powerful nation. On December 1, 1981, Ronald Reagan signed a "finding" that national security required the launching of a covert operation against Nicaragua, but as Robert McFarlane, who later served as national security adviser, conceded, the administration had established no framework for setting goals, assessing costs, or evaluating success or failure. Although Nicaragua for a time became Reagan's principal foreign policy interest, the administration never made the decision to commit the military power it would have taken to overthrow the Sandinista government, because the Pentagon did not believe that the American people would support another long, bloody guerrilla war.[36] So the United States settled for lesser objectives—the isolation and delegitimation of the Nicaraguan revolution—which could be pursued without either American casualties or an American presence on the TV screen.

No administration in American history ever lavished such attention, skill, and money on manipulating public opinion as did the Reagan administration. Ronald Reagan became famous as the Teflon president to whose genial person failure never stuck. Yet eight years of intensive efforts not only failed to elicit majority support for a popular president's policies in Central America and southern Africa, but the shocking game plan to confuse and circumvent public opinion in the United States became public knowledge. The alarmed and angry response of organized minorities of citizen activists to the Reagan worldview on nuclear weapons, supporting right-wing dictators, and dealing with the Soviet Union forced the administration to make major shifts in rhetoric and policy. The unraveling of the Iran-Contra scandal, which began with the disclosure by an obscure Lebanese journal that the United States had tried to buy back its hostages in the hands of Islamic fanatics by secretly shipping arms to Iran, almost destroyed Reagan's personal credibility. The Reagan government believed that controlling information was the key to the exercise of power, but it lost control. How did this happen?

The Reagan presidency began in a burst of patriotic fervor triggered by the return of the hostages from Iran. Jimmy Carter's last act, the completion of the hostage deal, permitted the new administration to begin on a note of triumph. President Reagan started with a number of other advantages over recent administrations.

First, he had the appearance of a big electoral mandate. It was not until the final days of the 1980 campaign, the polls showed, that the voters finally lost all patience with Jimmy Carter, and though only one out of four registered voters cast their ballot for Reagan, this was enough to assure a decisive victory in electoral votes. Second, Reagan was the beneficiary of the concerted attack on the media that had begun in the Vietnam War. The rise of modern investigative journalism and the "shouting matches" on television between reporters and presidents had brought the beleaguered elites of the 1970s to despair: TV was destroying presidents, undermining respect for authority, even making the country "ungovernable."[37] Members of the press began censoring themselves—"all totally subconscious," in the words of Benjamin C. Bradlee, executive editor of the Washington *Post*. "We've been kinder to President Reagan than any President that I can remember since I've been at the *Post*." Reading recent history and the election returns, members of the media concluded, according to Bradlee, "we've got to really behave ourselves here. . . . We've got to not be arrogant . . . be fair. I suspect in the process that this paper and probably a good deal of the press . . . didn't use the same standards on him that they used on Carter and on Nixon."[38] Third, disposed as they were to treat the commander in chief with greater deference, reporters found Reagan a refreshing personality who made good copy and even better pictures. He appeared to be a genuinely nice man who enjoyed life, could tell jokes on himself, and who behaved with exceptional grace and courage when he was struck by an assassin's bullet only a few weeks after assuming office.

But perhaps the biggest advantage that the Reagan administration had over its predecessors in selling its policies was its understanding of news management. The press has of course always been used as an instrument of presidential persuasion. But in the Reagan years the manipulation of public opinion—"public diplomacy," as it was called—was elevated to what one National Security Council official called a "new art form."[39] "This was a PR outfit that became President and took over the country," Leslie Janka, former deputy press secretary in the Reagan White House, concludes. The "first, last and overarching activity" of the Reagan administration was "public relations."[40] If the professionals in the media saw "giving the man a break" as the only way to be decent and "responsible," and, incidentally, the best tactic for getting exciting presidential footage for the evening news or a bit of classified gossip for a column, the professional opinion managers in the White House took pride in their skill at manipulating the media. Michael Deaver, a close family friend of the Reagans, James Baker, and Richard Darman, all veterans of political campaigns, saw the art of governance as the continuation of electoral politics. "Implementing policy depends on getting your media operation and your political operation together," James Baker explained, "but so does running a successful political campaign." The "key" to selling the president's message in Congress "is to sell it publicly." Because Reagan had no clear foreign policy framework or strategy upon taking office, policy was the product of a continuing clash between zealous underlings promoting confrontation and political advisers urging the avoidance of risky foreign policy moves that would alarm the public.

Enormous energy was expended at the highest levels in the White House on the crafting of appearance. Baker, Deaver, and others boasted to reporters how they manipulated the media and the public. They would meet at 8:15 in the morning at the White House to set the "line of the day" so that the White House "spin" would blanket the news. According to a participant, the agenda was usually the same: "What are we going to do today to enhance the image of the President? What do we want the press to cover today and how?"[41] Regular calls were made to the television networks in the hopes of influencing the lead story. After an unfavorable story White House anger was communicated in the hopes of getting a better one next time. Michael Deaver provided "visually attractive, prepackaged news stories" to make it easy for television to sell what one of Reagan's press aides called "the ultimate presidential commodity . . . the right product."[42] Reagan's advance men roamed the world, setting "toe marks" in places like the DMZ in Korea and the military cemetery in Bitburg so that the president might stand in the most flattering light. The access of the media to the president was sharply controlled. He was produced to make news and withdrawn from view to squelch news.

Calls from the White House to dress down or butter up magazine editors and television producers were hardly new. Other presidents knew how to chill or warm the hearts of the men, and occasional woman, assigned to cover them. John F. Kennedy, for example, took an almost obsessive interest in what people wrote about him, and he was adroit in letting editors know how attentive he was— and how much he cared. What marked the Reagan presidency as a new era in American foreign policy was the professionalization of its propaganda efforts and its extraordinary emphasis on opinion management.

The servants of the Reagan administration were masters of the subtleties of persuasion. Deadly missiles became "peacekeepers." Veterans of Somoza's National Guard who had participated in the killing and torturing of tens of thousands of Nicaraguans were likened to the Founding Fathers of the United States. Millions of Americans who supported the movement for a nuclear freeze were accused of being dupes or agents of Moscow. Any serious foreign adversary was either a "Marxist-Leninist," a "Communist," or a "terrorist." There was no room for nuance. The world was divided between the armies of light and the armies of darkness. Some presidential statements were so preposterous as to be incredible on their face, for example, the assertion that the Russian language has no word for "freedom" (the word is "svoboda"). Like much advertising, presidential rhetoric was not intended to be believed literally but to create a mood, in this case a feeling of righteous wrath and moral superiority.

Misinformation, that is, deliberately misleading stories designed to frighten or confuse foreign leaders, was planted in the American press. National Security Adviser John M. Poindexter's disinformation campaign to keep the Libyan leader Moammar Gadhafi "off balance" produced false stories in the Wall Street Journal and other newspapers.[43] The Pentagon developed a program to insert false data about military technology in technical journals to mislead the Russians, and, incidentally, the American subscribers. The White House engaged in covert propaganda to change American hearts and minds, employing CIA veterans of secret wars.

Nevertheless, on the propaganda front the administration kept running into booby traps. Four women religious workers had been murdered in El Salvador just before Reagan took office. The killings caused Roman Catholic bishops in the United States to take a stand against the death squads in El Salvador and to question whether the United States should be aiding a government that was unwilling or unable to control them. Reagan's off-the-cuff remark that the women might have been working for the guerrillas with its implicit suggestion that perhaps they got what they deserved did not go over well. A White Paper issued only a few weeks after Reagan took office, which tried to make the case that the Soviet Union was heavily involved in El Salvador, and was supplying "staggering" amounts of arms to the guerrillas, as Jeane Kirkpatrick put it, failed to convince either European governments or a majority of Americans. The principal author of the White Paper admitted in an interview with the Wall Street Journal that the administration's brief, which allegedly was based on captured guerrilla documents, was "full of mistakes" and in part "misleading" and "over-embellished." A CIA employee whose job it was to monitor arms traffic from Nicaragua to El Salvador resigned because the White House was giving out false information; after the spring of 1981, he said in a series of television interviews, the arms flow into El Salvador "just disappeared."[44]

A carefully orchestrated campaign to accuse the Soviets of chemical warfare in Afghanistan and elsewhere by spreading outlawed agents causing a toxic "yellow rain" failed to persuade the public. The evidence was so sparse that the bizarre refutation of a prominent Harvard biologist was sufficient to stall the campaign; "yellow rain," he insisted, was caused not by noxious chemicals but by deposits of bee excrement. Another campaign launched by Alexander Haig accused the Soviet Union of being the orchestrator of international terrorism, but this also foundered. Administration zealots promoted articles by journalist Claire Sterling that claimed the KGB had been behind all international terrorism, including the attempt on the pope's life in May 1981. But Lincoln Gordon, a former president of Johns Hopkins University serving as a member of a CIA review panel, concluded that there was no credible evidence for her claim. (The charge of Soviet involvement in the attempted assassination of John Paul II lost all credibility when a key witness changed his story.) The Gordon panel discovered that some details of Sterling's story of the Soviet connection to the Italian Red Brigades had actually come from a news story planted in the Italian press as part "of an old, small-scale CIA covert propaganda operation," a piece of "blowback" in the jargon of the intelligence world. The CIA concluded that Sterling's thesis was wrong. But, as Bob Woodward, who investigated the incident, observes, "as far as the American public was concerned, the Soviets still stood publicly branded by the Secretary of State as active supporters of terrorism. And the record was never corrected."[45]

When the Soviets shot down a Korean airliner on September 1, 1983, killing all 269 passengers on board, Ronald Reagan charged that the attack was "deliberate murder," a "terrorist act." It was almost certainly a tragic blunder caused by the Soviet gunner's confusing the airliner with a U.S. military plane in the area. Within hours American intelligence had the evidence that the Soviets had not intended to fire on a civilian aircraft. The administration did not, however, moderate its rhetoric, but used it over the next few weeks to push through votes in the House for producing binary nerve gas shells and funds for the B-1 bomber. Reagan also used the false accusation to support his resistance to being drawn into arms negotiations that he wished to avoid while the peace movement in Europe and the Freeze movement in the United States were gathering strength. "What can be the scope of legitimate mutual discourse with a state whose values permit such atrocities?"[46] Apart from hyperbolic abuse, however, Reagan did little to retaliate, so far had the calculus of war changed since the sinking of the *Maine*. The *New York Times* praised the president for being "shrewd and moderate" and displaying "dignified, justified anger." *Time* found his television speech "stirring and statesmanlike." A year later State Department officials proudly told a *Times* reporter that "a basic kind of anti-Soviet mood" had been created by the incident, which had been useful to the president in pushing his foreign policy.[47]

The assault on Grenada on the morning of October 25, 1983, two days after 241 marines had been killed in a bombing in Beirut, was skillfully used to deflect attention from a foreign policy disaster and to create a moment of euphoria. America is back standing tall, said the president, after a marine amphibious unit of 1,250 heavily armed men and two Ranger battalions defeated 636 Cuban construction workers and 43 soldiers. The Marxist revolution on the tiny island, which had prompted the president to make a TV speech some months before, warning that Grenada was a Communist menace to the hemisphere, had already devoured its leader and had been abandoned in disgust by Castro. Virtually everything that could go wrong with the U.S. military operation did; two-thirds of all casualties were caused by "friendly fire" or by accident. Under cover of victory the president withdrew the demoralized marine contingent from Lebanon; the 241 deaths became instant history along with the vital interests that the departing marines had supposedly been defending.

The press was barred from covering the Grenada invasion. But the comic-opera aspects of the engagement quickly came to light. The medical students, whose rescue was the original pretext for the invasion, dropped to their knees and kissed American soil as the TV cameras recorded their carefully choreographed arrival ceremony, but a few days later a number of them told the press that they had been in no danger. By March the Associated Press had figured out that more medals had been issued by the army than the number of soldiers wounded in the assault. (One hundred fifteen soldiers were reported wounded but the Pentagon issued 152 Purple Hearts.[48])

The cartoon "Doonesbury" likened the war to the Special Olympics for the handicapped. But neither facts nor cracks could dispel what the press called Grenada High. After spending trillions on the military the American people had finally been given a clear-cut old-fashioned victory, not much of one, but the first since MacArthur's triumph at Inchon thirty-three years before.

The most elaborate campaign to manipulate public opinion was a covert propaganda operation to elicit support for the administration's policy in Central America. In 1982 a CIA specialist in clandestine media operations was assigned to the National Security Council to establish a "public diplomacy" program. The CIA is barred by the National Security Act of 1947 from conducting operations within the United States. Under Executive Order 12333, signed by Ronald Reagan, the Agency is prohibited from activities "intended to influence United States political processes, public opinion . . . or media." Since the earliest days of the Reagan administration, however, officials in the bowels of the State Department and the Pentagon had been writing memos lamenting the "propaganda gap," which they believed had brought defeat in Vietnam. American laws that prohibited the conduct of propaganda campaigns aimed at American citizens put the guardians of the Republic at a serious disadvantage. (Giap, the victorious Vietnamese Communist general, according to one memo by an external relations official at the Agency for International Development, was actually a "dismal" battlefield commander who won only by his skill in using "propaganda and disinformation." The prime need was to "counter the Soviet-orchestrated effort to influence the United States Congress, the national media, and the general public."[49]) At a National Defense University forum on "low-intensity warfare" a deputy assistant secretary of the air force declared: "The most critical special operations mission we have . . . is to persuade the American people that the communists are out to get us. . . . If we win the war of ideas, we will win everywhere else."[50]

In January 1983 Reagan signed National Security Directive 77, entitled "Management of Public Diplomacy Relative to National Security," and a special planning group was set up within the National Security Council to take charge of campaigns to influence the media, Congress, and the voter on controversial issues of foreign policy. Walter Raymond, Jr., described by one U.S. government official as "the CIA's leading propaganda expert," was put in charge of the Central America campaign, working closely with CIA Director William Casey, Oliver North, and National Security Advisers Robert McFarlane and John Poindexter. As one NSC official told the investigative reporters Robert Parry and Peter Kornbluh, "They were trying to manipulate public opinion . . . using the tools of Walt Raymond's trade craft which he learned from his career in the CIA covert operation shop."[51] "Public diplomacy" was more than a "vast psychological warfare operation," as one participant described it. The White House campaign pressured reporters and news executives to put the right "spin" on the Nicaragua story. It secretly funded through "private-sector surrogates" television and newspaper ads attacking those in Congress who opposed giving aid to the Contras. (The campaign targeted Maryland Congressman Michael Barnes, a leading opponent of the administration's Central America policy, who was defeated after a barrage of secretly funded TV ads painted him as a Montgomery County Sandinista.) Professors were commissioned to write scholarly articles supporting the administration's case without acknowledgment of their government connection. White House clandestine operatives, in an effort to combat the increasingly damaging reports of U.S. religious figures about Contra atrocities, arranged to have an associate of Oliver North dressed up as a Roman Catholic priest testify on Sandinista human rights violations before a House subcommittee. The FBI harassed CISPES, the leading citizens' organization protesting the U.S. involvement in El Salvador, breaking into their offices and stealing their documents and correspondence. Despite a cable from the U.S. Embassy in Managua stating that there was "no verifiable ground" for charging the Sandinistas with anti-Semitism, White House officials organized a drive to influence Jewish opinion in the United States, using the false charges.

No administration ever put so great a premium on secrecy—the promiscuous use of classification, mandatory polygraph examinations to stop leaks, prepublication review for 128,000 government officials on anything they would ever write for the rest of their lives —and none was so quickly or so thoroughly exposed. On one level the story of the Reagan administration's bungled campaign to persuade the public to support its military and paramilitary operations in Central America is a triumph of democracy. Not only did the administration fail to sell either its rhetoric or its wars in Central America, but the exposé of its illegal and deceptive campaigns to win the hearts and minds of the voter was spread across the front pages and broadcast in a thousand sound bites even while Reagan was still in office.

From 1981 to 1986 public opinion polls were remarkably consistent in showing a high level of dissatisfaction with the Reagan policy in Central America. Less than one-third favored the overthrow of the Sandinista government. Americans opposed giving aid to the Contras in Nicaragua by a 2–1 margin. A consistent majority kept saying in one poll after another that Reagan's handling of foreign policy in general was either "only fair" or "poor." The willingness of thousands of Americans to travel to the war zones of Nicaragua as representatives of churches and organizations such as Witness for Peace, and the defiance of U.S. immigration laws by the Sanctuary movement, a church-based effort to hide illegal immigrants threatened with deportation to the war zones of Central America, sent signals that an invasion of Nicaragua would meet serious resistance in the United States. The polls showed that the war in Central America was much more unpopular than the Vietnam War was when U.S. ground troops were first committed to Indochina. The opposition was more organized, tougher, and more mainstream.

The weight of public opinion succeeded in setting limits to the escalation of an unpopular "low-intensity war." If the "public diplomacy" campaign failed to change the minds of the American people, the propaganda campaign against the Sandinistas, aided greatly by the panic and defiance of the Sandinista government, did induce Congress at a critical moment to vote $100 million to support the Contras' war of harassment. As long as the war effort was pursued without the visible involvement of Americans, the opposition was manageable. The secret strategy, as Speaker Jim Wright later revealed, was to goad the Sandinistas by economic squeeze and military pressure into closing newspapers and jailing opponents, in short to cause the Nicaraguan Marxists to undermine the legitimacy and appeal of their revolution themselves. And this is what happened.

Despite the lack of public support, the war in Central America continued. After eight years the United States seemed no closer to defeating the guerrillas in El Salvador or to overthrowing the Sandinistas in Nicaragua than it was on Inauguration Day, 1981. The Reagan administration left office with Nicaragua still in the hands of the Sandinistas, but its economy was crippled by war and its people dazed and demoralized. El Salvador had sunk into a morass of violence and poverty with no end in sight. Public opinion set limits to the prosecution of these wars, but it was not sufficiently aroused to compel the administration to end the U.S. intervention.

In Eisenhower's time when the shooting down of the U-2 spy plane blew the CIA's cover story and the chief executive decided to take personal responsibility for an official lie, it sparked weeks of debate. The country was still shocked at the thought that a president would lie in the national interest, and no less shocked that he would admit it. By the time Ronald Reagan left office, however, a pattern of deception over eight years provoked a different public reaction. Memoirs of close associates, such as David Stockman and Donald Regan, well-documented front-page news stories, and the prolonged televised Iran-Contra hearings revealed the extraordinary efforts of the administration to mislead, misinform, and manipulate the voters. By 1987 considerable negative information about the genial, tough-talking Great Communicator was already in the public domain. Not only had he paid a foolish ransom to the very "state terrorists" with whom he swore he would never deal, but his top national security advisers had used the payment for the arms to subsidize the Contras in direct violation of the will of Congress. In each case he denied what he had done until he had no recourse but to plead forgetfulness. Public disappointment was immediate and great. The president had betrayed his image. Popular approval for his foreign policy fell to 29 percent within a few weeks of the initial disclosures. But public outrage was feeble and short-lived compared with that occasioned by the Watergate scandals of the early 1970s. The Iran-Contra scandal was not played in either Congress or in the press as a constitutional crisis, even though it raised issues of the unlawful exercise of executive power at least as profound as those raised by the misdeeds of Richard Nixon. Ronald Reagan apologized for his bad memory and for the *appearance* of having traded arms for hostages, and on January 20, 1989, the fortieth president flew into retirement about as popular as ever.

5.

The principal battlefield on which the Reagan administration confronted public opinion was the fight over nuclear weapons. The foreign policy initiative that most absorbed the administration's attention in its first four years was the campaign to place intermediate-range missiles in Europe. These missiles, originally opposed by the Joint Chiefs of Staff as being of little military value, came to be seen by the Carter administration as political glue to bind the fraying NATO alliance. The Reagan administration's defense experts were not enthusiastic about deploying Pershing and cruise missiles in Europe. The military reasons were not compelling, and there were already signs of mounting public opposition.

But they saw the issue as a test of American will. If the United States were forced to reverse its decision to deploy the missiles on the soil of Britain, West Germany, and Sicily because of the opposition of millions of Europeans and an all-out Soviet propaganda campaign, the Soviet Union, they believed, would score a great political victory. As Assistant Secretary of Defense Richard Perle put it, the campaign to put the missiles into Europe became the overriding foreign policy objective of Reagan's first term.[52] Victory was achieved, but the price was a historic shift in public attitudes about nuclear weapons in Europe and in the United States.

Having campaigned on the "window of vulnerability," the Reagan administration came into office committed to an extensive buildup in nuclear weapons, bombers, aircraft carriers, and new land-based and sea-launched missiles. On the theory that the United States would emerge as the victor in an intensified competition in high-technology weaponry and that a spending race would bankrupt the Soviet Union long before it would harm the U.S. economy, the new administration proposed to spend almost $2 trillion dollars over five years to build up both nuclear and conventional forces. Plans were announced to increase the nuclear stockpile 13 percent. Critics calculated that thirty-seven thousand new nuclear warheads would be added to the stockpile. Most of the money, however, went to so-called conventional forces into which tactical and battlefield nuclear weapons were thoroughly integrated.

When Ronald Reagan took office the American people had been living with nuclear weapons for thirty-six years. For most of this period the prospect of nuclear holocaust surfaced as a public issue only intermittently. But there was a steady stream of nuclear images that relentlessly pervaded the society on many different levels. Hollywood remade H. G. Wells's myth of the mad scientist blowing up the world in some version or other every few years. Typically, in these films made for adolescents, atomic rays escaped from the laboratory and produced hideous, oversized spiders or other slimy monsters. The films drove home the point that society was at the mercy of mysterious contamination spread by a scientific priesthood.[53]

For the first nuclear generation the words of the Bhagavad-Gita uttered in awe by J. Robert Oppenheimer as he watched the first atomic fireball rising over Alamogordo were searing, unforgettable: "I am become Death/The destroyer of worlds." For the next generation the black humor of Dr. Strangelove—a patriotic cowboy riding an atomic bomb onto its target in the U.S.S.R., a crazed nuclear intellectual planning a new arms race even as nuclear bombs are exploding all around him—gave audiences shivers along with the belly laughs. The irrationality of threatening all human life on the planet in the name of protecting freedom was too monumental to confront except as a cosmic joke. For most Americans the proposition that nuclear weapons were keeping the peace was a theological belief, for on that credo hung a whole worldview about national security in the modern world. Not to believe it would lead citizens to doubt their own government at a profound level.

Since nuclear deterrence was in essence a strategy of psychological warfare, American leaders issued menacing statements from time to time to induce Soviet caution. But such statements—John Foster Dulles's "massive retaliation," General Curtis LeMay's threat to bomb the Vietnamese "back into the Stone Age"—frightened not only the intended targets but the American people too. A nuclear arms race required periodic campaigns to alert the country to the Soviet threat in order to create the climate for large military budgets. As the arms race grew more intense and more expensive, so did the rhetoric of bomber gaps, missile gaps, windows of vulnerability, and the like. The campaigns all succeeded in creating wide popular support for increased military spending. But there was a "down side," as the nuclear strategists well knew. A dynamic arms race meant that the people would never feel secure. There would never be enough at any level of armaments. By the 1970s the clues of despair were turning up in strange places. You could find them in children's drawings, in films, popular songs, and in the increasingly apocalyptical cast of fundamentalist religion, which was attracting more and more Americans from mainstream churchgoing. The most popular nonfiction book of the decade was Hal Lindsey's *The Late Great Planet Earth*, which predicted a nuclear Armageddon, a purifying, punishing fire that would settle the cosmic battle between good and evil once and for all.

The theorists of deterrence understood early in the nuclear age that public opinion was the weak spot in nuclear strategy. In democracies the people might not always accept the idea that they had to be readier than the Soviets to go to the brink of nuclear war. A democratic people would clutch at any hope that the nuclear shadow over their lives might be lifted, and so the Soviet Union could use American hopes for peace as its ultimate weapon for world domination. In his book *Nuclear Weapons and Foreign Policy* Henry Kissinger had warned that if citizens "no longer sense a real nuclear threat, popular support for the maintenance of forces could fade."[54] It was this concern that had prompted Acheson and Dulles to be extremely wary of negotiations with the Soviets. The very act of sitting down with the enemy, they feared, would produce "euphoria" and false hopes and weaken national resolve. Aware of the risk that the public might at some point stop supporting a security system based on booby-trapping the planet, Kissinger suggested that some day "governments might feel themselves compelled to provide for deterrence without the consent of the governed."[55] The Bomb did not fit well with popular democracy. The nuclear guardians did not doubt where duty lay; the people must be protected by nuclear weapons whether they liked it or not.

In 1957, the year Kissinger's book appeared, the first popular antinuclear movement in the United States was gaining force, a campaign sparked by the Nobel laureate Linus Pauling and other scientists to stop nuclear tests in the atmosphere. Pauling estimated in a scholarly article in 1958 that tests already conducted would cause a million cases of leukemia and as many as five million genetically defective children. The Hiroshima Maidens, survivors of the first atomic bomb, toured the United States to dramatize the mutilating effects of radiation. An antinuclear mood was building that the Pentagon and the weapons makers considered extremely dangerous.

The dangers of nuclear contamination, most dramatically the mounting evidence of strontium-90 in milk, created a new public awareness that the arms race itself had costs even if nuclear war, against the weight of history, was somehow to be postponed until the end of time. The concern about low-level radiation mobilized the political pressure that led to the 1963 treaty to ban nuclear tests in the atmosphere. The test ban diffused the concern, and as this measure of environmental protection was being implemented, the public was largely unaware that the pace of nuclear testing was actually increasing at a dramatic rate. But the tests were underground, out of sight and largely out of mind.

Nuclear concerns rose again in the early 1960s when the Kennedy administration briefly pushed a campaign to build fallout shelters. Nuclear strategists argued that civil defense was a crucial component of nuclear strategy. The individual American had to feel that he or she had a chance to survive if deterrence should fail; otherwise the people might turn against the strategy. Nelson Rockefeller, a longtime enthusiast of civil defense, met with Kennedy in May 1961 to urge a massive fallout shelter program, which, according to the governor of New York, would "stiffen public willingness to support

U.S. use of nuclear weapons if necessary."[56] At the height of the Berlin crisis of July 1961 Kennedy urged every American to build a shelter. Suddenly merchants of survival appeared everywhere. Swimming pool contractors offered to build shelters. Banks, having judged Armageddon to be at least a half decade away, offered five-year construction loans. *Life* printed a euphoric article by Edward Teller that assured the country that 99 percent of the population could survive and the editors advised sipping hot tea as a cure for radiation sickness. When a hasty survey showed that a quarter of shelter owners would shoot their neighbors rather than share their scant air and water supply with them, grisly articles began appearing in popular magazines quoting clergymen about when it was moral to shoot the folks next door and when it was not. The United States Employment Service issued a booklet on how to find a job "in the post-attack environment." The unintended effect of the civil defense scare was to dramatize the hopelessness of surviving a nuclear war. The growing antinuclear movement was given a new push.

In the Cuban missile crisis of October 1962, nuclear fear reached its high point and then quickly receded. The face-down between the United States and the Soviet Union over the deployment of Soviet missiles in Cuba made nuclear war appear imminent, to the highest officials and ordinary citizens alike. (At the height of the crisis Under Secretary of State Ball told his wife to turn their basement into a fallout shelter.[57] There was a run on peanut butter and toilet paper in Georgetown.) The brush with Armageddon taught leaders in both countries that basing national prestige on brandishing nuclear weapons took too great a toll on the leaders themselves. The margin for error was narrowing. It was not possible to live at such a pitch. The United States and the Soviet Union began to talk about managing their competition through arms control agreements, and negotiations on arms control began despite increasing Soviet support for the armies of North Vietnam.

In November 1967 the army announced plans to put ABM bases near Boston, Chicago, Pittsburgh, Seattle, and six other cities. The leading antinuclear peace organization, SANE, launched a campaign of full-page newspaper advertisements warning that "mad" generals, "The People Who Brought You Vietnam," were about to put H-bombs in people's backyards. The prospect of having nuclear antimissile missiles near their homes to shoot down incoming nuclear missiles was forcing Americans once again to think about the unthinkable. In response to the protest the army promised to put the missiles in unpopulated areas. In 1972 President Nixon signed the Antiballistic Missile Treaty, and the issue disappeared. Great publicity was focused on the SALT I negotiations to set limits on offensive missiles. Meanwhile, the superpowers kept turning out nuclear warheads at the rate of three or more a day. From 1962 to 1978 the nuclear arms race acquired more momentum than ever, but official talk about the weapons was controlled and reassuring.

The effect of all this on the public was what the psychiatrist Robert Lifton called "numbing," an analgesic forgetfulness about the nuclear horror, a defense mechanism to allow individuals to shut out fear and go on living. The mind leapt at the good news. Despite all the apocalyptical talk the nuclear war had not happened. And now the superpowers were trying to address the danger. To be sure, psychiatrists and pediatricians continued to report the helpless feelings of schoolchildren who believed that the nuclear war was no more than ten years away. But the years between the Cuban missile crisis and the revival of the Cold War in the late 1970s could be called the era of the Great Denial. In his 1973 best-seller *The Denial of Death*, the psychiatrist Ernest Becker argued that American society, confronted with the death of everything, was increasingly unable to deal with mortality on any level, one sign being the worship of youth, another the increasing insistence that coffins be closed at funerals. The historian Spencer Weart documents "the worldwide collapse of interest in nuclear war" during these years manifested in the sharp decline in articles on the subject in newspapers, magazines, catalogs of nonfiction books, novels, and films. "From their peak around the time of the Cuban crisis, all these measures plunged by the late 1960s to a quarter or less of their former numbers. Even comic books with 'Atom' in the titles faded from the newsstands."[58]

Ironically, Ronald Reagan did more than any other single individual to revive the antinuclear movement and create what Richard Perle called "the nuclear allergy." The new administration announced plans to increase its spending on nuclear weapons by 40 percent. Officials regularly talked about "winning" nuclear wars. Eugene Rostow, the head of the Arms Control and Disarmament Agency, declared, "We are living in a prewar and not a postwar world." Richard Pipes, a Harvard history professor called to service in the White House, said that the Soviets had a choice of changing their system "or going to war." A high Pentagon official who was pushing for revival of civil defense suggested that anyone with a shovel could dig a hole and survive a nuclear attack. The annual Defense Department "defense guidance statement," leaked to the

New York Times, stated that "protracted nuclear war is possible"—
up to six months. The secretary of state thought that nuclear weapons could be used to fire "a shot over the bow" to keep the Soviets
in line. Reagan himself mused about how the superpowers could
arrange a limited nuclear war in Europe.[59] The tough talk was designed to ease the passage of unprecedented military appropriations
and to dissuade the Soviets from challenging the new administration while it was preoccupied with domestic economic problems.
But the effect was to bring millions into the streets in Europe and
to stimulate an unprecedented explosion of antinuclear sentiment
in the United States.

The embers of antinuclear passion were already smoldering. In
the 1970s, during the years of the Great Denial, the energy crisis
and the increasing visibility of ecological problems had given a boost
to a variety of citizens' movements concerned with the environment. The most confrontational wing of the movement focused on
the dangers of nuclear power plants, and it was gaining considerable
momentum. Ostensibly driven by concerns about fallout and nuclear accidents caused by "the peaceful atom," not the arms race, it
attracted large numbers whose anxieties had been fed by years of
talk about nuclear holocaust. Because the antinuclear movement
was an environmental movement and not in the business of criticiz-
ing the nation's foreign policy, the activists' patriotism was not questioned. (Instead they were attacked as hysterical, uninformed, and
antibusiness.) The near meltdown of a nuclear reactor at Three
Mile Island on March 28, 1979, gave the movement a huge boost.
It produced a solid week of alarmed front-page news. As half the
residents of the surrounding area fled, Walter Cronkite voiced the
fears that were now gripping much of the country. Human beings
were "tampering with natural forces."[60] No one could say where it
would all end. The polls showed that almost half the country was
uneasy about nuclear power plants. At this point Helen Caldicott,
an Australian pediatrician who had become a full-time activist,
sought to gather the "antinukes" into the peace movement. "When
compared to the threat of nuclear war," she reiterated in speech
after speech, "the nuclear power controversy shrinks to paltry dimensions."[61]

The way to end the nuclear arms race, Caldicott, Randall Forsberg, a peace researcher in Boston, and a growing number of
church leaders declared, was for the superpowers simply to "freeze"
their nuclear weapons stockpiles. The idea had been around for
years, first suggested in the early 1970s by Gerard Smith, Nixon's

arms negotiator. For an arms proposal it was refreshingly simple and moderate, a way to end the arms race and preserve nuclear deterrence at the same time. The freeze gained national attention when a nonbinding referendum was put on the ballot in western Massachusetts in November 1980 and won 59 percent of the vote in the year of Ronald Reagan's triumph. Various peace organizations, including the American Friends Service Committee, Fellowship of Reconciliation, and Women's International League for Peace and Freedom came together to promote a "mutual freeze on the testing, production, and deployment of all nuclear warheads, missiles and delivery systems."[62] Soon resolutions supporting the freeze were passed in town meetings and city councils across the country. A national campaign for the freeze was supported by such mainstream organizations as the Wilderness Society, the American Association of University Women, the National Conference of Black Mayors, and the YWCA and was endorsed by prominent former national security officials, including Robert McNamara and William Colby.

In a matter of months these efforts produced a new national organization with chapters across the country and a burst of peace activism involving more Americans than any previous campaign in the nation's history. To an unprecedented degree the peace activists of the 1980s felt themselves to be part of an international movement. The peace movements of Europe offered an encouraging example for American activists. Having mobilized millions for street demonstrations, the movements succeeded in producing a permanent change in public attitudes on nuclear weapons even though the battle of the intermediate-range missiles was eventually lost. (Or, more accurately, lost and then won when Reagan and Gorbachev signed an agreement in 1987 for their removal.)

The Roman Catholic bishops in the United States, resisting pressures from prominent laymen close to the administration, issued a pastoral letter stating that it was immoral to use nuclear weapons except in response to a nuclear attack and that it was even immoral to stockpile the weapons, except temporarily, as part of a process of getting rid of them. Some bishops went further, calling for an unequivocal condemnation, unilateral disarmament, tax resistance, and refusal to participate in making the weapons. Attacked for their lack of credentials on military and strategic matters, the bishops asserted their right to speak out; The Bomb raised the supreme moral issue facing humankind. The only credentials citizens needed to participate in the debate about survival, they seemed to be saying, was moral sense and a searching mind. The example inspired millions of normally diffident Americans to take some small step to express their feelings about nuclear catastrophe. The Freeze movement attracted many people because it seemed to offer a way to take some control over their future. It was as much a movement for democracy as for peace. Nine states and more than fifty cities, including Philadelphia, Chicago, Galveston, and Miami, passed referenda calling for the freeze. In June 1982 almost one million people marched for peace in Central Park. Some opinion polls showed that nearly eight out of ten Americans favored a bilateral, verifiable freeze, and members of Congress in both houses rushed to support it.

At first the president and his top advisers aimed withering fire at the freeze. On October 4, 1982, Reagan accused the movement of being "inspired by not the sincere, honest people who want peace, but by some who want the weakening of America and so are manipulating honest . . . and sincere people." Foreign agents, he said a month later, were sent to "help instigate" the freeze.[63] Top officials such as Robert McFarlane went around the country with a softer but equally dismissive message: The freeze advocates were getting in over their heads. Ordinary citizens could not understand the technical aspects of arms control and therefore they should not interfere. But despite the president's insistence that the United States was dangerously "behind," a majority of citizens appeared to believe that the differences in the nuclear forces were meaningless. Enough is enough. Polls showed that support for military spending and for the president's approach to the nuclear issue were sharply declining.

Ronald Reagan was a supremely successful politician because he was unusually sensitive to shifts in public opinion. Famous as the Great Communicator, he could be an equally adept listener. In 1983 he abruptly shifted rhetoric and pronounced himself "the leader of the peace movement." Gone were the nuclear fulminations. In March the president announced plans to build a high-technology shield to protect the American people from incoming missiles, thus rendering nuclear weapons "impotent and obsolete." The president appeared to endorse the Roman Catholic bishops' moral denunciation of deterrence. The speech stunned Reagan's closest aides. One of the few who saw the speech before it was delivered, Dr. George Keyworth, the president's science adviser, conceded that the Strategic Defense Initiative was designed to head off the Freeze movement. "I think the Freeze movement in the United States told us something, and I think what it said was that the public is frightened. . . . I think people in many ways are telling us to go out and find something new, give us some hope."⁶⁴ As the 1984 election approached, the president took every occasion to re-peat his new antinuclear credo: "Nuclear war cannot be won and must not be fought."

Two years later the Freeze movement was in decline; by the end of the Reagan presidency it was dead. The story of its success and ultimate disappearance demonstrates the potentiality and the limits of citizens' movements to change foreign policy. Despite the initial enthusiasm, support for the freeze proved to be wide but not deep. Joining the movement did not require changing any attitudes about the Soviet Union, nuclear deterrence, or the role of the United States in the world. Congressmen found no difficulty voting for a Freeze Resolution and for the MX missile a few days later. Because the movement was so apolitical, it was easy to diffuse and to co-opt. Reagan was reelected in a landslide.

But the real message of the freeze was heard. In order to parry the thrust of the movement the president adopted antinuclear rhet-oric, which eventually propelled him toward nuclear arms reduc-tion and a fundamental attack on the legitimacy of nuclear weapons. Because of public pressure the president found himself navigating an unfamiliar course with uncertain goals. At the Reyk-javik summit in 1986 he publicly endorsed total nuclear disarma-ment, causing his aides to wonder whether he had taken leave of his senses. The successful outcome of the negotiations with the Soviet Union in 1987 for a treaty to destroy the intermediate-range missiles in Europe came as a great surprise to the craftsmen of the U.S. "zero-option" proposal, which had been designed as propa-ganda and was thought to be nonnegotiable. The president, having been forced into a new game, declared victory. The military buildup had worked. "Peace through strength." But the spending of money had yet to produce a significantly more impressive military force; building weapons and outfitting forces takes years. By 1983, the year Reagan changed his rhetoric, the "military balance," judged by Rea-gan's own election year criteria, had not improved; arguably, it was worse.

But the Interpreter of Last Resort announced that American strength and confidence had returned. In an age when no nation can afford the test of nuclear battle, the calculation of power rests almost exclusively on perception and appearance. The assertion that America was back, standing tall, made it so. As the opinion analyst Daniel Yankelovich puts it, public opinion communicates popular values of the time, not policy options. In voting for Reagan the public was voting for "strength" but not belligerence, and certainly not for war. In responding to the people's aspirations for peace, Ronald Reagan changed the discourse on national security. However cynical the intent to manipulate public opinion may have been, the shift created a new political reality. The hopes and fears of the people were acknowledged and given legitimacy by the president of the United States, and these now set the limits on the uses of American military power.

CONCLUSION

Battleground of Democracy

Throughout American history, leaders have taken public opinion more seriously than have the people themselves. For most of these two hundred years, presidents have worried about what the people thought, but popular sentiment was rarely a serious bar to presidential action in foreign policy. In the nuclear age, however, the power of public opinion has increased dramatically. Presidents now wield life-and-death power over every citizen, but they feel compelled to make ever greater efforts to court public opinion because the consent of the governed has been withdrawn from time to time in dramatic and unprecedented ways. In the 1980s the American people caught bad cases of the "nuclear allergy" and the "Vietnam syndrome" that limited the president's power to engage in nuclear missile rattling and thwarted presidential hopes for a decisive victory in Central America. A nationwide protest movement against apartheid in South Africa forced a change of rhetoric in the Reagan administration and caused Congress to vote sanctions against that racist government.

The increasingly frantic effort to sell American foreign policy to Americans has taken its toll. The hyperbole that was used to persuade one generation to go to war—to make the world safe for democracy, to end war itself—created a backlash of cynical isolationism in the next. The overselling of the Soviet Union during World War II and in the Nixon-Kissinger era was overcompensated in the Truman and Reagan eras by extreme anti-Soviet rhetoric from the White House that fed public rage, fear, frustration, and confusion. This atmosphere of contrived alarm made the public vulnerable to demagogic appeals, disarmed responsible criticism of military expenditures, and narrowed the spectrum of politically permissible debate in Congress and in the media on alternative foreign policy and national security strategies. It also created its own backlash in the early 1980s, a fear of war that gave rise to revived demands for relaxation of tension and control of the arms race. The marketing of nuclear policy has been accomplished largely through secrecy and obfuscation—secrecy about war plans, obfuscation about the effects of radiation, official silence about the profound moral questions raised by nuclear weapons and nuclear strategy. The mystique of secrecy and technological mystery associated with these weapons has eroded the self-confidence of ordinary citizens in their own judgment and, in the words of Yale political scientist Robert Dahl, has caused the most fateful decisions to escape "the control of the democratic process."[1]

The never-ending struggle between people seeking to influence foreign policy and presidents who govern by neutralizing, deflecting, or co-opting public opinion has produced seesaw rhetoric and drift in basic policy ever since the original Cold War consensus collapsed in the Vietnam War. As the world for which that consensus was created becomes increasingly unrecognizable, the fundamental values and purposes to be served by U.S. foreign policy are forgotten or become confused. Presidents treat national security policy as a commodity to be sold rather than as a set of inescapably controversial ideas to be debated and understood. The most dangerous result of government by hyperbole, propaganda, and denial is a depoliticized and increasingly shockproof electorate.

Ironically, public opinion plays a more important role today in setting limits to presidential power in foreign affairs than ever before, but by and large citizens do not *feel* empowered. What the United States is and what it should seek to be and do in a world on the threshold of the twenty-first century have not been clearly articulated by recent presidents, and the people are divided and uncertain about how to live in a global system in which the Cold War is pronounced to be over, enormous sums with which to fight it continue to be spent, and America's allies and protectorates, notably Japan, hold awesome power over the American economy. Public opinion sets limits to foreign military adventures and military spending, but the federal system envisages no positive role for the people in setting the foreign policy agenda. The machinery of electoral politics does not encourage the participation of citizens in confronting the most fundamental choices facing the nation.

People feel disempowered because too often electoral politics has become incapable of articulating or presenting the important decisions that will determine the quality of life for themselves and their children. The most important public questions facing the United States—what its economy should look like and how it is to fit into the world economy, how the environment is to be protected—are now inextricably linked to political and economic developments far removed from American shores. But the American political process is still controlled by the artificial compartmentalization of "foreign" and "domestic" policy. This outmoded way of looking at national policy inhibits public consideration of nonmilitary, cooperative approaches to international politics. Because politicians are prepared to seek office with demagogic attacks on the opposition for being "soft" on Russia or "soft" on Japan or "soft" on some other irritating foreign power with adverse interests, presidents are cautious about explaining to the electorate the realistic limits to American power. It is more tempting to bring an audience to its feet with the rhetoric of nostalgia and denial. So, too, presidents find it easier to order a new weapons system or a limited military operation than to take the risks of diplomacy. Failures of diplomacy, like Yalta, become the political slogans of the opposition, while military disasters are patriotically forgotten.

Unless citizens are armed with deeper understanding of the implications of foreign policy decisions and an awareness of a wider range of policy alternatives, they are easy marks for demagogic rhetoric. To have either political significance or staying power the consent of the governed should be reasonably informed, at least not deliberately misinformed. But in an age of propaganda, media hype, and disinformation, the message most people hear is that issues of war and peace are too complicated to think about—as long as the president seems to know what he is doing.

Polls show that Americans understand that the relative power of the United States is declining from its historic peak at the end of World War II, but politicians do not know how to talk about what this means. Conventional political advice to candidates is to say as little as possible about foreign policy except to be for peace, strength, standing up to (and cautious negotiation with) the Soviets, and the flag. When circumstances permit, a candidate may make a crowd-pleasing gesture such as going to Korea in search of peace in 1952 or to the Great Wall of China in 1972. The most urgent national security issues—whether the United States is wasting its resources in the arms race, whether it is failing to invest adequately in its physical infrastructure, industrial base, or its children, whether it is making commitments to other nations it cannot and should not fulfill, whether action should or can be taken to reverse the trends in the world economy that threaten American power and prosperity, whether the nation is neglecting ecological perils that threaten all human life—do not make good nine-second sound bites. At issue now is the future of the nation-state itself—what the United States is and what it is becoming in a global environment that is at once more intrusive and less controllable by any single nation, however rich, however powerful. Possible answers to the fundamental dilemmas are not debated because the questions, if they are noted at all, are consigned to op-ed pages. Candidates concentrate on the "manageable" issues which tend to be either bogus, trivial, or holdovers from another time. Thus there is nothing even approaching a consensus on what the national interest is.

As it has become harder to manage popular sentiment, the efforts to manipulate public opinion have become more cynical. As a result, the rituals for expressing consent attract a smaller percentage of the electorate. (A bare 50 percent of eligible voters showed up at the polls in the 1988 presidential election.) But where does the responsibility lie? Does this mean that people are too lazy, uninformed, or uncaring to act as citizens? Or is it because they do not believe that their participation matters?

Is it really true, to return to Dean Acheson's arch comment, that if leaders accede to the popular view they will always "go wrong"? There is a widespread assumption in the corridors of power that the average citizen doesn't grasp the big picture. Unlike investment bankers, ordinary people worry about themselves rather than America's world responsibilities. But who had a better sense of the national interest with respect to nuclear weapons production and planning—the complacent experts or the "hysterical" public? Who had a better understanding of the uses of power in the contemporary world and the ranking of priorities—those specialists in national security who planned military interventions in desperately poor countries or the millions of citizens who opposed them?

Let me state plainly, even at the risk of caricaturing them, the two premises that undergird Walter Lippmann's argument. (On occasion he himself was no less plain.) The people are too ignorant, too susceptible to emotional appeal, too short-sighted to be right. By contrast, the leaders are too experienced, too dispassionate, too disciplined to be wrong. Both propositions are at variance with much historical experience. The opinion analyst Daniel Yankelovich distinguishes between "mass opinion," which he defines as "the

volatile, confused, ill-formed, and emotionally clouded public responses to an issue when underlying value conflicts remain unre-
solved," and "public judgment," which is the product of considered
second thoughts after people "have pondered an issue deeply
enough to resolve all conflicts and trade-offs and to accept responsibility for the consequences of their beliefs."[2] When the public
reaches a judgment, the responses to polls vary little even when the
wording of questions is designed to produce the answer the pollster
wants. Mass opinion, on the other hand, remains volatile and is
easily influenced by the way questions are posed, even by the order
in which the questions are asked.

Before the United States entered World War II solid, stable majorities had come to favor aiding Britain even if it meant risking a
war that most Americans of course wished to avoid. As the public
learned more about Hitler and the implausibility of staying neutral,
the American people supported whatever steps Roosevelt proposed.
In the 1980s Yankelovich shows that the shift in public attitudes
about nuclear weapons reflected a similar learning process. As one
might expect, when it became evident that the United States was
vulnerable to Soviet missiles, public support for the first use of
nuclear weapons against a Soviet attack on Europe with nonnuclear
arms dropped precipitously from what it had been in 1949. In polls
taken in the 1980s an overwhelming majority of Americans found
the idea of initiating a nuclear attack against a nonnuclear threat so
irrational and so contrary to professed American values that they
assumed, contrary to fact, that the United States had no such policy. At the end of the 1980s the public appears to have come to the
judgment that Soviet foreign policy, while still the object of considerable suspicion, is not the overriding threat to national security.
An in-depth poll conducted by the Americans Talk Security Project
in 1988 showed that Americans considered an uncontrolled arms
race a greater threat than the Soviet Union, and America's unre-
solved economic and environmental problems a greater hazard
than any military threat. Large majorities subscribed to the commonsense view often ridiculed as "simplistic" by hard-line experts:
Sooner or later a nuclear arms race will result in a nuclear war.[3]
The respondents understood the idea—intuitively grasped in personal relations but the very opposite of most strategic thinking down
through the ages—that undermining the security of another is not
a good way to assure your own security.

The commonsense view of the public on nuclear weapons con-
trasts sharply with the "expert" opinion that has prevailed all

through the years of the Cold War: The United States can deter Soviet expansion only by demonstrating to the Kremlin by the weapons it builds, by what it says about them, and by death-defying bravado that it is less hesitant to resort to nuclear war than its enemies. Particularly after the Challenger and Chernobyl disasters of the 1980s, the public showed increasing skepticism about the rationality of a system that depends upon neither Soviet leaders nor American leaders *ever* succumbing to irrationality or making a serious miscalculation. As Yankelovich (writing in collaboration with the industrialist Sidney Harman) points out, the national security manager's time frame is likely to be shorter than the public's. He looks at a foreign policy problem with the next budget hearings or the next election in mind. Citizens are more likely to think of their children and grandchildren. The foreign policy elite have children too, but their official role carries with it an overriding obligation to be disciplined risk takers. It was precisely this self-image that prompted President John F. Kennedy in the Cuban missile crisis of 1962 to court risks of nuclear war, which he estimated at between one out of three and even, to avoid the *appearance* of doing under pressure of the Soviet missiles in Cuba what he had already decided to do unilaterally to improve U.S. security, that is, to remove obsolete, vulnerable missiles from Turkey.

This brings us to Lippmann's second assumption, largely a tacit one, that democratic leaders need to be insulated from the power of mass opinion because they will make wiser and steadier decisions if that happens. It is inconceivable that he would write such a book as *The Public Philosophy* in the post-Vietnam, post-Watergate world. (In the Vietnam War Lippmann found himself a leading symbol of the opposition to that war, and his respect for President Johnson and the diehards in his administration declined to the vanishing point.) Any attentive citizen would have to be an amnesiac to trust in the free reign of elected leaders on life-and-death issues, given the revelations of what recent presidents have said and done. Richard Nixon recounts eight separate incidents when the United States made plans for a game of nuclear bluff in a foreign policy crisis that involved no threat of nuclear attack. Four of them, he said, occurred in his own presidency.[4] No one can read about Nixon's final days in the White House or Lyndon Johnson's rage and believe that the nation is always blessed with wise, dispassionate leaders. (After Canadian prime minister Lester Pearson had made a mildly critical comment on the Vietnam War in the course of a state visit, the president picked him up by the shirt collar and accused him of "pissing on my rug."[5]) The best, the brightest, and the electable are still human beings. The conviction of the Founding Fathers that wielding unchecked power is an unhinging experience for ordinary mortals is corroborated by much twentieth-century experience.

For the first twenty years of the postwar era a self-selected foreign policy aristocracy was in charge of American foreign policy. The bankers and lawyers Henry Stimson brought into government in 1940 co-opted their friends and business associates and created a talent pool of generally like-minded men. As late as 1964 the list of eligibles for high office in matters relating to national security was still dominated by the heirs of Henry Stimson. Friends and protégés of one another, they shared the experiences of upper-class life, a coherent worldview, and a common ethos. "He who serves, reigns" —the motto of Groton School, which Acheson, Harriman, and others attended—captures the sense of duty, noblesse oblige, and dedication to service of this American ruling class. The Establishment put together a grand strategy over a two-year period, and this strategy produced a Pax Americana among the industrial nations and an unprecedented growth spurt in the world economy.

But the American Century lasted about twenty years. However their conduct of the Cold War may ultimately come to be judged, the postwar foreign policy elite had certain advantages in avoiding errors that are not available to their successors. They did not lack either a coherent vision or a set of shared values. Their objectives were clear. Men like Acheson and Harriman saw themselves as defenders of civilization, and they had a rather precise conception of what that civilization was. In developing the war-prevention strategy of the postwar era—what I have called the Four Pillars: nuclear deterrence, NATO and the other alliances, the Truman Doctrine, and the liberal economic order of Bretton Woods—the Establishment had a model.[6] They were quite self-consciously seizing the torch from Britain's faltering hands. When it became clear that British power was failing, the mission of the United States was to take over Britain's role as imperial peacekeeper, organizer of the global balance of power, and banker to the world.

But with the collapse of the Cold War consensus in the mid-1960s and the fading away of the Establishment, leaders today labor under two handicaps that the Acheson generation did not have. First, they no longer share the same ethic of service, and they no longer hold one another accountable to a common vision. Consider the following description by a recent subcabinet official in the Reagan administration: "Presidential appointees have their own futures uppermost in mind. Subsequent careers and incomes hinge on their media images and the contacts and friendships they establish with Washington insiders. The rule of thumb is lay low, don't make enemies, and don't take on the media."[7]

Second, foreign policy elites today are bereft of a model on which to base American strategy. Indeed, for the first time in the two-hundred-year history of the United States no manifest destiny beckons. In each of the four periods discussed in this book there was an almost irresistible inner logic to national security policy. In the Federalist period steering clear of the Napoleonic wars for as long as possible was a compelling option for a nation without an army or a navy. The conquest of North America in the nineteenth century was simply to accept nature's invitation and the logic of nation building. What other destiny so commended itself to a restless and energetic people? Colonial expansion at the turn of the century was to fall in with the fashion of the times. In World War I and World War II the power of the New World redressed the balance of the Old; the United States moved to keep the Continent of Europe from falling under the sway of a single power when Britain was no longer able to play the classic role. And when World War II was over, the United States easily slipped into Britain's role as number-one nation.

Undoubtedly, there is a manifest destiny for America today more compelling than any in our history: to mobilize the still enormous power, resources, and imagination of the American people to help save the planet. But the elites in charge of foreign policy do not yet grasp the dimensions of the task, much less a strategy for action. The dimness of vision and the lack of the compelling ethos of service that marked the Establishment make it especially dangerous to let elites, however well intentioned and well educated, experiment with national security without the constraints of public opinion. As the protective cocoon once offered this nation by the seas and the air above dissolves, the nation's once phenomenal economic edge disappears, and the atmosphere itself turns hostile, and the risks that confused leaders will do irreparable harm grow.

Thus popular participation is becoming more necessary but also more possible. Within national boundaries it is becoming harder to maintain authoritarian control with either the ideologies of the Right or of the Left. Borders are becoming porous, and despite the elaborate investment in propaganda, the scandals of oppression have become harder to hide. True, global communications conglomerates—Rupert Murdoch, Bertelsmann, Time-Warner—are rapidly concentrating their control of mass media across the planet and are in a position to influence the thoughts of many more people than any political or religious leader of the past. But the more significant development is the rise of technologies, such as personal computers, fax, and satellites, that open up multiple sources of information and varieties of direct person-to-person communication.

In the end, the argument for limiting citizen participation and for manipulating public opinion is rooted in the same fear that is always present when people give up freedom or allow it to be taken away: the fear of disorder. A number of writers on contemporary politics, such as Samuel Huntington, consider the protests of the Vietnam era as evidence of an "excess" of democracy. But direct action and massive protests occur only when citizens feel excluded from orderly participation in the decisions that most deeply affect them, and then only when the decisions elicit feelings of peril or outrage. Under our system aroused public opinion makes itself felt only after foreign policy appears to be going badly. The people react to unpopular policies that have already been carried out by punishing the policy makers. Such expressions of popular sentiment always affect future decisions, but they do not decide them. The punishment process is a disorderly business. The more channels there are for orderly participation in the making of important decisions before they are presented as *faits accomplis* the less disorder there is likely to be. The difficult question is how to create the structures for subjecting foreign policy to democratic control. The starting point is, first, to take the goal seriously and, second, to respect the constitutional structures already in place.

In the present political climate, however, popular participation is more feared than encouraged by our most vocal politicians, academics, and savants. The nation is still living in a backlash of cynicism about democracy occasioned by what Huntington calls the "creedal passion" of the 1960s and 1970s when moral questions threatened to engulf the technical and managerial questions with which elites are far more comfortable. Whenever questions of morals and values are admitted into the realm of debate, the fewer grounds there are for excluding the participation of ordinary citizens, for they are as expert on these matters as the experts. The most important questions facing the society involve profoundly difficult value choices that will determine what sort of a society the United States is to be in the twenty-first century. Facing many different risks—nuclear war, the debt crisis, growing class divisions, ecological disaster, the effects of worldwide impoverishment, mis-education, and lack of opportunity for many in the next generation —how does a nation as spread-out and diverse as the United States develop a common strategy? Where does a nation put energy and resources? And how does it decide to do it? What risks are Americans prepared to take in the process of adapting to a radically chang-ing world environment? And how are the risks and burdens of inevitable austerity to be shared? Neither the president nor any other hired executive can answer these questions for the people. If we cannot figure out practical ways for these choices to be made democratically, the Constitution will have all the relevance of a dead creed.

It is ironic that so many policy makers and writers on national security have preferred to celebrate democracy abroad rather than to implement it at home. Not believing their own professed ideol-ogy, they have in the Cold War years often considered dictatorship a Soviet advantage and democracy an American handicap. Yet So-viet president Mikhail Gorbachev is frantically experimenting with democratic forms not primarily to impress the West but to shake the Soviet Union out of its economic paralysis and to mobilize the Soviet people for the computer age. For Gorbachev a measure of democracy is a tool for regenerating Soviet society. Dictatorships in Latin America are also fading because of a new understanding that societies dependent upon either terror or the flimsy structure of personalized rule can neither motivate nor control their popula-tions. They are inherently unstable because they cannot compete in an integrated world.

Because democracy is so highly valued an ideal virtually every-where and dictatorships face increasing difficulties in controlling subversive notions like human rights, personal dignity, and political choice, it is becoming harder to govern modern nations by repres-sive means, even as the technology of repression is being perfected. From South Korea to Chile to Poland to South Africa people are demanding more participation in the decisions that control their lives, and leaders, realizing that the guarantee of personal freedom is the bedrock of legitimacy, are ever so slowly falling back before this wave of grass-roots democracy.

All governments miscalculate at times and act against their own interests. But the mistakes of rulers like Hitler, Stalin, or Pol Pot, who hear no opinions contrary to their own, have murderous con-sequences for their society. The feedback mechanisms of democatracy are indispensable for preserving the nation from the errors of its leaders. However, the strongest argument for democracy is ideological. The state exists for the benefit of the people, not the other way around. People do not feel free under the authoritarian rule of unaccountable leaders, and if they do not feel free, they are not fully human.

The United States is of course neither a one-party dictatorship nor an authoritarian regime, but rather an aging democracy. Yet it is ironic that in the midst of this worldwide popular pressure there should be so little sentiment for renewing the institutions of popular participation in the nation that gave birth to modern democracy. What the people want is still the source of political legitimacy, and politicians always present themselves as defenders of the people against the "interests" or "big business" or "union tycoons" or the "media" or the white-wine-sipping liberals who are too rich and protected to care about the criminals on the street. But populism and democracy are not the same. William Schneider, a political analyst at the American Enterprise Institute, argues that the most important force in U.S. politics for the past twenty years "has been an antiestablishment populism."[8] True. But it has not been put to the service of either greater equality or greater participation. In 1988 George Bush successfully ran a populist campaign in behalf of transferring resources from the poor to the rich just as Ronald Reagan had done twice before.[9] Even a candidate with an office in the White House can run against entrenched power.

Conducting foreign policy as it was conducted in the time of Dean Acheson or Dwight Eisenhower is no longer a real option, if only because the role of the press has changed and the secrecy needed to defuse public anxiety and anger can no longer be maintained. The level of political sophistication of the public is higher. It would be a formidable task today to sell a reactionary autocrat like Syngman Rhee as "the George Washington of Korea" or the confused, vengeful Vietnamese leader Ngo Dinh Diem as "the Winston Churchill of Asia" because sooner or later they would expose themselves on television. To market official truth so at variance with reality or to engineer consent to policies that mock American values or to bypass public opinion altogether, government must now so thoroughly misinform the public as to poison the wellsprings of democracy. In the late twentieth century, secrets are hard to keep because information has become such a marketable commodity. Extraordinary efforts to keep secrets continue, but they often fail. The result, unfortunately, is not full disclosure of the sort needed for citizens to come to judgment—a fair sample of facts and issues—but an official truth based on self-serving misstatements that are never corrected and outrageous lies that produce neither admissions nor apologies even when they are exposed.

The choice, therefore, is to make the foreign policy process more democratic or much less so.

The continuing struggle to shift the public mood is the battle-ground of democracy. Public opinion, as Joseph Schumpeter pointed out, is not the "motive power" of the political process but rather the "product" of contending forces.[10] In foreign policy matters the shock troops are the national security elites, business, labor, and church lobbies, advocacy groups, reinforced by opinion leaders, national and local. These need not be either famous or well informed. A letter writer to a newspaper qualifies as an opinion leader and so within a small circle does a family member. The extent of one's influence, however, depends on reach and credibility. But TV talk, much less the writing of pundits, does not greatly influence public opinion unless it is validated by great events and is in sync with struggles taking place within the political institutions themselves. Thus the battle to shape public opinion is a fight to define the historical moment. If enough people see the world as the president sees it, he will always win. The opposition has the uphill task of convincing enough citizens that the man they have elected to lead the nation misperceives the historical moment. It happens now much more frequently than in the past, but only when the president has been challenged in Congress, in the courts, in the streets, or by a concerted attack in the press. When this happens, to return to the battlefield analogy, masses of troops move in one direction or another, and this is enough to decide the battle.

Walter Lippmann turned Thomas Jefferson on his head to make the argument that a nation can either be a "successful democracy" or have an active foreign policy. Not both. To have a government run by the people—which for Jefferson meant preferably farmers— "you must fence off these ideal communities from the abominations of the world. If the farmers are to manage their own affairs, they must confine affairs to those they are accustomed to managing."[11] But things have changed since Lippmann's day. With neither a model to imitate nor a road map for exercising national power, the lawyers, bankers, and industrialists whom Lippmann assumed to have the expertise so lacking in other citizens seem to be immobilized by the rapid and surprising changes that are taking place across the planet.

At the same time more and more citizens are acquiring direct knowledge of other countries, greater sophistication about global problems, and increasing opportunities for direct contact with non-Americans. The opposition to the Reagan administration policy in Central America was fed by thousands of ordinary Americans—business people, local officials, physicians, specialists on environment, prisons, cattle, and a variety of other matters. Many of them were churchgoers who were concerned about the moral implications of American military activities abroad and decided to examine the national security threat for themselves. They returned to their own communities with facts and personal witness to challenge the credibility of a president who proclaimed small, impoverished countries to be a threat to American democracy. Many thousands of Americans, notably students, business people, and professionals of all sorts, traveled to the Soviet Union in the 1980s and built a wide variety of long-term relationships with people who had been pronounced to be either agents, foot soldiers, or captives of the Evil Empire. The reaction of American visitors to a variety of experiences in Russia was mixed, but this direct involvement made it possible for them to put official rhetoric and inflammatory characterizations into context and to see the officially proclaimed enemy as human beings. The empathy generated by human contact and professional and commercial association made thousands of Americans aware that international relations is more than the Cold War chess game. All this challenged the credibility of the Interpreter of Last Resort, and Ronald Reagan, moving quickly to catch up with his people, walked the streets of Moscow, smiling and patting the heads of children.

Municipalities are now playing a much more activist role in foreign policy, at times diverging sharply from the foreign policy of the federal government. While the Reagan administration was promoting "constructive engagement" with South Africa, seventy cities, thirteen counties, and twenty-two states moved more than $20 billion in assets out of South Africa.[12] Private groups have given medical, technical, and food supplies to local groups in Nicaragua in amounts almost matching congressional appropriations for the Contras.[13] More than one thousand cities in the United States are now establishing their own relations with local communities in foreign countries, including those designated as adversaries, making it possible to deal city to city on issues of trade, technical assistance, immigration, and refugees. There are new opportunities for citizens to involve themselves in actually carrying out foreign policy for

their own communities. The radical reduction in the costs of transportation and communication is democratizing international relations. The technology exists for bringing what Lippmann called the
"unseen environment" into the homes of America via cable, satellites, and VCRs. People are less dependent on stereotypes for simplifying reality than when Lippmann wrote. The technology also
exists for encouraging popular education and discussion of the connections between foreign and domestic policy issues on a national
scale. But education for participation and education for consent are
not the same.

By their very nature, war planning and war prevention as they
have been historically conceived, and especially since the birth of
the nation-state system in the seventeenth century, are highly centralized elite activities. As long as the chief business of nation-states
is to prevent, prepare for, and fight wars, the citizen's primary role
is to be a resource, not a decision maker. There is no room at the
chessboard for those whose fate hangs on the skill of the players.
But in the forty-fifth year of the nuclear age there is a growing
awareness of the suicidal consequences of even so-called "conventional" wars, of the limits of military power to effect desired political
change, especially for great nations with many connections and
much to lose, and of the transcendent importance of the nonmilitary components of national security, chiefly economic development and ecological health. The awakening to the potentially
catastrophic consequences of man-made ecological degradation—
the pollution of the seas, the fouling of the air, the destruction of
the ozone layer—is making the concept of security less abstract and
dramatizing the reality that the security of people and traditional
notions of national security are not always the same.

Large areas of the globe are facing starvation and disease, the
effects of which travel far more rapidly than in earlier times when
countries were more isolated. (The AIDS epidemic probably started
in Zaire.) Distant tragedies that once engaged the compassion of
only a few now affect everyone. Decisions about the rain forest in
Brazil can determine the air quality in Chicago. The entire planet
is threatened with temperature changes that could conceivably spell
the end of human life. In such a world it is increasingly bizarre to
think of the overriding security threat to Americans as primarily a
military one. To be sure, traditional national security bureaucracies
are ingenious in finding ways to adapt new realities to old ways of
thinking. Even as the Cold War is declared over, won, or irrelevant,
the search for new enemies is on. Nonetheless, though the potential

targets for military operations are boundless, the uncontrollable destructiveness of modern war, its cost, and the constraints of public opinion sharply limit what military power can accomplish. Unlike traditional war planning and war-prevention strategies, the national security tasks of the new century call for much greater decentralization and much greater participation of the population as a whole.

Public opinion polls continue to expose the fact that a shocking number of Americans have an abysmal ignorance of geography and history, including their own. One requirement for the adaptation of American domestic institutions to the demands of the new century is to break down the barriers of ignorance that separate Americans from their six billion neighbors. True patriotism can be built only on knowledge, empathy, and understanding of the real world rather than the fear, contempt, and immobilizing complacency that passes for realism.

In a democracy citizens are expected to set the parameters of policy not because of their technical or political knowledge but because a society cannot be democratic if it does not reflect their values and preferences. When citizens have the chance to learn what is happening over a period of time, it is not obvious that majorities are more error-prone than elites who read the same headlines and feel the same emotional tugs. The argument for making the conduct of foreign policy accountable to the people does not require romanticizing public opinion. Irrationality, inconsistency, and ignorance are liberally distributed in every human community. Ultimately, the case rests on Winston Churchill's famous aphorism: Democracy is the worst form of government, except for all the rest.

NOTES

Introduction

1. See Almond, *American People and Foreign Policy*, 1950 ed., Chap. 1.
2. LaFeber, "American Policymakers, Public Opinion, and the Outbreak of the Cold War, 1945–1950," in Nagai and Iriye, 60.
3. Acheson, *Present at the Creation*, 375.
4. Tocqueville, *Democracy in America*, 1969 ed., 1:228.
5. Acheson, *Citizen Looks at Congress*, 50–51.
6. Lippmann, *Public Philosophy*, 21–29.
7. See essay of Samuel Huntington in Crozier, Huntington, and Watanuki, *Crisis of Democracy*, 27.
8. Pearson, "Democracy and the Power of Division," in Jacobsen, 27.
9. "Federalist No. 6," in Hamilton, Jay, Madison, *The Federalist*, 31.
10. Hughes, *Domestic Context of American Foreign Policy*, 23–24. See also, Page, Shapiro, and Dempsey, "What Moves Public Opinion?"; Bardes and Oldendick, "Public Opinion and Foreign Policy."

CHAPTER ONE

1. Morison, *Oxford History* 2:57.
2. Malone, *Jefferson and His Time* 2:310.
3. Bailey, *Diplomatic History*, 5th ed., 4.
4. Ibid., 5.
5. Eugene P. Link, *Democratic-Republican Societies*, 46.
6. Bowers, *Jefferson and Hamilton*, 211.
7. Ibid., 212.
8. Ibid.
9. Ibid.
10. Malone, *Jefferson and His Time* 2:424.
11. Ibid., 486.
12. Bowers, *Jefferson and Hamilton*, 221.
13. Ibid., 216.
14. DeConde, *Entangling Alliance*, 228.
15. Ibid., 58.
16. Eugene P. Link, *Democratic-Republican Societies*, 177n.
17. Ammon, "Formation of the Republican Party in Virginia," 300.
18. Quoted in DeConde, *Entangling Alliance*, 94.
19. Morison, *Oxford History* 2:58.
20. Bowers, *Jefferson and Hamilton*, 220.
21. Ibid.
22. Bailey, *Diplomatic History*, 5th ed., 76.
23. DeConde, *Entangling Alliance*, 99.
24. Apr. 19, 1794, in *Letters of John Adams* 2:156.
25. DeConde, *Entangling Alliance*, 98.
26. Bowers, *Jefferson and Hamilton*, 24–42.
27. Eugene P. Link, *Democratic-Republican Societies*, 127n.
28. Bowers, *Jefferson and Hamilton*, 229.
29. Apr. 15, 1794, in *Letters of John Adams* 2:155.
30. Jensen, *New Nation*, 107–8.
31. Eugene P. Link, *Democratic-Republican Societies*, 7.
32. Ibid., 160–61.
33. Buel, *Securing the Revolution*, 103.
34. For who was a citizen, see calculations of Allan Nevins on the percentage who voted in early elections, cited in Lippmann, *Public Philosophy*, 33n.
35. *Gazette of the United States*, Apr.

19, 1794, quoted in Buel, *Securing the Revolution*, 101.
36. Buel, *Securing the Revolution*, 107.
37. Stewart, *Opposition Press*, 169; see also Eugene P. Link, *Democratic-Republican Societies*, 19–22.
38. Eugene P. Link, *Democratic-Republican Societies*, 72.
39. Ibid., 94.
40. See Hall, *Organization of American Culture*, Chaps. 4 and 5.
41. Nevins, *American Press Opinion*, 3.
42. Malone, *Jefferson and His Time* 2:425.
43. Leonard D. White, *Federalists*, 110.
44. Graber, *Public Opinion*, 22.
45. McMaster, *History of the People* 2:377.
46. Zinn, *People's History*, 95.
47. DeConde, *Entangling Alliance*, 56.
48. Wills, *Inventing America*, 282.
49. Graber, *Public Opinion*, 110.
50. Wills, *Inventing America*, 210.
51. Ibid., 225.
52. *Writings of Thomas Jefferson* (Lipscomb), 5:94.
53. Graber, *Public Opinion*, 110.
54. Wills, *Inventing America*, 282.
55. Bowers, *Jefferson and Hamilton*, 248.
56. LaFeber, *American Age*, 46.
57. Buel, *Securing the Revolution*, 106.
58. LaFeber, *American Age*, 47–48.
59. Buel, *Securing the Revolution*, 107.
60. Ibid., 108.
61. Cobbett, *Porcupine's Works* 4:444n; see also Buel, *Securing the Revolution*, 113–24.
62. Buel, *Securing the Revolution*, 106.
63. Ibid., 108.
64. Graber, *Public Opinion*, 47.
65. Page Smith, *John Adams* 1:3
66. Graber, *Public Opinion*, 43.
67. Gay, *Enlightenment* 3:4.
68. Ibid., 559.
69. See Morgan, *Inventing the People*, 59–78.
70. Morgenthau, *Scientific Man*, 19.
71. Graber, *Public Opinion*, 51, 46.
72. *Works of John Adams* 9:376.
73. Morison, *Oxford History* 2:70–71.
74. Cited in Lippmann, *Public Opinion*, 172n.

75. Graber, *Public Opinion*, 67.
76. LaFeber, *American Age*, 50.
77. *Centinel*, July 14, 1798 (Boston, Mass.).
78. *Works of John Adams* 8:613.
79. Ibid. 1:523–27.
80. Graber, *Public Opinion*, 75.
81. *Works of John Adams* 9:278
82. Richardson, *Messages and Papers of the Presidents* 1:273.
83. Bowers, *Jefferson and Hamilton*, 425–26.
84. *Writings of Thomas Jefferson* (Ford), 10:86–89.
85. Graber, *Public Opinion*, 78.
86. *Works of John Adams* 10:113; I am indebted to Anna Nelson for the observation about the self-confidence of revolutionaries in power.

CHAPTER TWO

1. Rogin, *Fathers and Children*, 108.
2. McMaster, *History of the People* 1:383.
3. Rogin, *Fathers and Children*, 109.
4. Quoted in Lippmann, *Public Opinion*, 170.
5. Dec. 20, 1787, in Koch and Peden, *Selected Writings of Thomas Jefferson*, 440–41.
6. Rogin, *Fathers and Children*, 107.
7. To Nathaniel Niles, Mar. 22, 1801, in *Writings of Thomas Jefferson* (Ford), 8:24.
8. Van Alstyne, *Rising American Empire*, 87.
9. Ibid., 20.
10. Bailey, *Diplomatic History*, 5th ed., 165.
11. Graber, *Public Opinion*, 134.
12. Malone, *Jefferson and His Time* 4:256; see also Kaplan, *Entangling Alliances with None*, Chap. 1.
13. Graber, *Public Opinion*, 135.
14. *Writings of Thomas Jefferson* (Ford), 9:418–21.
15. Graber, *Public Opinion*, 139.
16. *Writings of Thomas Jefferson* (Ford), 9:418.
17. Malone, *Jefferson and His Time* 4:281.
18. Bailey, *Diplomatic History*, 5th ed., 105.
19. Ibid., 110.

20. Malone, *Jefferson and His Time* 4:318.
21. Quoted in LaFeber, *American Age*, 55.
22. Malone, *Jefferson and His Time* 4:320; see also Sofaer, "Executive Power," 1–57.
23. McMaster, *History of the People* 2:630.
24. Bailey, *Diplomatic History*, 5th ed., 104.
25. *Writings of Thomas Jefferson* (Lipscomb), 10:417.
26. Quoted in Graber, *Public Opinion*, 143.
27. Graber, *Public Opinion*, 148.
28. Malone, *Jefferson and His Time* 4:326.
29. Ibid., 338.
30. Lyon, "Directory and the United States," 520.
31. Bailey, *Diplomatic History*, 5th ed., 110.
32. Jefferson to Du Pont de Nemours, cited in ibid., 117.
33. To Du Pont de Nemours, Dec. 31, 1815, in *Writings* (Monticello ed.), 14:371.
34. Henry Adams, *History of the United States* 1:189.
35. Graber, *Public Opinion*, 196.
36. Arthur M. Schlesinger, *Imperial Presidency*, 15.
37. Graber, *Public Opinion*, 168–78.
38. Ibid.
39. Fisher, "Francis James Jackson," 93–113.
40. See Mayo, *Henry Clay*, 427–66.
41. Graber, *Public Opinion*, 219n.
42. Nevins, *American Press Opinion*, 53.
43. Stagg, *Mr. Madison's War*, 50.
44. See Hatzenbuehler and Ivie, *Congress Declares War*, Chap. 1.
45. Graber, *Public Opinion*, 195.
46. Morison, Commager, and Leuchtenburg, *Growth of the Republic* 1:362.
47. Hatzenbuehler and Ivie, *Congress Declares War*, 12.
48. Brown, *Republic in Peril*, 168.
49. Stagg, *Mr. Madison's War*, 59–60.
50. Ibid., 72.
51. Graber, *Public Opinion*, 208–12.
52. Ibid., 199.
53. Morison, Merk, and Freidel, *Dissent in Three Wars*, 3. Also see Cress, *Citizens in Arms*, 172–73.
54. LaFeber, *American Age*, 63.

CHAPTER THREE

1. Thomas, "Just Say No," 44.
2. Ibid.
3. Persons, "Public Opinion—A Democratic Dilemma," in Hague, 171.
4. Hobsbawm, "Some Reflections on Nationalism," in Nossiter, Hanson, and Rokkan, 388.
5. Ginsberg, *Captive Public*, Chap. 1.
6. Ibid., 17.
7. Rogin, *Fathers and Children*, 310.
8. Jackson to Calhoun, May 5, 1818, in *American State Papers, Military Affairs* 1:702.
9. *Niles' Weekly Register* 14 (Aug. 8, 1818), 399
10. LaFeber, *American Age*, 77. Under the Adams-Onís Treaty the United States did recognize Spain's claims to Texas. On the public relations aspect of this incident, see Drinnon, *Facing West*, 108–11.
11. Tabbel and Watts, *Press and the Presidency*, 79.
12. Ibid.
13. LaFeber, *American Age*, Chap. 3.
14. Meyers, *Jacksonian Persuasion*, 18–19.
15. Pessen, *Jacksonian America*, 176.
16. Tocqueville, *Democracy in America*, 1986 ed., 1:259–60.
17. Martineau, *Society in America* 1:154.
18. Morison, *Oxford History* 2:162.
19. Tocqueville, *Democracy in America*, 1969 ed., 2:506.
20. Tabbel and Watts, *Press and the Presidency*, 75.
21. Remini, *Andrew Jackson, 1822–1832*, 291–99.
22. Tabbel and Watts, *Press and the Presidency*, 80.
23. Martineau, *Society in America* 1:147.
24. Morison, *Oxford History* 2:161.
25. Rogin, *Fathers and Children*, 103.
26. Arthur M. Schlesinger, *Age of Jackson*, 347.
27. Remini, *Andrew Jackson, 1833–1845*, 274–92.

28. Rogin, *Fathers and Children*, 3–4.
29. Ibid., 3.
30. Jordan, *White Over Black*, 90–91.
31. Wills, *Inventing America*, 284.
32. Dippie, *Vanishing American*, 57.
33. LaFeber, *American Age*, 54; De Conde, *This Affair of Louisiana*, Chap. 7.
34. Dippie, *Vanishing American*, 57.
35. Ibid., 58.
36. Rogin, *Fathers and Children*, 6.
37. Ibid., 128.
38. Ibid., 165–70.
39. Satz, *American Indian Policy*, 12.
40. Ibid., 18.
41. Filler, *Removal of the Cherokee*, 41.
42. Satz, *American Indian Policy*, 51.
43. Ibid., 39.
44. Dippie, *Vanishing American*, 64.
45. Satz, *American Indian Policy*, 16.
46. Dippie, *Vanishing American*, 62.
47. Tocqueville, *Democracy in America*, 1969 ed., 1:328.
48. Rogin, *Fathers and Children*, 120.
49. Ibid., 119–20.
50. Ibid., 116.
51. Satz, *American Indian Policy*, 50.
52. Rogin, *Fathers and Children*, 206.
53. Zinn, *People's History*, 145–46.
54. Remini, *Andrew Jackson, 1833–1845*, 314.
55. Ibid., 297–98.
56. Ibid., 574.

CHAPTER FOUR

1. Bailey, *Man in the Street*, 256. See also May, *Making of the Monroe Doctrine*. For Polk's reinterpretation, see Graebner, *Empire on the Pacific*, 110–11.
2. Morison, *Oxford History* 2:143.
3. Merk, *Manifest Destiny and Mission*, 54.
4. Graebner, *Empire on the Pacific*, 71.
5. Ibid., viii.
6. Ibid., 150–71.
7. LaFeber, *American Age*, 109.
8. For a description of the Oregon negotiation, see Pletcher, *Diplomacy of Annexation*, 395–420.
9. Belohlavek, *"Let the Eagle Soar!"* 226.
10. Bailey, *Diplomatic History*, 5th ed., 251.
11. Ibid., 249.

12. Merk, *Manifest Destiny and Mission*, 77; Pletcher, *Diplomacy of Annexation*, 89, 113–14.
13. Reeves, *American Diplomacy*, 284; see also Pletcher, *Diplomacy of Annexation*, 286–90.
14. Zinn, *People's History*, 149.
15. Ibid., 148.
16. *Diary of James K. Polk* 1:384–87.
17. Schroeder, *Mr. Polk's War*, 33–34.
18. Johannsen, *Halls of the Montezumas*, 11, 68, 186.
19. Merk, *Manifest Destiny and Mission*, 53.
20. Ibid., 57.
21. Schroeder, *Mr. Polk's War*, 27, 53.
22. Ibid., 53. See also Merk, *Manifest Destiny and Mission*, 247.
23. Van Alstyne, *Rising American Empire*, 106. See also Weinberg, *Manifest Destiny*.
24. McPherson, *Battle Cry of Freedom*, 51.
25. Merk, *Manifest Destiny and Freedom*, 122.
26. Ibid., 123.
27. See Weinberg in McDonald, *Mexican War*, 58.
28. Ibid., 62; Pletcher, *Diplomacy of Annexation*, 526–29.
29. Merk, *Manifest Destiny and Mission*, 185.
30. LaFeber, *American Age*, 113–14.
31. J. H. Smith, *War with Mexico* 2:181.
32. Vidal, *Fact and Fiction*, 179; McPherson, *Battle Cry of Freedom*, 47–77.
33. LaFeber, *American Age*, 118.
34. Bailey, *Diplomatic History*, 5th ed., 281.
35. Webster to Tichnor, Jan. 16, 1851, in ibid., 285.
36. J. W. Oliver, *"Louis Kossuth's Appeal,"* 481–95.
37. Arthur M. Schlesinger, *Cycles of American History*, 152.
38. Ibid., 150.
39. Henderson, *"Southern Designs on Cuba,"* 371–85.
40. See LaFeber, *American Age*, 125–26.
41. Bailey, *Diplomatic History*, 8th ed., 428.
42. LaFeber, *American Age*, 137–39.
43. Nicolay and Hay, *Abraham Lincoln* 3:446.

44. Bailey, *Diplomatic History*, 5th ed., 344.
45. Merk, *Manifest Destiny and Mission*, 230.
46. Luthin, "Sale of Alaska," 171.
47. Tocqueville, *Democracy in America*, 1969 ed., 1:126.
48. Ibid.
49. Hilderbrand, *Power and the People*, 8–9.
50. Arthur M. Schlesinger, *Cycles of American History*, 120.
51. May, *Imperial Democracy*, 270.
52. Ibid., 266.
53. Pratt, *Expansionists of 1898*, 3.
54. Ibid., 4–5.
55. Merk, *Manifest Destiny and Mission*, 232.
56. Arthur M. Schlesinger, *Cycles of American History*, 120–21, 153.
57. See Pratt, *Expansionists of 1898*.
58. Arthur M. Schlesinger, *Cycles of American History*, 144.
59. Van Alstyne, *Rising American Empire*, 178–79.
60. May, *Imperial Democracy*, 13–24.
61. Burnham, *Current Crisis*, 45.
62. Ibid., 180.
63. May, *Imperial Democracy*, 22.

CHAPTER FIVE

1. Karp, *Politics of War*, 5.
2. Burnham, *Current Crisis*, 45.
3. LaFeber, *American Age*, 150–54.
4. Healy, *U.S. Expansionism*, 115.
5. Hogan, *Panama Canal*, 24.
6. May, *Imperial Democracy*, 33.
7. Karp, *Politics of War*, 30.
8. Ibid., 13.
9. Ibid., 12.
10. See Pratt, *Expansionists of 1898*, Chap. 6.
11. Karp, *Politics of War*, 13.
12. Ibid., 36.
13. Burnham, *Current Crisis*, 46.
14. Russett, "Economic Decline, Electoral Pressure and the Initiation of Internal Conflict," in Russett, Starr, and Stall, *Choices in World Politics*.
15. Karp, *Politics of War*, 68.
16. Pratt, *Expansionists of 1898*, 209.
17. Bailey, *Diplomatic History*, 5th ed., 482.
18. Ibid., 478.
19. Ibid., 438.
20. Beisner, *Twelve Against Empire*, 40.
21. Ibid., 41.
22. Bailey, *Diplomatic History*, 5th ed., 438.
23. Morison, Merk, and Freidel, *Dissent in Three Wars*, 69.
24. Roosevelt to Lodge, Dec. 27, 1895, in *Letters of Theodore Roosevelt*, 504.
25. Karp, *Politics of War*, 36.
26. See ibid., 97–108; Hilderbrand, *Power and the People*, 8–29.
27. Hilderbrand, *Power and the People*, 8–14.
28. Wilkerson, *Public Opinion*, 18.
29. May, *Imperial Democracy*, 29.
30. Fitzgerald, "Rewriting American History," 66.
31. Beisner, *Twelve Against Empire*, 41.
32. Wilkerson, *Public Opinion*, 131.
33. Ibid.
34. Millis, *Martial Spirit*, 83–84.
35. Burnham, *Current Crisis*, 83.
36. Hilderbrand, *Power and the People*, 14.
37. Ibid., 13.
38. May, *Imperial Democracy*, 144.
39. Ibid., 118.
40. Millis, *Martial Spirit*, 130.
41. Wilkerson, *Public Opinion*, 92.
42. Hilderbrand, *Power and the People*, 18.
43. Roosevelt to Diblee, Feb. 16, 1898, in *Letters of Theodore Roosevelt*, 774.
44. A contemporary investigation of the tragedy is reported in *The Washington Post*, July 21, 1983, A23.
45. Hilderbrand, *Power and the People*, 21.
46. LaFeber, *American Age*, 189.
47. Bailey, *Diplomatic History*, 5th ed., 509.
48. William Allen White, *Autobiography*, 292.
49. Millis, *Martial Spirit*, 112.
50. May, *Imperial Democracy*, 244.
51. Ibid., 266.
52. Merk, *Manifest Destiny*, 253.
53. May, *Imperial Democracy*, 258–59.
54. Ephraim K. Smith in LaFeber, *American Age*, 201.
55. Beisner, *Twelve Against Empire*, 157.
56. Bailey, *Diplomatic History*, 5th ed., 475.

57. See Bain, *Sitting in Darkness*, and Roth, *Muddy Glory*.

CHAPTER SIX

1. Hilderbrand, *Power and the People*, 120–21.
2. Millis, *Road to War*, 38. See also Leuchtenburg, *Perils of Prosperity*, 13.
3. Halberstam, *Powers That Be*, 296.
4. Alexander, *Western Mind in Transition*, 73–74.
5. LaFeber, *American Age*, 219.
6. Seymour, *American Diplomacy*, 5.
7. Annual Address to Congress, Dec. 8, 1914, in *Public Papers of Woodrow Wilson* 1:224–26.
8. LaFeber, *American Age*, 255.
9. *War Memoirs of Robert Lansing*, 349.
10. Millis, *Road to War*, 5.
11. Ibid., 310.
12. David M. Kennedy, *Over Here*, 11.
13. Millis, *Road to War*, 63–64.
14. Ibid., 68.
15. Child, *German-Americans in Politics*, 23.
16. Barnet, *Roots of War*, 319.
17. Halberstam, *Powers That Be*, 297.
18. Child, *German-Americans in Politics*, 89.
19. David M. Kennedy, *Over Here*, 24.
20. Hilderbrand, *Power and the People*, 142.
21. See Millis, *Road to War*, 314–54.
22. Huntington, *Soldier and the State*, 144.
23. Tansill, *America Goes to War*, 54.
24. Ibid., 58–59.
25. Bailey, *Diplomatic History*, 5th ed., 616.
26. Tansill, *America Goes to War*, 180.
27. Seymour, *American Diplomacy*, 29.
28. Ibid., 57.
29. Tansill, *America Goes to War*, 275.
30. Hilderbrand, *Power and the People*, 123.
31. Millis, *Road to War*, 173.
32. Ibid., 195.
33. Child, *German-Americans in Politics*, 75–77.
34. Millis, *Road to War*, 193–94.
35. Letter of July 23, 1916, quoted in Seymour, *American Diplomacy*, 76–77.
36. Curti, *Peace or War*, 249. For accounts of the peace movement in World War I, see Chatfield, *Peace Movements in America*; Benedetti, *Peace Heroes*.
37. Millis, *Road to War*, 203.
38. Ibid., 214.
39. Tansill, *America Goes to War*, 385–387.
40. Ibid., 357.
41. LaFeber, *American Age*, 224.
42. Finnegan, *Against the Specter*, 24–25.
43. Ibid., 6.
44. Isaacson and Thomas, *Wise Men*, 70.
45. Millis, *Road to War*, 95.
46. Finnegan, *Against the Specter*, 95.
47. Ibid., 28.
48. Ibid., 30.
49. Ibid., 37.
50. Seymour, *American Diplomacy*, 23.
51. Millis, *Road to War*, 346.
52. Ibid., 347.
53. Bailey, *Diplomatic History*, 5th ed., 645.
54. Millis, *Road to War*, 404.
55. Arthur S. Link, *Brief Biography*, 112.
56. Ibid.
57. Millis, *Road to War*, 442–43.
58. Buitenhuis, "Selling of the Great War," 140.
59. Buchanan, "Editors Examine American War Aims," 256.
60. However, Creel opposed the campaign to ban the speaking of German and persuaded Wilson to speak out against mob violence. Thompson, *Reformers and War*, 228.
61. Shaffer, "Censorship," 29.
62. Buitenhuis, "Selling of the Great War," 145; Mock and Larson, *Words That Won the War*, 65.
63. Cornebise, *War As Advertised*, 10.
64. Ibid., 65.
65. Ibid., 94.
66. Bernstorff, *My Three Years in America*, 53.

CHAPTER SEVEN

1. Wilson's famous phrase "a little group of willful men" was actually uttered before the fight over the League arose.
2. Gene Smith, *When the Cheering Stopped*, 37–39.

3. Ibid., 50.
4. Fleming, *United States and the League*, 28.
5. Bailey, *Wilson and the Great Betrayal*, 2.
6. Ibid., 6.
7. Arthur S. Link, *Revolution, War, and Peace*, 106.
8. Gene Smith, *When the Cheering Stopped*, 55.
9. Ibid., 55–56.
10. Fleming, *United States and the League*, 34.
11. Ibid., 123.
12. Bailey, *Diplomatic History*, 5th ed., 668.
13. Nevins, *Henry White*, 456.
14. Fleming, *United States and the League*, 134.
15. Ibid., 9.
16. Arthur S. Link, *Revolution, War, and Peace*, 74.
17. Fleming, *United States and the League*, 165–69.
18. C. O. Johnson, *Borah of Idaho*, 232–233; Bailey, *Diplomatic History*, 5th ed., 669n.
19. Stromberg, "Uncertainties and Obscurities," 139.
20. Coben, "Study in Nativism," 65.
21. Ibid.
22. Manheim, *Déjà Vu*, 217.
23. Coben, "Study in Nativism," 65.
24. Allen, *Only Yesterday*, 48.
25. Coben, "Study in Nativism," 63.
26. Allport, *Nature of Prejudice*, 406.
27. See Barnet, *Roots of War*, 251; Kallen, *Culture and Democracy*, 154–155.
28. Coben, "Study in Nativism," 52.
29. Ibid., 60.
30. Dubin, "Elihu Root," 439.
31. Helbich, "American Liberals," 574.
32. Ibid., 595.
33. Lancaster, "Protestant Churches and the Fight for Ratification," 598.
34. Bailey, *Wilson and the Great Betrayal*, 21ff.
35. Gene Smith, *When the Cheering Stopped*, 59.
36. Ibid., 58.
37. Bailey, *Wilson and the Great Betrayal*, 125.
38. Fleming, *United States and the League*, 339.
39. Bailey, *Wilson and the Great Betrayal*, 128.
40. Gene Smith, *When the Cheering Stopped*, 143.
41. Bailey, *Diplomatic History*, 5th ed., 677.
42. Bailey, *Wilson and the Great Betrayal*, 338.
43. Steel, *Walter Lippmann*, 149.
44. Colorado statute: Murphy, "Normalcy, Intolerance, and the American Character," 448.
45. Ibid., 451.

CHAPTER EIGHT

1. Jonas, *Isolationism in America*, 115, 1.
2. See Revel, *How Democracies Perish*.
3. Lippmann, *Public Philosophy*, 24.
4. Burns, *Roosevelt*, 385.
5. Sherwood, *Roosevelt and Hopkins*, 133.
6. Leigh, *Mobilizing Consent*, 33.
7. Divine, *Roosevelt*, 3–4. A succinct summary of the opinions of other historians, not his own.
8. Beard, *President Roosevelt*; Tansill, *Back Door to War*. But see Feis, *Road to Pearl Harbor*; Wohlstetter, *Pearl Harbor*.
9. Divine, *Roosevelt*, 52.
10. Ibid., 55.
11. Divine, *Illusion of Neutrality*, 84.
12. Bailey, *Diplomatic History*, 5th ed., 709.
13. Murphy, "Normalcy, Intolerance, and the American Character," 456.
14. Ibid., 458.
15. Divine, *Roosevelt*, 8–10; Rosenman, *Working with Roosevelt*, 108.
16. Ted Morgan, *FDR*, 166.
17. Landecker, *President and Public Opinion*, 12.
18. See Watt, "Roosevelt and Neville Chamberlain."
19. Divine, *Roosevelt*, 13.
20. Landecker, *President and Public Opinion*, 14–16.
21. Rauch, *Roosevelt*, 47.
22. Rosenman, *Working with Roosevelt*, 167.
23. See Borg, "Notes on Roosevelt's 'Quarantine Speech,' " 424–33.
24. Leigh, *Mobilizing Consent*, 35.
25. Ibid., 16.

26. Landecker, *President and Public Opinion*, 19.
27. Divine, *Illusion of Neutrality*, 219–220.
28. Jonas, *Isolationism in America*, 208.
29. Jonas, *United States and Germany*, 222.
30. Paul Johnson, *Modern Times*, 146.
31. Jonas, *Isolationism in America*, 92.
32. Ibid., 91.
33. Ibid., 76.
34. Townsend, *Asia Answers*, 267, 271.
35. Brinkley, *Voices of Protest*, 119.
36. Alsop and Kintner, *American White Paper*, 44–46.
37. Landecker, *President and Public Opinion*, 35.
38. Ibid., 30
39. Divine, *Roosevelt*, 28.
40. Sherwood, *Roosevelt and Hopkins*, 167; for relations with press, see Steele, *Propaganda in an Open Society*, 67–97.
41. Leigh, *Mobilizing Consent*, 48.
42. Cole, *America First*, 30.
43. See Morse, *While Six Million Died*; Wyman, *Abandonment of the Jews*; Ted Morgan, *FDR*, 584.
44. Cole, *America First*, 144.
45. Goodhart, *Fifty Ships*, 73–74.
46. Ibid., 145–46.
47. Ibid., 179.
48. Bailey, *Diplomatic History*, 5th ed., 770.
49. Pusey, *Way We Go to War*, 68.
50. Sherwood, *Roosevelt and Hopkins*, 188.
51. Bailey, *Diplomatic History*, 5th ed., 772n.
52. Adler, *Isolationist Impulse*, 285.
53. Divine, *Roosevelt*, 41.
54. British War Cabinet minutes, 19 August 1941 CAB 65 84 (41), British Public Record Office, cited in LaFeber, *American Age*, 382.
55. Sherwood, *Roosevelt and Hopkins*, 298–99.
56. Ted Morgan, *FDR*, 602–3.
57. Ibid., 610.
58. Ibid., 615.

CHAPTER NINE

1. See Bureau of the Budget, *U.S. at War*, 434ff.
2. Polenberg, *War and Society*, 2.
3. Ibid., 185.
4. Lippmann, *Public Opinion*, 75.
5. Leigh, *Mobilizing Consent*, 52.
6. Personal communication.
7. Pimlott, *Public Relations and American Democracy*, 71.
8. See Steele, *Propaganda in an Open Society*, 33–67.
9. Koppes and Black, *Hollywood Goes to War*, 52.
10. Steele, "Preparing the Public for War," 1645.
11. Ibid., 1644–49.
12. Dower, *War Without Mercy*, 36.
13. Koppes and Black, *Hollywood Goes to War*, 59.
14. Weinberg, "What to Tell America," 78.
15. Bruner, "OWI and the American Public," 129.
16. Fussell, *Wartime*, 140, 179.
17. Zinn, *People's History*, 408.
18. Leigh, *Mobilizing Consent*, 67.
19. Ibid., 82.
20. Ibid., 72.
21. Lasswell, *Propaganda Technique*, 28.
22. Koppes and Black, *Hollywood Goes to War*, 67.
23. Feller, "OWI and the Home Front," 62.
24. Dower, *War Without Mercy*, 15–16.
25. Ibid., 322.
26. Polenberg, *War and Society*, 60–61.
27. Dower, *War Without Mercy*, 54–55.
28. Ibid., 49–50.
29. Koppes and Black, *Hollywood Goes to War*, 40. See also Steele, *Propaganda in an Open Society*, 147–71.
30. Ibid., Chap. 1.
31. Ibid., 33–34.
32. Bruner, "OWI and the American Public," 133.
33. Levering, *American Opinion*, 17.
34. Ibid.
35. Ibid., 43–56.
36. Kennan, *Memoirs, 1925–1950*, 83.
37. Koppes and Black, *Hollywood Goes to War*, 204.
38. Levering, *American Opinion*, 104.
39. Ibid., 112.
40. "Joint Chiefs of Staff Memorandum for Information No. 121," in LaFeber, *American Age*, 401.
41. Stoler, "The 'Second Front,' " 136–140.

42. Grigg, *Victory That Never Was*, 21.
43. Levering, *American Opinion*, 86; see also Davis, *American Experience of War*, 187ff.
44. Levering, *American Opinion*, 89.
45. Wyman, *Abandonment of the Jews*, 289.
46. Ibid., 299.
47. I am indebted to Kai Bird's forthcoming book on John McCloy for the Churchill quote.
48. Wyman, *Abandonment of the Jews*, 315–16, 321n.
49. Cantril, *Human Dimension*, 53–54.
50. See Levering, *American Opinion*, Chap. 6.

CHAPTER TEN

1. Lee, "Army 'Mutiny' of 1946," 555.
2. Ibid., 567.
3. Barnet, *Roots of War*, 29.
4. Feis, *Churchill, Roosevelt, Stalin*, 472.
5. "Memorandum for the Acting Secretary of State." I am grateful to Joan Garces for calling my attention to this document.
6. Dallek, *Roosevelt and American Foreign Policy*, 433.
7. Truman, *Year of Decisions*, 509–10.
8. Millis, *Forrestal Diaries*, 129.
9. Almond, *American People and Foreign Policy*, 1977 ed., 73.
10. Millis, *Forrestal Diaries*, 100.
11. Landecker, *President and Public Opinion*, 74.
12. Truman, *Year of Decisions*, 97.
13. Freeland, *Truman Doctrine*, 65.
14. Isaacson and Thomas, *Wise Men*, 338.
15. *Public Papers of the Presidents, Harry S. Truman*, 3:238.
16. Isaacson and Thomas, *Wise Men*, 256.
17. Barnet, *Roots of War*, Chaps. 3, 4, and 5.
18. LaFeber, *American Age*, 412.
19. Isaacson and Thomas, *Wise Men*, 28.
20. Cook, *The Nightmare Decade*, 69–70.
21. Isaacson and Thomas, *Wise Men*, 547.
22. See "Joint Chiefs of Staff Memorandum for Information No. 121," 11.

23. Freeland, *Truman Doctrine*, 7.
24. Ibid., 24.
25. Stimson and Bundy, *On Active Service*, 592–93.
26. Isaacson and Thomas, *Wise Men*, 262.
27. Ibid., 282.
28. Ibid., 303, 325.
29. Ibid., 315.
30. June 7, 1945, in Truman, *Off the Record*, 44.
31. Truman, *Year of Decisions*, 79–82.
32. Sherwin, *World Destroyed*, 172.
33. Isaacson and Thomas, *Wise Men*, 269.
34. *Time*, June 11, 1945.
35. "Memorandum for the Chief of Staff."
36. *New York Times*, Feb 10, 1946, 30.
37. Gaddis, *Origins of the Cold War*, 315 n.
38. Ibid., 312.
39. Ibid.
40. Acheson, *Present at the Creation*, 375. "If we made our points clearer than truth, we did not differ from most other educators and could hardly do otherwise."
41. Harriman and Abel, *Special Envoy*, 552.
42. Acheson, *Present at the Creation*, 374.
43. See Isaacson and Thomas, *Wise Men*, 355–56.
44. Freeland, *Truman Doctrine*, 49.
45. LaFeber, "American Policymakers, Public Opinion, and the Outbreak of the Cold War," in Nagai and Iriye, 75.
46. Ibid., 60.
47. Ibid., 60–75.
48. Boyer, *By the Bomb's Early Light*, 5.
49. Ibid., 7.
50. Ibid., 9.
51. Weart, *Nuclear Fear*, Chap. 6.
52. NSC 30, in Etzold and Gaddis, *Containment*, 341–43.
53. Isaacson and Thomas, *Wise Men*, 457 n, 458.
54. Djilas, *Conversations with Stalin*, 182.
55. Freeland, *Truman Doctrine*, 81.
56. LaFeber, "American Policymakers, Public Opinion, and the Outbreak of

the Cold War," in Nagai and Iriye, 50.

57. Jones, *Fifteen Weeks*, 159.
58. Acheson, *Present at the Creation*, 219.
59. Freeland, *Truman Doctrine*, 89.
60. Jones, *Fifteen Weeks*, 162.
61. Gaddis, *Origins of the Cold War*, 350.
62. Ibid., 351.
63. Steel, *Walter Lippmann*, 439.
64. Freeland, *Truman Doctrine*, 87.
65. Ibid., 89.
66. Steel, *Walter Lippmann*, 419.
67. Isaacson and Thomas, *Wise Men*, 409.
68. Divine, *Foreign Policy*, 1:170.
69. See Jones, *Fifteen Weeks*, Chap. 6.
70. Isaacson and Thomas, *Wise Men*, 403.
71. Feb 20, 1947, in Kennan Papers, Princeton University.
72. Acheson, *Present at the Creation*, 233.
73. Divine, *Foreign Policy*, 1:161.
74. Freeland, *Truman Doctrine*, 79.
75. See Acheson, *Present at the Creation*, 316–17.
76. Richard Powers, *Secrecy and Power*, 282.
77. Ibid., 278.
78. Ibid., 288.
79. "Strategic Guidance to Facilitate Planning."
80. Richard Powers, *Secrecy and Power*, 289.
81. Ibid., 277.
82. Divine, *Foreign Policy*, 1:200–201.
83. Freeland, *Truman Doctrine*, 140.
84. Divine, *Foreign Policy*, 1:172.
85. *Public Papers of Franklin D. Roosevelt*, 1939, 202–3.
86. Ibid., 1941, 387.
87. Freeland, *Truman Doctrine*, 138.
88. Ibid., 140.
89. Exchange between Patterson and Howard, Aug. 15, 16, 1947, in papers of Robert Patterson, Library of Congress.
90. Ranelagh, *The Agency*, 115.
91. Freeland, *Truman Doctrine*, 227.
92. Office of Education, *Annual Report*, 1947.
93. *New York Times*, Nov. 29, 1947.

94. HUAC hearings, Feb. 5, 1948, 18, 22–24, 32.
95. Harper, *Politics of Loyalty*, 49.
96. Freeland, *Truman Doctrine*, 209.
97. Ibid., 238; Isaacson and Thomas, *Wise Men*, 427.
98. Divine, *Foreign Policy*, 1:172.
99. Isaacson and Thomas, *Wise Men*, 440.
100. Jean Edward Smith, *Papers of General Lucius D. Clay*, 2:568–69.
101. Divine, *Foreign Policy*, 1:173.
102. Wilcox, *Congress and Foreign Policy*, 138.
103. Divine, *Foreign Policy*, 1:183–84.
104. Ibid., 275.
105. Ibid., 254–57.

CHAPTER ELEVEN

1. See Talbott, *Master of the Game*.
2. Etzold and Gaddis, *Containment*, 385.
3. U.S. Department of State, *Foreign Relations*, 1:237–92 at 237–38. NSC 68 is reprinted in Etzold and Gaddis, *Containment*, 385–442.
4. Wells, "Sounding the Tocsin," 132.
5. Ibid., 124.
6. Etzold and Gaddis, *Containment*, 404.
7. Steel, *Walter Lippmann*, 212.
8. Baughman, *Henry R. Luce*, 112.
9. Barnet, *Roots of War*, 244.
10. Weart, *Nuclear Fear*, 105.
11. Almond, *American People and Foreign Policy*, 1960 ed., 88.
12. Martineau, *Society in America*, 1:7.
13. Bryce, *American Commonwealth*, 2:351.
14. Etzold and Gaddis, *Containment*, 432.
15. See Kennan, *Memoirs, 1950–1963*, 256–57.
16. Evangelista, "Stalin's Postwar Army Reappraisal," 110–38.
17. Weart, *Nuclear Fear*, 124.
18. Ibid., 130.
19. Ibid., 116.
20. Zion, *Autobiography of Roy Cohn*, 76–79.
21. Peter H. Irons, "American Business and the Origins of McCarthyism," in Griffith and Theoharis.
22. Caute, *Great Fear*, 350–51.

23. Kampelman, *Communist Party vs. the CIO*, 138.
24. O'Neill, *American High*, 212.
25. Frady, *Billy Graham*, 237; Swanberg, *Luce and His Empire*, 290–91.
26. Bagdikian, *The Media Monopoly*, 45.
27. Baughman, *Henry R. Luce*, 145.
28. Cooney, *American Pope*, 146–47.
29. Ibid., 166.
30. Ibid., 167.
31. Almond, *American People and Foreign Policy*, 1960 ed., 180; see also Gustafson, "Church, State, and the Cold War," 52.
32. Schrecker, *No Ivory Tower*, 111.
33. Ibid., 116.
34. Halberstam, *Powers That Be*, 190–91. See also Barnouw, *History of Broadcasting*, 2:246–57.
35. Wills, *Reagan's America*, 253.
36. Ibid., 254.
37. Skinner, "Hollywood's Cold War Anti-Communist Films," 35–40.
38. Lasch, *New Radicalism in America*, 290.
39. Pells, *Liberal Mind*, 11.
40. Fox, *Reinhold Niebuhr*, 219.
41. Ibid., 285.
42. Pells, *Liberal Mind*, 129.

CHAPTER TWELVE

1. Siegel, *Troubled Journey*, 80.
2. Isaacson and Thomas, *Wise Men*, 508.
3. Ibid.
4. Siegel, *Troubled Journey*, 77.
5. Foot, *Wrong War*, 46–49.
6. Ibid., 47.
7. Ibid., 69.
8. See Barnet, *Alliance: America, Europe, Japan*, Chap. 1.
9. Siegel, *Troubled Journey*, 81.
10. Foot, *Wrong War*, 51.
11. Ibid., 69.
12. Isaacson and Thomas, *Wise Men*, 530.
13. Connally papers, Sept. 29, 1950, Harry S. Truman Library.
14. Foot, *Wrong War*, 96.
15. Isaacson and Thomas, *Wise Men*, 540.
16. Ibid., 537.
17. Mueller, *War, Presidents and Public Opinion*, 51 n.
18. Isaacson and Thomas, *Wise Men*, 542.
19. Foot, *Wrong War*, 107.
20. Ibid., 114.
21. See Truman, *Memoirs*, 2:440–450.
22. Meeting of State-Defense Policy Review Group, March 16, 1950, in U.S. Department of State, *Foreign Relations*, 1:198.
23. Sanders, *Peddlers of Crisis*, 63.
24. Ibid., 64–65.
25. Wells, "Sounding the Tocsin," 146.
26. *New York Times*, June 29, 1950.
27. Mueller, *War, Presidents and Public Opinion*, 39.
28. See Caridi, *Korean War and American Politics*, Chap. 8, for review of contemporary assessments of the Korean War issue in the 1952 election.
29. Taft, *Foreign Policy for Americans*, 48–60.
30. Divine, *Foreign Policy*, 2:9.
31. Ibid., 2:25.
32. Sulzberger, *Long Row of Candles*, 771.
33. Divine, *Foreign Policy*, 2:43.
34. Ibid., 2:73–74.
35. Thompson, "Exaggeration of American Vulnerability," 4.
36. Divine, *Foreign Policy*, 2:51, 53.
37. Ibid., 2:83.
38. Ambrose, *Eisenhower*, 2:97.
39. Ibid., 2:135.
40. Ibid., 2:123.
41. Ibid., 2:243.
42. Weart, *Nuclear Fear*, 185.
43. Ambrose, *Eisenhower*, 2:491.
44. Ibid., 2:38.
45. Ibid., 2:71.
46. Weart, *Nuclear Fear*, 169.
47. Ibid., 149, 150.
48. Ambrose, *Eisenhower*, 2:111.
49. The term "back alley war" is Dean Rusk's.
50. Arthur Schlesinger, *Imperial Presidency*, 156.
51. Prados, *Presidents' Secret Wars*, Chaps. 2–7; Ranelagh, *The Agency*, Chaps. 4, 5, 6.
52. Ambrose, *Eisenhower*, 2:226.
53. Prados, *Presidents' Secret Wars*, 97.
54. Schlesinger and Kinzer, *Bitter Fruit*, 86.
55. Ibid., 87.

56. Ibid., 154–55.
57. See Siegel, *Troubled Journey*, Chap. 6.
58. Ambrose, *Eisenhower*, 2:434.
59. Nixon, *Six Crises*, 356.
60. See Phillips, *Night Watch*.
61. *Report on the Covert Activities of the Central Intelligence Agency*, Sept. 30, 1954, in Ranelagh, *The Agency*, 277.
62. Arnson, *Press and the Cold War*, 160.
63. Holm, *Informing the People*, 26.
64. Gallup, *Gallup Poll*, 3:1743, 1759.
65. Theodore H. White, *America in Search of Itself*, 174.
66. Mueller, *War, Presidents and Public Opinion*, 196.
67. Quoted in Chomsky, *Towards a New Cold War*, 140.
68. Quoted by Douglas H. Rosenberg, "Arms and the American Way," in Russett and Stepan, 170.
69. See Karnow, *Vietnam: A History*.
70. Ibid., 366–75.
71. Ibid., Chap. 10.
72. Siegel, *Troubled Journey*, 171–72.
73. Mueller, *War, Presidents and Public Opinion*, 54–55.
74. *Military Review* (February 1987), 78.
75. Thomas Powers, *Vietnam: The War at Home*, 57.
76. Memorandum for the president from Horace Busby, "Vietnam News—What's Missing?" July 21, 1965, LBJ Library.
77. Thomas Powers, *Vietnam: The War at Home*, 136.
78. Karnow, *Vietnam: A History*, 547.
79. Ranney, *Channels of Power*, 5.
80. Roberts, *Washington Post*, 5.
81. Gitlin, *Whole World Is Watching*, 205.
82. Hallin, *Uncensored War*, 59.
83. Memorandum for the president from John P. Roche, Feb. 26, 1968, LBJ Library.
84. Memorandum on "Public Affairs" (First Draft), Mar. 3, 1968, LBJ Library.
85. Karnow, *Vietnam: A History*, 481.
86. See Gitlin, *The Sixties*, 171–92.
87. Thomas Powers, *Vietnam: The War at Home*, 164–95.
88. Gitlin, *The Sixties*, 283.
89. Siegel, *Troubled Journey*, 178.
90. Thomas Powers, *Vietnam: The War at Home*, 116.
91. *New York Times*, Apr. 22, 1966.
92. Thomas Powers, *Vietnam: The War at Home*, 118.
93. *New York Times*, Apr. 5, 1967.
94. Weigel, "The Long March."
95. Karnow, *Vietnam: A History*, 479.
96. Gitlin, *The Sixties*, 303.

CHAPTER THIRTEEN

1. Karp, *Liberty Under Siege*, 3.
2. Ibid., 9.
3. Sussman, *What Americans Really Think*, 54.
4. Samuel Huntington in Crozier, Huntington, and Watanuki, *Crisis of Democracy*, 76.
5. See Burnham, "Thoughts on the 'Governability Crisis' of the West," 46; Samuel Huntington, in Crozier, Huntington, and Watanuki, *Crisis of Democracy*, 59–115.
6. Lippmann, *Public Philosophy*, 20.
7. Garthoff, *Détente and Confrontation*, 564.
8. Wills, *Reagan's America*, 441. See also Sanders, *Peddlers of Crisis*, 216–217.
9. Karp, *Liberty Under Siege*, 59.
10. Schulzinger, *American Diplomacy*, 322.
11. Sussman, *What Americans Really Think*, 99.
12. Potomac Associates poll. See Free and Watts, "Internationalism Comes of Age . . . Again," 46.
13. Russett and Deluc, " 'Don't Tread on Me,' " 386–87.
14. Gergen, "Hardening Mood Toward Foreign Policy," 12.
15. See Chace, *Solvency: The Price of Survival*; Paul Kennedy, *Rise and Fall of the Great Powers*.
16. Yankelovich and Kagann, "Assertive America," 699.
17. Ibid. See also Gallup poll quoted in Reilly, *American Public Opinion*, 16.
18. Tocqueville, *Democracy in America*, 1:125–26.
19. Wills, *Reagan's America*, 344.
20. This is Garry Wills's characterization

of the public perception of Jimmy Carter. See Wills, *Reagan's America*, 350.

21. Theodore White, *America in Search of Itself*, 416.
22. For a description of the committee's activities, see Sanders, *Peddlers of Crisis*; Barnet, *Real Security*.
23. Murray Marder, "Carter to Inherit Intense Dispute on Soviet Intentions," Washington *Post*, Jan. 2, 1977.
24. See Wills, *Reagan's America*, 336.
25. Ibid., Chap. 38.
26. 1980 *Presidential Debates Official Transcription Record* (Education Fund, League of Women Voters), 361, 399.
27. *Vital Speeches*, June 15, 1981, 516.
28. FitzGerald, *America Revised*, 142.
29. Washington *Post*, Sept. 22, 1985, A9.
30. Goldman and Fuller, *Quest for the Presidency*, 413.
31. Washington *Post*, Dec. 19, 1985.
32. Ibid., Oct. 10, 1985.
33. Gutman, *Banana Diplomacy*, 31, 61.
34. Harris poll cited in *Central America and the Polls*, Washington Office on Latin America, 5.
35. Hertsgaard, *On Bended Knee*, 114.
36. See Gutman, *Banana Diplomacy*.
37. The characterization of pre-Reagan press relations as "a shouting match" is David Gergen's. See Hertsgaard, *On Bended Knee*, 19.
38. Hertsgaard, *On Bended Knee*, 3.
39. This is the characterization of National Security Council official Walter Raymond, Jr., as quoted in Parry and Kornbluh, "Iran-Contra's Untold Story," 9.
40. Hertsgaard, *On Bended Knee*, 6.
41. Ibid., 35; see also Kornbluh, *Nicaragua: The Price of Intervention*, Chap. 4.
42. Hertsgaard, *On Bended Knee*, 6.
43. Washington *Post*, Oct. 2, 1985.
44. See Bonner, *Weakness and Deceit*, 255–61; Pearce, *Under the Eagle*, 242–44; McMahan, *Reagan and the World*, 123–59.
45. Woodward, *Veil*, 129. See also Chomsky and Herman, *Manufacturing Consent*, 300.

46. *New York Times*, Sept. 3, 1983.
47. Bernard Gwertzman, "Downing of a jet a year ago said to lead to U.S. gains," *New York Times*, Aug. 31, 1984.
48. Wills, *Reagan's America*, 356; Luttwak, *Pentagon and the Art of War*, 51–58, 268–69; Gabriel, *Military Incompetence*, 149–86.
49. Parry and Kornbluh, "Iran-Contra's Untold Story," 8.
50. Ibid., 10.
51. Ibid., 4.
52. Personal communication.
53. See Weart, *Nuclear Fear*, 195.
54. Quoted in Lifton and Falk, *Indefensible Weapons*, 147.
55. Quoted in ibid., 147. The apt description of nuclear stockpiles as "booby traps" is Carl Sagan's.
56. Memo of McGeorge Bundy in Weart, *Nuclear Fear*, 254.
57. Ball, *Past Has Another Pattern*, 304–305.
58. Weart, *Nuclear Fear*, 262.
59. Barnet, *Alliance: America, Europe, Japan*, 413–15.
60. Weart, *Nuclear Fear*, 371–73.
61. Caldicott, *Nuclear Madness*, 61.
62. *Loeb, Hope in Hard Times*, 68. See Solo, *From Protest to Policy*.
63. Washington *Post*, Oct. 5, 1982.
64. "Crossroads," CBS-TV, Aug. 15, 1984.

CONCLUSION

1. Dahl, *Controlling Nuclear Weapons*, 3.
2. Yankelovich and Harman, *Starting with the People*, 9.
3. *Americans Talk Security*.
4. Rosenblatt, "The Atomic Age," 48–49.
5. LaFeber, *American Age*, 584.
6. Barnet, "The Four Pillars."
7. Paul Craig Roberts, "The Milquetoast Presidency," *New York Times*, Dec. 1, 1988, A35.
8. William Schneider, " 'Rambo' and Reality," in Oye, Lieber, and Rothchild, 45–51.
9. See article of Garry Wills in *Time*, Nov. 21, 1988.

10. Ginsberg, "Opinion Mongering," 278.
11. Lippmann, *Public Opinion*, 170–72.
12. Shuman, *Building Municipal Foreign Policies*, 3 (as updated).
13. Personal communication from Quest for Peace, the organization that monitors aid by U.S. citizens for Nicaragua.

BIBLIOGRAPHY

Acheson, Dean. *A Citizen Looks at Congress.* New York: Harper & Bros., 1957.
———. *Present at the Creation: My Years in the State Department.* New York: Norton, 1969.
Adams, Henry. *History of the United States.* Book 1. New York: Albert & Charles Boni, 1930.
Adams, John. *Letters of John Adams Addressed to His Wife.* Edited by Charles F. Adams. 2 vols. Boston: C. C. Little and J. Brown, 1841.
———. *The Works of John Adams.* 10 vols. Boston: Little, Brown, 1850–56.
Adler, Selig. *The Isolationist Impulse.* New York: Free Press, 1957.
Alexander, Franz. *The Western Mind in Transition.* New York: Random House, 1960.
Allen, Frederick Lewis. *Only Yesterday.* New York, London: Harper & Bros., 1931.
Allport, Gordon W. *The Nature of Prejudice.* Reading, Mass.: Addison Wesley, 1979.
Almond, Gabriel A. *The American People and Foreign Policy.* Var. eds. New York: Harcourt, Brace; New York: Frederick Praeger; Westport, Conn.: Greenwood.
Alsop, Joseph, and Robert Kintner. *American White Paper.* New York: Simon and Schuster, 1940.
Ambrose, Stephen E. *Eisenhower.* 2 vols. New York: Simon and Schuster, 1983, 1984.
———. *Rise to Globalism: American Foreign Policy, 1938–1980.* New York: Penguin, 1980.
American State Papers, Military Affairs. Vol. 1. Holland, Mich.: T. Wierenga, 1981.
Americans Talk Security. Winchester, Mass.: Americans Talk Security Project, 1988–89.
Arnson, James. *The Press and the Cold War.* Indianapolis: Bobbs-Merrill, 1978.
Bagdikian, Ben. *The Media Monopoly.* Boston: Beacon Press, 1983.
Bailey, Thomas A. *A Diplomatic History of the American People.* Var. eds. New York: Appleton-Century-Crofts; Englewood, Cliffs, N.J.: Prentice-Hall.
———. *The Man in the Street: The Impact of American Public Opinion on Foreign Policy.* New York: Macmillan, 1948.
———. *Woodrow Wilson and the Great Betrayal.* New York: Macmillan, 1945.
———. *Woodrow Wilson and the Lost Peace.* New York: Macmillan, 1944.
Bain, David H. *Sitting in Darkness: Americans in the Philippines.* Boston: Houghton Mifflin, 1984.
Ball, George. *The Past Has Another Pattern.* New York: Norton, 1982.
Bardes, Barbara A., and Robert W. Oldendick. "Public Opinion and Foreign Policy: A Field in Search of a Theory." Manuscript, 1987.
Barnet, Richard J. *The Alliance: America, Europe, Japan—Makers of the Postwar World.* New York: Simon and Schuster, 1983.
———. *Real Security.* New York: Simon and Schuster, 1981.
———. *Roots of War.* New York: Pelican, 1973.
Barnouw, Erik. *The History of Broadcasting in the United States.* Vol. 2. New York: Oxford University Press, 1966–77.

Bauer, Theodore W., et al. *National Security Policy Formulation*. Washington, D.C.: National Defense University, 1977.

Baughman, James L. *Henry R. Luce and the Rise of the American News Media*. Boston: Twayne, 1987.

Beard, Charles A. *President Roosevelt and the Coming of the War*. Hampden, Conn.: Anchor Books, 1968 (1948).

Beisner, Robert. *Twelve Against Empire*. Chicago: University of Chicago Press, 1986.

Belohlavek, John M. *"Let the Eagle Soar!"* Lincoln: University of Nebraska Press, 1985.

Benedetti, Charles di, ed. *Peace Heroes in Twentieth-Century America*. Bloomington: Indiana University Press, 1986.

————, ed. *Peace Movements in America*. New York: Schocken Books, 1973.

Bernstorff, Johann. *My Three Years in America*. New York: Scribner's, 1920.

Blum, John Morton. *V WAS FOR VICTORY*. New York: Harcourt Brace Jovanovich, 1976.

Bonner, Raymond. *Weakness and Deceit: U.S. Policy and El Salvador*. New York: Times Books, 1984.

Bowers, Claude G. *Jefferson and Hamilton: The Struggle for Democracy in America*. Boston: Houghton Mifflin, 1929.

Boyer, Paul. *By the Bomb's Early Light: American Thought and Culture at the Dawn of the Atomic Age*. New York: Pantheon, 1985.

Braestrup, Peter. *Big Story: How the American Press and Television Reported and Interpreted the Crisis of Tet 1968 in Vietnam and Washington*. Boulder, Colo.: Westview Press, 1977.

Brinkley, Alan. *Voices of Protest*. New York: Knopf, 1982.

Brown, Roger H. *The Republic in Peril: 1812*. New York: Columbia University Press, 1964.

Bryce, James. *The American Commonwealth. 2 vols*. New York: Putnam, 1959.

Buel, Richard, Jr. *Securing the Revolution: Ideology in American Politics, 1789–1815*. Ithaca: Cornell University Press, 1972.

Bureau of the Budget. *U.S. at War*. Washington, D.C.: Government Printing Office, 1946.

Burnham, Walter Dean. *The Current Crisis in American Politics*. New York: Oxford University Press, 1982.

Burns, James MacGregor. *Roosevelt: The Lion and the Fox*. New York: Harcourt, Brace, 1956.

Caldicott, Helen. *Nuclear Madness: What You Can Do!* New York: Bantam, 1979.

Cantril, Hadley. *The Human Dimension: Experiences in Policy Research*. New Brunswick: Rutgers, 1967.

Caridi, Ronald J. *The Korean War and American Politics*. Philadelphia: University of Pennsylvania Press, 1969.

Caute, David. *The Great Fear*. New York: Simon and Schuster, 1978.

Chace, James. *Solvency: The Price of Survival*. New York: Vintage, 1982.

————, and Caleb Carr. *America Invulnerable: The Quest for Absolute Security from 1812 to Star Wars*. New York: Summit Books, 1988.

Chatfield, Charles, ed. *Peace Movements in America*. New York: Schocken, 1973.

Chester, Edward. *Sectionalism, Politics and American Diplomacy*. Metuchen, N.J.: Scarecrow Press, 1975.

Child, Clifton J. *The German-Americans in Politics*. New York: Arno Press, 1970.

Chomsky, Noam. *Towards a New Cold War*. New York: Pantheon, 1982.

————, and Edward Herman. *Manufacturing Consent*. New York: Pantheon, 1988.

Cobbett, William. *Porcupine's Works*. Vol. 4. London: Cobbett & Morgan, 1801.

Cohen, Bernard C. *The Press and Foreign Policy.* Princeton: Princeton University Press, 1963.

————. *The Public's Impact on Foreign Policy.* Boston: Little, Brown, 1973.

Cole, Wayne S. *America First: The Battle Against Intervention, 1940–1941.* Madison: University of Wisconsin Press, 1953.

————. *Roosevelt and the Isolationists, 1932–1945.* Lincoln: University of Nebraska Press, 1983.

Cook, Fred J. *The Nightmare Decade: The Life and Times of Senator Joe McCarthy.* New York: Random House, 1971.

Cooney, John. *The American Pope.* New York: Times Books, 1984.

Cornebise, Alfred E. *War As Advertised: The Four Minute Men and America's Crusade, 1917–1918.* Philadelphia: American Philosophical Society, 1984.

Cress, Lawrence D. *Citizens in Arms.* Chapel Hill: University of North Carolina Press, 1982.

Crozier, Michel, Samuel Huntington, and Joji Watanuki. *The Crisis of Democracy: Report on the Governability of Democracies to the Trilateral Commission.* New York: Random House, 1965.

Curti, Merle. *Peace or War.* New York: Garland, 1936.

————. *The Roots of American Loyalty.* New York: Russell and Russell, 1967.

Dahl, Robert. *Controlling Nuclear Weapons: Democracy Versus Guardianship.* Syracuse: Syracuse University Press, 1985.

Dallek, Robert. *Franklin D. Roosevelt and American Foreign Policy: 1932–1945.* New York: Oxford University Press, 1979.

————. *Ronald Reagan: The Politics of Symbolism.* Cambridge: Harvard University Press, 1984.

Davis, Elmer. *Report to the President.* Edited and with an Introduction by Ronald T. Farrar. Austin, Tex.: Association for Education in Journalism, 1968.

Davis, Kenneth S. *The American Experience of War: 1939–1945.* London: Secker & Warburg, 1967.

DeConde, Alexander. *Entangling Alliance: Politics and Diplomacy under George Washington.* Westport, Conn.: Greenwood Press, 1958.

————. *This Affair of Louisiana.* New York: Scribner's, 1976.

Deibel, Terry. *Presidents, Public Opinion, and Power: The Nixon, Carter and Reagan Years.* New York: Foreign Policy Association, 1987.

Dippie, Brian. *The Vanishing American.* Middletown, Conn.: Wesleyan University Press, 1982.

Divine, Robert A. *Foreign Policy and U.S. Presidential Elections.* 2 vols. New York: New Viewpoints, 1974.

————. *The Illusion of Neutrality.* Chicago: University of Chicago Press, 1962.

————. *Roosevelt and World War II.* Baltimore: Johns Hopkins Press, 1969.

Djilas, Milovan. *Conversations with Stalin.* London: Pelican Books, 1969.

Dower, John. *War Without Mercy.* New York: Pantheon, 1986.

Drinnon, Richard. *Facing West: The Metaphysics of Indian-Hating and Empire-Building.* Minneapolis: University of Minnesota Press, 1980.

Etzold, Thomas H., and John Lewis Gaddis, eds. *Containment: Documents on American Policy and Strategy, 1945–1950.* New York: Columbia University Press, 1978.

Feis, Herbert. *Churchill, Roosevelt, Stalin.* Princeton: Princeton University Press, 1957.

————. *The Road to Pearl Harbor.* Princeton: Princeton University Press, 1950.

Filler, Louis. *Removal of the Cherokee Nation.* Huntington: R. E. Krieger, 1962.

Finnegan, John Patrick. *Against the Specter of a Dragon: The Campaign for American Military Preparedness, 1914–1917.* Westport, Conn.: Greenwood Press, 1974.

FitzGerald, Frances. *America Revised*. New York: Vintage, 1980.

Fleming, D. F. *The United States and the League of Nations*. New York: Russell & Russell, 1968.

Foot, Rosemary. *The Wrong War*. Ithaca: Cornell University Press, 1985.

Foster, H. Schuyler. *Activism Replaces Isolationism: U.S. Public Attitudes, 1940–1975*. Washington, D.C.: Foxhall Press, 1976.

Fox, Richard. *Reinhold Niebuhr*. New York: Pantheon, 1985.

Frady, Marshall. *Billy Graham*. Boston: Little, Brown, 1979.

Freeland, Richard M. *The Truman Doctrine and the Origins of McCarthyism*. New York: New York University Press, 1985 (1972).

Fromm, Erich. *Escape From Freedom*. New York: Farrar & Rinehart, 1941.

Fussell, Paul. *Wartime: Understanding and Behavior in the Second World War*. New York: Oxford University Press, 1989.

Gabriel, Richard A. *Military Incompetence*. New York: Hill and Wang, 1985.

Gaddis, John Lewis. *The United States and the Origins of the Cold War, 1941–1947*. New York: Columbia University Press, 1972.

Gallup Poll, the. *Public Opinion*, 2 vols. New York: Random House, 1972.

Garthoff, Raymond. *Détente and Confrontation*. Washington, D.C.: Brookings Institution, 1985.

Gay, Peter. *The Enlightenment: An Interpretation*. Vol. 3. New York: Knopf, 1969.

Gillon, Steven M. *Politics and Vision: The ADA and American Liberalism, 1947–1985*. New York: Oxford University Press, 1987.

Ginsberg, Benjamin. *The Captive Public: How Mass Opinion Promotes State Power*. New York: Basic Books, 1986.

Gitlin, Todd. *The Sixties: Years of Hope, Days of Rage*. New York: Bantam, 1987.

———. *The Whole World Is Watching: Mass Media in the Making and Unmaking of the New Left*. Berkeley: University of California Press, 1980.

Goldman, Peter, and Tony Fuller. *The Quest for the Presidency 1984*. New York: Bantam, 1985.

Goodhart, Philip. *Fifty Ships That Saved the World*. Garden City, N.Y.: Doubleday, 1965.

Graber, Doris A. *Public Opinion, the President, and Foreign Policy*. New York: Holt, Rinehart & Winston, 1968.

Graebner, Norman A. *Empire on the Pacific*. Santa Barbara, Cal.: ABC-Clio Reprint edition, 1983.

Green, David. *Shaping Political Consciousness: The Language of Politics in America from McKinley to Reagan*. Ithaca: Cornell University Press, 1987.

Griffith, Robert, and Athan Theoharis, eds. *The Specter*. New York: New Viewpoints, 1974.

Grigg, John. *1943: The Victory That Never Was*. New York: Hill and Wang, 1980.

Gutman, Roy. *Banana Diplomacy*. New York: Simon and Schuster, 1988.

Hague, John A., ed. *American Character and Culture in a Changing World*. Westport, Conn.: Greenwood, 1979.

Halberstam, David. *The Powers That Be*. New York: Dell, 1980.

Hall, Peter D. *The Organization of American Culture, 1700–1900*. New York: New York University Press, 1982.

Hallin, Daniel. *The Uncensored War: The Media and Vietnam*. Berkeley: University of California Press, 1986.

Hamilton, Alexander, John Jay, and James Madison. *The Federalist*. New York: Modern Library, no date.

Harper, Alan. *The Politics of Loyalty*. Westport, Conn.: Greenwood, 1969.

Harriman, W. Averell, and Elie Abel. *Special Envoy to Churchill and Stalin, 1941–1946*. New York: Random House, 1975.

Hatzenbuehler, Ronald L., and Robert L. Ivie. *Congress Declares War*. Kent, Ohio: Kent State University Press, 1983.

Healy, David. *U.S. Expansionism: The Imperialist Urge in the 1890s*. Madison: University of Wisconsin Press, 1970.

Hersh, Seymour. *The Price of Power*. New York: Summit Books, 1983.

Hertsgaard, Mark. *On Bended Knee: The Press and the Reagan Presidency*. New York: Farrar, Straus & Giroux, 1988.

Hilderbrand, Robert C. *Power and the People: Executive Management of Public Opinion in Foreign Affairs, 1897–1921*. Chapel Hill: University of North Carolina Press, 1981.

Hobsbawm, Eric. "Some Reflections on Nationalism" In *Imagination and Precision in the Social Sciences*, edited by T. J. Nossiter, A. H. Hanson, and Stein Rokkan. London: Faber and Faber, 1972.

Hofstadter, Richard. *Anti-Intellectualism in American Life*. New York: Vintage, 1964.

Hogan, J. Michael. *The Panama Canal in American Politics*. Carbondale: Southern Illinois University Press, 1986.

Holm, Lewis M., et al., eds. *Informing the People: A Public Affairs Handbook*, New York: Longman, 1981.

Hughes, Barry B. *The Domestic Context of American Foreign Policy*. San Francisco: W. H. Freeman, 1978.

Huntington, Samuel. *The Soldier and the State*. New York: Vintage, 1964.

Irons, Peter H. "American Business and the Origins of McCarthyism." In *The Specter*, edited by Robert Griffith and Athan Theoharis. New York: New Viewpoints, 1974.

Isaacson, Walter, and Evan Thomas. *The Wise Men: Six Friends and the World They Made*. New York: Simon and Schuster, 1986.

Jacobsen, Harold K., ed. *America's Foreign Policy*. New York: Random House, 1965.

Jefferson, Thomas. *The Writings of Thomas Jefferson*. Edited by Paul Leicester Ford. 10 vols. New York: G. P. Putnam & Sons, 1892–99.

———. *The Writings of Thomas Jefferson*. Edited by Andrew A. Lipscomb. 20 vols. Thomas Jefferson Memorial Association, 1903–1904.

Jensen, Merrill. *The New Nation*. New York: Knopf, 1950.

Jewell, Malcolm. *Senatorial Politics and Foreign Policy*. Lexington: University of Kentucky Press, 1962.

Johannsen, Robert W. *To the Halls of the Montezumas: The Mexican War in the American Imagination*. New York: Oxford University Press, 1985.

Johnson, C. O. *Borah of Idaho*. Seattle: University of Washington Press, 1967.

Johnson, Paul. *Modern Times*. New York: Harper & Row, 1983.

Johnson, Walter. *The Battle Against Isolation*. Chicago: University of Chicago Press, 1944.

Jonas, Manfred. *Isolationism in America, 1935–1941*. Ithaca: Cornell University Press, 1966.

———. *The United States and Germany: A Diplomatic History*. Ithaca: Cornell University Press, 1984.

Jones, Joseph. *The Fifteen Weeks*. New York: Harcourt, Brace & World, 1964.

Jordan, Winthrop D. *White Over Black: American Attitudes Toward the Negro, 1550–1812*. New York: Norton, 1968.

Kallen, Horace M. *Culture and Democracy in the United States*. New York: Arno Press, 1970.

Kampelman, Max. *The Communist Party vs. the CIO*. New York: Arno, 1971.

Kaplan, Lawrence. *Entangling Alliances with None: American Foreign Policy in the Age of Jefferson*. Kent, Ohio: Kent State University Press, 1987.

Karnow, Stanley. *Vietnam: A History*. New York: Viking, 1983.

Karp, Walter. *Liberty Under Siege*. New York: Holt, 1988.

———. *The Politics of War*. New York: Harper & Row, 1979.

Kennan, George F. *Memoirs, 1925–1950*. London: Hutchinson, 1968.

———. *Memoirs, 1950–1963*. Boston: Little, Brown, 1972.

Kennedy, David M. *Over Here: The First World War and American Society*. New York: Oxford University Press, 1980.

Kennedy, Paul. *The Rise and Fall of the Great Powers*. New York: Random House, 1987.

Kluger, Richard. *The Paper: The Life and Death of the New York Herald Tribune*. New York: New York Press, 1986.

Koch, Adrienne, and William Peden, eds. *The Life and Selected Writings of Thomas Jefferson*. New York: Modern Library, 1944.

Koppes, Clayton, and Gregory Black. *Hollywood Goes to War*. New York: Free Press, 1987.

Kornbluh, Peter. *Nicaragua: The Price of Intervention*. Washington, D.C.: Institute for Policy Studies, 1987.

Kusnitz, Leonard A. *Public Opinion and Foreign Policy: America's China Policy, 1949–1979*. Westport, Conn.: Greenwood Press, 1984.

LaFeber, Walter. *The American Age*. New York: Norton, 1989.

———. "American Policymakers, Public Opinion, and the Outbreak of the Cold War, 1945–1950." In *The Origins of the Cold War in Asia*, edited by Yonosuke Nagai and Akira Iriye. New York: Columbia University Press, 1977.

Landau, Saul. *The Dangerous Doctrine*. Boulder, Colo.: Westview Press, 1988.

Landecker, Manfred. *The President and Public Opinion*. Washington, D.C.: Public Affairs Press, 1985.

Lansing, Robert. *War Memoirs of Robert Lansing, Secretary of State*. Westport, Conn.: Greenwood Press, 1970 (1935).

Lasch, Christopher. *The New Radicalism in America*. New York: Knopf, 1965.

Lasswell, Harold D. *Propaganda Technique in the World War*. New York: Garland Publishers, 1972.

Leigh, Michael. *Mobilizing Consent*. Westport, Conn.: Greenwood Press, 1976.

Leuchtenburg, William E. *The Perils of Prosperity, 1914–32*. Chicago: University of Chicago Press.

Levering, Ralph B. *American Opinion and the Russian Alliance*. Chapel Hill: University of North Carolina Press, 1976.

———. *The Public and American Foreign Policy 1918–1978*. New York: Morrow, 1978.

Lifton, Robert Jay, and Richard Falk. *Indefensible Weapons*. New York: Basic Books, 1982.

Link, Arthur S. *Woodrow Wilson: A Brief Biography*. Cleveland: World, 1963.

———. *Woodrow Wilson: Revolution, War, and Peace*. Arlington Heights, Ill.: AHM Publishing, 1979.

Link, Eugene P. *Democratic-Republican Societies, 1790–1800*. New York: Columbia University Press, 1942.

Lippmann, Walter. *Public Opinion*. New York: Free Press, 1965 (1922).

———. *The Public Philosophy*. New York: Mentor, 1955.

Loeb, Paul. *Hope in Hard Times*. Lexington, Mass.: Lexington Books, 1987.

Luttwak, Edward N. *The Pentagon and the Art of War*. New York: Simon and Schuster, 1984.

McDonald, Archie P., ed. *The Mexican War: Crisis for American Democracy*. Lexington, Mass.: D. C. Heath, 1969.

McMahan, Jeff. *Reagan and the World*. New York: Monthly Review Press, 1984.

McMaster, J. B. *A History of the People of the United States.* Vols. 1, 2. New York: D. Appleton, 1883, 1885.

McPherson, James M. *Battle Cry of Freedom: The Civil War Era.* New York: Oxford University Press, 1988.

Malone, Dumas. *Jefferson and His Time.* Vol. 2, *Jefferson and the Rights of Man.* Boston: Little, Brown, 1951.

———. *Jefferson and His Time.* Vol. 4, *Jefferson the President: First Term, 1801–1805.* Boston: Little, Brown, 1970.

Manheim, Jarol. *Déjà Vu: American Political Problems in Historical Perspective.* New York: St. Martin's Press, 1976.

Manoff, Robert Karl, and Michael Schudson, eds. *Reading the News.* New York: Pantheon, 1986.

Martineau, Harriet. *Society in America.* 2 vols. Garden City, N.Y.: Anchor, 1986.

May, Ernest. *Imperial Democracy.* New York: Harcourt, Brace & World, 1961.

———. *The Making of the Monroe Doctrine.* Cambridge: Harvard University Press, 1975.

Mayo, Bernard. *Henry Clay.* Boston: Houghton Mifflin, 1937.

Merk, Frederick. *Manifest Destiny and Mission in American History.* New York: Knopf, 1963.

———. *The Monroe Doctrine and American Expansionism: 1843–1849.* New York: Knopf, 1966.

Meyers, Marvin. *The Jacksonian Persuasion: Politics and Belief.* Stanford: Stanford University Press, 1957.

Millis, Walter. *The Martial Spirit.* New York: Arno Press, 1931.

———. *Road to War: America 1914–1917.* Boston: Houghton Mifflin, 1935.

———, ed. *The Forrestal Diaries.* New York: Viking, 1951.

Mock, James R., and Cedric Larson. *Words That Won the War: The Story of the Committee on Public Information.* Princeton: Princeton University Press, 1939.

Moore, Jonathan. *Campaign for President: The Managers Look at 1984.* Dover, Mass.: Auburn House, 1985.

Morgan, Edmund S. *Inventing the People: The Rise of Popular Sovereignty in England and America.* New York: Norton, 1988.

Morgan, Ted. *FDR.* New York: Simon & Schuster, 1985.

Morgenthau, Hans J. *Scientific Man vs. Power Politics.* Chicago: University of Chicago Press, 1946.

Morison, Samuel Eliot. *The Oxford History of the American People.* Vol. 2. New York: Mentor, 1972.

———, Henry Steele Commager, and William E. Leuchtenburg. *The Growth of the American Republic.* 2 vols. New York: Oxford University Press, 1969, 1980.

———, Frederick Merk, and Frank Freidel. *Dissent in Three American Wars.* Cambridge, Mass.: Harvard University Press, 1970.

Morse, Arthur. *While Six Million Died.* Woodstock, N.Y.: Overlook Press, 1968.

Mueller, John E. *War, Presidents and Public Opinion.* New York: Wiley, 1973.

Nagai, Yonosuke, and Akira Iriye, eds. *The Origins of the Cold War in Asia.* New York: Columbia University Press, 1977.

Nevins, Allan. *Henry White: Thirty Years of American Diplomacy.* New York and London: Harper Brothers, 1930.

———, ed. *American Press Opinion.* Port Washington, N.Y.: Kennikat Press, 1969.

Nicolay, John, and John Hay. *Abraham Lincoln.* Vol. 3. New York: Century, 1917.

Nixon, Richard M. *Six Crises.* Garden City, N.Y.: Doubleday, 1962.

Nossiter, T. J., A. H. Hanson, and Stein Rokkan, eds. *Imagination and Precision in the Social Sciences.* London: Faber and Faber, 1972.

O'Neill, William L. *American High*. New York: Free Press, 1986.

Osgood, Robert E. *Ideals and Self-interest in America's Foreign Relations*. Chicago: University of Chicago Press, 1953.

Oye, Kenneth A., Robert J. Lieber and Donald Rothchild, eds. *Eagle Resurgent: The Reagan Era in American Foreign Policy*. Boston: Little, Brown, 1987.

Page, Benjamin, Robert Shapiro, and Glenn Dempsey. "What Moves Public Opinion?" Manuscript, March 1986.

Paterson, Thomas G., ed. *Cold War Critics: Alternatives to American Foreign Policy in the Truman Years*. Chicago: Quadrangle Books, 1971.

Pearce, Jenny. *Under the Eagle: U.S. Intervention in Central America and the Caribbean*. Boston: South End Press, 1982.

Pearson, Lester. "Democracy and the Power of Division." In *America's Foreign Policy*, edited by Harold K. Jacobsen. New York: Random House, 1965.

Pells, Richard H. *The Liberal Mind in a Conservative Age*. New York: Harper & Row, 1985.

Persons, Stow. "Public Opinion—A Democratic Dilemma." In *American Character and Culture in a Changing World*, edited by John A. Hague. Westport, Conn.: Greenwood, 1979.

Pessen, Edward. *Jacksonian America*. Albany: State University of New York Press, 1967.

Phillips, David Atlee. *The Night Watch*. New York: Atheneum, 1977.

Pimlott, J. A. R. *Public Relations and American Democracy*. Port Washington, N.Y.: Kennikat Press, 1951.

Pletcher, David M. *The Diplomacy of Annexation: Texas, Oregon, and the Mexican War*. Columbia: University of Missouri Press, 1973.

Polenberg, Richard. *War and Society*. Philadelphia: Lippincott, 1972.

Polk, James K. *The Diary of James K. Polk During His Presidency, 1845 to 1849*. Vol. 1. Chicago: A. C. McClurg, 1910.

Potter, David. *Lincoln and His Party in the Secession Crisis*. New Haven: Yale University Press, 1942.

Powers, Richard. *Secrecy and Power: The Life of J. Edgar Hoover*. New York: Free Press, 1987.

Powers, Thomas. *Vietnam: The War at Home*. New York: Grossman, 1973.

Prados, John. *Presidents' Secret Wars*. New York: Morrow, 1986.

Pratt, Julius. *Expansionists of 1898*. Baltimore: Johns Hopkins Press, 1936.

Public Papers of the Presidents of the United States, Harry S. Truman. Vol. 3 (1947). Washington, D.C.: Government Printing Office, 1963.

Pusey, Merlo. *The Way We Go to War*. Boston: Houghton Mifflin, 1969.

Ranelagh, John. *The Agency: The Rise and Decline of the CIA*. New York: Simon & Schuster, 1986.

Ranney, Austin. *Channels of Power: The Impact of Television on American Politics*. New York: Basic Books, 1983.

Rauch, Basil. *Roosevelt from Munich to Pearl Harbor*. New York: Barnes & Noble, 1967.

Reeves, Jesse S. *American Diplomacy under Tyler and Polk*. Gloucester, Mass.: P. Smith, 1907.

Reilly, John E., ed. *American Public Opinion and U.S. Foreign Policy 1979*. Chicago: Council on Foreign Relations, 1983.

Remini, Robert V. *Andrew Jackson and the Course of American Democracy, 1833–1845*. New York: Harper & Row, 1984.

———. *Andrew Jackson and the Course of American Freedom, 1822–1832*. New York: Harper & Row, 1981.

Revel, Jean-François. *How Democracies Perish*. Garden City, N.Y.: Doubleday, 1983.

Richardson, James D., ed. *A Compilation of the Messages and Papers of the Presi-*

dents, 1789–1897. Vol. 1. Washington, D.C.: Government Printing Office, 1896–99.

Risjord, Norman K. *The Old Republicans.* New York: Columbia University Press, 1965.

Roberts, Chalmers. *The Washington Post.* Boston: Houghton Mifflin, 1977.

Robinson, John P., and Robert Meadow. *Polls Apart.* Cabin John, Md.: Seven Locks Press, 1982.

Rogin, Michael Paul, *Fathers and Children.* New York: Knopf, 1975.

Roosevelt, Franklin D. *The Public Papers and Addresses of Franklin D. Roosevelt.* 1939 vol., *War—and Neutrality.* Compiled by Samuel I. Rosenman. New York: Macmillan, 1941.

——. *The Public Papers and Addresses of Franklin D. Roosevelt.* 1941 vol., *The Call to Battle Stations.* Compiled by Samuel I. Rosenman. New York: Harper & Bros., 1950.

Roosevelt, Theodore. *The Letters of Theodore Roosevelt.* 8 vols. Edited by Elting E. Morison. Cambridge: Harvard University Press, 1951–54.

Rosenberg, Douglas H. "Arms and the American Way: The Ideological Dimension of Military Growth." In *Military Force and American Society,* edited by Bruce Russett and Alfred Stepan. New York: Harper and Row, 1973.

Rosenman, Samuel. *Working with Roosevelt.* New York: Harper & Bros., 1952.

Roth, Russell. *Muddy Glory: America's "Indian Wars" in the Philippines, 1899–1935.* West Hanover, Mass.: Christopher Publishing House, 1981.

Russett, Bruce, Harvey Starr, and Richard Stall. *Choices in World Politics.* New York: W. H. Freeman, 1989.

Russett, Bruce, and Alfred Stepan, eds. *Military Force and American Society.* New York: Harper & Row, 1973.

Sanders, Jerry W. *Peddlers of Crisis.* Boston: South End Press, 1983.

Satz, Ronald. *American Indian Policy in the Jacksonian Era.* Lincoln: University of Nebraska Press, 1974.

Sayre, Nora. *Running Time: Films of the Cold War.* New York: Dial Press, 1982.

Schlesinger, Arthur M., Jr. *The Age of Jackson.* Boston: Little, Brown, 1945.

——. *The Cycles of American History.* Boston: Houghton Mifflin, 1986.

——. *The Imperial Presidency.* Boston: Houghton Mifflin, 1973.

Schlesinger, Stephen, and Stephen Kinzer. *Bitter Fruit.* Garden City, N.Y.: Doubleday, 1982.

Schneider, William. " 'Rambo' and Reality: Having It Both Ways." In *Eagle Resurgent: The Reagan Era in American Foreign Policy,* edited by Kenneth A. Oye, Robert J. Leiber, and Donald Rothchild. Boston: Little, Brown, 1987.

Schrecker, Ellen W. *No Ivory Towers.* New York: Oxford University Press, 1986.

Schroeder, John H. *Mr. Polk's War: American Opposition and Dissent, 1846–1848.* Madison: University of Wisconsin Press, 1973.

Schulzinger, Robert D. *American Diplomacy in the Twentieth Century.* New York: Oxford University Press, 1984.

Seymour, Charles. *American Diplomacy During the World War.* Westport, Conn.: Greenwood Press, 1975 (1934).

Sherwin, Martin. *A World Destroyed.* New York: Knopf, 1975.

Sherwood, Robert E. *Roosevelt and Hopkins.* New York: Harper & Bros., 1948.

Shuman, Michael H. *Building Municipal Foreign Policies.* Manuscript, 1988.

Siegel, Frederick. *Troubled Journey.* New York: Hill and Wang, 1984.

Smith, Gaddis. *Morality, Reason, and Power: American Diplomacy in the Carter Years.* New York: Hill and Wang, 1986.

Smith, Gene. *When the Cheering Stopped.* New York: Morrow, 1964.

Smith, Jean Edward, ed. *The Papers of General Lucius D. Clay: Germany 1945–1949.* 2 vols. Bloomington: University of Indiana Press, 1974.

Smith, J. H. *The War with Mexico*. Vol. 2. New York: Macmillan, 1919.

Smith, Page. *John Adams*. Vol. 1. Westport, Conn.: Greenwood Press, 1969.

Smith, Perry. *The Air Force Plans for Peace, 1943–1945*. Baltimore: Johns Hopkins Press, 1970.

Solo, Pam. *From Protest to Policy: Beyond the Freeze to Common Security*. Cambridge: Ballinger, 1988.

Stagg, J. C. A. *Mr. Madison's War*. Princeton: Princeton University Press, 1983.

Steel, Ronald. *Walter Lippmann and the American Century*. Boston: Atlantic Press, 1980.

Steele, Richard W. *Propaganda in an Open Society: The Roosevelt Administration and the Media, 1933–1941*. Westport, Conn.: Greenwood Press, 1985.

Stewart, Donald. *The Opposition Press of the Federalist Period*. Albany: State University of New York Press, 1969.

Stimson, Henry, and McGeorge Bundy. *On Active Service in Peace and War*. New York: Octagon Books, 1971.

Sulzberger, C. L. *A Long Row of Candles*. New York: Macmillan, 1969.

Sussman, Barry. *What Americans Really Think: Why Our Politicians Pay No Attention*. New York: Pantheon, 1988.

Swanberg, W. A. *Luce and His Empire*. New York: Scribner's, 1972.

Tabbel, John, and Sarah Miles Watts. *The Press and the Presidency*. New York: Oxford University Press, 1985.

Taft, Robert A. *A Foreign Policy for Americans*. Garden City, N.Y.: Doubleday, 1951.

Talbott, Strobe. *The Master of the Game*. New York: Knopf, 1988.

Tansill, Charles C. *America Goes to War*. Boston: Little, Brown, 1938.

———. *Back Door to War: The Roosevelt Foreign Policy 1933–1941*. Westport, Conn.: Greenwood Press, 1975.

Thompson, John S. *Reformers and War: American Progressive Publicists and the First World War*. Cambridge: Cambridge University Press, 1987.

Tivnan, Edward. *The Lobby: Jewish Political Power and American Foreign Policy*. New York: Simon and Schuster, 1987.

Tocqueville, Alexis de. *Democracy in America*. Var. eds., 2 vols. Garden City, N.Y.: Doubleday Anchor.

Townsend, Ralph. *Asia Answers*. New York: Putnam, 1936.

Truman, Harry S. *Memoirs*. Vol. 1, *Year of Decisions*. Garden City, N.Y.: Doubleday, 1955.

———. *Memoirs*. Vol. 2, *Years of Trial and Hope*. Garden City, N.Y.: Doubleday, 1956.

———. *Off the Record: The Private Papers of Harry S. Truman*. Edited by R. H. Ferrell. New York: Harper & Row, 1980.

U.S. Department of State. *Foreign Relations of the United States*, 1950, Vol. 1. Washington, D.C.: Government Printing Office.

Van Alstyne, R. W. *The Rising American Empire*. New York: Norton, 1974.

Vandenberg, Arthur H., Jr. *The Private Papers of Senator Vandenberg*. Boston: Houghton Mifflin, 1952.

Vidal, Gore. *Matters of Fact and Fiction*. New York: Random House, 1977.

Weart, Spencer. *Nuclear Fear: A History of Images*. Cambridge: Harvard University Press, 1988.

Weinberg, Albert K. *Manifest Destiny: A Study of Nationalist Expansion in American History*. Baltimore: Johns Hopkins Press, 1935.

Westerfield, H. Bradford. *Foreign Policy and Party Politics: Pearl Harbor to Korea*. New Haven: Yale University Press, 1955.

White, Leonard D. *The Federalists: A Study in Administrative History*. Westport, Conn.: Greenwood Press, 1978 (1948).

White, Theodore. *America in Search of Itself*. New York: Harper & Row, 1982.
White, William Allen. *The Autobiography of William Allen White*. New York: Macmillan, 1946.
Wilcox, Francis O. *Congress, the Executive, and Foreign Policy*. New York: Harper & Row, 1971.
Wilkerson, Marcus. *Public Opinion and the Spanish-American War*. New York: Russell & Russell, 1967.
Williams, William Appleman. *Empire as a Way of Life*. New York: Oxford University Press, 1980.
Wills, Garry. *Inventing America: Jefferson's Declaration of Independence*. Garden City, N.Y.: Doubleday, 1978.
———. *Reagan's America*. Garden City, N.Y.: Doubleday, 1987.
Wilson, Woodrow. *The Public Papers of Woodrow Wilson*. Vol. 1. Edited by Ray S. Baker and William B. Dodd. New York: Harper, 1925.
Wittner, Lawrence S. *Rebels Against War: The American Peace Movement, 1933–1983*. Philadelphia: Temple University Press, 1984.
Wohlstetter, Roberta. *Pearl Harbor: Warning and Decision*. Stanford: Stanford University Press, 1962.
Woodward, Bob. *Veil*. New York: Simon and Schuster, 1987.
Wyman, David. *The Abandonment of the Jews*. New York: Pantheon Books, 1984.
Yankelovich, Daniel, and Sidney Harman. *Starting with the People*. New York: Houghton Mifflin, 1988.
Zinn, Howard. *A People's History of the United States*. New York: Harper & Row, 1980.
Zion, Sidney. *The Autobiography of Roy Cohn*. Secaucus, N.J.: Lyle Stuart, 1988.

SELECTED ARTICLES AND STUDIES

Ackerman, William. "U.S. Radio: Record of a Decade." *Public Opinion Quarterly* (Fall 1948).
Adler, Les K., and Thomas G. Paterson. "Red Fascism: The Merger of Nazi Germany and Soviet Russia in the American Image of Totalitarianism, 1930's–1950's." *American Historical Review* (Feb.–Apr. 1970).
Ammon, Harry. "Formation of the Republican Party in Virginia." *Journal of Southern History* 19 (Feb.–Nov., 1953): 300.
Anderson, Kurt. "America's Upbeat Mood." *Time* (Sept. 24, 1984).
Angell, Norman. "Public Opinion in Foreign Policies." *Annals of the American Academy of Political and Social Science* (July 1916).
Apple, R. W. "New Stirrings of Patriotism." *New York Times Magazine* (Dec. 11, 1983).
Bagdikian, Ben H. "Patriotic Television?" *The Quill* (Feb. 1980).
Barnet, Richard J. "The Four Pillars." *New Yorker* (Mar. 7, 1987).
Berger, Henry. "Bipartisanship, Senator Taft, and the Truman Administration." *Political Science Quarterly* (Summer 1975).
Bonafede, Dom. "The Selling of the Executive Branch—Public Information or Promotion?" *National Journal* (June 27, 1981).
Borg, Dorothy. "Notes on Roosevelt's 'Quarantine Speech.' " *Political Science Quarterly* 72 (1957): 424–33.
Bruner, Jerome S. "OWI and the American Public." *Public Opinion Quarterly* (Spring 1943).
Buchanan, Russell. "American Editors Examine American War Aims and Plans in April, 1917." *Pacific Historical Review* (Sept. 1940): 256.
Buitenhuis, Peter. "The Selling of the Great War." *The Canadian Review of American Studies* 7, no. 2 (Fall 1976): 139–46.

Burnham, Walter Dean. "Thoughts on the 'Governability Crisis' of the West." *Washington Quarterly* (July 1978): 46.

Cable, John N. "Vandenberg: The Polish Question and Polish Americans, 1944–1948." *Michigan History* (Winter 1973).

Caridi, Ronald J. "The G.O.P. and the Korean War." *Pacific Historical Review* 37 (1968).

Clifford, Clark. "American Relations with the Soviet Union." (Sept. 1946). In Arthur Krock, *Memoirs*.

Clinton, David. "The Marshall Plan: A Non-Presidential Consensus?" In Richard A. Melanson, *Foreign Policy and Domestic Consensus*.

Coben, Stanley. "A Study in Nativism: The American Red Scare of 1919–1920." *Political Science Quarterly* 79, no. 1.

Dorman, William A. "The Media: Playing the Government's Game." *Bulletin of the Atomic Scientists* (Aug. 1985).

Dubin, Martin David. "Elihu Root and the Advocacy of a League of Nations 1914–1917." *Western Political Quarterly* (Sept. 1966).

Duff, John B. "The Versailles Treaty and the Irish-Americans." *Journal of American History* (Dec. 1968).

Elowitz, Larry, and John W. Spanier. "Korea and Vietnam: Limited War and the American Political System." *Orbis* (Summer 1974).

Evangelista, Matthew A. "Stalin's Postwar Army Reappraisal." *International Security* 7, no. 3.

Feller, A. H. "OWI and the Home Front." *Public Opinion Quarterly* (Spring 1943): 62.

Fisher, Josephine. "Francis James Jackson and Newspaper Propaganda in the United States, 1809–1810." *Maryland Historical Magazine* 30 (1935): 93–113.

FitzGerald, Frances. "Rewriting American History." *New Yorker* (Feb. 26, 1979): 66.

Free, Lloyd, and William Watts. "Internationalism Comes of Age . . . Again." *Public Opinion* (May/Apr. 1980): 46.

Gergen, David. "The Hardening Mood Toward Foreign Policy." *Public Opinion* (Feb./Mar. 1980): 12.

Ginsberg, Benjamin. "Opinion Mongering." *The Nation* (Oct. 3, 1988): 278.

Gustafson, Merlin. "Church, State, and the Cold War, 1945–52." *Journal of Church and State* (Winter 1966).

Hallin, Dan. "The Myth of the Adversary Press." *The Quill* (Nov. 1983).

Harris, Huntington, and Paul M. Lewis. "The Press, Public Behavior, and Public Opinion." *Public Opinion Quarterly* (Spring 1948).

Helbich, Wolfgang J. "American Liberals in the League of Nations Controversy." *Public Opinion Quarterly* (Winter 1967–68).

Henderson, G. B. "Southern Designs on Cuba, 1854–1857." *Journal of Southern History* 5 (1939): 371–85.

Horsman, Reginald. "American Indian Policy and the Origins of Manifest Destiny." *Historical Journal* (1969).

Kornbluh, Peter. "Reagan's Propaganda Ministry." *Propaganda Review* (Summer 1988).

Ladd, Everett Caril. "The Freeze Framework." *Public Opinion* (Aug.–Sept. 1982).

Lancaster, James L. "The Protestant Churches and the Fight for Ratification of the Versailles Treaty." *Public Opinion Quarterly* (Winter 1967–68).

Lapham, Lewis H. "The New Patriotism." *Harper's* (Jan. 1984).

Lee, R. Alton. "The Army 'Mutiny' of 1946." *Journal of American History* (Dec. 1966).

Leffler, Melvin P. "From the Truman Doctrine to the Carter Doctrine: Lessons and Dilemmas of the Cold War." *Diplomatic History* (Fall 1983).

Lipset, Seymour M. "Feeling Better: Measuring the Nation's Confidence." *Public Opinion* (Apr.–May 1985).

Lunch, William L. and Peter W. Sperlich. "American Public Opinion and the War in Vietnam." *Western Political Quarterly* (Mar. 1979).

Luthin, R. H. "The Sale of Alaska." *Slavonic Review* 16 (1937): 171.

Lyon, E. W. "The Directory and the United States." *American Historical Review* 43 (1938): 520.

Manoff, Robert Karl. "Covering the Bomb: The Nuclear Story and the News." *Working Papers* (May–June 1983).

Masland, John W. "Pressure Groups and American Foreign Policy." *Public Opinion Quarterly* (Spring 1942).

Maxwell, Kenneth R. "Irish-Americans and the Fight for Treaty Ratification." *Public Opinion Quarterly* (Winter 1967–68).

May, Ernest. "American Imperialism: A Reinterpretation." In *Perspectives in American History*, Vol. 1, 1967.

Melanson, Richard A. "The Grenada Intervention: Prelude to a New Consensus?" In Richard A. Melanson and Kenneth W. Thompson, *Foreign Policy and Domestic Consensus.*

Morgenthau, Hans J. "National Interest and Moral Principles in Foreign Policy." *The American Scholar* (Spring 1949).

Morrow, Lance. "Yankee Doodle Magic." *Time* (July 7, 1986).

Murphy, Paul. "Normalcy, Intolerance, and the American Character." *Virginia Quarterly Review* (Summer 1964).

Myers, Robert C. "Anti-Communist Mob Action: A Case Study." *Public Opinion Quarterly* (Spring 1948).

Oliver, Bryce. "Thought Control—American Style." *New Republic* (Jan. 13, 1947).

Oliver, J. W. "Louis Kossuth's Appeal to the Middle West—1852." *Mississippi Valley Historical Review* 14 (1928): 481–95.

Parry, Robert, and Peter Kornbluh. "Iran-Contra's Untold Story." *Foreign Policy*, no. 72 (Fall 1988).

Paterson, Thomas G. "Presidential Foreign Policy, Public Opinion, and Congress: The Truman Years." *Diplomatic History* 3 (1979).

Rielly, John E., ed. "American Public Opinion and U.S. Foreign Policy." The Chicago Council on Foreign Relations 1975, 1979, 1983, and 1987.

Rosenblatt, Roger. "The Atomic Age." *Time* (July 29, 1985): 48–49.

Russett, Bruce. "The Americans' Retreat from World Power." *Political Science Quarterly* (Spring 1975).

———. "Economic Decline, Electoral Pressure, and the Initiation of Internal Conflict." In *Choices in World Politics* (New York: W. H. Freeman, 1979).

———, and Donald R. Deluc. " 'Don't Tread on Me': Public Opinion and Foreign Policy in the Eighties." *Political Science Quarterly* (Fall 1981): 386–87.

Shaffer, Ronald. "Censorship." *Mankind* 5, no. 11 (1976).

Skinner, James M. "Cliché and Convention in Hollywood's Cold War Anti-Communist Films." *North Dakota Quarterly* 46, no. 3 (Summer 1978).

Small, Melvin. "Public Opinion." In *Encyclopedia of American Foreign Policy.*

———. "When Did the Cold War Begin?: A Test of an Alternative Indicator of Public Opinion." *Historical Methods Newsletter* (Mar. 1975).

Sofaer, Abraham D. "Executive Power and the Control of Information." *Duke Law Journal* (Mar. 1977): 1–57.

Steele, Richard W. "The Great Debate: Roosevelt, the Media, and the Coming of the War, 1940–1941." *Journal of American History* (June 1984).

———. "Preparing the Public for War: Efforts to Establish a National Propaganda Agency, 1940–41." *American Historical Review* 75 (June–Oct. 1970).

Stoler, Mark A. "The 'Second Front' and American Expansion, 1941–1943." *Military Affairs* (Oct. 1975): 136–40.

Stromberg, Roland N. "Uncertainties and Obscurities about the League of Nations." *Journal of the History of Ideas* (Jan.–Mar. 1972).

Thomas, Keith. "Just Say No." Review of *Inventing the People: The Rise of Popular Sovereignty in England and America*, by Edmund S. Morgan. *New York Review of Books* (Nov. 24, 1988): 44.

Thompson, John A. "The Exaggeration of American Vulnerability: The Anatomy of a Tradition." (Unpublished manuscript.)

Washington Office on Latin America. "Central America and the Polls." 1984.

Watt, Donald. "Roosevelt and Neville Chamberlain: Two Appeasers." *International Journal* 28, no. 2 (Spring 1973).

Weigel, George. "The Long March." *Wilson Quarterly* (New Year's, 1987).

Weinberg, Sidney. "What to Tell America: The Writers' Quarrel in the Office of War Information." *Journal of American History* 55, no. 1 (June 1986): 78.

Weisman, Steven R. "Reagan's Magic Prevails." *New York Times Magazine* (Apr. 29, 1984).

Wells, Samuel F., Jr. "Sounding the Tocsin." *International Security* 4, no. 2 (Fall 1979).

Yankelovich, Daniel, and Larry Kagann. "Assertive America." *Foreign Affairs: America and the World* (1980): 699.

GOVERNMENT DOCUMENTS

Department of State Division of Public Studies. "Current Outlook of U.S. Public Opinion." (Mar. 9, 1951.)

———. "Monthly Survey of American Opinion on International Affairs." (1943–1951.)

———. "Popular Attitudes on MacArthur Dismissal and Far East Policies." (May 8, 1951.)

"Joint Chiefs of Staff Memorandum for Information No. 121." Aug. 22, 1943, in Records of the Joint Chiefs of Staff, Soviet Union, Pt. I, 1942–1945.

"Memorandum for the Acting Secretary of State." Feb. 21, 1944. Sec. 1-B, National Archives.

"Memorandum for the Chief of Staff." Mar. 14, 1946. ABC 092 (18 July 1945). Sec 1-B, National Archives.

"Memorandum for the President: Viet Nam News—What's Missing?" July 21, 1965, Horace Busby, LBJ Library.

Memorandum on "Public Affairs" (First Draft), Mar. 3, 1968, LBJ Library.

"A Report to the National Security Council on Public Statements with Respect to Certain American Weapons." Psychological Strategy Board, Feb. 28, 1952.

Roche, John P. "Memorandum for the President: Possible Public Reaction to Various Alternatives." (Feb. 26, 1968.)

"Strategic Guidance to Facilitate Planning." Apr. 12, 1946. ABC 092 (18 July 1945). Sec. 1-B, National Archives.

INDEX

abolitionism, 91, 95
Acheson, Dean, 209, 253, 261, 271,
    272, 274, 279, 298, 325, 390, 405
  elitism of, 15, 255–56, 290, 291, 402
  Korean War and, 308, 309–10, 311,
    312, 313, 314, 320
  loss of China and, 310, 336
  NSC 68 and, 285
  opinion polling disdained by, 263
  postwar order and, 253, 254–55,
    258
  Sino-Soviet split and, 309
  Truman Doctrine and, 266–69, 270
  Vandenberg manipulated by, 273
  Vietnam War and, 336, 350
Adams, Abigail, 31, 44, 50
Adams, Henry, 67, 137
Adams, John, 30, 31, 32, 36, 38, 43–
    51, 52, 53, 74, 77
  ideology of, 43–44
  military spending under, 47–49
  peace policy of, 50–51
  XYZ Affair and, 46–47
Adams, John Quincy, 59, 63, 75, 76,
    77, 79, 85, 94, 107
Adams, Samuel, 26, 35
Adams, Samuel Hopkins, 160
Adams, Sherman, 321
Addams, Jane, 150
Adler, Julius, 330

Afghanistan invasion (1979), 361, 363,
    364, 365, 366, 382
Agee, James, 235
Agnew, Spiro, 343
Aguinaldo, Emilio, 137
Air Force, U.S., 250, 265, 302
Alamo, battle of (1836), 94, 95, 98
Alaska, 110–11, 115
Albania, 328
Albert, Heinrich, 151
Alexander, Franz, 142
Alien Act (1798), 34, 47, 49
All Mexico movement, 102–3, 104
Allport, Gordon W., 172
Almond, Gabriel, 290
Alsop, Joseph, 270, 281, 295, 308–9,
    312
Alsop, Stewart, 281, 295
Ambrose, Stephen, 323
Amerasia, 275
America First Committee, 200, 207–8,
    212
American Board of Commissioners for
    Foreign Missions, 86, 87
American Century, 227, 356, 361, 405
"American Century, The" (Luce), 227
American character, traits of, 290
American Civil Liberties Union
    (ACLU), 192
American Club of Minneapolis, 177

American Commonwealth, The (Bryce), 144
American Defense Society, 153, 174, 185, 192
American exceptionalism, 112, 113, 174, 371
American Federation of Labor (AFL), 131, 242, 360
American Friends of Cuba, 131
American Hebrew (Zuckerman), 239–240
American Humanity League, 150
American Institute of Public Opinion, 187
Americanism Commission, 298
Americanization movement, 173
American Labor Party, 228
American Legion, 173, 192, 298, 320
American Legion, 236
American Mercury, 237–38
American Minerva, 36
American Peace Society, 86, 102, 141, 150
American People and Foreign Policy, The (Almond), 290
American Revolution, 23–24, 26, 27, 30–33, 35, 38, 42–44, 54, 64, 69, 83, 159, 211
Americans for Democratic Action (ADA), 306, 308
American Society of Newspaper Editors, 320, 334
Americans Talk Security Project, 403
American Truth Society, 150
American Vigilante Patrol, 174
Ames, Fisher, 31, 35, 45
anarchists, 170, 171
Andropov, Yuri, 372
Angell, Norman, 141
Angola, 352, 356, 363
Annexation Club, 115
Antiballistic Missile Treaty (1972), 391–92
anti-Communism, 271, 290, 317, 369
in Cold War, 273–84, 292–304
McCarthyism, 172, 192, 292–93, 302, 322, 346
nuclear fear and, 294–96
in post–World War I period, 170–172
of Reagan, 303, 369
Truman Doctrine and, 266–69, 270
wartime alliance with Soviets and, 236, 237, 238
Anti-Imperialist League, 136, 137

antinuclear movement, 390–97
atmospheric testing and, 340–41, 390
Catholic bishops in, 394–95
civil defense program and, 390–91
domestic ABM bases and, 391
Freeze movement and, 381, 383, 393–97
inadvertently revived by Reagan, 392–93
anti-Semitism, 202, 232, 385
and plight of Jews in World War II, 207–8, 242–43
in Soviet Union, 239–40
Anti-Slavery Society, 102
antiwar movement (Vietnam era), 340–42, 344, 346–51, 352
American life denounced by, 347, 349
election of 1968 and, 348–49
established peace movement and, 346
failure to win war and, 348–49
Johnson administration's tactics against, 341–42, 345–46
moral concerns of, 342
prominent figures in, 349–50
radical activists in, 346–47
street theater in, 347–48
supporters of North Vietnam in, 349
Tet offensive and, 342–43, 345
at universities, 340–42
war possibly prolonged by, 350
see also pacifism; peace movement
appeasement era, 187–204, 250
actions considered by FDR in, 194–196
assessments of FDR's performance in, 189–90
defeatism in, 199–200
Depression and, 192–93
failure of public opinion in, 187–88, 189, 190
isolationism in, 191, 193, 197–202, 204
pacifism in, 187–88, 191–93
public opinion polls in, 196–98
Arbenz Guzmán, Jacobo, 329–30
Argentina, 118, 358
aristocracy, 24, 25, 35, 77
Arizona, 108, 156
Armed Neutrality Convention, 40
Armenians, slaughter of, 127
arms control, 323, 330, 365, 366, 368, 383, 391, 392, 395

arms race, 266, 322–23, 363, 371, 388, 389, 390, 392, 394, 400, 403
Armstrong, John, 65
Army, U.S., 34, 38–39, 48–49, 53, 67, 94, 98, 128, 144, 152, 214, 217, 250, 278, 322, 375, 383
Aron, Raymond, 157
Articles of Confederation, 24, 28, 32, 39, 53
Assignment in Utopia (Lyons), 236
Associated Press (AP), 144, 252, 383
Association of Radio News Analysts, 252
Atlantic Monthly, 113, 305, 330
atomic bomb, 258, 275, 292, 388
  as public relations challenge, 264–266, 267
  in World War II, 188, 241, 242, 254, 264–65, 289, 295, 314, 390
  see also nuclear weapons
Atomic Energy Commission, 323
Atoms for Peace, 324
"attentive public," 12
Aurora, 41
Auschwitz, 242–43
Austin, Moses, 94
Austria, 105–6, 147, 324

Bache, Benjamin Franklin, 33, 41
Bailey, Thomas, 125, 156
Baker, James, 377, 380
Baker, Newton, 159–60
balance-of-power diplomacy, 256
Baldwin, Hanson, 264
Balkans, 251, 260, 267
Baltimore Board of Trade, 130
Baltimore Federal Republican, 63
Baltimore Sun, 146–47
Bancroft, George, 80–81
Baptists, 88
Barbary pirates, 39
Bard, Ralph, 252
Barnes, Michael, 385
Barrett, Edward W., 286–87
Barrie, J. M., 144
Baruch, Bernard, 203, 252–53, 257, 314
Baruch Plan, 295
Battle of Britain, 206, 235
Bay of Pigs invasion (1961), 332–33, 334
Beard, Charles A., 159, 175, 190, 201
Beard, Mary, 175
Beast of Berlin, 233
beat generation, 347

Becker, Ernest, 392
Beirut bombing (1983), 383
Belgium, 144–45, 161
Bell, Daniel, 354
Bemis, Samuel Flagg, 40
Bennett, James Gordon, 80
Bennett, William J., 374
Bentley, Elizabeth, 273–74, 300
Benton, Thomas Hart, 97, 108
Benton, William, 207
Berle, A. A., Jr., 205
Berlin crisis (1948), 265, 283, 322
Berlin crisis (1961), 391
Bernays, Edward L., 222, 329–30
Bernstein, Leonard, 302
Bernstorff, Johann Heinrich, Count, 149, 155, 161
Beveridge, Albert, 113–14, 134
Biddle, Charles, 33
Biddle, Francis, 214
Bill of Rights, 304
bipartisan foreign policy, 211, 219, 287
  and building of postwar consensus, 272–84
  unraveling of, after 1948 election, 311
Black, Gregory, 232
blacklists, 302, 303
blacks, 38, 54, 150, 157, 161, 169, 336
  civil rights movement and, 292, 342, 347, 349, 352
  Cuban revolution of 1890s and, 130, 131
  World War II and, 225, 228
  see also slavery
Blackwood's, 109
Blair, Francis P., 79
Bledsoe (judge), 159
Blount, James H., 116
Blount, William, 52
Boer War, 125
Bohlen, Charles, 254, 270, 271, 293
Bolitho, William, 164
bomber gap (1950s), 331
Boorstin, Daniel, 347
Borah, William E., 165, 168, 179, 180, 191, 196, 202, 203, 204, 273
"Born in the U.S.A.," 375
Boston *Atlas*, 104
Boston *Columbian Centinel*, 31, 63–64
Boston *Herald*, 116, 191
Boston Merchants Association, 130
Boston Tea Party, 74
Boston Times, 100

Boston *Transcript*, 95
Bourke-White, Margaret, 238
Bourne, Randolph, 168
Bowles, Chester, 207
Bradlee, Benjamin C., 379
Bradley, Omar, 314
Brandegee, Frank B., 167
Brazil, 358
Breckinridge, Henry, 147
Breckinridge, John, 58
Bretton Woods Conference (1944),
    257, 274, 405
Brewer, Roy, 303
Brewster, Kingman, Jr., 207
Brewster, Owen, 314
Brezhnev, Leonid, 358, 365, 366
"British Aggressions in Venezuela"
    (Scruggs), 124
British Guiana, 122, 124–25, 128
Brodie, Bernard, 265
Brown, David, 47
Brown University, 191
Bryan, William Jennings, 119, 121,
    123, 205
  in election of 1900, 131, 136, 137–38
  Spanish-American War and, 131,
    136
  in Wilson cabinet, 144, 148, 149
Bryant & Sturgis, 101
Bryce, James, Lord, 144, 148, 187,
    290
Buchanan, James, 106
Budenz, Louis, 275, 300
budget deficits, 14, 357, 361, 363
Buell, Elias, 33
Buffon, Georges-Louis, 83–84
Bullitt, William, 178–79, 182, 193
Bundy, McGeorge, 255, 341
Bureau of Intelligence, 226
Bureau of Investigation, 171, 192
Burke, Edmund, 16
Burnham, James, 305, 306
Burnham, Walter Dean, 116, 118, 121,
    129, 359
Burns, James MacGregor, 189, 321
Burns, William J., 192
Busby, Horace, 341–42
Bush, George, 368, 409
Bush, Vannevar, 315, 322
Butler, Hugh, 255
Byrnes, James, 252, 264

Caddell, Patrick, 361
Caldicott, Helen, 393
Calhoun, John C., 94, 97, 98, 107

California, 81, 96, 136
  acquisition of, 93, 101, 104, 112–13
California, University of, 302
Canada, 24, 54, 57, 61, 98, 110, 275,
    292
  fishing rights disputes with, 123
  plans for conquest of, 67, 68
Canning, George, 62
Cantril, Hadley, 197, 224, 226, 243
Capra, Frank, 229, 230
Caribbean:
  expansionism in, 106, 107–8, 109
  see also Cuba
Carnegie, Andrew, 136, 141, 176, 282
Carnegie Endowment, 150
Carr, A. Z., 283
Carroll, Charles, 79
Carter, Jimmy, 14, 358–61, 364, 367–
    368, 371, 379, 387
  in election of 1976, 358–59, 360
  in election of 1980, 368, 370, 379
  energy crisis and, 360–61
  ideology of, 359
  Iranian hostage crisis and, 361, 368,
    378
  Panama Canal Treaty and, 360
  Soviet brigade in Cuba and, 366
Casablanca Conference (1943), 234
Case, Francis, 269
Casey, William, 384
Cass, Lewis, 88, 89
Castillo Armas, Carlos, 329
Castlereagh, Robert Stewart, Lord, 76
Castro, Fidel, 347, 364, 366, 383
  covert operations against, 332–33,
    334, 355
Catholicism, 168–69, 185, 201, 236,
    243–44, 297, 360, 381
  anti-Communism and, 300–301
  antinuclear movement and, 394–95
Catron, John, 95
Cavell, Edith, 161
CBS, 240, 336, 363
censorship, 226, 278
  of films, 232–34
  in World War I, 157–59
Central America, 111, 399
  expansionism in, 106–7
  Reagan policy on, 376–78, 381–82,
    384–86, 411
  see also specific countries
Central Intelligence Agency (CIA),
    217, 322, 356, 365, 368, 386
  anti-Castro operations of, 332–33,
    334, 355

covert operations of, as principal
    weapon in Cold War, 325
covert propaganda campaigns of,
    381, 382, 384–85
Guatemala coup and, 329, 330
investigations of, 352, 355
Mossadegh coup and, 329
Soviet Union infiltrated by, 327–28
"Century of the Common Man, The"
    ((Wallace), 227
Chamberlain, Joseph, 123
Chamberlain, Neville, 194
Chamber of Commerce, 296, 297
Chambers, Whittaker, 300
Chemical Warfare Service, 192
Cherokee Indians, 84–88, 90, 91
Chesapeake, 60
Chiang Kai-shek, 207, 235, 303, 308,
    310, 311
Chicago Daily News, 213
Chicago *Herald*, 116
Chicago *Tribune*, 128, 196, 236
Chickasaw Indians, 90
Chile, 355, 356, 358
China, Imperial, 134, 176
China, People's Republic of, 285, 308,
    323, 324, 327, 328, 336
    in Korean War, 301, 313–14, 315,
        316
    normalization of relations with, 13,
        354, 358
    Soviet split with, 309, 331, 358
    Vietnam War and, 339, 343, 345,
        349, 356
China, Republic of, 195, 201, 207,
    231, 235, 251, 262, 269, 308, 323
    loss of, 309, 310, 311, 312, 318, 339
China Lobby, 231, 310
Choctaw Indians, 90
Christian Anti-Communism Crusade,
    369
Christian Enquirer, 116–17
Christian Register, 176
Christian Science, 92
Christian Science Monitor, 308, 330
Church, Frank, 366
churches:
    Communism issue and, 299–301,
        322
    expansionism and, 116–17, 135
    political activities of, 37
    see also specific denominations
Churchill, Winston, 242, 243, 255,
    324, 413
    destroyer swap and, 208–9

Lend-Lease program and, 212–13
postwar order and, 260, 266
war against Nazis sought by, 187,
    189
wartime propaganda and, 235, 237
Church Peace Union, 176
Cigarmakers' Union, 131
Cincinnatier Freie Presse, 145
Cisneros, Evangelina, 129
Citizens' Committee for the Marshall
    Plan, 271
civil defense, 331, 390–91, 392
civil rights movement, 292, 342, 347,
    349, 352
Civil War, 104, 108–9, 118, 122, 168,
    183, 208, 242, 299
Clark, Abraham, 31
Clark, George Rogers, 30
Clark, Tom, 275, 279–80
Clay, Henry, 75, 77, 80, 93, 97, 107
    Indian rights and, 86–87
    War of 1812 and, 63, 65, 67
Clay, Lucius, 281–82
Clayton, Will, 269
Clemenceau, Georges, 164
Clemson, Thomas G., 98
Cleveland, Grover, 116, 120, 136
    presidential campaigns of, 123–24
    Venezuela–British Guiana border
        dispute and, 122, 124–25
Clifford, Clark, 270, 276, 279, 350
    Truman Doctrine and, 268, 269
    Truman's campaign strategy and,
        280–82
Cline, Ray, 368
Clinton, DeWitt, 65
Coalition of the Kings, 28
Cobb, Frank, 146, 157
Cobbett, William, 42, 46
cognitive dissonance, 244–45
Colby, William, 394
Cold War, 12, 183, 188, 236, 245, 252,
    254–351, 355, 363, 372, 400, 404,
    405, 408
    advisers' alarmist prose in, 261–62
    bipartisan foreign policy in, 272–84,
        287, 311
    breakdown of consensus on, 336,
        351, 354, 358, 360
    business community in, 296–98, 299
    churches in, 299–301, 322
    consumption issue in, 326
    covert operations in, 325, 327–30,
        332–34, 355, 356, 365
    crisis atmosphere in, 281–82

Cold War (*cont.*)
domestic Communism and, 273–81, 282–83, 292–93, 297, 317, 322
easing of tensions in (1950s), 321–322, 330
under Eisenhower, 321–32
election of 1948 and, 280, 281, 283
empire building in, 357
Greek insurgency in, 266–69, 270
hysteria in, 271, 292–304, 311
as ideological struggle, 270–71
intellectuals in, 304–7
labor movement in, 297–99, 303
Molotov-Truman meeting and, 259
Mossadegh affair in, 328–29
national media in, 302–4
NSC 68 in, 285–86, 287, 291, 308, 322
nuclear weapons in, 264–66, 267, 270–71, 281, 285, 286, 289–90, 291, 294–96, 301, 322–25
opponents of anti-Soviet policy in, 262–63
permanent mobilization in, 256, 263, 285, 286–87
"preventive war" issue in, 290–91, 297
propaganda in, 239, 278–81, 303–4, 315–16, 318
public opinion in, 260–61, 262, 263–264, 266, 267, 285, 286–90, 292–307
universities in, 301–2
see also Korean War; Truman Doctrine; Vietnam War
Collier's, 296
Collot, Victor, 45
Columbian Star and Christian Index, 88
Columbia University, 348
Comintern, 240, 244
Commission on National Goals, 332
Committee on Nothing at All, 175
Committee on Public Information, 157–58, 159–62, 217, 223, 226, 227, 229
Committee on the Present Danger, 316, 368
Committee to Aid the NLF, 349
Committee to Defend America by Aiding the Allies, 205–7, 209, 316
Commons, John R., 175
Common Sense (Paine), 25
communication technology, 406–7

Communism, 174, 200, 212, 245, 258, 261, 262, 285, 289, 328, 330, 357, 359, 362, 377
containment of, 257, 271, 293, 310, 318, 325, 358
domestic, 273–81, 282–83, 292–93, 297, 317, 322, 346
Domino Theory and, 319, 356
Greek insurgency and, 266–69
labor movement and, 242, 277, 292, 297, 298–99
Red Scare and (1919–20), 170–72, 185, 192
in Vietnam, 336, 337, 338
in Western Europe, 271, 292, 356
"world," as mistaken notion, 358
see also anti-Communism
Communism and the Conscience of the West (Sheen), 300
Communist Labor Party, 171
Communist Party of Iran, 328
Communist Party USA, 170, 171, 236, 273–76, 298, 302, 303, 317
Conant, Charles A., 114
Conant, James Bryant, 206, 209, 302, 315–16
Conelrad, 295
Confessions of a Nazi Spy, 232
Congregational Church, 127
Congress, U.S., 13, 14, 31, 39, 41, 47, 50, 51, 55, 60, 63, 69, 81, 90, 108, 115, 124, 166, 180, 250, 263, 273, 279, 299, 302, 308, 315, 353, 377, 380, 399, 400
in appeasement era, 194, 195, 196
CIA and, 352, 355, 356
Contra aid and, 385, 386, 387
elections of 1810 and, 64–65
foreign aid and, 257, 273, 276, 280, 281
Freeze movement and, 395, 396
Hawaiian Islands annexation and, 136–37
information withheld from, by presidents, 327, 328
Louisiana Purchase and, 57–58
Mexican War and, 96, 97, 100, 103, 104
military spending and, 48, 49
power lost by, in wartime, 183
propaganda and, 222, 223, 227–28, 384, 385
Spanish-American War and, 130, 131, 132, 133

Truman Doctrine and, 267–68, 269, 270
Vietnam War and, 339, 342, 351
war-making power of, 105, 198–99
War of 1812 and, 64–65, 66, 67, 68
World War I and, 143, 145, 146, 149, 150, 153, 154, 156, 167
World War II and, 208, 209, 210, 212, 218, 249
XYZ Affair and, 46
see also House of Representatives, U.S.; Senate, U.S.
Congress for Cultural Freedom, 306–7
Congress of Industrial Organizations (CIO), 242, 298–99, 360
Connecticut Gazette, 27
Conscience of a Conservative, The (Goldwater), 337
conscription, 350, 354, 355
in peacetime, 251, 281, 365
in Vietnam War, 14, 342
in World War I, 154, 157, 159–61
in World War II, 211, 212
Constitution, U.S, 12, 14, 17, 34, 35, 53, 57, 62, 66, 89, 92, 114, 159, 173, 184, 210, 220, 280, 408
Lowell's proposal for replacement of, 68
overseas annexations and, 130, 135
public opinion and, 262, 263
study groups on, 33
war-making power and, 105, 198–99
Constitution, U.S.S., 45
Constitutional Convention, 33, 37, 61
constitutions, twentieth-century, 220
containment doctrine, 257, 271, 293, 310, 318, 325, 358
Continental Congresses, 43
continentalism, 103
Contras, 378, 385, 386, 387, 411
Coolidge, Calvin, 192, 205
Cooper, James Fenimore, 90
Corwin, Edward S., 210
Cottrell, Leonard, 289–90
Coudert, Frederic R., 153
Coughlin, Father Charles E., 201–2
Council of Economic Advisers, 262
Council of National Defense, 153
Council on Foreign Relations, 331, 359
covert operations, 278, 355, 356, 365, 378
against Castro, 332–33, 334, 355
Doolittle's justification of, 333–34

under Eisenhower, 325, 327–30, 333
press passive, misled, or manipulated in, 329, 330, 333
public opinion misled in, 329
Reagan's propaganda initiatives, 381–87
under Truman, 327–28
Cowles, Gardner, 228
Cox, James, 181
credibility gap, 341
Creek Indians, 45, 83, 90
Creel, George, 157–58, 217, 223, 226, 227, 229
Creelman, James, 128
Crime of the Century, 304
Crisis of Democracy, The, 343
Crockett, Davy, 86, 94
Croly, Herbert, 175
Cronin, Father John F., 297
Cronkite, Walter, 324, 343, 393
Cuba, 54, 136, 369
attempted annexation of, 107–8, 109
Central American insurgencies and, 376, 377
covert operations against, 332–33, 334, 355
missile crisis in, 188, 366, 391, 404
revolution in (1890s), 125–29, 130–133
Soviet brigade in, 366
Curti, Merle, 174
Curtiz, Michael, 238
Custodial Detention Program, 275
Czechoslovakia, 197, 203
coup in (1948), 276, 281–82, 322

Dahl, Robert, 400
Daily Worker, 275, 311
Damrosch, Walter, 175
Dana, Richard Henry, 101
Daniels, Josephus, 193
Darman, Richard, 374, 380
Darwin, Charles, 113
Daughters of the American Revolution (DAR), 173, 192
Davies, Joseph E., 238–39, 240
Davis, Elmer, 209, 224, 225, 243
Davis, Jefferson, 97, 109
Davis, Richard Harding, 128
Deaver, Michael, 377, 380
Debs, Eugene V., 159, 170
Declaration of Independence, 79, 173, 280

DeConde, Alexander, 29
defeatism, 199–200, 208, 220, 223, 277
defense bonds, 223–24
Defense Department, U.S., 354, 377, 392–93
    see also Joint Chiefs of Staff; Pentagon
Defenseless America (Maxim), 152–53
democracy, 11, 12, 13, 25, 26, 31, 39, 62, 73, 84, 109, 158, 175, 178, 200, 220, 221, 222, 227, 228, 236, 239, 269, 290, 306, 309, 323, 330, 357, 385
    abroad, U.S. attitudes toward, 408
    Adams's views on, 43–44
    cynicism about, 407
    failure of, in appeasement era, 187–188
    foreign policy strategists hampered by, 15–16, 285, 287, 356, 410
    Freeze movement and, 395
    imperialism and, 112, 136
    inculcating principles of, 279
    insulation of leaders from mass opinion in, 404–6
    Jacksonian, 76, 80
    Jefferson's views on, 53–54
    land needed for, 153–54
    and likelihood of war, 17
    Lippmann's views on, 188, 288, 404, 410
    nuclear strategy and, 389–90
    public opinion sampling as pulse of, 197
    repression hindered by, 408–9
    and social upheavals of mid-1970s, 352, 354
    see also electoral politics; public opinion
Democratic Party, 58, 93, 97–98, 116, 118, 122, 123, 125, 135, 155, 166, 184, 203, 204, 219, 222, 238, 244, 276, 312–13, 325, 330–31, 343–44, 350, 352, 368
    bipartisan foreign policy and, 272–284
    election of 1952 and, 318, 319
    expansionism and, 107, 108
    industrialization and, 119, 121
    League of Nations and, 179, 180, 181
    politics of foreign adventure and, 120, 121
    Wallace and, 282–83
Democratic Review, 103

Denby, Charles, 134
Denial of Death, The (Becker), 392
Denmark, 40
Depression, Great, 186, 187, 236, 292, 304
    appeasement and, 192–93
Dernberg, Bernhard, 150
Descent of Man, The (Darwin), 113
Des Moines Register, 178, 206
détente, 354, 358, 359, 363, 365, 366–367, 368, 372
deterrence doctrine, 14, 256, 264, 265–66, 267, 318, 324, 389, 390, 394, 395, 396, 405
Detroit News, 123
Dewey, George, 133–34, 135, 136, 137
Dewey, John, 227, 294
Dewey, Thomas E., 272, 283, 284, 311, 320
Dickinson (senator), 104
Dieckhoff, Hans Heinrich, 199
Dilling, Elizabeth, 273
disarmament, 278, 295, 327, 359, 396
Disney, Walt, 324
Divine, Robert, 193, 283
Djilas, Milovan, 266
Dr. Strangelove, 388–89
Dominican Republic, 109, 111
Domino Theory, 319, 356
Donovan, William, 210
Doolittle, James, 333–34
Dos Passos, John, 191
Douglas, Stephen A., 97, 107, 108
Douglas, William O., 260
Dower, John, 230–31
draft, see conscription
Drucker, Peter, 288
Dryfoos, Orvil, 333
Dudman, Richard, 333
Dulles, Allen, 209, 330
Dulles, John Foster, 312, 320, 324, 330, 389, 390
    ideology of, 318–19
Du Pont de Nemours, Pierre-Samuel, 60
Durant, Will, 175
Duranty, Walter, 238

Early, Stephen, 208
Eastern Europe, 296, 301, 318, 320
    Nazi atrocities in, 231–32
    postwar order and, 252, 257, 262, 365
    see also specific countries
East Indies, 40–41

Eastman, Max, 306
Eaton (secretary of war), 88
Eberhart, Sylvia, 289–90
Ecclesiastical Review (Kelly), 240
Economic Consequences of the Peace,
   The (Keynes), 176
economy, 147, 369, 370, 400
   foreign dimension to problems in,
      363–64
   inflation and, 357, 358, 361, 363–64,
      368
   and prosperity of Eisenhower era,
      325–26, 330
   slowdown of, in mid-1970s, 356–58
   transformed in late nineteenth
      century, 118–19, 120, 121–22
Eddy, Mary Baker, 92
Eden, Anthony, 195, 243
Edison, Thomas A., 154
education, 44, 62, 292, 294
   textbook reform and, 373–74
Einstein, Albert, 201
Eisenhower, Dwight D., 217, 241,
      250, 283, 321–32
   arms negotiations and, 323, 330
   Committee on the Present Danger
      and, 316
   critics of, 331–32, 347
   in election of 1952, 318, 319, 320,
      325, 335
   era of good feelings under, 330–31
   Korean War ended by, 322
   McCarthy and, 322, 327
   military spending under, 324, 331
   national security policy of, 322–25,
      327–28, 331, 333
   nuclear weapons as viewed by, 322–
      323
   permissive public mood and 327–28,
      333
   prosperity under, 325–27, 330
   relaxing of Cold War tensions
      under, 321–22, 330
   secrecy surrounding foreign policy
      initiatives of, 325, 327–30, 333
   televised appearances of, 320–21,
      335
   U-2 incident and, 386–87
   Vietnam War and, 336–37
Eisler, Gerhard, 304
elections:
   of 1796, 42–43
   of 1798, 49
   of 1800, 50
   of 1810, 64–65
   of 1812, 64, 65
   of 1824, 77
   of 1828, 76, 77, 83, 86, 87
   of 1832, 77, 89–90
   of 1844, 93
   of 1888, 123–24
   of 1892, 120
   of 1896, 122
   of 1900, 131, 136, 137–38
   of 1912, 184
   of 1916, 12–13, 146, 152, 153, 154–
      155, 157
   of 1918, 166
   of 1920, 181–82, 190
   of 1932, 191, 202, 304
   of 1936, 197, 202
   of 1938, 203
   of 1940, 207, 209, 210–11, 272
   of 1942, 219
   of 1944, 228, 231, 260, 272
   of 1946, 262, 263, 272, 274
   of 1948, 263, 272, 274, 276–77, 280–
      284, 287, 317, 357
   of 1950, 311
   of 1952, 317–21, 325, 335
   of 1956, 327, 331
   of 1960, 93, 332, 335
   of 1964, 337–38, 369
   of 1966, 342
   of 1968, 348–49, 350, 351
   of 1972, 343, 350, 354
   of 1976, 350, 353, 358–59, 360
   of 1980, 359, 368–69, 370, 379
   of 1984, 374, 396, 397
   of 1988, 409
electoral politics, 11, 12–13, 34, 117
   absence of serious debate in, 401–
      402
   expansionism and, 76–77
   and feelings of disempowerment,
      400–401
   in Jacksonian era, 76–78
   in one-party countries, 220
   voter turnout in, 121, 353, 402
Electra: The National Preparedness
   Magazine, 153
Eliot, Charles W., 143
El Salvador, 267, 376–78, 381–82, 385,
   386
Elsey, George, 269, 274, 313
Emancipation Proclamation, 280
Embargo Act (1807), 60–61, 66
Emerson, Ralph Waldo, 90, 102
Employee Loyalty Program, 279, 283,
   297, 303

energy crisis (1970s), 360–61, 363, 372, 393
Enlightenment, 44
Erskine, David, 62
Erskine, John, 160
Escape from Freedom (Fromm), 289
Espionage Act (1917), 158–59, 231
Essex Register, 63
Ethiopia, 195, 363
Europe, *see* Eastern Europe; Western Europe; *specific countries*
European Recovery Program, *see* Marshall Plan
Evarts, Jeremiah, 86
Everett, Edward, 90, 103
evolution, 113, 373
expansionism, 61, 80–81, 92–117, 406
　Alaska and, 110–11, 115
　California and, 93, 101, 104, 112–13
　in Central America and Caribbean, 106–8, 109, 111
　and changes in political culture, 76–77
　Civil War and, 108–9
　and closing of American frontier, 143
　democracy and, 53–54, 112, 136
　Hawaiian Islands and, 108, 109, 112, 114, 115–17, 121, 136–37
　Indians and, 81, 82–91
　Louisiana Purchase and, 56–59
　Manifest Destiny and, 81, 99–100, 105, 112, 115, 120, 136
　Mexican War and, 96–105, 106
　Oregon and, 81, 93–94, 103
　Philippines and, 113, 114, 133–34, 135, 136, 137
　and politics of foreign adventure, 119–38
　population pressures and, 54
　in post-bellum period, 109–10
　religious outlook and, 116–17, 135
　slavery and, 93, 95, 97–98, 100, 106, 107, 108
　Texas and, 93, 94–105
　and vulnerability to popular unrest, 74–75
　see also imperialism; Spanish-American War
extermination camps, 232, 242–43
Eyes of the Navy, 234

"Fall of a Nation" (Herbert), 153
fallout shelters, 331, 390–91
Falwell, Jerry, 373

Fay, Sidney B., 159
Federal Bureau of Investigation (FBI), 201, 214, 352, 385
　domestic Communism and, 273–76, 292, 293, 300, 303, 317
Federal Civil Defense Administration, 294–95
Federal Council of Churches, 174, 176, 301
Federalists, 23–69, 350, 406
　demise of, 69
　French Revolution and, 23, 27–32
　ideology of, 25
　Indian policy under, 83–85
　Jay Treaty and, 39–43
　Logan mission and, 49, 50
　Louisiana Purchase and, 57
　Madison's offensive against, 65–66
　Napoleonic wars and, 59–67, 68
　political societies and, 33–36
　War of 1812 and, 65, 67, 69
　western frontier and, 52–53, 56, 57
Fenno, John, 27, 36
Ferguson, Adam, 44
Filene, Edward A., 167
filibusterers, 106–7, 126–27
films, 292
　New Patriotism and, 374–75
　about nuclear weapons, 388–89
　propagandistic, 229, 230, 232–34, 235, 238–39, 303–4, 316, 325
　see also Hollywood
Finland, 237
Fiske, John, 113
FitzGerald, Frances, 373
Florida, 24, 30, 45, 47, 52, 54, 55–56, 67
　Jackson's campaign in, 75, 76
Flynn, Ed, 218
Foch, Ferdinand, 164
Fonda, Jane, 295, 340
Ford, Gerald R., 355, 360, 366
Ford, Henry, 150, 154, 282
Ford Motor Company, 199
Foreign Affairs, 262
foreign aid, 273, 276, 316
　as goal of Truman Doctrine, 267, 269–70, 271–72
　Marshall Plan, 267, 269–73, 277, 278–80, 281, 297, 311
foreign policy:
　bipartisanship in, 211, 219, 272–84, 287, 311
　as continuation of domestic politics, 121

importance of money in, 286
as means to presidential power and
 prestige, 183, 367
as metaphor for struggle to define
 American identity, 25
public opinion in making of, 11–19,
 399–413
revolutionary changes in, after
 World War II, 256
as trap for presidents, 14, 367–68
see also specific topics
Foreign Policy Association, 175
foreign policy Establishment, 254–56,
 335, 355, 405, 406
Formosa, 308, 310, 311, 323
 see also China, Republic of
Formosa Resolution, 327
Forrestal, James, 252, 254, 285
 domestic Communism and, 277,
  278
 postwar order and, 257, 258, 261,
  262, 270–71
Forsberg, Randall, 393
Fortress America, 262, 291
Fortune, 202, 226, 296
Founding Fathers, 54, 69, 75, 221,
 405
Four Freedoms, 227, 235
Four Minute Men, 160–61
Four Policemen, 251, 255
Fourteen Points, 168, 183
Fowler, Henry, 368
Fox, William T. R., 265
France, 74, 107, 108, 109, 112, 114,
 134, 135, 197, 251, 271, 277, 292
 American ships seized by, 45, 60,
  62–63, 64, 67
 Indochina and, 323, 336
 Jackson and, 81–82
 Louisiana territory and 54, 55–59
 Napoleonic wars and, 59–64, 67, 68
 U.S. relations with, in earliest days
  of Republic, 24–32, 34, 35, 37–38,
  40–43, 45–59
 in World War I, 147, 148, 161, 164,
  165, 242
 in World War II, 203, 205–8, 223,
  233, 235
France, Anatole, 199
Frank, Jerome, 200–201
Frankel, Max, 344
Frankfort *Argus*, 79
Frankfurter, Felix, 175
Franklin, Benjamin, 46, 47, 54
Freedom Train, 280

*Freeman's Journal and Catholic
 Register*, 159
free silver issue, 119, 122, 123, 125
Freeze movement, 381, 383, 393–97
Frelinghuysen, Theodore, 86
Frémont, John Charles, 101
French and Indian War, 83
French Army of the Mississippi, 30
French Directory, 45, 49
French Revolution, 23, 25, 26–32, 37,
 38, 74, 127
 demonstrations of solidarity with,
  26–28
 Genet's campaign to gain support
  for, 29–30, 32
 Reign of Terror in, 26–28
 Washington's Neutrality
  Proclamation and, 28–29, 31, 32
Freneau, Philip, 36–37, 45
Freud, Sigmund, 182, 201, 221, 288
Frick, Henry Clay, 167
Fries, Amos, 192
Fromm, Erich, 172–73, 289
Frost, Robert, 188
Fuchs, Klaus, 296
Fulbright, J. William, 349–50

Gabler, Mel, 374
Gabler, Norma, 374
Gaddis, John Lewis, 260
Gadhafi, Moammar, 381
Gadsden Purchase (1853), 108
Gaither, H. Rowan, 331
Galbraith, John Kenneth, 306, 347
Gallatin, Albert, 33
Gallup, George, 197, 198, 237, 289
Gallup polls, 210, 226, 236, 244, 252,
 253, 260, 262, 276, 277, 314, 316,
 321, 335–36, 362
Galsworthy, John, 144
Garfield, James A., 132
Garner, John, 203, 204
Garrison, William Lloyd, 127
Gavin, James, 349
Gazette of the United States, 27
General Electric, 324
General Motors, 199
Genet, Edmond, 29–30, 32
Genghis Khan, 220
George III, King of England, 24, 28,
 65
German-Americans, 201
 World War I and, 145–46, 149, 177,
  231
German Democratic Republic, 285

German Federal Republic, 262, 294,
 364, 388
 rearmament of, 293, 294, 310
Germania-Herold, 149
German Republican Society of
 Philadelphia, 33
Germany, 252, 258
 division of, 365
Germany, Imperial, 114, 135, 142,
 170, 201
 Versailles Treaty and, 175–76
 in World War I, 143–45, 147–56,
 160–62, 164, 165
Germany, Nazi, 208–9, 225, 250, 288,
 295, 301, 320
 aggression of, leading to World War
 II, 196, 197–98, 199, 204–5
 American fifth column and, 277,
 278
 appeasement of, 187–204; *see also*
 appeasement era
 atrocities of, 231–32, 242–43, 294,
 299
 danger of, perceived by FDR, 194–
 195
 Hitler-Stalin Pact and, 236–37, 239
 in North Atlantic fighting, 212–14
 propaganda against, 229–30, 231–34
 propaganda campaigns of, 220, 223
 reputed plans of, for Western
 Hemisphere, 214
 war declared on U.S. by, 215, 219
 see also Hitler, Adolf; World War II
Germany, Weimar, 172
Gerry, Elbridge, 46, 50
Ghent, Treaty of (1814), 68
GI Bill of Rights, 326
Gibson, Charles Dana, 159
Ginsberg, Benjamin, 74
Godfrey, Arthur, 324–25
Godkin, E. L., 120, 136
Goebbels, Joseph, 217, 277, 344
Goering, Hermann, 199
Goldmann, Nahum, 243
Goldstein, Robert, 159
Goldwater, Barry, 337, 338, 339, 369
Gompers, Samuel, 131, 185
Goodwin, William J., 200
Gorbachev, Mikhail, 394, 408
Gordon, Lincoln, 382
government:
 changed by World War II, 216–17
 distrust of, 192, 353
 expanded in Eisenhower era, 326
 growth in spending by, 357

Graebner, Norman, 93
Graham, Catherine Macauly, 26
Graham, Rev. Billy, 299, 300
Grant, Ulysses S., 104, 111
Great Britain, 18, 46, 76, 91, 96, 98,
 107–10, 112, 114, 116, 125, 135,
 142, 166, 190, 199, 235, 277, 293,
 357, 388, 406
 American sailors impressed by, 59,
 64, 66, 68
 American ships seized by, 28, 59–
 60, 62, 63–64, 66, 67
 animosity toward, in late nineteenth
 century, 121, 122–25
 in appeasement era, 194, 195, 197
 destroyer swap with, 208–10
 in effort to crush French
 Revolution, 28–32
 Greek insurgency and, 266, 268
 Indians and, 30, 61, 64, 75, 83
 Irish struggle against, 47, 177
 Jackson and, 81, 82
 Jay Treaty with, 39–43, 45, 78, 177
 Napoleonic wars and, 59–67, 68
 Oregon and, 93–94
 postwar order and, 251, 255, 256,
 259, 405
 propaganda to generate support for,
 235
 secret military operations of, in
 Soviet Union, 327–28
 U.S. Civil War and, 109, 122
 U.S. relations with, in earliest days
 of Republic, 24–32, 34–43, 45, 52,
 54–56, 59
 Venezuela–British Guiana border
 dispute and, 122, 124–125
 War of 1812 and, 59–69
 in World War I, 144, 147–51, 155,
 156, 159, 161, 164, 187, 242
 in World War II, 189, 203, 205, 206,
 208–10, 212–13, 214, 228, 233,
 235, 237, 243, 403
Great Dictator, The, 232
Great Illusion, The (Angell), 141
Great Society, 338, 339
Greece, 127, 273, 312
 insurgency in, 266–69, 270
Greeley, Horace, 100, 101, 129
Greer, 214
Gregory, Thomas Watt, 174
Grenada invasion (1983), 383–84
Grenville, William, Lord, 40
Grew, Joseph, 258
Grey, Sir Edward, 142, 144, 148, 152

group narcissism, 172–73
Groves, Leslie, 296
Gruening, Ernest, 338
Gruson, Sydney, 330
Guam, 136, 137, 249
Guatemala:
  coup in (1954), 329–30
  Cuban exiles trained in, 333
Gunga Din, 235

Haig, Alexander, 369, 376, 377, 382
Haiti, 56, 190
Halberstam, David, 355
Haldeman, Isaac M., 176
Hale, William Bayard, 141–42, 150–51
Hallin, Daniel, 344–45
Halsey, William, 230
Hamilton, Alexander, 16–17, 34, 36,
    45–49, 55, 78, 82, 112, 174
  French Revolution and, 27–30
  ideology of, 25, 35, 37–38, 39
  Jay Treaty and, 40–42
  Jefferson's conflict with, 37–38
Hammond, George, 29
Hand, Learned, 175
Hanna, Mark, 205
Harding, Warren G., 165, 168, 181–
    182, 272
Harman, Sidney, 404
Harper's, 113, 305
Harriman, W. Averell, 254, 255–56,
    258, 259, 261, 272, 278, 279, 309,
    319, 405
Harrison, Benjamin, 116, 124, 136
Harrison, William Henry, 64
Harris polls, 363, 364, 377
Harsch, Joseph, 308
Harvard University, 68, 125, 127, 136,
    302, 342
Harvey, George, 164, 177
Harvey's Weekly, 164, 177
Hastings, Philip, 321
Hatch, Orrin, 360
Hawaiian Islands, 108, 109, 112, 114,
    121
  annexed by McKinley, 136–37
  planters' scheme for annexation of,
    115–17
Hawthorne, Nathaniel, 75, 99, 108
Hay, John, 125, 135
Hays Office, 232–34
Hearst, William Randolph, 128, 129,
    134, 191, 300
Heatter, Gabriel, 225
Helvétius, Claude-Adrien, 44

Hemingway, Ernest, 187, 191
Henry, John, 65
Henry, Patrick, 34
Herberg, Will, 299
Hershey, Lewis B., 234
Hill, Isaac, 77
Hiroshima bombing, 188, 264–65, 289,
    295, 314, 390
Hiroshima Maidens, 390
Hiss, Alger, 274, 292
History of the American People
    (Wilson), 181
History of the United States (Adams),
    67
history textbooks, 373–74
Hitchcock, Ethan Allen, 96
Hitler, Adolf, 150, 182, 189, 197–206,
    208, 209, 212–14, 229, 232, 233,
    240, 242, 272, 288, 291, 308, 403
  campaign to alert Americans to
    danger of, 205–7
  danger of, perceived by FDR, 194–
    195
  Johnson compared to, 347
  propaganda campaigns of, 172, 188,
    217, 223, 274, 277, 278
  public misperception of, 187–88
  Soviet Union invaded by, 236, 237
  Stalin compared to, 236, 237, 238–
    239, 275, 305
  war declared on U.S. by, 215, 219
Hitler-Stalin Pact (1939), 236–37, 239
Hobsbawm, Eric, 74
Ho Chi Minh, 336
Hodgkinson, John, 28
Hollywood, 292, 388–89
  anti-Communism and, 303–4, 369
  World War II and, 230, 232–34, 235,
    238–39
  see also films
Hollywood Ten, 303
Holocaust, 232, 242–43, 294, 299
Hook, Sidney, 305, 306, 307
Hoover, Herbert, 181, 217, 257, 262,
    291
Hoover, J. Edgar, 273–76, 277, 298
Hopkins, Harry, 195, 203, 215
House, Edward, 142, 143, 145, 146,
    149, 151, 153, 155, 183, 194, 196
House of Morgan, 187, 203
House of Representatives, U.S., 31,
    40, 55, 62, 67, 86, 97, 136, 171,
    212, 218, 219, 262, 272, 313, 314,
    327, 342, 353, 382–83
  Alaska acquisition and, 110–11

House of Representatives, U.S. (*cont.*)
  Appropriation Committee, 171
  Foreign Affairs Committee, 103
  Judiciary Committee, 198
  military spending and, 286, 287
  Un-American Activities Committee
    (HUAC), 274–75, 279, 303
  see also Congress, U.S.; Senate,
    U.S.
Howard, Roy, 278
Howard, Sidney, 192–93
How Democracies Perish (Revel), 188
Howe, Julia Ward, 127, 129
How We Advertised America, 158
Hughes, Charles Evans, 154, 155, 181
Hughes, Emmet John, 319
Hulcy, D. A., 297
Hull, Cordell, 195, 198, 203, 204, 211,
    235
Human Nature and Politics (Wallis),
    221
human rights concerns, 294, 329, 358,
    364, 367, 385
  Cuban revolution and, 127, 128–
    129, 131–32
Humphrey, Hubert, 306
Humphreys, Robert, 319
Hungary, 267, 301
  revolution in (1848), 105–6
Huntington, Samuel, 343, 354, 407
Hutcheson, Francis, 44
Hutchins, Robert, 201, 207
hydrogen bomb, 327
  see also nuclear weapons

Ickes, Harold, 189, 213, 215, 223, 272,
    273
Ikle, Fred, 377
Illinois State Register, 103
immigrants, 80, 146, 386
  German, 145–46, 149, 177, 201, 231
  Irish, 47, 122–23, 155, 176–77
  Japanese, 230
  nativism and, 168–69, 191–92
  radical movements and, 170–72, 185
  Versailles Treaty opposed by, 176–
    177
  Wilsonian vision rejected by, 184
Imperial Democracy (May), 112–13
imperialism, 111–17, 122, 126, 128,
    138, 175, 235
  democratic ideals and, 112, 136
  domestic conflicts defused by, 119–
    122
  enthusiasts of, 113–14

Hawaiian Islands annexation
    scheme and, 115–17
  national security and, 114–15
  pressures of mass opinion in, 112–
    113, 114
  Venezuela–British Guiana border
    dispute and, 122, 124–25
  see also expansionism
impressment, 59, 64, 66, 68
Independent Gazetteer, 42
India, 41, 119
Indian Bureau, 87
Indians (Native Americans), 24, 34,
    39, 45, 48, 52–53, 58, 82–91, 98,
    373
  British and, 30, 61, 64, 75, 83
  in colonial period, 82–83
  confused legal status of, 85
  expansionism and, 81, 82–91
  in Federalist era, 83–85
  images of, 82, 88–89
  in Jacksonian era, 82, 83, 85–91
  Jackson's Florida campaign and, 75,
    76
  marshaling public support for
    removal of, 87–88
  political opposition to removal of,
    86–87, 89–90
  separatist movement among, 64
  slavery issue compared to, 91
individualism, 79, 290
Indonesia, 328
industrialization, 118–19, 121–22
inflation, 357, 358, 361, 363–64, 368
intellectuals:
  in Cold War, 304–7
  Korean War and, 317
  in 1930s, 304–5
intermediate-range missiles, 387, 394,
    396
International Monetary Fund (IMF),
    274
International Review, 165
International Socialist Review, 158
International Workers of the World
    (IWW) (Wobblies), 170, 184, 185,
    192
Iran, 260, 312, 356, 361, 372
  hostage crisis in, 14, 361, 363, 368,
    378
  Mossadegh affair in, 328–29
Iran-Contra scandal, 14, 344, 378, 387
Ireland, 47, 159, 166
Irish-Americans, 47, 122–23, 155,
    176–77

Irving, Washington, 61
isolationism, 146, 182, 189–90, 270
  in appeasement era, 191, 193, 197–202, 204
  Asia-only, 207, 316
  conservative, 200, 262
  defeatism and, 199–200
  Fortress America policy and, 291
  of Left, 200
  in mid-1970s, 362–63, 364
  of New Dealers, 200–201
  after outbreak of World War II, 206, 207–8, 209, 211, 212, 213, 214, 231, 232, 236–37
  in post-Revolutionary period, 25–26
  in post–World War II period, 252, 253, 256, 262
  in Taft's 1952 campaign, 317–18
  see also pacifism
Israel, 18, 282
Italian-Americans, 177
Italy, 251, 388
  fascist regime in, 187, 195, 196
  Communism in, 271, 277, 292, 356
  in World War I, 164, 177
I Was a Communist for the FBI, 304

Jackson, Andrew, 52–53, 75–91, 101, 111
  expansionist vision of, 81
  Farewell Address of, 90
  foreign policy issues and, 81–82
  inauguration of, 78–79, 80
  Indian removal and, 82, 83, 85–91
  military career of, 75–76, 83
  in presidential elections, 76, 77, 83, 86, 87, 89–90
  press network of, 79–80
  purchase of Texas attempted by, 94
  War of 1812 and, 65, 67, 68
Jackson, C. D., 320
Jackson, Francis James, 62
Jackson, Robert, 234
Jacobin Club, 35
Jacobson, Eddie, 282
James, William, 124–25, 127–28, 137
Janka, Leslie, 379
Japan, 135, 143, 186, 196, 242, 250, 311, 351, 363, 364, 400
  atomic bomb dropped on, 188, 264–265, 289, 295, 314, 390
  China occupied by, 194, 195, 201, 207
  FDR's desire to go to war with, 214–215

Hawaiian Islands acquisition and, 116, 136
  intensity of feelings against, 230–31, 232
  occupation of, 249
  Pearl Harbor attacked by, 98, 188, 189, 190, 212, 215, 218, 219, 224, 230, 231, 251, 331
  propaganda against, 229–31
  propaganda campaigns of, 201, 228, 277
Japanese-Americans, 230
Jay, John, 39–40
Jay Treaty (1794), 39–43, 45, 78, 177
Jefferson, Thomas, 24–30, 40, 46, 47, 49, 50, 52–59, 62, 64, 74, 76, 81, 107, 159, 184, 221, 288, 306, 410
  Barbary pirates and, 39
  French Revolution and, 26–30, 32
  Hamilton's conflict with, 37–38
  ideology of, 25, 35, 37–38, 53–54
  Indians and, 83–84
  involvement in European wars opposed by, 38, 52, 55
  Louisiana Purchase and, 56–59, 84, 210
  Napoleonic wars and, 60–61
  press and, 36
  War of 1812 and, 66–67, 68
  western frontier and, 53–54, 55
Jenner, William, 311
Jensen, Richard, 117
Jersey Chronicle, 43
Jews, 185, 201, 202, 244, 282, 385
  plight of, in World War II, 207–8, 232, 242–43
  see also anti-Semitism
jingoism, 99–100, 127, 130, 172
John Paul II, Pope, 382
Johnson, Edwin C., 249
Johnson, Hiram, 166, 178, 179
Johnson, Louis, 287
Johnson, Lyndon B., 14, 61, 255, 306, 331, 354, 360
  credibility gap of, 341
  domestic policy of, 338, 339
  in election of 1964, 337–38
  in election of 1968, 348–49, 351
  Vietnam War and, 12–13, 317, 336, 337–43, 345–51, 365–66, 367, 377, 404–5
Johnston, Eric, 296
Joint Army-Navy Board, 223
Joint Chiefs of Staff, 260, 275, 323, 387

Joint Chiefs of Staff (*cont.*)
  Korean War and, 308, 311, 312, 314
Jones, John Paul, 39
Jones, Joseph, 266–67
Jordan, Winthrop, 83
Josselson, Michel, 307
Journal des Débats, 113
Justice Department, U.S., 158, 171,
  174, 192, 234, 279–80

KAL 007 incident (1983), 382–83
Kaltenborn, H. V., 224, 264
Kant, Immanuel, 167
Karp, Walter, 118, 352
Kaufman, Irving, 296
Kearny, 214
Kearny, Stephen, 101
Kefauver, Estes, 319
Kellogg-Briand Pact (1928), 191
Kelly, Ignatius, 240
Kendall, Amos, 79
Kennan, George, 238, 254, 279, 285,
  349
  alarmist prose of, 261–62
  Korean War and, 308–9
  strident anti-Communism opposed
    by, 269, 271, 281, 293
Kennedy, Edward, 368
Kennedy, John F., 332–37, 367, 369,
  380, 404
  Bay of Pigs invasion and, 332, 334
  civil defense program of, 390–91
  in election of 1960, 93, 332, 335
  Inaugural Address of, 332
  as master of television, 335–36
  permissive public mood and, 333
  Vietnam War and, 336, 337, 341,
    345
Kennedy, Joseph P., 291
Kerr, Walter, 240
Keynes, John Maynard, 176
Keyserling, Leon, 287
Keyworth, George, 395
KGB, 328, 382
Khomeini, Ayatollah, 14
Khrushchev, Nikita, 188, 294, 324, 331
King, Martin Luther, Jr., 346, 350
Kipling, Rudyard, 144
Kirkpatrick, Jeane, 377, 381
Kissinger, Henry, 331, 356, 358–59,
  361, 363, 368
  nuclear strategy and, 389–90
Kitchen Cabinet, 79
Knights of the Golden Circle, 106
Knowland, William, 328

Know-Nothing Party, 168–69
Knox, Frank, 189, 213, 223
Knox, Henry, 50, 85
Koch, Howard, 238
Koestler, Arthur, 306
Koppes, Clayton, 232
Korean War, 97, 102, 296, 307, 308–
  315, 330, 339
  atomic bomb considered in, 314
  Chinese intervention in, 301, 313–
    314, 315, 316
  crossing of the 38th parallel in, 311–
    313
  election of 1952 and, 317–21
  ending of, 316, 322
  as political opportunity for Truman
    administration, 308
  public opinion in, 14, 308–9, 313,
    314, 315, 316–17, 321
  U.S. military setbacks in, 309, 311,
    313–14
Kornbluh, Peter, 385
Kossuth, Louis, 106
Kriesberg, Martin, 289
Krock, Arthur, 270

Labor League of Hollywood Voters,
  303
labor movement, 119, 184–85, 192,
  225
  Cold War and, 297–99, 303
  Communists in, 242, 277, 292, 297,
    298–99
Ladies' Home Journal, 240
LaFeber, Walter, 108
La Guardia, Fiorello H., 177, 223,
  224, 240
Lambert, Gerard, 321
Lamont, Thomas, 239
Lane, Franklin K., 173
Lansing, Robert, 143, 147, 170, 179,
  180
Lasch, Christopher, 307
Lasky, Melvin, 307
Lasswell, Harold, 221–22, 226–27,
  288–89
Late Great Planet Earth, The
  (Lindsey), 389
League for the Preservation of
  American Independence, 177
League of Free Nations Association,
  175
League of Nations, 163–85, 190–91,
  202, 260, 264–66, 270–71
  American identity and, 184

Article X and, 166, 176, 180, 181, 183
and breakup of political coalition, 184
election of 1920 and, 181–82
history of idea for, 144, 146, 167–68
lessons drawn from rejection of, 182
liberals' views on, 175–76
postwar xenophobia and, 168–74
psychohistorians' analyses of, 182
public opinion on, 167, 168, 177–78, 179, 180, 182–83
Senate vote on, 165–67, 174–75, 177, 178–79, 180–81, 183
separation of powers and, 183
League of Nations Association, 205
League of Women Voters, 174
League to Enforce Peace, 153, 167
Leahy, Francis, 195, 230
Lee, Ivy, 222
Lehrer, Tom, 324
LeMay, Curtis, 324, 389
Lend-Lease program, 212, 257
L'Enfant, Pierre Charles, 74
Lenin, V. I., 114, 173, 293, 347
Lewis, John L., 298
Lewis, Meriwether, 84
Liberty Bonds, 172, 161
Liebman, Rabbi Joshua Loth, 299
Life, 153, 225, 227, 233, 238, 241–42, 244, 300, 306, 318–19, 391
"Life Is Worth Living," 299–300
Lifton, Robert, 392
Lilienthal, David, 276
Liliuokalani, Queen of Hawaii, 115
Lincoln, Abraham, 75, 97, 103, 118, 131, 178, 183, 184
expansionism and, 108–9
war-making power and, 104–5
Lincoln, Levi, 58
Lindbergh, Charles A., 199–200, 206, 208, 218
Lindsey, Hal, 389
Link, Arthur S., 156
Lippmann, Walter, 73, 183, 260, 269–270, 284, 308, 312, 412
on democracies, 188, 288, 404, 410
on public opinion, 15–16, 221, 355, 402, 404
Literary Digest, 168, 171, 196–97
Little Sarah, 32
Litvinov, Maksim, 239
Livingston, Robert, 55, 56, 57
Lloyd George, David, 164, 190
Locke, John, 33, 44

Lodge, Henry Cabot, 149
imperialism and, 117, 120, 122–25, 134
League of Nations and, 165, 166, 167, 168, 174, 177, 180, 181
as Wilson's archantagonist, 165–66, 182
World War I and, 156–57
Logan, George, 49–50
Lonely Crowd, The (Riesman), 290
Long, Breckinridge, 207–8
Long, Russell, 349
Longfellow, Henry Wadsworth, 90
Longworth, Alice Roosevelt, 165
Los Angeles *Examiner*, 300
Los Angeles *Mirror*, 333
Los Angeles Times, 180
Louis XVI, King of France, 27–28, 30
Louisiana, 24, 30, 45, 52, 54, 55
Indians relocated to, 84–91
purchase of, 56–59, 68, 84, 110, 210
L'Ouverture, Toussaint, 56
Love, Kennett, 329
Lovett, Robert A., 240, 254, 279, 291, 315
Lowell, A. Lawrence, 167
Lowell, James Russell, 102
Lowell, John, 68
Lowell, Robert, 341
loyalty oaths, 279, 283, 297, 302, 303
Luce, Clare Boothe, 189, 300
Luce, Henry, 206, 209, 227, 288, 296, 300, 310, 344
Ludlow Amendment, 198–99
Ludwig III, King of Bavaria, 145
Lusitania, 148–49, 150
Lyons, Eugene, 236

McAdoo, William G., 151
MacArthur, Arthur, 137
MacArthur, Douglas, 137, 231, 249, 339
dismissal of, 314–15, 316
in Korean War, 308–15
McCann, Thomas, 330
McCarthy, Eugene, 348–49
McCarthy, Joseph R., 290, 292–93, 302, 322, 327, 330
Korean War and, 308, 309, 310
McCarthyism, 172, 192, 292–93, 302, 322, 346
McCloy, John J., 152, 243, 254, 274, 310, 315
McCullers, Carson, 306
MacFadden, Bernarr, 120

McFarlane, Robert, 378, 385, 395
McGovern, George, 348, 368
McKean, Thomas, 49
McKenney, Thomas L., 87–88
McKinley, William, 61, 113, 122
  in election of 1900, 137–38
  Hawaiian Islands annexed by, 136–137
  Philippine insurgency and, 137
  presidential manner of, 126
  press relations of, 126, 130
  Spanish-American War and, 126, 130–36
MacLeish, Archibald, 223, 224
McNamara, Robert S., 337, 341, 342, 394
McNarney, Joseph T., 249
McNaughton, John, 350
McNutt, Paul V., 230
Maddox, 338, 345
Madison, James, 27, 31, 32, 35, 36, 46, 56, 61–69, 74, 221
  ideology of, 61–62
  Jay Treaty and, 40, 41
  Neutrality Proclamation and, 28–29
  public contempt for, 63
  War of 1812 and, 54, 61
Mahan, Alfred, 113, 134
Mahon, George, 287
Mailer, Norman, 347, 348
Main, Jackson, 35
Maine, 132
Manifest Destiny, 81, 99–100, 105, 112, 115, 120, 136
Manifest Destiny and Mission (Merk), 103
Mao Tse-tung, 285, 309, 313, 331
March of Freedom, The, 98
Marcuse, Herbert, 347
Marie Antoinette, Queen of France, 30
Marine Corps, U.S., 222, 225, 383
Marshall, C. B., 312
Marshall, George C., 137, 241, 271, 278, 281, 282, 283, 312
  Truman Doctrine and, 267–68, 269
Marshall, John, 67–68, 89
Marshall Plan (European Recovery Program), 267, 269–73, 277, 279–280, 281, 297, 311
Martin, Joseph, 272, 273, 314, 316
Martineau, Harriet, 78, 79, 80, 100, 290
Marx, Karl, 112, 129
Marxism, 175, 244, 347

Masaryk, Jan, 281
Mason, Stevens Thomson, 41
Massachusetts Bay Colony, 82
mass culture, 220, 233, 290
Masses, 158
massive retaliation doctrine, 318, 389
"mass opinion," 402–3
Mather, Increase, 26
Matthews, Francis P., 297
Maxim, Hudson, 152–53
May, Ernest, 112–13, 126, 127, 135
Mayer, Louis B., 303
Mead, Margaret, 226
Meany, George, 242
media:
  attacked in 1970s, 379
  in Cold War, 302–4
  global communications and, 406–7
  manipulated by Reagan White House, 379–83, 385
  see also press; television
Mellett, Lowell, 234, 235
Mellon, Andrew, 167
Melville, Herman, 98, 102
Menjou, Adolphe, 303
Menken, S. Stanwood, 174
Mennonites, 117
Merk, Frederick, 102–3, 110
Mexican War, 96–105, 350
  antiwar faction and, 97–98, 100–102
  declaration of war in, 97
  events leading to, 93, 94–97, 98, 100, 101
  legacy of, 104–5
  national identity and, 100–101
  peace treaty in, 104
  public opinion in, 98–99, 102–3, 104
  territories annexed in, 101, 104, 106
Mexico, 45, 47, 81, 107, 108, 112, 136, 166, 194,
  reputed German operations in, 156, 214, 320
  revolution in (1910), 144, 293
Meyers, Marvin, 77
MGM, 235
Michigan, University of, 340, 353
Middle East, 18, 268, 282, 319, 364
Midway Islands, 110
Military Review, 340
military spending, 14–15, 216, 219, 286–87, 298, 315, 332, 354, 355, 362, 365, 389, 392
  under Adams, 47–49
  under Eisenhower, 324, 331
  under Reagan, 370–71, 388

Miller, Francis, 209
Millis, Walter, 186–87, 209
Mindszenty, József Cardinal, 301
missile gap (1950s), 332
missionaries, Indian removal and, 86, 87–88, 89–90
Mission to Moscow (Davies), 238–39
Mississippi River, 34, 41, 45, 52, 53, 55
Modern Arms and Free Men, 316
Mohammad Reza Pahlavi (Shah of Iran), 329
Molotov, V. M., 274, 282
    second front issue and, 240–41
    Truman's belligerence toward, 259
Mondale, Walter ("Fritz"), 374
Monroe, James, 26, 54, 65, 75
    Indian removal and, 84–85
    in Paris peace mission, 55, 56, 57
    War of 1812 and, 66–67
Monroe Doctrine, 92, 94, 108, 122, 124, 376
Montesquieu, Charles-Louis de Secondat, Baron de la Brède et de, 44, 54
Montgomery, Robert, 335
Moral Majority, 373
Morgan, Edmund S., 44, 73
Morgan, J. P., 130, 150, 151–52, 171
Morgenthau, Henry, Jr., 195, 213, 243
Morison, Samuel Eliot, 41, 42, 45, 68, 80
Morris, Gouverneur, 30, 57
Morrison, Norman, 342
Morse, Jedidiah, 127
Morse, Wayne, 338
Mossadegh, Mohammed, 328–29
Motion Picture Alliance for the Preservation of American Ideals, 303
Motion Picture Industrial Council, 303
Mott, John, 116
Moultrie, William, 31
Moyers, Bill, 335
Moynihan, Patrick, 364
Mrs. Miniver, 235
Munich Pact (1938), 188, 197, 203
municipalities, foreign policy roles assumed by, 411–12
Münter, Erich, 151–52
Murphy, George, 303
Murray, Philip, 298
Murray, William Vans, 29
Murrow, Edward R., 206
Mussolini, Benito, 232

Nagasaki bombing, 264–65, 295
Napoleon I, Emperor of France, 37, 53–59, 67, 68, 74, 84, 134
    Louisiana sold by, 56–59
    Madison misled by, 62–63, 65
Napoleonic wars, 59–67, 68, 406
    British blockade of France in, 59
    congressional hawks and, 64
    impressment of American sailors in, 59, 64, 66, 68
    seizures of American ships in, 59–60, 62–64, 66, 67
    U.S. embargo in, 60–61, 66
    War of 1812 and, 59–61, 62–67
Nation, 176
National Association of Manufacturers (NAM), 297
National Clay Products Industries Association, 185
National Committee of Soviet-American Friendship, 244
National Council of Churches, 301, 360
National Defense Act (1916), 154
National Defense University, 384
National Education Association, 302
National Gazette, 27, 36
National German-American Alliance, 145
National Grange, 191
National Intelligencer, 59
nationalism, 92–93, 103, 105–6, 172, 184, 185
    Jacksonian, 80
    "new," 363, 370
    patriotism vs., 376
    Reagan and, 370, 371
    of recent immigrants, 184
    superpatriotism and, 172–74
    Trilateral Commission and, 359–360
National Protective Society, 153
national security, 11, 188, 212, 216, 217, 355, 356, 360
    Eisenhower's policy of, 322–25, 327–28, 331, 333
    and exemption from political scrutiny, 13–14
    imperialism and, 114–15
    premises of, challenged by antiwar movement, 341
    Reagan's rhetoric and, 370, 371
    shift in public opinion on (1964–80), 362–63
National Security Act (1947), 384

National Security Council (NSC), 265, 278, 377, 384
National Security Directive, 77, 384
National Security League, 153, 173, 174, 185
Nation's Business, 296
Native American Party, 168–69
Native Americans, *see* Indians
nativism, 168–69, 191–92
Navy, U.S., 31, 39, 47–48, 63, 66, 137, 152, 153, 193–94, 195, 198, 208, 213, 214, 224, 250
Navy League, 153
NBC, 336
"Negroes and the War," 228
Nelson, Donald, 296
neoconservatives, 16, 370, 372
Netherlands, 277
Neutrality Act (1935), 195, 213, 214
  "cash and carry" amendment to, 203–4, 205
Neutrality Proclamation (1793), 28–29, 31, 32
Nevins, Allan, 36, 230
New Deal, 202, 203, 216, 218, 219, 222, 227, 228, 236, 239, 257, 273, 276, 280, 292, 296, 297, 298, 325
  isolationism and, 200–201
New Frontier, 332
New Hampshire Patriot, 77
New Left, 342, 351
New Look, 324, 331
New Mexico, 101, 104, 108, 136, 156
"new nationalism," 363, 370
New Orleans, 52, 54–56, 57
  battle of (1814), 68, 75
New Patriotism, 372–76
New Republic, 174, 175–76, 304, 305
Newsweek, 330, 365
New York Board for the Emigration, Preservation, and Improvement of the Aborigines of America, 87
New York Chamber of Commerce, 125
New York *Daily News*, 237
New York Democratic Society, 33
New Yorker, 305
New-Yorker Staats-Zeitung, 145
New York *Evening Post*, 116, 120
New York Herald, 102, 105
New York Herald Tribune, 206
New York *Journal*, 128, 129, 132, 134
New York *Journal of Commerce*, 98, 125
New York Stock Exchange, 364

New York *Sun*, 102, 127, 134
New York Times, 175, 238, 264, 279, 308, 352, 363, 383, 393
  covert operations and, 329, 330, 333
  Vietnam War and, 317, 344, 345
  World War I and, 141–42, 145, 150–151
  World War II and, 241–42, 243, 252
New York Tribune, 100, 101, 108, 115, 120, 121, 129
New York *World*, 123, 128, 132, 133, 146, 151
Nguyen Ngoc Loan, 342
Nicaragua, 107, 267, 361, 377, 381, 382
  Contra war in, 378, 385, 386, 387, 411
Nicholas, Wilson Cary, 57
Nicholson, Commodore, 29
Niebuhr, Reinhold, 306
Niemöller, Pastor, 233
Niles, David, 226, 243
Niles' Weekly Register, 75–76
Nineteen Eighty-Four (Orwell), 288
1919 (Dos Passos), 191
Nitze, Paul, 285–86, 287, 312, 368
Nixon, Richard M., 360, 367, 369, 379, 404
  in election of 1960, 332
  in election of 1968, 350, 351
  international diplomacy of, 354, 358, 363, 365, 366
  nuclear weapons and, 391–92
  Vietnam War and, 13, 14, 340, 343, 350, 351, 354–55, 366
  Watergate and, 343–44, 351, 352, 367, 387
Non-Partisan Committee for Peace through Revision of the Neutrality Act, 205
Norris, Chuck, 375
Norris, Kathleen, 157
North, Oliver, 384
North American Review, 88, 114
North Atlantic Treaty Organization (NATO), 256, 318, 324, 356, 364, 387, 405
Northwest Territory, 39–40, 48
Norton, Charles Eliot, 136
Norway, 208
"Notes on the Next War" (Hemingway), 187
Notes on the State of Virginia (Jefferson), 83–84
Noyes, David, 283

NSAM, 328, 345
NSC 4, 278
NSC 30, 265
NSC 34, 309
NSC 68, 285–86, 287, 291, 308, 322
nuclear energy, 324, 393
Nuclear Test Ban Treaty (1963), 390
nuclear war, 13, 14, 358, 392–93, 396
nuclear weapons, 182, 275, 281, 292,
    322–25, 387–97, 412
  arms control and, 323, 330, 365,
    366, 368, 383, 391, 392, 395
  arms race and, 266, 322–23, 363,
    371, 388, 389, 390, 392, 394, 400,
    403
  buildup of, 322, 324, 327, 388,
    392
  campaign to make Americans
    comfortable with, 324–25
  civil defense and, 331, 390–91, 392
  in Cold War, 264–66, 267, 270–71,
    281, 285, 286, 289–90, 291, 294–
    296, 301, 322–25
  Cold War hysteria related to fear of,
    294–96
  deterrence doctrine and, 14, 256,
    264, 265–66, 267, 318, 324, 389,
    390, 394, 395, 396, 405
  disarmament and, 278, 295, 327,
    359, 396
  Eisenhower's views on, 322–23
  Great Denial era and, 392, 393
  Korean War and, 314
  massive retaliation doctrine and,
    318, 389
  NSC 30 and, 365
  Operation Candor and, 323, 324
  opposition to, 381, 390–97; see also
    antinuclear movement
  postwar order and, 252, 255, 258,
    260
  public opinion on, 266, 267, 289–90,
    335–36, 362, 370, 388–97, 399,
    402, 403–4
  Reagan's policy on, 378, 387–88,
    392–97
  SDI and, 395–96
  secrecy and obfuscation
    surrounding, 400
  of Soviets, 285, 286, 291, 296, 316,
    365, 366, 368, 371, 403
  testing of, 323–24, 327, 336, 340–41,
    390
  Vietnam War and, 323, 337, 339,
    343, 365–66, 389

  in World War II, 188, 241, 242, 254,
    264–65, 289, 295, 314, 390
Nuclear Weapons and Foreign Policy
    (Kissinger), 389–90
Nye, Gerald, 232
Nye Committee, 151, 187

Observations Concerning the Increase
    of Mankind (Franklin), 54
Ochs, Adolph, 142, 145
Office of Facts and Figures, 224,
    226
Office of Government Reports, 223
Office of War Information (OWI),
    224–29, 234, 242
  domestic pamphlet program of,
    228–29
  film industry and, 229, 235, 239
  ideology of, 228
  Republicans' attacks on, 228
Ohio River, 45
oil, 268, 269, 282, 356, 358, 361, 364
  energy crisis of 1970s and, 360–61,
    363, 372, 393
  Mossadegh's nationalization of,
    328–29
Oklahoma, University of, 302
O'Leary, Jeremiah, 155
Olney, Richard, 122
Olympics (1984), 374
One World (Willkie), 227
Operation Ajax, 329
Operation Candor, 323, 324
Operation Success, 329
"opinion leaders," 12, 305, 350, 363,
    410
Oppenheimer, J. Robert, 388
Oregon, 81, 93–94, 103
Orlando, Vittorio, 164
Ortega y Gasset, José, 288
Orwell, George, 288, 375–76
Oscar II, 150
Osceola, 89
Ostend Manifesto, 108
O'Sullivan, John, 99, 103
Otto, Louis-Guillaume, 59
Ottoman Empire, 127
Our Country (Strong), 113
Our Friend the Atom, 324

pacifism, 117, 185, 207, 301
  in democracies, 188
  in 1930s, 187–88, 191–93, 199
  World War I and, 141, 144, 149,
    150, 154, 156–57, 158, 176

pacifism (*cont.*)
　see also antiwar movement
　　(Vietnam era); isolationism; peace
　　movement
Packard, Vance, 347
Page, Walter Hines, 148, 149
Paine, Thomas, 25, 33, 46, 49, 371
Palestine, 282
Palmer, A. Mitchell, 171–72, 192
Panama Canal, 142, 360
Panay, 195, 198
panic of 1893, 119, 120
Papen, Franz von, 150
Paris Peace Conference (1918–19),
　163–64, 178–79, 190
　see also Versailles Treaty
Parkman, Francis, 89
Parliament, British, 73
Parran, Thomas, 222
Parry, Robert, 385
Partisan Review, 305
Patriotic Societies, 33
patriotism, 184–85, 413
　meaning of, as issue in Vietnam
　　era, 349
　nature of, changed by World War I,
　　174
　of Reagan era, 372–76
Patterson, Robert, 249, 278
Pauling, Linus, 340–41, 390
peace movement, 192, 195, 346, 347
　of 1980s, 383, 393–97
　in World War I, 150, 156–57
　see also antiwar movement
　　(Vietnam era); pacifism
Peace Ship, 150
Peale, Norman Vincent, 299
Pearl Harbor attack (1941), 98, 188,
　189, 190, 212, 218, 219, 230, 231,
　251, 331
　information withheld about, 224
　Magic intercepts and, 215
Pearson, Lester, 404–5
Pegler, Westbrook, 236
Pelley, William Dudley, 201
Pells, Richard, 306
penny press, 99–100, 129
Pentagon, 275, 286, 339, 371, 378, 381,
　384, 390
　demobilization after World War II
　　and, 249, 250
　postwar order and, 257, 258
　see also Defense Department, U.S.;
　　Joint Chiefs of Staff
People's Party, 119, 305

Perle, Richard, 388, 392
permanent mobilization, 14, 250, 251,
　256, 263, 285, 286–87
Persons, Stow, 73
Phantom Public, The (Lippmann), 288
Philadelphia *Daily Advertiser*, 28
Philadelphia *Inquirer*, 196
Philadelphia *Ledger*, 105
Philby, Kim, 328
Philippines, 113, 114, 249, 277, 358
　insurgency in, 128, 136, 137
　Spanish-American War and, 133–
　　134, 135, 136
Phillips, David Atlee, 333
Pierce, Franklin, 107–8
Pinchot, Amos, 200
Pinckney, Charles Cotesworth,
　45
Pinkney, William, 63
Pipes, Richard, 392
Pius XII, Pope, 301
Plain Words, 171
Plattsburgh Movement, 152
Pledge of Allegiance, 299
Podhoretz, Norman, 370
Poindexter (senator), 170
Poindexter, John M., 381, 385
Point Four Program, 267
Poland, 197–98, 204, 205, 267
　postwar order and, 257–58, 262
political action committees (PACs),
　353
political parties, 353
　formation of, 29
　in Jacksonian era, 76, 77
　newspapers' ties to, 99, 129
　in post-bellum period, 118
　radical, lack of, 304–5
　realignment of 1896 and, 121
　third parties and, 119
political societies, 33–36, 78
Polk, James K., 75, 93–94, 96–105
　election of, 93
　Oregon territory and, 93–94
　war with Mexico provoked by, 93,
　　96–97, 100, 101
Popular Front, 236, 298
popular sovereignty doctrine, 73–74
populism, 16, 69, 107, 113, 119, 122,
　123, 158, 288, 352, 409
Porcupine's Gazette, 46
Portugal, 46, 356
Postman, Neil, 344
postwar order (1940s), 227, 249–66,
　405

deterioration of U.S.-Soviet
relations and, 244, 245, 252, 257–
258, 259
isolationism and, 252, 253, 256, 262
public opinion and, 244, 251, 252,
253, 256, 260–61, 262, 263, 276,
277, 283
reconstruction aid and, 256–57,
262, 267–70, 271–72
U.S. as guiding power of, 255
U.S. military capability and, 250–
252, 257, 260, 264–66, 263
see also Cold War
Potomac Associates, 363
Power and Beauty of Superb
Womanhood, The (MacFadden),
120
Preparedness Parade (1916), 154
Presbyterian Banner, 135
presidents, 37, 47, 273
and collapse of imperial presidency,
352, 354
credibility of, 334, 335, 341, 344, 371
exemption from political scrutiny
sought by, 13–14
foreign policy as means to power
and prestige for, 183, 367
foreign policy as trap for, 14, 367–68
information withheld from
Congress by, 327
power of, over domestic vs. foreign
policy, 111
press relations of, 334–35
public opinion as constraint on, 196
public opinion as viewed by, 12
war-making power of, 13, 198–99
see also specific presidents
press, 98, 110, 191, 210, 226, 252, 371,
409
change in nature of (1890s), 129–30
covert operations and, 329, 330, 333
as instrument of foreign policy, 278
Jackson's relations with, 79–80
McKinley's relations with, 126, 130
market pressures and, 344
misinformed by Reagan
administration, 381–87
national security Establishment's
relations with, 335
penny, 99–100, 129
in post-Revolutionary period, 36–37
president's relations with, 334–35
Reagan's relations with, 379–80
Spanish-American War and, 127,
128–30, 131, 132, 134

"spin" and, 12, 344, 345, 380, 385
Third World politics and, 364–65
Vietnam War and, 342–45
World War I and, 144, 145, 148,
150, 151, 156, 157–59
World War II and, 206, 237
yellow, 128–30, 135
see also media; television; specific
publications
press conferences, 335, 344, 372
"preventive war," 290–91, 297
Proctor, Redfield, 132–33
Production Code, 232–33
Progressive Citizens' Association, 280
Progressive Movement, 152, 184, 251,
304
Progressive Party, 280, 282, 291
propaganda, 172, 185, 220–40, 329
in Cold War, 239, 278–81, 303–4,
315–16, 318
covert, under Reagan, 381–87
disillusionment with, 191–92
against Japan vs. Germany, 230–31
ministries of, 334
in morale building, 223–24
new social science and, 221–22
on nuclear energy, 324
presidential credibility and, 334
prohibited when aimed at U.S.
citizens, 384
in totalitarian societies, 220–21
in Vietnam War, 384
in World War I, 150–51, 159, 160–
162, 173–74, 187, 217, 223, 226,
227, 229, 231
in World War II, 188, 201, 207, 217,
222–40, 253, 274
Protestantism, 244, 299–300, 301, 322
expansionism and, 116–17
League of Nations and, 176
Providence Journal, 151
psychological warfare, 220, 224, 278
see also propaganda
psychopathology of politics, 288–89
"public judgment," 403
public opinion, 175
direct action and protests as
expressions of, 407
expert opinions vs., 402, 403–4
fathoming of, 17, 18; see also public
opinion polls
feelings of disempowerment and,
400–401
growing ease of popular
participation and, 406–7

public opinion (*cont.*)
    increase in impact of, 16, 399, 400
    irreconcilable goals and, 17
    knowledge and, 17–18, 288, 289–90, 401, 402, 409, 410–12, 413
    leaders' judgments inferior to, 355–356
    as legitimating principle of government, 11, 220–21
    in making of foreign policy, 11–19, 399–413
    "mass opinion" vs. "public judgment," 402–3
    modes of expression of, 12
    molding of, 12, 16, 18, 99, 399–400, 407, 409–10; *see also* propaganda
    moral or value judgments and, 407–408
    new social science and, 221, 288–89
    pessimism about, 287–90
    presidents constrained by, 196
    resistant to use of force, 356
    sophistication of techniques for handling of, 222
    veto power of, 15, 355
    vulnerable to mass manipulation, 289–90
    see also specific topics
public opinion polls, 18, 196–97, 210, 334, 357, 368, 370, 401, 403, 413
    in appeasement era, 196–98
    increased interest in (mid-1970s), 361–62
    Korean War and, 309, 313, 314, 315, 316, 317
    on lack of confidence in basic American institutions, 352–54
    in marketing of policies, 362
    mood shifts of 1970s and, 362–67
    on nuclear power plants, 393
    on nuclear weapons, 335–36, 362, 395, 403
    and pessimism about voice of people, 289–90
    in policy-making decisions, 243–44
    postwar order and, 252, 253, 260, 262, 283
    on Reagan, 377, 385–86
    on Vietnam War, 338, 339, 343, 346
    in World War II, 212, 226, 233, 234, 237, 243–44
Public Philosophy, The (Lippmann), 355
public relations, 222
Public Studies Division, 263–64

Puerto Rico, 109, 136, 137
Pulitzer, Joseph, 128
Pullman, George, 130
Puritans, 82–83

Quakers, 87, 117, 176
Quebec, 45

racism, 107, 136
    in anti-Japanese propaganda, 230–231
Rafshoon, Gerald, 361
Rambo, 374–75, 376
Randolph, Edmund, 41
Randolph, John, 64
Rankin (operation), 241
Rankin, Jeannette, 218
Rather, Dan, 344
Raymond, Walter, Jr., 384–85
Reader's Digest, 222, 233, 236, 237–38, 300, 306
Reagan, Ronald, 15, 75, 365, 368–97, 399, 405–6, 409
    and advantageous timing of administration, 378–80
    anti-Communism of, 303, 369
    Central America policy of, 376–78, 381–82, 384–86, 411
    conflicts within national security bureaucracy of, 369, 376, 377, 380
    domestic policy as focus of, 369
    in election of 1980, 368–69, 370, 379
    in election of 1984, 374, 396, 397
    Grenada invasion and, 383–84
    Iran-Contra scandal and, 14, 344, 378, 387
    Korean airliner incident and, 382–383
    misinformation campaigns of, 381–387
    new public mood created by, 371–376
    nuclear weapons policy of, 378, 387–88, 392–97
    Panama Canal Treaty opposed by, 360
    press conferences of, 372
    press relations of, 379–80
    public relations as overriding concern of, 378, 379–87
    rhetoric of, 381
    salesmanship of, 371–72
    secrecy in administration of, 385
    textbook reform and, 373–74

Reciprocal Trade Agreements
    Program, 272–73
Red Channels, 302
Red Network (Dilling), 273
Red Nightmare, 304
Red Scare (1919–20), 170–72, 185, 192
Reed, Daniel, 218
Reed, James A., 166, 172
John Reed Society, 305
Regan, Donald, 387
Regnery, William, 207
Reick, W. C., 133
Reid, Whitelaw, 130
religion, *see* churches; *specific
    denominations*
Remarque, Erich Maria, 191
Remington, Frederic, 128
Removal Act (1830), 87, 90
Republican Party, 26, 29, 31, 40, 41,
    43, 45, 46, 47, 55, 117, 123, 124,
    129, 130, 131, 146, 154, 165, 166,
    167, 181, 183, 184, 204, 205, 209,
    219, 222, 231, 236, 244, 276, 279,
    330–31
    bipartisan foreign policy and, 272–
        284
    election of 1946 and, 272, 274
    election of 1948 and, 283
    election of 1952 and, 317–19, 325
    imperialism and, 122
    industrialization and, 119, 121–22
    Korean War and, 309, 310, 311, 312,
        314
    Madison and, 64, 65, 66
    Marshall Plan and, 270, 281
    OWI attacked by, 228
    and politics of foreign adventure,
        119, 120, 122
Reston, James, 224, 270
Reuther, Walter, 298
Revel, Jean-François, 188
Review of Reviews, 115
Revolt of the Masses, The (Ortega y
    Gasset), 288
Revolutionary War, *see* American
    Revolution
Reykjavik summit (1986), 396
Reynolds, Quentin, 233
Ribbentrop, Joachim von, 239
Richmond *Dispatch*, 125–26
Richmond *Enquirer*, 98
Richmond Whig, 101
Ridgway, Matthew, 349
Riesman, David, 290, 347
Rinehart, Mary Roberts, 160

Rittenhouse, David, 33
Rivers, Mendel, 314
Rives, John C., 79
RKO, 235
Road to War (Millis), 186–87
Robinson, Bill, 323
Roche, John, 345–46
Rockefeller, David, 359
Rockefeller, John D., 130, 171, 222
Rockefeller, Nelson, 331, 332, 390–91
Rockwell, Norman, 229
Rocky Mountain News, 157
Rogin, Michael, 83
Rome, bombing of, 243–44
Roosevelt, Eleanor, 194, 195, 222,
    233, 306
Roosevelt, Elliott, 230
Roosevelt, Franklin D., 75, 153, 178,
    181, 182, 188–245, 256, 267, 272,
    273, 274, 278, 320, 321, 403
    and campaign to alert Americans to
        dangers of Hitler, 205–7
    "cash and carry" arms trade and,
        203–4, 205
    danger of Hitler perceived by, 194–
        195
    death of, 254
    destroyer swap and, 208–10
    diplomatic relations with Soviet
        Union established by, 236
    in election of 1940, 12–13, 210–11
    as father figure, 218
    ideology of, 190–91
    interventionist vs. isolationist critics
        of, 189–90
    isolationism of, 191, 193, 197
    Lend-Lease program and, 212
    navy as interest of, 193–94
    neutrality policy of, 204–5
    and plight of European Jews, 207–8,
        242–43
    postwar order and, 227, 245, 251,
        255
    public opinion and, 18, 146, 189,
        190, 196, 197–202, 205–15
    second front issue and, 240–42
    Stalin's dealings with, 251, 255, 257–
        258
    and war in North Atlantic, 212–14
    wartime propaganda and, 222–40
Roosevelt, James, 203, 233
Roosevelt, Theodore, 75, 119–20, 137,
    155, 162
    imperial vision of, 114, 117, 126, 137
    in preparedness movement, 152, 153

Roosevelt, Theodore (*cont.*)
  Spanish-American War and, 120–
    121, 125, 132, 133–34
  Wilson attacked by, 159, 164–65,
    166
  World War I and, 142–43, 144–45,
    149, 152, 153, 193
Root, Elihu, 148, 154, 175, 181
Roots of American Loyalty (Curti),
  174
Roots of the Modern American Empire
  (Williams), 113
Roper surveys, 321, 336
Rosenberg, Anna, 197, 226
Rosenberg, Ethel, 296
Rosenberg, Julius, 296
Rosenman, Samuel, 196, 243
Rosenwald, Lessing, 208
Rostow, Eugene, 368, 392
Roundup, 241
Rousseau, Jean-Jacques, 33, 44
Rowse, A. L., 194
Rush, Benjamin, 44
Russell, Richard, 338
Russett, Bruce, 121
Russia, Imperial, 109, 119, 127
  Alaska sold by, 110–11, 115
  see also Soviet Union
Russian American Company, 110
Russian Revolution (1917), 170, 185,
  239, 293
Rustin, Bayard, 346
Ryerson, Donald M., 160

Sackville-West, Sir Lionel, 123
St. Louis *Post-Dispatch*, 333
St. Louis *Westliche Post*, 145
SALT I Treaty, 392
SALT II Treaty, 365, 366, 368
Samoan Islands, 137
SANE, 391
San Francisco *Chronicle*, 116
San Francisco *Examiner*, 116, 128
Santa Anna, Antonio Lopez de, 94,
  95, 103
Saturday Evening Post, 158, 295
Save America First (Frank), 200–201
Scheer, Robert, 342
Schenck, Joseph, 234
Schenck, Nicholas, 234
Schlesinger, Arthur, Jr., 114, 306, 327
Schneider, William, 409
Schumpeter, Joseph, 118, 410
Schwimmer, Rosika, 150
Scott, Hugh D., 312

Scott, Winfield, 90, 102, 104
Screen Actors Guild, 303
Scruggs, William L., 124
secular-humanism, 374
Sedition Act (1798), 34, 47, 49
Sedition Act (1918), 159, 171, 185
Selective Service, 211, 212, 234, 281,
  342, 354
  see also conscription
Seminole Indians, 75
Senate, U.S., 35, 37, 41, 55–56, 57–
  58, 67, 75, 86, 97, 108, 110, 116,
  136, 202, 205, 210, 213, 219, 222,
  232, 255, 272, 308, 312, 316, 327,
  342, 353, 365
  Cuban insurrection and, 131, 133
  Foreign Relations Committee, 111,
    166, 180, 271, 309, 349–50
  League of Nations and, 165–67,
    174–75, 177, 178–79, 180–81, 183
  McCarthy censured by, 322
  Naval Committee, 209
  Oregon treaty and, 94
  Spanish-American War and, 165
  Vietnam War and, 349–50
  see also Congress, U.S.; House of
    Representatives, U.S.
separation of powers, 183
Sergeant York, 234
Seward, William H., 104, 108–10
Seymour, Charles, 302
Shahn, Ben, 229
Shanley, Bernard, 323
Shays, Daniel, 33
Sheean, Vincent, 233
Sheen, Monsignor Fulton J., 299–300
Shelley, Percy Bysshe, 92–93
Sherrill, Henry Knox, 301
Sherrod, Robert, 225
Sherwood, Robert E., 189, 206, 211,
  213
Shirer, William L., 206, 233, 303
Shoup, David, 350
Silver Shirts, 201
Skinner, Otis, 160
slavery, 38, 103, 105, 169
  abolitionism and, 91, 95
  expansionism and, 93, 95, 97–98,
    100, 106, 107, 108
  Indian issue compared to, 91
Sledgehammer, 241
Slidell, John, 96, 104
Smith, Al, 202
Smith, Gerard, 393–94
Smith, Robert, 62, 65

socialism, 297, 328
Socialist Party, 171
Social Structure of Revolutionary America, The (Main), 35
Society of the Cincinnati, 36
Solarium, 325
Somoza, Anastasio, 329
Sons of Liberty, 33
South Africa, 125, 399, 411
Soviet Union, 175–76, 196, 217, 313, 328, 343, 357, 381, 384, 396, 399, 411
  Afghanistan invaded by, 361, 363, 364, 365, 366, 382
  American Communists and, 277–78
  anxiety about Bomb displaced onto, 295–96
  balance of power between U.S. and, 356, 365, 368, 396
  Central American insurgencies and, 377, 381
  China's split with, 309, 331, 358
  conquest goal ascribed to, 293, 294, 300, 316, 319, 365, 389, 404
  consumer goods lacked in, 326
  containment of, 257, 271, 293, 310, 318, 325, 358
  Cuban missile crisis and, 391
  democratic reforms in, 408
  détente with, 354, 358, 359, 363, 365, 366–67, 368, 372
  Greek insurgency and, 266–69
  international terrorism ascribed to, 382
  Korean airliner shot down by, 382–383
  major shifts in public opinion on, 363, 365–67
  nuclear arsenal of, 285, 286, 291, 296, 316, 365, 366, 368, 371, 403
  plans for war against, 275
  as portrayed in TV commercials, 376
  postwar order and, 245, 250–66; *see also* Cold War
  propaganda to generate support for, 235–40, 244–45, 253
  Reagan's nuclear strategy and, 388, 392, 393, 396
  Reagan's rhetoric against, 369, 372, 374, 378, 382–83
  second front issue and, 240–41
  secret U.S. military operations in, 327–28
  Sputnik launched by, 331

  strains in U.S. alliance with, 240–241, 244, 245, 252, 257–58, 259
  as trade partner, 296, 358
  Vietnam War and, 365–66, 391
  as viewed in NSC 68, 286
  in World War II, 200, 212, 228, 236–237, 240–41, 244
  see also Russia, Imperial
Spain, 26, 83
  Cuba and, 107–8, 126–29, 130–33, 134, 136
  North American territories of, 24, 30, 34, 41, 45, 52–58, 61, 75, 76, 94
Spanish-American War, 124, 125–36, 165
  annexation issue in, 130, 133
  declaration of, 133
  events leading to, 125–33
  peace treaty in, 136
  Philippines taken in, 133–34, 135, 136
  press and, 127, 128–30, 131, 132, 134
  public opinion in, 112–13, 120–21, 125, 130–31, 132, 134–35
  U.S. role in global politics changed by, 142, 143
Speaking Frankly (Byrnes), 252
Spellman, Francis Cardinal, 211, 300, 301
Spider Web Chart, 192
"spin," 12, 344, 345, 380, 385
Spock, Benjamin, 342
sports, 120
Spring-Rice, Sir Cecil, 143
Springsteen, Bruce, 375
Sputnik, 331
Stalin, Joseph, 220, 264, 274, 276, 285, 286, 288, 291, 296, 299, 301, 309, 311
  denunciation of, 294
  FDR's dealings with, 251, 255, 257–258
  Greek insurgency and, 266, 268
  Hitler compared to, 236, 237, 238–239, 275, 305
  hyperbolic response to, 292, 293, 294
  postwar order and, 251, 255, 257–258, 259, 260
  pro-Soviet propaganda and, 236–240
  Truman's hard line aided by, 271, 281, 282, 283

Stalin, Joseph (*cont.*)
   World War II and, 200, 228, 236–42, 252
Stallone, Sylvester, 374, 375
Standard Oil, 199
Starnes, Joe, 228
Stassen, Harold, 312
State Department, U.S., 15, 36, 108, 147, 148, 173, 189, 191, 203, 204, 216, 254, 258, 260, 261, 271, 273, 282, 285, 290, 291, 293, 311, 329, 338, 377, 383, 384
   Greek insurgency and, 266–69
   Korean War and, 309, 310, 312
   public opinion surveyed by, 263–64, 267, 286–87
   suspected Communists in, 274–75
   Vietnam War and, 340
Steffens, Lincoln, 157
Stegner, Wallace, 201
Stephens, Alexander Hamilton, 100
Stephenson, Sir William, 214
Stepinac, Archbishop, 301
Sterling, Claire, 382
Stevens, John L., 115
Stevenson, Adlai E., 206, 319–20, 321, 331
Stimson, Henry L., 189, 198, 213, 217, 218, 223, 256–57, 405
Stockman, David, 387
Stockton, Robert, 101
Stoeckl, Édouard de, 110
Stoler, Mark, 241
Stone, William J., 145
Strategic Air Command (SAC), 324–325
Strategic Defense Initiative, 395–96
Strong, Caleb, 68
Strong, Josiah, 113
Stuart, R. Douglas, Jr., 207
Studebaker, John, 279
Students for a Democratic Society (SDS), 342, 346, 348
Sullivan, Gael, 276, 277
Sulzberger, Arthur Hays, 330
Summer Olympics (1984), 374
Sumner, Charles, 111
superpatriotism, 172–74, 191–93
Supreme Court, U.S., 89, 203, 231, 280, 354
Survey, 184
Survival under Atomic Attack, 294–295
Sweden, 40
Swing, Raymond Gram, 224–25, 259

Swope, Herbert Bayard, 257
Szulc, Tad, 333

Taft, Robert A., 272, 291, 308
   in election of 1952, 317–18, 319
   World War II and, 200, 207, 212, 214, 218
Taft, William Howard, 167
Taft-Hartley Act (1947), 298
Taiwan, *see* China, Republic of
Talleyrand-Périgord, Charles-Maurice de, 46, 49, 55, 57
Tammany Hall, 35–36, 76, 155
Tarbell, Ida, 157, 175
Tarkington, Booth, 160
taxes, 14, 286, 287, 332, 353, 369
   bomb defenses and, 322, 323
   covert operations and, 328
   Vietnam War and, 339, 346
   World War I and, 158
Taylor, Maxwell, 331
Taylor, Zachary, 96, 97, 98, 102, 104
teach-ins, 340–41, 342
Team B report, 368
Tecumseh, 64
Teheran Conference (1943), 251
television, 363, 376, 379, 385, 409
   Eisenhower's use of, 320–21, 335
   entertainment as primary function of, 344
   first presidential debates on, 332
   Johnson's credibility gap and, 341
   Kennedy as master of, 335–36
   as most widely used source of news, 336
   nature of news coverage on, 344–345
   Reagan and, 380
   as resource for presidents to persuade public, 334
   Vietnam War and, 340, 342–43, 344–45, 347–48, 349
Teller, Edward, 331, 391
Tenskwatawa, 64
Terkel, Studs, 186
terrorism, 364, 382
Tet offensive (1968), 342–43, 345
Texas, 156
   annexation of, 93, 94–105
   slavery issue and, 93, 95, 97–98, 100
   see also Mexican War
textbook reform, 373–74
Third World, 114, 358
   press coverage of, 364–65

Soviet intervention in, 363, 365
  *see also specific countries and
    regions*
Thomas, Charles, 170
Thomas, Keith, 73
Thomas, Norman, 200
Thompson, Dorothy, 201
Thoreau, Henry, 102
Three Mile Island, 393
Thurston, Lorrin, 115
Tibet, 328
Time, 233, 241–42, 259, 262, 264, 300,
  306, 330, 333, 383
Times (London), 109, 133
Tippecanoe, battle of (1811), 64
Tito (Josip Broz), 266, 301, 309
Tocqueville, Alexis de, 15, 31, 77, 78,
  79, 80, 88, 92, 111, 290, 292, 367
Tonkin Gulf Resolution (1964), 338,
  345, 349
Torrijos, Omar, 360
totalitarianism, 220–21, 275, 277, 279,
  285, 306, 408–9
Townsend, Ralph, 201
Treasury Department, U.S., 256
Trilateral Commission, 343, 359–60
Trist, Nicholas, 104
Truman, Harry S., 14, 97, 212, 253–
  317, 325
  advisers to, 254–56
  bipartisan foreign policy consensus
    and, 272–73
  Cold War hysteria and, 293
  covert operations under, 327–28
  demobilization and, 250, 252, 253
  domestic Communism and, 273–75,
    278–79, 297, 300
  election of 1948 and, 276–77, 280–
    284, 287, 317, 357
  election of 1952 and, 317, 319, 320
  European policy of, 315–16
  ideology of, 254
  Korean War and, 308, 312, 313,
    314–15, 317
  MacArthur fired by, 314–15
  military spending and, 287
  nuclear weapons and, 264, 265
  postwar order and, 252, 253–66
Truman Doctrine, 254, 256, 266–70,
  280, 292, 297, 303, 310, 356, 361,
  405
  Congress and, 267–68, 269, 270
  critics of, 270
  foreign aid program as goal of, 267,
    269–70, 271–72

Trumbo, Dalton, 200
Tully, Grace, 210
Tumulty, Joseph, 149, 154, 157, 181
Turkey, 273, 312, 404
  Truman Doctrine and, 266–69
Twentieth-Century Fox, 234
Tydings, Millard, 311

Ukraine, 328
ultranationalism, 172–74
Uncensored War, The (Hallin), 344–45
Union Carbide, 199
Union League Club, 131, 154
United Automobile Workers, 298
United Electrical Workers, 298
United Freemen of Mingo Creek, 33
United Fruit Company, 329–30
United German Societies of New
  York, 149
United Nations, 182, 251, 258, 261,
  267, 273, 298, 309, 364, 377
  creation of, 259, 260
United Press International (UPI), 333
United States Journal, 93
universities, 371
  in Cold War, 301–2
  Vietnam War opposed at, 340–42
U.S. News & World Report, 308, 330
U-2 incident (1960), 386–87

Valera, Eamon de, 177
Vallandigham, Clement, 208
Van Buren, Martin, 90, 91, 95
Vance, Cyrus, 350–51
Vandenberg, Arthur, 259, 268, 270,
  273, 283, 311
Vanderbilt, Cornelius, 153
Vanderbilt, William K., 154
Van Rensselaer, Stephen, 87
Venezuela, 122, 124–25, 128
Versailles Treaty (1919), 30, 163–64,
  165, 176–77, 181, 201
  Senate defeat of, 180
  see also League of Nations
Veterans of Foreign Wars, 311
Victoria, Queen of England, 109
Viereck, George Sylvester, 201, 231
Vietnam, North:
  bombing of, 338, 339, 340
  U.S. supporters of, 349
"Vietnam syndrome," 371, 376, 399
Vietnam War, 13, 14, 49, 61, 206, 255,
  267, 306, 319, 330, 336–51, 352,
  355–56, 358, 359, 367, 371, 372,
  379, 386, 391, 404–5

Vietnam War (*cont.*)
America split by, 350–51
conscription in, 14, 342
escalation of, 317, 339–40, 341, 345, 349
moral critique of, 342
nuclear weapons considered in, 323, 337, 339, 343, 365–66, 389
opposition to, *see* antiwar movement
plans for selling of, 345–46
propaganda gap in, 384
Rambo and, 374–75
Reagan's views on, 376
Senate hearings on, 349–50
shift of public opinion in, 340–51, 362–63
Soviet Union and, 365–66, 391
television and, 340, 342–43, 344–45, 347–48, 349
Tet offensive as turning point of, 342–43, 345
Vietnamization of, 321, 340, 351
Viguerie, Richard, 360
Villa, Pancho, 194
Vinson, Fred, 283
Virgin Islands, 137
Voice of Liberation, 329
Voltaire (François-Marie Arouet), 44
Vo Nguyen Giap, 384
Vyshinsky, Andrey, 239, 282

Walk East on Beacon, 304
Walker, Robert J., 110
Walker, William, 106–7
Wallace, George, 349, 350
Wallace, Henry, 284, 302, 306, 308
Communist ties ascribed to, 274, 280–81, 282–83, 291, 300, 302
in election of 1948, 276–77
postwar vision of, 227, 228
Truman's anti-Soviet policy opposed by, 262–63, 270
World War II and, 223, 230, 240
Wallis, Graham, 221
Wall Street Journal, 158, 237, 369, 381–82
Walsh, David I., 209
Wanamaker, John, 148
Ward, Barbara, 361
War Department, U.S., 67, 192
Warner, Harry, 238
Warner, Jack, 238, 304
Warner Brothers, 234

War of 1812, 54, 59–69, 75, 76, 78, 98, 147, 187, 350
ambivalence about, 67–68, 69
declaration of war in, 66, 67
end of, 68
events leading to, 59–61, 62–67
secession threats in, 68, 69
territorial goals of, 67
War on Poverty, 354
War Without Mercy (Dower), 230–31
Washburn, Israel, 110
Washington, George, 23–43, 48, 52, 75, 85, 92, 167, 181, 277
army and, 38–39
ideology of, 25–26, 35
ineffective in managing public opinion, 44–45
Jay Treaty and, 40–43
Neutrality Proclamation of, 28–29, 31, 32
political clubs and, 33–35
press and, 36–37
Washington *Daily Union*, 96, 103
Washington *Federalist*, 60
Washington *Globe*, 79–80
Washington *Post*, 173, 275, 343–44, 345, 379
Watergate, 343–44, 351, 352, 367, 387
Watson, James E., 177
Wayne, Anthony, 48
Wayne, John, 250, 303, 360
Weart, Spencer, 295, 392
Weber, Max, 74
Webster, Daniel, 94, 97, 105–6
Webster, Noah, 33, 36
Wehrmacht, 199, 234
Weigel, George, 350
Weinberger Doctrine, 15
welfare state, 354, 357–58
Welles, Orson, 218, 238, 302
Welles, Sumner, 196
Wellington, Arthur Wellesley, Duke of, 102
Wells, H. G., 144, 388
Western Europe:
communism in, 271, 292, 356
missile deployment in, 387–88
permanent stationing of U.S. troops in, 315–16, 318
see also specific countries
West Indies, 40, 42, 45, 48, 81
Westmoreland, William, 342–43
Wheeler, Burton K., 207, 232
Wheeler, Joseph, 341
Wherry, Kenneth, 310

Whig Party, 81, 94, 350
Mexican War and, 97, 100, 101–2, 103, 104
Whiskey Rebellion, 34
White, Harry Dexter, 273–74
White, Henry, 165
White, William Allen, 133, 205–7, 209, 210, 316
White Cliffs of Dover, The, 235
Whitman, Walt, 98
"Why America Fights Germany," 160
Whyte, William, 347
Why We Fight, 229
"Wild West, The," 324
Wilhelm II, Kaiser of Germany, 142, 144, 145, 149, 154, 156, 161, 187, 201
Wilkinson, James, 53
Williams, Roger, 82
Williams, William Appleman, 113
J. B. Williams Company, 303
Willkie, Wendell, 209, 210–11, 227, 228, 232, 241, 311, 320
Wills, Garry, 38, 369, 371
Wilmot, David, 100
Wilson, Edmund, 304
Wilson, Mrs. Woodrow, 178, 179, 180, 181
Wilson, Woodrow, 61, 141–85, 187, 193, 204, 227, 251, 254
arms exports and, 147
in election of 1912, 184
in election of 1916, 12–13, 146, 154–155, 157
ideology of, 143–44
illness of, 178, 179–80, 181, 182
League of Nations and, 144, 146, 163–68, 172–83, 190, 202
Lodge as archantagonist of, 165–66, 182
neutrality policy of, 141, 143–49, 154–56
at Paris peace talks, 163–64, 165, 179
preparedness movement and, 153–154
public opinion as viewed by, 143, 146, 148–49
as public speaker, 177–78, 179
war entered by, 156–57
Winchell, Walter, 201
"window of vulnerability," 368, 388
Winter, Ella, 240
Winthrop, John, 82, 112, 371
Wirthlin, Richard, 370, 377

Wise Men, 254–56
Wohlstetter, Albert, 265
Wolcott, Oliver, 28, 45
Woman on Pier 13, The, 304
Women's Peace Party, 150
Wood, Leonard, 149, 152
Wood, Robert E., 200, 207, 208
Woodward, Bob, 382
Woolf, Leonard, 168
Worcester, Samuel, 89
Works Projects Administration (WPA), 200, 222
World Court, 191, 202
World Federalists, 295
World War I, 13, 98, 141–62, 190, 195, 199, 201, 206, 208, 209, 212, 218, 233, 235, 237, 242, 243, 251, 252, 304, 406
American identity altered by, 169–170, 172, 173–74
conscription in, 154, 157, 159–61
economic considerations in, 147
FDR's views on, 193–94
German sabotage and intrigue in, 151–52
information management in, 157–159
mobilization for, 157–62, 173–74
paying for, 158
peace movement and, 150, 156–57
peace talks in, 142, 155–56, 163–64, 165, 178–79, 190
postwar order and, 167; see also League of Nations
preparedness movement in, 152–154
propaganda in, 150–51, 159, 160–162, 173–74, 187, 217, 223, 226, 227, 229, 231
public opinion in, 144–46, 148–53, 157–62
shock at outbreak of, 141–42
submarine warfare in, 148–49, 150, 154, 155, 156
superpatriotism at end of, 172–74, 191–93
TR's attacks on Wilson during, 164–165
U.S. arms shipments in, 147–48, 151, 203
U.S. entry into, 156–57, 214
U.S. neutrality in, 141, 142–44, 145, 146–47, 148–49, 154–56
Versailles Treaty and, 30, 163–64, 165, 176–77, 180, 181, 201

World War I (*cont.*)
  as viewed in 1930s, 186–87
  war debts from, 187, 262
World War II, 13, 25, 98, 110, 125,
    137, 183, 186–246, 299, 305, 326,
    403, 406
  American society transformed by,
    188
  appeasement and, *see* appeasement
    era
  atomic bomb in, 188, 241, 242, 254,
    264–65, 289, 295, 314, 390
  cross-Channel invasion in, 241–42
  defeat of League of Nations and,
    182
  demobilization after, 14, 249–52,
    253, 262, 294, 316
  destroyer swap in, 208–10
  dislocations after, 277
  as educational experience, 217–18
  failure of public opinion leading to,
    187–88, 189, 190
  FDR's personal authority in, 218–19
  as "the Good War," 186
  mobilization for, 219–20, 225
  North Atlantic fighting in, 212–14
  outbreak of, 204
  partisan politics during, 218
  plight of Jews in, 207–8, 232, 242–43
  priority of European vs. Pacific war
    in, 231, 311
  propaganda in, 188, 201, 207, 217,
    222–40, 253, 274
  public opinion in, 205–15, 212, 226,
    233, 234, 237, 243–44

  reconstruction aid after, 256–57,
    262, 267–70, 271–72; *see also*
    Marshall Plan
  second front issue in, 240–42
  U.S. arms trade in, 203–4, 205
  U.S. domestic politics changed by,
    216–17
  U.S. entry into, 198, 215, 218
  U.S. neutrality in, 204–5
  see also postwar order
Wright, Jim, 386
Wriston, Henry, 316
Wyman, David, 243

xenophobia, 146, 168–74
XYZ Affair, 46–47, 50

Yale University, 127, 302
Yalta Conference (1945), 188, 253,
    257–58, 274, 283, 312, 320, 367
Yamamoto Isoroku, 224
Yankelovich, Daniel, 396–97, 402–3,
    404
yellow press, 128–30, 135
Yemen, 363
Young America, 107
"Your Flesh *Should* Creep" (Alsop),
    295
Yugoslavia, 301, 309

Zanuck, Darryl, 234
Zeal for American Democracy
    program, 279
Zimmermann, Arthur, 156, 214
Zuckerman, William, 239–40

Richard J. Barnet is a Senior Fellow of the Institute for Policy Studies in Washington, D.C. He is the author of *The Alliance; Real Security; The Lean Years; Global Reach* (with Ronald E. Müller); and six other books. He writes frequently for *The New Yorker* and lives in Washington, D.C.